THE

TEXT-BOOK

OF

ASTROLOGY

(SECOND EDITION)

BY

ALFRED JOHN PEARCE,

Author of THE WEATHER GUIDE-BOOK,
THE SCIENCE OF THE STARS,

Editor of URANIA (1880), FUTURE (1892-1894),
and STAR LORE (1897-1903), etc.

IN FIVE BOOKS:

GENETHLIACAL ASTROLOGY, MUNDANE ASTROLOGY,
ASTRO-METEOROLOGY, MEDICAL ASTROLOGY, AND ELECTIONS.

TABLES OF HOUSES FOR LONDON AND NORTHAMPTON, TABLES OF RIGHT ASCENSION AND DECLINATION, AND OF ASCENSIONAL DIFFERENCE FOR LONDON AND WASHINGTON.

"TRUTH IS NEVER REFUTED."—PLATO.

ISBN: 0-86690-560-X
Current Printing: 2006
Cover Design: Jack Cipolla

Published by:
American Federation of Astrologers, Inc.
6535 S. Rural Road
Tempe AZ 85283.
Printed in the United States of America

PREFACE TO THE SECOND EDITION.

FARADAY, one of the most conspicuous examples of that typically philosophical mind which Great Britain has produced, uttered, toward the close of his life, his well-known warning against presumptuous judgment as the besetting intellectual vice of his time—a vice to which the educated class were almost wholly given over and from which professed philosophers were not exempt.

No science has suffered so severely from presumptuous judgment as Astrologia Sana. The mildest advocacy for an impartial investigation of it is held to be evidence of a mental obliquity, notwithstanding the fact that for ages it commanded the enlightened belief of the most learned and the most highly gifted of mankind.

The religious world may believe, with Professor Smyth and the Abbé Moigno, that astronomy began 2170 B.C., and that the first astronomers were instructed supernaturally; but this involves the belief that a knowledge of astrology was also revealed to man as Josephus averred, for astronomy and astrology were originally one and the same science. The late astronomer, R.A. Proctor (an opponent of astrology) declared that "astrology was the nursing mother of astronomy."

It is often asked: "Why is it the great majority of learned men of the nineteenth and the present century have denied that there is any truth in astrology?" The reply is: "Because they had never investigated it, being too prejudiced against it to do so." The vexed question of the truth of astrology cannot be solved by à *priori* arguments. It must be thoroughly and impartially examined before an opinion on its merits or demerits can be justified. As Bacon said:

"All idols must be abjured and renounced with firm and solid resolution, and the understanding must be freed and cleared of them, so that the access to the kingdom of man, which is founded on the sciences, may resemble that to the Kingdom of Heaven, where no admission is conceded except to children."

It is puerile to say that as orthodox scientists do not recognize astrology there can be nothing in it worthy of study. It has been well said that if there were not successive generations of men the world would stand still. No great or learned man, who had attained the age of forty years, accepted Harvey's doctrine of the circulation of the blood, in his day. It was the great and learned men who despised the persecuted

Galileo, who laughed at Newton, who could perceive no wisdom in Bacon and Locke, who repudiated Linnaeus and Hahnemann, and would have strangled modern astronomy, geology, chemistry, magnetism and homeopathy.

The author entertains the greatest respect for the learned astronomers and philosophers of the present day. At the same time a protest must be entered against those astronomers and philosophers who presume to decide by autocratic authority so important a question as that of the truth of the most ancient of all sciences, with the merits of which they are totally unacquainted. As for the attacks of purely literary men, however brilliant they may be in their own department, they are without the pale of natural science, and are, therefore, incompetent to form an opinion as to the truth of Astrologia Sana.

Sir David Brewster presumptuously assumed the absurdity of astrology, instead of investigating it; in fact, in his article on the subject in the *Edinburgh Cyclopaedia*, there was neither a single sentence of reasoning nor a single fact presented in evidence against it; for he simply set up a phantom of his own for the amusement of knocking it down, and thereby only betrayed his utter ignorance of the subject and his unreasoning prejudice against it. "These be thy gods, O Israel."

Some materialistic opponents think to crush astrology with the dictum that "it is opposed to common sense." Before the science can be tried by this standard, knowledge and justness are essential—for "common sense" is usually a cloak to cover a vast amount of common prejudice. Without entering into the logical definition of what common sense is, I may ask such self-satisfied critics what is their common sense? If it is opposed to scientific sense it is simply common ignorance. "Common sense," about a century since, ridiculed the idea of traveling at the rate of fifty miles per hour by means of the locomotive steam engine. The really scientific Dr. Lardner's "common sense" led him to ridicule the idea of crossing the Atlantic Ocean in a steam-ship, he pronounced it visionary; but nevertheless he subsequently availed himself of a steam-ship when he emigrated to America. Sir Humphrey Davy's "common sense" led him, in the course of his lecture at the Royal Institution, to compare the project of lighting up towns with gas conveyed by pipes to that of the Yorkshireman who proposed to dissipate London fogs by setting up windmills. Such "common sense," which draws conclusions from à *priori* reasoning, is the most fallacious and gratuitous mode of judging an experimental science.

The planetary Heavens are the macrocosm and man is the microcosm.

Astronomers boast that one of the greatest charms of astronomy is that it enables them to predict eclipses of the Sun and Moon, etc., exactly, and that their predictions are accepted with as little doubt as if they were the records of past events. On the other hand, when an astrologer foretells great earthquakes, destructive storms, floods, droughts, scarcity or plenty, etc., in regions through which the line of central eclipse (of the Sun) passes, coinciding, or nearly so, with the maximum of planetary action, his prediction when fulfilled is most unfairly stigmatised as a mere "lucky hit." In both cases, the predictions of the astronomer and the astrologer are based upon astronomical phenomena and computations: the reason why the forecasts of the former are lauded as achievements of true science, and those of the astrologer are branded as "pseudo-science," or even as "imposture," is, in fairness, impossible to comprehend. It is the outburst of sheer prejudice. Many have been the failures of the predictions—especially in relation to comets—many have been the mistakes of astronomers; yet, because they can predict the moment of an eclipse (which the ancient astrologers could and did accomplish thousands of years before Newton and, moreover, the return of comets, also, modern astronomy is held to be an exact science—the νομος is received, the λογος is rejected!

Even Sir David Brewster, who ridiculed astrology, yet enthusiastically declared: "The planets and Constellations are truly the only objects in the Universe which all nations have witnessed and all peoples admired. They presided over the horoscope of our birth, and they will throw their pale radiance over the green mounds beneath which we are destined to lie."

The author trusts that all who love TRUTH for its own sake will do their best to demand a fair field and no favour for Astrologia Sana, and aid in circulating this work. No study can be more interesting nor more fascinating, and few can be more useful. None other can surpass it in leading "from Nature up to Nature's GOD."

A. J. P.

PREFACE TO THE 2006 REPRINT

The A.F.A. is pleased to publish this reprint of A.J. Pearce's *The Text-Book of Astrology*, a classic work of English astrology, first published as a combined edition in London in 1911, and previously reprinted by the A.F.A. in 1970.

Alfred John Pearce (1840-1923) was the son of a homeopathic physician. He originally intended to pursue medicine as a career, but was unable to complete his studies due to a lack of funds. However, he later practiced medicine as an assistant to other physicians. As a homeopath he remained unreconciled to vaccination and other harsh procedures employed by the allopathic physicians of his time.

Pearce became interested in astrology, and by 1875 he had acquired sufficient stature as an astrologer to be offered the position of Editor of the popular annual *Zadkiel's Almanac*. He thus became Zadkiel II and held that position for 48 years.

His major work, *The Text-Book of Astrology*, gives an excellent presentation of traditional astrology and is filled with numerous examples he had collected over the years. Pearce accepted Claudius Ptolemy (2nd century) as the principal ancient authority on astrology. And since Ptolemy did not mention Horary Astrology in his book the *Tetrabiblos*, Pearce did not favor it; he characterized it as "a system of divination . . . not really worth serious consideration, except in cases of the deepest anxiety and perturbation of the mind on the part of the querent…." However, he did favor Elections, thus agreeing in that respect with the famous French astrologer J.B. Morin (1583-1656).

Pearce's book is devoted to reading character in the natal horoscope and predicting definite events. It is devoid of the psychological trend set in motion by his younger contemporary Alan Leo (1860-1917). It contains explicit instructions for calculating and interpreting primary directions (with many auxiliary tables at the end of the book), and for interpreting solar revolutions. It also has chapters on Mundane Astrology, Meteorological Astrology, and much information on Medical Astrology with many actual cases that he had collected. There is a wealth of information on notable events and persons of the 19th century and earlier, providing much information for astrological research. There is even a reproduction of the chart for the foundation of the Greenwich Observatory.

Thus, *The Text-Book of Astrology* offers an excellent introduction to traditional astrology in all its branches. And it precedes the complications introduced by esotericism, new planets, asteroids, and satellites, and vague psychological interpretations.

James Herschel Holden, M.A., FAFA
July 2006

James Herschel Holden
Historian, Linguist, and Astrologer

James Herschel Holden, M.A. FAFA, has been Research Director of the American Federation of Astrologers since 1982.

He has had a life-long interest in the history of astrology and astronomy and has translated a number of astrological works from the Classical Era, Medieval and Modern times. In recent years, he has translated several Books of J.B.Morin's *Astrologia Gallica*, namely Books 13, 14, 15,16, 17, 22, 23, 24, and 25. They are available from the American Federation of Astrologers.

Trained as a linguist, he has a degree in English literature with a minor in foreign languages (Latin, German, French, and Russian), and as a scientist (he holds a second B.A. in pure mathematics with a minor in physics), Holden has translated numerous astrological books and articles from Latin, Greek, French, German, Spanish, and Italian.

Some of the translations are: Albumasar's *Book of Flowers*, Abu 'Ali's *The Judgments of Nativities*, Māshā'allāh's short *Book of Nativities*, Sahl ibn Bishr's five books on Horary and Electional Astrology, Porphyry's Introduction to the Tetrabiblos, Paul of Alexandria's Introduction, Rhetorius the Egyptian's *Compendium of Astrology*, and Brahy's autobiography. Currently, he is working on a new translation of Julius Firmicus Maternus's *Mathesis*.

He is also the author of *A History of Horoscopic Astrology* and *Astrological Pioneers of America*, also available from the American Federation of Astrologers, and numerous articles published in A.F.A's *Journal of Research*, including "The Classical Zodiac,"and "An Astrological Theory of Personality.

In his spare time, he also functions unofficially as the translator for AFA correspondence received and sent in foreign languages and as a Foreign Correspondent of the Italian astrological Organization CIDA (Centro Italiano di Astrologia).

CHAPTER I.

INTRODUCTION.

> "It is a gentle and affectionate thought,
> That, in immeasurable heights above us,
> At our first birth the wreath of love was woven
> With sparkling stars for flowers."—SCHILLER'S
> *Wallenstein* (Coleridge's Translation).

THE HISTORY of Astrology is coeval with that of the earliest civilisation. It formed the basis of all ancient religions and mythology, and was indissolubly interwoven with the sacred truths of the Christian religion.

Godfrey Higgins, the talented author of the "Anacalypsis" and an opponent of astrology, stated that, "Among all the ancient nations of the world, the opinion was universal, that the planetary bodies were the disposers of the affairs of men."

Simplicius relates that Calisthenes, who accompanied Alexander to Babylon, sent to Aristotle from that capital a series of astronomical observations, which he had found preserved there, extending back to a period of 1,903 years from Alexander's conquest of the city. Epigenes states that these observations were recorded on tablets of baked clay. They must have extended, according to Simplicius, as far back as 2234 B.C., and would therefore seem to have been commenced and continued for many centuries by the primitive Chaldaean people. The Chaldaean astrologers were highly honoured in Persia, at the court and by the people, as related by Plato in one of his dialogues. The Druids held the astrology of the ancient Chaldaeans in equal honour, for it was, in fact, their religion.

Cicero passed the following eulogy,[1] on the Chasdim:

"Chaldaei cognitione astrorum sollertiaque ingeniorum antecellunt."

Josephus states that astrology was practised by the antediluvians,

---

[1] Cicero de Div. I., 41.

who had it from Adam, who received his information thereof from God himself. He further states that Seth having received instruction in its principles from Adam, and foreseeing the flood, engraved the rudiments of the science upon two permanent pillars of stone; and that the remains of those pillars he (Josephus) himself had seen. He also relates that the science was taught by Enos and Noah, who preserved it to the days of Abraham.

Eusebius informs us that Abraham was thoroughly versed in the Chaldaean astrology.

There can be no doubt that the secret religion of the Chaldaeans was that of Aur, literally the light, metaphorically the doctrine from which Abraham was called to worship the true God alone, and not, as they did, namely, to mix with that the worship of the Host of Heaven. Abraham had learned the great secret of the *Aurim* and *Thummim*—which meant the Doctrines and Perfect Laws, and which has remained to this day a perfect mystery, inscrutable to the ablest of our philologists, and the most learned of our divines, owing to their ignorance of astrology.[2]

Zoroaster, legislator of the *Magi*, or wise men of Chaldaea, adopted astrology. He was the originator of *magia*, or magic, which, at first, was a good principle, being the worship of the Deity.

Aristotle says that the Chaldaean *Magi* were prior to the Egyptian priests—who were contemporaneous with Moses.

Manetho, an ancient historian, says that there was a temple at Heliopolis, dedicated to the Sun, or Mithra, where the *Magi* instructed the priests of Isis in the mysteries of their religion; and that there was one Moses, a priest at this temple, who afterwards became the leader of a number of enslaved Jews, and from this it is evident that Moses was well acquainted with the Chaldaic philosophy.

Godfrey Higgins says:

"Though the adoption of the astronomical and astrological emblems of the Magi and the Egyptians may be no proof of the wisdom or sagacity of Moses, they are sufficiently clear proofs of the identity of his religion with the religion of the Magi, &c., before their corruption. What are we to make of the brazen serpent set up by Moses in the Wilderness, and worshipped by the Israelites in the time of Hezekiah? What of the Cherubim under the wings of which the God of the Jews

---

[2] See *Zadkiel's Almanac*, 1868, pp. 62-71; also the *Anacalypsis* by Godfrey Higgins, Book II. Chaps. 1 and 2.

dwelt? These Cherubim had the faces of the beings which were in the four cardinal points of the zodiac, when the Bull was the equinoctial sign, viz., the ox, the lion, the man and the eagle.[3] These were clearly astrological.

"The secret meaning of all these emblems, and of most parts of the books of the Pentateuch, of Joshua and Judges (almost the whole of which was astrological, that is, magical allegory), was what in old times, in part at least, constituted the Jewish Cabala, and was studiously kept from the knowledge of the vulgar."

Moses was brought up in the court of Rameses II.

The Rev. John Butler, B.D., maintained:

"That Moses did particularly understand astrology is apparent by his predictions of the tribes as to what should betide them for the time to come; for it was not by revelation, nor dream, nor vision, that he spake those things, for when it was so the Scripture was wont to say how it was so; and no such thing being alleged now, it follows that he spake merely of his natural knowledge, and besides, the phrase savours of mere natural prophecy."

The ancients believed that the planets had, under their special care, the affairs of men. Philo was of this opinion, and even Maimonides declares that the planets are endued with life, knowledge, and understanding; that they acknowledge and praise their Creator. "On this opinion," says Godfrey Higgins,[4] "all judicial astrology, magic, was founded—a science, I believe, almost as generally held by the ancients as the being of a God is by the moderns."

Phornutus says, "For the ancients took those for gods whom they found to move in a certain and regular manner, thinking them to be the causers of the changes of the air and the conservation of the universe.[5] These then are gods which are the disposers and formers of all things."

As to the probable origin of the ancient belief that the planets were animated beings, Godfrey Higgins says:

"If a person will place himself in the situation of an early observer of the heavenly bodies, and consider how they must have appeared to him in his state of ignorance, he will at once perceive that it was

[3] See a picture of them in Parkhurst's Heb. Lex.

[4] *Anacalypsis*, Book I. Chap. I.

[5] Godfrey Higgins adds, "And this is the meaning of Genesis . . . which is as visible as the noon-day sun in every part of the Old and New Testament."

scarcely possible that he could avoid mistaking them for animated or intelligent beings. To us, with our prejudices of education, it is difficult to form a correct idea of what his sensations must have been, on his first discovering the five planets to be different from the other stars, and to possess a locomotive quality, apparently to him subject to no rule or order. But we know what happened; he supposed them animated, and to this day they are still supposed to be so, by the greatest part of the world.

"Persons are apt to regard with contempt the opinion that the planetary bodies are animated or rational beings. But let it not be forgotten that the really great Kepler believed our globe to be endowed with living faculties; that it possessed instinct and volition—an hypothesis which M. Patrin has supported with great ingenuity. Among those who believed that the planets were intelligent beings were Philo, Origen, and Maimonides.[6]

"There can be no doubt that judicial astrology, or the knowledge of future events by the study of the stars, was received and practised by all the ancient Jews, Persians, and many of the Christians, particularly the Gnostics and Manicheans. The persons now spoken of thought that the planets were the signs—that is, gave information of future events, not that they were the causes of them[7]—not that the events were controlled by them, for between these two there is a great difference. Eusebius tells us, on the authority of Eupolemus, that Abraham was an astrologer, and that he taught the science to the priests of *Heliopolis* or *On*. This was a fact universally admitted by the historians of the East. Origen was a believer in this science as qualified above; and M. Beausobre observes, it is thus that he explained what Jacob says in the prayer of Joseph: HE HAS READ IN THE TABLES OF HEAVEN ALL THAT WILL HAPPEN TO YOU, AND TO YOUR CHILDREN."

In the Para papers[8] we read that:

"It is in the planetary system one finds the key that unlocks this great pantheon of granite gods, rends the veil of the temple that encloses the 'holy of holies,' and reveals many a sublime truth of which these solemn and silent images have so long been the misunderstood interpreters."

---

[6] Faber, Pag. Idol., Vol. I., p. 32.

[7] "It is not meant to say that, at a very early period, the planets were not believed to be the active agents of a superior power, they probably were."—Note by Higgins.

[8] Page 100; Paris, 6, Rue Montpensier, Palais Royal.

The first verse of Genesis records that, "In the beginning God created the heavens and the earth." This should be, " In the first place God created the planets and the earth." The words "ath he shemim" import, *ath*, the original matter, *he-shemim*, of the disposers. It is the plural of *shem*, the *disposer* or *placer*. It has been falsely rendered "heaven." In the 19th Psalm we have the same word *heshemim* rendered the "heavens," and followed by a verb in the plural. "The heavens declare the glory of (AL) God." That the *planets* were here, also, signified, is certain, for David says: "There is no speech or language where *their* voice is not heard." In the 4th verse of the same Psalm we read: "In them hath he set a tabernacle for the Sun." This means among the *planets*. In the same verse we are told: "Their line has gone out through all the earth." What does this mean? Aquila (the astrologer) renders it canon, a line or *thread* spread out at length. It really meant, therefore, the "*thread of destiny*," just as the Parcae, or *Destinies*, held distaffs, spinning the thread of human life.

Godfrey Higgins says:

"The word *esmim* in the Hebrew, and *esmin* in the Chaldee, do not mean the heavens or heavenly bodies generally, but the planets only, the disposers, as Dr. Parkhurst, after the Magi, calls them.

"The conduct of Christian expositors, with respect to the Hebrew words *smim* and *rasit*, has been as unfair as possible. They have misrepresented the meaning of them, in order to prevent the true *astrological* character of the book [of Genesis] from being seen. But that the first does mean *disposers*, the word *heavens* making nonsense, and the words relating to the stars in the 16th verse [of the first chapter], showing that they cannot be meant, put it beyond a question. My reader may, therefore, form a pretty good judgment how much Parkhurst can be depended upon for the meaning of the second, from the striking fact that, though he has filled several columns with observations relating to the opinions of different expositors, he could not find room for the words, *the opinion of the Synagogue is, that the word means* WISDOM, or *the Jerusalem Targum says it means* WISDOM. But it was necessary to *conceal* from the English reader, as already stated, the *countenance it gives to judicial astrology*, and the doctrine of Emanations."

In the 14th verse of the first chapter of Genesis we read that: "God said, Let there be lights in the firmament of the *heaven* to divide the day from the night, and let them be for signs, and for seasons, and for days and years." The word translated "lights" should have been rendered "instruments of light"; and "in the firmament of the heaven" should read "in the expanse of the heavens." "Let them be for signs," should be "let them be for signs of the future "—the word is *latheth*, and it signifies *sign of the future.*[9]

Adam Clarke, commenting on Genesis XLIX, says,

"It has been conjectured that the eleven stars that bowed down to Joseph might possibly refer to the *signs of the zodiac*,"[10] which were very anciently known in Egypt, and are supposed to have had their origin in Chaldaea. On this supposition, Joseph's eleven brethren answered to eleven of the signs, and himself to the twelfth."

General Vallancey, well known for his antiquarian researches, has endeavoured, in his *Collectanea Hibernica*,[11] to trace out the analogy between the twelve signs of the zodiac and the twelve sons of Jacob, which Dr. Hales[12] has altered a little and placed in a form in which it becomes more generally applicable:

"1. REUBEN—'Unstable (or rather pouring out) as water'—the sign *Aquarius*, represented as a man pouring out water from an urn.

2. SIMEON and LEVI—'The united brethren'—the sign *Gemini*, or the twins.

3 JUDAH—'The strong lion'—the sign *Leo*, or the lion.

4. ASHER—'His bread shall be fat'—the sign *Virgo*, generally represented holding a full ear of corn.

5. ISSACHAR—'A strong ass,' or *ox*; both used in husbandry—the sign *Taurus*, the bull.

6. and 7. DAN—'A serpent biting the horse's heel'—*Scorpio*, or the scorpion. On the Celestial sphere the scorpion is actually represented as biting the heel of the horse of the archer (*Sagittarius*), and *chelae*, 'his claws,' originally occupied the space of *Libra*.

8. JOSEPH—'His bow remained in strength'—the sign *Sagittarius*, the archer, or *bowman*, usually represented, even in the Asiatic zodiacs, with his bow bent, and the arrow drawn up to the head—the bow in full strength.

9. NAPH-TALI—By a play on his name *Taleh*; the ram, the sign *Aries*, according to the Rabbins.[13]

---

[9] See *Zadkiel's Almanac*, 1871, pp. 44-7.

[10] The number of the apostles also corresponds to that of the signs of the zodiac.

[11] Vol. VI., part 2 page 343.

[12] *Analysis* Vol. II., p. 165.

[13] See Buxtorf's Rab. Lex

10. ZEBULON—'A haven for ships—denoted by *Cancer*, the crab.

11. GAD[14]—'A troop or army'—reversed *Dag* a fish, the sign *Pisces*, the fishes.

12. BENJAMIN—'A ravening wolf'—*Capricornus*, which, on the Egyptian sphere, was represented by a goat, led by *Pan*, with a wolf's head."

The Reverend F. Fysh called attention[15] to Deuteronomy XXXII., 8, "When the Most High divided to the nations their inheritance when he separated the sons of Adam, he set the bounds of the people according to the number of the children of Israel." The Septuagint has, "according to the number of the *angels of God*." This difference is explained by a reference to *Genesis* XXXVII., 9. The twelve signs of the zodiac are plainly referred to. The meaning appears to be that however numerous the nations are, they are all under one or other of the twelve signs.

In Deborah's song of triumph we are told that "the stars in their courses [i.e. *exaltations*] fought against Sisera." Parkhurst renders this passage, " The stars from their *elevations* fought against Sisera." He then asks, " How so?" and replies, "By having their *influence* on the atmosphere supernaturally increased, so as to occasion those heavy rains which swelled the river *Kishon*, so as to sweep away the army of Sisera, as mentioned in the text." Josephus' account is, that a violent hailstorm blew in the face of the enemy; this hailstorm was caused by the electrical state of the atmosphere; and this electrical state of the atmosphere was caused by *planetary influence*. Parkhurst says, "But the modern philosopher will object that the *stars*, including the planets, have no natural influence or efficiency at all in causing rain. I answer, this is certainly more than he knows. One of the principal causes of rain is an alteration of the state of the atmosphere." Parkhurst then quotes Boerhave, "Perhaps, also, the different aspects of the planets may contribute to this effect—*i.e.*, of uniting the primary particles of water, which floated before separately in the atmosphere—and so occasion rain, snow, and hail."

---

[14] The name of Gad signified the planet Jupiter. Pisces is Jupiter's "night-house." The literal translation of *Genesis* XXX., 12 and 13, is, "And bare Zilpah, servant to Leah, to Jacob, a son; and said Leah 'cometh Gad,' and she called the name of him Gad." The authorised translation has it "a troop cometh"; but the word *Gad* is in the Vulgate translation. Aberbanel expounds this passage without any scruple, "This *Gad* is the star *Jupiter*."

[15] *Zadkiel's Almanac* for 1869, page 49.

Much has been made by religious opponents of astrology of the injunction of Jeremiah, "Be not dismayed at the signs of heaven; for the heathen are dismayed at them"; and the following passage has also been quoted against astrologers, "Let now the astrologers, the star-gazers, the monthly prognosticators, stand up and save thee" (Isaiah XLVII., 13). But these passages are not in the least condemnatory of astrology as a sinful pursuit. They merely prove that the heathen were dismayed at the signs of the heavens because they were ignorant of the true God, and accordingly worshiped the planets as gods in order to propitiate them. Although the astrologers could foresee impending calamities by the signs in the heavens, yet they were powerless to prevent their occurrence. Besides, these very injunctions prove that there *are* signs in the heavens! St. Paul, in his soul-stirring appeal, delivered on *Mars'* hill at Athens, quoted the following sentence from the *Phenomena* (a poem teaching astrology) of Aratus, and yet he did not take occasion to condemn astrology: "for we are also His offspring." Late in the autumn of 1909, the excavators of the Berlin Archaeological Society, engaged on the site of Pergamos, Asia Minor, unearthed the remains of a Temple of Demeter, which was built about 262 B.C. A marble altar was dedicated "To the Unknown God"; this is said to be the first confirmation of the passage in St. Paul's Areopagus speech.

Jesus Christ's prophecy: "Great earthquakes shall be in divers places, and famines, and pestilences; and fearful sights and great signs shall there be from Heaven; And there shall be signs in the Sun, and in the Moon, and in the Stars," was exactly fulfilled at the destruction of Jerusalem. Josephus relates that "a comet in the form of a sword hung over Jerusalem for a whole year."

At the birth of our Saviour, his star appeared, and by means of it the *Magi*, or "wise men," were divinely guided to the place of His birth; and they were the first, with the exception of the shepherds, to worship him. Even in returning, the wise men (who were astrologers, as Bishop Porteous proved), were again divinely guided, for "they were warned of God, in a dream, not to return to Herod." The three presents which were offered to the infant Saviour by the wise men, were *gold*, *frankincense*, and *myrrh*; three things consecrated by the ancients to the Sun, as the history of the Chaldaeans, Arabs, and all Eastern nations demonstrates.

In the Bible we are told that, "One star differeth from another star in glory." The pure practice of celestial philosophy in course of time became corrupted into the worship of the heavens, or *Zabaism*, and afterwards into idolatry, or the worship of the images found to resemble certain qualities of the planets in honour of which they were instituted. At first, men began to attribute the effects which they perceived were produced by the celestial bodies, to the powers of those bodies as gods or demons of an inferior rank to the great FIRST CAUSE, whose majesty was gradually lost sight of to some extent. It has been doubted by some writers whether the ancient gods were named from the planets. This doubt could only arise in the minds of those persons who have only examined the writings of the poets of Greece and Rome. It is dispelled by a proper study of the mythology of the ancient inhabitants of India, Phoenicia, and Egypt.

Bunsen has observed in his work on Egypt, that "Chaeremon is said to have stated that *the most ancient Egyptian Deities are the Planets*, the constellations of the zodiac, and others, with the Decans and Horoscopi." Here we have an element of pure Egyptian astrology, tinged perhaps with the zodiacal system, borrowed from the Greeks, and with a Stoical colouring. For the Stoics corrupted the ancient mythology, if not as radically as the Neo-Platonists, still with a total want of either poetical feeling or historical sense. Porphyry describes Chaeremon as "a lover of truth, a man of accuracy, and as much respected among the Stoic Philosophers."

The Hindu Gods *Balàrama*, *Subhadra*, *Jagannatha*, are (*Balàrama*) "the Sun in his exaltation"; (*Subhadra*) "the glorious mover in the circle"—a title exactly suited to the moon; and (*Jagannath*) "the Living God, the shield or protector." *Buddha* means wisdom; the word has been generally held to signify the Sun; but the distinction between *Chrisna*, also the Sun, and Buddha, has not been well understood. The secret lies in the character of the planet "ruling" the Sun, or "disposing of him," as astrologers term it, by having the Sun in his, or her, house. To understand this it must be borne in mind that each of the planets known to the ancients had, from the earliest foundation of astrology, or the AUR CHASDIM, one or more of the twelve zodiacal signs under its special rule. During the 2,160 years that the vernal equinox was found to be in the sign *Gemini* (the day-house of Mercury), the Sun was named, universally, *Buddha*, and was worshipped accordingly under that appellation. Astrology teaches that Mercury rules the brain. The Indian name of Mercury was *Buddha*. After 2,160 years from the first period of Buddha, or the Sun in Gemini, the precession of the equinoxes brought the vernal equinox into the sign *Taurus*; and then, as this is the house of Venus, the Sun partook of her character and became, instead of Buddha, that female being, known in Scripture as the "Heifer Baal." After another period of 2,160 years the vernal equinox fell in the sign *Aries*, the *ram*; accordingly, the Sun then became *Bal-aram*, because in that sign the Sun has his exaltation or chief power. Porphyry says,[16] "Hence a place near to the equinoctial circle was assigned to Mithra, as an appropriate seat, and on this account he bears the sword of Aries, which is a martial sign. He is likewise carried in the Bull, which is the sign of Venus; for Mithra, as well as the Bull, is the Demiurgus and Lord of Generation." The Greeks affixed the horns of the Bull to Bacchus, who was the Sun in Taurus, or Baal-chus, shortened into Ba-chus, the word chus signifying *black*, hence the black Baal. To the statue of Jupiter[17] they affixed a ram, because they would distinguish the two gods. In fact the Sun in these three signs, Gemini, Taurus, and Aries, was found everywhere. In Aries the Sun was called *Chrishna*, from which, probably, the Greeks formed their *Krios*, a ram, from the Chaldee, *Kresa*, a throne, or seat of power; in allusion to the power of the Sun when in Aries, his exaltation.[18] The romantic legend of *Sakya Buddha*, which has been lately translated from the Chinese-Sanscrit by Mr. Samuel Beal, contains a mass of striking evidence of the complete interweaving of astrology with religious tradition, and earthly sovereignty in the East. The struggle between *Buddha* (Mercury) and *Mâra* (Mars) is in strict harmony with astrological principles, for Mars is always at enmity with Mercury; and the victory achieved by Buddha over worldly allurements and the "terrible array" of Mâra's hosts, is singularly suggestive of the triumph of our Saviour over Satan.

A celebrated Persian philosopher lived in the reign of Darius Hystaspis, whose Persian name was Gushtasp. The "Ancient Universal History" relates of this personage that "in the reign of Gushtasp, King of Persia, a celebrated astrologer flourished whose name was Gjannasp, surnamed Al Hakim or the Wise. The most credible writers say that he was the brother of King Gushtasp, and his confidant and chief minister. He is said to have predicted the coming of the Messiah, and some treatises under his name are still current in the East." Dr. T. Hyde, writing of this philosopher, cites a passage from a very ancient

---

[16] "Cave of the Nymphs," Sect. ii., page 190, ed. Taylor.

[17] "Thorwaldsen one day dining with Bunsen at Rome, and becoming wearied of the theological conversation of his host, threw open the window, which commanded a noble prospect of the city, over which the planet Jupiter was shining with great splendour, and filled his glass 'to the honour of the ancient gods.'"—*Fraser's Mag*, Nov. 1875.

[18] See *Zadkiel's Almanac* 1868, pp. 62-71.

author who wrote an account of the very famous Persian doctors, as follows:

"Of these the sixth was Gjamasp, an astrologer, who was counsellor to Hystaspis. He is the author of a book entitled 'Judicia Gjamaspis,' in which is contained his judgment on the planetary conjunctions. Therein he gave notice that Jesus should appear; that Mohammed should be born; that the Magian religion should be abolished, etc. Nor did any astrologer ever come up to him."

In China astrology was established at the earliest periods of its existence as an Empire, and even Emperors were chosen on account of their astronomical skill. In the year 2513 B.C., this was the case with Chueni.

We are informed by Tillotson that a belief in astral influence was common for some thirteen hundred years before Christ.

In the book of Job we read, "Canst thou bind the sweet influences of Pleiades, or loose the bands of Orion?"

Hermes, the first great Egyptian astrologer, lived at a period anterior to that of Moses. The "*Tetrabiblos* or *Quadripartite*, being four books of the Influence of the Stars," written by Claudius Ptolemy, about the year 126, appears to have been chiefly based upon the teachings of Hermes.

Proctor, in his philippic[19] against astrology, was constrained to admit that "although astronomers now reject altogether the doctrines of judicial astrology, it is impossible for the true lover of that science to regard astrology altogether with contempt. Astronomy, indeed, owes much more to the notions of believers in astrology than is commonly supposed."

Proctor bears testimony to the fact that Seneca, "who was well acquainted with the uniform character of the planetary motions, seems to have entertained no doubt respecting their influence."

Tacitus, he says, "expresses some doubts, but seems on the whole inclined to believe in astrology. 'Certainly' he (Tacitus) says, 'the majority of mankind cannot be weaned from the opinion that at the birth of each man his future destiny is fixed; though some things may fall out differently from the predictions, by the ignorance of those who profess the art; and that thus the art is unjustly blamed, confirmed as it is by noted examples in all ages.'"

---

[19] *Vide* "Belgravia" for November and December, 1876.

Cicero's argument—"What contagion can reach us from the planets whose distance is almost infinite?"—was quoted by Mr. Proctor, but he omitted to mention the following observation of Cicero: "If the office and business of prophecy cannot be performed without the gift of prophecy, yet, notwithstanding that the prophet may prophesy falsely, it is sufficient for the establishment of his prophet power that he shall have once prophesied truly. But innumerable are such examples; therefore the existence of the powers of divination[20] must be conceded. . . . We see it, and hear it, and read of it, and have inherited it from our forefathers: before the beginning of philosophy—which is not so long ago—it was not doubted of in common life; and since philosophy has appeared no philosopher has thought otherwise—at least none worthy of esteem. I have spoken of Pythagoras, Democritus, of Socrates, and others." If we substitute the words "astrological science" for "prophet power," in the foregoing argument, we shall have a complete answer to those modern philosophers who rail against astrology.

In the common cant of the day, it is said that the Copernican system of astronomy overthrew astrology!

Pythagoras anticipated the discoveries of Copernicus, for he taught the diurnal revolution of the earth, and its annual motion round the Sun, which he supposed to be the centre of the planetary system; he did not regard these theories as antagonistic to judicial astrology, but accepted the prevailing belief, in his day, that "the stars do rule mankind."

Anaxagoras, who anticipated many of the discoveries made by means of the telescope, who thought that the Sun was a mass of fire, and that the Moon contained seas, mountains, and rivers, was also a believer in astrology. He foreshadowed, as it were, the molecular theory of our own age, and the infinitesimality and micrological nature of all motion and all things.

Pliny and others relate that Anaxagoras foretold the fall of a meteoric stone, about the second year of the 78th Olympiad, which occurred near the Egos, in Thrace. "It happened," says Pliny, "in sight of many, in the day time, a comet blazing at the time, and this stone was as big as a wain could carry, and was kept for a monument."

---

[20] The first men who reasoned of the stars were the first *divines*. In all nations which have emerged from barbarism the divines or priests have ever been astrologers. Hence Claudius Ptolemy was called "the *divine* Ptolemy."

Anaximander, the disciple of Thales (a renowned astrologer), regarded the planets as unconnected with the earth. He taught that the fixed stars were centres of other systems, perhaps more extensive and glorious than our own. He considered the Sun as a body of fire, and he taught that the earth moved round the centre of the universe. Pliny relates that he "foretold the earthquakes that overthrew Lacedaemon." He, too, was a great and renowned astrologer, a fact which has been concealed by Sir David Brewster, for fear astrology should gain credit thereby, I presume.

Democritus advanced the very same explanation of the whiteness of the milky way that Herschel discovered by means of his powerful telescopes, which separate that immense nebula into its component stars; and he maintained, though from an erroneous theory, that the number of the planets was not known, and that more would be discovered in succeeding ages. This prediction was fulfilled after an interval of more than 2,000 years.

It is impossible that Pythagoras, Anaximander, Anaxagoras, and the many other great men of old time who believed in and practised astrology, could have been blind to its falsity, if it were a false science as its enemies assert; and it would have been equally impossible for those ancient philosophers to have foretold events by means of "the signs in the heavens" had astrology no foundation in fact. Had Anaxagoras discovered that astrology was a delusion, he would not, most assuredly, have shrunk from publicly proclaiming such a discovery, for he did not shrink from incurring the penalty of death—afterwards mitigated into banishment, at the instance of his friend Pericles—for having promulgated his theories in regard to the Moon. The ancient philosophers before-named *examined* astrology; and were, therefore, in a far better position to judge of its claims to scientific truth, than was R. A. Proctor, who proved himself, by the blunders[21] he committed in his tirade against it, completely ignorant of its laws and principles.

---

[21] One of the errors consisted of Mr. Proctor's statement that "Jupiter occupied the house of wealth"—which is the *second* house, at the birth of H.R.H. the Prince of Wales; whereas that planet was *rising* at the moment (10h. 48m, a.m. of November 9th, 1841), given in the official bulletin. Another error consisted of Mr. Proctor's statement that the Sun was in the sign Cancer at the Prince's birth, when, in fact, as every schoolboy knows, the Sun is in Scorpio during the first twenty-one days of November. These errors, although they were pointed out in *Zadkiel's Almanac* for 1878, are to be found reproduced in the reprint of Mr. Proctor's paper on Astrology in his book entitled *Myths and Marvels of Modern Astronomy*.

Eudoxus, born 368 B.C., was distinguished for a knowledge of astrology, medicine, and geometry. He was the first who regulated the year among the Greeks.

Hippocrates, who devoted much study to astrology and prognostics declared that the physician who was ignorant of astrology was not worthy to be called a physician. It is a remarkable fact that the study of prognostics generally has been neglected by the medical profession since astrology fell into disuetude; and as the *Medical Press and Circular*[22] once stated, "some have gone so far as to say that the science of prognosis has advanced little since the time of Hippocrates."

Nigidius Figulus, the intimate friend of Cicero, obtained the hour of birth of Augustus Caesar, and declared that the ruler of the earth was born to the world!—as Suetonius relates.

The days of the week and the hours of each day, were assigned to the seven planets[23] (including the Sun and Moon). The Egyptians also assigned the months to the planets in regular order.[24]

The Romans dedicated the months as follows:

December was sacred to Saturn, the Sun being in his house (Capricornus), and Saturn being at the greatest distance from the Sun.

January was sacred to Janus, whose double face had its origin in the fact of the Sun in two successive signs being ruled by Saturn. It is remarkable that he and Saturn are said to have *governed together* in Italy.

February was sacred to Neptune, by which was meant Jupiter in his character as a sea-god, for his chariot was drawn by *Hippocampi*, which were *horses* in their foreparts and *fishes* in their hinder; thus exemplifying the two houses of Jupiter, *Sagittarius* the Archer, drawn

---

[22] "The Prognosis of Disease" (leading article), Nov. 7, 1877. Hippocrates predicted the advent of plague at Athens, and it is related that when it broke out in Greece, he dispelled it by "purifying the air with fires into which were thrown sweet scented herbs and flowers, along with other perfumes."

[23] *Vide Zadkiel's Almanac* for 1876, pp. 57-62. In the *Contemporary Review*, March, 1875, Mr. R. A. Proctor wrote on "Saturn and the Sabbath of the Jews" to show that the Oriental belief that Saturn's day (Saturday) was unfortunate, *dies infaustus*, when it was unlucky to undertake any work, was the origin of the Sabbath of the Jews. "The observance was derived from an Egyptian, and primarily from a Chaldean source."

[24] Godfrey Higgins says: "Throughout all the nations of the ancient world the planets are to be found appropriated to the days of the week" (*Anacalypsis*, Vol. I. page 6).

with partly the body of the horse, and *Pisces* the fishes. Two days in the month, the lst and 13th, were sacred to Jupiter.

March was named after *Mars*, the first day being sacred to him. The *Equiria* were games held on the 14th day, in honour of Mars.

April was sacred to Venus, to whom the lst and 23rd days were dedicated.

May[25] was so named from *Maia*, the Mother of Mercury, whose birth was said to have occurred on the 15th day. The 14th was sacred to Mercury, the Sun being in his house, *Gemini*.

June was named from Juno, who was the same as Diana, or Luna, the Moon. The first day was sacred to her. The Sun is then in her house, *Cancer*.

July was sacred to Jupiter, meaning Jupiter Ammon, being an Egyptian term for the Sun, the greater light being then in his own house (*Leo*). The *Ludi Apollinares* were eight days of festival held in his honour this month.

August was sacred to Ceres, the goddess of corn, who is drawn with a bunch of wheat in her hand, to represent the sign *Virgo*, the house of Mercury. The 13th day was sacred to *Vertumnus*, the god of change—the astrological character of Mercury.

September was under the protection of Vulcan, the husband of Venus, who was herself termed Vulcanus; thus Plautus: "*Vulcanus, Sol, Luna, Dies, dei quatuor, scellestiorem nullum illuxere alterum*"—Venus, the Sun, Moon, and Jupiter, four deities who never shine upon the unfortunate (a very good astrological aphorism). The Sun is this month in the house of Venus (*Libra*). It is remarkable that the 25th day was sacred to Venus and Saturn, and the 27th to Venus the mother. Saturn has dignities in Libra, which is the sign of his exaltation.

October was under the protection of Mars, in whose honour the *Armilustrium* festival and sacrifices took place on the 19th day, when the Romans assembled their army. The Sun is this month in the house of Mars, Scorpio.

November was under the protection of Diana, goddess of hunting; the 14th day was set apart for the trial of horses, *Lectisternia*, festival was held, also the *Neptunalia* games, all of these being allusions to

[25] "The worship of the equinoctial Sun in the sign Taurus, the remains of which are to be found in our May-day festivals, carries it back at least for 4,500 years before Christ" (*Anacalypsis*, Vol. I., page 9).

Jupiter, and the sign of the Archer (♐), which is his house. On the first day a solemn banquet, in honour of Jupiter, took place. These observances had relation to the Sun's passage this month through Sagittarius, the house of Jupiter.

The Greeks and Romans perverted the Chaldaean astrology into a mere system of divination, and rendered it almost entirely unfit for any genethliacal purpose. The Arabian astrology is a most superstitious mass of symbolical and allegorical trash—as Wilson averred. The mean, crafty, and selfish policy of the Egyptians, who, in order to keep the people ignorant of the grand truths of astrology, converted all their knowledge and observation into hieroglyphics, or transcribed it in the so-called "sacred letters" which belonged to an alphabet made use of by the priesthood only, the key of which once being lost all their learning was lost with it—this selfish policy contributed to cause astrology to be mixed up with many absurdities, and its original meaning to be almost entirely forgotten.

CHAPTER II.

INTRODUCTION.—Continued.

"Thence oblique
Brancheth the circle where the planets roll,
To pour their wished influence on the world."—DANTE

AMONG modern votaries of astrology we find on record the honoured names of Bacon (Lord Verulam), Roger Bacon, Baron Napier of Merchistoun (the inventor of logarithms), Flamstead (the first Astronomer Royal, and founder of Greenwich Observatory), Kepler, Archbishop Usher, Melancthon, Sir Elias Ashmole (founder of the Ashmolean Museum), Sir Christopher Heydon, Dr. Mead, Dr. Partridge, Dr. Blagrove, Cardan, Placidus, Burton, and the Rev. Dr. Butler.

Kepler—of whom it has been justly recorded that, "the history of philosophy affords no more remarkable instance of sincere, uncompromising love of truth"—honestly avowed that[1]: "a most unfailing experience of the excitement of sublunary natures by the conjunctions and aspects of the planets, has instructed and compelled my unwilling belief."

Flamstead transmitted to posterity a demonstration of his interest in astrology in the form of a map of the heavens, drawn by his own hand, for the moment of the laying of the foundation-stone of Greenwich Observatory. It may be seen among his MSS., carefully preserved, at the Royal Observatory. No remarks were appended to the figure (which is in the form of a square) by Flamstead, but the following phrase has been pencilled in the inner square by some learned astronomer hostile to astrology, viz., "*Risum teneatis amici.*"

The just renown, stability, and usefulness of the Royal Observatory, have amply vindicated Flamstead's judgment and foresight.

The following is a *fac simile* of Flamstead's figure:

---

[1] Extract from a work of Kepler's quoted in *Observations on the Life of Kepler*, published by the Society of Useful Knowledge, 1830.

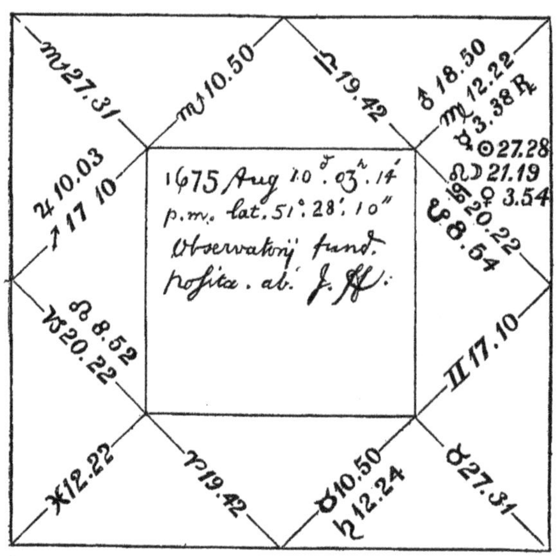

Figure l.
N.B.—Approximate place of ♅ is 29° ♓ 45′ retrograde.
Approximate place of ♆ is 13° ♒ 23′N retrograde.

Ramesey's "Rules for Electing Times for all Manner of Works,"[2] collected from writings of the ancients, contain the following precept: "Endeavour, therefore, at the beginning of thy work to fortify the lord of the ascendant, and cusp of the ascendant itself." Again, "have a special care that the Moon be not with Saturn, or dragon's tail, or Saturn in the ascendant or fourth house [of the heavens], for this will impedite the work and cause delays therein; and if the affliction be by Mars, and the ascendant be a sign of short ascension, it causeth fires therein."

An inspection of the figure shows the benefic planet Jupiter rising in his own sign *Sagittarius*, the eighteenth degree of which is placed on the cusp of the ascendant. On the meridian the fortunate star *Spica Virginis* is posited (but not marked in by Flamstead). The Sun and Moon are located in the fixed sign *Leo*, separating from the trine aspect of Jupiter, which planet receives, also, the assistance of the trine of Venus. Mercury—the planet having dominion over science and art—is posited in his own sign *Virgo*, elevated above the Sun and

[2] *Astrology Restored*, edit. 1653.

Moon, and "ruling" the ninth house of the heavens (that of science). Neither of the malefic planets (Mars and Saturn) is found in an angle. Hence it is manifest that Flamstead followed the wise precepts of the ancients as to "elections," and no amount of invective can "rail the seal from off the bond." As Solomon said: "To everything there is a season, and a time to every purpose under the heavens."

A passage in one of Flamstead's letters[3] may be quoted with a recommendation to the earnest consideration of the opponents of astrology:

"If you would particularly advise your colleague, Dr.___, to have a care of discoursing of things he is not acquainted with, and has only false, imperfect, or prejudiced information of, you would oblige me much."

In a paper on "Coincidences and Superstitions," which was printed in the *Cornhill Magazine* (December, 1872), the following anecdote was related in order to illustrate the prejudiced and narrow-minded ideas of the writer thereof:

"An old woman came to Flamstead, the first Astronomer-Royal, to ask him whereabouts a certain bundle of linen might be which she had lost. Flamstead determined to show the folly of that belief in astrology which had led her to Greenwich Observatory (under some misapprehension as to the duties of an Astronomer-Royal). He 'drew a circle, put a square into it, and gravely pointed out a ditch, near her cottage, in which he said it would be found.' He then waited until she should come back disappointed, and in a fit frame of mind to receive the rebuke he intended for her; but 'she came back in great delight, with the bundle in her hand, found in the very place.'"

No authority is given for the statement that Flamstead intended to rebuke the woman's faith in astrology; and the description given of the drawing of the figure of the heavens stamps it as "an invention of the enemy." The plain truth of the matter is that Flamstead drew the figure for the moment of consultation, and based his judgment and advice upon the rules of horary astrology. In all probability the planet which was significator of the lost bundle of linen was posited in the sign *Scorpio*, which, in horary questions as to lost or stolen goods, has always been held to indicate "a place of unclean water, such as a sink, ditch, or gutter." It is very probable that Flamstead, like Bacon, and others, believed not in *horary* astrology.

---

[3] Letter of Flamstead to the Rev. Dr. Wallis, June 24, 1701 (page 55, Vol. 33, Flamstead MS.).

The Rev. Dr. Butler *examined* astrology for the purpose of overthrowing it, but in the course of his studies he became convinced of its truth, and wrote a vindication of it. In his Introduction[4] he says:

"Myself must also needs acknowledge that some years since I also was one of those enemies to the noble science, who buffeted in the dark I knew not what, until sorely tempted to take a few lines reading in this subject, although it was with a serious purpose, to take up the after occasion to throw dirt at it; yet by this means attaining to understand who it was I spoke to, it begat in me a reverence to those gray hairs, which, as unjustly as ignorantly, I had despised."

Butler's three propositions were: "1. That there *is* an astrology in the Heavens. 2. That this astrology, man (in the state of corruption) may attain in some measure to understand. 3. That this understanding may be lawfully and fairly compassed by natural means, without any diabolical helps."

Bacon wrote of the state of the science in his day as follows:

"Astrology is so full of superstition that scarce anything sound can be discovered in it; though we judge it should rather be *purged*[5] than absolutely *rejected. But we receive astrology as a part of physics*, without attributing more to it than reason and the evidence of things allow, and strip it of its superstructure and conceits. Thus we banish that empty notion about the horary reign of the planets, as if each resumed the throne thrice in twenty-four hours, so as to leave three hours supernumerary; and yet this fiction produced the division of the week, a theory so ancient, and so universally received. . . . We will add one thing more, which if amended, and improved, might make for astrology, viz., *that we are certain the celestial bodies have other influences besides light and heat*. . . . So that, on the whole, we must register as needed, an astrology in conformity with these principles, under the name of *Astrologia Sana*. . . . Let this astrology be used with greater confidence in prediction, but more cautiously in election, and in both cases with due moderation."

---

[4] "AÃIAΣTPOΛOÃIΓA, or the most Sacred and Divine Science of Astrology. I. Asserted, in three Propositions, showing the excellency and great benefit thereof, when it is rightly understood and religiously observed. II. Vindicated, against the calumnies of the Rev. Dr. More. By John Butler, B.D., A Protestant Minister of the True, Antient, Catholick, and Apostolick Faith of the Church of England. London, M.C.D. LXXX."

[5] This was done by Zadkiel I as far back as 1830, when he published his *Herald of Astrology*. Partridge, in his *Opus Reformatum*, published in 1693, exposed the errors of Gadbury and others.

It may not be out of place here to mention a recent instance of planetary influence confounding the speculations of a philosopher. In the *Cornhill Magazine* (July, 1877), in a paper on "The Planet of War," by Proctor appeared the following words:

"But if Mars were in truth the Planet of War; if his influence, poured from near at hand upon the nations of the earth, excited them to war and bloodshed, we might well fear that the coming months would bring desolation on many terrestrial fields. Moreover, twice, during his time of greatest splendour his rays will be closely conjoined with those of the malignant planet Saturn."

At the time the foregoing paragraph was written, Proctor shared the belief of the Russian commanders that the crusade against Turkey would be but a military promenade, and would be ended in a few weeks. The fearful holocaust of victims to the unsuccessful attempts to take Plevna by storm (the sacrifice of life being greater than any known for centuries past) attested the power of Mars and the validity of his right to be called "the Planet of War." The war was foretold by the present editor of *Zadkiel's Almanac* (for 1877).[6] After the contributor to the *Cornhill Magazine* had exhausted the whole of his ingenuity and resources for arguments against the influence of Mars, it was an exceedingly cruel fate to have them scattered to the winds by means of the very circumstance to which he appealed as a test (Mars' nearest approach since 1798).[7] Perhaps the words of Longfellow (in his poem addressed to the planet Mars) recurred to his mind:

> "O Star of strength, I see thee stand,
> And smile upon my pain!"

Lavater said, "The true philosopher looks first to the positive proofs of the proposition—the superficial mind first examines the negative objections." Had Proctor *examined* first the *positive* proofs of planetary influence, before writing against astrology, he would never have brought upon himself a defeat so signal and crushing.

---

[6] See pages 19, 21, 23, 25, 27, and 42 of *Zadkiel's Almanac* for 1877; also pages 11, 39 to 43 of *Zadkiel's Almanac* for 1878. The conjunction of Mars and Jupiter in 0° 1′ 56″ of *Capricorn* (the sign ruling Bulgaria), which took place on March 1st, 1877, foreshadowed the religious crusade entered upon by Russia against Turkey and predicted in that annual.

[7] Mars was in *perigee* on September 7th, 1877; and in exact *conjunction* (in ♓ 13° 45′ 21.4″) with Saturn, at 11h, 28m, 20s p.m., (G. M. T.) of November 3rd, 1877.

Dean Stanley, in his sermon (1878),[8] said:

"It is a deplorable recoil from the progress which either now or formerly has substituted the barbarian desire for destruction, for the civlised desire for reform and improvement. Yet still in all these cases there remains a permanent solution when even the failures disappear and the success comes at length. The nineteenth century may close in darkness, but the twentieth century will dawn in light. The prophets whom we stone, our sons will honour." Alluding to the terrible catastrophe caused by the capsizing of the *Eurydice*, during a sudden squall, the Dean said: "The calamities of this world, so it would seem, come not by accident, but by *fixed laws*, by a *combination of causes* which, on looking back, seems irresistible."

Opponents of astrology would do well to ponder over these words of Dean Stanley, and examine the proofs of planetary influence in the light of their meaning. It has been frequently asked by our opponents why Sir Isaac Newton rejected astrology? Newton's biographer says of him that, "A desire to know whether there was anything in judicial astrology first put him upon studying mathematics. He discovered the emptiness of that study as soon as he erected a figure." This, to say the least, was certainly a very sudden discovery; and if he really did no more than merely erect a figure of the heavens, we can easily understand how and why the great Newton may be quoted as an opponent of astrology. This science is altogether founded on *experience*; hence if any man, however high may be the order of his genius, would not condescend to give it even a cursory examination, he could, of course, know nothing of it from his own experiments, and could not fairly lay claim to a right to deny its truth.

The medical student, who, on inspecting a mere drawing of the human skeleton, should declare that he had discovered the emptiness of the study of medicine, would be justly regarded as no authority whatever on the subject. We may, therefore, form the same opinion of Sir I. Newton's alleged discovery of the emptiness of astrology. *He did not examine, therefore he could not understand*, he could not justly condemn—for "*ne damnent qua non intelligunt*."

It must be noted, too, that at the time of this *ipse dixit* of Newton against astrology, he was not twenty-four years old. As it is known that Sir Isaac did not rashly bring forward any of his great discoveries, but allowed nearly forty years to elapse from the time of their first

[8] Sermon preached in Westminster Abbey, on Good Friday, 1878, reported in the *Daily Telegraph* of April 20th, 1878.

conception till their publication, the fact of his ever having given any such opinion about the principles of a science which he had not studied, may be reasonably doubted.[9]

Cardan, a physician of Milan, born in 1501, who was a very learned man, and a celebrated algebraist, who gave rules for resolving cubic equations, which still bear his name, was also an astrologer of high repute. He was sent for to cure the Archbishop of St. Andrews of a painful disorder which had baffled all the physicians of France and Germany; and having succeeded, he returned through London, where he calculated the nativity of King Edward.

Didacus Placidus de Titus, an Italian monk, who published many elaborate works on Mathematics, was a renowned astrologer. He wrote the *Primum Mobile*, and gave therein the nativities of thirty eminent men of Europe to demonstrate the truth and reality of astrology.

Among the English astrologers we find almost every name of any note in the mathematical world, from the days of the Conquest down to those of Lord Bacon. To begin with, we find the name of Oliver of Malmesbury, in the year 1060, who is the oldest English writer on mathematics. We next find Herbert of Lorraine, 1095. John of Hexham, and Simeon of Durham, come next in order, in 1160 and 1164, respectively, who wrote of comets; Sigidius of St. Albans, in 1224, physician to the King of France, and an author on astronomy. Roger Bacon, born in 1214, who was the friend of Fisacre and Shirewood, both known as mathematicians, and of Robert Grouthead the Bishop of Lincoln. Roger Bacon was the most extraordinary man of his day, and spent the enormous sum, in those times, of £2,000 in experiments, instruments, and scarce books. In his works he spared neither the ignorance nor the want of morality of the clergy, who found, consequently, no difficulty in persuading the vulgar that he was possessed with the devil. In 1256 died the famous John of Halifax; his name was really John Holywood, but he was known on the continent as Sacrobosco. "His work on the Sphere was for centuries almost as general an object of study as Euclid himself." It was written from Ptolemy's *Almagest*, translated into Latin from Arabia by order of the Emperor Frederick II. Before Newton, he was one of the ablest men England ever produced. Michael Scot, the famous wizard of Scotland in 1290; Duns Scotus, in 1304; William Grizaunt, 1350; Clinton Langley and John Killingworth, 1360; John Estwood, 1365; John

[9] There is some reason to believe that there may be a work on astrology in the possession of Oxford University, by Newton.

Chylmack, 1390; and King Richard II, in 1392—who, it is asserted by Sherbrun wrote "something in Astronomy or Astrology, now (1675) extant in his Majesty's library at St. James's." The poet, Geoffrey Chaucer, wrote a treatise on the Astrolabe, in 1410. "John Walter, 1410, wrote astronomical tables for the purposes of Astrology; and appears to have been more esteemed than we might now suppose to have been the case"—says a modern writer. The good Duke of Gloucester (1440) composed astrological tables of directions. Robert Recorde, the physician, a man whose memory deserves much greater fame than has been accorded to it, on several accounts; he was the first who wrote on arithmetic, astronomy, and the sphere, in English, the first to introduce algebra into England, and the first Englishman who adopted the system of Copernicus. Dr. Dee, who professed magic also, by way of showing that this was an exception, and not the rule with astrologers; he died in 1572.[10]

Baron Napier, to whom the world is indebted for the invention of logarithms, and of whom, one of his contemporaries wrote: "He was a general scholar, and deeply read in all divine and human histories," was, also, a great astrologer.

"James Bassantin, a Scotch astronomer, son of the Laird of Bassantin, in Merse, was born in the reign of James IV. He was educated at the University of Glasgow, travelled through Germany and Italy, and then fixed his abode in the University of Paris, where he taught mathematics with great applause. Having acquired some fortune, he returned to Scotland in 1562, where he died in 1568. From his writings he appears to have been no contemptible astronomer, considering the times, but like most of the mathematicians of that age, he was addicted to judicial astrology. Sir James Melvil, in his memoirs, says that his brother Sir Robert, when he was exerting his abilities to reconcile the two Queens, Elizabeth and Mary, met with one Bassantin, a man learned in the high sciences, who told him that 'all his travel would be in vain, for,' said he, 'they will never meet together; and next, there will never be anything but dissembling and secret hatred for awhile, and at length captivity and utter wreck to our Queen from England.' He added 'that the kingdom of England at length shall fall of right to the crown of Scotland; but it shall cost many bloody battles, and the Spaniards shall be helpers and take a part to themselves for their labour.' Sir James Melvil is an author of

[10] See *The Life of Dr. John Dee* by Charlotte Fell Smith. Constable, London, 1909, l0s. 6d.

credit, therefore we may believe that Bassantin did utter this prediction."[11]

Tycho Brahe not only carefully studied the comet of 1577 as an astronomer, but as an astrologer predicted, from its appearance, that: "In the North, in Finland, there should be born a Prince who should lay waste Germany, and vanish in 1632." Gustavus Adolphus, it is well known, was born in Finland, overran Germany, and died in 1632.

Poets, from time immemorial, have sung the praises of astrology, viz., Aratus, Aeschylus, Manilius, Virgil, Horace, Homer, Propertius, Macrobius, Chaucer, Dante, Milton, Dryden, Campbell, Byron, Scott, Schiller, Shakespeare, etc.

Horace asked: "Why does one brother like to lounge in the forum, to play in the campus, and to anoint himself in the bath so well, that he would not put himself out of the way for all the wealth of the richest plantations of the East; while the other toils from sunrise to sunset for the purpose of increasing his fortune?" Horace very correctly attributes this diversity of character to the influence of genius, and the *natal star*.

Dryden was skilled in astrology. He foretold danger of an accident to his son Charles in his thirty-third year, who was drowned near Windsor, while swimming across the Thames, having survived two severe accidents in his eighth and twenty-third years, both of which accidents his father had also predicted from his nativity. It is related in the "Life of Dryden," that the poet told his wife that their son Charles was born in an unlucky hour, because the Sun, Venus, and Jupiter were all below the horizon, and the ruler of the ascendant was afflicted by the quartile aspect of both Mars and Saturn.

---

[11] *Imperial Cyclopaedia*, Vol. I., page 391.

CHAPTER III.

GENETHLIACAL ASTROLOGY.

"In my stars I am above thee—Some
Are born great, some achieve greatness,
And some have greatness thrust upon
Them."–SHAKESPEARE.[1]

BACON, whose advocacy of an *Astrologia Sana* has been already alluded to, rejected, what he regarded "as all idle figment," namely, "the doctrine of horoscopes, and the distribution of houses, though these are the darling inventions of astrology, which have kept revel, as it were, in the heavens. And lastly, for the calculation of nativities, fortunes, good or bad hours of business, and the like fatalities, they are mere levities, that have little in them of certainty and solidity, and may be plainly confuted by physical reasons." The absurd and mischievous mixing of horary (or symbolical) astrology with genethlialogy on the part of some of the English astrologers of the middle ages may have led Bacon to the conclusion above named. When, however, genethliacal astrology is stripped (as Partridge, and Zadkiel I. and II. stripped it) of the admixture referred to, it can no longer be "confuted by physical reasons"; and, on the contrary, by the Baconian method of induction, its truth can be demonstrated.

Sir Francis Galton wisely observes:[2]

"I have no patience with the hypothesis occasionally expressed and often implied, that babies are born pretty much alike, and that the sole agencies in creating differences between boy and boy, and man and man, are steady application and moral effort. It is in the most unqualified manner that I object to pretensions of natural equality. The experiences of the nursery, the school, the university, and the professional careers, are a chain of proof to the contrary. I acknowledge freely the great power of education and social influences in develop-

---

[1] *Twelfth Night*, Act II., Scene 4.

[2] *Hereditary Genius: An Inquiry into its Laws and Consequences*. By Sir F. Galton, F.R.S.

ing the active powers of the mind, just as I acknowledge the effect of use in developing the muscles of the blacksmith's arm, and no further. The eager boy when he first goes to school and confronts intellectual difficulties, is astonished at his progress; he glories in his newly-developed mental grip and growing capacity for application, and, it may be, fondly believes it to be within his reach to become one of the heroes who have left their mark upon the history of the world. The years go by, he competes in the examinations of the school and college, over and over again with his fellows, and soon finds his place amongst them. He knows that he can beat such and such of his competitors; that there are some with whom he runs on equal terms, and others whose intellectual feats he cannot even approach."

Galton proceeds, further, to illustrate the fact of genius being innate, or congenital, instead of hereditary—although he does not suspect the true cause:

"In statesmanship, generalship, literature, science, poetry, art, just the same enormous differences are found between man and man. I am sure that no one who has had the privilege of mixing in the society of the abler men of any capital, or who is acquainted with the biographies of the heroes of history, can doubt the existence of grand human animals; of natures pre-eminently noble, of individuals born to be kings of men."

Galton relates of the Lord Chancellors, that:

"Lord Harwicke was the son of a small attorney at Dover, in narrow circumstances; Lord Eldon (whose brother was the great Admiralty judge, Lord Stowell), was son of a coal-fitter; Lord Truro Tenterden, the Chief Justice of Common Pleas), was son of a barber. Others were sons of clergymen of scanty means; others have begun life in alien professions, yet notwithstanding the false start, have easily recovered lost ground in after life. Lord Erskine was first in the navy, and then in the army, before he became a barrister. Lord Chelmsford was originally a midshipman. It is a mere accident if a man is placed in his youth in the

[3] This is one of the many instances of what the world loses in consequence of the neglect of astrology; for a clever astrologer can always indicate the occupation for which a person is best fitted, on inspection of the figure of the heavens for the moment of his birth. Kepler was brought up as a waiter in a German public-house; Ben Jonson was a mason: Lord Clive was a clerk; Inigo Jones was a carpenter; Turner, the greatest of English landscape painters, was a barber; Hugh Miller was a bricklayer; Sir William Herschel was educated especially for a musician.

profession for which he has the most special vocation."[3]

To believers in astrology it is curious and interesting to perceive how closely Galton has reasoned to the true cause of the similarity of the personal features, characters, and careers of twins,[4] without ever suspecting it. Astrologers find that the closer the approximation of the respective moments of birth of twin children, the closer is the similarity of their personal appearance and character, and the closer is the correspondence of the events of their lives. It is well-known to *accoucheurs* that the intervals between the births of twins vary very greatly. In some cases the interval has not exceeded three or four minutes, while in other cases it has been known to extend to hours, and even days. Every four minutes' interval of time brings another degree of right-ascension on the meridian. Consequently, a difference of half an hour in the times of birth would make a great difference in the part of the sign of the zodiac ascending, and (as one degree of arc represents one year of life, in "primary directions") would alter the periods of occurrence of the subsequent events. The whole sign of Aries only takes (in the latitude of London), about fifty-two minutes in ascending. Hence, it is evident that a difference of half an hour might give *Aries* ascending at the birth of one child, and *Taurus* at the birth of the second. In signs of long-ascension the difference would not be so great. In one case Saturn might be culminating or rising, and in the other might be cadent, which would make a great difference in the chances of life, and prospects and health of the two children. Galton says:

"The steady and pitiless march of the hidden weakness of our constitution, through illness to death, is painfully revealed by the histories of twins. We are too apt to look upon illness and death as capricious events, and there are some who ascribe them to the direct effect of supernatural interference, whereas the fact of the maladies of two twins being continually alike shows that illness and death are necessary incidents in a regular sequence of constitutional changes beginning at birth,[5] upon which external circumstances have, on the whole, very small effect. In cases where the maladies of the twins are continually alike the clock of life moves regularly on governed by internal mechanism. When the hand approaches the hour mark,[6] there is a sud-

[4] *The History of Twins, as a Criterion of the Relative Powers of Nature and Nurture*, by Francis Galton, F.R.S.

[5] Just as astrologers have ever taught.

[6] Or, as the astrologer would say, "when the fatal train of 'arcs of primary direction' comes up."

den click, followed by a whirring of wheels; the moment that it touches it the stroke falls. Necessitarians may derive new arguments from the life-history of twins."

Proctor cited the case of Jacob and Esau, as telling against astrology, because, being twins, their fortunes "should manifestly have been similar, which was certainly not the case, if their history has been correctly handed down to us." Taking the account given in the Bible of their births as correct, a considerable interval must have occurred between their respective moments of birth; so the objection that their fortunes were not similar cannot be fairly urged against the doctrine that twins born very near together, in point of time, have similar fortunes, similar tastes, &c.—a fact which Galton's researches have incontestably proved.[7]

In the course of a letter to the *Times* of May 31st, 1910, Sir Francis Galton wisely observed:

"It is now generally admitted that the apparent vacancy of space is a plenum of ether, that vibrates throughout like a solid."

Sceptics in regard to astrology are mostly like Proctor, who declared that he would not inquire whether astrology was true or not. They hate the very name of astrology, and their object appears to be not to discover any truth which is distasteful to them, because of their narrow-minded views and prejudices instilled into them by their teachers who were in the habit of repeating the parrot-like cry that astrology is an "exploded" science, notwithstanding that when challenged they cannot say who exploded it.

As Sir Oliver Lodge recently said: "They should always mistrust negation, which commonly signified blindness and prejudice."

Believers in astrology are often told that public and scientific opinion is against it, but, as Max Muller once wisely observed:

"What is public opinion to a scholar and lover of truth?"[8]

The Rev. Dr. Butler says:

"Some men do come into the world in a lucky hour, so as whether they be wise or foolish, yet shall they be buoyed upon the wings of fate, for matter of wealth, or honour, or pleasure, in all that they take

---

[7] See the article on Twins, etc. (in answer to the criticism of the *Referee* of July 30th, 1893) in FUTURE, September, 1893.

[8] Essay on "The Lesson of Jupiter," in the *Nineteenth Century*, October 1885, by Professor Max Müller. Commented upon by the author in STAR LORE, October, 1898.

to; while wiser and better men, smitten by an unlucky time of birth, shall be as unworthily disparaged, and in all purposes shall be as unhappy. Some shall be lucky in the van of their contrivances, and as unfortunate in the rear; and others again contrarily. Astrology shows us plainly the wonderful contrivance of God in Nature, that we see it with our eyes, as it were, written in great and plain characters on fair paper."

CHAPTER IV.

THE ALPHABET.

> "Heaven's golden alphabet—
> And he that runs may read."—YOUNG.

THE Alphabet of Astrology comprises thirty-two symbols, representing the Sun, Moon, planets, signs of the zodiac, certain differences of longitude called aspects, and the Moon's nodes.

The first division comprises nine characters:

☉ The Sun.	♀ Venus.	♄ Saturn.
☽ The Moon.	♂ Mars.	♅ Uranus.
☿ Mercury.	♃ Jupiter.	♆ Neptune.

The second division comprises twelve symbols:

NORTHERN.	SOUTHERN.
♈ Aries.	♎ Libra.
♉ Taurus.	♏ Scorpio.
♊ Gemini.	♐ Sagittarius.
♋ Cancer.	♑ Capricornus.
♌ Leo.	♒ Aquarius.
♍ Virgo.	♓ Pisces.

The third division comprises eight characters:

☌ Conjunction, when two heavenly bodies have the same longitude.

s ⚹ Semi-sextile, when their difference of long. is 30°, or 1 sign.			
s □ Semi-quartile,	"	"	45°, or 1½ signs.
⚹ Sextile,	"	"	60°, or 2 signs.
□ Square,	"	"	90°, or 3 signs.
△ Trine,	"	"	120°, or 4 signs.
ss □ Sesquiquadrate,	"	"	135°, or 4½ signs.
☍ Opposition,	"	"	180°, or 6 signs.

There are other aspects, viz., the vigintile (18°), the quindecile (24°), the decile (36°), the quintile (72°), the tredecile (108°), the biquintile (144°), and the quadrasextile (150°). All these aspects were suggested by Kepler, and their influence is undeniable, with the exception of the vigintile, quindecile, and the tredecile, which require confirmation. When two or more heavenly bodies are in equal or parallel declination (north or south), the effect of their combined influences is as great as when in conjunction. When at parallel distances in proportion to their semi-arcs from either the upper or lower meridian, they are in mundane parallel.

The *major* aspects are: the conjunction, parallel declination, mundane, and rapt parallel, sextile, square, trine, and opposition.

The *minor* aspects are: the vigintile, quindecile, semi-sextile, decile, semi-quartile[1], quintile, tredecile, sesquiquadrate, biquintile, and quadrasextile.

The fourth division comprises two symbols:

☊ The Moon's north node.	☋ The Moon's south node.

BENEIFIC ASPECTS.	UNFAVOURABLE.
Conjunction[2], Trine,	Opposition[3], Quadrature,
Sextile, semi-sextile,	Sesquiquadrate, semi-quartile,
biquintile, decile, quintile.	quadra-sextile.

When the student has committed the foregoing symbols to memory, it will be advisable for him to learn the signs which are opposed to each other, viz.:

♈	is opposite to	♎	♋	is opposite to	♑
♉	"	♏	♌	"	♒
♊	"	♐	♍	"	♓

The following table will enable the student to determine the zodiacal position of a heavenly body whose longitude is reckoned from the first point of Aries:

[1] The *mundane* semi-quartile when formed, by *direction*, by a planet angular at birth to the ascendant and mid-heaven, is powerful.

[2] The Conjunction of the Sun, Moon, or Mercury, with Mars or Saturn is unfavourable.

[3] The opposition of the Sun or Moon with Jupiter is less evil than with Mars or Saturn.

From	♈	0° 0′	Entering	♏	210° 0′
Entering	♉	30° 0′	″	♐	240° 0′
″	♊	60° 0′	″	♑	270° 0′
″	♋	90° 0′	″	♒	300° 0′
″	♌	120° 0′	″	♓	330° 0′
″	♍	150° 0′	″	♈	360° 0′
″	♎	180° 0′			

CHAPTER V.

ON THE RIGHT-ASCENSION, DECLINATION, &c., OF THE HEAVENLY BODIES.

"The virtue and motion of the sacred orbs,
As mallet by the workman's hand, must needs
By blessed movers be inspired."—DANTE.

THOSE of my readers who may happen to have forgotten the outlines of astronomy which were taught them at school or college, will do well to look them up again; and those who possess a copy of my "Weather Guide Book" will find (in the first chapter) some remarks on the Sphere, &c.

"RIGHT-ASCENSION" and "DECLINATION": If the Equator be taken as the great circle of reference, the first point of Aries is chosen as the origin. The abscissa of any heavenly body, whose position is thus referred, is called its "right-ascension" (R.A.); and its ordinate is called its "declination" (dec.) The R.A. varies from 0° to 360°, and is measured from the first point of *Aries* in the direction of west to east. The declination varies from 0° to 90°, and is either upper or under, *i.e.*, north or south.

"ASCENSIONAL DIFFERENCE": When the Sun is on the Equator it rises in a right sphere, and its arc above the earth is exactly twelve hours, one half of this (diurnal semi-arc) is six hours. When, however, the Sun has *north* declination it is more than six hours, from the time of sunrise, coming to the zenith (at noon). The difference between six hours and the Sun's diurnal semi-arc, is its "ascensional difference." It depends on the amount of declination, for in proportion as the Sun declines to the north, it rises in a sphere which is declined towards the north—an *oblique* sphere; it rises before six o'clock and sets as much after six o'clock, p.m., and the day exceeds the night in duration. When the Sun declines from the Equator towards the south, it rises after six o'clock, and sets before six o'clock p.m.—the day is then shorter in duration than the night. In all cases the difference between sunrise and six o'clock is the Sun's ascensional difference. This ascensional difference added to the Sun's right-ascension if it has south declination, but subtracted therefrom if it has north declination, gives its "oblique ascension."

"LONGITUDES" and "LATITUDES": If the Ecliptic be taken as the great circle of reference, the first point of *Aries* is chosen as its origin. The abscissa of any heavenly body, whose position is thus referred, is called its "longitude " (long.); and its ordinate is called its "latitude" (lat.). The longitude varies from 0° to 360°, and is measured from the first point of ♈ in the direction of west to east. The latitude varies from 0° to 90°, and is either upper or under, *i.e.*, north or south.

"ASPECTS" or CONFIGURATIONS: Two heavenly bodies have either the same longitude, or else different longitudes. If they have different longitudes their difference of longitude is the remainder left after subtracting the less from the greater. Since the long. of two heavenly bodies may have any value from 0° to 360° the difference of longitude of two heavenly bodies may have any value from 0 to 360°. But if this difference exceed 180°, we add 360° to the smaller value, and then deduct the other from it. Certain differences of longitude of two heavenly bodies (Sun, Moon, or planets) have been termed "aspects between the two bodies." They are in all fifteen, as stated in Chapter V. The first two aspects occur when the difference of long. is either 0° or 180°. In the former case the two bodies are in "conjunction," in the latter case they are in "opposition." The remaining thirteen aspects occur when the difference of long. is of the following magnitudes: 18°, 24°, 30°, 36°, 45°, 60°, 72°, 90°, 108°, 120°, 135°, 144°, and 150°, or the 20th, 15th, 12th, l0th, 8th, 6th, 5th, 4th, and 3rd parts of the whole circumference, and the difference between a semi-circumference and the 5th, 8th, l0th, and 12th parts respectively.

"DIRECT " and "RETROGRADE" MOTION: When a planet moves forward in the zodiac in the order of the signs, its motion is "direct." When a planet appears to move in the contrary manner, its motion is "retrograde."

"STATIONARY" POSITIONS: When a planet appears to stand still in the heavens, it is said to be "stationary," and its effect is then very powerful.

"ELEVATIONS": The Sun, Moon, or planet nearest to the zenith at the moment of birth, is "elevated" above the rest. An elevated planet when in aspect to another is the more powerful of the two.

"GEOCENTRIC" and "HELIOCENTRIC" POSITIONS: The position of a heavenly body as seen from the Earth's centre, is termed "geocentric"; and that which has relation to the Sun's centre is termed "helio-centric." The geocentric positions, only, are considered in genethliacal astrology, because they have relation solely to the earth.

"RAPT MOTION": The apparent daily motion of the heavens from east to west is called "rapt motion."

"MUNDANE" ASPECTS: These consist of the conjunction, parallel, semi-sextile, semi-quartile, sextile, quintile, square, trine, sesquiquadrate, biquintile, and opposition. When two heavenly bodies are two houses apart they are in mundane sextile; when three houses apart they are in quartile; when at equal distances from the meridian (and having semi-arcs of the same value) they are in mundane parallel; a planet exactly culminating is in mundane square to the ascendant; a planet rising is in mundane trine to another planet situated on the cusp of the 9th or 5th house; the remaining aspects are determined in like manner, in proportion to the semi-arcs of the heavenly bodies.

The mundane aspects are wholly independent of the zodiac; a planet on the upper meridian is in mundane square to another on the ascendant, and at the same time may have a sextile in the zodiac with it.

All the mundane aspects were demonstrated by Placidus, who, however, affirmed that they were known and referred to by Claudius Ptolemy, because he writes of the sextile of the Sun and Venus, an aspect which Venus can never form with the Sun in the zodiac. There can be no doubt that they are powerful, but they are inferior to zodiacal aspects. Wilson was as much prejudiced against the mundane aspects as Placidus was in favour of them. Reference to figure 2 will render them easily understood.

CHAPTER VI.

ON DIVIDING THE HEAVENS.

"Between two worlds life hovers like a star,
'Twixt night and morn, upon the horizon's verge."—BYRON

THE ancient inhabitants of Hindostan, Chaldaea, Persia, Egypt, &c., divided that portion of the heavens visible at a given moment of time into six equal parts, which they called "Mansions," or "Houses." The opposite portion, invisible from being below the horizon, were also divided by them into six equal and corresponding mansions, and these twelve divisions (corresponding in number to the signs of the zodiac) they termed the TWELVE HOUSES.

Claudius Ptolemy adopted the same method, and in addition suggested the construction and use of the *zodical planisphere.*

Regiomontanus divided the heavens into twelve equal parts in the equator, but not in the zodiac. This division was commended by Morinus as the most exact extant, yet he complained of its deficiency, and claimed to have supplied its defect by an invention of his own. Although the method of Regiomontanus was called "Modus Rationalis," it is not correct, and is inferior to that of Placidus. It is, therefore, unnecessary to reproduce it here; but those of my readers who are curious in this matter will find a description and criticism of it given by Partridge in his valuable work, *Defectio Geniturarum.*

The true method is that of Claudius Ptolemy, Placidus, Oxley, and Zadkiel; it is the *semi-arc* method (which is the *true motion* in Nature), consisting each (house) of *two temporal hours*, either of the place or star—that is, by a proportional division of the motions of the moveable arcs from one *angle* to another. A diurnal arc is always equal to an *opposition aspect*, although it may measure more or less than 180°; a planet rising is always on the horizon *opposite* to that where it sets. Of course, there can only be 180° between the two points when the planet is on the *equator*; but when in other places, its diurnal arc must measure either more or less than 180°, and more or less than twelve hours. But, whatever may be its arc from horizon to horizon, the space of the *house*, in which it is located, will always be one-sixth of that arc (or what has been called its "double horary time"), which is one-third of its semi-arc. And as its *whole* arc is equal to an *opposition* aspect (though it may not be exactly of the value of 180°), so is its *semi-arc* equal to a *square* aspect (though not exactly 90°); and, therefore, a planet on the horizon is in mundane square aspect to another planet on either meridian.

The term "Chakravartis," in Sanscrit, literally means "turners of the wheel"—and it is applied to kings who have great power and dominion.[1] The wheel, so constantly introduced in the ancient Budhistic and Brahminical religions, was an emblem of the circles formed by the heavenly bodies.

The "Chart," or "Figure of the Heavens," is simply a scheme, or plan, presenting an accurate picture of the heavens—*i.e.*, the positions and longitudes of the Sun, Moon, and planets, and, in some instances, certain of the fixed stars also—for the moment at which a child is born. It shows what planets may be rising, southing, setting, or on the lower meridian, &c. In *mundane* astrology the figure of the heavens is drawn for the required time.

It has two hemispheres—the upper being the *diurnal*, and the lower the nocturnal hemisphere—which are divided, of course, by the horizontal line. It has two other grand divisions, effected by the line drawn from the upper to the lower meridian. These four divisions are the *east*, *south*, *west* and *north angles* respectively; the *south* angle being *above* the earth, and the *north* angle *below* it. In the *northern* hemisphere of the globe, the *east* angle is on the left hand side of the figure, and the *west* on the right. But in the *southern* hemisphere this arrangement is reversed, the *east* angle is on the *right* hand side of the figure (a point which must be borne in mind when the student has to erect a figure for a *southern* latitude). The most powerful angle is the *south*, the next in order of power is the *east*, then come the *west* and the *north*. The distance between the meridian and the horizon is always the same, measured by *oblique* ascension, namely, 90°, or one-fourth of the circle.

For the purpose of illustrating the subdivisions which have now to be made, let us suppose that the first degree of *Aries* (the first point of the zodiac) is *ascending*; the opposite point (the first degree of *Libra*) will be *descending*; the first degree of Capricornus will be on the upper meridian; and the first point of Cancer on the lower meridian. If

[1] "Chakravartin" is rendered "a universal monarch" by Mr. Beal who translated the Chinese version of the " Abhinishkramana Sutra."

the Sun be rising in the first point of *Aries*, then he is crossing the equator, and the days and nights are equal, it is the *vernal equinox*. The Sun rises, accordingly, at six o'clock, culminates at twelve (noon), sets at six in the evening, and arrives at the *imum cali* at midnight. At eight a.m., the Sun will have risen 30° (he is, therefore, in mundane *sextile* aspect to the mid-heaven, and in mundane *semi-sextile* to the ascendant), and this being one-twelfth part of the circle, the Sun has passed through *one house* (and is on the cusp of what is called the *twelfth house*). In two hours more the Sun arrives at the *sextile* of the ascendant and *semi-sextile* of the mid-heaven, and has passed through *two houses* (or 60°). He is now on the cusp of the *eleventh house*. At noon he has passed through a *third house* (he is in *conjunction* with the mid-heaven). Each *quadrant* of the heavens is, therefore, subdivided into *three houses*, making in all TWELVE HOUSES.

When the Sun is not on the equator, the proportions of his *semi-arc* must be taken (in *trisections*) to find the time at which his centre will pass the cusp (*i.e.*, the beginning) of any of the minor houses.

The houses which are next in rotation to the angles are called *cadent*. They are the 12th, 9th, 6th, and 3rd houses. The ancients regarded a planet located in a cadent house as extremely weak, in nativities, but I think this is a mistake—at least in regard to the 12th and 9th houses (a star located in either of these houses is *above* the earth). The power of any celestial body is increased by being angular. The houses next in order of succession, are called *succedent*. They are the 11th, 8th, 5th, and 2nd. In nativities, the power of a planet posited in the 2nd house has been much exaggerated by the ancient and some of the modern astrologers. In fact, too much reliance has been placed on the power of the houses in nativities, an error which Zadkiel I. and Wilson pointed out, and cautioned their readers against.

The following figure is inserted with the view of making the text clearer:

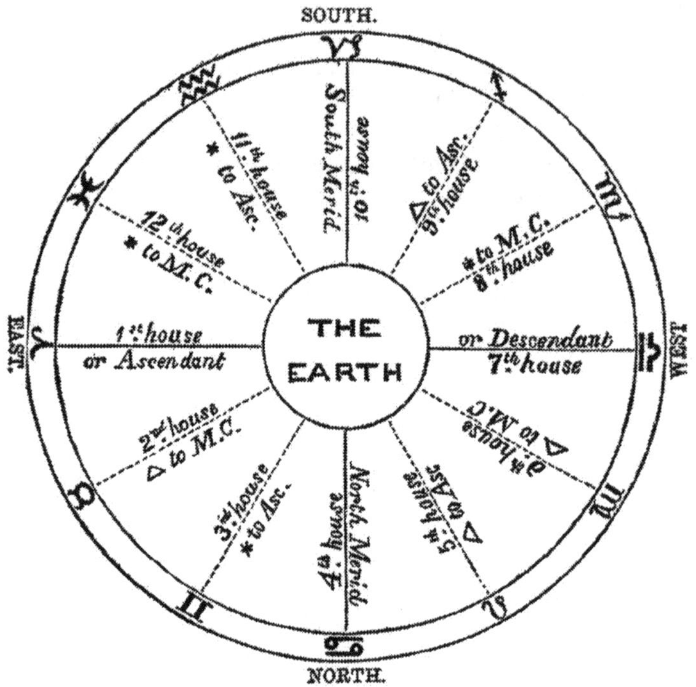
SOUTH.
NORTH.
EAST.
WEST.
THE EARTH
10th house
South Merid.
11th house
* to Asc.
12th house
* to M.C.
1st house
or Ascendant
2nd house
△ to M.C.
3rd house
* to Asc.
4th house
North Merid.
5th house
△ to Asc.
6th house
△ to M.C.
7th house
or Descendant
8th house
* to M.C.
9th house
△ to Asc.

Figure 2

CHAPTER VII.

ON CASTING A FIGURE OF THE HEAVENS.

"I'll know the stars, which yet alone to gain
Is knowledge mean, unequal to the pain;
For doubts resolved, it no delight affords,
But fills soft empty heads with rattling words;[1]
I'll search the depths, the most remote recess,
And flying Nature to confession press;
I'll find what sign and constellation rule,
And make the difference 'twixt the wise and fool,
My verse shall sing what various *aspect* reigns
When kings are doom'd to crowns, and slaves to
chains."—MANILIUS.[2]

A MAP of the Heavens should be drawn in the *circular* form.

Rule A, 1°. Draw a circle (with a diameter of four inches is a convenient size) to represent the heavens; within which draw a smaller circular (of one inch in diameter) to represent the earth. Then draw a straight line, horizontally, through the outer circle to represent the horizon. Next, draw a vertical line, at right angles from the first, to represent the meridian. The four quadrants thus formed must next be subdivided, each into three parts. Mark the *Midheaven* (*above* the earth) with the letter S, or the letters M.C. (*medium-cali*) and the lower meridian I.C. (*Imum cali*). If the figure to be drawn is for a northern latitude, mark the *left*-hand extremity of the horizontal line E, or *ascendant*; and the opposite point, W. It will be advisable to mark off the numbers of the various houses on the edge of the outer circle, bearing in mind that the ascendant is the first house.

---

[1] These words will apply to some of the nineteenth century (*soi-disant*} "really scientific" men, who mistake mere *learning* for *knowledge*.

[2] "The Five Books of Manilius; containing a system of the Ancient Astronomy and Astrology, together with the Philosophy of the Stoicks," were translated and published by Mr. Thomas Creech, in the year 1700.

2°. Observe either in the *Nautical Almanac or Zadkiel's Ephemeris*, for the year of birth, the amount of *Sidereal Time* at the *mean noon preceding* the time of birth given. Write this down—correcting it for the longitude of the birthplace if far from Greenwich by adding 9.86^{s} per hour if the longitude is west, and subtracting if it is east. Note how far the given time differs, in hours, minutes, and seconds from the preceding noon (or twelve hours in the day, by a good clock or chronometer). *Add* this to the *sidereal time* already written down; and *add*, also, the correction for the difference between *mean* and *sidereal* time,[3] at the rate of 9.86^{s} per hour elapsed since noon. If the sum exceed twenty-four hours, deduct that amount. The sum is the *Right-ascension* of the *meridian* at the given time of birth.

[Note.—Some of the old *Ephemerides* (White's are the best of those prior to 1840) do not give the *sidereal* time at noon. In such case, the *right-ascension* of the *Sun* must be found for the noon preceding the birth (and if not given it can be readily calculated from the *Tables of Right-Ascension*, by observing the *longitude* of the Sun at noon), and this right-ascension (in degrees and minutes) can be converted into time by multiplying it by 15 (as one hour answers to 15°), if a table for reducing degrees to time[4] be not at hand. The value obtained in this manner must now be corrected for *equation of time*; and the amount (always given in White's *Ephemeris* daily at noon) must be added or subtracted according to whether the clock is *fast* or *slow*. Next, add the time elapsed since noon (and the correction for reduction of *mean* to *sidereal* time) in the manner before described.]

3°.—With a "Table of Houses" for the nearest latitude, if one be at hand, enter the first column and find the nearest *riqht-ascension* to that which you have obtained, and mark the values therein given on the cusps of the houses, the numbers of which are found at the heads of the respective columns, entering on the opposite houses the same degrees of the opposite signs. [If no "Tables of Houses" can be procured calculated to within 2° or 3° of the latitude of the birthplace, this process will have to be effected by means of a method which will be found in the *Formulae for Computing Longitude, &c.*]

4°.—Place the Sun, Moon, and planets in the figure (after having by the rule of proportion, reduced their longitudes from the noon pre-

---

[3] A Table to Reduce *Mean* to *Sidereal* Time is given in Chambers' *Mathematical Tables*.

[4] A table is given for this purpose in Chambers' *Mathematical Tables*.

ceding the birth, as given in the *Ephemeris*,[5] to the time of birth), taking care to place them in the proper *houses*, which may easily be done if it is remembered that the degrees pass over the cusps of the houses from left to right. The Moon's ascending ("dragon's head"), or descending ("dragon's tail") *node*, need not be marked in the figure, unless the Moon happens to be very near one of them.

B.—How to Cast a Figure of the Heavens for a Southern Latitude.

Rule 1°. Compute the R.A, of the meridian in the usual manner (taking care to correct the sidereal time for the *longitude* of the birth-place), by adding 9.86^s for each hour, and proportional parts thereof for the minutes and seconds, of *West* longitude, or by *subtracting* the same for *East* longitude.

2° Draw the figure, taking care to number the houses from *right to left*, making the angle on the *right* hand the ascendant and that on the *left* the descendant, or 7th house. Mark the upper meridian M.C. and the lower I.C.

3° Compute the longitudes to be inserted on the various houses by the rule given in the appendix, viz., *Oblique ascension given to find ecliptic longitude*.[6]

4° Find the Greenwich mean time corresponding to the given time at the place of birth, and compute the longitudes of the Sun, Moon, and planets thereto.

C.—The Speculum.

The "Speculum" is a table containing the latitudes, declinations, right-ascensions, meridian distances, and semi-arcs, of the Sun, moon, and planets, and should always be appended to a Nativity. The *data* referred to may be calculated from the *Nautical Almanac* for the year of birth, or from the "Tables" given in this work. The planets' *latitudes* are given in the *Ephemeris*, and can be reduced to the time of

---

[5] When an old *Ephemeris* is used, care must be taken to ascertain if it is calculated to *mean* or *apparent* time. If to the latter, rectification will be required, which is effected in the same way as that already described in the *Note* to 2°, when dealing with the Sun's R. A. *Zadkiel's Ephemeris* is computed for *mean* time, and requires, therefore, no such rectification.

[6] "Tables of Houses" for many northern and a few southern latitudes (cities of importance) are given in my FUTURE (June 1893 to July 1894). A set of these numbers may be had of the author, price 6s. 6d.

birth given by proportion, in the same way as their longitudes. The student can, of course, make his speculum include other data than those mentioned above, if he desire to make it very complete.

D.—To Draw a Map of the Heavens by Means of a Terrestrial Globe.

Rule 1°. Raise the north pole (if the latitude of the birthplace be north) to the degree of the latitude of the place. Bring the hour and minute of the right-ascension of the meridian to the brass meridian. The degree of the ecliptic, culminating, will now be seen on the meridian; and that which is rising will be seen on the eastern horizon.

2°. Reduce the pole to the degree given in the "Table of the Poles of Houses" for the eleventh house, add two hours to the R.A. on the zenith, and bring the sum of R.A. to the eastern horizon; when the longitude of the ecliptic on the eleventh house will be found to be cut also by the horizon.

3°. Alter the pole to the degree of the pole of the twelfth house (found by the Table of Poles), add four hours to the R.A. of the mid-heaven, and bring the amount thus gained to the eastern horizon; when the longitude of the ecliptic to be placed on the cusp of the twelfth house, will be found to be cut by the horizon.

4°. Leave the pole at the last-named elevation, add eight hours to the R.A. on the meridian, and bring the value thus obtained to the eastern horizon; and the longitude of the ecliptic to be marked on the cusp of the second house will be found to be cut by the horizon.

5°. Reduce the pole again to the same elevation as for the eleventh house, add ten hours to the R.A. on the meridian, and bring the sum thus gained to the eastern horizon; when the longitude to be marked on the cusp third house will be found to be cut by the horizon.

6°. On the cusps of the houses opposite to those above enumerated, insert the corresponding degrees of the opposite signs, and the map will then be ready for the insertion of the Sun, Moon, and planets.

E.—The True Moment of Birth.

The true moment of birth may be taken as that when the child first *cries*. It sometimes happens that the infant is born asphyxiated or unconscious; in such cases the moment at which the funis is severed by the accoucheur must be taken as the true (astrological) time of birth. When the birthplace is remote from London the *local* mean time must be taken.

CHAPTER VIII.

CALCULATION OF NATIVITIES

How just and wise,
And good, is the Contriver of the skies;
At whose command the stars in order met,
Who times appointed when to rise and set;
That Heaven's great secrets may be hid no more,
And man, instructed, gratefully adore.—MANILIUS.

THE FIGURE OF THE HEAVENS is usually termed the Horoscope, whereas the degree of the zodiac ascending is really the horoscope. The late Dr. Richard Garnett contributed to the *Classical Review*, July, 1899, a most valuable paper "On Some Misinterpretations of Greek Astrological Terms,"[1] in which he wrote as follows:

"Even those who may consider the correct definition of astrological terms in a Greek dictionary, a matter of slight intrinsic importance, will allow that it may be discussed with profit if it serves to draw attention to the necessity of bringing the chief Greek-English lexicon to a level with the philological requirements of the day.

"The misconceptions of astrological terms in Liddell and Scott's, and other dictionaries proceed chiefly from the omission to note the astrological significance of the word ᾷρυ, which in Manetho and similar writers means neither an *hour* nor a *season*, but *the degree of the zodiac ascending at any nativity*. Manetho uses the term perpetually, and never in any other sense. Whether his Latin translator understood him or not is uncertain, but unquestionably he invariably renders ᾧρυ by *hora*, which if taken literally involves sheer absurdity. Where Manetho, for example, says (VI. 321):

ετ χᾲὶ ὤᾳ̂ὶ ἐν τετρᾲπεδετστ κυθεὐροτς,

the translator makes him say Si etiam *horam* in quadrupedibusreperias. The occurrence of an hour in a quadruped must be highly exceptional; but what Manetho means, is, 'should the

[1] Vide my STAR LORE, September, 1899, pp. 37-40, for a fuller quotation, by the kind permission of Dr. Garnett, from the paper.

degree ascending be in a quadrupedal sign,' such as *Leo*, for example. That ὥρη denotes the degree ascending here and elsewhere is patent from inumerable passages. A great part of Manetho's third book is occupied with the description of the supposed effects of planets when occupying the angles of a nativity, *i.e.*, rising, southing, setting, or opposed to the meridian."

In the *Medical Press and Circular* December 26th, 1877, three cases of puerperal convulsions were quoted from the clinical records of the Rotunda Hospital, Dublin. In the second case, the time of birth of the child was stated as 3h. 40m. p.m. of November 20, 1877. As this case affords a means of verifying the aphorism attributed to Claudius Ptolemy, relating to children insusceptible of nurture, the figure of the heavens may be taken as the first example. In order to avoid the possibility of dispute as to the true right ascension of the meridian, it shall be computed from the *Nautical Almanac* for 1877, wherein, at page 183, the sidereal time at Greenwich mean noon of November 20th is given, thus:

Sidereal Time, G.M. noon	15h.	58m.	25.28
Add correction for long. of Dublin 25m. 21s. W.			4.17
Sidereal time at Dublin	15	58	29.45
Add the time of birth	3	40	0.00
Add difference of mean and sidl. time 3h. 40m.			36.14
R.A. of M.C. 294° 46′ 24″=	19	39	5.59

Declinations

☉ 19° 50′ 12″ S.	♀ 25° 28′ 48″ S.	♄ 8° 25′ 30″ S.
☽ 23° 56′ 49″ N.	♂ 4° 54′ 36″ S.	♅ 12° 23′ 18″ N.
☿ 21° 33′ 57″ S.	♃ 23° 24′ 40″ S.	♆ 11° 39′ 1″ N.

Referring to the Tables of Right Ascension it will be found that 294° 46′ will give the sign *Capricornus* 22° 56′ on the upper meridian. "Tables of Houses" for Dublin[2] give *Aquarius* 14° on the cusp of

[2] "Table of Houses" for Dublin and for every degree of longitude in Great Britain, St. Petersburg, Adelaide, Brisbane, Paris, Rome, Washington, Cairo, Benares. etc., were given in my FUTURE, 1892-94.

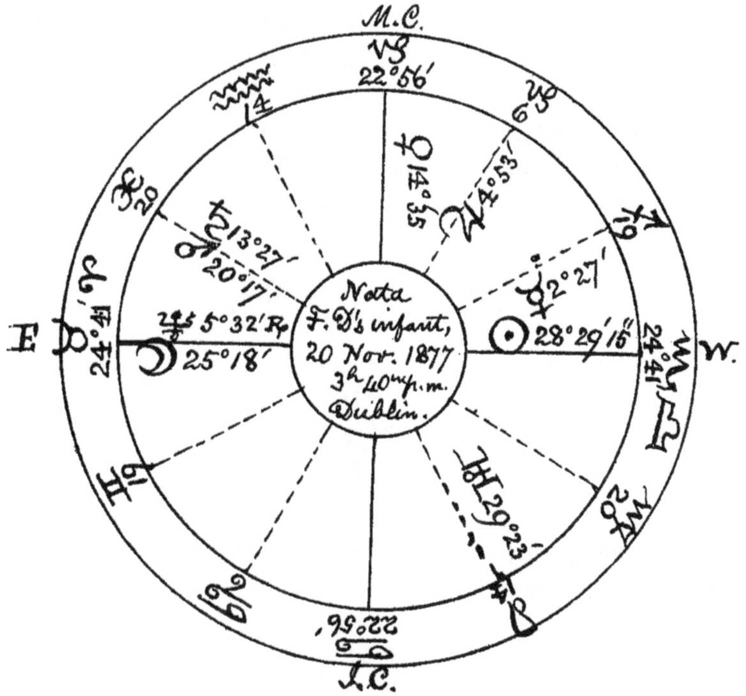

Figure 3

the eleventh house, *Pisces* 21° on the twelfth, *Taurus* 24° 41′ on the ascendant, *Gemini* 19° on the second, and *Cancer* 6° on the third house. The sign *Aries* is intercepted in the twelfth house, and its opposite, *Libra*, in the sixth.

The *longitudes* of the Sun, Moon, and planets may be readily found, by proportion, from those given of them at the noon preceding and that following the time of birth in *Zadkiel's Ephemeris* for 1877. The time of birth being Dublin mean time must be first reduced to the corresponding Greenwich mean time by adding the longitude of Dublin 25m 21s to it. This makes 4h 5m 21s G.M.T. after noon on the 20th of November, 1877. The Sun's longitude at noon of the 20th day was Scorpio 28° 18′ 56″, and on the 21st, 29° 19' 33"; his motion in the twenty-four hours was therefore 1° 0′ 37″. Then, by the golden rule of three:

As the ternary proportional logarithm of 24h (a.c.)		9.12494
To " " "	4h 5⅓m	1.64364
So " " "	1° 0′ 37″	.47268
To " " "	10′ 19″+ =	1.24126
Long. of ☉ at noon	28 18 56	
Long. of ☉ at birth is ♏	28 29 15	

For the Moon's longitude:

As prop. log. of 12h (a.c.)		8.82391
To "	4h 5⅓m	1.64364
So ☽ motion 6° 39′ 25″		1.43240
To "	2° 16'+ =	1.89995
Long. of ☽ at noon	23 ♉ 2	
	25 ♉ 18	

The ancient aphorism given in the *Tetrabiblos* is as follows:

"If either of the two luminaries [Sun and Moon] be in an angle, and one of the malefics [Mars and Saturn] be either in conjunction with that luminary, or else distant in longitude from each luminary in an exactly equal space so as to form the point of junction of two equal sides of a triangle, of which two sides the two luminaries form the extremities; while at the same time no benefic planet may partake in the configuration, and while the rulers [or disposers] of the luminaries may be also posited in places belonging to the malefics, the child then born will not be susceptible of nurture but will immediately perish."

In the nativity under consideration, the Sun is in the descendant or western angle, the Moon is close to the ascendant by longitude, although already risen having 4° 59′ of north latitude, and within three degrees of exact opposition with the Sun; and the evil planet Uranus is in quadrature (90° aspect) with both Sun and Moon. The Sun in the martial sign Scorpio. The malefic planets, Mars and Saturn, are elevated above the Moon, and neither the Sun (hyleg) nor the Moon has any adequate assistance from either Jupiter or Venus, the latter planet being in semi-quartile with the Sun.

The child, a female, lived "only for about twenty hours, and was very puny and feeble. Very great difficulty was experienced in establishing respiration, artificial respiration being kept up for nearly five hours before natural respiration was fairly established." The mother,

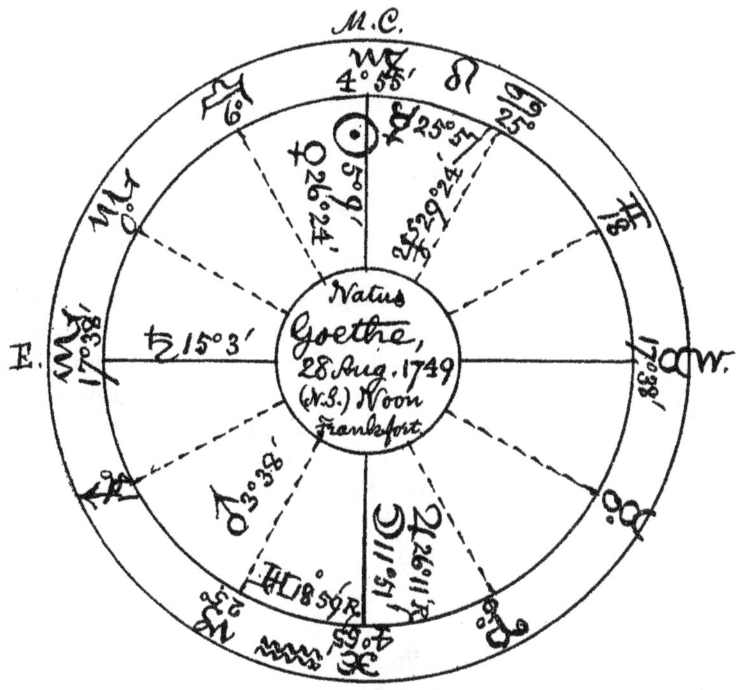

Figure 4

LATITUDE		
☽	4°	7′N.
☿	1	38N.
♀	1	9N.
♂	4	22S.
♃	1	37S.
♄	2	8N.
♅	0	45S.
♆	0	20S.

DECLINATION		
☉	9°	38′N.
☽	3	19S.
☿	14	23N.
♀	2	30N.
♂	27	47S.
♃	3	1S.
♄	14	30S.
♅	15	41S.
♆	19	57N.

who was only nineteen years old, recovered from a very dangerous attack of convulsions.

The truth of Ptolemy's aphorism is supported in this instance in a remarkable manner, for the afflicting planet Uranus was unknown to that ancient and renowned astronomer and geographer; and it is found to be distant in an almost exactly equal space of ninety degrees of the ecliptic from each luminary, the Sun, hyleg, being in the western angle of the heavens. Despite all that surgical skill could do for the child, she was insusceptible of nurture, and did immediately perish.

EXAMPLE II.—Goethe, in his autobiography[3] relates that:

"On the 28th August, 1749, at mid-day, as the clock struck twelve, I came into the world, at Frankfort-on-the-Maine. My horoscope was propitious. The Sun stood in the sign of the Virgin, and had culminated for the day. Jupiter and Venus looked on him with a friendly eye, and Mercury not adversely; while Saturn and Mars kept themselves indifferent. The Moon, alone just full, exerted the power of her reflection all the more, as she had reached her planetary hour. She opposed herself therefore to my birth, which could not be accomplished until this hour was passed. These good aspects, which the astrologers managed, subsequently, to reckon very auspicious for me, may have been the causes of my preservation; for, through the unskilfulness of the midwife, I came into the world as dead, and only after various efforts was I enabled to see the light."

Parker's *Ephemeris* for 1749—a copy of which may be inspected at the British Museum—gives the Sun's longitude at noon of the 17th of August (O.S.)[4] as Virgo 5° 10′. The Table of Right Ascension gives R.A. 157° 0 ′ corresponding to this longitude; the clock was 0m 53s fast, therefore 13′ 15″ must be subtracted therefrom, and as the longitude of Frankfort-on-the-Main is, in time, 34m 45s East of Greenwich, 1′ 25″ must also be subtracted, thus making the R.A. of the Midheaven 156° 45′ 20″, which gives Virgo 4° 55′ as the longitude to be placed on the upper meridian.

The latitude of Goethe's birthplace is 50° 6′ 43″ N. The ascendant is, accordingly *Scorpio* 17° 38′.

In Goethe's nativity the Sun is hyleg and is, happily, free from affliction by Saturn, Mars, Uranus, and Neptune. The ascending position of Saturn delayed the birth and danger of asphyxia followed. It is open to doubt whether his coming into the world "as dead" was owing to the unskilfulness of the midwife, for every skillful obstetric physician meets with such cases occasionally. Indeed, it was a very fortunate circumstance that the birth did not take place half an-hour earlier, when Saturn was exactly on the Eastern horizon (or ascendant), for in such case Goethe would have been liable to suffer from some chronic

---

[3] "The Autobiography of Goethe." *Truth and Poetry. From my Own Life*. Translated from the German by John Oxenford. Bohn. Vol. I. Book I. Chap I.

[4] The Germans had adopted the New Style.

ailment, or deformity, or to serious accidents, from time to time.

EXAMPLE III.—In the first volume of the "Life of the Prince Consort," the time of birth is given of Prince Albert, to the nearest hour, in a letter written by the Dowager Duchess of Coburg-Saalfeld to the Duchess of Kent: Rosenau, August 27th, 1819. The date will of itself make you suspect that I am sitting by Louischen's bed. She was yesterday morning safely and quickly delivered of a little boy. . . . at six the little one gave his first cry in this world."

White's Ephemeris for 1819 gives the longitude of the Sun at noon of the 25th of August as *Virgo* 1° 23′ 51″; his right ascension may be found by the following process:

Logarithm Cosine of O.E. 23° 27′ 58″	9.9625058
Tangent 28° 36′ 9″ (from ♎ 0° 0′ 0″)	9.7366150 +
Tangent of 26° 34′ 23″ =	9.6991208

Then 180° 0′ 01″ - 26° 34′ 23″ = 153° 25′ 37″
or 10h 13m 42s.5 = R.A. of Sun.

Subtract for Equation of Time			
	31 0	or	2 4.0
	152°54 37	or	10 11 38.5
Subtract for long. of Rosenau, 11° 2′E.			
	1 49		7.25
	152 52 48	or	10 11 31.25
Add time elapsed since noon			
	270 51 0	or	18 3 24
Add diff. mean and sidl. time			
	44 30	or	2 57.98
	424 28 18		28 17 53.23
Subtract the circle			
	360 0 0	or	24 0 0
The R.A. of the Mid-heaven is			
	64 28 18	or	4 17 53.23

The longitudes of the Sun, Moon, and planets have now to be computed by proportion from *White's Ephemeris* for 1819, for 17h 17m 12s of August 25th, Greenwich Solar Time, and entered in the figure of the heavens. The declinations and right-ascensions can be readily found by means of the Tables of R.A. and declin. given in this work, and entered in the Table or Speculum attached to the diagram.

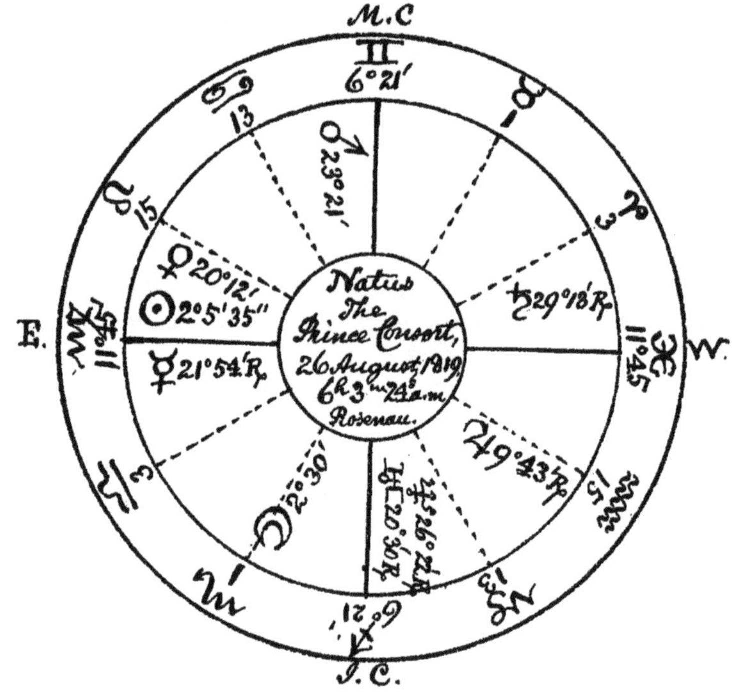

Figure 5

The Speculum

	Lat.	Declin.	Rt. Asc.	Mer. dist.	Semi-Arc.
☉		10° 44′ N	154° 5′	89° 37′	103°11′
☽	1°50′S	14 3 S	209 38	34 50	107 32
☿	4 10 S	0 36 S	170 54	73 34	90 43
♀	15 N	15 46 N	142 58	78 30	109 52
♂	0 9 S	12 9 N	82 46	18 18	120 59
♃	0 56 S	18 44 S	312 27	67 59	114 6
♄	2 29 S	2 35 S	0 16	64 12	86 53
♅	0 8 S	23 16 S	259 39	15 11	121 9
♆	1 16 N	22 9 S	266 4	21 36	119 21

For example, Uranus is in longitude 20° 30′ of *Sagittarius*, and in latitude 0° 8 South, what is his declination?

(a.) The Table of Declination headed "Sagittarius with South latitude," gives the declin. corresponding to 20° without lat. as 23° 5′, and

21° gives 23° 10′, difference 5′. Now say: as 60′ of long. are to 5′ of declin., so are 30′ to 2′ 30″ +. Opposite the long. of 20° and in the column headed 1° of lat., we find 24° 5′ of declin. Now say: as 60′ of lat., are to 60′ of declin., so are 8′ of lat. to 8′ of declin.+. Then as the differences so found are both *plus*, they must be added together, thus to 8′ + 3′ (rejecting the seconds) = 11′, and this added to 23° 5′ = 23° 16′ as the declination of Uranus at the time of birth.

(b.) Let it now be required to find the right-ascension of Uranus. Reference to the Table of R.A., "Sagittarius with South latitude," shows that 20° of Sagittarius without latitude is (adding 180° to the 79° 7′ given) 259° 7′, and that of 21° is 260° 12′, difference 65′. Now say: 60′ : 65′ : : 30′ : 32′ 30″ +. On a line with 20° of Sagittarius and in the column headed 1° of lat. it is seen that the R.A. is 259° 2′ difference 5′. Then say: 60′ : 5 : : 8 : 0′ 40″-. As the first difference is *plus* and the second *minus*, the latter must be subtracted from the former: 32′ 30″ - 0′ 40″ = 31′ 50″ *plus*, or 32′, which, added to 259° 7′, gives the R.A. of Uranus as 259° 39′.

(c.) The meridian distance is £ound by taking the difference between the R.A. of the nearer meridian and that of the planet. In this case, Uranus being below the horizon, we must subtract the R.A. of the lower meridian (obtained by adding180° 0′ 0″ to that of the upper meridian) 244° 28′ from 259° 39′ and thus find the meridian distance of Uranus to be 15° 11′.

(d.) The Semi-arc of a celestial body is found by adding the logarithm tangent of its declination to the log. tang. of the Pole of the Ascendant (which is the latitude of the birthplace) and the sum is the log *sine* of the ascensional difference, which must be added to 90° if the planet is below the horizon, and in south declination, or above the earth and in north declination; and subtracted if the celestial body is above the horizon and in south declination, or below the horizon and in north declination. When, in computing primary directions the body directed changes its hemisphere, its opposite semi-arc can be found by subtracting the one given in the speculum from 180°.

Let it be required to find the Semi-Arc of Uranus:

Logarithm tangent of	50° 17′N. lat. of Rosenau	10.0805519
"	23° 15½′ declin. of Uranus	9.6332727
"	sine of 31° 9′ 28″ asc diff. =	9.7138246

As Uranus is below the horizon and in south declination, 31° 9′ + 90° = 120° 9′ his (nocturnal) semi-arc.

The declinations, right ascensions, meridian distances, and semi-arcs of the other celestial bodies being computed and entered in the table, the speculum is completed, and is ready as the basis for the calculation of the arcs of primary direction. The reason for adopting the rectification of the stated time of birth, six o'clock a.m. to six hours, three minutes and twenty-four seconds a.m. will be given in the chapter on Rectifying a Nativity.

The aspects in the Prince Consort's horoscope are: Sun sextile Moon; Moon applying to par. dec. Venus and semi-quartile Uranus; Mercury semi-sextile Venus, quartile Mars and Uranus, sesqui-quadrate Jupiter; Venus trine Uranus, sextile Mars; Mars separating from opposition with Uranus and applying to opposition with Neptune, and sesqui-quadrate Jupiter; Jupiter semi-quartile Neptune; Saturn quartile Neptune; and Uranus within six degrees of conjunction with Neptune. Midheaven (M.C.) proximate trine of Jupiter.

EXAMPLE IV.—H.R.H. the Duke of Connaught opened the first South African Parliament on the fourth day of November, 1910, at noon, Capetown meantime, latitude 33° 56′ South, and longitude 1h 13m 55s East of Greenwich.

Sidereal Time at Greenwich mean noon	14h 51m 24.19s
Correction for 1h 13m 5s E.	12.15
R.A. of the Midheaven, 222° 48′ 1″ =	14 51 12. 04

The longitudes of the Sun, Moon, and planets have now to be computed from *Zadkiel's Ephemeris* (pp. 46, 47 of *Zadkiel's Almanac* for 1910) for 11h 46m 5s a.m. of November 4th, Greenwich mean time, and placed in the respective signs, and houses, in the figure 6.

The Midheaven is *Scorpio* 15° 16′, and the Ascendant is *Aquarius* 20° 31′. The Sun has passed the upper meridian and is in the ninth house, in 11° 7′ 50″ of the sign *Scorpio*. The Moon is in the tenth house, in *Sagittarius* 6° 42′. Mercury is in the ninth house, in 6° 8′ of *Scorpio*, very near Venus in 5° 39′ of the same sign. Mars has just separated from Jupiter (their conjunction having taken place at 3h 34m a.m. of the same day), and is in 28° 35′ of Libra, Jupiter being in 28° 27′ of the same sign, in the ninth house. So that five of the celestial bodies are within a space of 38° 15′, and near the upper meridian. This augurs a brilliant future for United South Africa, under the British flag. Nevertheless, Saturn in the third house, and Uranus in the twelfth, seems to pre-signify some trouble with a neigh bouring, ambitious nation, and from secret foes, from time to time. Jupiter, ruler of the eleventh and second houses, being in conjunction with Mars,

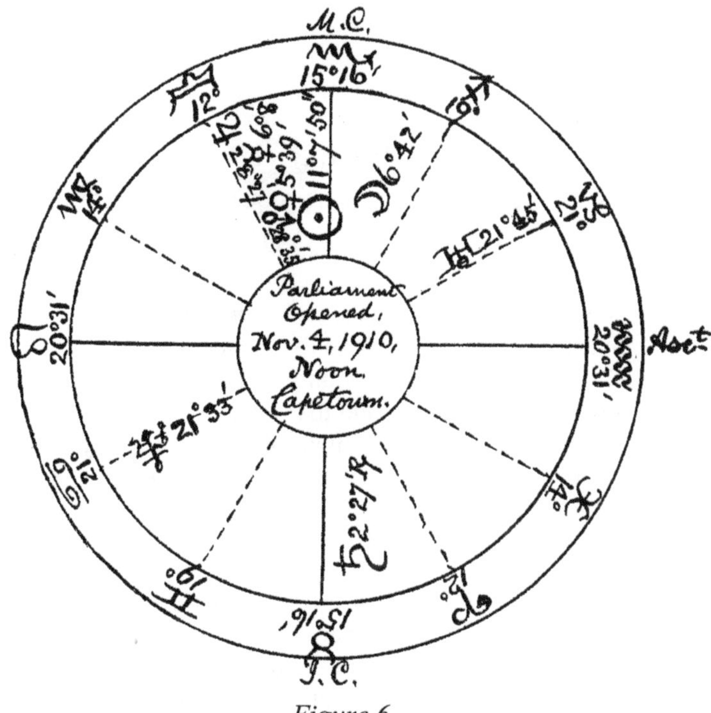

Figure 6

pre-signifies some serious squabbles in Parliament over financial measures, and some racial antagonism for a time. Applied science, music, art, and literature, will be advanced greatly in South Africa.

Before proceeding further, the student is advised to make himself master of the foregoing rules for casting horoscopes.

"Tables of Houses" for Prague, lat. 50° 5′ N., Taunton, lat. 51° 1′ N., Buckingham, 52° N., Nottingham, 52° 57′ N., Dublin, 53° 23′ N., York, 53° 57½′ N., Newcastle-on-Tyne, 54° 59′ N., Edinburgh, 55° 57′ N., Aberdeen, 57° 9′ N., Wick, 58° 27′ N., St. Petersburg, 59° 56½′ N., Adelaide, 34° 56′ S., Brisbane, 27° 28′ S., Paris, 48° 50′ N., Rome, 41° 54′ N., Washington, 38° 54′ N., Lat. 35° 0′ N., Cairo, 30° 2′ N., and Benares, 25° 19′ N., were all given in FUTURE, June 1893 to July 1894, inclusive, enabling students to cast horoscopes readily for any place in Great Britain, and Europe, and two important places in the Southern Hemisphere.

The formulae for computing the longitudes of the eleventh, twelfth, first, second, and third houses, are given in the appendix.

CHAPTER IX.

THE SIGNS AND CONSTELLATIONS OF THE ZODIAC.

> Now *constellations* Muse; and *signs* rehearse;
> In order let them sparkle in thy verse;
> Those which obliquely bound the burning zone,
> And bear the summer and the winter Sun—
> Those first: then those which roll a different way
> From west, nor Heaven's diurnal whirl obey,
> Which nights serene disclose, and which create
> The steady rules, and fix the laws of Fate.—MANILIUS.

The zodiac is a band or belt measuring about 14° in breadth, but, as Venus sometimes appears to have double her real or heliocentric latitude, it is more correctly considered to be 18° in breadth. The ECLIPTIC, or path of the Sun, passes exactly through the centre of the zodiac, longitudinally.

The ancients divided the zodiac into *ten signs—Libra* being omitted altogether, *Virgo* and *Scorpio* being merged into one thus: Virgo-Scorpio. Hence the similarity of their symbols, ♍ ♏.

Claudius Ptolemy hands down to posterity the division of the zodiac into *twelve equal parts*, of 30° each. He says[1]: "The beginning of the whole zodiacal circle (which in its nature as a circle can have no other beginning or end, capable of being determined), is, therefore, assumed to be the sign Aries, which commences at the vernal equinox." Ptolemy speaks of "the ambient" as producing the effects attributed to the respective signs of the zodiac, when in the ascendant at a Nativity.

The first sign, *Aries*, extends 30° in *longitude* from the equator and 11° 29′ in *declination*. The fifth sign, *Virgo*, has the same value in declination from the equator, yet experience proves that the general character of the respective influences of the stars in these signs is totally different.

---

[1] *Tetrabiblos* Book I., Chap. xii.

That the names assigned to the various divisions of the zodiac are appropriate is abundantly proved by the experience of ages, although, at first sight, they may appear to be fanciful and arbitrary.

Ptolemy writes of the influences of the signs of the zodiac as follows:[2]

"It is the *general* tendency of the quadrant comprised between the vernal equinox and the summer tropic to produce good complexions, advantageous stature, fine constitutions, and fine eyes; with a temperament abounding in heat and moisture.

"The quadrant from the summer tropic to the autumnal equinox tends to produce an ordinary complexion, proportionate stature, a healthy constitution, large eyes, a stout person, with curled hair, and a temperament abounding in heat and dryness.

"The quadrant from the autumnal equinox to the winter tropic causes yellowish complexions, slender, thin, and sickly persons, with a moderate growth of hair, fine eyes, and a temperament abundantly dry and cold.

"The other (remaining) quadrant, from the winter tropic to the vernal equinox, gives a dark complexion, proper stature, straight hair on the head and some on the body, a goodly figure, and a temperament abounding in cold and moisture.

"To speak, however, more particularly, all constellations of human form, both those within and those without the zodiac, act in favour of giving a handsome shape to the body, and due proportion to the figure, while those not of human form vary its due proportions, and incline it towards their own shape, assimilating it, in some measure, to their own peculiarities, either by enlarging or diminishing its size, by giving it additional strength or weakness, or by otherwise improving or disfiguring it. Thus, for example: *Leo*, *Virgo*, and *Sagittarius* enlarge the person; and *Pisces*, *Cancer*, and *Capricorn* tend to make it diminutive; and thus, again, the upper and anterior parts of *Aries*, *Taurus*, and *Leo*, increase its strength, and their lower and posterior parts render it weaker; while, on the other hand, *Sagittarius*, *Scorpio*, and *Gemini* act conversely, for their anterior parts produce greater debility, and their posterior parts give greater vigour. In like manner *Virgo*, *Libra*, and *Sagittarius*, contribute to render the person handsome and well-proportioned, and *Scorpio*, *Pisces*, and *Taurus*, incline it to be misshapen and disfigured.

---

[2] Book III., Chap. xvi.

"The other constellations also operate on similar principles; and all these influences it is necessary to bear in mind, in order that the peculiar properties, observed in their joint temperament, may be so compounded as to authorise an inference therefrom, concerning the form and temperament of the body."

R. A. Proctor wrote:

"The zodiacal twelve are in some respects the most important and interesting of all the constellations. If we could determine the origin of these figures, their exact configuration as at first devised, and the precise influences assigned to them in the old astrological systems, we should have obtained important evidence of the origin of astronomy itself. It seems highly probably that the date to which all inquiries into the origin of the constellations and the zodiacal signs seems to point—viz., 2170 B.C.—was the date at which the Chaldean astronomers definitely adopted the new system, the luni-solar, instead of the lunar division of the zodiac and of the time."

Reference to the *Tetrabiblos* of Claudius Ptolemy will show the precise influences assigned to the zodiacal constellations by the ancient Chaldaean astrologers. As before stated the *Tetrabiblos* was based chiefly upon the teachings or writings of Hermes.

The Chaldaeans and Egyptians depicted the events of the early ages of the world, their mystic religion, in the emblematical figures of the constellations. The Greeks and Romans replaced several of the Chaldean constellations by others emblematical of their own history.

Eratosthenes says:

"That the constellation of Argo was placed in the heavens by Divine Wisdom. That the Argo was the first ship that ever was constructed—that it was built at a period of most remote antiquity—that it was an ORACULAR VESSEL—that it was the *first* ship that ventured upon the sea, which had never been previously crossed; and that it was placed in the sphere as a commemorative token to posterity."[3]

The Greeks themselves, so far from claiming for any of their philosophers the honour of the sphere, assigned it with general consent to the Centaur Chiron, the incidents of whose life prove him, through all the mist of fable to have been one of the many personages whom tradition has substituted for Noah.[4] They fully acknowledged that the

[3] Eratos. Catast., XXXV.

[4] See Jacob Byrant's *Heathen Mythology*; and Faber's *Origin of Pagan Idolatry*.

Argo was the ship in which Danaus with his colony sailed from Egypt to Greece. This was many years before the poetic fiction of Jason and his voyage through the Black Sea in search of the Golden Fleece. Now the Egyptian account is that the Argo was the ship in which Osiris with the goddess Isis sailed upon the waters of the great deluge.[5]

The people of Hindostan have a tradition in which the names and circumstances are almost identical. The ship in their language is Argha, and the persons who sailed in it were Iswara and Isi; whilst the voyage, also, was on the waters of the deluge. The Persians have preserved the account, with slight alteration, calling the ship Arg.

Thus we see the same tradition preserving the knowledge of the one mighty event, extending through Southern Asia from Hindostan to Egypt evidently emanating from one origin, whence it has spread throughout the world, entirely independent of, though to the fullest extent confirming the account given in the Pentateuch by the inspired prophet of the Jews.

The very *position* of the constellation in the sphere proves that it was not of Grecian origin. Its principal star *Canopus* is only 37° from the South Pole, and the greater part of the constellation is still nearer to it. The whole is, therefore, invisible to Greece, which undoubtedly received the tradition from Egypt, whence the Greeks and all their science came. As to the sphere itself, the southern half is principally occupied with *aquatic* animals, and water appears streaming upon it in all directions. In the midst of the waves is the ship called, variously, Argo, Argha, Arg, Ark, in Egypt, Persia, Hindostan, or by the Jews. Near is a *dove* which seems flying towards it, and at a little distance, a raven perched on the back of a serpent. Farther off, as if he had just left the ship, is the fabulous Centaur, who with a lance pierces an animal, and appears to bear it towards a smoking altar. The whole is an undeniable portraiture of the mighty catastrophe—the Great Deluge! A marvellous confirmation of the Mosaic account. Further, that those who framed it must have lived in a southern latitude, and at a time when men's minds were deeply impressed with the awful circumstances of the terrible event, is an inference which suggests itself to the mind without effort or research.

The *teraphim* were images formed for the purposes of worship, and for *divining future events*. They were made by astrologers, under *certain constellations*. Among other reasons why Rachel stole her fa-

[5] Plutarch *de Isid.*

ther's images, this is thought to be one, viz., that Laban might not, by consulting with those images, discover what way Jacob took in his flight.[6]

It is manifest, therefore, that the *teraphim* had been constructed long after the first knowledge of the particular properties of the various constellations existed, constituting, as such knowledge did constitute, without doubt, the first principles of astrology. As Laban lived about six hundred years after the flood, it follows that the influences of the constellations of the zodiac were known within a very few generations of that catastrophe, or about 2,200 years before Christ. At the present day, tradition, history, experience, and common sense are alike set at nought, and men are allowed to substitute for real ennobling knowledge and divine truth, their own shallow, and absurd speculations.

Proctor observed that, "In Egypt there are temples of vast antiquity, having a dome, on which a zodiac—or more correctly, a celestial hemisphere—is sculptured with constellation figures. And we now learn, from ancient Babylonian and Assyrian sculptures, that these Egyptian zodiacs are, in all probability merely copies (more or less perfect) of yet more ancient Chaldaean zodiacs. One of these Babylonian sculptures is figured in Rawlinson's *Ancient Monarchies*. It seems probable that in a country where Sabaeamsm, or star worship, was the prevailing form of religion, yet more imposing proportions would be given to such zodiacs than in Egypt."[7] "Indeed," continues Mr. Proctor, "there have not been wanting those who find in the ancient constellations the record of the early history of Man. According to their views Orion is Nimrod—the 'Giant,' as the Arabic name of the constellation implies—the mighty hunter, as the dogs and hare beside him signify. The figure now called Hercules, but of old Eugonasin, or the kneeler, and described by Aratus as 'a man doomed to labour,' is Adam. His left foot treads on the dragon's head, in token of the saying, 'It shall bruise thy head'; and Serpentarius, or the serpent bearer, is the promised seed."

It is stated in the *Anacalypsis* that,

"When the French possessed Italy they examined thc chair of St. Peter and found upon it the *signs of the zodiac*. There is, also, a published account, written by a Roman of eminence, before the time of

---

[6] See *Ecclesiastical Rites, used by the Ancient Hebrews*, by Thomas Goodwyn. 1628.

[7] The *Student*, June, 1868.

the French invasion, which states that the same thing was observed, and much discussed on the chair being formerly taken down to be cleaned. The zodiac had been forgotten, or the chair would not have been again taken down. This is the chair of St. Peter, with its zodiacal chain, on which the Pope is supposed to sit to rule the Empire of his *first* crown, of the *planets*. It must not be forgotten that the triple crown is emblematical of his three kingdoms. The illustrious Spaniard did not err far when he said that the life of Jesus was written in the stars.

"Irenaeus was Bishop of Lyons. He was one of the first fathers of the Church who suffered martyrdom, and generally accounted one of its most eminent and illustrious early writers. He was an Asiatic, but was sent as bishop to Gaul. He founded or built a church in that country. This church is yet remaining in Lyons, though in the course of almost 2,000 years, no doubt it has undergone many alterations. On the floor, in front of the altar, may been seen a Mosaic pavement of the zodiac, though a considerable part of it is worn away.

"Persons who do not look deeply into these matters, are easily blinded by being told that it is the remains of an old temple. But Irenaeus had no power to get possession of Roman pagan temples. The pretence is totally void of foundation. The style of building, its records, &c., all show what its priests say is true, viz., that it was built by Irenaeus. On many other churches, which never were Roman temples, both in Britain and elsewhere, similar marks of the esoteric religion, which I have partly unfolded, may be seen."

Modern authors have described the special influences exerted by the respective *signs of the zodiac*. The following may be accepted as a fair description of them:

ARIES (♈) produces a spare and strong body, of stature rather above the average; face long; eyebrows bushy; neck long; shoulders thick and powerful; complexion sallow or swarthy; hair black or sandy; disposition irritable. The first half of the sign gives a stronger constitution, and a greater muscular development, than the latter half.

TAURUS (♉) gives a middle stature; a thick, well set body; a broad forehead; full face and prominent eyes; neck and lips thick; nose and mouth wide; complexion swarthy; dark or black hair, often curly; disposition melancholy; slow to anger, but, when provoked, furious.

GEMINI (♊) usually produces a tall and straight body; complexion dark sanguine; hair blackish; eyes hazel, sight quick; a smart, active appearance; disposition fickle, understanding good.

CANCER (♋).—Moderate stature, upper part of body somewhat large; small round face, with pale, delicate complexion; brown hair; small gray eyes; effeminate in constitution and disposition, subject to chest affections.

LEO (♌).—A large, fair stature, broad shoulders; prominent and large eyes; hair generally light, and often yellowish; oval, ruddy countenance; of a high, resolute, haughty, and ambitious temper.

VIRGO (♍).—Middle stature, rather slender, but very neat and compact; dark sanguine complexion; dark hair; small, shrill voice (but if Mercury ascend in this sign, the native will be a great orator), witty, ingenious and studious, but of a fickle disposition.

LIBRA (♎).—Tall and elegantly formed, rather slender; hair brown, smooth, and glossy, yet sometimes jet-black; face having generally great beauty; fine clear sanguine complexion; blue sparkling eyes; good tempered, amiable, and high principled.

SCORPIO (♏).[9]—Strong, corpulent, robust body; of middle stature; dark complexion; dark brown curling and bushy hair; neck thick; mind and disposition active, yet reserved and thoughtful.

SAGITTARIUS (♐).—A well-formed person; inclined to tallness; sanguine complexion, oval face and handsome; high forehead; chestnut or bright-brown hair, growing off the temples, bald early in life; long Grecian nose; fine, clear eyes; jovial, active, and intrepid disposition, very fond of horses and hunting.

CAPRICORN (♑).—Slender make, in some cases ill-formed or crooked; a long, thin face, generally plain; thin beard; chin long and protruding; black, lanky hair; narrow chest; disposition subtle, collected, calm, witty, and yet melancholy.

AQUARIUS (♒).—Middle stature, stout, well-set, robust, and strong; long and fleshy face; good, clear, delicate, and sanguine complexion; sandy or darkish flaxen hair; hazel eyes; of prepossessing appearance, and good disposition.

PISCES (♓).—Stature short, body fleshy, crooked, or stooping,

---

[9] Virgil makes the following allusion to the claws—χηλᾲδ, chelae—of Scorpio, in the first Georgic:

> "Quo locus Erigonen inter, Chelasque sequentes
> Pauditur: ipse tibi jam brachia contrahit ardens
> Scorpius, et coeli justlâ plus parte reliquit.

Ovid alludes to the same sign, as follows:

> "Porrigit in spatium signorum membra duorum."

round shouldered; brown hair, large, round, pale face, (but if ☉ be rising, a good complexion); in disposition indolent and dull, prone to drinking, more or less.

The foregoing descriptions rarely answer exactly. For the ascending sign (although it has chief influence over the form of the body), will, if a planet be within 5° of the Eastern horizon, or in close *aspect* with it, have its influence considerably modified thereby.

Some authors instruct the student to consider, in addition to the ascending sign, "the sign occupied by the Moon, and that in which the lord of the ascendant is placed." This can only apply to horary (symbolical) astrology, and *not* to nativities, except when the Moon or the "lord" of the ascendant happens to be rising, or in close aspect to the horizon, at birth. The late John Varley gave the following "elementary notions of the twelve signs":

"The sign *Aries*, amongst its various classes of human physiognomy, gives one that much resembles that of a *ram*; and it signifies that class of animals, and their attributes.

"*Taurus* gives very powerfully that of the *bull*, with tufted hair on the forehead.

"*Gemini*, though a beautiful and human sign, yet occasionally gives to persons born when it is rising a strong resemblance in the head and neck to the characteristic forms of goats, kids, and deer; and therefore, being a bicorporal sign, or one of plurality, in very ancient times it was represented by two kids; but, subsequently, the human character of the sign has been recognised by the introduction of the *Twins*, representing the two stars Castor and Pollux."

[These two stars were in the sign Gemini at the time when the constellations so far agreed with the signs whose names they bear, that the beginning of Aries was at or near the commencement of the constellation so-called, and the place of the Sun at the vernal equinox.]

"*Cancer* is found occasionally to give, among other characterists of the sign, a crabbed, short-nosed class of persons, greatly resembling a crab in features, when viewed in front; these persons resemble crabs, also, in the energy and tenacity with which they attack any object.

"*Leo* produces the physiognomies most resembling a lion, especially in the nose and retreating chin; such as the profile of King George III exhibits; and the sign is particularly significant of such animals as the lion.

"*Virgo* has been found to be well-suited to the signification of a class of cool, discreet, studious women."

An ancient zodiac, sculptured on one of the temples of Thebes, represents this sign as a virgin with a distaff in her hands, to denote the *industrious* character of women born under Virgo. The same figure is found in the zodiac in the great temple of Tentyra.

"*Libra*, independently of its appearing in the world's horoscope, to mediate the zodiac horizontally, and to balance, as it were, the sign Aries, has been found to signify straight lines and regular buildings, and the sublime uninterrupted horizon line of the sea; it represents also the blue colour of the sky and distances.

"*Scorpio* has been occasionally found to afford to one class of human form when it is rising, a near approach to serpents, in the expression of the countenance, especially in the eyes and mouth; and when doing or saying cruel and bitter things, they are apt to be assimilated to the nature of snakes, scorpions, etc.

"*Sagittarius* has been observed to represent, not only such rapid motions as belong to the flying arrow, but the centaurion form was suggested by the first portion of the sign, signifying the deliberation or temperate resolves of humanity, with happy termination, in a greater degree than the latter half, which often exhibits more of the excessive impulses and nature of a race-horse, an animal most specifically described by Sagittarius; and persons born while the latter half of the sign is rising, are subject to the constant apprehension of vicissitudes or violent accidents.

"*Capricornus* is found to give gray-eyed human beings a most perfect resemblance in the eyes to the full-grown goat; and in others, both dark and fair, the under lip somewhat resembles that of these animals. Capricorn from reflecting as it were, the watery sign Cancer, which is opposite to it in the zodiac, and from the former location of the famous fishy star Fornalhaut in it (which left the sign about the period of the great plague at Athens), caused so many persons born under the sign to partake in their physiognomy of the character of fish, that it was anciently represented by a goat with a fish's tail."

[In the zodiac of Thebes, before alluded to, the goat is drawn in full, and without the tail of the fish, as generally seen in less ancient zodiacs.]

"*Aquarius* is, by many persons, erroneously termed a watery sign; but it is, in fact, the third sign of the aerial trigon; and as it is an amiable, peaceful, and uranian sign, and as the air was perceived to be the bearer of vapours, clouds, and even waterspouts, Aquarius was represented by the figure of the water-bearer, which also denoted one who followed a useful and domestic, rather than any destructive occupation.

"*Pisces* was found to signify persons who were employed in fishing, and in other watery concerns; and likewise shallow streams in which fish are readily seen. It is a sign under which many fishmongers are born, or in which planets are located at their birth; and some of the persons born when it is rising approximate to fishes in their eyes, which are somewhat conspicuous and phlegmatic.

"It must be borne in mind that all the signs indicate various classes of individuals, and that by the entrance of illustrious fixed stars into them their characters are reduced or exalted, as in the instance of Scorpio, which was once termed the accursed sign, but since the celebrated star Minerva, the north balance, and other eminent stars have been located therein, this sign has been the ascendant of many of the most illustrious heroes, legislators, surgeons, astronomers, painters, engravers, etc. It was the ascendant of Edward III., and the Black Prince, of Lord Nelson, Lord Byron, Jenny Lind, and many distinguished officers employed by the late Duke of Wellington. The sign is so strictly *martial* that no planet except Mars has any dignities in it; and it was probably on this account singled out as having no friendly signification to the harmonies of nature.

"There have been many other interpretations given of the names of the signs. The most common is that which alludes to the animals produced in the various months, as the Sun proceeds through some of the signs. Another originates in the ideas of the Sun's motion, and its effects, as that at the summer solstice he begins, like a crab, to move backwards towards southern declination; that his fiery heat, when in Leo, resembles a raging lion; that the harvest time is alluded to when he enters the sign Virgo, who is represented (latterly) holding an ear of corn in her hand. In Libra he is said to balance the days and nights; and in Scorpio, to produce an unpleasant effect (by means of the weather), as if like a scorpion, he left a string behind.

"These, and the explanations of the other signs are ingenious evasions, invented by the enemies of judicial astrology, or by persons entirely ignorant of it; and serve only to mislead persons of enquiring mind from the true zodiacal origin on their appellations."

Ptolemy relates that the signs Aries, Gemini, Leo, Libra, Sagittarius, and Aquarius were denominated *masculine*, and the remainder *feminine*, in alternative order, "as the day is followed by the night, and as the male is coupled with the female."

The signs have been divided into four *triplicities*, thus: *fiery*, ♈, ♌, ♐; *earthy*, ♉, ♍, ♑; *airy*, ♊, ♎, ♒; and *watery*, ♋, ♏, ♓.

The *bicorporal* signs are ♊, ♓, and the first half of ♐. The *fruitful* signs are ♋, ♏, ♓; the *barren* signs are ♊, ♌, and ♍.

The signs of *long-ascension* are ♋, ♌, ♍, ♎, ♏, ♐. The signs of *short-ascension* are ♑, ♒, ♓, ♈, ♉, ♊. The last-named are so-called because they ascend in a shorter period of time (owing to the diurnal motion of the earth being, when they ascend, nearly parallel with its orbit) than the others. A *trine* aspect falling in signs of *short-ascension*, is equal to a *square* in its effects, according to Ptolemy. This, if it were true, would only apply, *per se* to *mundane* positions, and not to differences of longitude in the zodiac. It is not true, even in regard to mundane positions, and could only receive (apparent) support from experience when the two bodies in aspect happened also to be in equal, or parallel, declination.

Signs of voice are ♊, ♍, ♒, and the *first* half of ♐, because, it is said, when either of these signs ascends at a birth, and Mercury is strong, the native will prove a good orator.

The "houses" of the planets are readily shown by the following table. It is exactly the same as that found in the mummy-case of the Archon of Thebes, in ancient Egypt, as may be seen in the British Museum.

♌	☉		☽	♋
♍		☿		♊
♎		♀		♉
♏		♂		♈
♐		♃		♓
♑		♄		♒

The sign *Leo* is the only house (or chief essential dignity) of the Sun, just as Cancer is the only house of the Moon. The planets had each *two* houses assigned to them. Some modern authors have assigned *Aquarius* to Uranus, thus either robbing Saturn of his "day-house," or forcing upon him a partner. However, until *experience* teaches us in what signs Uranus and Neptune are most powerful, I must decline to endorse so hasty an attempt to provide for one of the "houseless wanderers."

The sign *Aries* is said to govern the head and face of man, and the diseases it produces (when evil planets are located in it) are the small-pox, measles, ringworm, apoplexy, palsy, &c.

Taurus rules the neck and throat, and its diseases are consumption (laryngeal or bronchial), scrofula, croup, quinsy, diphtheria, bronchocele, &c.

Gemini governs the arms and shoulders, and its diseases are brain fevers, corrupt blood; fractures of the head and arms, &c.

Cancer rules the chest, breasts, and stomach. The diseases under its influence are cancer, asthma, bronchitis, inflammation and consumption of the lungs, cough, expectoration of blood, gastric catarrh, and fever.

Leo governs the heart and spine, and its diseases are spinal affections, convulsions, acute fevers, pestilence, smallpox, measles, jaundice, and all inflammatory complaints.

Virgo rules the intestinal canal, the spleen, the abdomen, and diaphragm; its diseases are colic, melancholia, dysentery, enteric fever, &c.

Libra governs the reins and loins; its diseases are affections of the kidneys, diabetes, tabes dorsalis, &c.

Scorpio rules the generative organs, inguinal regions, bladder, &c.; its diseases are haemorrhoids, fistula, ruptures, scurvy, &c.

Sagittarius governs the hips and thighs, and the os sacrum; its diseases are sciatica, coxalgia, gout, rheumatism, and fever; and its accidents are broken bones of the lower extremities chiefly.

Capricorn rules the knees; its accidents are sprains, dislocations, and broken limbs; its diseases are articular rheumatism, hysteria, cutaneous eruptions, &c.

Aquarius governs the legs and ankles; its diseases are gout, cramp, rheumatism, and corrupt blood; its accidents, broken legs.

Pisces rules the feet and toes; its diseases are affections of the feet, gout, lameness, ulcers, and rheumatism.

This, of course, only applies to nativities in which one or more of the evil planets—Mars, Saturn, Uranus, and Neptune—may be in conjunction, opposition, parallel declination, or quartile with the Sun or Moon, or ascending degree, whichever may be hyleg, and when, at the same time, the hyleg receives no support from either Jupiter or Venus. In a less degree, the sesquiquadrate and semi-quartile aspects affect the health. The mundane parallel also is prejudicial when the evil planet happens to be elevated above the hyleg, or close to the cusp of the eighth or sixth house, or ruler of the sign on either of those houses.

CHAPTER X.

THE SUN

"Most glorious orb! that wert a worship, ere
The mystery of thy making was reveal'd !
Thou earliest minister of the Almighty,
Which gladden'd on their mountain-tops the hearts
Of the Chaldaean shepherds, till they pour'd
Themselves in orisons!"—BYRON.

THE SUN was believed by the ancients to revolve around the earth. The Ptolemaic system of astronomy was founded on this belief. It has been rightly observed that, "Ptolemy's order, false as it was, enabled observers to give a plausible account of the motions of the Sun and Moon, to foretell eclipses, and to improve geography."[1] Inasmuch as Ptolemy's system of astronomy portrayed the actual phenomena of the heavens as they appear to observers on the earth, it follows that his astrology is quite as applicable to modern and improved astronomy as to his own, for the heavenly bodies act upon the earth, its atmosphere, and mankind, according to their apparent or *geocentric* positions, without reference to their true or heliocentric places. The Sun's distance from the earth is now computed at 92,350,000 miles, in mean value. Astronomers have differed, in the past, so greatly as to the Sun's distance, that it has been variously stated to be from 28 to 96 millions of miles.

The Sun has always been held to rule the first day of the week—Sunday. "It is a curious fact that the Hebrew words expressing the seven first cardinal numbers, are all formed of one syllable that signifies a star, and of, one or more, others that imply the character or quality of that star. ATCHED, or ASHSHED, *one*, is a corruption of the words Ash, *fire*, and Shed, *to pour forth*; whence SHEDDAI, the name of God, the 'All Bountiful'; and the words signify 'The All Bountiful Fire'; which is perfectly characteristic of the Sun. It is, then, a direct reference to the Sun, whose rule was over IAUM ATCHED 'day one.'"[2]

---

[1] *Spectacle de la Nature.*

[2] *Zadkiel's Almanac* for 1849, p. 59.

The first deity worshiped was BELUS, which was the Sun, called in Scripture BAAL; hence the Buddhist terms Bal and Bali, denoting a species of magic by which it is pretended that diseases are cured. The Greek mythologists elaborated from this lord or chief of the Sabaean idolatry both Jupiter and Apollo, the former as king of heaven, the latter as the local deity of the Sun.

The figure of Brachma, with four faces, denotes the Sun, the four seasons, and the four triplicities of the zodiac, viz., the airy, fiery, earthy, and watery.

Mr. Coleman says, "This deity"—Surya, or the Sun—"is pictured of a deep golden complexion, with his head encircled by golden rays of glory. He presides over ADIT-WAR, or Sunday; from *Adit*, the first, and *War*, day." Many ages before Christianity—in the remotest times of Britain and Gaul—the first day of the week was set apart, more particularly, for the instruction of the laity, and distinguished by the name of *the day of the Sun*. A Saronide, or preacher, delivered his sermon from a jube, or pulpit. The discourse delivered was termed Sab-aith, or "the word of the teacher, or wise man." Hence the day itself came to be termed the Sabaith-day. The assembly was called Sabat—a term since most absurdly applied by the French to signify a nocturnal assembly of witches and conjurors. In the word Sabbatines is still preserved the original unperverted sense of instructive discourses.[3] The divines, or theologians, were styled Faidhes (hence the Latin, *Vates*), who on the day of the Sun, or of Apollo,[4] preached the faith, or so much of the tenets of religion as they chose to communicate to the people. The name, however, of the Drudical Sab-aith day having happily merged into that of *Sabbath*, was received by the Christians. Not only the change of the day (from the Jewish Sabbath, Saturn's day, the seventh day of the week), but the primordial appellation of it, Sunday, still collaterally retained in our language demonstrates its origin.

When Constantine desired to hand over the people, who followed the Drudical religion, to the power of the Christian priests, he issued this decree: "Let all judges and townspeople, and the occupations of all trades, rest on the venerable day of the Sun, &c.

Eusebius gives an ancient Oracle, which he had copied from Por-

---

[3] See *Etymological Vocabulary*, p. 97; also *The Way to Things by Words and to Words by Things*. London, 1766.

[4] Apollo—the radiance of the Sun. Apollo and Sol, in the Celtic, have exactly the same meaning; an emanation from the eye of heaven.

phyry, in which we are clearly told that the *Magi* named the days of the week from the planets.[5]

The Sun is said to possess "a hot and dry nature, though inferior, in this respect, to Mars," and to possess, also, the peculiar power of destroying the nature and influence of any planet with which he may happen to be in conjunction, and appropriating its qualities to himself. This is termed *combustion* (when the planet is within 8° 30′ of the Sun). A planet within 17° of the Sun is said to be "under the Sun's beams," but this is not so great an affliction as the former position. There can be no doubt that a planet gradually loses its power as well as its light as it approaches the Sun, and slowly regains it as it recedes from the great luminary. The ancients held that a planet within 17′ of the centre of the Sun was thereby fortified, and this position they termed "cazimi," but a planet so situated is undoubtedly in the worst state of combustion.

When the Sun is afflicted at birth his influence becomes malefic, and when an evil direction of his to the ascendant or Moon (if either be hyleg) comes into operation, it materially assists in the destruction of life. When the Moon is hyleg, an evil direction to the Sun, even when the latter is free from malefic influence at birth, is somewhat dangerous to life.

For success, or prosperity in the world to be attained, it is essential that the Sun, as well as the Moon, shall be free from affliction at birth. When both the Sun and Moon are afflicted the person then born has a long struggle against adverse fate. It is better to have the Sun and Moon free from even the good aspects of Saturn.

The Sun, at birth, in benefic aspect with Jupiter, pre-signifies good fortune, and a good constitution (if the Moon and ascendant be free from affliction).

The Sun in good aspect with Mars, pre-signifies success in war, surgery, chemistry, etc., and the stronger the position of Mars, the greater will be his fame.

The Sun in the midheaven and free from affliction, leads to public life; and if the Sun have the declination, or trine with Jupiter, eminence in the Church, or the law or in medicine.

The Sun rising at a birth, confers courage, ambition, and good fortune. But if afflicted by Saturn, liability to consumption or paralysis or to misfortune. Afflicted by Mars, there is rashness and sternness,

[5] Pr. E.5, 14.

unless Jupiter assist the Sun by good configuration. The Sun is said to govern the heart, spine, arteries, the right eye of a man and the left eye of a woman. His diseases, accordingly, are: Affections of the heart and the eye, acute fever, disordered brain, spinal complaints, etc. His angel is called Michael.

The Sun describes, generally, when rising at a birth, a person of large, strong and good build, high forehead, inclined to baldness, large eyes, sharp sight, yellowish or light-brown hair, and much beard.

If the Sun be well dignified, the disposition is noble, generous, proud, magnanimous, humane, and affable, friendly, and generous to an enemy; one of few words; and fond of luxury and magnificence. If ill-dignified, pride, arrogance, and want of sympathy.

The Sun in the Twelve Signs

☉ in ♈ describes usually one of good stature, strong, and well-made; a good complexion; yellowish, flaxen, or sandy hair; courageous, and martially disposed; likely to succeed in the army or in the medical profession; fortunate, and victorious over his enemies.

☉ in ♉ represents a rather short, well-set person; dark complexion; not very attractive features; large nose; broad face; strong, bold, proud, fond of opposing others, and often gaining the victory.

☉ in ♊ confers a well-proportioned body; complexion sanguine; hair brown; of a good, affable, and kind disposition, rather deficient in firmness and resolution; and not particularly fortunate.

☉ in ♋ represents a moderate stature (if afflicted, deformed, or diminutive); brown hair; disposition harmless and cheerful, somewhat indolent and addicted to pleasure.

☉ in ♌ gives a strong, well-made person; of a sanguine complexion; light-brown or yellow hair; full round face and large eyes; honest and upright in conduct, ambitious, and fond of pleasure.

☉ in ♍ describes a tall person, slender, and comely; plentiful hair of a brown colour; mind ingenious, artistic or scientific; disposition cheerful and agreeable.

☉ in ♎ represents a straight, tall body; a pleasing personality; prominent eyes; light hair; pimpled face in age; disposition amiable; fond of pleasure, just, and luxurious.

☉ in ♏ gives a square, fleshy body; broad face and mouth; complexion freckled or sunburnt; hair brown and curling; mind ingenious; disposition rugged and may be overbearing; fortunate upon the sea and in the practice of medicine, chemistry, engineering, &c.

☉ in ♐ represents a tall, well-proportioned body, a very comely person; oval face; sanguine complexion; light-brown curling hair; disposition generous, lofty, proud, aiming at noble ends, bold, and capable of great deeds; a good sportsman.

☉ in ♑ describes a mean stature; a sickly complexion; oval face; lank brown hair; disposition just and upright, generally good-natured, hasty, and autocratic.

☉ in ♒ gives a middle stature; a corpulent body; of fair proportions; round, full face; light-brown hair; clear complexion; good disposition, though tinctured with pride and ambition; artistic or scientific.

☉ in ♓ describes a short, fleshy person; round face; good complexion; light-brown or flaxen hair; a harmless disposition, may be his own enemy by reason of extravagance, and indulgence in feasting and pleasure.

The Sun when afflicted in *Aries*, or afflicting the Moon or ascendant, is said to cause conjunctivitis, acne, and vertigo. When so situated in *Taurus*, quinsy and other diseases of the throat. In *Gemini*, epidemic fever, or scurvy. In *Cancer*, smallpox, measles, dyspepsia, and dropsy. In *Leo*, neuralgia of the head, calculus, and acute fever. In *Virgo*, diarrhoea, dysentery, dyspepsia, etc. In *Libra*, fever, calculus, and renal disease. In *Scorpio*, diseases of the kidney, prostate, etc. In *Sagittarius*, sciatica, fistula, and acute fever. In *Capricornus*, articular rheumatism, and intestinal affections. In *Aquarius*, disordered blood, calculus, and strangury. In *Pisces*, affections of the kidneys, dropsy, etc.

CHAPTER XI.

THE MOON.

"To the blanc Moon
Her office they prescrib'd."—MILTON.

THE MOON, the earth's satellite, was said by the ancients to be "feminine, cold, moist, and phlegmatic." Her influence, is, strictly speaking, convertible as to its character, being fortunate or unfortunate according to her position, relative to the Sun and planets at her birth. Her position in the heavens at a nativity, is of much importance; her proximity to the earth and the rapidity of her motion render her a very powerful significator in all branches of astrology. The critical years in the life of man, the crises in disease, the period of gestation, the rise and fall of the tides—all attest the verity of her influence.

The second day of the week (Lunae dies) is ruled by the Moon—hence the term Monday. In Hebrew SHEMIN, TWO, or ASHNEM, is compounded of Ash, *fire* (the stars being termed the fires of heaven), and NEM, *slumber*, meaning "the star of slumber," which evidently applies to the Moon as ruler of the night, the time for slumber. Thus SHEMIN, two, clearly indicated the rule of the Moon over "Day two." The Moon was worshipped under the name of Diana by the Ephesians, whence arose the cry, "Great is Diana of the Ephesians"; she was also worshiped throughout the whole of Asia. The oracle of Themis (the goddess of oracles being Ar-Temis, Diana, the Moon) was the most ancient, and was consulted by Deucalion after the flood. Among the most ancient Orphic hymns is one addressed to the Moon under this title:

ΑᾳΟΥΣΑ ΚΑΔΟΥ'Σ ΚΑΡΗΟΥ'Σ ύκό γᾲιης
Thou bringest from the earth the goodly fruits.

"Does not," asks Parkhurst, "this exactly agree with the precious things put forth by the streams of light from the Moon, Heb., IARACHIM, of which Moses speaks, Deut. xxxiii., 14 ?" This proves the belief of the ancients in the power of the Moon over vegetation, a fact beyond question.[1]

[1] Dr. Goad says: "In felling trees for timber the ancients have told us that it

The ancients considered the full moon fortunate; but when the Moon was horned they considered it so malignant that a child born under certain aspects at that time would soon die, or if it lived, it would be guilty of crimes as great as its temper was black. This led the Hebrew wise women to write upon the walls of their bed chambers, "Let not Lilith enter here"—this demon, *Lilith*, being certain influences of the Moon.

When the Moon ascends at a birth the stature of the child usually becomes tall, complexion pale, face round, eyes gray, brow lowering, arms short, body smooth, inclined to corpulence, and temperament phlegmatic. If impeded by (*i.e.*, in evil aspect with) the Sun, a blemish usually appears on or near one of the eyes; and if she be occidental, and in evil aspect to Mars, the sight is defective. I have known cases wherein the full Moon rising at birth, without any aspect to the evil planets, has produced great defect in sight, although no hereditary predisposition of this nature existed.

If the Moon be dignified (*i.e.*, angular, or in the signs ♋ or ♉) at birth, the person will be more graceful, of refined and engaging manners, good easy disposition, ingenious, and given to traveling; rather unstable, however, and of little forecast, providing only for the present; prone to frequently change his employment or pursuits.

If the Moon be unfortunate (*i.e.*, cadent, or located in either ♑ or ♏ and having no assistance from the fortunes, ♃ or ♀) at birth, the native is inclined to be slothful, improvident, and may be given to dissipation. When oriental[2] the Moon inclines to corpulence; when occidental to leanness and deformity.

The Moon is said to govern the stomach, the intestinal canal, the left eye of a man and the right eye of a woman. Her diseases are: rheumatism, consumption, palsy, colic, lunacy, scrofula, and dropsy.

must be a winter work in regard to the Sun. That oaks cut down in spring-time will presently rot. They teach withal that it is of an infinite concern to add the Moon's observation as well as the Sun's; Infinitum refert et Luvaris ratio, Pliny, xvi, 39. The elm, the pine, the nut, and all other timber trees must follow the same rule, that if in the felling you join both observations together, *viz.*, the depth of winter, *i.e.*, the winter solstice and the last days of the Moon (interlunium) the stuff will last to perpetuity." [*Astro-Meteorologica*, 1699, p. 17.] Montgomery Martin's work on the Colonies records some very interesting facts in regard to lunar influence. The ancients knew nothing of "dry rot," but they, poor simpletons, believed in astrology!

[2] This refers to the increase of light of the Moon; she is occidental when decreasing in light (*i.e.*, after the full).

The angel of the Moon is called Gabriel.

THE MOON IN THE TWELVE Signs.

The Moon in *Aries* represents middle stature, round face, light-brown or flaxen hair; temperament rash, variable, and passionate; not a fortunate person.

☽ in ♉ describes a well-formed body, middle stature, poor, complexion; brown or black hair; gentle and obliging in disposition; a fairly fortunate person.

☽ in ♊ gives a tall, well-set person, very comely; brown hair; good complexion; one who is subtle, crafty, ingenious and variable; unsettled in life, usually.

☽ in ♋ represents middle-sized persons, well-proportioned, and fleshy; face round and full; complexion pale and dusky; hair brown; of a pleasant, merry, easy disposition, free from passion; fortunate and highly respected; but of a roving and indolent nature.

☽ in ♌ describes a person strong, robust, above the middle height, large boned; full face; large eyes; brown hair; sanguine complexion; disposition ambitious; hardly fortunate.

☽ in ♍ gives a person of tall stature; dark brown or black hair; oval face; dark, ruddy complexion; of an ingenious fancy, inventive, retiring, melancholy; often unstable, and rarely fortunate.

☽ in ♎ describes a tall, neatly formed person; smooth light-brown hair; fine sanguine complexion; merry disposition; beloved and respected.

☽ in ♏ gives an indifferent person, short, fleshy, muscular; dark brown or black curling hair; dark complexion; disposition quarrelsome, in some instances malicious; of ingenious mind.

☽ in ♐ denotes a handsome person; oval face; bright brown hair; sanguine complexion; disposition open and generous, passionate, ambitious and fond of sports; usually fortunate.

☽ in ♑ represents low stature, and a weakly *physique*; thin face; dark brown, lank hair; weak in the knees; an unsettled character (unless the Moon be well aspected).

☽ in ♒ gives a middle-sized, corpulent body; brown hair; clear, sanguine complexion; disposition affable, inoffensive, kind, and irresolute; mind ingenious; conduct good.

☽ in ♓ describes a short stature; face and body plump; complexion pale; hair bright brown; inactive easy disposition, given to the pleasures of the table, merry, and "happy go lucky."

Observations on the Moon's Application to, and Separation from the Planets.[3]

If the Moon apply to SATURN, at birth, and increase[4] in light, it signifies widowhood to the mother, and much misfortune.

If the Moon increase in light and apply to JUPITER, or be joined to him, it signifies rich, faithful, honest, and jovial persons—unless Mars be in square or opposition to her, for this would modify the good influence of ♃.

If the Moon apply to MARS or be conjoined with him, in a nocturnal geniture, it signifies crafty, violent, dangerous persons, often subject to be deceived; by day, weak, feeble constitutions, subject to diseases of the eyes and stomach, and likely to die a violent death.

If the Moon be carried to or conjoined with the SUN, in whatever part of the heavens it may fall, it signifies unhappy persons, unfortunate or sickly.

If the Moon be carried to VENUS, or if the Moon be increasing in light and conjoined with Venus, it signifies noble parents, but the native may be separated from their affection, he will be fortunate, however; but if the Moon be decreasing, she signifies power and happiness in youth, but subject to scandal, and dissipated if Mars behold Venus without the help of Jupiter.

If the Moon separate from Saturn and apply to JUPITER, it signifies rich and happy persons.

The full Moon separating from SATURN and applying to MARS, signifies much sickness and infirmity, and the native will die in early youth (if ☽ be hyleg).

If the Moon separate from SATURN and apply to the SUN, it is very unfortunate, and signifies many calamities,[5] and a liability to lunacy, dropsy, etc.

The Moon separating from SATURN and applying to VENUS, signi-

---

[3] These are the (condensed) aphorisms of J. Angelus and Regiomontanus—compiled at Venice in the fifteenth century.

[4] At the birth of King Edward VII. the Moon applied to (the square of) Saturn, but was decreasing in light; Queen Victoria was widowed at 42 years.

[5] At the birth of the emperor Francis Joseph of Austro-Hungary, the Moon was separating from the conjunction of Saturn and applying to the Sun in the 11th house) in the sign Leo, and he suffered defeat in Italy, in 1859, at Sadowa, in 1866, and lost his son by tragic death, and his Empress by assassination.

fies noble, happy, rich, and wealthy persons, but licentious; if the Moon decrease in light it denotes gain, but dissipation also.

The Moon separating from SATURN and applying to MERCURY, and increasing, she signifies obscure persons, writers of libels, studious of celestial sciences and the arts, good speakers, and physicians; but if the Moon decrease in light, she impedites the speech, or hearing, the body is sickly, cough, dropsy, and colic result.

If the Moon separate from JUPITER and apply to MARS, in a nocturnal geniture, and be increasing, it denotes magistrates, men in power, but not free from danger and sickness.

The Moon separating from JUPITER and applying to the SUN, it destroys the patrimony, causes the native to separate himself from his parents, and become an exile or a captive (especially if ☽ be in ♑, ♒, ♈, or ♏).

If the Moon increasing or at the full, separate from JUPITER and apply to a good aspect of VENUS, it signifies noble, powerful persons, but they soon lose their parents; they gain by their wives' dowry.

If the Moon separate from JUPITER and apply to SATURN, and be increasing or at full, it causes the native to be adopted by a stranger; it gives tutors, or persons employed in watery places, sailors, etc.; but if the Moon be decreasing, it signifies servitude, misfortune, captivity, frequent sickness (chronic) and misery, and, if it be a nocturnal geniture, a violent death.

If the Moon separate from JUPITER and apply to MERCURY, she signifies judges, collectors of money, interpreters of law, religious and fortunate persons.

If the Moon separate from MARS and apply to the SUN, it signifies very great evils, misfortunes, shortness of life, imbecility, and violent death in a strange land.

The Moon separating from MARS and applying to VENUS at full, or increasing, denotes adulterous persons; also jewellers, painters, perfumers, dealers in metals, innkeepers, etc. (according to the nature of the sign); if the Moon be decreasing in light, it signifies fortunate, happy persons, gaining wealth by female influence, but sometimes suffering disgrace through wantonness.

The full Moon separating from MARS and applying to MERCURY in a nocturnal geniture, signifies great persons in public authority, but wicked and malicious; if the nativity be diurnal, and the Moon at the full, it signifies judical condemnation and a violent death.

If the Moon separate from MARS and apply to SATURN, it denotes sluggish, dull persons, good for nothing; if the Moon be full or increasing, destroyers of their estates, and vicious; if the Moon be decreasing, it denotes privation, lunacy, epilepsy, and a violent death.

If the Moon separate from MARS and apply to JUPITER, it signifies powerful, rich, fortunate persons; but, if she be decreasing in light, it renders the native vicious, and consequently unhealthy.

If the Moon, in a diurnal geniture, separate from the SUN and apply to VENUS, it signifies barrenness, hinders marriage, inclines to vice; yet, in general, good fortune; in a nativity by night, it signifies many wives, living in good repute, and gaining a fortune.

The Moon separating from the SUN and applying to MERCURY in a diurnal geniture, signifies danger to life, evil manners, atheistical mind, etc.; in a nocturnal geniture, it signifies public notaries, writers, inventors, students of occult science and mysteries, gainers of estates.

The Moon separating from the SUN, in a diurnal geniture, and applying to SATURN, destroys the estate, separates one from his parents, and brings him to want and misery, but in process of time he may gain an estate by miserly economy; in a nocturnal geniture, it signifies want, destruction of estate, much sickness and affliction.

The Moon separating from the SUN and applying to JUPITER, by day, signifies a good estate, good fortune, and happiness beyond pleasure; in a nocturnal geniture, the native obtains an estate by his own industry, travels early in life, is deceived and disappointed in youth, but in age lives in high repute.

If the Moon proceed from the SUN to MARS, in a diurnal geniture, it signifies sudden death, and the parents often die a violent death; the native is liable to blindness or defects in the sight; in a nocturnal geniture, it signifies cruel, violent persons, their employment connected with fire, iron, or metals, and subject to continual labour.

The Moon parting from VENUS and applying to MERCURY, if she be increasing or at full, signifies stewards of noble women, and gaining preferment by female aid; it also denotes dyers, jewellers, armourers, musicians, lovers of arts and sciences, but inclined too much to pleasure; if the Moon be decreasing, it signifies vicious, abandoned persons, of various employments.

The Moon separating from VENUS and applying to SATURN, at the full, or increasing in a nocturnal geniture, gives a wife of infamous character; in a diurnal nativity, and the Moon decreasing, the native is licentious, and brings disgrace and ruin on himself.

If the Moon separate from VENUS and apply to JUPITER, it signifies noblemen, magistrates, and courteous, amiable persons; if the Moon decrease, it signifies gain by the good friendship of ladies, happiness, attainment of property or of an honourable office in the Church.

The Moon separating from VENUS and applying to MARS, in a diurnal geniture, at full or increasing, signifies misery, imprisonment, or sudden death, through a love affair; in a nocturnal geniture, it signifies cruel persons in great power, but subject almost daily to dangers and mischances.

If the Moon be transferred from VENUS to the SUN, it separates the native from his parents through a bitter dispute, consequent privation, troubles, and indiscreet attachments; but after youth be past, in process of time, he increases his substance, and easily attains his desires.

If in a diurnal geniture the Moon increasing separate from MERCURY and apply to SATURN, it denotes deafness, stammering, or some impediment in the speech; it gives employment as an interpreter, or tailor, and a disposition to inquire into occult arts and sciences; but if the nativity be by night, it signifies watermen, or men employed about the water, and if malevolent stars afflict them, it denotes imprisonment and ill-fortune.

If the Moon be transferred from MERCURY to JUPITER, it signifies great men, ambassadors, treasurers, stewards of noblemen, priests, rich and happy persons.

If the Moon be increasing or at full, and pass from MERCURY to MARS in a diurnal geniture, it signifies irreligious, perjured, wicked persons, having a tendency towards theft, fraud, and murder, liable to die by the hand of justice; if it be a nocturnal geniture, it signifies captains, governors of cities, men in power, but offending in divers ways, deposed, banished, or executed.

If the Moon separate from MERCURY and apply to the SUN, it signifies men of dull understanding, having an impediment in their speech, deaf, poor, wandering and inconstant, yet in process of time these evil effects will be qualified, and after youth be passed, they gain a livelihood by sundry employments.

If in a nocturnal geniture the full Moon separate from MERCURY and apply to VENUS, it signifies men employed in a public capacity, gaining credit and honour in all their actions, and increase of happiness, orators, poets, gaining chiefly by the good offices of ladies, artists, druggists, and jewellers, but living moderately, neither abounding nor in want, votaries of pleasure; in a nocturnal geniture, the Moon decreasing and applying to Venus, signifies wealthy persons, having the chief government over towns and cities (especially if the Moon and Venus be free from the beams of the Sun); in a diurnal geniture the Moon decreasing and applying to Venus, and in the tenth house it signifies religious persons, builders of churches, prelates; in any other part of the figure this conjunction signifies moderate estates, occupation in arts or with metals, perfumers, engravers, choristers, students of celestial science and occult arts, and gaining livelihood by such pursuits.

The Moon when afflicted in *Aries*, or afflicting the hyleg therefrom, is held to indicate convulsions, lethargy, weakness of sight, or pains in the knees. In *Taurus*, pains in the legs and feet, tumours, intestinal obstruction, or quinsy. In *Gemini*, gout, surfeits, and obstructions. In *Cancer*, dyspepsia, carcinoma, convulsions, epilepsy, or dropsy. In *Leo*, affections of the heart, quinsy, scrofula, and spinal complaints. In *Virgo*, cholera, diarrhoea, colic, dysentery, obstructions, and debility. In *Libra*, renal affections, and pleurisy. In *Scorpio*, affections of the genito-urinary organs, smallpox, dropsy, and debility of the heart. In *Sagittarius*, sciatica, and intestinal affections. In *Capricornus*, calculus, gout in the lower extremities, etc. In *Aquarius*, hysteria, and ulcers in the legs. In *Pisces*, cold taken at the feet, dropsy, and effects of intoxication.

CHAPTER XII.

THE PLANET MERCURY.

"Tis Jove's world-wandering herald, Mercury."—SHELLEY

MERCURY is the chief significator, next to the Sun and Moon, in genethlialogy.

The cardinal number *four* in Hebrew, ARABO, is compounded of AR, *light*, *i.e.*, the light or star, and RABO, *activity*, *business* or *employment*; thus meaning "the active star," or "the star of employment," in allusion to the doctrine that Mercury rules over *business* and employment, and influences activity of mind and body. Arabo means a finger, and also a locust, both influenced, astrologically, by Mercury. The name of the wandering Arabs is taken from this word, all persons born under Mercury's influence having a Bohemian tendency, and being fond of moving from place to place. The root of the word RAB, means to strive or contend in words, to dispute, a well-known characteristic of mercurial persons. The word ARABO, *four*, alluded, therefore, to Mercury, who rules over "Day four" (Mercurii dies), or Wednesday.

The name of Buddha is formed from Budhuha or Budahu—the name of the planet Mercury. Hermes was the Greek name of Mercury, and the great Hermes Trismegistus, *i.e.*, ter maximus, thrice great by reason of his virtues and great learning, lived about the time of Moses and is thought to be the same. Hermes in Greek means "the interpreter of the gods," and Mercury was ever represented as the messenger of the gods. Homer, in his hymn to Mercury, says[1]:

"Hermes, nothing loth
Obeyed the Aegis-bearer's will—for he,
Is able to persuade all easily."

The sixth hieroglyphic in Mr. Upham's work on Buddhism[2] represents Buddha as born of a virgin, this being an allusion to the sign Virgo, the chief dignity and "house," of Mercury, or the sign in which

[1] Shelly's translation.

[2] *History and Doctrines of Buddhism.*

he has most power. The fourth hieroglyphic in the same work, exhibits the twin children of Buddha, an allusion to the sign Gemini, the twins ("the pair" in Buddhist astronomy), the other house of Mercury. The Hebrew BUD, which signifies alone, single, solitary, agrees in a remarkable manner with the character of Buddha, and also persons born under the rule of the planet Mercury; such persons, being given to a contemplative or studious life, were led to seek retirement and to dwell alone—"far from the busy haunts of men."

The late Prince Consort was born when the planet Mercury was rising in the sign of Virgo.[3] His high talents, wisdom, and love of retirement were in exact accord with the character of the influence of Mercury. "In his early youth," says his biographer,[4] "Prince Albert was very shy, and he had long to struggle against that feeling. He disliked visits from strangers, and at their approach would run to the farthest corner of the room, and cover his face with his hands; nor was it possible to make him speak a word. If his doing so was insisted upon he resented to the utmost, screaming violently."

Mercury in *Gemini*, *Virgo* or *Sagittarius* and in any aspect with Jupiter (more particularly the conjunction and parallel of declination) at birth, renders the native liberal, generous, humane, jovial, amiable, and of good mental capacity. The quartile and opposition when formed between Mercury and Jupiter, are said to produce "a weak judgment, and an inclination to view things through a false medium"; in my opinion this is an error, for I have never found an instance of its verity, and I am satisfied that any aspect of Mercury, or the luminaries, to Jupiter is better than none. If Jupiter happen to have familiarity with Saturn, that observation would, probably, hold good, but in such case, it would be due to Saturn's influence vitiating to some extent that of Jupiter.

Mercury in conjunction or evil aspect with Mars, at birth, the native is inclined to violence and rashness, yet is he possessed of acuteness and discrimination; but when the evil aspects of Saturn also coincide, and when no assistance is rendered by Venus or Jupiter, he may descend to the level of a thief, swindler, or murderer. Mercury in conjunction or benefic aspect with Mars, at birth, the native proves a first-rate mechanic, or painter, or surgeon, brave, skillful, ingenious, possessing a fund of caustic humour, a penetrating wit, a talent for mathematics.

[3] See page 52.

[4] *Life of the Prince Consort*, Vol. I.

Mercury in conjunction with the Sun is said to destroy the abilities of the person then born, rendering him shallow, superficial, devoid of good judgment, and, though qualified for business, incapable of the pursuit of the higher branches of science. This effect, however, can only take place when Mercury is afflicted and receives no assistance from the fortunes—at least such is my opinion. Inasmuch as Mercury is never more than 28° distant from the Sun, no aspects can be formed between those bodies, except the mundane and zodiacal parallels. The mundane parallel, when there is more than 17° distance between them, of the Sun and Mercury from the mid-heaven, is said to cause "great and boundless ambition, and if the other parts of the figure concur, the native may rise to considerable eminence."

When Mercury is in conjunction, par. dec., or sextile with Venus, the person then born is fond of poetry, music, and drawing; when the conjunction happens in the ascendant, and the Moon separates from good aspect of Venus and applies to Mercury, the native will prove eminent in either music, poetry, or painting. Mars assisting this configuration, inclines the native to painting and sculpture. Robert Burns was born with Mercury and Venus ascending in Aquarius.

Mercury in good aspect or parallel declination with the Moon produces excellent abilities, and the native proves successful in either literature or science. A benefic aspect of Saturn to this configuration is of great service in imparting to the native that application and steadfastness of purpose which are indispensable to the attainment of success and distinction. Mercury and the Moon in conjunction, or mutual evil aspect, the native, though possessing great abilities, is rather unsettled. Culpeper says that to understand the character of a person born when the Moon and Mercury are conjoined, you have only to look at a weather-vane!

Whenever Mercury and the Moon are weak, and unconnected with each other or the ascendant and one of them afflicted, the person then born is very liable to mental derangement. Mercury being a convertible planet may, when aspected by evil planets, operate as a malefic; and when aspected by the fortunes, as a benefic. Notwithstanding that this is the well-known and observed character of Mercury, ancient authors have declared—and some modern writers have repeated it—that "he is in nature cold, dry, and melancholy." When strongly posited at birth, *i.e.*, when in the ascendant or third house or in either Gemini or Virgo, and more than 17° from the Sun, Mercury produces the most pointed wit, ingenuity, and inventive genius.

When ascending at a birth, and free from the rays of other planets, he denotes a rather tall, straight, spare body; narrow face, deep forehead, long, straight nose, eyes neither black nor gray, thin lips and chin, with but little beard, brown complexion; hazel or chestnut coloured hair; the extremities long and slender; the walk quick and energetic; and the manners refined. It has been stated that, "If orientally posited (unless in ♊) as regards the Sun, the stature will be shorter, with sandy hair and sanguine complexion, somewhat sunburnt, the limbs and joints large and well set, with small gray eyes; but if occidental, the complexion will be quite sallow, lank body, small, slender limbs, hollow eyes, of a red cast, and of a dry constitution."

Mercury strongly posited, at a birth, the person will possess a strong imagination and retentive memory, will be likely to become an excellent orator or a good logician. He will be given to the attainment of learning, an encourager of the liberal arts, of a sharp, witty, and pleasant conversation, of an unwearying fancy, aud curious in pursuit of all natural knowledge; with an inclination to travel or trade into foreign countries. If bred to mercantile pursuits, he will be ambitious of excelling all others in the merchandise, and will prove successful in obtaining wealth.

If Mercury be neither accidentally nor essentially dignified, and be not in aspect to either of the fortunes, the native will be wanting in resource and effort, a talebearer, and hardly capable of acquiring anything beyond a superficial knowledge of any trade or profession.

Mercury above the horizon, at a birth, inclines to oratory; below, to arts, sciences, and occult studies.

Mercury governs the brain, intellect, tongue, hands and feet. The diseases he produces are: mania, apoplexy, convulsions, impediments of speech, coryza and dry cough. His angel is Raphael.

Mercury in the Twelve Signs.

☿ in ♈ gives middle stature, spare and angular; long neck, oval face, light-brown curling hair, dusky or brown complexion; choleric disposition.

☿ in ♉ describes a person of middle stature, full face, and brown hair, swarthy complexion; inert and obstinate in disposition.

☿ in ♊ represents a tall, slender, well-set person, swarthy complexion, dark brown hair, hazel eyes, prominent nose, long hands and feet; of great ingenuity and activity of mind, a lover of science and art, a good orator, well-calculated for a barrister, or author, possessing a clear and incisive intellect.

☿ in ♋ gives low stature, bad complexion, sad brown hair, thin face, sharp nose, and small eyes; erratic disposition.

☿ in ♌ represents large stature, not corpulent but rather lean, large prominent eyes, dark brown or black hair, swarthy complexion, a prominent nose; a hasty and proud disposition, ambitious, and apt to be dogmatic.

☿ in ♍ describes a full stature, rather above the medium height, well-proportioned body, indifferent complexion, oval or thin face, dark brown or black hair, intellectual expression, and high forehead; witty, ingenious, profound, and active in disposition, one who readily acquires knowledge, industrious, a good orator, a great projector, and an able negotiator.

☿ in ♎ gives a tall, handsome person, smooth, light-brown hair, gray or blue eyes, sanguine complexion; a just and good nature and disposition, a promoter of learning, and accomplished.

☿ in ♏ represents short stature, well-set, broad shoulders, swarthy complexion, sad brown hair curling and bushy; one who is subtle and careful of his own interests, fond of company and the fair sex, but intellectual and capable of acquiring knowledge, especially of chemistry, medicine, or engineering.

☿ in ♐ describes a person inclined to tallness, well-formed, oval face, sanguine and clear complexion, chestnut hair growing off the temples, prominent Grecian nose; disposition impulsive good-natured, aiming at noble ends, and fond of pleasure and outdoor games and sport; a good equestrian.

☿ in ♑ denotes short stature, thin face, brown hair, dusky complexion, large nose, thick lower lip, may be bow-legged or lame; of a peevish melancholy and nervous disposition, rather unfortunate.

☿ in ♒ confers but indifferent stature, fleshy, large face, clear complexion, brown hair; ingenious, witty, kind, and humane disposition, love of research and invention.

☿ in ♓ gives short stature, brown hair, thin face, pale complexion; disposition good-natured yet melancholy, and, in some cases, addicted to strong drink.

CHAPTER XIII.

THE PLANET VENUS.

"Cynthiae figuras aemulatur Mater Amorum."—GALILEO.
"The Mother of Love imitates the aspects of Diana."

"Lo! in the painted oriel of the West,
Whose panes the sunken sun incarnadines,
Like a fair lady at her casement, shines
The evening star, the star of love and rest."—LONGFELLOW.

NEXT after the Sun, says Aberbanel, the ancient Fathers accounted Venus to be the most propitious. It was early recognised that Venus was the chief cause of generation, and the mother of love—the universal passion. Hence, her influence being held to be propitious and second only to that of the Sun, this beautiful planet was especially worshiped throughout the whole East, as it is affirmed by Rabbi Kapal Ben-Samuel. The worship of Venus led the Turks to hold Friday (Venus's day) in the same veneration that we hold Sunday. The stone (Bractan) which is set up at Mecca, measuring four feet long by two feet broad, and said by Gaffarel to be only a talisman, has engraved upon it the figure of Venus with a crescent.

In Hebrew Shish, *six*, is an abbreviation of ASH-ISH, "*the star of Being or Existence*," the precise character of Venus. On the sixth day the Creation was finished, and Job says "the morning stars sang together, and all the sons of God shouted for joy." Venus influences music and singing. The influence of Venus was thus recognised over the sixth day (Veneris dies) of the week.

The Greek name of Venus was Aphrodite, derived from ΦΕΡΩ, *fero*, to bear, bring forth, or produce—and *not* (as the poets imagined) from ΑΦΟΣ, *aphros*, froth of the sea, etc. Venus's chief dignity is in the watery sign Pisces, hence a fish was affixed to her statue. Her "night-house" is Taurus, hence ASH-TAROTH, "The Star of Taurus," called Αστᾷςτη Astarte, viz., VENUS. As a modern writer[1] has ob-

[1] R. J. Morrison, R.N.

served: "Ignorance of the grand astrological fact that the sign Tanrus is the house of Venus, and also the exaltation of the Moon, is at the bottom of all the confusion of the learned world when treating on the subject. This was one of the grand mysteries, which could not be known or understood by any but the Chaldei, or first Freemasons, who took care to teach it to the Royal Arch Masons, only. This is clear from the words of Godfrey Higgins'[2] who says 'The Masons, or Chaldei, or Culdees, were the judicial astrologers at Rome in the time of the Emperors. They could be of no small consequence when they were employed by Julius Caesar to correct the calendar.'"

Venus is the brightest planet of the Solar system. Her orbit, being smaller than that of the earth, she can never appear more than 48° distant from the Sun. When Venus has chief dominion over the mind and disposition, she inclines to music, poetry, painting, sculpture, drawing, amusement, and dancing; she confers a good-humoured, witty, kind, and charitable disposition. Men born under the influence of Venus are general favourites—especially with the fair sex—but they are rather deficient in firmness and resolution. But if Venus be much afflicted, the very good nature of the man sometimes leads him into awkward scrapes.

Venus in the ascendant (near the horizon) at a man's birth, strengthens his constitution, promotes his welfare, confers upon him a good personality, depth of affection, a tender heart, and a love of pleasure. In person he is, usually, handsome, well-formed, but not tall in stature, of fair and clear complexion, bright sparkling eyes of a dark hazel or black, hair bright-brown or chestnut, shining and plentiful, generally has dimples in either the cheek or chin, and sometimes in both; voice musical. Women born with Venus rising, and unafflicted, display the most amiable, engaging, and fascinating qualities, they are very neat and elegant, and frequently very beautiful. If Venus be afflicted, there is a tendency to dissipation. A friendly ray of Saturn to Venus is exceedingly useful in steadying the character. The sextile, trine, or par. dec. of Jupiter with Venus, the former being in the mid-heaven, and the latter in the ascendant, not only confers amiable qualities of mind[3] and disposition, but good fortune also (unless the Sun and Moon be afflicted by Saturn). The conjunction of Venus and Jupiter in the ascendant, at a birth, is of similar import.

Venus is said to govern the reins, spine, the tubili seminiferi, the

[2] *Anacalypsis*, page 768.

[3] Provided Mercury be configurated with them.

neck, throat, and breasts. Her diseases are: those affecting the spine, generative organs, and breasts, hysteria and diabetes; some authors say hernia and fistula also. Venus is friendly to Mars. Her angel is called Anael.

VENUS IN THE TWELVE SIGNS.

♀ in ♈ represents a person of middle stature, rather slender, good complexion, light hair, with a mark or scar in the face; one who is sensitive, merry and affectionate.

♀ in ♉ gives a comely person, short in stature, fleshy, sanguine complexion, and brown hair; a mild disposition, kind, humane, and very affectionate.

♀ in ♊ gives a stature inclined to tallness, slender, well-formed body, rather fair, intellectual expression of features; a loving, just, humane disposition, and good natural abilities.

♀ in ♋ forms persons of short stature, inclined to corpulence, round face, delicate or pale complexion, light hair; an inactive, easy-going, and pleasure-loving disposition.

♀ in ♌ designates a tall well-made person, a clear complexion, round face, full prominent eye, light flaxen hair; a disposition somewhat hasty but soon appeased, generous, large-minded, having proper pride and dignity.

♀ in ♍ represents a tall well-proportioned body, sad brown or black hair, dark sanguine complexion, oval face; in disposition thoroughly amiable, aspiring, sensitive, and active, endowed with excellent qualities and conversational powers, often with eloquence.

♀ in ♎ gives a tall, elegant person, brown hair, sanguine complexion, often freckled, dimpled cheeks; one who is kind, affectionate, and generally beloved, very artistic and clever.

♀ in ♏ represents a well-set, short, stout person, face broad, complexion dusky, hair sad brown, curling, and plentiful; in disposition contentious, emotional, and affectionate, but inert.

♀ in ♐ gives a well-formed person, clear sanguine complexion, bright-sparkling eyes, oval face, brown hair; in disposition amiable, "merry even to a fault," generous, humane, and very sensitive; and clever; a general favourite, and usually fortunate.

♀ in ♑ gives but a mean stature, pale sickly complexion, face thin and lean, hair dark or black; in disposition good-natured, but careful; voice musical; not very fortunate.

♀ in ♒ represents a handsome well-proportioned person, rather stout, light brown hair, clear and sanguine complexion; in disposition very courteous, kind, humane, and affable; one who is gifted, and much admired.

♀ in ♓ gives middle stature, a fleshy body, moderately good complexion, round dimpled face, brown or flaxen hair; in disposition thoroughly good-natured, mild, quiet, and inoffensive, fond of pleasure; generally fortunate.

"Alma Venus!

Quae mare navagerum, quae terras frugiferentes
Comelebras; per te quoniam genus omne animatum.
Consipitur, visitque exortum lumina. solis."—LUCRETIUS.

"Blest Venus! thou the sea and fruitful earth
Peoplest amain. To thee whatever lives.
Its being owes, and that it sees the Sun."

The ancient temples of Venus crowned heights and headlands at many places in Asia and Greece.

The moral conception of Aphrodite Urania—the "heavenly"—-as goddess of the higher and purer love and fruitfulness was but slowly developed in the course of ages.[4]

The ancients found by long observation that the planets Venus and Mars were "friendly," and this explains why the goddess Aphrodite was associated with Are, Mars, both in worship and legend.

[4] See the "Dictionary of Classical Antiquities," p. 39.

CHAPTER XIV.

THE PLANET MARS.

"Is it the tender star of love,
The star of love and dreams?
Oh no! from that blue tent above
A hero's armour gleams."—LONGFELLOW.

THE Hebrew, ASH-LESH, means the STAR OF FLAME, or FLAMING STAR. SHELESH, the number three, means, also, a general or commander of an army; the *third* day of the week is under the rule of Mars, "the god of war," who influences all military men.

The *red* deity, Mara, of the Buddhists, is evidently the planet Mars. The final letter *a* seems to be a mere termination, for a vast number of other names have the same terminal letter; and, if we substitute for it the European final letter *s*, we have the word Mars, which planet is red in the heavens, and has always been represented as a fiery, evil planet. Mars was drawn with a battle-axe or spear in one hand, and a cock or horned goat in the other. This shows that the Buddhist planet—deity Mara was Mars, the god of war, to whom the cock was dedicated; the horned goat shows that it was the planet Mars, because Capricornus (the horned goat) is the sign in which Mars is exalted—his chief dignity. The Buddhists also assigned the third day of the week to Mars (Angaharu).

The mythology of the Egyptians, Greeks, and Romans was originally a method of handing down astrological truths, from generation to generation, before the era of letters. The hieroglyphics of Buddha's life and adventures are similar in character to the Egyptian hieroglyphics, and may have been derived from the latter. Buddhism is nothing more nor less than a crystallisation of Sabeism, or planet-worship.

Mungula is the Hindu name of Mars. "He is painted of red or flame colour. His *vahan* (vehicle) is a ram. Those who are born under this planet are subject to losses and misfortunes; but it is considered fortunate to engage in battle on Mungul-war, or Tuesday, over which day he presides. Like many other martial personages, Mungula is said to be of a fierce and arbitrary disposition."[1]

The scape-*goat*[2] which was sent into the wilderness (Leviticus, Chap. xvi.), bears a striking analogy to the astrological allegory that the angel of Mars dwelt in a desert place. There is a curious instance of the connection existing between astrology and the Buddhist mythology in Bodhisatwa's reply to Mara's challenge to Buddha. The first three lines are thus rendered[3]:

> "Thou, although supreme in the world of Desire
> Hast no authority or power in the Spiritual world.
> Thou art only acquainted with the wretched beings in Hell."

Mars, in astrology, is friendly with Venus, hence the allusion in the first line quoted above.

It has been supposed that HERCULES typifies the Sun, his twelve labours being symbolical of the passage of the Sun through the twelve signs of the zodiac, his extraordinary strength denoting the potent effect of the solar rays. It is not so, however. Hercules is the personification not of the Sun, but of the planet Mars. Hyginus says, "The third planet is Mars, which others called Hercules." Macrobius says, "Maro with the ripeness of profound learning, refers the Salii to Hercules, because the priests consider that god the same as Mars." The same is affirmed in the "Menippea" of Varo, entitled "The other Hercules," in which, after much discourse about Hercules, this god was proved to be Mars. The star which all others call Mars, is called Hercules by the Chaldaeans.

Ptolemy says, " Mars ascending, gives a fair ruddiness to the person, with large size, a healthy constitution, blue or grey eyes, a sturdy figure, and a moderate growth of hair, with a temperament principally of heat and dryness. When occidental, he makes the complexion simply ruddy, and the personal figure of moderate stature, with small eyes; the body without hair, and the hair of the head light or red, and straight; the bodily temperament being chiefly dry."

Mars describes, when rising, one of a middle stature, strong well-set body, rather muscular than corpulent, the face round, the eyes hazel, sharp and piercing, a dark reddish complexion, the hair sometimes red, sandy or flaxen; not infrequently a scar on the face es-

[1] Coleman's *Mythology of the Hindus*.

[2] In Thibet the same rite was practised.

[3] De Sig. Coeli, 2, page 80.

pecially if he be ascending near the cusp; the countenance full of confidence and boldness, and the disposition active and intrepid. Experience has shown me that some men are of large stature who were born with the planet Mars ascending, and others of short stature. In every instance, irrespective of sex, with but one exception, has the ruddiness of Mars been imprinted either on the complexion or the hair, often in both. In the case of the lady who is an exception to the rule, Mars was rising in Sagittarius, at her birth, in sextile to Jupiter, Venus being in (mundane) sextile to the ascendant from the third house and the sign Pisces.

The Martialist is remarkable for acuteness of perception, an incisive intellect, but possessing some rashness as well as judgment. He is possessed of great mechanical skill, high courage, having a contempt for death, impatience of control or submission, and but little respect for social and in some cases moral laws when they interfere with his liberty of action.

A good aspect of Mars to the Sun, Moon, or Mercury, is necessary to produce "pluck," resolution, and self-reliance—qualities which are so greatly needed in the battle of life, when distinction and success are to be won. Persons devoid of martial influence are mean-spirited, dejected, helpless creatures. Evil aspects of Mars to the significators are apt to produce evil qualities, such as dissimulation, revenge, obstinacy, and violence. Mars-men make excellent soldiers, surgeons, chemists, butchers, iron-workers, cutlers, etc.

Mars was termed by the ancients the lesser infortune, in contradistinction to Saturn, who was called the greater infortune. It is found that the effects of Mars' influence by "direction" come most certainly and closely to time. Mars is, in nature, hot and dry, and the instigator of quarrels and war. He is said to rule the left ear, head, face, sense of smell, the imagination, reins, gall, reproductive organs, kidneys, etc. His diseases are the smallpox, acute fevers, measles, scarlatina, erysipelas, jaundice, diabetes, and carbuncle; accidents, burns, gunshot wounds, wounds in battle, surgical incisions, haemorrhages, etc. His place in a nativity or solar revolution is held to be very unfortunate.

When Mars is rising or oriental of the Sun, at a nativity, the native will be above the middle stature, very hairy, and of a clearer complexion. When occidental, the native will be short, of a ruddier complexion, a small head, with yellow hair, and a dry constitution.

The angel of Mars is called Samael.

MARS IN THE TWELVE SIGNS.

Mars in ♈ represents middle stature, well-set body, big-boned, swarthy complexion, "beetling brows," light or red curling hair; countenance fierce and austere; mind and disposition valorous, intrepid, confident, enterprising, ambitious, and warlike, one who gains preferment and distinction in martial pursuits.

♂ in ♉ makes the native rather short, corpulent, of swarthy complexion, a scar in the face; in disposition vicious, profligate, and perfidious (unless ♂ be well aspected).

♂ in ♊ describes a tall person, well-made, of sanguine complexion, dark brown or black hair (red, if ♂ be near Aldebaran); mind and disposition very ingenious, but fickle; and, through frequent changes of residence and employment, the native is likely to prove unfortunate.

♂ in ♋ was said to produce "short stature, an ill-made, misshapen body;[5] thick brown hair; mind and disposition contentious, unamiable, not highly gifted, and the native is usually unfortunate." This is much overdrawn.

♂ in ♌ signifies large stature, a muscular and well-made body, ruddy or sunburnt complexion, large, prominent eyes, flaxen or sandy hair; disposition choleric, hasty, free, magnanimous, and proud, delighting in out-door exercise and sport.

♂ in ♍ designates a middle-sized person, dark brown or black hair, dark ruddy complexion, a scar or blemish in the face; in disposition, nervous, irritable, mutable, conceited, and impatient of subjection; one who is not very fortunate.

♂ in ♎ represents a well-proportioned person, tall, and commanding; oval face, sanguine complexion, countenance full of expression and vivacity; in disposition luxurious, fond of personal adornment and voluptuous.

♂ in ♏ gives a well-set, muscular, square built figure, inclined to corpulence, a broad face, swarthy complexion, black curling hair, countenance bold and resolute; temper fiery and revengeful; one who possesses genius, well fitted for a commander, or surgeon, successful in his undertakings and of invincible courage. [Lord Nelson was born

[5] The Duke of Connaughi was born with Mars rising in Cancer, and he is neither short in stature nor deformed; but, fortunately, Mars was in sextile aspect with Jupiter. The poet Byron had Mars in the ascendant, in Cancer, at the moment of his birth—at two o'clock p.m.

with Mars exactly rising in Scorpio.] Liable to hernia.

♂ in ♐ gives a rather tall, well-made body, compact and fleshy; complexion sanguine, hair brown and growing off the temples, a fine forehead, quick eye; in disposition jovial, martial, self-reliant, rash, large of soul, generous, active, enterprising, ambitious of renown; one who is fond of outdoor exercise and sport; liable to gun-shot wounds, and hernia.

♂ in ♑ represents a mean stature, rather lean; bad complexion, thin face, small head, black lank hair; one who is very ingenious, witty, penetrating, courageous, commanding, and generally successful.

♂ in ♒ gives a well-set, middle-sized body; fair complexion, sandy hair; disposition turbulent, controversial, unruly; and not fortunate.

♂ in ♓ gives but a small stature, corpulent body; indifferent complexion, light brown or sandy hair; in disposition artful, mischievous, not very industrious, prone to excesses and quarrelsomeness.

Mars, when configurated with Mercury, invariably sharpens the intellect. As before observed, Lord Nelson was born with Mars rising in Scorpio; I have known several clever surgeons who were born with Mars rising in *Aries*, *Virgo*, *Sagittarius*, *Scorpio*, and *Pisces*, respectively.

When Mars afflicts the "hyleg," at birth, from the sign *Aries*, the health is too likely to suffer from feverish ailments, congestion of the brain, or apoplexy. Mars in *Taurus* causes throat affections, bronchitis, and calculus. In *Gemini*, eruptions on the skin. In *Cancer*, haematemesis, and if in quartile or opposition, or conjunction with Saturn, abscess of the breast. In *Leo*, hypertrophy of the heart, or kidney disease. In *Virgo*, intestinal irritation, etc. In *Libra*, a liability to diabetes. In *Scorpio*, hernia, calculus, and cystitis. In *Sagittarius*, sciatica, or fracture of the thigh, or gunshot wounds. In *Capricorn*, gout in the knees, or synovitis. In *Aquarius*, eczema, or gout in the legs. In *Pisces*, gout in the feet.

CHAPTER XV.

THE PLANET JUPITER.

"—Jupiter, the lustrous, lordeth now,
And the dark work, complete of preparation,
He draws by force into the realm of light."—SCHILLER'S *Wallenstein*.

The Hebrew CHEMASH, or the cardinal number *five*, affixed to the fifth day of the week (Jovis dies) Thursday, is evidently formed of CHEM, *warmth*, and ASH, *a star*, meaning "the star of warmth, the exact character of, Jupiter," "in-whom," said Claudius Ptolemy, "warmth is predominant." By reversing the first letter we have MESHECH, to anoint with oil, the root being cognate with MECH, *fat*; whence the term MESCHICH, the anointed, the "Messiah"; because anointing with oil was part of the ceremony of the investiture of priests as well as kings. Here we have a reference to the influence of Jupiter over priests, religion, and holy things; and olive oil was generally employed, because, the olive was held to be under this planet's influence. Again, Shemach, formed from Chemash by reversing the first and last letters, signifies Joy, and is a direct corruption of ASH-MACH, literally "The Star of Joy," which is the emphatic title of Jove, whence we derive jovial, joy, jolly, etc. Here is ample evidence that the word *five* alluded to the day of Jupiter, who rules "Day five."[1]

The character of Jupiter's influence is the same all over the world. This planet has been deified and worshipped under several names, but has ever been regarded as a mild and benevolent deity, the character of Vishnu in Buddhism. The chackra, or thunderbolt of Mara (Mars) is also common to Vishnu (Jupiter), demonstrating that it was early observed that these two planets are the chief causes of thunder, and it is a fact that when they are configurated or conjoined there is more heat and violent thunder than at other times. This was the opinion of Pliny. The Buddhist name of Jupiter was Braspaty or Braspatia, and he was held to rule the fifth day of the week (Thursday).

The more modern Hebrew name of Jupiter was *Tsedeq*, Justice, be-

[1] See *Zadkiel's Almanac* for 1849, page 56, "Origin of the Days of the

cause of the just character of persons born under his influence. GAD, as before remarked, was also a Hebrew name of Jupiter, to which Aben Ezra bears testimony, for he says that the Targum expressly retained this word as being the most proper for expressing this star.

The Jupiter man is easily distinguishable by his generosity, sincerity, and courtesy of manner. He is manly and noble, and far removed from the nervous manner of the Saturnine, as from the boldness of the Martialist character.

When Jupiter is in good aspect with the luminaries, or ascending at a birth, he confers a sound, healthy constitution, of great vitality, and capable of withstanding the effects of very evil "directions." When posited in the tenth house, and near the upper meridian he confers honour and dignity; on merchants, great success in trade and speculations; and generally raises those born in poverty to comparative wealth.

At the birth of H.M. Queen Victoria, Jupiter was in the tenth house (meridian). At the birth of King Edward VII, Jupiter was ascending and in sextile aspect with Venus.

When Jupiter is in the ascendant at a nativity, he produces an erect stature rather above middle height, a handsome rosy complexion, oval face, high forehead, large gray eyes, soft, thick, brown hair, short neck, capacious chest, broad shoulders, strong and well-proportioned limbs. The native is sober and manly in address, and of excellent manners. His disposition is good, amiable, generous, faithful, prudent, just, honest, religious, and liberal, hating all mean and sordid actions.

Jupiter is considered a masculine, hot, moist, airy, social planet, the author of temperance, justice, and moderation; and he is termed the greater fortune. He is said to govern the lungs, the blood, and viscera; and his diseases are such as affect those organs, and plethora. The name of his angel is Zedekiel, or Zadkiel.

JUPITER IN THE TWELVE SIGNS.

Jupiter in ♈ designates a person of middle stature, of a rosy complexion; light brown or flaxen hair; piercing eyes; a high nose; oval face, subject to pimples; disposition noble, free, generous, with becoming pride, courteous, and polite.

♃ in ♉ gives middle stature, a well-set, compact, strong body; swarthy complexion, brown rugged hair, inclined to curl or frizzle, round face, not handsome; disposition good, manners, amiable, judgment sound, and temper benevolent and humane; addicted to pleasure.

♃ in ♊ forms a well-composed, rather tall person, sanguine complexion, brown glossy hair, full handsome eyes; manners graceful and obliging, disposition generous, but somewhat fickle, a great admirer of the fair sex, a lover of science and art; but if ♃ be near any of the violent fixed stars of Gemini the disposition will be somewhat rash, and unstable.

♃ in ♋ gives middle stature, pale complexion, fragile appearance, dark brown hair, oval face; disposition busy, loquacious, fond of maritime pursnits, but maybe lacking in courage unless ♂ aspect ♃ or the luminaries.

♃ in ♌ represents a strong, robust constitution; tall, well-made body; light-brown or yellowish curling hair, prominent eyes, sanguine complexion; a noble-minded, courageous, ambitious, and magnanimous person.

♃ in ♍ gives a full-sized person, well made, often handsome; brown or blackish hair; sanguine but not fair complexion; in disposition ambitious, excitable, studious, industrious, and speculative.

♃ in ♎ confers complete symmetry in form and figure, good stature; oval and handsome face, rosy complexion, light brown hair, large eyes; disposition mild, fascinating, obliging, and fond of pleasure.

♃ in ♏ makes the body compact, stout, middle sized, and robust; fleshy face, dull complexion, dark curling bushy hair; a lofty, resolute, and ambitious character; fortunate upon the sea and in the practice of medicine, surgery, or chemistry.

♃ in ♐ represents a tall, upright, well-made, handsome person; sanguine complexion, fine clear eyes, oval face, chestnut hair, thick beard; manners courteous and highly accomplished, disposition generous, free, just and humane, very fond of horses, hunting, and all out-door sports and exercises.

♃ in ♑ gives but a mean stature, small head, pale complexion, lean face, little beard, dark hair; disposition rather harmless and indolent; a person usually unfortunate.

♃ in ♒ gives middle stature, compact, corpulent body; fair complexion, brown hair; disposition cheerful, obliging, kind, humane, just, busy, and not extravagant.

♃ in ♓ signifies middle stature, a full fleshy body; dark complexion, light brown hair; disposition eminently good, studious, and kind; talents of a high order; one who is fortunate upon the seas.

CHAPTER XVI.
THE PLANET SATURN.

"The empire of Saturnus is gone by;
Lord of the secret birth of things is he;
Within the lap of earth, and in the depths
Of the imagination dominates;
And his are all things that eschew the light."—SCHILLER'S *Wallenstein*.

THE ancient inhabitants of India, Phoenicia, and Egypt, seem to have studied very carefully the character of Saturn's influence, and their esoteric doctrines comprise the very essence thereof. The root of the name Saturn is evidently the ancient Hebrew term *Sater*, to hide or conceal.

SHEBO, the cardinal number *seven*, is composed of ASH, *a star*, and SHEB, old age; thus expressing the chief character of Saturn as "the star of old age." Shebo signifies, also, to be full or have plenty, in allusion to Saturn's rule over the produce of the earth; just as the Latins had *saturo*, to sate or saturate, from Saturnus. In allusion to this power of the star of agriculture, recognised by all astrologers, Virgil calls a sickle "Saturni deus curvus"—the crooked tooth of Saturn, whence ♄, the planet's symbol. SHEB, to return, or to restore, is applied (I. Sam. vii., 17) to the *end* of the year[1] and its beginning again; so it implies the end of a week of days, and its beginning again. It also signifies "hoary hairs," which are under Saturn's influence. Here is ample proof that the word SHEBO (seven) had reference to Saturn, the ruler of "Day seven," or Saturday.

The other name of the planet, KRONOS, appears to have originated from the Hebrew word *Kron*, a born—an emblem of power in the East.

Moses decidedly set apart Saturn's day as the sacred or Sabbath day, it being *dies infaustus*, or an unlucky day for the beginning of

[1] Claudius Ptolemy says, "Saturn, moving in the last sphere, regulates the final old age."—*Ashmand's Translation*, page 205.

any work. In Scotland no one will marry on a Saturday.

The Chaldees observed that Saturn when potent at a nativity rendered the person then born "mystical," and "confederate in secrecy." Sater or Seater signifies the god of secrecy. The same term in the Chaldee signifies to destroy or demolish; and, it being observed that infants born when Saturn was in power and elevation, almost invariably died in infancy, the fable arose that Saturn devoured his own children. The priests, with the aid of the poets, personified the doctrines they taught, and the truths they learned by experience and observation, in fables and apologues before the invention of letters.

Lemprière says: "Saturn always devoured his sons as soon as born"; "It was usual to offer human victims on his altars"; again, "The god is generally represented as an old man, bent through age and infirmity. In his left hand he holds a child, which he raises up, as if instantly to devour it."

The Hindu name of the planet Saturn is Sani (the Buddhist name is Henahura). "He is described of a dark colour, and clothed in black. His vahan is by some called a black vulture, or raven. He is old, ugly, lame, of an evil disposition, has long hair, nails, and teeth, and is of the sudra (husbandmen) caste. It is unfortunate to be born under this planet, and the ills of life are ascribed to his influence, as he is supposed to be skilled in all kinds of wickedness. He presides over the day of the week Sanis-war, or Saturday."[2]

The influence of Saturn is the most lasting and malignant of all the planets. A modern author[3] has aptly contrasted the influences of Mars and Saturn, thus: "Mars may be compared to a fever, violent indeed, but short in its duration; while Saturn resembles a consumption, which, though hardly perceptible in its progress, is hard to be averted by any effort of human skill." If placed in the mid-heaven at a nativity, Saturn, unless extremely well aspected, eventually causes ruin or disgrace, mostly. A similar effect results from the affliction by Saturn of both the Sun and Moon; and in this case, if either luminary be hyleg, the infant lives but a very short time, the closer the aspects the shorter its life.

When Saturn is exactly on the upper or lower meridian, ascendant, or descendant, the ascendant being hyleg, and having no assistance from the fortunes, the infant then born seldom lives long.

---

[2] Coleman's *Mythology of the Hindus*.

[3] Zadkiel, *Handbook of Astrology*, Vol. I., page 17.

Saturn ascending subjects the native to blows, bruises, falls, broken bones, and other accidents; to nervous affections, catarrh, rheumatism and debility. Saturnine people are melancholy, hypochondriac, penurious, secretive, and fond of solitude. They are capable of great endurance, and are noted for their patience as well as for their obstinacy; they are also bashful, firm in friendship, but strong in enmity, grave, austere, often ascetic, and very stupid if Saturn afflicts Mercury.

Saturn's benefic aspects to Mercury and the Sun and Moon, confer prudence, patience, subtlety, and faithfulness on the native. He is not given to change, and will be likely to remain in one place or one employment for the whole of his life; and he will prove fortunate in mining operations, agriculture, and building.

Saturn ascending produces a middle stature, a swarthy or pale complexion, small black deeply-set eyes, lean face, broad forehead, lowering brow, thick nose and lips, his head and shoulders stooping, large ears, broad shoulders, black or dark brown lank hair, thin beard, small and lean thighs and legs. If well dignified, (i.e. in ♎, ♑, or ♒), the native will possess acute perceptive facilities, strong imagination, and great application; in disposition and manners he will be austere, reserved, and taciturn.

Claudius Ptolemy wrote that:

"Saturn, when oriental, acts on the personal figure by producing a yellowish complexion and a good constitution; with black and curled hair, a broad and stout chest, eyes of ordinary quality, and a proportionate size of body, the temperament of which is compounded principally of moisture and cold. Should he be occidental, he makes the personal figure black or dark, thin and small, with scanty hair on the head; the body without hair, but well shaped; the eyes black or dark; and the bodily temperament consisting chiefly of dryness and cold."[4]

Saturn is said to govern the bones, spleen, teeth, joints, and right ear, and those born under his rule are said to have bad teeth, and to suffer greatly with toothache. He is also said to govern the memory. His diseases are such as proceed from taking cold, obstructions, all nervous disorders, melancholia, epilepsy, ague, black jaundice, catarrhs, the various forms of consumption, atrophy, fistula, leprosy, palsy, apoplexy, dropsy, etc.

---

[4] *Ashmund's Translation*, page 149.

SATURN IN THE TWELVE SIGNS.

Saturn in ♈ represents middle stature; a ruddy complexion, full face, little beard, dark hair, deep voice, large eyes; disposition quarrelsome, fretful, and austere.

♄ in ♉ gives middle stature; dark complexion, rough dark hair, disposition avaricious, secretive, and envious.

♄ in ♊ gives a tall and fairly well-proportioned body; oval face, dark complexion, though sanguine, hair black or dark brown; mind ingenious but crafty; disposition perverse, selfish, and austere.

♄ in ♋ represents a weak, infirm, deformed body, of small stature; face pale, thin, and of sad expression, hair sad-brown, eyes languid, dull and heavy; disposition reserved and unsociable.

♄ in ♌ gives moderately large stature, broad strong shoulders; hair brown, countenance austere, eyes deeply set; disposition passionate and brooding, yet true to a friend.

♄ in ♍ designates a tall, spare body; hair black or very dark brown, and plentiful; face long, thin, and of grave appearance, a long head; disposition melancholy, reserved, nervous, speculative, and avaricious.

♄ in ♎ gives a tall and fairly good-looking person; hair auburn or brown; face oval, nose and forehead prominent, complexion tolerably clear; disposition proud, contentious, argumentative, and may be extravagant.

♄ in ♏ represents a short, square, and muscular body; black or dark hair, bushy; dark complexion, plain face, prominent nose; disposition petulant, subtle, inconstant, and envious; mind ingenious, profound, and clever; unfortunate on the sea.

♄ in ♐ gives good stature, well-proportioned and handsome person; hair brown, beard thin, complexion sanguine, eyes deeply set, prominent nose; disposition affable, obliging, generous, honest and upright, merciful to an enemy, and constant to a friend, profuse in promises through excess of good nature.

♄ in ♑ produces low stature, a thin ungainly body; sallow complexion, small eyes, blackish hair; disposition peevish, covetous, and discontented, due, largely, to bad health; mind ingenious.

♄ in ♒ gives large stature, corpulent strong body; hair dark brown; complexion good, teeth distorted; disposition sober, manly, graceful, and courteous; mind acute and ingenious.

♄ in ♓ gives low stature, corpulent body; dark hair, pale complexion; disposition fickle, merry for a Saturnian, and very careful and cautious.

Saturn when occidental in *Aries* and afflicting the Sun, Moon, or ascendant, is said to indicate a liability to deafness, toothache, and nasal catarrh. In *Taurus*, bronchocele and bronchial and laryngeal affections. In *Gemini*, rheumatism of arms and shoulders, and disorders of the blood. In *Cancer*, pulmonary phthisis, asthma, and cancer of the breast. In *Leo*, affections of the heart, spine, and liver. In *Virgo*, phthisis abdominalis, enteric fever, and disorders of the bowels. In *Libra*, disorders of the kidneys and rheumatism. In *Scorpio*, affections of the genito-urinary organs, haemorrhage, palsy, gout, and fistula. In *Sagittary*, sciatica, gout, and hip-joint disease. In *Capricorn*, gout of the lower extremities, hemiplegia, and rheumatism. In *Aquarius*, deafness, toothache, quinsy, and cramp. In *Pisces*, scrofula, ulcers on the feet, dropsy, and marasmus.

Dante, *Convito*, II., 14, makes the planet Saturn the symbol of astrology. He says:

"The heaven of Saturn has two properties by which it may be compared to Astrology. The first is the slowness of its movement through the twelve signs; for its revolution requires twenty-nine years and more. The second is that it is the highest of all the planets. And these two properties are in Astrology; for in completing its circle, that is in learning it, a great space of time passes; both on account of the experience necessary to judge rightly in it. And, moreover, it is the highest of all, for, as Aristotle says at the beginning of his treatise on the Soul, science is of high nobility from the nobleness of its subject, and from its certainty; and this, more than any of the above-mentioned is noble and high, from its noble and high subject, which is the movement of the heavens; and high and noble from its certainty, which is without any defect, as one that proceeds from a most perfect and regular source. And if any one thinks that there is any defect in it, the defect is not on the side of the Science, but as Ptolemy says, it comes from our negligence, and to that it should be attributed."[5]

---

[5] Vide "The Divine Comedy of Dante Alighieri. Translated by Henry Wadsworth Longfellow." London: George Routledge and Sons, 1877, p. 680.

CHAPTER XVII.
THE PLANET URANUS.

"Full often learn the art to know
Of future weal, or future woe,
By word, or sign, or star."—SCOTT.

URANUS was discovered on the 13th of March, 1781, by Sir William Herschel, and was first called the *Georgium Sidus* or Herschel, names which have fallen into disuse, and was unknown to the ancients. His influence is found to be very powerful in nativities when he is in an angle or in aspect to the Sun or Moon. The existence of Uranus having been unknown to the ancients accounts for most of the errors of the old writers on nativities.

The singular death of AEschlyus was very probably due to the influence of Uranus being conjoined with that of Saturn or Mars. It had been foretold to AEschylus that he would be in danger of death by the fall of a house or other building about a certain (named) period. He, in order to avoid the threatened danger, went away from all buildings, to pass his time in the fields until the evil influence should be passed over. AEschylus was killed, while sitting in the fields, by the fall of a tortoise which an eagle dashed against his bald pate, probably mistaking it for a stone, and desiring to break the shell thereon. The remarkable nature of the death induces modern astrologers to surmise that the planet Uranus was a joint cause of it. If so, the astrologer who foretold the death of AEschylus could not predict the nature of it so approximately as if the existence of Uranus and the peculiar character of his influence had been known.

Godfrey Higgins relates the following circumstance:

"Soon after the discovery of the last of the primary planets [Uranus], an astrologer called on a friend of the author's, who was well known to be a skillful calculator, and requested him to calculate for him the periodical motions of the newly-discovered planet; observing it was very probable that the want of the knowledge and use of its mo-

---

[1] *Anacalypsis*, Vol. I., page 208.

tions was the cause that, in judicial astrology, the predictions so often failed."[1]

If Uranus be ascending at a nativity, he produces great eccentricity, and independence of thought and opinion. When free from the rays of evil planets, his influence is not wholly evil, for persons born under his influence exhibit a great love of truth; they are remarkable for a love of romance, a tendency to Bohemianism, a love for antiquarian researches, metaphysics, and occult science. Uranus seems to be very inimical to conjugal happiness, for even his good aspects to the Sun, at birth, delay marriage or prevent it entirely, to women; and his conjunction, quartile; or opposition, with the Moon seems to cause unhappiness in love and marriage, to men, or delays their marriage.

When Uranus becomes stationary near the place of the Sun or Moon at birth, or in evil aspect to either, strange and unexpected events ensue, and generally danger to or death of a relation.

His good aspects at birth, or by direction, produce sudden events of an advantageous nature, and often in a manner quite unlooked-for. If Uranus be posited near the cusp of the second house, at birth, and in evil aspect to the Sun or Moon, the person then born is liable to experience sudden, strange, and severe pecuniary losses, and he should ever avoid speculative transactions. If posited near the cusp of the 8th house, the property of the partner in marriage either will be almost *nil*, or be diminished by some strange mischance.

When Uranus is located in the 10th house and near the meridian at birth, the native generally either loses one of his parents early in life, or makes an unfortunate marriage. He or she is subject to sudden and strange reverses of fortune (unless ♅ be well aspected by the fortunes), and suffers by speculation. If posited in the 4th house, and near the lower meridian, the father of the child when born usually dies early, and the latter part of the life of the child is sad or unfortunate.

King Victor Emmanuel I. of Italy was born when Uranus was ascending in the sign Sagittarius, and in trine aspect to Venus. The ex-Queen Isabella, of Spain, was born with Uranus ascending in the 7th deg. of Aquarius, and in opposition to the Moon. The late Commander Morrison, R.N., was born with Uranus exactly rising in the last degree of Leo, and in sextile to the Sun and Mars.

Uranus when located in *Sagittary*, and affecting the Sun, Moon, or ascendant, I have found to produce sciatica, or gout of the lower extremities. In *Taurus*, a liability to diphtheria, and to bronchitis and laryngitis. A lady who was born when Uranus and Saturn were nearly conjoined in Taurus, in the eighth house, and afflicting the Moon, suffered for many years with a peculiar constant cough, the slightest movement of air producing a most exhausting paroxysm of coughing. She eventually died of phthisis laryngea.

No attempt will be made in these pages to describe the personal characteristics of the Uranus "native" as varied by the transit of the planet through the twelve signs of the zodiac. Any such descriptions found in astrological books must, necessarily, be largely if not wholly, fanciful. For, before a mere outline of such delineation could be justified, it would be imperative that, at fewest, a hundred exact and well-authenticated times of birth stated as observed and recorded to the hour and minute, for Uranus in each decanate of every sign. This would involve the careful comparison of 3,600 Uranian nativities in which the planet was alone rising at the moment of birth, and not more than five degrees above or below the ascending degree, measured by its (the planet's) oblique-ascension. I do not possess any such desirable data, although my study of the ancient science has extended over fifty years—from May, 1860, to the time of writing (January, 1911).

However, a few cases of notable Uranians may now be presented: 1°—The founder and original editor of *Zadkiel's Almanac*—R. J. M.—was born, according to the entry made by his father in the family Bible, at $9^{h} 45^{m}$ a.m. of the 15th of June, 1795, in lat. 51° 40′ N., and long. 0° 6′ W. This time the author rectified to one minute earlier, making the R.A. of M.C. 49° 38′ 15″, which gives *Taurus* 22° 4′ on the upper meridian, and *Virgo* 1° 36′ on the ascendant. The planet Uranus had lately risen in 29° 53′ of *Leo*, and was 3° 17′ above the eastern horizon, measured by oblique-ascension.[1] There was no other planet in or near the ascendant; but, inasmuch as Mars, in *Gemini* 29° 1′ was very nearly in sextile with Uranus and Mercury, in 15° 32′ of *Cancer* was nearly in semi-quartile with the ascending planet, this cannot be said to be a wholly Uranian horoscope.

In stature Zadkiel I. was very tall, being over six feet in height, and was well built. His head was large and well balanced. His temperament was very energetic, sanguine, and somewhat impulsive. He possessed a clear, active brain, of good scientific calibre. He was free from prejudice, independent in thought and opinion, ingenious, brave, self-reliant, original, and not materialistic; and was predisposed towards spiritism. His disposition was frank, courteous,

[1] A diagram of the horoscope was given in my FUTURE, December, 1893.

light-hearted, sociable, sincere, generous, and yet careful. He possessed in a high degree "the courage of his opinions," and ever fearlessly proclaimed what he believed to be the truth. He wrote largely on astrology for nearly half a century, and wrote a work, in 1857, entitled "The Cycloid System of Astronomy."

When Uranus is very close indeed—within one degree—to the ascending degree, a child then born usually meets with several accidents in the course of his life. Zadkiel I., although he was engaged in several actions at sea—for he was a commander in the Royal Navy—in his early years was, I believe, never wounded. He was once bitten in the foot by a dog, and had to submit to a slight surgical operation in consequence, at 39 years of age, under the influence of Ascendant quartile Mars in the zodiac, 38° 59′, by primary direction. He died in his sleep at 78 years and 8 months of age, in the early morning of February 5th, 1874, under Sun quartile Mercury, zodiac, conversely, 78° 28′ by primary direction (followed by two other evil directions)—Mercury having the parallel declination of Mars at birth.

2°.—The DUKE OF ORLEANS was born at 1h 50m p.m. of the 6th of February, 1869, at Twickenham. R.A. of M.C. 343° 55′ 56″, *Pisces* 12° 34′ on the upper meridian, and *Cancer* 14° 20′ on the ascendant. Uranus was retrograde in *Cancer* 14° 10′, within one degree of (above) the eastern horizon, no other planet being in the ascending sign. Mars was within two degrees of the quintile aspect with Uranus, and Jupiter was within three degrees (applying) of the quartile with the ascending planet. The Sun was in mundane trine with ♅.

The Duke of Orleans is not tall, and is stout in build. He met with an accident while hunting, on the 26th of April, 1895 (arc = 26° 13′), fracturing a leg (the tibia), under the primary direction of Ascendant parallel Uranus, in the zodiac, conversely 26° 22′ and M.C. par. ♂ zod., con. 26°46′. Again, he was much shaken in a motor-carnage collision, on the 20th of June, 1899 (arc = 30° 22′), under the primary direction of ☉ □ ♄ zod. 30° 33′. In the year 1890[2] the author foretold that this direction would "in his 31st year, cause the Duke some misfortune."

3°.—THE CROWN PRINCE RUDOLF, of Austria-Hungary, was born at 10h 15m p.m. of the 21st of August, 1858, at Vienna.[3] R.A. of

[2] See *Zadkiel's Almanac* for 1891, p. 57.

[3] The author gave the time of birth in Urania (April, 1880). p. 128, on the authority of Mr. A. G. Trent, who had examined the official record of it.

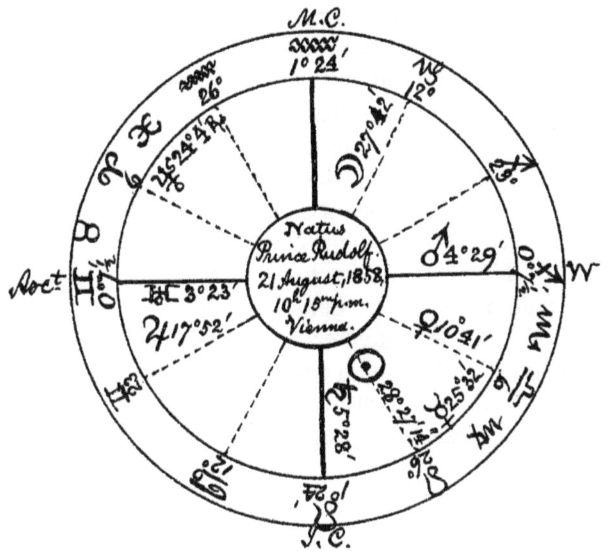

Figure 7

	Lat.	Declin.	Rt. Ascn.	Mer. dist.	Semi-Arc.
☉		12° 1′ 17″ N	150° 36′ 47″	26° 58′ 13″	76° 12′ 21″
☽	3 28 S	24 1 36 S	300 31 50	3 6 44	60 3 23
☿	2 20 S	0 32 34 S	174 54 38	51 16 4	90 36 28
♀	0 12 S	4 25 0 S	189 44 54	66 6 20	94 57 40
♂	2 36 S	23 35 59 S	241 59 57	118 21 23	119 17 12
♃	0 39 S	22 14 46 N	81 52 22	41 46 2	62 44 32
♄	0 25 N	19 19 4 N	127 56 42	4 18 8	66 53 22
♅	0 10 S	20 40 51 N	61 23 13	62 15 21	64 59 48
♆	1 15½ S	3 24 54 S	355 10 11	51 31 37	86 10 8
Reg.	0 28 N	12 39 32 N	150 12 28	26 33 54	75 26 3

M.C. 303° 38′ 34″, *Aquarius* 1° 24′ on the Midheaven, and *Gemini* 0° 7½′ on the ascendant. Uranus in Gemini 3° 23′, in opposition with Mars in *Sagittarius* 4° 29′ on the cusp of the descendant, and in mundane quartile with Saturn in *Leo* 5° 28′, in the fourth house. Uranus is 2° 44′ below the eastern horizon, measured by oblique ascension. The Moon (hyleg) is 3° 7′ cadent from the Midheaven, in 27° 42′ of *Capricornus*, in parallel declination with Mars, separating from the trine with Mercury, and applying to opposition with Saturn. The Sun is in conjunction with Regulus, a martial star of the first magnitude, in the fifth house, and within two degrees of quartile to the ascending degree. This nativity is a violent one, and the presence of Uranus in the ascendant increases the violence of Mars and Saturn, and indicates the mysterious and violent nature of the tragedy which ended the life of the Prince at 30½ years of age. The presence of Mars so close (really 0° 56′ *below* the western horizon) to the cusp of the house of marriage, and the fatal primary direction of the Sun to the opposition of the Moon by converse motion 30° 55′, preceded by Moon opposition Regulus 30° 29′, mundo, accounts for it, astrologically speaking. Cardan wrote that when the infortunes are in angles it denotes a public death or a sudden one. It is said that a shot wound was found behind the ear, and that the skull was fractured; but every attempt having been made to hush up the tragedy, the sad affair remains a mystery. The arc for death (1° = 1 year of life) is 30° 27′.

As Uranus is powerful when in Gemini, this may be the sign of his exaltation. Americans have good reason to remember the power of this planet, in 1775-1776, and again in 1860-1865, which were the last two of his periodical visits to Gemini, the sign ruling America.

4°.—THE EARL OF ROSEBERY, K.G., was born at 3 o'clock precisely, in the morning of the 7th of May, 1847, in London. This very interesting horoscope was given in STAR LORE, April 1897. The R.A. of the M.C. is 269° 10′ 42″, the sign *Sagittarius* 29° 42′ culminating, and *Pisces* 28° 3′ ascending, *Aries* being intercepted in the first house, or division of the heavens. Uranus is seen in the ascendant in *Aries* 16° 1′, near to Mercury in 20° 42′ of the same sign, the former planet being but 8° 38′ below the eastern horizon, measured by oblique-ascension, and both Uranus and Mercury are in sextile aspect with both Venus and Jupiter in the third house. This is a rare and very happy combination of auspicious influences, conferring clearness, depth, and breadth of intellect, eloquence, and good nature. A mediaeval author—Morinus—averred that Mercury in mutual sextile with both Venus and Jupiter gave "wisdom and eloquence, and a proper person to be an ambassador or statesman." The noble Earl has evinced that independence of thought and judgment characteristic of Uranians, in his zealous endeavours for the welfare of Great Britain, apart from party politics. His recent writings and speeches have demonstrated his honesty of purpose, and have verified what I wrote in 1897, when presenting his lordship's nativity, namely: "Earl Rosebery is deservedly popular among thoughtful and unprejudiced people, and is far superior in honesty of purpose and generosity to the great majority of his opponents." He is a great force in the political world, and all true Britons are proud of him.

5°.—VISCOUNT WOLSELEY, K.P., etc., was born at 11h 55m p.m. of the 4th of June, 1833, at Golden Bridge House, Co. Dublin, *Aquarius* 17° 20′ on the ascendant, and Uranus in 22° 32′ of the same sign less than five degrees below the eastern horizon. The nativity will be found in FUTURE, June, 1892. Uranus had the approximate sextile aspect with both Venus and Jupiter. These configurations, and the entry of Mercury into the sign *Gemini*, within four degrees of the sextile of Mars, together conferred on the gallant General a scientific mind, an energetic and resolute nature, resourcefulness, high courage, and martial skill. Lord Wolseley entered the army in March, 1852; he was severely wounded in the Burmese War, in his twentieth year (under the primary direction of Moon opposition Mars, mundo, 19° 34′). At the siege of Sebastopol he was again so severely wounded in the face that he lost his right eye, and was at first thought to have expired. As a commander Lord Wolseley was particularly fortunate. "It is careers like his which lead men to believe in a lucky star," said a writer in the *Review of Reviews* on the gallant General's military career.

6°.—The late PRINCE FRANCIS OF TECK, the second son of the Duke and Duchess of Teck, and brother to Queen Mary, was born at 11 o'clock in the evening of the 9th of January, 1870, at Kensington Palace, as certified by the doctors Farre and Hill.

The R.A. of the M.C. is 94° 3′ 35″ *Cancer* 3° 43′ culminating and *Libra* 2° 51′ ascending. Uranus is in the tenth house, in *Cancer* 20° 1′, in opposition to the Sun in the fourth house, in *Capricornus* 19° 33′ 49″, and in quartile with the Moon (hyleg) in *Aries* 20° 27′ in the seventh house. The Moon is separating from conjunction with Neptune in *Aries* 16° 50′. The hyleg has no support from Jupiter, and her configuration with Venus is the semi-quartile. As in the case of F.D.'s infant, Uranus is afflicting both Sun and Moon, and in this instance, is in the tenth house elevated above the luminaries. The early death of the estimable Prince Francis, after an illness of a few weeks took place on the 22nd of October, 1910, from blood poisoning, following on an operation on his throat, nine days beforehand. The arc for the fatal event is 40° 48′, and the primary direction of the Moon to the zodiacal parallel of Neptune, conversely, in the sixth house, measures closely thereto—40° 35′—and is immediately followed by Ascendant opposition Venus, mundo, conversely, 41° 21′. If the birth took place only two minutes before eleven o'clock, this direction would be brought up exactly to the terminus vitae, and Venus's influence when found in the fatal train of primary arcs is usually associated with poisoning in some form. The lamented Prince was forward in every good work, and he is sadly missed.

7°.—PRINCE LEOPOLD, Duke of Albany, was born at 1h 10m p.m. of the 7th of April, 1853, London. The R.A. of the M.C. is 33° 3′ 30″, *Taurus* 5° 21′ culminating, and *Leo* 20° 13′ ascending. The author gave the horoscope in *Zadkiel's Almanac* for 1885. Uranus was in the tenth house, in *Aries* 7° 17′, elevated above all the other celestial bodies, and but 2° 1′ from the upper meridian, his meridian passage taking place at 1h 17m p.m. Saturn was in *Aries* 16° 54′. This royal duke possessed great abilities, Mercury being in trine with Jupiter, and the Moon with Venus in the ninth house. A train of evil directions came into force in his thirty-first year, and his health failing, he was advised to go to the South of France early in 1884. On the 27th of March of that year the Prince was seized with giddiness while ascending some steps, fell, and struck his head; during the night he becanie rapidly worse and expired, at Cannes. The fatal primary directions were Sun conjunction Saturn zodiac 30° 47′ (last contact), Midheaven conjunction Mars, zodiac, conversely, 30° 50′, and Sun semi-quartile Mars, zodiac, 31° 5′. Mars, Saturn, Uranus, and the Sun were all in Aries, the sign ruling the head, and whether the rupture of a blood vessel in the head was the cause of the fall, or *vice versa*, a point on which the surgeons in attendance were not agreed, the death was of a martial (haemorrhagic) nature, and partly due to a fall, under Saturnine influence, and in a foreign land, as the hyleg (the Sun) and Mars were cadent in the ninth house.

8°.—A gentleman who was born on the 9th of April, 1848, at 5h 30m a.m. in lat. 55° 15′ N., and long. 2° 11′ W., had the Sun rising in conjunction with Uranus in *Aries* and nearly in parallel declination with Saturn. He lost the sight of his right eye by an accident. He died suddenly on the 1st of November, 1875.

9°.—PRINCE CHRISTIAN VICTOR was born at 5 o'clock p.m. of the 14th of April, 1867, at Windsor Castle. Uranus is within two degrees (cadent) of the upper meridian (southing at 4h 52m p.m.) in *Cancer* 4° 50′, and in quartile to the ascending degree (*Libra* 4° 42′), Mars is in the tenth house, in *Cancer* 24° 58′, in quartile to the Sun. As neither Sun nor Moon occupied any hylegliacal place the ascending degree is hyleg. The Prince went out to South Africa in October, 1899, with his regiment, and, unfortunately, succumbed to enteric fever at Pretoria, in October, 1900. Mars and Uranus being in *Cancer*, the sign ruling

Africa, and Saturn in *Scorpio*, which rules the Transvaal, the sad fatality is accounted for, astrologically speaking.

It may be of interest to students to note that Uranus was in the tenth house at the birth of Mr. W. E. Gladstone (whose horoscope was given in STAR LORE, June, 1898), and at that of Ruskin (STAR LORE, December, 1900). Uranus was in the fourth house at the birth of Bismarck (S. L., Feb. 1898), Cecil Rhodes, the Prince Imperial of France, and Mr. Lloyd George. Uranus was in tbe third house at the birth of Zola (S. L., 1902). Uranus was in the sixth house (in *Aries*) at the birth of Lord Randolph Churchill, (S. L., June, 1899).

It is remarkable that a transit of Uranus (in *Gemini* 8°) over the Midheaven of the horoscope of the late Dr. Richard Garnett coincided with a sudden impulse on his part to study astrology as a key to mythology, in January, 1861. And in May, 1861, the author hall his interest awakened in regard to astrology in connection with medicine and surgery, by a remarkable case of illness of a patient of his father's, when Uranus was in *Gemini* 10½°, in transit over the cusp of the seventh house of his (the author's) nativity, in trine aspect to the degree in the Midheaven and in opposition to the place of Mercury in his ascendant.

At the birth of the Pretender, son of James II., namely at 9h 30m a.m. of June 10th (old style), 1688, Uranus was close to the Midheaven in *Taurus* 20°. The astrologers of that day, being unaware of the existence of Uranus, would pronounce his nativity a fortunate one, for the Sun and Venus were both entering the tenth house, and they would be at a loss to account for his misfortunes. The Pretender spoke of himself, so related Sir Walter Scott, in this wise: "that for him it was no new thing to be unfortunate, since his whole life, from his cradle, had been a constant series of misfortunes."

In like manner the nativities of Buckingham and Laud afford instances of the power of Uranus. Gadbury gave absurd reasons for their violent deaths.

If Uranus when close to the upper meridian happens to be in close trine aspect with the Sun, Moon, Jupiter, or Venus, there is every reason to anticipate success, in the long run, despite some occasional difficulties; and that even a serious crisis may eventually end successfully.

CHAPTER XVIII.
THE PLANET NEPTUNE.

"All Nature is but art, unknown to thee;
All chance direction, which thou canst not see;
All discord, harmony, not understood;
All partial evil, universal good."—POPE.

IT having been observed for several years that the motion of Uranus was not always as it was calculated to be, after allowance had been made for all known causes of disturbance, Mr. Adams, of Cambridge, England, and M. Le Verrier, of Paris, began, unknown to each other, an inquiry into the source of this apparent anomaly. They soon arrived at the conclusion that a great planet revolved outside the orbit of Uranus. The difficult problem was to ascertain the position of such planet amongst the stars, with the view of discovering it by means of the telescope. Several eminent astronomers declared their opinion that the place of the latent planet could not be discovered by calculation. Adams and Le Verrier, however, finally succeeded in solving the problem, and assigned nearly the same position to the planet. Adams, however, did not announce his conclusions publicly, and much of the credit was given to the French astronomer, who had declared the position of the new planet to the Academy of Sciences at Paris in the summer of 1846; and on the 23rd of September of that year, Dr. Galle, of the Royal Observatory, Berlin, acting upon the urgent representations of Le Verrier, contained in a letter received on that date, turned the great telescope of the Observatory to that part of the heavens indicated by Le Verrier, when a bright telescopic star appeared in the field of view at a point where no such object was marked in the map of that part of the heavens. It proved to be the predicted planet, named by the common consent of Le Verrier, Adams, and the chief astronomers of Europe—the planet Neptune. Its period of revolution is 60,118 days, or a little over 164½ years, which is twice the period of Uranus.[1]

[1] The above particulars were given in Dr. Hind's "Introduction to Astronomy"; London, Bell and Daldy.

It is claimed that the discovery of Neptune affords "a remarkable confirmation of the truth of the Newtonian laws of gravitation."

In the first edition (1879) of this work, the author stated that: "Sufficient time has not yet elapsed to enable astrologers to determine the precise nature of Neptune's influence. Until more experience shall have been gained as to its influence, it may be accepted that its general character is fortunate, and that persons born under its sway are healthy and good-natured."

CASE 1.—Not long after the above sentence was published, my attention was directed to the case of a male child born at 3h 50m p.m., Greenwich mean time, at Edinburgh, July 13th, 1879. R.A. of M.C. 165° 36′. The Moon was then in *Taurus* 15° 53′ (and, having 4° 56′ of north latitude was really *above* the western horizon) and separating from conjunction with Neptune in *Taurus* 11° 47′. The child died five days after birth. The moon was hyleg, and was not afflicted by either Saturn, Mars, or Uranus, so that there is nothing to account, astrologically speaking, for the early death, unless Neptune is of malefic nature. The Sun had the quartile of Saturn, but was not in any hylegliacal situation; this might weaken the heart, but would not *per se* cause so early a death. It was owing to a malformation and internal obstruction that the child succumbed, and the sign *Taurus*, which contained the Moon and Neptune, is one connected with such congenital affliction.

The surgeon in attendance at the birth of this infant kindly furnished the particulars.[2]

Further investigation soon confirmed the view that Neptune's influence is quite as malefic as that of Uranus—when afflicting the Sun, Moon, or Mercury, and receiving no assistance from either Venus or Jupiter.

2.—A youth, who was "born between 7h 30m and 8h p.m., and most probably very close to the former time, of the 23rd of August, 1859, in lat. 52° 5′ N., and 9m 20s W.," went to Bath, on a visit, in 1885, and was drowned on the 29th of November (1885), but how the sad event took place was never known. He left his brother at half-past nine o'clock, and said he would walk home in a few minutes. His body was found three days afterwards, washed on the bank of the river Avon, at Teverton. His watch stopped at ten forty-five. The arc for death 26° 16′. Taking 7h 30m p.m. local mean time as the proba-

[2] Vide URANIA, August, 1880, p. 237.

ble moment of birth, the R.A. of the M.C. is 264° 4′, *Sagittarius* 24° 33′ culminating, and *Pisces* 15° 33′ ascending at the birthplace. Neptune was alone in the ascendant, in *Pisces* 26° 27′, retrograde, and in quartile with the Moon in the fourth house, in *Gemini* 29° 0′, and in parallel with Mercury in *Virgo* 9°27′ retrograde in the sixth house. The ascending degree is hyleg; and Neptune is 6° 33′ below the eastern horizon, measured by oblique ascension, (thus: his semi-arc 93° 22′—86° 48′, his merid. dist. = 6° 33). The death took place under the primary direction of Ascendant parallel Saturn, in the zodiac 26° 25′, followed by Ascendant □ ♄ zodiac 27° 55′; Saturn being, at birth, in the sixth house, in *Leo* (the sign ruling Bath) 17° 47′, with Mars in 19° 30′ of the same sign, the ruler of the eighth house (*Scorpio* being thereon), and with Venus in 20° 38′ of the same sign (*Leo*). A sign of the "watery triplicity" ascended at birth with Neptune therein in quartile with the Moon in the house of the grave, and practically in *Cancer*, a watery sign, and the third watery sign (*Scorpio*) is found on the cusp of the house of death; and the end of this youth's life was by drowning.

3.—The Duke of Brabant, first-born of King Leopold I. of Belgium, was born at 4h 30m a.m. of the 24th of July, 1833, at Brussels. He died on the 4th of May, 1834. The R.A. of the M.C. is 8° 21′, *Aries* 9° 6′ culminating, and *Leo* 2° 12′ ascending. The Sun had just risen in *Leo* 0° 57′, separating from parallel declination and opposition with Neptune in *Capricornus* 28° 7′, less than five degrees below the western horizon. The Moon was in the fourth house, in *Scorpio* 4° 22′, separating from quartile with both the Sun and Neptune. Zadkiel I. gave this nativity in the Horoscope, June 7th, 1834, and Neptune not having then been discovered, attributed the early death of the child to the mundane semi-quartile of the Sun (hyleg) with Mercury. The contra-parallel of the Sun with Neptune was very close, the Sun's declin. being 19° 58′ N., and that of Neptune 20° 7′ S.

4.—*Nata*, November 28th, 1876, 8h 45m p.m., in lat. 51° 31′ N. and long. 0° 22′ W. The Moon in the tenth house in *Taurus* 2° 21′ in conjunction with Neptune in 3° 2′ of the same sign, and separating from opposition with Mars in *Libra* 29° 34′. This young lady fainted and fell, and died immediately of heart failure in February, 1898. She had suffered from weak digestion and anorexia. The time of her birth was accurately observed and recorded.

5.—*Nata*, November 14th, 1851, at 7 o'clock a.m. in lat. 50° 51′ W., and long. 0° 28′ E., Virgo 6° 30′ culminating, Scorpio 18° 16′ ascending, and Pisces 6° 30′ on the lower meridian, Neptune being in Pisces 6° 28′, just within the fourth house, and in mundane quartile to the Sun in the ascendant, and in sesquiquadrate to the Moon near the cusp of the ninth house. This lady was seized with paralysis (partial) in 1888, and suffered for ten subsequent years from neuritis in her lower extremities, and if her feet were touched the pains were agonizing and like electric shocks.

6.—*Nata*, January 30th, 1847, 6 p.m., in lat. 52° 20′ N, and long, 1° 22′ W. The sign *Leo* 24° 50′ ascending. Neptune in the seventh house, in *Aquarius* 27° 10′, only 2° 57′ above the western horizon (measured by oblique descension), and in opposition to the ascending degree (the hyleg). Saturn was also in the seventh house, in *Pisces* 0° 37′, but was 7° 55′ above the horizon. Mars was on the cusp of the fifth house in *Sagittarius* 22° 26′. This poor woman suffered from a large tumour which prevented her child from being born *per vias naturales*, and she died on the 3rd of February, 1880, two days after the Cesarean operation.

7.—*Nata*, September 27th, 1862, 11h 51m a.m. Greenwich mean time, in lat. 50° 40′ N. R. A. of M.C. 183° 13′, Libra 3° 30′ on the upper meridian, and *Sagittarius* 6° 29′ on the ascendant. The Sun in *Libra* 4° 6′ 21″ in opposition with Neptune in *Aries* 2° 25′ on the lower meridian (cadent only 0° 25′), and supported by Jupiter in *Libra* 7° 1′, but afflicted by the zodiacal parallel of Mars. This lady met with an accident by falling on the ice in February, 1888, under the primary direction of Ascendant quartile Saturn 25° 23′, and has suffered, more or less, ever since, and has undergone a serious operation. Here the hyleg has both opposition and mundane parallel with Neptune, a double affliction greater than his (the Sun's) parallel with Mars.

Although Neptune is more of a malefic than a benefic planet, it does not follow that when he is exactly rising at a birth, the child is of a nature more malefic than benefic; but, when at the same time the ascending degree is hyleg, Neptune does render the health more or less delicate.

In the chapter on Neptune, in the first edition of this work, the author (in 1879) gave the description (furnished by the husband) of a young lady who was born when Neptune alone was rising in 17° 52′ of the sign *Pisces*, and in trine aspect with the Moon: "Height, 5ft. 3½ in.; eyes very large and of a blue colour; high forehead, oval face, light complexion; light brown hair; good figure, and, generally speaking, handsome; voice musical."

A young lady who was born when Neptune was in the ascendant in *Aries* 28° 54′, only five degrees below the horizon, the Moon in 25° 20′ of *Aquarius* applying to sextile aspect with the planet, has black hair; very large eyes of a dark brown colour, almost black, and black eyebrows; slenderly built, and of good figure; and very prepossessing personality; and is in height 5 ft. 5 in. Her father had black hair, her mother dark auburn. Her father died when she was only four-and-a-half years old under the primary direction of Ascendant conjunction Neptune in her nativity.

Neptune in the tenth house, near the meridian, and at the same time in quartile with Uranus, causes difficulties and changes in employment, business, or profession; and, unless the nativity is fortunate otherwise, loss of business or employment, with years of consequent troubles. Two notable instances of this effect have fallen under my notice, one sufferer having been born in June, 1869, and the other in January, 1870. In the former case the mother died five years after the birth of her son, and in the latter instance, the mother very nearly died of fever five years after the birth of her son, also.

Neptune in the second house of a nativity, unless very well configurated, usually involves the owner thereof in financial losses and difficulties from time to time, and brings heavy expenses upon him.

Neptune does not incline towards melancholy and despondency like Saturn; neither does he incline to excitability like Mars and Uranus. Neptune gives an inclination to scientific studies and pursuits, but not so much of the mechanical kind as Mars and Uranus do; and not so much ingenuity is conferred by Neptune, as by Mars and Uranus, when in conjunction or aspect with Mercury.

Again, Neptune usually inclines to foreign travel, and several Neptunians whom I have known have travelled almost to every civilised country. This propensity to roam abroad seems to be more pronounced in persons who were born when Neptune was rising or in the ninth house, in either the first or twelfth sign of the zodiac.

I have not found that Neptunians and Uranians are particularly inclined to occult studies and pursuits—not more so than are Saturnians—although occultists and psychics seem disposed to believe that the two most distant planets are of such nature.

Uranus does, usually, confer independence and originality of thought and action, and inclines to romanticism.

CHAPTER XIX.

THE FIXED STARS.

"And taught the fix'd
Their influence malignant when to shower."—MILTON.

THE FIXED STARS are so called because they *appear* to remain stationary, to keep the same distance from each other, and to have no annual revolution around the Sun. The stars have an apparent motion from east to west, in circles parallel to the equinoctial.

When a star ascended with the Sun, or descended when the Sun rose, the ancient poets wrote of it as rising or setting *cosmically*. When a star rose at sunset, or set with the Sun, it was said to rise and set *acronically*. When a star first became visible in the early morning, after having been in such close proximity to the Sun as to be hidden by his rays, it was said to *rise heliacally*[1]; and when a star first became invisible in the evening, on account of its proximity to the Sun, it was said to *set heliacally*.

The time of the rising and setting of the fixed stars varies according to the latitudes of the places of observation; and the refraction in high latitudes is very great.

The longitudes of the fixed stars increase at the annual rate of 50.25″.[2] Their latitudes vary but very little. The right-ascsenions and

[1] The ancients reckoned the commencement of the *Dog Days* from the heliacal rising of Sirius, and their length to be about forty days. Hesiod says that the hottest season of the year (*Dog Days*) ended about fifty days after the Summer Solstice. Sirius rose heliacally at Alexandria in the time of Hesiod about four days after the Summer Solstice. The Dog Days now begin on the 3rd of July, or twelve days after the Summer Solstice, and end on the 11th of August; hence they nowadays have no reference whatever to the heliacal rising of Sirius, for this star rises heliacally at London about the 26th of August. At the beginning of the nineteenth century our Almanacs made the Dog Days begin at the *cosmical* rising of Procyon, viz., on the 30th of July, and continue to the 7th of September; but they are now made to depend upon the Sommer Solstice.

[2] Sir John Herschel gave the precession of the equinoxes as 50.1″. From the

declinations of most of the principal stars are given annually in the *Nautical Almanac*; and, by means of their annual differences their places, may be readily computed for many years in advance. White's *Ephemeris*, from 1792 to 1839, gave the places of the principal stars. The stars of the first magnitude have the greatest power; those of less than the fourth magnitude (except when in a cluster, like the Pleiades) have no appreciable influence.

When a fixed star whose latitude does not exceed 8° 30′ happens to be in conjunction with the Sun at birth, or when the Sun is directed to its conjunction, certain effects are distinctly traceable.

When a fixed star whose latitude does not differ greatly from that of the Moon or any planet which may happen to be in conjunction with it, certain effects are produced.

When a star of the first or second magnitude happens to be exactly culminating or ascending its influence is undeniable.

Stars having north latitude affect us most; and, *per contra*, stars having great south latitude affect the denizens of the southern hemisphere most. The Sun, the Moon, or a planet may have the parallel declination of a star with which, on account of its great latitude, it can never be in (zodiacal) conjunction. In such case—provided that the star's latitude be *north*—the effects of this parallel would probably be nearly as great as if the star were in the zodiac.

The conjunction, opposition, and zodiacal and mundane parallel should only be considered in regard to the fixed stars; they are said, in astrology, to cast no rays, *i.e.*, they do not operate on the planets or angles of the heavens by sextile, square, trine, etc. Aldebaran, Regulus, Rigel, Arista, Hercules, the North Scale, Fomalhaut, Antares,[3] or Orion's Shoulder culminating, give great honour, preferment, and good fortune; and the same in a lesser degree when they ascend. Rigel, or Orion's foot, is said to confer great and lasting honours, good fortune, and happiness. Although situated in the sixteenth degree of Gemini, it *rises* with 27° of Cancer and sets with 14° of

---

declination of the zodiac which La Gentil brought from India, it appears that the star Aldebaran was forty minutes before the vernal equinox in 3012. Taking the precession of the equinoxes at 50.1″ we shall find that the value obtained will differ only 39″ from that given by the Indian astronomers—a fact which proves that their calculation was correct and founded upon observation.

[3] This word is probably compounded of ᾀυτς pro and ᾆςες Mars, signifying Mars's deputy or lieutenant, or one acting for Mars.

Taurus. At the Prince Consort's birth Rigel was in the tenth house.

The Sun conjoined with Aldebaran, Hercules, Regulus, Antares or any eminent star of the nature of Mars, is said to threaten a violent death, or frequent sickness. These same stars are also said to bring the native military preferment, or distinction in surgery, but in the end to cause disgrace or ruin.

Napoleon I. had the Sun with Regulus.

The Sun with the Pleiades, Hyades, Castor, Pollux, Praesepe, or the Asselli, is indicative of evil, and liability to a violent death.[4] The South Scale[5] and the Knee of Ophiucus are, when conjoined with the Sun, indicative of trouble and disgrace. The North Scale and Arista conjoined with the Sun give the most eminent and permanent good fortune. All eminent fixed stars with the Sun in an angle give advancement and success; those of the nature of Mars cause violent death, or ultimate ruin, in consequence of the native's own conduct; those of the nature of Saturn bring disgrace, ruin, and great calamity. The Pleiades and Praesepe with the Sun in an angle often produce blindness.

The Moon conjoined with Aldebaran or Pollux threatens a violent death; with the Pleiades, Praesepe, or Antares, blindness or injuries to the eyes (when in an angle). When the Moon happens to be conjoined with Pleiades, and Saturn, or Mars with Regulus, and the Moon combust, total blindness sometimes ensues. The Moon with Antares, in opposition to Saturn with Aldebaran, threatens a violent death, maybe strangulation. If Mars, instead of Saturn be with Aldebaran, the death will be by a blow or fall—particularly if they are in an angle. The Moon with Cor Hydrae, and also in conjunction, parallel declination, square, or opposition with Mars or Saturn, death may be due to drowning or poison if Mars be angular. The Moon with Antares and Saturn, danger of drowning or assassination. The Moon with Aldebaran or Antares in the ascendant or mid-heaven, gives honours and preferment, attended, however, with danger.

In *Zadkiel's Almanac* for 1886 was presented "a chapter of accidents," in which I mentioned that the nativity of a child who died, at fourteen months old, from the effects of being accidentally scalded, showed the Moon in conjunction with Mars in the midheaven and in

---

[4] The Pleiades are, I think, not so evil, their influence is "mild," as described in the book of Job.

[5] I have repeatedly observed that persons born when the Moon was with the South Scale, were very unfortunate.

I.—Eminent Fixed Stars near the Ecliptic, with their Longitudes and Latitudes computed for January 1st, 1911.[6]

Name.	*Magnitude.*	*Longitude.*	*Latitude.*	*R.A.*	*Declination.*	*Nature.*
β Arietis	2.7	2 ♉ 43 34	8 29N	1 49 43	20 22 23N	♄ ♂
α Arietis, Ram's following horn	2.2	6 ♉ 25 5	9 58N	2 2 9	23 2 37N	♄ ♂
η Tauri, brightest of the 7 stars	3	23 ♉ 45 2	4 2N	3 42 12	23 49 57N	♂ ☽
γ Tauri, Hyades	3.9	4 ♊ 33 41	5 49S	4 14 44	15 24 53N	♂ ☽
ϵ Tauri Oculus, Tauri	3.7	7 ♊ 13 16	2 35S	4 23 25	18 59 7N	♀
α Aldebaran	1.1	8 ♊ 32 49	5 29S	4 30 49	16 19 57N	♀
β Tauri, Bull's North Horn	1.8	21 ♊ 20 2	5 22½N	5 20 40	28 32 6N	♂
γ Geminorum, Bright foot of Gemini	1.9	7 ♋ 51 49	6 45S	6 32 35	16 28 39N	☿ ♀
α Geminorum, Castor	2	19 ♋ 00 13	10 5N	7 28 56	32 5 9N	♂ ♀ ♄
β Geminorum, Pollux	1.2	21 ♋ 59 23	6 40N	7 39 53	28 14 34N	♂
γ Cancri, North Assellus	4.8	6 ♌ 17 58	3 11N	8 38 9	21 47 23N	♂ ☉
δ Cancri, South Assellus	4.5	7 ♌ 28 43	0 4N	8 39 38	18 29 2N	♂ ☉
α Leonis, Regulus	1.3	28 ♌ 35 33	0 28N	10 3 38	12 24 11N	♂
α Virginis, Spica	1.2	22 ♎ 35 42	2 3S	13 20 29	10 41 45S	♀ ♂
α Librae, South Scale	2.9	13 ♏ 50 16	0 21N	14 45 56	5 40 18S	♄ ♀
β Librae, North Scale	2.8	18 ♏ 7 24	8 31N	15 12 11	9 3 18S	♃ ♂
β Scorpii, Frons Scorpii	2.7	1 ♐ 56 22	1 1N	16 0 14	19 33 45S	♄ ♀
α Scorpii, Antares	1.3	8 ♐ 30 42	4 33S	16 23 55	26 14 7S	☿ ♂
η Ophiuchi, Right Knee of Ophiuchus	2.6	16 ♐ 43 1	7 13N	17 5 14	15 36 59S	♄ ♀
ς Capricorni, Capricorn's Tail	3	22 ♒ 17 16	2 35S	21 42 6	16 32 6S	♄

[6] The stars in the above list whose R.A. and declin. are not given in the *Nautical Almanac*, are taken from the Catalogue of 1,500 stars presented in Dr. Loomis's "Introduction to Practical Astronomy." Praesepe is described in the old works on Astrology as "in the Claw of the Crab." Even Wilson repeated this wretched blunder. The cluster is in the middle of the Crab and in *Leo* 6°.

II.—Eminent Fixed Stars not Included in Table I., with their Diurnal Semi-arcs, computed for Greenwich, January 1st, 1911.

Name.	*Magnitude.*	*R. A.*	*Declination.*	*Semi-Arc diurnal.*	*Nature.*
α Caput Andromedae	2.1	0 3 46	28 36 1N	132 52	♃ ♀
γ Pegasi, Algenib	2.9	0 8 38	14 41 19N	109 5	♂ ☿
β Ceti, S. end of Whale	2.2	0 39 7	18 28 41S	65 22	♄
β Andromedae, Mirach	2.4	1 4 44	35 9 4N	151 28	♀
γ Andromedae, Almach	2.2	1 58 25	41 54 22N	-	♀
β Persei, Caput Algol	2.4	3 2 28	40 36 59N	-	♄ ♃
α Aurigae, Capella	0.2	5 10 7	45 54 40N	-	☿ ♂
β Orionis, Rigel	0.3	5 10 16	8 8 12S	79 31	♃ ♂
γ Orionis, Bellatrix	1.7	5 20 22	6 16 15N	97 53	☿ ♂
δ Orionis	2.3	5 27 28	0 21 48S	89 33	♃ ♄
ε Orionis	1.7	5 31 42	1 15 25S	88 26	♃ ♂
α Orionis, Betelguese	1	5 50 22	7 23 33N	99 19	♂ ☿
β Aurigae	2.1	5 53 1	44 56 29N	-	♂ ☿
μ Geminorum	3.2	6 17 35	22 33 42N	121 13	☿ ♀
α Canis Majoris, Sirius	1.4	6 41 14	16 35 32S	68 11	♃ ♂
α Canis Minoris, Procyon	0.5	7 34 39	5 27 18N	96 45	☿ ♂
α Hydrae, Alphard	2.2	9 23 13	8 16 13S	79 33	♄ ♀
β Leonis, Denebola	2.2	11 44 31	15 4 9N	109 38	♄ ♀ ☿
η Virginis	4	12 15 21	0 10 17S	89 47	☿ ♂
δ Virginis	3.7	12 51 6	3 52 52N	94 51	♂ ☿

Name.	*Magnitude.*	*R. A.*	*Declination.*	*Semi-Arc diurnal.*	*Nature.*
ϵ Virginis, Vendemiatrix[7]	3	12 57 44	11 26 12N	104 37	♄ ♀ ☿
α̨ Bootis, Arcturus	0.3	14 11 35	19 38 36N	116 27	♃ ♂
α̨ Coronae, North Crown	2.3	15 30 54	27 0 39N	129 30	♀ ☿
α̨ Serpentis	2.8	15 39 51	6 42 13N	98 26	♄ ♀ ♂
δ Scorpii	2.5	15 55 2	22 22 8S	59 6	♄ ♀
δ Ophiuchi	3	16 9 39	3 28 lS	85 40	♄ ♀
α̨ Ophiuchi	2.1	17 30 46	12 37 19N	106 13	♄ ♀
α̨ Lyrae, Vega	0.1	18 33 53	38 41 53N	-	♀ ☿
α̨ Aquilae, Altair	0.9	19 46 24	8 37 50N	100 55	♄ ☿
β Aquarii	3.3	21 26 51	5 57 58S	82 31	♄
α̨ Piscis Australis, Fomalhault	1.3	22 52 43	30 5 56S	43 41	♀ ☿
α̨ Pegasi, Markab	2.6	23 0 18	14 43 32N	109 8	♂ ☿
β Pegasi, Scheat	2.3	22 59 26	27 36 1N	130 43	♄

[7] Vendemiatrix is placed, in Wilson's "Dictionary of Astrology," in the eighth degree of the sign Virgo, with 10° latitude *South*, whereas this bright star is really in the sign Libra, and has 16° 13 of latitude *North*. The lists of stars as given in the old works on astrology are all inaccurate.

parallel declination with Antares. The birth took place at 4h 30m p.m. of the 28th of September, 1873, at Rishton.

Another instance of the influence of eminent fixed stars was given in the nativity of a gentleman who was born in 1846, his ascendant being *Leo* 21° 53′, Mercury in the ascendant was in 27° 23′ of the ascending sign very close to Regulus, and in opposition with Saturn in *Aquarius* 26° 11′ retrograde. The Sun in *Virgo* 14° 6′ was very near Mars in 15° 10′ of the same sign. This gentleman was nearly killed by a serious accident, in 1879, and was shot at only a few months previously, under the primary directions of Sun rapt parallel Mars 32° 44′, and Sun parallel Saturn 32° 44′.

VARIABLE stars exhibit periodical changes of brilliancy. The bright star Capella is believed to have increased in brightness during the last century. On the other hand, one of the seven bright stars of Ursa Major has diminished in lustre.

Professor Pickering showed that no theory hitherto advanced accounts satisfactorily for the variability of the lustre of such a star as Algol, except that of an opaque satellite.

The ancient astrologers declared that Algol is the most evil of all the fixed stars, and that when it is in the line of right-ascension of the Sun or Moon in a violent nativity it pre-signifies "a murderer who will come to an untimely end!" In Robespierre's nativity (two o'clock a.m. of May 6th, 1758, at Arras) the Sun in *Taurus* 15° 24′ was in the line of R.A. of Caput Algol, and in parallel declination with Aldebaran, and also in quadrature with Mars, which evil planet was in opposition to the ascendant, and Regulus also was in opposition to the ascendant. Here is an extraordinarily violent nativity, and Robespierre, after sending many victims to the guillotine, was himself executed, at the end of July, 1794, in the thirty-seventh year of his age.

IRREGULAR or Temporary Stars have occasionally shone forth with a lustre far surpassing that of stars of the first magnitude, or even that of Venus and Jupiter, remaining for a short period, and then disappearing slowly. The most celebrated star of this kind is that bright one in Cassiopaeia, one of the circum-polar constellations, which appeared in 1572, and was observed by Tycho Brahé, the famous astronomer and astrologer, who handed down to posterity a concise and valuable description of the various changes it passed through while

* Vide *Zadkiel's Almanac* for 1879, pp. 67-71 art. "The Star of Bethlehem."

visible.* During the early part of its appearance it surpassed the brightness of Sirius. It was seen at noon by strong-sighted persons; and was at first white, then yellow, and finally very red in colour. It has been supposed to have heralded our Saviour's birth—the Star of Bethlehem—as its period was computed to be just about 315 years; and it was expected to re-appear in the year 1887, but has not yet been observed.

Another temporary star came suddenly into view in Ophiuchus in 1604, and was observed by the great astronomer and astrologer, John Kepler. It exceeded Jupiter in splendour. It did not change colour, and was always white. It remained visible until March, 1606.

Daniel's declaration:

> They that be wise shall shine as the brightness of the firmament;
> And they that turn many to righteousness, as the stars for ever and ever.

is occasionally taken as a text by preachers, but to understand and explain its true meaning astrological knowledge is indispensable. The proficiency of Daniel in the interpretation of visions is directly attributable to the Almighty. In his visions we meet with several references to astrological ideas. The constellation-sign of the Ram is appropriately taken as typical of the Medo-Persian power. The mention of Gabriel, the angel of the Moon, the messenger, and *Mikal*, the angel of the Sun, the "prince" of Israel, is the outcome of the Chaldaean doctrine of the spirits of the spheres. The multitudinous celestial spirits were believed to have been the spirits of just men made perfect and received into the starry heavens, so that in *Daniel* viii. 10, we find stars = saints, and "they that be wise shall shine," etc., as already quoted. Manilius held the Milky Way to be the souls of illustrious men, and Heraclitus is reported to have believed that the soul is a spark taken from the stellar essence. Modern popular theology has confounded the heaven of stars into which the early Christians believed that the soul is taken, with the New Jerusalem, which is merely an allegorical vision of the perfected Church.

Let the religious world ponder over the fact that the crucifixion was accompanied by portents, and that the visit of the Magi—astrologers—was divinely guided by the Star of Bethlehem, and cease to neglect and ignore *astrologia sana*—divine study that it really is.

CHAPTER XX.

THE IMPORT OF THE NATIVITY.

> "In the eternal volume of the sky
> The stars displayed, are characters on high,
> Where Man may read his future and his fate
> If dim the tale seem 'tis his sunken state
> Unfit by sin, that bright page to descry
> Writ by the finger of the Deity."[1]

THE Map or Figure of the Heavens being drawn for the true moment of birth, the next proceeding is to form an opinion or judgment upon the indications afforded by the configurations and relative positions of the Sun, Moon, and planets.

Ptolemy says,[2] respecting the "distribution of the doctrine of Nativities":

"The questions of the periods subsequent to the birth relate first to the duration of life (which is distinct from the question of rearing), then to the shape and figure of the body, to the bodily affections, and to injuries or defects in the members. After these, further inquiry is instituted as to the quality of the mind, and the mental affections; then as to the fortune, in regard to rank and honours, as well as wealth. In succession to these, the character of the employment or profession is sought out; then the questions relative to marriage and offspring, and to consentaneous friendship, are to be considered; then, that concerning travel; and lastly, that concerning the kind of death which awaits the native. The question of death, although depending, in fact, upon the same influence as the question of the duration of life, seems yet to find its proper situation in being placed last in the series.

"On each of the foregoing points of inquiry, the doctrine and precepts to be followed shall be thoroughly and succinctly detailed; but all idle conceits, promulgated by many persons without any founda-

---

[1] "Fragment of Chaucer Modernised"; from *Miscellaneous Poems,* by R. J. Gilman, Esq.

[2] Book III., Chap. iv.

tion capable of sustaining the test of reason, shall be utterly avoided, in deference to the only true agency, which is derived from primal Nature herself. It is only upon clearly effective influences that this treatise is established; and all matters which are open to an authorised mode of inquiry by means of the theory of the stars, and their positions and aspects with regard to appropriate places, shall be fully discussed here; but the divination by lots and numbers,[3] unregulated by any systematic causation, must remain unnoticed."

THE PARENTS.

"In conformity with nature," says Ptolemy, "the Sun and Saturn are allotted to the person of the father; and the Moon and Venus to that of the mother; and the mode in which these luminaries and planets may be found posited, with reference to each other as well as to other planets and stars, will intimate the situation of affairs affecting the parents."

If there happens to be a planet in the mid-heaven and, if neither the Sun nor Moon is there, it represents the mother; if there is a planet in the fourth house, it is the significator of the father.

Ptolemy says "That the degree of the fortune and wealth of the parents will be indicated by the doryphory,[4] or attendants of the luminaries. If the luminaries be accompanied (either in the same signs in which themselves are placed, or in the signs next following), by the benefics, and by such stars or planets as are of the same tendency as themselves, a conspicuous and brilliant fortune is presaged: especially should the Sun be attended by matutine stars and the Moon by vespertine," etc.

The following observations, respecting the mother of the native are from Ptolemy:

"If Mars be succedent to the Moon or Venus, or in quartile or op-

---

[3] This is an allusion to the ancient practice of divination by lots. Reference to *Acts* iv., 24 to 26, will show that the Apostles practised this form of divination. Joseph's cup, which was found in Benjamin's sack, was the silver cup used for divining, just as the Mussulmen in India, at the present day, practice divination.

[4] Δοξυρηξιᾳ. This word has been heretofore rendered "*satellitium*," and "satellites," but as these terms do not seem sufficiently precise in their meaning, and are already in use to signify the minor orbs which revolve around a principal planet, I have ventured to Anglicise the Greek word the usual signification of which is a body-guard.—Note by Ashmand.

position to them, or if Saturn be similarly aspected to the Moon only, and both of them be void of course or retrograde, or cadent, adverse accidents and disease will attend the mother; should they, on the other hand, be swift in motion and placed in angles, they portend that her life will be short, or grievously afflicted. Their position in the oriental angles, or succedent houses, particularly denotes the shortness of her life; and in those which are occidental, her affliction. In the same manner, should Mars be thus aspected to the Moon (and should that luminary at the same time be oriental), the mother's sudden death, or some injury in her face or eyes, will be produced; and, if the Moon be then occidental, death will be occasioned by miscarriage, in parturition, by inflamation, or by wounds. Such are the effects which ensue from these aspects made by Mars to the Moon; but, should he make them to Venus, death will then take place from fever, some latent disease, or sudden sickness. Saturn's aspect [quartile or opposition] to the Moon, when she is oriental, inflicts on the mother disease and death from extreme colds, or fevers; but, should the Moon be occidental, the danger arises from affections of the uterus, or from consumption."

My own experience has shown me, repeatedly, that when the Moon is afflicted at the birth of a child, the mother has a bad time after her accouchement. This is the more likely to result when the Moon happens to be posited in the 4th or 8th house, and afflicted. For example:

Case 1.—A male child, "H. R. P.," was born February 28th, 1875, lat, 54° 54′ N., long. 1° 24′ W. The Moon was in the 4th house, in 13° 9′ of Sagittary, and less than 5° separated from the conjunction with Mars. The mother was seized with metritis, and her life was despaired of by her medical attendants and nurse, and she only recovered after being as near death as it is possible for anyone to be without actually succumbing.

2.—A male child (stillborn), April 30th, 1878, at 3h p.m., London. The Moon in the 8th house, in Aries, in aspect to Mars (culminating) and Uranus. Venus setting, in conjunction and par. dec. with Saturn, and also in square to Mars. The mother suffered seriously from haemorrhage, and died, of fever, May 15th, 1878.

3.—A male child, "T. H. B.," was born April 24th, 1874, in Sunderland. The Moon was in the 10th house, in the 19th deg. of Leo, in opposition to Saturn, and in square to Mars (in the 8th house). The mother died in April, 1877. The child died in August, 1874.

4.—A male child, "J. Y." born October 26th, 1874, at 6h 25m a.m., in Sunderland. The Moon in square and par. dec. with Saturn, and in square to Uranus (in the 10th house). The mother died (of pneumonia) two days afterwards; the child lived only 35 hours.

5.—A male child, "A," born February 16th, 1878, at 4h 45m p.m., London. The Moon, in the 7th house, in exact square to Mars in the 4th house. The mother died three weeks after the child's birth. She was a strong and perfectly healthy young lady, and had never been ill since childhood.

6.—A male child, " A. B.," born at 11h a.m., of April 4th, 1864, in London. The Moon conjoined with Venus, in the 9th house, applying to the square of Uranus, and 150° from Saturn. The mother died in a few days, of fever.

7.—A female child, "D," born March 10th, 1875, at 11h p.m., in Sunderland. The Moon in the 6th house, in sesqui-quadrate to Mars, and applying to the square of Uranus. The mother died in a fortnight, of fever.

8.—A female child, "R.," born November 18th, 1872, at 9h 5m p.m., Sunderland. The Moon in the 12th house, in opposition to Saturn; Venus in the 5th house, in square to Mars. The mother died in a fortnight, of puerperal mania.

9.—A male child, born February 16th, 1828, at 7h 20m a.m., Rochdale. The Moon in square to Mars. The mother died, January 29th, 1832.

10.—Miss C., born June 6th, 1843, at 4h 3m a.m.; lat. 51° 8′ N., long. 1° 12′ W. The Moon in trine to Saturn, and applying to the opposition and par. dec. with Uranus, and the square of Mercury. The mother died between two and three hours after the birth.

11.—Mrs. H., born February 17th, 1824, at 6h 52m p.m., lat. 53° 40′ N, long. 2° 27′ W. The Moon in conjunction with Mars, and in square to Uranus and Venus (conjoined). The mother died, December 10th, 1829.

12.—Mr. J. R., born August 10th, 1840, at 4h 54m a.m. The Moon in opposition to Mars. The mother died, May 25th, 1844.

13.—Miss S., born August 18th, 1838, London. The Moon "under the Sun's beams," and in par. dec, with Mars. Venus in par. dec. with Mars, and in (mundane) square to Saturn. The mother died, May 31st, 1843.

Now let us proceed to investigate the doctrine that the Sun and Saturn represent the father:

Case 14.—Dr. C. T. P., born August 11th, 1815, at 7h a.m. London. The Sun nearly in opposition with Saturn, and in trine with Mars; and Uranus close to the lower meridians. The father died in June, 1820.

15.—Dr. A., born February 3rd, 1837, at 4h a.m., lat. 51° 25′ N. The Sun in square to Saturn, and in opposition to Mars and Jupiter. His father died during Dr. A.'s infancy.

16.—The Princess Beatrice, born April 14th, 1857, at 1h 45m p.m., Buckingham Palace. The Sun in conjunction with Jupiter and Mercury, and applying to conjunction with Mars (within 14°). The Prince Consort died on December 14th, 1861.

17.—The ex-Queen Isabella of Spain, born October 10th, 1830, at 2h p.m. The Sun in par. dec. with Mars and Mercury. Her father died, September 29th, 1833.

18.—Le Comte de Paris, born August 24th, 1838, at 2h 45m p.m., Paris. The Sun in semi-quartile to Mars, and in opposition to Uranus. His father died July 13th, 1842.

19.—A male child, born March 9th, 1862, at 6h 45m a.m., Hastings. The Sun in opposition to Saturn, and square to Uranus. His father, a fisherman, was drowned in the evening of the same day, while endeavouring to enter Portsmouth harbour during a gale. It will be observed that the Sun was in Pisces, a "watery" sign.

20.—E. M. H., born September 17th, 1822, at 9h 37m a.m., near Rotherham. The Sun in sesqui-quadrate to Saturn (angular), in semi-quartile to Mars (angular), applying to quartile with Uranus. Her father died, June 28th, 1827.

21.—Mr. J. K,. born January 4th, 1844, at 1h 39m p.m., Liverpool. The Sun within 4° of the rapt parallel of Mars, and applying to conjunction with Saturn. His father died, October 23rd, 1847.

22.—Mr. D. Le V., born September 8th, 1828, at 4h a.m., Jersey. The Sun in semi-quartile to Saturn, in sesqui-quadrate with Uranus, and in conjunction with Mercury and Jupiter. His father died, January 22nd, 1834.

23 to 25.—Three children born, respectively, May 7th, 1868, at 5h 55m p.m.; November 9th, 1871, at 11h 20m p.m.; and October 3rd, 1869, at 5h 40m p.m. In the nativity of the first-born the Sun in par. dec. with Saturn. In the second, the Sun in semi-quartile with Mars and Saturn (conjoined). In the third, the Sun in square with Uranus.

Their father died, September 8th, 1873.

26.—Mrs. F., born April 6th, 1822, at 9h 25m p.m, The Sun in par. dec. with Mercury and Saturn, in trine with Mars, in opposition with the Moon, and separating from the square of Uranus. The father died in February or March, 1829.

27.—A male child, S., born April 23rd, 1877, at 10h 25m p.m., Sunderland. The Sun in square with Mars and in trine with Jupiter. His father died, September 23rd, 1877.

The foregoing nativities present a formidable array of facts in support of the aphorism of Ptolemy in respect to the probable fate of the parents, as indicated by the configurations of the Sun and Saturn in the one case, and of the Moon and Venus in the other. It cannot, however, be affirmed that the aphorism is always true, namely, that when the Sun and Saturn are afflicted the father will inevitably die early, and when the Moon and Venus are afflicted at the birth of a child, that the mother will soon die. The threatened evil may fall in some other way.

Medical men may take the horoscope of a child and consider it as a figure for the decumbiture of the mother, and watch the effects of the configurations of the Moon, her positions in the figure, and the aspects she forms on the critical days of the following four weeks.

I cannot coincide with Wilson's view that the luminaries are significators of the parents only in a general way; and that if the luminaries are in good or evil condition, the native and everything belonging to him will be the same. In some cases, the early death of the father may be a positive benefit to the child; and many people who have lost both parents early in life have prospered greatly through the kind care of relatives or friends. There can be no doubt that the mid-heaven of a nativity bears some relation to the parents; and in rectifying a nativity we have occasionally to take an evil aspect of Saturn or Mars to the ascendant or mid-heaven, to account for the death of a parent.

THE DURATION OF LIFE.

Ptolemy's rule in regard to children who are insusceptible of nurture, has been quoted already, in the eighth chapter. In regard to the probable duration of life Ptolemy says:

"Of all events whatsoever which take place after birth, the most essential is the continuance of life; and as it is, of course, useless to consider, in cases wherein the life of a child does not extend to the period of one year, what other events contingent on its birth might otherwise have subsequently happened, the inquiry into the duration of life consequently takes precedence of all other questions. The discussion of this inquiry is by no means simple, nor easy of execution; it is conducted in a diversified process, by means of the governance of the ruling places."

The prorogatory, or HYLEGIACAL places are, says Ptolemy:

"The sign on the angle of the ascendant, from the fifth degree above the horizon, to the twenty-fifth degree below it; the thirty degrees in dexter sextile thereto, constituting the eleventh house; also the thirty degrees in dexter quartile; forming the mid-heaven above the earth; those in dexter trine making the ninth house; and, lastly, those in opposition, belonging to the angle of the west.

"Among these places, the degrees which constitute the mid-heaven are entitled to preference, as being of a more potent or paramount influence; the degrees in the ascendant are next in virtue; then the degrees in the eleventh house, succedent to the mid-heaven; then those in the angle of the west; and lastly, those in the ninth house, which precedes the mid-heaven."

Ptolemy says that "the Sun, the Moon, the Ascendant, and the Part of Fortune are to be considered as the four principally liable to be elected to the office of prorogator"—or hyleg.[6] Zadkiel I. held that "the Sun is always hyleg and has chief rule over the life, when in any of the hylegliacal places; but if he be not there, and the Moon be, then she is hyleg. When neither luminary is such, I prefer to consider the ascending degree as the hyleg."

I think it is very doubtful whether the Sun is hyleg when in the first half of the eleventh house. I prefer to consider the Sun hyleg only after he has passed his semi-quartile to the M.C. in the eleventh house. The same remark applies to the Moon.

The nativity of Philip III., of Spain, computed by Placidus, is mentioned by Wilson,[7] and he claims that the prolonged course of the disease of which that monarch died, and which he says was due to the direction of the Moon to the declination of Mercury seven years before his death, shows that, "there is a strong probability that the luminaries, and particularly the Moon, are at all times aphetical; and that there is more probability of their being so than even the horoscope." Nevertheless, Wilson admits that, "the direction of the horoscope to the

---

[6] Vide "Star Lore," November, 1897, art. "The Hylegliaca.l Places."

[7] *Dictionary of Astrology*, page 312.

square of Saturn was apparently the more immediate because of death." Wilson also states that "the Sun in the nativity had the declination of Mars, and was in zodiacal square to the Moon, so that the luminaries mutually afflicted each other by the interchange of the evil effects of the two infortunes; and although they were both under the earth, I have no doubt that they were both hylegliacal." If the luminaries were both hylegliacal, how is it that Philip attained the age of 42 years and 11 months? The Moon had the declination of Saturn and was hastening to the opposition of Mars; it is true that she had the sextile of Jupiter, but this weak aspect could not overcome either the affliction of the Sun or her own.

The "Part of Fortune" is an absurdity in nativities, and cannot be hyleg under any circumstances. Zadklel I. never regarded it as hyleg.

A modern writer propounded the absurd idea that the Sun is always hyleg in a man's nativity, and the Moon in a woman's; the ascendant never being hyleg under any circumstances whatever! Comment on such an absurdity would be superfluous; suffice it to say that no facts in evidence of its verity were presented for examination.

My own experience leads me to believe that the limit of 5° above the ascendant, should be extended to 15° (measured by oblique ascension), as a hylegliacal place for the Sun. It certainly seems more in accordance with reason that the luminaries should be more hylegliacal when they happen to be above than when below the horizon. We know that the Moon is the chief ruler over the physical faculties, and that in order to enjoy the possession of a perfectly sound and healthy "constitution," it is necessary that the Moon be absolutely free from affliction at birth.

At the birth of the late Prince Consort the Moon had the sextile of the Sun—a configuration of which Schiller writes thus:

> "And Sun and Moon, too, in the sextile aspect,
> The soft light with the veh'ment—so I love it."[8]

This happy aspect, combined with the approximate parallel declination of the Moon and Venus, tended to strengthen the physique and vital stamina. The mundane quartile of Venus, the zodiacal quartile of Jupiter, and the zodiacal semi-quartile of Uranus to the Moon could produce nothing prejudicial to the health, beyond occasional attacks of malaise arising from plethora; and, in fact, the aspects of Venus and Jupiter to the Moon would help to fortify the constitution. But, on

[8] Schiller's *Wallenstein*, Coleridge's Translation.

the other hand, both the Sun (hyleg) and the Moon had the quadra-sextile of Saturn; and the ascending planet, Mercury, had the quartile of Mars (in the midheaven) and Uranus (in the northern angle), and was applying to the opposition of Saturn (in the western angle), receiving assistance only from Venus by semi-sextile aspect. Hence the Prince succumbed in his 43rd year to a malady (typhoid fever) plainly indicated by the affiiction of Mercury in Virgo, and by the affliction of the Sun and Moon by Saturn. The affliction of Mercury was also indicative of the attacks of croup from which the Prince suffered in early life.

In the nativity of Goethe the Sun was hyleg, and, happily, free from affliction. The narrow escape, which Goethe himself records, from asphyxia at birth, was indicated by the evil Saturn ascending.

The following cases will be found to illustrate the result of the hyleg being much afflicted at birth:

Case 1.—A male child, born February 2nd, 1871, at 5h 21m p.m., Sunderland. The Moon (hyleg) in the 11th house, in 10° 5′ of Cancer in opposition to Saturn (in 5° 39′ of ♑), in square to Mars (in 7° 55′ of ♎), and having the par. dec. of Saturn, Jupiter, and Uranus. The Sun had the trine of Jupiter. The child died on May 23rd, 1873, of broncho-pneumonia.

2.—A male child, born August 26th, 1873, at 10h 30m p.m., Sunderland. The ascendant was hyleg. Uranus in conjunction with Mercury, on the nadir, in mundane square to the ascendant. Saturn and Mars in par. dec. with ascendant. This child died, December 29th, 1874, of whooping cough and bronchitis.

3.—A female child, born December 15th, 1866, at 6h 40m p.m., London. The Moon (hyleg) on the zenith in mundane square to Mars (rising), in sesqui-quadrate to Saturn, in square to Uranus, and in sextile to Jupiter. The child died in January, 1871, of malignant scarlatina (a martial disease).

4.—A female child, born December 19th, 1869, at 7h 35m a.m., Sunderland. The Sun (hyleg) rising in conjunction with Saturn, in opposition to the Moon, and having the par. dec. of Mars and Uranus. This child died, January 25th, 1872. Sixteen days before her death she was attacked with measles, crysipelas followed, and hydrocephalus supervened.

5.—A male child, born June 9th, 1871, at 10h 35m a.m., Sunderland. The Sun (hyleg) in square to Mars and the Moon, and in par. dec. with Saturn, Uranus, Jupitcr, and Venus. The Moon, setting, in opposition to Mars. This child died of smallpox in July, 1871.

6.—A female child, born June 29th, 1871, at 2h 45m a.m., Sunderland. The Sun (hyleg) in conjunction with Jupiter, in opposition to Saturn, in square to Mars, and in par. dec. with Saturn, Uranus, Jupiter, and Mercury. The Moon in semi-quartile to Saturn, in square to Venus, and in sesqui-quadrate to the Sun. The child died of atrophy (congenital), August 31st, 1871.

7.—A male child, born July 4th, 1872, at 4h 30m a.m., Sunderland. The Sun (hyleg) in opposition to Saturn, and in par. dec. with Saturn, Uranus, and Venus. The Moon in conjunction with Mars, in the 12th house. Mercury rising in opposition to Saturn. This child died of phrenitis following measles, November 28th, 1873.

8.—A male child, born August 7th, 1873, at 9h 5m a.m., Sunderland. The Sun (hyleg) in close square to Mars. The Moon in the 4th house in exact conjunction with Saturn. This child died of convulsions, August 14th, 1873.

9.—A male child, born September 1st, 1872, at 10h p.m., Sunderland. Mars and Uranus on the lower heaven in mundane square to the ascendant (hyleg) and Saturn in par. dec. with the ascendant. The child died of diphtheria, June 30th, 1874.

10.—A male child, born April 30th, 1875, at 1h 40m a.m., Sunderland. The Moon (hyleg) in exact conjunction with Saturn, in the ascendant. This child died of marasmus and bronchitis, February 15th, 1876.

11.—A female child, born March 29th, 1859, at 7h a.m., London. The Moon (hyleg) in opposition and par. dec. with Saturn and in square to Mars (rising). The child died, October 16th, 1864.

12.—A male child, born October 17th, 1866, at 1h 10m a.m., London. The ascendant was hyleg—the Moon being on the cusp of the 6th house, in conjunction with Jupiter and more than 6° separated from the opposition of Mars. Saturn was on the nadir, in mundane square, and also in par. dec. with the ascendant. The child died in convulsions, April 7th, 1867.

13.—A female child, born May 7th, 1860, at 4h 45m a.m., Northampton. The Sun (hyleg) rising in mundane square to Mars (on the zenith), in mundane square and zodiacal sextile to Jupiter (on the nadir and in opposition to Mars), and also in zodiacal square and in par. dec. with Saturn (in Leo). The Moon in opposition to Uranus. This child died of spinal disease, August 12th, 1862.

14.—A female child, born February 21st, 1876, at 11h 15m a.m., Sunderland. The Sun (hyleg) in conjunction with Saturn, and in par. dec. with Mars. The Moon in the 8th house in square to Mars. Uranus on the nadir in mundane square to the ascendant. The child died of scarlatina, October 26th, 1876.

15.—A female child, born August 13th, 1878, at 0h 7m 16s a.m., Edinburgh, the Moon (hyleg) on the zenith, eclipsed, in opposition to Uranus and Mars, and in semi-quartile to Saturn. This child died of diarrhoea, August 25th, 1878. The doctor describes her as of average size and healthy when born.

The foregoing cases are beyond dispute. The exact moment of birth was taken for the purpose of scientific inquiry, in every instance, by a medical gentleman. All the children—with one exception—were apparently healthy, and of average size when born. Cases of children born prematurely, and those whose moments of birth were not observed by a professional man, have not been given, or the list could have been considerably augmented. The sole aim being the elucidation of truth, all cases in which the data were open to any doubt, have been rigidly excluded. We wait with confidence for a thorough examination of this question. The result cannot be doubtful. Opponents of the ancient science of astrology never appeal to facts, but content themselves with empty declamation against what they term the "superstition" of believing in it. If we ask one of them to produce facts in proof of his assertion that it is a false science, he forthwith beats a retreat, and refuses to break a lance with us. To such a carpet-knight the words of the Marquis of Montrose are exceedmgly appropriate:

"He only fears his fate too much
Or his deserts are small,
Who dares not put it to the touch
To gain or lose it all."

CHAPTER XXI.

PHYSICAL CONSTITUTION AND TEMPERAMENT.

"The stars o'er man's poor trivial body ride,
And raise or lower it easier than a tide."—THE ACHILLEAD.

THE form and temperament of the body are to be judged, said the ancients, from the ascendant or planet rising at birth, and the Moon's position and configuration. The particular influences of the Sun, Moon, planets, and signs of the zodiac, and the effects imputed to them, respectively, on the form and temperament of the human body, have already been described.

It now remains for us to consider how far the description given by the best authors may be relied upon. In regard to stature the testimonies are very conflicting.

Ptolemy says[1]:

"Men of tall stature have their lords of nativity in elevation, and their ascendants in the beginnings of signs; but the lords of men of short stature will be found in declination [or in obscure situations]. It must also be seen whether the signs be right or oblique."

This aphorism cannot hold good in regard to the so-called "lord" of the ascending sign unless he happen to be within 5° above or below the Eastern horizon. Even in this case, I cannot, from my own experience, vouch for its accuracy; indeed I regard this question of stature as one that has never been satisfactorily solved. I have known tall men who were born with *Cancer* or *Scorpio* ascending; and I have known men of very short stature who were born with *Leo* rising, whereas we are told that *Cancer* and *Scorpio* produce short stature, and that *Leo* produces tallness. I have never known but one very tall person born with Venus rising. Ramesey avers that "the Martialist doth seldom exceed in height," and is usually of low stature. I have known several Mars-men who were tall—one of them was born with Mars and Jupiter rising in *Scorpio*. Generally speaking, I have observed that the su-

[1] Aphorism, LII.

perior planets[2] give tall stature; Venus short stature; Mercury and the Moon, according to their configurations; and the Sun, usually, tall stature.

In judging of personal appearance, from the nativity, the difficulty lies in balancing fairly the opposing influences, and in comprehending the complex rules of the ancients. The ever-varying face of the heavens renders this problem, like every other in judicial astrology, very difficult of solution; indeed, when the fallible nature of human judgment is also considered, the wonder is, not that astrologers sometimes fail to correctly describe persons whom they have never seen, merely from an inspection of their nativities, but, rather, that they ever succeed.

As Wilson observed:

"That the position of the heavens has such effect is abundantly manifest, from the resemblance of children born nearly together, whereas the offspring of the same parents, born at a distant period under a different constitution of the heavens, are essentially and sometimes wholly unlike both in body and mind."[3]

The difficulty lies in comprehending the rules of the ancients as handed down to us by Claudius Ptolemy, for he appears to revel in that mysticism of which the Magi were so enamoured.

The nativities of the late Prince Consort and the late King Edward VII. are well marked, and are forcibly illustrative of the fact that the ascending planet and sign impress their characters upon the person and nature.

Diseases and accidents are judged from the planets which may happen to be rising or setting, and those in configuration with the ascending degree or luminaries. Ptolemy tells us to consider also the planets (if any) in the sixth house. His reason is that the 6th house, in nativities, is "inconjunct with the ascendant." The same remark would also apply to the eighth house. But since the quadra-sextile aspect (five houses, or 150° distance in longitude) has been discovered to have some influence, the cusps of the sixth and eighth houses can no longer be considered as inconjunct with the ascendant. Any apparent effect arising from an infortune posited on the cusp of the sixth

[2] Saturn sometimes produces short stature, when rising at a birth, owing to spinal curvature, or some defect in the legs; also, when in opposition to the Moon, and located on the upper meridian. A gentleman, well known to the author, who was born with Saturn rising in Cancer, is considerably above the middle height.

[3] *Dictionary of Astrology*, page 151.

would, therefore, be traceable to its mundane aspect to the ascendant; and, for the same reason, similar effects should be traceable to an evil planet located on the cusp of the eighth house.

Ptolemy held that oriental planets signify accidents rather than disease. The author's experience has shown that oriental planets sometimes produce diseases as well as accidents. For example:

"J. P. L.," born February 26th, 1847, at 3h 23m a.m., lat 53° 47′ N. Mars was in the ascendant, at this man's birth, in the sign Capricorn, and in square to Uranus. He broke a thigh at twenty years old. Disease of the knee-joint came on in his twenty-third year, necessitating amputation.

In regard to blindness Ptolemy says:

"Blindness of one eye will ensue, when the Moon may be in the ascendant or descendant, either operating her conjunction [with the Sun] or being at the full: it will also happen should she be configurated with the Sun in any other proportional aspect, and be at the same time connected with any one of the nebulous collections in the zodiac; such as the cloudy spot of Cancer, the Pleiades[4] of Taurus, the arrow-head of Sagittarius, the sting of Scorpio, the parts about the mane of Leo, or the urn of Aquarius. Moreover, both eyes will be injured should the Moon be in an angle, and in her decrease, and Mars or Saturn, being matutine, ascend in succession to her; or, again, if the Sun be in an angle, and these planets pre-ascend before him, and be configurated with both the luminaries, whether the luminaries be in one and the same sign, or in opposition; provided, also, the said planets, altogether oriental of the Sun, be occidental of the Moon. Under these circumstances, therefore, Mars will cause blindness by a stroke or a blow, or by the sword, or by burning; and, if he be configurated with Mercury, it will be effected either in a place of exercise or sport, or by the assault of robbers. Saturn, however, under the same circumstances, produces blindness by cataract, or cold, by a white film, or by other similar disorders."

Let us examine the truth of these remarks in the light of facts.

Case 1.—The lady whose time of birth is given in Case 13 had the Moon in 11° 10′ of Leo, with 4° 8′ N. lat., very near the Asselli, under the beams of the Sun (operating her conjunction), and in square with Saturn. Loss of sight of the right[5] eye resulted from a series of ab-

[4] There is reason to doubt this effect, as far as regards the Pleiades.

[5] The Moon is said to govern the left eye of a man, and the right eye of a woman.

scesses beginning in the 8th year.

2.—Mr. R. H., born June 2nd, 1826, at 7h p,m., Leeds. The Moon, on the cusp of the sixth in opposition with Mars and semi-quartile with Saturn. This gentleman lost the sight of his left eye, but I do not know either the date or the cause of the privation.[6]

3.—Mrs. A. D., born March 17th, 1817, at 0h 28m p.m., lat. 50° 44′ N. This lady became totally blind, gradually, from 48 to 54 years of age, and remained so until her death in 1878; she also suffered from cancer of the breast, the sign Cancer rising at her birth. The Moon, operating her conjunction, in Pisces, in semi-quartile with Mars, and in square with Uranus.

4.—The late King George V., of Hanover, born May 27, 1819, at 4h 40m p.m., Berlin. The Moon in square with Mars; the Sun in semi-quartile with Mars, and near the mundane square of Saturn. The Moon, moreover, was within 5° of the semi-quartile of the Sun. Mars was in the 6th house, and in Aries, which rules the head. The injury to the eye, in 1832, which eventually caused blindness, occurred under the primary directions of ☉ s. □ ☽ m., con. 13° 19′, and ☉ s. □ ♂ m., con. 13° 24′. It must not be overlooked that Mars was in mundane parallel to Mercury, at birth, producing, as Ptolemy avers, "blindness by a stroke or a blow, in a place of exercise sport." The injury occurred while the late king was playing with a purse, receiving a blow on the eye from it.

5.—Natus, May 29th, 1812, at 2h a.m., in lat. 53° 48′ N. Saturn on the upper meridian in par dec. with the Sun. The Moon separating from her conjunction with the Sun, and applying to conjunction with Mars. This man was born blind; and his lower limbs were defective from birth, being drawn up under him and paralysed (♄ in ♑).

The next point investigated by Ptolemy is privation of the faculty of speech. He says:

"If Saturn and Mercury, in conjunction with the Sun, be in the before-mentioned angles, the native will have some defect in the tongue, and stammer or speak with difficulty; especially if Mercury be occidental, and both he and Saturn configurated with the Moon. Should Mars, however, be found together with them, he will for the most part remove the defect in the tongue, after the Moon shall have completed her approach to him."

A cousin of the author's was born (January 4th, 1834, 10h 55m

[6] Vide *Star Lore*, October, 1897, p. 154 for this horoscope.

p.m., London) a deaf mute. Saturn was in the ascendant in square with the Sun, in the 4th house. Mercury was conjoined with Mars and Venus; and the Sun, Mars, Mercury and Venus were in parallel declination with each other. Many physicians and surgeons were consulted, but none of them could effect a cure. His intellect was of a high order, and he possessed considerable technical skill.

Ptolemy next proceeds to instruct his disciples in the causes of paralysis, etc., thus:

"Should the malefics be in angles, and the luminaries, either together or in opposition" be brought up to them; or, if the malefics be brought up to the luminaries, especially when the Moon may be in her nodes, or in extreme latitude, or in obnoxious signs, such as Aries, Taurus, Cancer, Scorpio, and Capricorn, the body will then be afflicted with excrescences, distortions, lameness, or paralysis.

"If the malefics be in conjunction with the luminaries, the calamity will take effect from the very moment of birth; but, should they be in the mid-heaven, in elevation above the luminaries, or in opposition to each other, it will then arise out of some great and dangerous accident; such as a fall from some height or precipice, or an attack of robbers, or of quadrupeds. And thus, if Mars hold dominion, he will produce the misfortune by means of fire or wounds, through quarrels or by robbers; and if Saturn, it will be caused by a fall, by shipwreck, or by convulsive fits or spasms.

"Mercury, also, will contribute to the increase of the evil; thus, if he be in familiarity with Saturn, he will much augment the coldness, and promote the continuance of rheumatism, and the disturbance of the fluids, especially in the chest, throat, and stomach. If in familiarity with Mars, he will tend to produce greater dryness, and will increase ulcers, abscesses, loss of hair, erysipelas, tetters, blackness of bile, insanity, epilepsy, and similar disorders.

"Under the circrunstances above detailed, the disease or hurt will be incurable, provided there shall be not one of the benefics in configuration with the malefics which effect the evil, nor with the luminaries posited in angles; and even though the benefics may be so configurated, the misfortune will still be incapable of remedy, if the malefics be well fortified, and in elevation above them."

Here we have some well-defined rules to guide us in our judgment in respect to disease; the question arises: Are they borne out by experience? Let us ascertain:

Case 1.—James R. T ., born August 13th, 1861, at 0h 30m a.m.,

Monkwearmouth. Suffered from epilepsy from birth; had been under medical treatment with no permanent benefit. Occasionally he became maniacal. The Sun in conjunction with Mars, in Leo, and in square with the Moon, in Scorpio. Mercury in par. dec. with the Moon, which luminary partakes of the nature of Mars and the Sun by reason of her configuration with them. Saturn vitiates both Jupiter and Venus by his conjunction with them.

2.—"F. W.," born November 24th, 1870, at 6h a.m., London. The Sun in the ascendant, in conjunction with Mercury, and in par. dec. with Saturn and Uranus. Mars in the mid-heaven, elevated above all the heavenly bodies. The Moon in conjunction with Saturn, in square with Mars, in opposition with Jupiter, having the par. dec. with Mercury, Saturn, Jupiter, and Uranus. He suffered with attacks of epilepsy every fortnight, often coming on when he was asleep. Medical treatment proved of no avail.

3.—"E. M.," born November 11th, 1857, at 5h a.m., Northampton. The Moon (hyleg) in conjunction with Mars. Saturn on the upper meridian, in mundane square with Venus, rising. The evil Saturn was elevated above all the heavenly bodies. This child died, May 23rd, 1861. He never had the proper use of his limbs, and he was so weak that he was always in the recumbent posture. He suffered much with his throat, being only able to swallow liquids (♅ in ♉, in the eighth house).

4.—"A. C.," born June 6th, 1831, midnight, Northampton. Uranus conjoined with Jupiter, rising, in opposition to Saturn, setting; Mars in the sixth house in square with the Moon, and in par. dec. with the Sun. The Sun on the lower meridian in mundane square with Saturn (in Leo), Uranus and Jupiter (in Aquarius). He was paralysed from 3 years and 10 months old, when he had a severe fall and broke a thigh and also lost his speech and hearing for eleven years.

5.—"B.," born June 18th, 1838, at 9h 5m p.m., Northampton. Saturn on the upper meridian, in opposition with the Moon. She had paralysis of the lower extremities from birth.

6.—"A. D. M.," born August 7th, 1855, at 2h 40m p.m., South Shields. The Moon in Gemini, in par. dec. with Mars and Saturn. Mars had risen, in Cancer, just before birth, and Saturn was in Gemini, and in the 12th house, receiving the application of the Moon. This young man was run over by an engine, on the Hartlepool line, and lost an arm and a leg. On the day of the accident (July 6th, 1866), the Sun was passing over the exact place of Mars at birth. The "direction" operating was Asc. par. ♄ zod., con. 10° 57′.

A young lady who was born when Saturn was exactly setting in the sign *Leo*, in opposition to the ascending degree (hyleg) suffered from birth until she was over nineteen years of age, with a spinal complaint, which kept her lying down, and was pronounced incurable by several specialists who treated the case from time to time without success. The author encouraged the parents of the poor sufferer to hope for a cure being effected by the *vis medicatrix natura* in her twentieth or twenty-first year, when she would have a long train of benefic primary directions coming into operation in her favour. She recovered at twenty years old almost suddenly, and is strong and well now.

The cases enumerated above furnish us with ample evidence of the truth of Ptolemy's observations respecting the major bodily diseases and accidents. It is open to the opponents of astrology to bring counter evidence—if they can find any. The important question of physical well-being is indicated, or contra-indicated, by the relative positions of the Sun, Moon, and planets, is deserving of the most extended observation on the part of philosophers and the medical profession.

CHAPTER XXII.

THE MIND AND DISPOSITION.

"How little do we know that which we are!
How less what we may be!"—BYRON.

MERCURY has chief dominion over the mental faculties; the sentient, and also the passions, are governed by the Moon and the ascendant. The manners and disposition are also chiefly influenced by the ascendant and the Moon. That the planet Mercury rules the rational and intellectual faculties has been recognised in all ages of the world, and it has ever been known that in order to be possessed of *mens sana in corpore sano*, both Mercury and the Moon must be strong, free from affliction, and connected either with each other or with the ascendant, and with Jupiter, Mars, or Venus.

The mutual configuration of the Moon with Mercury is, undoubtedly, very desirable. The angular position especially in the ascendant is the best "dignity" that Mercury can possess. Experience teaches us that Mercury is stronger zodiacally, when located in either *Gemini* or *Virgo* than when in other signs, but it by no means follows that he is weak when in Sagittary or Pisces. At Sir Isaac Newton's birth Mercury was in Sagittary and in quartile with Jupiter and Saturn conjoined in Pisces.

When Mercury and the Moon happen to be configurated with several planets, the person then born will (it is averred by some authors) be very unsettled and unstable in disposition—"Everything by turns, and nothing long." Whether this is true or not, it is observed that such a variety of configurations confers versatility of talent, and a love of change of occupation.

The parallel of declination, the conjunction, the sextile, and the trine, are the happiest bonds of connexion between the Moon and Mercury, for they produce, more or less, according to the position and other configurations of these two bodies, good abilities, ingenuity, readiness of resource, a pretty wit, and energy. The square and opposition are better than no aspect between the Moon and Mercury, but they sometimes cause obstinacy, cynicism, and fickleness in addition to good abilities; chiefly if Mars or Saturn be evilly configurated with one of them. The "dispositors," or planets ruling the signs containing Mercury and the Moon, may be disregarded, unless they happen to be in configuration with one or the other; and the oriental position of one of them is better than the occidental.

The general influence of the signs—excepting the equinoctial strangely omitted by Claudius Ptolemy—when ascending, or, containing Mercury and the Moon, is thus described:

"The tropical signs [Cancer and Capricornus] generally dispose the mind to enter much into political matters, rendering it eager to engage in public and turbulent affairs, fond of distinction, and busy in theology; at the same time, ingenious, acute, inquisitive, inventive, speculative, studious of astrology and divination.

"Bicorporal signs [Gemini, Sagittarius, and the first half of Pisces] render the mind variable, versatile, not easy to be understood, volatile, and unsteady; inclined to duplicity, amorous, wily, fond of music, careless, full of expedients, and regretful.

"Fixed signs [Taurus, Leo, Scorpio and Aquarius] make the mind just, uncompromising, constant, firm of purpose, prudent, patient, industrious, strict, chaste, mindful of injuries, steady in pursuing its object, contentious, desirous of honour, avaricious, and pertinacious."

Ptolemy enjoins his disciples to consider "the configuration made with the Sun and the angles by stars bearing any relation to the point in question," in addition to "such stars as hold any influence over Mercury and the Moon."

The retrograde position of Mercury is said by some authors to impair the native's abilities. That this aphorism is unsound can be proved by a reference to the Prince Consort's nativity, wherein Mercury will be found to be retrograde. The proximate quartile aspect of both Mars and Uranus with Mercury in the same nativity supports the observation of Wilson, that he had "never observed that the nature of an aspect," to Mercury, "made much difference, whether a square or sextile."

The abilities of a person born when Mercury is "combust" or "under the sunbeams," are also said, by some authors, to be impaired; and, on the other hand, that the abilities of persons born when Mercury is in "cazimi" (within 17′ of the Sun's centre) are of the highest order.

At the Right Hon. W. E. Gladstone's birth (December 29th, 1809),

Mercury was (at noon) in 6° 45′ of ♑, and the Sun was in 7° 27′ of ♑; hence Mercury was combust. The great mental abilities of Mr. Gladstone cannot he denied, and this fact induces very grave doubt as to the truth of the axiom that the combustion of Mercury impairs the abilities of the native.*

The Earl of Beaconsfield, K.G., was born December 21st, 1804; Mercury (at noon) in 13° 2′ of ♑, the Sun in 29° 31′ of ♐, hence Mercury was under the sunbeams. Moreover, Mercury had the close square aspect with both Saturn and Uranus (nearly conjoined in Libra).†

According to the teachings of some authors the noble Earl should possess very mean abilities indeed, owing to the position and aspects of Mercury. In justice to Ptolemy it must be stated that he draws no distinction between the nature of the aspects to Mercury, for he uses only the terms "conciliated" and "connected," and nowhere speaks of any difference in the influence of the square and sextile, etc., in relation to Mercury.

At Goethe's birth Mercury was less than ten degrees separated from the Sun, and had the parallel declination of Saturn.

At the birth of the late Sir Robert Peel, Mercury was only five degrees distant from the Sun, and in trine aspect with Jupiter.

At the birth of Napoleon I., Mercury was within seventeen degrees of the Sun, and in quartile with Uranus.

At the birth of Lord Nelson, Mercury was less than fourteen degrees from the Sun.

Mercury when in conjunction, sextile or trine with Saturn, is said to indicate "sound judgment, and a careful, constant wit." Upon this aphorism, Wilson remarks: "I am certain the *conjunction* with Saturn would be productive of quite a contrary effect." In this opinion Wilson was decidedly mistaken, as reference to Goethe's nativity (wherein ☿ had par. dec. with ♄) will prove. Any aspect of Saturn with Mercury contributes to *solidity* of intellect, and gives a love for antiquarian studies, patience, and laboriousness; and (if mixed with Jupiter) probably a tendency to asceticism. Jupiter in aspect with Mercury gives candour, generosity, and good abilities. Mars configurated with Mercury gives courage, se1f-confidence, mechanical dexterity, and sometimes brashness. Many eminent sur-

* The horoscope was given in "STAR LORE," June 1898.

† Earl Beaconsfield's horoscope was presented in my "Science of the Stars."

geons were born when Mercury and the luminaries were configurated with Mars. Unless Jupiter or Venus be configurated with Mercury, his familiarity with Mars is apt to produce want of tenderness, as in the case of vivisectionists.

The Sun in conjunction or parallel with Mercury, indicates pride, conscientiousness, and ambition.

Venus in aspect with Mercury confers taste, elegance, love of luxury, music, fascination of manners, and amiability; but if there are cross aspects of the infortunes to Venus and Mercury, the motives of the person then born are liable to misconstruction; and, unless Jupiter should be configurated with them or with the Moon, or predominant, the talents are liable to be perverted.

Uranus in configuration with Mercury, inclines the native to the study of astrology, astronomy, and applied sciences, and renders his mental abilities ingenious and original.

Neptune gives as much romance to the mind and nature, when configurated with Mercury, as Uranus gives, but less ingenuity.

At the birth of H.R.H. the Duchess of Argyll, Mercury was retrograde, in Pisces, in close conjunction with Saturn, in square with Mars, and in trine with Jupiter. The Moon was in sextile with Jupiter, in square with Mars, in opposition with Mercury, and in par. dec. with Saturn. Venus was in square with the ascending degree. This amiable Princess, it is well known, is highly gifted.*

In the nativity of George III., June 4th, 1738, at 7h 46m a.m., Mercury was conjoined with Saturn; Mars (on the upper meridian) was in square with the ascendant and the Moon, and the Moon and Mercury were neither connected with each other nor with the ascendant. Under evil primary directions the king became insane, and, but for Mercury having the sextile of Jupiter, and the conjunction with Venus, he would have become insane much earlier in life. It is most important that Mercury and the Moon be connected either with each other or with the ascendant, for otherwise there is always a risk, temporarily at least, of insanity under the combined influence of a train of evil directions. Saturn inclines to melancholia, Mars to mania; and the combination of their evil influences induces either epilepsy or alternate fits of melancholy and fury.

The observations of Ptolemy on diseases of the mind and body, are so confused that, although there is much truth in many of them, it is

---

* This horoscope was given in *Zadkiel's Almanac*, 1890.

very difficult to sift the wheat from the chaff. It is just possible, however, that Ptolemy is not so much to blame for the confusion to be found in his writings, as handed down to us, for the Greeks and Romans corrupted the Egyptian astrology. The edition of the *Elzevirs*, dated in 1635, was printed in double columns, one containing Proclus's Greek paraphrase, the other the Latin translation of Leo Allatius, II, a Greek by birth, celebrated for his works in both languages, who was appointed keeper of the Vatican Library, by Pope Alexander VII., with whom he was in high favour. Melancthon after having been at the pains of correcting and republishing, in 1553 (with his own emendations), the edition of Camerarius, containing the reputed oriental text, still deemed it advisable, in the following year, to edit Proclus's paraphrase.

A few cases have fallen under the author's notice. They are these:

Case 1.—Adah P., an idiot, born January 13th, 1858, at 0h 21m p.m., Northampton. Mercury on the upper meridian in opposition with Saturn, in square with Mars; and in par. dec. with Uranus (rising), and unconnected with the Moon. Saturn being in Cancer and opposed to the Sun, the child suffered from chronic dyspepsia.

2.—"B.," born June 18th, 1838, at 9h 5m p.m., Northampton. This woman was idiotic from birth. Mercury in conjunction with Mars, and the Moon in opposition with Saturn (culminating).

3.—"J. N. S.," born September 25th, 1843, at 7h a.m., London. The Moon and Mercury nearly conjoined, in the ascendant, in square with Saturn (in the northern angle). The Moon had the trine of Jupiter. The Sun in square with Mars, in opposition with Uranus, and in conjunction with Venus. This gentleman, who was well educated, and possessed good musical talent, fell a victim to melancholia, and died, of abscess of the brain, in a lunatic asylum, in his 31st year.

4.—"R. J.," born April 9th, 1848, at 5h 30m a.m., lat. 55° N. This gentleman who was highly educated, suffered with religious mania, and died suddenly, in asylum, in his 28th year. Mercury was in conjunction and par. dec. with Saturn and Venus, in Pisces, and in square with Mars. The Moon had separated but 7° from the conjunction with Mars, and was applying to the conjunction with Jupiter. The Sun had just risen in close conjunction with Uranus. At the autopsy the heart and lungs were found to be perfectly healthy (☽ ☌ ♃ in ♋); and the doctors said that he had died from exhaustion through having refused all kinds of food.

"The diseases of the body act through the vital principle upon the mind," as Dr. Sharp wrote:* "and, on the other hand, the disorders of the mind act through the same medium upon the body. These are the only instances we are cognisant of in which matter and spirit meet and act upon each other; in all other cases, so far as we know, matter acts only upon matter, and spirit upon spirit."

Hahnemann, the founder of homeopathy, observed that certain symptoms manifested themselves "at the new or full Moon," and some "when the moon is waning." Jahr[1] directs certain medicines to be given at the decline of the Moon, and others at the next full Moon. Dr. Sharp repudiated "the re-introduction of astrological considerations among the reasons for prescribing remedies for disease," but expressed himself as "ready to adopt whatever is demonstrated, or concede whatever is rendered highly probable." Dr. Sharp admitted that, "for many centuries a belief had been maintained that the action of drugs is under the government of the Sun, Moon, and planets." Also that, "All the details of this misbelief are given with perfect good faith, and with entire confidence, so lately as the middle of the seventeenth century; in one of the most popular medical books of the time—by 'popular,' I here mean among medical men; this is the Pharmacopaeia of John Schröder (1656)." If Dr. Sharp had carefully compared the directions for the administration of herbs given in Culpeper's *Herbal*, with the symptoms produced in the healthy and cured in the diseased by certain drugs, used by homeopathic (and some allopathic) physicians, he could not have failed to be struck with the manifest correlation of the homeopathic with the astrological law. Medicine was invented by the Egyptians in order to overcome the apparently fatal influence of the evil planets, when in certain relative positions; and, as Ptolemy relates, "they combined the medical art with astronomical prognostication." Since the spread of homeopathy, and the improvement of the medical art generally, a knowledge of astrology and of the relation of certain drugs to the Sun, Moon, and planets, is not so indispensable as formerly. Even at the present day, however, such knowledge would be of great use to the doctors, and of great benefit to their patients; and, in regard to the treatment of the insane, a knowledge of astrology would be found to be of immense service.

---

* *Essays on Medicine, being an investigation of Homeopathy and other Medical Systems*. Leath and Ross. Tenth Edition, page 137.

[1] *Clinical Guide*, article, "Worm Affections."

[2] July 22nd, 1876.

The *Lancet*[2] once stated that:

"The progressive explorations of physiological and pathological science develop intimate bonds of union between mind and body hitherto undiscovered, and not even supposed to exist.[3] Mind and body are inseparable,[4] at least during life; they are mutually dependent for energy; the strength of the one is the power of the other; the weakness of one is the impotence of both."

No better evidence of this truth can be obtained than that afforded by a study or the genethliacal branch of astrology.

In the *Psychologie Morbide* of Dr. J. Moreau (de Tours), Médecin de l'Hospice de Bicêtre, the author thus speaks of two twin brothers who had been confined, on account of monomania, at Bicêtre:

"Physically the two young men are so nearly alike that the one is easily mistaken for the other. Morally their resemblance is no less complete, and is most remarkable in its details. Thus, their dominant ideas are absolutely the same. They both consider themselves subject to imaginary persecutors, the same enemies have sworn their destruction, and employ the same means to effect it. Both have hallucinations of hearing. They are both of them melancholy and morose; they never address a word to anybody, and will hardly answer the questions that others address to them. They always keep apart and never communicate with one another. An extremely curious fact, which has been frequently noted by the superintendents of their section of the hospital, and by myself, is this: From time to time, at very regular intervals of two, three, and many months, without appreciable cause, and by the purely spontaneous effect of their illness, a very marked change takes place in the condition of the two brothers. Both of them, at the same time, and often on the same day, rouse themselves from their habitual stupor and prostration; they make the same complaints, and they come of their own accord to the physician with an urgent request to be liberated. I have seen this strange thing occur, even when they were some miles apart; the one being at Bicêtre, and the other living at Saint-Anne."

There is another curious French case of insanity in twins, described by Dr. Baume, in the *Annales Médico-Psychologiques*.[5]

---

[3] Except by the Astrologers.

[4] See *The Human Body and its Connection with Man*, by Dr. Garth Wilkinson; also by the same author, *Human Science and Divine Revelation*.

[5] 4 Série, Vol. I.,1863, page 312.

Trousseau gives a remarkable case, in his important work *Clinique Médicales*, in the chapter on Asthma, of twin-brothers "so extraordinarily alike," and who had "a yet more remarkable pathological resemblance." He says:

"These twins were also asthmatic, and to a frightful degree. Though born in Marseilles, they were never able to stay in that town, where their business affairs required them to go, without having an attack. Still more strange, it was sufficient for them to get away only as far as Toulon in order to be cured of thc attack caught at Marseilles. They travelled continually and in all countries, and they remarked that certain localities were extremely hurtful to them, and that in others they were free from all asthmatic symptoms."

Who will say that this is not strongly corroborative of the truth of astrology?

The similarity of twins is an incontrovertible proof of the influence of the ambient. If Mercury be strong in both nativities the countenance of twins born nearly together will be illuminated by wisdom, and *vice versá*. It is a mistake to think that either religion or education can ever change the original impress of nature. The leonine man will ever be leonine in the expression of his countenance, and in many of the *traits* of his character; the Saturnine man will never become jovial looking; the Mercurialist will always be mercurial. Lord Verulam once observed that "a fine person is a perpetual letter of recommendation."The Almighty has, however, in some notable instances conferred the highest intellect upon men whose bodies and countenances could lay no claim to symmetry—as was the case with Swift, Pope, Voltaire, Goldsmith, Johnson, and Aesop. Goethe tells us in his *Autobiography* that Lavater was to a certain extent disappointed with his personal appearance at their first interview.

The remarkable horoscopes of twins born on the 9th June, 1890, at an interval of one hour and a half, one dying in infancy and the other surviving that period, were given in STAR LORE, March, 1897, pp. 32, 33.

In FUTURE, August and September, 1893, pp. 121, 130, there are some remarks on twins.

Emerson in his "Essay on Beauty" wrote that:

"Astrology interested us, for it tied man to the system. Instead of an isolated beggar, the farthest star felt him and he felt the star. However rash and however falsified by pretenders to it, the hint was true and divine, the soul's avowal of its large relations, and that climate, century, remote natures as well as near are part of its biography . . . a right and perfect man would be felt to the centre of the Copernican system."

Some persons born with either of the signs Aries, Taurus, Leo, Scorpio,[6] the latter half of Sagittary, and Capricorn, ascending (except when Mercury is in the ascendant and configurated with the Moon and the fortunes) have something nearly akin to the animal expression and character. When Mercury is powerful in a nativity, the cultivation of the mind and subordination of the passions to reason will cause a gradual transformation from the human to the divine expression. The divine physiognomical expression pourtrayed by the Greeks as appertaining to their heroes and divinities, marks "how high progressive life may go," as Pope says.

[6] Scorpio often gives features greatly resembling those of the eagle.

CHAPTER XXIII.

THE FORTUNE OF WEALTH AND RANK.

"Errors, like straws, upon the surface flow;
He who would search for pearls must dive below."—DRYDEN.

NAPOLEON I. and LOUIS NAPOLEON III., by their wonderful careers, exemplified the pre-signification of the major planets rising or culminating at birth. They "achieved greatness," by the power of their stars and the force of their intellect, and they both fell from their exalted positions, were made prisoners, and died in exile! A fitting commentary is afforded by the eventful career of those monarchs, on the meridional position of the planet Saturn; for at their births, and at the birth of Louis Phillippe, also, was the greater infortune culminating! The nativity of Napoleon the Great was computed by Worsdale, who stated that:

"The Emperor himself gave the time of his birth to an astronomer in Corsica, as having taken place at a quarter before ten o'clock in the forenoon of August 15th, 1769, at Ajaccio."

The time of birth of Louis Napoleon was given in the *Moniteur* of April 21st, 1808. as follows:

"Paris, le 20 Avril, 1808.—Aujourd'hui, mercredi 20 Avril á une heure du matin, S.M. la reine de Hollande est heureusement accouchée d'un Prince."

For Louis Phillippe's time of birth the author cannot vouch, but it was given as 9h 40m a.m., October 6th, 1773.

The great Solar Eclipse of October 9th, 1847, fell close to the place of the Sun in the nativity of Louis Phillipe (in opposition to Uranus), and foreshadowed his downfall.

Zadkiel I. foretold the fate of Louis Napoleon, in his *Almanac* for 1853, in the following words:

"But let him not dream of lasting honours, power, or prosperity. He shall found no dynasty, he shall wear no durable crown; but, in the midst of deeds of blood and slaughter, with affrighted Europe trembling beneath the weight of his daring martial hosts, he descends beneath the heavy hand of fate, and falls to rise no more."

King Francis I. of France, born September 12th, 1494, at 10h 37m p.m., in lat. 48° N ., whose horoscope was given by Placidus, had Saturn in the tenth house in Pisces 10° 22′ and in parallel of declination with the Moon, and Neptune on the lower meridian, fought against the Emperor Charles V. of Germany, whose horoscope was also given by Placidus, and suffered a great overthrow, and was himself wounded and taken prisoner by the victorious Germans. The German Emperor's nativity was the more fortunate one.

Ptolemy directs us to judge of the fortune of wealth by the "Part of Fortune" alone; "the position of which," he says, "is, in all cases, always as far removed from the ascendant as the Sun is distant from the Moon." This may have been an interpolation, however.

Wilson avers that the *pars fortuna* "is really nothing but a phantom hatched in the figurative brain of Ptolemy, which has no influence whatever, except influence can arise out of nothing." The author is in perfect accord with Wilson in this view.

Placidus once confessed that he had, with regard to the Part of Fortune, laboured a long time, and had never been able to find any truth in it.

The Part of Fortune is that point of the horoscope whereon the rays of the Sun and Moon converge, and where the Moon would be if the Sun were exactly rising. Effects (if any) connected with the Part of Fortune, are really traceable to the Sun and Moon. It must, therefore, be rejected from a rational system of genethlialogy.

If Venus and Jupiter be strong, and in good configuration with either the Sun or Moon in a nativity, the person then born will become wealthy, either through inheritance or by means of his own industry. The angular position is the strongest that the luminaries and the planets can have. The space extending from the cusp of the 2nd house to that of the 9th, via the ascendant, is the next best, and most fortunate for the luminaries and benefics to be placed in at birth. The most powerful angle is the south, the next is the east, then the west; and the fourth is held to be weakest of four angles.

Saturn and Mars angular also give advancement, but it is almost invariably attended with risks and dangers, and with reverses towards the end of life.

The Sun and Moon afflicted and cadent in the 6th or 3rd houses, and the planets weakly posited, threaten poverty, difficulties, and misery, difficult to overcome even by those who are gifted with indomitable resolution, and are blessed with health and strength.

Planets retrograde at birth are said to cause poverty and sickness, but this is very doubtful.[1]

It is important that the Sun and Moon be in good aspect with each other—sextile or trine—and if one of them be on the upper meridian, so much the better for the native's fortune. For persons who continue to reside in or near the place of their birth, it is important that the Sun and Moon, Jupiter and Venus be above the earth, in order to afford a prospect of lasting prosperity. Saturn with the Moon, especially when angular, is one of the worst positions; and, unless the Moon be configurated with Jupiter, or that benefic be ascending, ruin or disgrace may ensue. Fixed stars of a fortunate nature (Arista, North Scale, Rigel, etc.) ascending, culminating, or with one of the luminaries, promise riches or good fortune.

Saturn in benefic aspect with the Sun, Moon, and Jupiter gives riches by inheritance, gain by mines (if Saturn be in the fourth house), lands, legacies, agriculture, or navigation.

Jupiter gives wealth by means of the church, the law, offices of state, or University appointments.

Mars gives riches by military preferment, surgery, and all mechanical trades in which iron and sharp tools are used.

Venus gives wealth through the friendship or kind offices of ladies of position and influence and success in art, music, the drama, etc.

Mercury confers riches by means of science, art, literature, elo-

[1] "Had I faith in astrology, brother (which by the bye my father had), I would have sworn some retrograde planet was hanging over this unfortunate house of mine, and turning every individual thing in it out of its place."—LAURENCE STERNE (Tristram Shandy).

"But there is a fatality attends the actions of some men; order them as they will, they pass through a certain medium which so twists and refracts them from their true direction—that with all the titles to praise which a rectitude of heart can give, the doers of them are nevertheless forced to live and die without it."—STERNE.

"I had never more need that the heavenly bodies should befriend me, for my earthly path is darkened and confused."—LEICESTER.

"And shake the yoke of inauspicious stars,
From this world-wearied flesh."—SHAKESPEARE.

quence, travelling, etc.

From the position of the planets most strongly fortified in the horoscope, the *direction*, or part of the world in which fortune most likely of attainment, may sometimes be known.

Too much stress has been laid on the position of Jupiter in the 2nd house of a nativity. Hopes have thereby been raised only to be disappointed, of "wealth beyond the dreams of avarice." If the Sun and Moon be evilly configurated with Saturn, and have no assistance from Jupiter, the accidental position of Jupiter in the 2nd house can of little avail, and the native is more likely to meet with penury than wealth. The position of Jupiter in the 2nd house when happily configurated with the Sun, and receiving the bodily application of the Moon, especially in Cancer, Sagittarius, or Pisces, the luminaries being free from affliction, will bring good estate, or good fortune in trade. The career of an individual may be advantageously altered, in some cases, by emigration, as before stated. For example:

A gentleman, whose birth took place at midnight of September 29th, 1816, in Scotland, met with but little prosperity in the United Kingdom. He removed to Australia, and there prospered to such extent that he became one of the wealthiest and most highly respected citizens of Melbourne. At his birth the planets Mercury, Venus, and Jupiter, were located in the 4th house (the northern angle). By crossing the equator, and pitching his tent in a southern latitude (38°) he inverted his horoscope, and thereby brought the benefics nearly to the upper meridian of his nativity.

Here is another instance, and of a different kind, of benefit by emigration:

A gentleman, whose birth took place when the Moon was culminating in the sign *Capricorn*, in sextile to Jupiter (setting), and in trine to the Sun. He went to India (ruled by Capricorn), rose to distinction, and obtained a lucrative post under Government there.

RANK.—The Sun and Moon when angular, especially if, in Aries, Cancer, Capricornus, or Libra and well aspected by the benefics, or the benefics angular and well aspected by the luminaries, confer power, distinction, and greatness on the native. On the other hand, the luminaries far below the horizon, afflicted by the malefics, and no benefic angular, poverty, obscurity, and adversity from which the native will find it well-nigh impossible to emerge, at least in the hemisphere in which he was born, are likely to be endured.

Rank and authority proceeding from Saturn, may probably be derived from the possession of land, houses, mines, etc.

Rank and authority proceeding from Jupiter and Venus are pleasurable, and accompanied with honour and riches.

Rank and authority proceeding from Mars, are derived from the command of armies the gaining of victories by sea or land, distinction in surgery, engineering, etc.

Rank and authority proceeding from Mercury arise from distinction in literature, arts, sciences, and in the direction or management of great companies.

Planets when rising before the Sun, and setting after the Moon, are held to possess more efficacy in the promotion of rank and wealth.

The configurations and positions of the Sun, Moon, Jupiter and Venus at the births of Her Majesty Queen Victoria, the Prince Consort, and King Edward VII., are eminently illustrative of the power of the heavenly bodies in nativities.

The nativities of the late German Emperor, grandfather of the Kaiser, and of King George III. of Great Britain show the power of Mars when culminating at birth.

The unfortunate nativities of the members of the Bourbon family[2] (with one exception), illustrate the power of the malefic planets, when evilly configurated with the luminaries and powerfully situated, to bring misfortune even upon royal families. The exception is the nativity of Louis XVIII., in which Jupiter was rising, and, therefore, after all his vicissitudes of fortune, he died upon the throne.

The mutual sextile or trine aspect of the Sun and Moon, when they are free from affiiction, will give advancement, honour, dignity, and comparative wealth. On the other hand, the mutual quartile or opposition aspect of the Sun and Moon generally causes great difficulties and troubles to bar the way of advancement. Many great men have been born near full Moon, but then the fortunes have assisted the Moon, or have been angular at their births.

---

[2] The times of birth, and the positions of the luminaries and planets thereat, were given in a letter to the *Spectator*, and printed in the edition of that journal for February 22nd, 1862; they were also given in the authors' pamphlet, *A Defence of Astrology*, pages 24 to 26.

CHAPTER XXIV.

ON THE VOCATION.

"They marked the influence, and observed the power
Of every sign, and every fatal hour;
What tempers they bestowed, what fortunes gave,
And who was born a king, who doom'd a slave."—MANILIUS

TO those persons whose lot it is to labour for their daily bread, no question can be more important than that relating to the nature of the vocation best suited to their talents, and most favourable to their success. Many eminent men have been compelled to change their profession or business in consequence of the mistakes of their parents, or guardians, in having apprenticed them to trades or professions repugnant to their natures. Much light can sometimes be thrown on the natural bent of an individual, on the nature of the employment most fortunate for him, and, also, on the part of the world most favourable to his success, by a careful study of his nativity. It is not, however, always a point easily determined; there are, in some nativities, so many positions and configurations presented for consideration, that the induction (by which method alone can a safe conclusion be gained) becomes very difficult.

If one and the same planet be in the mid-heaven, and making its oriental appearance nearest to the Sun, it alone should be taken as the representative of the nature of the profession or employment. But here, again, a pretty wide field of inquiry is opened up, for this same planet may bear rule over a variety of trades and professions. For example, let us suppose Mercury alone is the significator. We find that he produces writers, superintendents of business, accountants, teachers, merchants, and bankers; and all who live by literature and furnishing instruction, as well as by stipend or salary. If Mercury be badly afflicted, the profession followed may be that of an informer, or contributor to the low-class journals.

If Saturn be in any way configurated with Mercury, persons then born will most probably become managers of the affairs of others, or employed in connection with places of worship.

If Jupiter and Venus be configurated with Mercury, persons then born will prosper as painters, artists, musicians, or jewellers. If Jupiter alone be configurated with Mercury, the legal or clerical profession will be well adapted to the genius of the person then born, or the woollen or grocery trade. If Venus be in conjunction with Mercury, a taste for music, the drama, etc., may lead the native to devote his talents to the pursuit of one of them as a profession; or he may become an astronomer, or astrologer, or both.

If Saturn join Mercury and Venus, success is promised in the manufacture or sale of ornaments and garments for women.

If Jupiter be joined with Mercury and Venus, the person then born is well adapted for the office of a magistrate, judge, or tutor.

Should Mercury and Mars be joined together, the person then born will, probably, do well as a sculptor, surgeon, engineer, ironmaster or ironworker, shipbuilder, or in any trade in which sharp tools are used. If Saturn afflict these planets, and at the same time afflict the Sun or Moon, there is a danger of becoming dishonest. If Jupiter be joined with Mercury and Mars, the person then born will distinguish himself in honourable warfare, or in business; and he will be greatly disposed to engage in foreign trade.

Venus and Mars being joint arbiters of the employment, favour success in dealing in perfumery, dyes, drugs, etc.; and, also, in art and the theatrical profession.

Saturn joined with Venus and Mars will incline people to be attendants on religious ceremonies, undertakers, grave-diggers, etc. If Jupiter join Mars and Venus, in signification, persons then born may become holders of sacred offices.

Venus alone ruling the employment, signifies dealers in perfumery, flowers, fruit, wines, colours, dyes, spices, and apparel (silk, especially, if ♀ be in ♎).

The signs of the zodiac appear to have some general influence over the nature of the employment. The signs Gemini, Libra, and Aquarius, are held to indicate scientific pursuits, Aries, Taurus, Leo, and Capricorn, give employment among metals, in business, trade, housebuilding; and as smiths or mechanics. The tropical and equinoctial (*i.e.*, the cardinal signs) give employment in matters of exchange, mensuration, agriculture, or of religion. The signs Taurus, Cancer, Virgo, Scorpio, Capricornus, and Pisces, incline to employment on the water, horticulture, shipbuilding, and agriculture.

The Moon regulating the employment, and, separating from the

Sun, forming an aspect with Mercury, inclines to the pursuit of traveling, or astronomy, or astrology, or teaching.

The magnitude and importance of the employment will be determined by the power, elevation, and aspects of the ruling planet or planets. If they be angular, or oriental of the Sun, they usually give eminence and authority; but if under the horizon, or occidental, they often render the employment of a subordinate character. If the benefics be rulers of the employment, or in aspect with the planet ruling, and elevated, they give important, lucrative, honourable, agreeable, and conspicuous positions. If, on the other hand, the malefics elevated above and in evil configuration with the ruling planet, the employment and position of the person then born may prove to be uncertain, poverty-stricken, insecure, and, probably, unhealthy also. In such case Saturn causes delay and difficulty; and, in some cases, through several pursuits being blended together. Mars produces mischief by rash and reckless conduct. Both Saturn and Mars when evilly configurated with the ruler of the employment indicate several enemies conspiring against the owner of the horoscope, and seeking to oust him from his post; and (unless the Moon be configurated with Mercury) these planets may prevent proficiency as well as good reward.

In regard to the learned professions, we may be assured that in order to command success in the law, Jupiter and Mercury must be strong, and either the Sun or Moon in conjunction, sextile, trine, or parallel, with Jupiter. To insure success in medicine, Mars must be strong in the nativity, and harmoniously configurated with either the Sun or Moon or Mercury. To succeed in the church, Jupiter, or one of the luminaries should be found in the ninth or tenth house of the nativity, and in harmonious configuration with Saturn.

In the remaining professions and trades, success may be predicated in like manner. The parts of the world most favourable to the native's career, may be judged according to the instructions given in the preceding chapter.

As a general rule the planet Mercury when in either the first, eleventh, tenth, or ninth house, bears chief sway over professions and trades. But, should another planet be making its oriental appearance nearest to the Sun, or be located in the tenth house, it must be taken to be the representative of the employment. If one planet be making its oriental appearance nearest the Sun, and another planet be on the upper meridian, that one must be taken which receives the application of the Moon. If both planets be configurated with the Moon, or if neither have any configuration with her, then that one which has the most fortunate aspects should be taken to represent the employment. If two or more planets be conjoined with Mercury, and have configuration with the Moon, the person then born will (especially if the Moon be angular) change his employment and residence, frequently.

In Goethe's nativity both Mercury and Venus are near the Sun and the mid-heaven. Mercury is seen placed in the ninth house, oriental of the Sun, having the parallel of declination of Saturn, the trine of Mars, and the semi-sextile of Venus; and separating from the opposition of Uranus. Venus is found in the tenth house, occidental of the Sun, having the parallel declination of the Moon, the opposition and par. dec. of Jupiter, and applying to the quartile with Mars. Venus's position is, therefore, the strongest, and her configuration with Mercury inclined Goethe to follow the pursuit of literature, and he developed that dramatic and poetic genius for which he is so justly and deservedly famed. The angular positions of the Sun, Venus, the Moon, and Jupiter, together, constitute this nativity a fortunate one, and clearly point to his high talents and brilliant career. The connection formed by Saturn and Uranus with Mercury, gave a mystical trait to his mind.

In *Urania*, May 1880, will be found a paper by a physician on "Successful Commanders," in which it was shown in the great majority of instances (eighteen) there was a trine aspect of the Moon with Mars on the birthday. In a few cases the trine had been completed on the day before the birth, and in others the day after. In the absence of information as to the natal hour it would be unfair to regard these cases as telling against the theory of martial influence on the careers of generals. Next to the trine came the mutual sextile of Mars and the Moon. In Soult's case there was an opposition of these two celestial bodies, but the Sun was in Aries and in proximate sextile with Mars at that great general's birth. In the case of Lord Napier of Magdala, the Moon was in opposition with Mars in the evening before his birthday, but the Sun in Sagittary was in sextile with Mars in Libra, and, probably, the birth took place about sunrise of December 6th, 1810. The quartile of the Moon with Mars was only found on the birthday of Count Moltke. Frederic the Great had the Sun, Mercury and Mars in the tenth house, for he was born at noon.

The Emperor Frederic William of Germany had the Sun in the martial sign *Aries* at his birth (two o'clock p.m.) and Mars in the tenth house. Moltke had the Sun in the martial sign *Scorpio*, and Prince Bismarck had the Sun in *Aries*, and Mercury in semi-quartile with Mars. No wonder that this triumvirate defeated Louis Napoleon in

1870, and consolidated the various kingdoms of Germany into a powerful, united, Empire.

Lord Roberts had the Sun in close trine with Mars at his birth, and Mars nearly in parallel with Jupiter, Mercury, Venus and Jupiter were all in their respective chief dignities.[1]

On the birthday of Lord Kitchener the Moon was just separating from the trine with Mars in *Leo*; and on his fiftieth birthday (1900) the Moon was in conjunction with Mars.

The zodiacal sign containing the ruler of the vocation, especially if it be on the meridian of the nativity, and if the ruler be dignified in it—as the Sun is in Leo, the Moon in Cancer, Mercury in Gemini and Virgo, Venus in Taurus and Libra, Mars in Aries and Scorpio, Jupiter in Sagittarius and Pisces, and Saturn in Capricornus and Aquarius—may be of use in indicating the country or city in which eminence and success may be achieved in the vocation.

The gentleman, whose nativity was mentioned earlier, who was born at 8h 20m p.m. of September 6th, 1840, in lat. 52° 58′ N., and long. 6° W., Capricornus 19° 24′ on the upper meridian, and the Moon in 16° 14′ of that sign, in trine with the Sun in Virgo 14° 16′, and in sextile with Jupiter in Scorpio 14° 15′, went out to India (ruled by Capricornus) in October, 1862, and succeeded well in that country. In this instance although the Moon is not dignified in ♑, she is well supported by the benefic aspects of both the Sun and Jupiter.

[1] Vide STAR LORE, March, 1900.

CHAPTER XXV.

MARRIAGE.

"Oh, happy they, the happiest of their kind,
Whom gentler stars unite."—THOMSON.

A GOOD knowledge of astrology, and due regard being paid to its premonitions, might prevent many unhappy marriages, and thus help to reduce the ever-increasing number of appeals to the Court for Divorce and Matrimonial Causes. Claudius Ptolemy laid down some very clear and concise rules on this subject. He advised persons about to marry to have a care that the Sun and Moon in their respective nativities are in concord. It would be well if persons contemplating matrimony would see to it that the places of the Sun and Moon in the one nativity are in sextile or trine aspect to the places of these luminaries in the other. Ptolemy advised that "mutual reception" should also be sought, but this is of no material consequence. Astrologers generally consider that it is of the happiest augury when the Moon in the bridegroom's nativity happens to be in sextile or trine to the Sun in the bride's nativity. On the other hand, the square or opposition aspect between the places of the luminaries in the two nativities, is too often associated with matrimonial strife; and the worst effects will follow, if at the same time the malefic planets afflict the luminaries in both nativities. Ptolemy says that if Venus be with the malefics, the separation will be on account of adultery, etc. Benefic planets partaking in the concord established between the places of the luminaries in both nativities, render the married pair happy and fortunate,[1] and if Mercury also partake in the happy configurations, their mutual affection will become notorious. If Venus in the one nativity be on the place of Mars in the other, the cohabitation (whether legal or illegal) will be lasting, and marked by entire love and concord.

For WOMEN, the SUN is to be chiefly regarded in estimating their chances of marriage and happiness. If the Sun be oriental (*i.e.*, be-

[1] While Napoleon the Great had Josephine by his side, he was fortunate, but when he put her away, his good fortune left him.

tween the ascendant and mid-heaven, or between descendant and lower meridian) a woman will marry in her youth; or, when elderly, with a young man. If the Sun be between the descendant and lower meridian she will marry late in life; or, when young, to an old man. If the Sun be in a double-bodied sign, or configurated with several oriental planets (in one sign) she will marry more than once. If Saturn configurated with the Sun, the husband will be "stedfast, advantageous, and industrious," says Ptolemy. My experience has shown that when Saturn is in square or opposition with the Sun, the husband may prove unsteady and improvident. Jupiter configurated with the Sun gives a good, benevolent, and honourable husband. Mars, says Ptolemy, gives a severe husband, "void of affection and intractable." Venus gives an amiable husband of handsome appearance, but he may be fond of pleasure. Mercury gives one who is provident and expert in his profession or business.

The configurations formed by Venus must not be disregarded for, says Ptolemy, "If Venus be found connected with Saturn, she will indicate dull and timid husbands; if with Jupiter, the husbands will be good, just, and modest; if with Mars, hasty and unfaithful; and if with Mercury, they will be very fond of children."

For MEN, the MOON must be chiefly considered, in regard to marriage. The Moon in her first or third quarter, at birth, the native will either marry when young (under thirty); or, after having passed his prime, a young woman. "If the Moon be found under the Sun's beams and configurated with Saturn, she then entirely denies marriage," says Ptolemy. If the Moon be in a sign of single form, or configurated with only one planet, the native will marry but once; on the other hand, if she be in a bicorporal sign (Gemini, first half of Sagittarius, or Pisces), or in aspect with several planets (in one and the same sign), the man will marry several times.

If the Moon make application to the benefics, the wives be good and true; but if she make application to evil planets, the wives may prove either unreliable or of a quarrelsome disposition. For example: If Saturn receive the Moon's application the wife will prove troublesome and morose, yet constant and industrious; if Jupiter receive it, the wife will be decorous, good, and economical; if Mars, autocratic and refractory; if Venus, cheerful, handsome, and agreeable; if Mercury, sensible, prudent, and clever; if Uranus or Neptune, independent, and difficult to understand.

Should Venus be connected with Jupiter, Saturn, or Mercury, she will render wives provident, and attached to their husbands and children; but, if she be found connected with Mars, they will be irascible, indiscreet, if not unsteady and inconstant.

Women, in whose nativities Venus is configurated with Jupiter or Mercury, are virtuous and well-conducted; but when Venus is with Mars only, they are liable to be led away, unless Mercury or the Moon is connected with Jupiter.

Saturn, Uranus, and Neptune[2] when in the seventh house of a nativity, bring either unhappiness in married life, or separation from or early death of the partner. The unhappiness may arise from poverty, and not from incompatibility of temper. The Sun afflicted by Saturn or Uranus in the nativity of a woman, and the Moon afflicted by either of these planets in the nativity of a man, usually brings some trouble and disappointment in love or matrimony.

Description of the Wife or Husband.—If a planet happens to be located near the cusp of the seventh house, it may be taken (with the sign in which it is posited) to describe the partner in marriage, approximately. If no planet happens to be so situated, then that which receives the application of the Moon must be taken in a man's nativity; and that which receives the application of the Sun in a woman's nativity. In some cases the planet to which the Sun applies indicates the nature of the profession or trade followed by the husband. Fortunate planets in the seventh house, denote a happy marriage; evil planets therein, show either trouble or separation. Fortunate planets in the eighth house show that the wife or husband, as the case may be, will be rich; unfortunate planets therein show loss or diminution of the estate.

The Probable Period of Marriage.—This is to be judged by the "directions." The planet to which the Moon applies is often the promittor. Venus does not always produce marriage, but she generally indicates a love engagement when the Sun, Moon, M.C., or Asc. is directed to her. Jupiter often brings marriage in the case of women, and so do the Sun and Mars by direction. In the nativity of H.R.H. the Duchess of Argyll, the Sun directed by converse motion to the place of Venus (☉ ☌ ♀ m., con. 22° 45′ = Dec., 1870), and to the parallel of Venus in the zodiac (☉ par. ♀ zod. 23° = March, 1871), operated to produce marriage, the latter arc measured exactly to the period of the happy event.

"Love at first sight " is produced by the harmonius configuration

[2] Unless well configurated with either Jupiter or Venus.

of the luminaries and the concurrence of the benefics, or of Venus and Mars, in the two nativities. The beauty and fascination of the eyes, to which love at first sight is so frequently due, are produced by the position of Venus in the ascendant or in configuration with the ascending degree. Shakespeare has pourtrayed the beauty of Juliet's eyes, and the effect produced on her enraptured lover Romeo. Samuel Lover in *Handy Andy*, says:

> "And as sages wise, of old,
> From the stars could fate unfold,
> Thy bright eyes *my* fortune told,
> Lady, lady, mine."

Venus ascending, or culminating, or in juxtaposition with either Sun or Moon, in the nativities of men, will render them great favourites with the fair sex. Goethe was born when Venus was culminating, in parallel declination with the Moon, and in semi-sextile aspect with Mercury; hence he was a great favourite with the hyleg, and so addicted to love-making that he averred that the happiest moment of a man's life was when an old love was terminating and a new love commencing!

Jupiter materially assists to bring marriage to women, particularly when approaching the meridian or in the seventh house, or receiving the application of the Sun or Moon. In such cases (unless Jupiter happens to be greatly afflicted, or the Sun afflicted by Saturn), the marriage usually proves happy and fortunate. The position of the Moon in the 10th house, and in trine aspect with Jupiter in the seventh is equally fortunate. For example:—A lady, born May 14th, 1815, at 5h p.m., lat. 53½° N., was married under the *primary direction* of M.C. △ ♃ zod. The Moon was in the 10th house of her nativity, in Leo 25° 9′, and Jupiter was in the seventh house, and in Aries 25° 56′—a close trine aspect.

2.—A lady, born May 15th, 1840, at 2h 30m p.m., lat. 52½° N., was married under the direction of M.C. △ ♃ m., on October 18th, 1862, to a noble lord whose social position was far superior to that in which she was born. At her birth the Moon was in conjunction with Jupiter in the 2nd house.

3.—Another lady who was born when *Virgo* 24° 55′ occupied the ascendant, Neptune being close to the cusp of the seventh, the house of marriage, in *Pisces* 24° 15′ was compelled to divorce her first husband, and married a second time, but none too happily.

4.—A lady who was born under *Leo* 18° 19′, had Neptune in the seventh house in Aquarius 24° 14′ near the Moon in 24° 37′ of the same sign, and near Venus in 27° 50′ also in the sign, was married to a handsome and kind gentleman, who unfortunately succumbed to fever less than eight years after the wedding day.

5.—A lady who was born when Venus in *Libra* 10° 32′ was close to the upper meridian, and applying to conjunction with Jupiter in 16° 22′ of the same sign in the tenth house, the latter benefic being in quartile with the Moon in *Capricornus* 16° 33′, which luminary was applying to the trine aspect with Mercury, ruler of the seventh house, married at twenty-six and a half years of age a wealthy gentleman, under the primary arc of direction of Sun conjunction Venus 26° 33′, preceded by Sun sextile Jupiter 26° 8′. She was widowed at 42 years of age under the primary direction of Sun parallel Saturn mundo 41° 56′. This lady was married a few years later to a nobleman, under Moon opposition Venus and Jupiter by primary direction. In her nativity the Sun was in a sign of single form, in conjunction with Regulus, and applying to Mars by sextile aspect.

6.—A lady who was born under *Leo* 15° 24’ had Neptune close to the cusp of the seventh house of her nativity in *Aquarius* 13° 15′, in proximate sextile with Saturn in *Sagittarius* 15° 10′, in the fifth house, and in proximate quartile with Jupiter in 11° 12′ of *Scorpio*, in the fourth house; the Moon in Pisces 14° 40′, separating from trine with Jupiter and applying to conjunction with Uranus; made an early and romantic marriage under the primary direction of Ascendant conjunction Venus. She was left a widow under the direction of Midheaven quartile Uranus in the zodiac, attended by Midheaven opposition Venus; and married a second time under Midheaven sextile Sun in the zodiac.

It must be borne in mind by the student that marrying is a voluntary act, and not so unavoidable as are accidents and serious illnesses; and, therefore, the time of marriage is difficult to forecast, especially when several primary directions favouring courtship and marriage fall near together, that is to say, within the space of four or five years.

CHAPTER XXVI.

CHILDREN.

"O Child! O new born denizen
Of life's great city! on thy head
The glory of the morn is shed,
Like a celestial benison!
By what astrology of fear or hope
Dare I to cast thy horoscope?"—LONGFELLOW.

IN estimating the probability of offspring, the 10th and 11th houses of the nativity are to be first examined; and if there be no planets located therein, then the opposite houses (the 4th and 5th) are to be considered.

The Moon, Jupiter, and Venus are held to be givers of children; the Sun, Mars, Saturn, and Uranus are said to deny children, or allot but one or two, one being liable to early death or to become a source of trouble and anxiety to the parents. Mercury either gives or denies children, according to the planets with which he may happen to be configurated. If the planets promising offspring happen to be located in bicorporal (Gemini, first half of Sagittarius or Pisces) or in Cancer, Virgo, or Scorpio, they are said to give twins, which is incompatible with the very doubtful doctrine that Gemini and Virgo are "barren" signs.

If no planets be located in either of the houses before-mentioned, those that may happen to be in benefic aspect to the degrees on the cusps of those houses, must be considered.

If the planets giving offspring be strongly situated the children born will attain to good positions in the world.

It is of the greatest importance that parents should understand the bent of their children's minds. This can only be known, in many instances, from the children's nativities. Lord Beaconsfield once observed:

"We are apt to believe that the character of a boy is easily read." Tis a mystery the most profound. Mark what blunders parents continually make as to the nature of their own offspring, bred too under their eyes, and displaying every hour their characteristics. How often in the nursery does the genius count as a dunce, because he is pensive; while a rattling urchin is invested with almost supernatural qualities, because his animal spirits make him impudent and flippant."[1]

"What has Horatio done," said the bluff sailor uncle of Lord Nelson, "that he, of all others, should be sent to rough it out at sea? But let him come, and the first time, go into action, a cannon-ball will knock off his head, and provide for him at once." Here we have a notable instance of wrong judgment. The sailor uncle was unaware of the fact that the great Nelson was born with Mars rising in Scorpio, and that his stars indicated a brilliant and victorious career.

It is hardly possible to deny the usefulness of astrology in regard to directing as well as understanding the natural bent of children's minds; and in saving several years of unavailing efforts to excel in a pursuit for which the youth is totally unfitted by nature. Let us bear in mind the following words of Ruskin:

"Every human action gains in honour, in grace, in all true magnificence, by its regard to things that are to come. It is the far sight, the quiet and confident patience, that, above all other attributes, separate man from man, and near him to his Maker, and there is no action or art whose mystery we may not measure by this test."[2]

Ruskin was born at 7h 30m a.m. of the 8th of February, 1819, in London. R.A. of M.C. = 249° 56′, *Sagittarius* 11°28′ on the upper meridian, and *Aquarius* 16° 28′ ascending. Jupiter had just risen in *Aquarius* 0° 20′, the Sun was in the ascendant in 18° 46′ of the same sign, and Saturn was also in the ascendant in *Pisces* 17° 15′. His horoscope was given in STAR LORE, December 1900. His biographer says that Ruskin had "a mood of playing with the occult, believing like so many that 'there is something in it,' and he declared that Saturn presided at his birth: another way of saying that an unfortunate influence seemed to have predominated over his life. Weak health, especially, has to be set off against a fair share of wealth: a certain ill-luck in little things and personal aims against the supreme gift of genius. The violent reaction of a too sensitive nervous system discounted his keen capacity for enjoyment; and renown, public notice, were much more

[1] *Coningsby*, Vol. I.

[2] *Seven Lamps of Architecture*, page 171.

[3] "Life and Work of John Ruskin," By the Rev. W. Gershom Collingwood.

trouble to him than it was ever worth."[3]

Aye, the nativity of Ruskin, whose fame will never die, affords good proof of the reality of the influence of the celestial bodies. As he wisely observed "there is something in it," nay, more there is a great deal in it—for it affects the greatest and meanest of mankind; at one time—"when the planets to disorder wander"—it shakes the earth with terrible effects; at another it brings glorious benefits. The following saying of John Ruskin is worthy of careful consideration by sceptics:

"Astronomy—by her ancient name Astrology, as we say Theology, not Theonomy: the knowledge of so much of the stars as we can know wisely; not the attempt to define their laws for them—not that it is unbecoming of us to find out, if we can, that they move in ellipses, and so on; but it is no business of ours. What effects their rising and setting have on man, and beast, and leaf; what their times and changes are, seen, and felt in this world, it is our business to know, passing our nights, if wakefully, by that divine candlelight, and no other."[4]

The rules found in several modern books on astrology with regard to judging as to the number of children likely to be borne to the husband, or by the wife; and the rules advanced as affording a reliable forecast as to the chances of life of the children, whether they will die in infancy or attain maturity; and the rules as to "fruitful" and "barren" signs (of the zodiac), are fanciful, and should be treated as unreliable by the student. Such rules could only be advanced by those practitioners who mix up *horary* with genethliacal astrology, a practice which has brought great confusion into the study and pursuit of the ancient science. One such rule is that: "If an evil planet or planets be in the fifth house of a nativity, the native will have very few children, or if many, most of them will die early in life. It generally indicates a world of trouble caused by children. If the ruler of the fifth house is in the sixth, eighth, twelfth, or second house, especially if an evil planet, it causes unhappiness with children, or else most of them will die."[5]

I have examined many hundreds of horoscopes and cannot find any real evidence of the truth of this rule. One lady, who had Mars in the fifth house, has reared six children to maturity and lost none, and is on the happiest terms with all of them.

---

[4] "Mornings in Florence," the straight gate, fifth morning.

[5] "Elements of Astrology," by L. D. Broughton, New York.

CHAPTER XXVII.

FRIENDS AND ENEMIES.

"Tell me, by what hidden magic
Our impressions first are led
Into liking or disliking,
Oft before a word is said."

FRIENDSHIP and enmity depend wholly on the concord or discord of the Sun, Moon, and planets in the nativities of two acquaintances. The benefics in the one nativity in the place of the Sun or Moon in the other, favour mutual friendship and esteem; and the person whose Sun or Moon is happily configurated with the benefic of the other, will benefit the more. On the other hand, the malefics in the one nativity in the place of the Sun or Moon in the other, some drawback is likely to result. Persons born under the same sign of the zodiac, or when the Moon occupied the same degree of longitude, often become very friendly, when they meet. Mars afflicting the luminaries causes misunderstandings. Saturn similarly placed is apt to give rise to some mistrust or dislike. Venus and Mercury, says Ptolemy, "produce communion by means of the arts and sciences, and by a mutual interest in literature," to which may be added, a mutual interest in sports and amusements.

The eleventh house of a nativity is believed to be symbolical of friends, the seventh of open enemies, and the twelfth of secret foes. This notion, so far as it relates to nativities, is very doubtful. The fact is that persons born when the Sun or Moon is afflicted usually meet with many enemies, and some mischief from them; whereas, those who are so fortunate as to be born when the Sun and Moon are happily configurated with the benefics, find troops of friends, and few enemies. In like manner, persons born when an ascending planet or planets meet with cross aspects are involved in misunderstandings, disputes, and quarrels which may be none of their seeking. The nativity of the Prince Consort is an instance of this, for the ascending planet Mercury is nearly in quartile with Mars and Uranus, and in opposition with Saturn. This accounts for the attacks of jealous and envious people, and of the Press, to which he was subjected at certain periods. The poet Keats was born when cross aspects prevailed; his fate was a melancholy one, for, being of a too sensitive nature, he could not survive the merciless criticism of which he was made the victim.

Fortunate planets ascending or culminating bring numerous friends. The signs containing the fortunes, or the angles in which they are located, will show in what part of the world the native will meet with the greatest number of friends who will advance his interests. The signs or angles containing the infortunes will show the parts of the world wherein the native would be likely to meet with the most inveterate opposition from public and private enemies.

Dr, Nobiling who wounded the Emperor of Germany, by shooting him in the neck, on the 2nd of June, 1878, was born on the 10th of April, 1848. At his birth Mars was in the place of Saturn at the Emperor's birth; and the Moon was in opposition to her place at the Emperor's birth. On the 2nd of June, 1878, Mars was passing over the Moon's place at Nobiling's birth.

Claudius Ptolemy said that "Saturn in one nativity in the place of Mercury in the other denotes friendship by science, art, business profits, or secret mysteries." This I have proved to be quite true.

"Nescio quid, certe est quod me tibis temperet astrum."

"What was the star I know not, but certainly some star it was that attuned me unto thee."

CHAPTER XXVIII.

TRAVELLING.

"The Heavens give safety to your purposes!
Lead forth, and bring you back in happiness."—SHAKESPEARE.

THE relative position of the Moon is chiefly to be considered in regard to travelling. When she is "cadent" in the ninth or third house more especially the person then born travels much. The ninth house is considered as indicating long journies; and the third house short journies (such as are completed in a day). The Moon in a sign of the watery triplicity usually brings travelling by water; and when so located in the ninth or twelfth house, a sea voyage, early in life. When, however, the Moon is cadent at birth, and in a fixed sign (with the, exception of *Scorpio*), the native does not usually travel much.

Claudius Ptolemy considered that Mars when occidental and declining from the meridian, and in quartile or opposition with the Sun or Moon causes travelling in foreign countries. This is doubtful, and the author's own nativity contradicts it, wherein Mars is in the ninth house in proximate mundane quartile with the Moon and exact sextile with the Sun.

If the benefics be configurated with the Moon, travelling is usually prosperous, profitable, and safe. If the malefics be evilly configurated with the Moon, they threaten troubles, losses, misfortunes, and bad weather in travelling.

The Moon located, at birth, in the sign Gemini, and oriental, gives a great propensity to travel. Both Mercury and the Moon cadent and in Aries, Cancer, or Capricornus, have the same effect; but when both are in fixed signs and angles there is little disposition to travel.

When either the Moon, Mars, or Mercury, is found, at birth, in the ninth or third house, a journey or sea voyage is made when the Moon or planet comes by primary direction (in mundo) to the cusp of that house.

Mercury ascending in Aries, Gemini, Cancer, Virgo, Libra, Sagittarius, Capricornus or Pisces, gives a disposition to travel, or trade, in foreign countries.

The parts of the world most fortunate for travelling in, may be judged either from the signs containing the Moon, Mercury, Jupiter, and Venus. The signs containing Saturn and Mars show the countries unfavourable to any continued stay in.

In travelling for health, consider first the position of Jupiter, unless he is much afflicted; and, next, that of Venus.

It is averred that if the planet afflicting the Moon be in Cancer, Scorpio, or Pisces, danger of shipwreck will result: and, if other testimonies concur, death by drowning. The afflicting planet being located in the twelfth house, is said to signify danger of being kidnapped or imprisoned.

Mr. J. W., born 6h a.m., May 3rd, 1824, in lat. 54° 51′ N., and long. 1° 28′ W., was severely shaken by the terrible collision at Abbot's Ripton, January 21st, 1876. At that period the following arcs were operating in his nativity; ☉ Par. ☿ zod. 51° 46′; ☽ □ ☉ zod.. 52° 8′; and ☉ par. ♅ zod. 52° 11′.

A relation of the author's at whose nativity the Moon was in the third house in *Scorpio* 9° 22′, separating from quartile with Saturn in Aquarius 8° 21′, always met with bad weather at sea, and more than once was nearly being shipwrecked.

CHAPTER XXIX.

THE KIND OF DEATH.

"There is no Death—what seems to us transition,
This life of mortal breath
Is but a suburb of the Life Elysian
Whose portal we call—Death."—LONGFELLOW.

THE TERMINUS VITAE is sometimes clearly foreshadowed by the nativity. In forecasting danger, the Christian astrologer does not forget that the issues of life and death are in the hands of our CREATOR—without Whose knowledge not even a sparrow falls to the ground. It is not then, in any atheistic or fatalistic spirit that the astrologer gives warning of times of danger to life. King David prayed: "Lord, let me know mine end, and the number of my days: that I may be certified how long I have to live." The foreknowledge that in certain cases life was destined, astrologically speaking, to be short, may undoubtedly save much human misery. Too often does a sudden and unexpected death leave the widow and the fatherless in abject poverty; whereas, could the danger of it have been foreseen, adequate provision might have been made for them. The invention of the medical art, as explained in a previous chapter, was due to the desire for a means of overcoming the apparently fatal influences of the evil planets. How often in everyday life do we hear of medical men lamenting that the initial stage of a chronic and fatal malady had not been foreseen or detected early enough to admit of preventive treatment. Life might in many instances be prolonged if the insidious attack could be foreseen; change of residence, of occupation, and of climate could be advised, where necessary, and other preventive measures taken.

Hufeland said that:

"A grand point in guarding against disease is that everyone should try to discover to what malady he is constitutionally most disposed, in order that this tendency may be destroyed, or at least that all opportunity of its being converted into disease may be removed. In this respect the ancients were more prudent than we are. They employed the medical art and physicians chiefly for determining their dietetic mode of life; and even their astrological, chiromantic, and other researches of like kind tended, at bottom, to define the moral and physical character of man, and to prescribe for him, accordingly, a proper mode of living and a regimen. They undoubtedly did much better in thus employing their physicians than if they had run to them every week to make them prescribe for them purgatives or emetics. But for this purpose a judicious, prudent, and acute physician is necessary; while, on the other hand, any empiric is capable of writing a prescription. These people, at any rate, had a surer means of distinguishing a false from a true prophet."[1]

Claudius Ptolemy says that had the ancients been of opinion that all expected events are unalterable and not to be averted, they would never have instituted any propitiations, remedies, and preservatives against the influences of the ambient, whether present or approaching, general or particular.

Goethe was seized with smallpox very early in life—the planet Mars being in semi-quartile aspect (in mundo) to the ascendant at his birth. But inasmuch as the hyleg was not afflicted, he did not die of that attack, and his health was not prejudiced by it in after life. Astrologers find that unless Mars afflict either the ascendant or luminaries, at birth (or in the fatal train of directions) there is little, if any, liability to take smallpox. The doctors are wrong in assuming that every child born will, if it live, certainly contract smallpox sooner or later if it be not vaccinated in infancy; and Parliament is not justified in passing penal laws, and retaining them on the Statute book, to enforce vaccination[2] to support a medical dogma based on a delusion, and on incomplete statistics manipulated by fanatical believers in the practice of the rite.

---

[1] Hufeland's *Art of Prolonging Life*, edited by Erasmus Wilson, F.R.S.; translation of 1794, pages 250, 251.

[2] But for the terror caused by exaggerated statements as to the fatality and sequelae of smallpox, and but for the fear of pitting, people would never submit to the insertion of lymph, taken from a diseased calf, into their system. The asserted modifying power of vaccination is, to say the least, open to grave doubt. In smallpox as in measles and scarlatina there are several varieties and while one person takes the disease in a mild form, another takes it in a malignant form. Jenner, in 1798 (in his *Inquiry into the Cause and Effects of the Variolae Vaccine*, pages 54, 55) recorded that, "About seven years ago a species of smallpox spread through many of the towns and villages of this part of Gloucestershire; it was one of so mild a nature that a fatal instance was scarcely ever heard of. This was before vaccination was practised.

The inexorable logic of facts is against the practice of vaccination.

The kind of death depends chiefly on the nature of the planets whose "directions" operate to cause death (astrologically speaking). The signs in which such planets were located at birth may be considered in forecasting the nature of the fatal illness, and the part of the body attacked.

URANUS threatens nervous breakdown, and a sudden death, of a peculiar nature.

SATURN indicates death by falls, crushing, or suffocation, when close to the ascendant or in the mid-heaven; and by chronic diseases arising from rheumatic fever, and its effects upon the heart, low or continued fever, ague, paralysis, epilepsy, or melancholia, when occidental. In a fixed sign and afflicting the hyleg cancerous disease.

JUPITER (when much afflicted in a nativity) may become a promittor in death, in such cases he signifies quinsy, apoplexy, pleurisy, inflammation of the lungs, liver-disease, spasms, and failure of the heart.

MARS indicates death by acute or eruptive fever, bronchitis, pneumonia, haemoptysis, and all kinds of haemorrhage; and (in women) abortion, and surgical extraction of the foetus. When oriental, Mars signifies burns, scalds, incised and gunshot wounds.

VENUS (when much afflicted at birth and concerned in the train of fatal directions) signifies death by poison, diseases of the stomach or liver, and excess in eating or drinking.

MERCURY indicates death (when oriental) by accidents of the nature of the planet with which he is in aspect (at birth); when occidental, by brain-disease, nervous disorders, whooping cough, etc., according to his configurations with the malefics. If with or afflicted by Mars and Saturn, by assaults of robbers.

The MOON signifies death by surfeits, obstructions, etc., according to her familiarity with the malefics. When in a watery sign and evilly configurated with Saturn, death may take place by drowning.

The SUN, when affiicted at birth and in quartile or opposition to the Moon or ascendant, whichever may be hyleg, causes death by apoplexy, paralysis, or fever.

Death occurs by violence when Mars and Saturn and evil fixed stars afflict the hyleg, and are in mutual quartile or opposition. Saturn, in such case, particularly when in *Taurus*, indicates death by hanging, or suffocation. Saturn in opposition to either the Sun or Moon rising, is said to threaten death in prison. Venus and Mercury conjoined with Saturn, the last-named afflicting the hyleg, death is threatened from poison, or through the treachery of a woman. Saturn in Virgo, and afflicting the Moon (hyleg), death will be caused by drowning or suffocation. If found near Argo, by shipwreck. If Saturn be in a tropical or quadrupedral sign, and the Sun be in conjunction or opposition, or Mars be so, death will be caused by the fall of buildings; and if Saturn be in the mid-heaven and so configurated with the Sun or Mars, death will result through falls from heights or precipices, especially if he be in an airy sign.

Saturn and Mars in Gemini, Virgo, Aquarius, or Sagittarius, and in square or opposition with the Sun or Moon threaten death by violence, in battle, or by suicide. If Mercury also be evilly configurated with Mars, death will be caused by highwaymen or burglars. Mars near *Caput Medusa* is said to threaten death by decapitation or mutilation. If Mars be in *Taurus* or *Scorpio* afflicting the hyleg, death may result from surgical amputation, burning, or scalding, or by the small-pox. If Mars be in opposition to the ascendant, and in Aries, Leo, or Sagittarius, it threatens death by fire or gunshot wounds, especially if near the *Asselli*; if in Aries, Taurus, Leo, Sagittarius, or Capricornus, and so situated, by falls or fractures. If Jupiter bear testimony, and be also afflicted "death may ensue from the wrath of princes and kings, and from judicial condemnation," wrote Claudius Ptolemy.

In the nativity of John Baptist Cardan (son of the great Cardan), who was beheaded on the scaffold by an executioner of justice for destroying his wife by poison. Jupiter was afflicted and aspected by Mars, and the Moon was afflicted by the parallels of the Sun and the infortunes,[3] and the Sun and Moon were with violent fixed stars. "Death will occur in foreign places," wrote Ptolemy, "when the planets controlling the anaretic places,[4] may be in cadent houses, and especially if the Moon be in one of the said places."

At the period of death a train of evil directions is usually found to be in operation, one evil direction, however powerful, rarely destroys life. When the Moon is hyleg, and is directed to the conjunction of an

[3] See *Opus Reformatum*, by Dr. Partridge, Physician to Queen Mary II., London, 1693.

[4] The 8th and 4th houses. If no planet be located in the 8th house, if there be one in the 4th, the latter often partakes in the signification of the kind of death. The presence of ♃ in the 8th does *not* promise a painless and natural death, if the hyleg is afflicted by Saturn or Mars.

evil planet, if her latitude, when she completes the aspect, differs greatly from that of the planet at birth, life will generally be saved, although a dangerous illness may result. If there be a direction of Jupiter or Venus to conjunction or trine, or parallel declination with the hyleg in the train of otherwise evil directions, or within two degrees thereof, life will be saved, provided that Jupiter or Venus be not badly afflicted at birth. Even a sextile of one of them has sometimes saved life.

The following cases are interesting and instructive:

Case 1—"H.L.," a lieutenant in a native infantry regiment of Bengal, was killed in a sortie from Lucknow, July 16th, 1857. He was born precisely at noon of November 5th, 1826, at Gloucester. At his birth the 11th degree of Capricornus was rising, Mars, Uranus, and the Moon being conjoined in that sign. The Sun was on the meridian and in mundane square with Saturn. Saturn, Mars, and Uranus were in parallel declination with the ascending degree. Any student who will take the trouble to cast this figure will find that the following directions correspond exactly to the period of death: ☉ par. ♄ zod. 30° 35′, ☉ par. ♅ zod 30° 42′. The sign Capricornus rules India, and the death took place in that country. [N.B.—The nativity requires no "rectification," and the time of birth is given just as the author received it from the sister of the unfortunate officer. The R.A. of the M.C. was 224° 10′.]

2.—"G.W.," born 0h 54m a.m., of June l0th, 1853, at Sunderland. Died of confluent smallpox (he was vaccinated in infancy), August 1st, 1871, at the sixteenth day. Uranus, Mars, and Saturn, nearly conjoined in Taurus. The 6th degree of Aries on the ascendant hyleg. At the time of death the following train of directions operated; Asc. par. ♂ zod. 17°58′, Asc. ☌ ♂ zod. 18° 32′, and Asc ☌ ♂ m. 19° 19′. The arc of Asc. ☌ ♄ zod. 21° 17′ was near at hand. [N.B.—The time of birth is given as found in the family Bible. Mars is the killing planet, and the fatal illness was martial.]

3.—"C.D.," born October 18th, 1838, at 6h a.m., Sunderland. At the birth, Mars was in the l0th house, in opposition to the Moon, and in par. dec. with both the Sun and Moon. The Sun was hyleg. This gentleman broke a blood-vessel in January, 1866, under Asc. □ ♂ m. 27° 15′. He died in the spring of 1869, of constipation, under the following train of evil directions: ☉ □ ♂ zod. 30° 10′, Asc. □ ☽ m. 30° 24′, and ☉ ☌ at par ♄ m., d.d. 31° 8′.

4.—Czar Alexander II. was born at l0h a.m., of the 29th of April,

1818, at Moscow, *Leo* 4° 42′ ascending. The Sun (hyleg) was in the tenth house in *Taurus* 8° 21′, in mundane semi-quartile aspect with both Mars and Saturn (the latter planet being ruler of the eighth, the house of death), and the mundane parallel of Saturn. The Moon was afflicted by the sesquiquadrate of Mars, the mundane parallel of Uranus, and was in opposition to the martial star Regulus. The *Asselli* were very near the ascending degree, which had the sesquiquadrate aspect of Uranus. The primary direction of Sun rapt parallel Mars 63° 12′ = July, 1881. As Zadkiel I. and the author have observed and maintained (for years previous to 1881) all directional parallels operate, as a rule, several weeks before they are exactly due. Moreover, if the Sun's semi-diameter 0° 16′ be subtracted from the arc of 63° 12′, we have 62° 56′ = March, 1881, as the arc of first contact of the Sun's limb with the parallel of Mars (the direction being computed to the Sun's centre) and the Czar was cruelly assassinated on the 13th of March, 1881, by the explosion of a bomb thrown at his feet by the assassin. Moreover, the dangerous direction of Sun parallel Saturn, in the zodiac, conversely, 63° 23′ closely followed the before-mentioned rapt parallel. It was the train of five evil directions (62° 20′ to 63° 52′) which led the author to foretell that: "The Czar of Russia will be in some personal danger about the 6th of March, 1881," and to say that "He will do well to prepare for the dread summons."[5] This warning was written in July, 1880, and published five months before the tragic death of "Alexander the Liberator" took place.

5.—King Humbert, of Italy, was born at 10h 30m a.m. of the 14th of March, 1844, at Turin, according to the official bulletin. R.A. of M.C. 329° 37′. His horoscope was given in STAR LORE, May, 1897. The Sun in Pisces 23° 57′, was in semi-quartile with Mars in Taurus 7° 5′, and was separating from conjunction with Jupiter in Pisces 13° 35′ and applying to Uranus in Aries 1° 46′. The Moon was in mundane quartile with Mars and applying to conjunction with Saturn. Regulus was close to the lower meridian. An attempt was made to assassinate King Humbert in April, 1897, when Sun parallel Saturn, zodiac, first contact, was operating in his nativity, by primary direction. In the evening of the 29th July, 1900, an anarchist shot the king, who died of his wounds ere he could be conveyed to the Palace. The author wrote, twelve months, beforehand, that in August, 1900, the king

[5] Vide *Zadkiel's Almanac* for 1881, pages 9 and 12, and 1882, pp. 53-63. *Punch* was candid and kind enough to acknowledge that the above forecast was a case of "hitting the bull's eye."

would be "plagued by insidious foes and should beware of anarchists." The arc for death, 1° = 1 year) is 56° 22′, and the primary directions then operating were: Sun parallel Uranus, m., con. 56° 14′, Mercury conjunction Mars, m. 56° 16′, Mercury conjunction Mars, zodiac, 56° 25′, and Ascendant par. ☉ zod, con. 56° 29′. The nativity shows Mars close to (above) the cusp of the twelfth, the house of secret enemies. Mercury, ruler of the ascending sign, was ruler of the nativity, being in the tenth house, elevated above the rest of the celestial bodies.

6.—Dr. D., born at 9 o'clock in the evening of the 26th of November, 1860, at Warsaw. R.A. of M.C. = 20° 57′, *Aries* 22° 39′ culminating, and *Leo* 10° 53′ ascending. The Sun in the fifth house in *Sagittarius* 4° 50′, in quartile with Mars in the eighth, in 3° 41′ of *Pisces*, in par. declin. with Moon in the tenth house, in *Taurus* 15° 37′; and applying to quartile with Saturn in *Virgo* 9° 3′, and to opposition with Uranus in *Gemini* 10° 17′. This learned and successful (in cure-work) physician lost his valuable life during the revolutionary outbreak in Russian Poland in the year 1907, by assassination! He was a diligent student of *astrologia sana*, and wrote in a medical periodical very highly of (the first edition of) the "The Text Book of Astrology."

The sceptic may remind us that the great majority of diseases, premature death, and deformity, are due to the violation of natural laws. A pure atmosphere, a plain and nourishing diet, plenty of out-door exercise, early hours, personal cleanliness, abstinence from excessive indulgence in stimulants, and a cheerful temperament are, undoubtedly, the best means of preserving health and of preventing disease.[6] Nevertheless, it is a fact that the diseases to which an individual is liable, or those which he inherits, are as a rule plainly indicated in the face of the heavens at the moment of his birth. It is the Martialist who rushes into danger, or excesses, who brings diseases or wounds upon himself. It is the Saturnine man who mopes and frets, and thereby renders himself liable to liver-disease, to melancholia, and suicidal mania. It is the Mercurial man who exhausts his nervous energies by that restless activity so characteristic of modern life. It is the Saturnine man who is so liable to catarrhs that despite his daily use of the cold bath and the exercise of the most unceasing vigilance, he "catches cold" from the slightest "draught of air," or the slightest wetting, and is the ready prey of the germs of phthisis. It is the Martialist who be-

[6] It is the pro-vaccinators who advance the absurd and monstrous doctrine that a healthy child, if unvaccinated, is a danger to society.

comes a victim to acute fevers. It is true that people who are blessed with the greatest amount of vitality—due largely to their having been born when Jupiter or Venus, or both were rising, or supporting the Sun and Moon—the greatest power of resistance, and who observe the conditions of health before-named, are almost proof against the attack of any kind of disease, and pass unharmed through the city decimated by yellow fever, plague, cholera, diphtheria, etc., as the case may be. But then it is also true that the face of the heavens as constituted at the birth of such persons, harmonises with the possession of so enviable a store of vitality and stamina. There are others who are born to a different fate, for they take whatever disease happens to be epidemic. It is a fact well-known to astrologers that persons born under the sign *Sagittary* have (unless the hyleg happens to be afflicted), a great love of out-door exercise and sports, and enjoy good health, strength, and vitality.

In the year 1588 the Duke of Guise, a few days before he and his brother were murdered, had a presentiment of personal danger; afterwards, a more direct caution warned him of the existence of a plot against his life. It was, however, the general opinion that no such attempt would be made. On the 22nd December, as the Duke sat down to dinner, he saw a note in his napkin. Opening it he read, "Take care; an evil turn is about to be played on you." He wrote underneath it, "They dare not," and flung the paper under the table. On the same day the Duc. d'Elboeuf told him there would be an attempt on his life the next morning, upon which Guise said, smiling, "I see, cousin, you have been looking at your *Almanac*. All the Almanacs this year are stuffed full of such threats."

CHAPTER XXX.

ON PRIMARY DIRECTIONS.

PRIMARY DIRECTIONS are arithmetical computations of the apparent motion of any point in the heavens or of any heavenly body, from the situation which it occupied at the moment of birth until it meets with the conjunction, parallel of declination, or aspect of some other body or point. The value thus obtained is termed the "arc of direction," and it is converted into time by allowing every degree of arc to represent one year of life, and every five minutes over and above the number of degrees to represent one month.

All directions of the midheaven are measured by an arc of right ascension. All directions of the ascendant in mundo by the semi-arc of the body directed, and in zodiaco by oblique ascension.

All the directions of the Sun, Moon, and planets are computed by means of their semi-arcs. Those directions which are taken in the zodiac, and for the sake of classification called zodiacal, are really mundane.

Primary directions are due to the revolution of the earth on its axis, and all those to be computed for a hundred years are formed within, comparatively, a few hours of the moment of birth.

The place of a heavenly body in a nativity is considered as if it were the body itself, for the various celestial bodies are found to impress their respective natures on the places held by them at the moment of birth as fully as if they were always located therein, although, by their proper motion, they may have passed (in the heavens) away from their respective places several or many degrees when the significator (the body directed to those places) arrives—thus, if the Sun be directed to conjunction with Jupiter, we mean to the radical place of Jupiter.

The speculum, or table of the latitudes, declinations, right-ascensions, meridian distances, and semi-arcs of the Sun, Moon, Mercury Venus, Mars, Jupiter, Uranus, and Neptune must be carefully computed, as directed in the seventh chapter, before any primary directions can be calculated. In fact, the "horoscope" is not complete without the speculum, and without it no proper judgment as to its import can be safely given.

The mundane directions of the Midheaven and ascendant should be calculated first, for they give the distance of each celestial body from the cusps of the various houses, and thereby facilitate the working of the mundane directions of the Sun, Moon and planets.

Many practising astrologers of the present day ignore mundane directions—no doubt because they are either too lazy to compute them or so imperfectly educated that they cannot understand the method of computing them. Students who read only such publications on astrology as omit all instruction in the Placidian system of directing, and substitute the old Arabian method of "secondary directions," only waste their time. The errors of such instructors is all the more glaring in that they fail to see and comprehend that the "Tables of Houses"—and the very *ascendant* of the figure of the heavens which they cast by the aid of such tables—are really MUNDANE!

MUNDANE DIRECTIONS OF THE MIDHEAVEN.

RULE 1.—To find the *Conjunction* of a celestial body with the Midheaven (M.C.), take its distance therefrom—or meridian distance—as the *arc of direction*, if such body is between the ascendant and midheaven. This is termed a *direct* direction.

2.—If the celestial body is between the midheaven and the descendant, its meridian distance is the *arc of direction* of Midheaven conjunction with such body *conversely*.

3.—For the *Sextile* aspect (two houses), if the celestial body is in the twelfth house, subtract two-thirds of its semi-arc from its meridian distance to find the *arc of direction* of the sextile.

If the celestial body is in the first or second house, subtract two-thirds of its *diurnal* semi-arc from its distance from the upper meridian. This is a *direct* direction.

N.B.—The *diurnal* semi-arc of a body so placed may be found by subtracting its *nocturnal* semi-arc from 180 degrees.

If the celestial body is in the seventh house, subtract two-thirds of its semi-arc from its meridian distance. This is a *converse* direction.

4.—To find the *Semi-quartile*, subtract one half of the semi-arc of the body directed from its meridian distance. If, however, the celestial body is less than half-way between the ascendant and midheaven at birth, subtract the meridian distance from two-thirds of its semi-arc, to find the arc of direction—a *converse* one.

If the celestial body is between the upper meridian and the *descendant*, (*i.e.* in the ninth or first half of the eighth house) subtract its meridian distance from two-thirds of its semi-arc. If it is near the cusp of the eighth or in the seventh house, subtract two-thirds of its semi-arc from its meridian distance, to find the *arc* of its semi-quartile to the M.C., conversely.

5.—For the *Opposition* to the M.C. take the planet's distance from the lower meridian as the *arc of direction*, if it is between the cusp of the seventh house and the lower meridian. If the celestial body is in the third, second, or first house, its meridian distance (from the I.C.) is the *arc of direction* of its opposition to the M.C., *conversely*.

6.—For the *trine*, if the planet is in the third or second house, subtract its merid. dist. from two-thirds of its semi-arc. If in the first house, subtract two-thirds of its semi-arc from its merid. dist. to find the *arc of direction*, *conversely*.

If the celestial body is in the sixth house subtract two-thirds of its semi-arc from its merid. dist. If in the seventh or eighth house, add one-third of its nocturnal semi-arc to the arc for its opposition to the ascendant.

Mundane Directions of the Ascendant.

Rule II.—For the *Conjunction* of the Sun or Moon or planet with the Ascendant: When the celestial body is in the third, second, or first house, subtract its meridian distance *(i.e.,* from the lower meridian, or I.C.) from its semi-arc to find the *arc of direction*. If the celestial body is in the fourth, fifth or sixth house, *add* its meridian distance to its semi-arc to find the *arc of direction*, because it has to pass the lower meridian.

2.—For the opposition: When the celestial body is in the ninth, eighth or seventh house, subtract its meridian distance from its semi-arc, to find the *arc of direction*. If it is eastward of the upper meridian, *add* its meridian distance to its semi-arc.

If the celestial body is in the fourth, fifth or sixth house, subtract its meridian distance from its semi-arc to find the *arc of direction* of its *opposition* to the ascendant, conversely. If it is eastward of the lower meridian, *add* its merid. dist. to its semi-arc.

3.—For the *sextile* of the ascendant: When the planet directed is in the third house, subtract its meridian distance from one-third of its semi-arc, to find the *arc of direction*. If it is in the second or first house, subtract one-third of its semi-arc from its meridian distance to find the arc of direction, conversely.

4.—For the *trine* aspect: If the celestial body is in the sixth or fifth house, subtract one third of its semi-arc from its meridian distance, to find the arc of direction. If the heavenly body is in the seventh or eighth house, add two-thirds of its *nocturnal* semi-arc to the arc of its opposition to the ascendant, to find the arc of direction. If it is in the ninth or tenth house, add one-third of its semi-arc to its meridian distance, and the sum is the arc of direction. If it is in the ninth house, subtract its meridian distance from one-third of its semi-arc. If it is in the eighth or seventh house, subtract one-third of its semi-arc from its meridian distance, to find the arc of direction conversely.

5.—The sesqui-quadrate above the horizon, in the eighth house is the same direction as the semi-quartile already formed to the Midheaven. To find the arc of direction of the sesqui-quadrate in the fifth house, if the celestial body is in the sixth house (at birth) subtract half of its semi-arc from his meridian distance. If in the seventh or eighth house, add half of its nocturnal semi-arc to the arc of its opposition to the ascendant. If the celestial body is in the fourth house subtract its meridian distance from half of its semi-arc, and the sum is the sesqui-quadrate, conversely. If in the third house, add half of its semi-arc to its meridian distance.

RULE III.—To direct the Sun, Moon, and planets to (mundane) *parallels from the* meridian.

1° Say: As the semi-arc of the Sun, Moon, or planet, is to the semi-arc of the celestial body directed, so is its meridian distance to the second distance (of the body directed) from the meridian.

2°.—Then: Take the difference between the second distance of the body directed so found from its meridian distance (at the time of birth), and the remainder is the *arc of direction*.

N.B.—If the body directed has to pass the meridian in order to form the parallel, then its second distance must be added to its first distance, and the sum is the arc of direction.

RULE IV.—*Rapt Parallels.* These are formed by the rotation of the earth on its axis. They require careful consideration. In the first place, the planet approaching the upper or lower meridian when the parallel is completed, must be directed.

1°. Say: "As the sum of the semi-arcs of both bodies is to the semi-arc of the celestial body directed, so is the difference of their right-ascensions to the second distance of the body directed."

2°. The difference of the first and second distances of the body directed, is the *arc of direction*.

[*Note.*—When the body directed happens to be in the opposite hemisphere to that in which the other body is located, the opposite place of the latter must be worked with as if it were really there. In such case its semi-arc will, of course, be the same; but its right ascension will require either 180° added to or subtracted from it—according to whether it is greater or less than half the circle—to obtain the value of the R.A. of its opposite place in the zodiac.]

In ascertaining the difference of right-ascension between the two celestial bodies, care must be taken to compute it in the order of the signs, adding the circle when necessary. For example: Let the Sun be in the third house with 332° 10′ of R.A., and Saturn in the fourth house with 8° 17′ of R.A.; in order to find the difference of their right-ascensions 360° must be added to that of Saturn, and the resulting difference will be 36° 7′.

If the celestial body directed is below the ascendant and has to rise before it can complete the rapt parallel with the one in the seventh or eighth house, the diurnal semi-arc of the former must be taken. In like manner if a celestial body in the seventh or eighth house at birth has to set before it can be directed to the rapt parallel with one in the first or second house, the nocturnal semi-arc of the former must be taken.

[It is usually best to work with half of each quantity, and then to double the product.]

MUNDANE DIRECTIONS OF THE SUN, MOON, AND PLANETS.

Rule.—1°. Say: "As the semi-arc of the fixed body is to that of the body directed so the distance of the latter from the cusp of the house to which it is nearest, to its second distance from the cusp of the house in aspect to the former."

2°. Subtract the second distance from the primary distance, and the difference will be the *arc of direction*.

[*Note.*—The body to be directed is always that one which (by the diurnal revolution of the earth) will arrive at the aspect of the other. When the body directed has to cross the horizon to form the required aspect, its opposite semi-arc must be taken.]

In enumerating these directions of the Sun, Moon, and planets, write the symbol of the Sun or Moon first; and those directions in which the planet's semi-arc is employed in the first position, term *converse*, and append this word, or its abbreviation *con.*, to such directions. For example, the Sun directed to the mundane parallel of Saturn in the nativity of the Prince Consort (see speculum) should be described as ☉ par. ♄ m., con. But, on the other hand, when Saturn is directed to the mundane parallel of the Sun, in the same nativity it should be described as ☉ par. ♄ m., d.d.

The Sun and Moon may be directed to aspects of their own places by taking the proportional parts of their semi-arcs when these aspects are formed in one and the same hemisphere.

The Sun and Moon may be directed to their own mundane parallels by doubling their meridian distances when East of the M.C., or in the 4th house.

CHAPTER XXXI.

EXAMPLES OF RULES FOR WORKING MUNDANE DIRECTIONS.

MUNDANE DIRECTIONS TO THE ANGLES.

EXAMPLE 1.—Required the arc of M.C. ☍ ♅, in the nativity of the Prince Consort.[1]

Right-ascension of ♅	259	39
Right-ascension of lower meridian	244	28
Arc of Direction	15	11

EXAMPLE 2.—Bequired the arc of Asc. ☍ ♄, in the same nativity.

Semi-arc of ♄	86	53
Meridian distance of ♄	64	12
Arc of Direction	22	41

N.B.—This is bringing ♄ to the cusp of the 7th house.]

EXAMPLE 3.—Required the arc of M.C. △ ♄ in the same nativity.

One-third of the semi-arc (*nocturnal*)[2] of ♄	31	2
Distance of ♄ from cusp of 7th house +	22	41
Arc of Direction =	53	43

EXAMPLE 4.—Required the arc of M.C. □ ♄, in the same nativity.

One-sixth of the semi-arc (nocturnal) of ♄	15	31
Distance of ♄ from cusp of 6th house +	53	43
Arc of Direction =	69	14

EXAMPLE 5.—Required the arc of Asc. △ ♃, in the same nativity.

Meridian distance of ♃	67	59
One-third of semi-arc of ♃	38	2
Arc of Direction =	29	57

[1] See page 50.

[2] This is found by taking the semi-arc *diurnal* of ♄ from 180°.

EXAMPLE 6.—Required the arc of M.C. ☌ ♂, in the same nativity.

Right-ascension of ♂	82	46
Right-ascension of M.C.	64	28
Arc of Direction or Merid. Dist. of Mars =	18	18

EXAMPLE 7.—Required the arc of M.C. ☍ ☽ *converse*, in the same nativity.

Right-ascension of lower meridian	244	28
Right-ascension of ☽	209	38
Arc of Direction =	34	50

DIRECT DIRECTIONS TO THE SUN AND MOON.—When the planets are directed to the places of the Sun and Moon, the process is called "*direct* direction." When the Sun or Moon is directed to the planets, it is termed "*converse* direction." The latter is the more powerful.

EXAMPLE 1.—Required the arc of ☉ △ ♃ d.d., in the nativity of the Prince Consort.

In this instance ♃ will have to be brought up to a distance outside the 5th house, from its cusp, proportionate (according to their semi-arcs) to the distance of the Sun outside the 1st house (which is in trine to the 5th). The distance of the Sun outside the first can be found by taking his meridian distance from his semi-arc, thus: 103° 11′ - 89° 37′ = 13° 34′, which is Ascendt. ☌ ☉ con. Then:

	.24166
As the semi-arc of ☉ 103°12′ (prop. log.) (a.c.)	9.75834
To the semi-arc of ♃ 114° 6′	.19799
So is distance of ☉ above ascendant 13° 34′	1.12280
To second distance of ♃ 15°0′ =	1.07913

The distance of ♃ £rom the cusp of the 5th house is 29° 57′, (Asc. △ ♃). Then 29° 57′ + 15° 0′ = 44° 57′ the *arc of direction* of ☉ △ ♃ d.d.

EXAMPLE 2.—Required the arc of ☉ ☌ ☿ d.d., in the nativity of the Prince Consort.

Constant log.[3] of ☉	0.88114
Log. of semi-arc *diurnal* of ☿ 89° 17′	.30450
Log. of second dist. of ☿ 11° 44′ =	1.18564

The distance of ☿ from the ascendant (asc, ☌ ☿) is 17° 9′. Then 17° 9′ + 11° 44′ = 28° 53′, the arc of direction.

[3] Found by adding the log. of the semi-arc to the log. of the merid. dist. of ☉.

[N.B.—In this case the *diurnal* semi-arc of ☿ is taken in the second term because ☿ must pass the horizon in order to arrive at the Sun's place. This conjunction is also the (mundane) parallel of ☉ and ☿.]

CONVERSE DIRECTIONS OF THE SUN AND MOON.

EXAMPLE 1.—Required the arc of ☽ △ ♃ converse, in the nativity of the Prince Consort.

As the semi-arc of ♃ 114° 6′, log. a.c.	9.80201
To the semi-arc of ☽, 107° 32′	.22373
So the distance of ♃ from cusp of 6th, 8° 5′	1.34768
To the second distance of ☽ 7° 37′ =	1.37342

The Moon has to pass the cusp of the 2nd house to form the trine aspect with Jupiter's place outside the cusp of the 6th. The Moon's distance from the cusp of the 2nd house is 36° 51′ (M.C. △ ☽). Therefore, 36° 51′ + 7° 37′ = 44° 28′ the *arc of direction* of ☽ △ ♃ conversely.

When one arc is computed, others may be obtained from it by merely adding or subtracting, as the case may be, the proportional part of the semi-arc of the body directed, provided that they are formed in the same hemisphere as the first. For example, the □ of ☽ to ♃ may be found by subtracting one-third of the semi-arc of ☽ from the previous arc, thus: 44° 28′ - 35° 51′ = 8° 37′ the arc of ☽ □ ♃ con. The sesquiquadrate may be found by adding one-sixth of the semi-arc of ☽ to the arc of the △, thus: 44° 29′ + 17° 56′ = 62° 24′ the arc of ☽ ss □ ♃ conversely.

PARALLELS DIRECT AND CONVERSE.

EXAMPLE 1.—Required the arc of ☉ parallel ♄ *direct* direction, in the nativity of the Prince Consort.

As the semi-arc of ☉ 103° 12′, log. *A.c.*	9.75834
To the semi-arc (*nocturnal*) of ♄ 93° 7′	.28625
So the meridian distance of ☉ 89° 37′	.30288
To the second distance of ♄ 80° 52′ =	.34747

The primary distance of ♄ from the lower meridian is 115° 48′, *ergo* 115° 48′ - 80° 52′ = 34° 56′ the *arc* of ☉ par. ♄ m. d.d.

In this instance ♄ forms the parallel (*below* the horizon) in the 6th house, therefore the nocturnal semi-arc of ♄ is taken in the third term; and, of course, the parallel of the ☉ and ♄ is ☉ ☍ ♄ also.

EXAMPLE 2.—Required the arc of ☽ parallel ♃ conversely in the same nativity.

As the semi-arc of ♃ 114° 6′ log. *a.c.*	9.80201
To the semi-arc of ☽ 107° 33′	.22373
So the merid. distance of ♃ + 67° 59′	.42287
To second distance of ☽ 64° 4′ =	.44861

Then 64 ° 4′ - 34° 50′ (primary meridian distance of ☽) = 29° 14′ the *arc of direction* of ☽ par. ♃ conversely.

EXAMPLE 3.—Required the arc of ☽ parallel ♅ direct direction, in the same nativity.

	.22373
As the semi-arc of ☽ 107° 32′, log (a.c.)	9.77627
To the semi-arc of ♅ 121° 9′	.17195
So the merid. distance of ☽ 34° 50′	.71328
To the second distance of ♅ 39° 15′ =	.66150

To form this parallel ♅ has to pass the lower meridian therefore the second distance must be *added* to the primary distance of ♅ from the nadir, thus: 15° 11′ + 39° 15′ = 54° 26′.

RAPT PARALLELS.

EXAMPLE 1.—Required the arc of ☽ Rapt Parallel ♀, in the nativity of the Prince Consort.

Semi-arc of ☽	107 32	R.A. of ♀	142 58
Semi-arc of ♀	109 52	R.A. of ☍ ☽	29 38
	2)217 24		2)113 20
	108 42		56 40

As ½ semi-arcs 108° 42′ log. *a.c.*	9.78098
To ½ semi-arc of ♀ 54° 56′	.51544
So ½ diff. of R.A. 56° 40′	.50194
To ½ second distance of ♀ 28° 38′	.79836
2	

Second distance of ♀ =	57 16
Merid. distance of ♀	78 30
Arc of Direction =	21 14

[Note.—In this instance the opposite place of the Moon is taken, as if she were in the 9th house, because the planet is applying to the upper meridian.]

CHAPTER XXXII.

ZODIACAL DIRECTIONS.

DIRECTIONS in the zodiac are of two kinds—"direct" and "converse." When they are made in the order of the signs they are termed *direct*; and when contrary to the order of the signs, they are termed *converse*. In the latter case the place of the moderator is supposed to be carried in a retrograde manner by the rotation of the earth on its axis. These zodiacal *converse* directions were formed shortly before birth.

TO DIRECT THE MID-HEAVEN IN THE ZODIAC.

RULE.—Find the right-ascension of the place of the aspect or parallel declination, and, if the direction be *direct*, deduct the R.A. of the M.C. from it; if *converse*, take the R.A. of the aspect from that of the M.C.

TO DIRECT THE ASCENDANT IN THE ZODIAC.

RULE.—Find the oblique ascension of the place of the aspect or parallel declination, and, if the direction be *direct*, deduct the oblique ascension of the ascendant (which is to be computed by adding 90° to the R.A. of the M.C.) from it. If the direction be *converse*, take the oblique ascension of the aspect from that of the ascendant.

TO DIRECT THE SUN, MOON OR PLANET FORWARDS IN THE ZODIAC.

RULE 1°. Find the right ascension, the meridian distance, the declination, and the semi-arc of the place of the aspect.

2°. Say: As the semi-arc of the Sun is to the semi-arc of the aspect so is the merid. dist. of the Sun to his second distance.

3°. The sum or difference of the primary and secondary distances of the aspect will be *the arc of direction*, according to whether the aspect falls on the same side of the meridian as the Sun is or the other side.

TO DIRECT THE SUN BY CONVERSE MOTION IN THE ZODIAC.

RULE.—1°. Find the right-ascension, meridian distance, declination, and semi-arc of the longitude in which the aspect

2° Say: As the semi-arc of the aspect is to the semi-arc of the Sun so is the merid. dist. of the aspect to the second distance.

3°. The sum or difference of the first and second distance of the Sun will be the *arc of direction*.

TO DIRECT THE SUN, MOON OR PLANET TO A PARALLEL OF DECLINATION BY DIRECT MOTION.

RULE. 1°. Find the longitude corresponding (in the Tables of Declination) to the declination of the celestial body to the parallel of which the Sun is to be directed.

2°. Find the right-ascension, meridian distance, and semi-arc of the parallel, and

3°. Say: As the semi-arc of the Sun is to that of the parallel so is his meridian distance, to the second distance.

4°. The sum or difference of the first and second distances will be the *arc of direction*.

TO DIRECT THE SUN TO A PARALLEL OF DECLINATION BY CONVERSE MOTION.

RULE.—1°. Find the longitude corresponding to the declination of the body to the parallel of which the Sun is to be directed.

2°. Find the right-ascension, meridian distance, and semi-arc of the parallel, and

3°. Say: As the semi-arc of the parallel is to that of the Sun so is the meridian distance of the parallel to the second distance.

4°. The sum or difference of the first and second distances of the Sun will be the arc of direction.

TO DIRECT THE MOON OR PLANET TO ANY ASPECT IN THE ZODIAC, BY DIRECT MOTION, WITH LATITUDE.

RULE. 1°. Find by reference to the *Nautical Almanac*, or *Zadkiel's Ephemeris* for the year of birth, the latitude the Moon or planet will have when the aspect is formed.

2°. Find the right-ascension, declination, and semi-arc corresponding to the longitude and latitude the Moon will have when she reaches the aspect.

3°. Say: As the semi-arc of the Moon or planet is to the semi-arc of the place of the aspect, so is the merid. dist. of the Moon or planet directed to the second distance.

4°. The sum or difference of the first and second distances of the aspect will give the *arc of direction.*

TO DIRECT THE MOON OR PLANET TO A PARALLEL OF DECLINATION BY DIRECT DIRECTION, WITH LATITUDE.

RULE. 1°. Find by reference to the *Nautical Almanac*, or the *Ephemeris*, for the year of birth, the longitude and latitude the celestial body has when it reaches the parallel of declination to which it is directed.

2°. Find the right-ascension, meridian distance, and semi-arc of the parallel.

3°. Say: As the semi-arc of the Moon is to the semi-arc of the parallel, so is the merid. dist. of the Moon (or planet) to the second distance.

4°. The sum or difference of the first and second distances will give the *arc of direction.*

TO DIRECT THE MOON (OR PLANET) TO A PARALLEL OF DECLINATION BY CONVERSE MOTION.

RULE.—1°. Find the longitude (without reference to latitude), in the *ecliptic*, corresponding to the declination of the body to the parallel of which the Moon (or planet) is to be directed.

2°. Find the right-ascension, meridian distance, and semi-arc of the longitude obtained.

3°. Say: As the semi-arc of the parallel is to that of the Moon or planet, so is the merid. dist. of the parallel to the second distance.

4°. The sum or difference of the first and second distances of the Moon (or planet) will give the *arc of direction* required.

Formerly the Sun and Moon were directed under their POLES, and this method is taught in *Zadkiel's Grammar of Astrology*, as well as the method already given of directing those bodies by means of their *semi-arcs*. The latter is the simpler method, and I advise the student always to follow it. The "crepusculine" and "obscure" arcs of Placidus and Wilson should be disregarded. The *semi-arc* method is the true motion in Nature.

The pole of the Sun, or Moon, is a certain elevation it has from the meridian towards the horizon; hence, if one of them happens to be *exactly on the meridian* it has no pole, and *the arc of direction must be found by right ascension*, as already shown in the method given for directing the mid-heaven in the zodiac. If the Sun or Moon be *exactly on the horizon*, it will have the polar elevation of the horizon, which is the latitude of the birthplace, and it must be directed by oblique ascension in the same manner as that given for directing the ascendant in the zodiac. Placidus taught that the Sun is to be directed by right-ascension when within 2° of the meridian at birth: and when within 3° of the ascendant (measured by oblique ascension) he advises that the Sun be directed by oblique ascension; and when within 3° of the western horizon, by oblique descension, and I advise students to follow his precept.

CHAPTER XXXIII.

EXAMPLES OF RULES FOR COMPUTING ZODIACAL DIRECTIONS.

ZODIACAL DIRECTIONS OF THE MID-HEAVEN.

EXAMPLE 1°.—Required the arc of the Mid-heaven directed to the square of Saturn, in the zodiac, in the nativity of the late Prince Consort.

The square aspect of Saturn falls in 29° 13′ of ♊. Reference to the "Tables of Right Ascension" will show that the 29th deg. of ♊ (without latitude) gives 88° 55′, and the 30th deg. gives 90° 0′. Then say: "As 60′ of long. are to 65′ of R.A., so are 13′ (difference of long.) to 14′ (difference of R.A.)." Add 14′ to 88° 55′ and write down the sum as the R.A. of the aspect, viz., 89° 9′. From the R.A. of the aspect subtract the R.A. of the Mid-heaven, 64° 28′, and the *arc of direction* of M.C. □ ♄ is found to be 24° 41′.

EXAMPLE 2.—Required the arc of M.C. 45° ☉ zod., in the same nativity. This aspect falls in 17° 6′ of ♋.

R.A. of 17° 6′ of ♋	108 32
R.A. of M.C.	64 28
Arc of Direction =	44 4

ZODIACAL DIRECTIONS OF THE ASCENDANT.

EXAMPLE 2.—Required the arc of direction of Ascendant opposition Saturn, in the nativity of the late Prince Consort.

The opposition falls in 29° 13′ of Virgo, the R.A. of which is 179° 17′, the declin. 0°19′ N. Then:

Log. tang. of 50° 18′	10.0805519
Log. tang. of 0°19′ +	7.7424841
Log. sine of asc. diff. 0° 23′=	7.8230360

R.A. of 29° 13′ of ♍	179 17
Asc. Difference	0 23

Oblique ascension of opposition =	178 54
Obl. asc. of ascendt. -	154 28
Arc of Direction[1] =	24 26

EXAMPLE 3.—Required the arc of the Ascendant directed to the parallel of Saturn, in the same nativity.

The declination of Saturn being 2° 35′ the parallel falls in 6° 30′ of Libra, the R.A. of which point is 185° 58′. Then:

To the R.A. of ♎ 6° 31′	185 58
Add the ascensional difference of ♄	3 07
Obl. asc. of parallel =	189 05
Obl. asc. of ascendt. -	154 28
Arc of Direction	34 87

EXAMPLE 4.—Required the arc of the Ascendant directed to the quartile of Uranus, in the same nativity.

This aspect falls in 20° 30′ of ♍; the R.A. of which point is 171° 7′, the declin. 3° 46′ N., and the asc. diff. 4° 33′. Then:

From the R.A. of 20° 30′ of ♍		171 17
Subtract the ascen. diff.	-	4 33
Obl. asc. of the aspect	=	166 44
Obl. asc. of ascendant	-	154 28
Arc of Direction	=	12 16

EXAMPLE 5.—Required the arc of the Ascendant directed to the sesqui-quadrate of Saturn in the zodiac, *conversely*, in the same nativity.

This aspect falls in 14° 13′ of Leo, the R.A. of which is 136° 42′, the declin. 16° 35′, and the asc. diff. 21° 1′. Then:

R.A. of 14° 13′ of Leo	136 41
Asc diff. -	21 00
Obl. asc. of aspect =	115 41
Obl. asc. of ascendant	154 28
Arc of Direction	38 47

THE SUN'S DIRECTIONS IN THE ZODIAC.

EXAMPLE 1.—Required the arc of the Sun directed to the parallel of Saturn in the nativity of the late Prince Consort.

The parallel falls in 6° 30′ of Libra, the R.A. of which is 185° 58′,

[1] This arc corresponds exactly with the arc for the father's death—24° 25′.

the merid. dist. 121° 30′, and the semi-arc 86° 53′.

As Sun's semi-arc 103° 12′, prop. log. (*a.c.*)	9.75834
To semi-arc of parallel 86° 53′	.31624
So Sun's merid dist. 89° 37′	.30288
To second dist. of parallel 75° 29′ =	.37746

Then, the merid. dist. of the parallel 121° 30′ - 75° 29′ = 46° 1′ the Arc of Direction.

THE MOON'S DIRECTIONS IN THE ZODIAC.

EXAMPLE 1.—Required the arc of the Moon directed to the quartile of Venus, in the nativity of the late Prince Consort.

The aspect falls in 20° 12′ of Scorpio, on reaching this longitude the Moon had 3° 13′ S. lat. The R.A. of 20° 12′ of Scorpio with 3° 13′ S. lat. is 226° 49′, the merid. dist. 17° 39′, the declin. 20° 54′ S., and the semi-arc 117° 22′.

As Moon's semi-arc, 107° 33′, prop. log. (*a.c.*)	9.77627
To semi-arc of asect 117° 22′	.18573
So Moon's merid. dist. 34° 50′	.71328
To second dist. of aspect 38° 1′ =	.67528

Then, the second dist. of aspect 38° 1′ - 17° 39′ (the primary merid. dist.) = 20° 22′, the Arc of Direction.[2]

EXAMPLE 2.—Required the arc of the Moon directed to the opposition of Saturn, by *converse* motion, in the nativity of the late Prince Consort.

The opposition falls in 29° 13′ of Virgo, the R.A. of which is 179° 17′, the merid. dist. 65° 11′, the declin. 0° 19′ N., and the semi-arc 89° 37′.

As semi-arc of aspect 80° 37′, prop. log. (*a.c.*)	9.69712
To semi-arc of Moon 107° 32′	.22373
So merid. dist. of aspect 65° 11′	.44114
To second dist. of Moon 78° 13′	.36199

Then, the second dist. of Moon 78° 13′—the Moon's merid. dist. 34° 50′ = 43° 23′ the *arc of direction.*[3]

EXAMPLE 3. Required the arc of the Moon directed to the parallel

[2] This arc corresponds closely to the period of the Prince Consort's *engagement.*

[3] This arc falls in the fatal train.

of Mercury by *converse* motion in the same nativity.

This parallel falls in 28° 30′ of Virgo (without latitude), the R.A. of which is 178° 38′, the merid. dist. 65° 50′, and the semi-arc 89° 17′.

As semi-arc of parallel 89° 17′, prop. log. (*a.c.*)	9.69550
To semi-arc of Moon 107° 32′	.22373
So merid. dist. of parallel 65° 50′	.43683
To second dist. of Moon 79° 29′ =	.35606

Then, 79° 17′ - 34° 50′ (the Moon's merid. dist.) = 44° 27′ the *arc of direction.*

THE PLANETS' DIRECTIONS IN THE ZODIAC.

EXAMPLE 1.—Required the arc of Saturn directed to the parallel of the Sun, without latitude, in the nativity of the late Prince Consort.

This parallel falls in 27° 54′ 25″ of *Aries*, and the R.A. of this point of the ecliptic is 25° 55′, and its meridian distance is 38° 33′.

Then, as Saturn's semi-arc, 86° 53′	.31634
(*a.c.*)	9.68366
To the Sun's semi-arc, 103° 11′	.24166
So is Saturn's merid. dist. 64° 12′	.44774
To the second distance 76° 15′=	.37306
38° 33′ -	
Arc of Direction = 38° 42′	

EXAMPLE 2.—Required the arc of Saturn directed to the parallel of the Sun, with latitude, in the same nativity.

When Saturn arrived at the parallel of the Sun's declination, (in May, 1822) his latitude was 2° 15′ south, and his longitude was *Taurus* 4° 0′. This gives the R.A. as 32° 30′, and the meridian distance 31° 58′.

As Saturn's semi-arc 86° 53′ (*a.c.*)	9.68366
To the Sun's semi-arc 103° 11′	.24166
So Saturn's merid. dist. 64° 12′	.44774
To the second distance 76° 15′ =	.37306
31° 58′ -	
Arc of Direction = 44° 17′	

EXAMPLE 3.—Required the arc of Saturn directed to the opposition of the Moon, in the same nativity.

The opposition falls in 2° 29′ of ♉, on reaching which longitude

Saturn had 2° 15′ S. lat. R.A. was 31° 4′; merid. dist. 33° 24′; declin. 10° 15′ N., and his semi-arc, 102° 34′.

As Saturn's semi-arc 86° 53′, prop. log. (*a.c.*)	9.68366
To semi-arc of aspect 102° 34′	.24427
So Saturn's merid. dist. 64° 21′	.44774
To second dist. of ditto 75° 47′=	.37567

Then, the second dist. 75° 47′ - 33° 24′ = 42° 23′ the *arc of direction.*[4]

EXAMPLE 4.—Required the arc of Mars quartile Moon in the zodiac, without latitude, direct, in the same nativity.

The quartile of the Moon's place falls in Leo 2° 30′. The R.A. of this longitude (*sine* lat.) is 124° 47′; the declination is 19° 37′; the semi-arc is 115° 24′; and the meridian distance is 60° 19′.

As Mars's semi-arc 120° 59′ prop. log.	.17255
(*a.c.*)	*9.82745*
To the semi-arc of the aspect 115° 24′	.19307
So is Mars's merid. dist. 18° 18′	.99282
To the second distance 17° 27′=	1.01334
60° 19′	

Arc of Direction = 42° 52′

[4] This arc measures to within one month of the period of death, arc = 42° 18′.

CHAPTER XXXIV.

ON EQUATING ARCS OF DIRECTION.

"A year for a day, and a day for a year."

VARIOUS methods of equating arcs of direction have been suggested and adopted by different authors. The Ptolemaic measure of time is the most correct, viz.: one degree = one year of life, and one-twelfth part of a degree (5′) = one month. The author adopted this measure—at the suggestion of Zadkiel I.—in the year 1862, and his experience afforded by the calculation of several hundreds of nativities proves that it comes nearer to the truth than any other.

The method of Placidus was this: "Add the R.A. of the Sun to the arc of direction; the sum will be the right-ascension of that part of the zodiac which when reached by the Sun (as shown in the *Ephemeris* for the year of birth) the direction comes into force, and the time must be equated by allowing a year for every day the Sun takes in reaching that point, and a month for every two hours."

The method of Naibod was to allow "for every degree of arc, one year, five days, and eight hours; and for every minute six days, four hours."

Maginus recommended (on the authority of Dr. Dee, who was a good mathematician) that the arc of direction should be considered as right-ascension, and measured according to the Sun's motion, in right-ascension, at the time of birth.

Some artists divide the arc by the Sun's mean motion; others by the rate of the Sun's motion on the day of birth.

It is no small recommendation in favour of the Ptolemaic measure that Zadkiel I. after having adopted the measure recommended by Placidus (termed by Wilson as the "most rational"), and followed it for many years, was compelled by the results of his great experience to discard it in favour of the Ptolemaic question.

EXAMPLE 1.—His late Royal Highness the Duke of Edinburgh and of Saxe-Coburg-Gotha was born at Windsor Castle on the sixth day of

August, 1844, at 7h 50m a.m., Greenwich mean time.

	h.	m.	s.
Sidereal time at noon, Aug. 6	8	56	32.62
Add time elapsed	19	50	
Add diff. mean and sidl. time		3	15.49
	28	49	48.11
Subtract long. of Windsor Castle		2	20.30
Subtracting the circle, 24h	4	47	27.81

The sidereal time so found is equivalent to 71° 51′ 57″, which is the right-ascension of the meridian at the moment of birth stated in the official bulletin. The apparent obliquity of the ecliptic was then 23° 27′ 31.4″. The exact longitude of the upper meridian may be readily found as follows:

Logarithm sine of obl. ecliptic	9.9625337
Logarithm cotang. of R.A. 71° 51′ 57″+	9.5152252
Logarithm cotang. 73° 16′ 39 ″=	9.4777589

Subtracting 60°, for two signs of the zodiac, we have 13° 16′ 39 ″ of *Gemini* to enter on the midheaven, or cusp of the tenth house. By means of the rule "Oblique ascension given to find the ecliptic longitude," given in the Appendix to this work, the ascendant is found to be *Virgo* 17° 13′. The oblique ascension of the ascendant is found by adding to the R.A. of the midheaven ninety degrees, thus 71° 51′ 57″ + 90° = 161° 51′ 57″.

The horoscope was given at page 101 of the first volume of FUTURE. The longitudes of the Sun and planets were, respectively: Sun in Leo 13° 52′ 23″. Moon in Taurus 15° 52′ 10″. Mercury in Leo 29° 19′, Venus in Cancer 23° 49′, retrograde. Mars in Leo, 13° 20′. Jupiter in Aries 3° 41′, retrograde. Saturn in Aquarius 3° 13′, retrograde. Uranus in Aries 6° 1′, retrograde. Neptune in Aquarius 22° 38′, retrograde. The Moon was hyleg, and she was in quadrature with both the Sun and Mars, and in mundane sextile with Venus. The Sun was only half-a-degree past conjunction with Mars. This rendered the Royal duke liable to feverish ailments, and his first attack of fever took place in February, 1863, arc = 18° 30′, under the operation of the primary direction of Moon rapt parallel Mars 17° 50′ and Sun rapt parallel Moon 18 ° 20′.

In December, 1862, Prince Alfred was elected King of Greece, but he declined the honour of becoming the monarch of that country, on the advice of his illustrious parents and the British Government. This honour was proffered under the influence in the nativity of the second son of Queen Victoria, of Ascendant parallel Jupiter, zodiac 18° 31′.

Early in the year 1868, the young prince visited Australia, and on the 12th of March a dastardly Fenian attempted to kill him by shooting him in the back. Zadkiel I. foresaw the danger and foretold that "the 12th of March (1868) is evil for a great personage." This narrow escape of death at the hands of an assassin was incurred under the primary directions of M.C. parallel Mars, zodiac, conversely, 23° 39′, and Moon parallel Saturn, mundo, con. 23° 46′. The arc for this dangerous experience is 23° 36′. It is noteworthy that in the nativity the Sun and Mars were together in the sign *Leo*, which from time immemorial has been held by astrologers to rule the back of the body, and the spine.[1] At the 23rd Solar revolution the Sun was in quartile and the Moon was in conjunction with Saturn, which malefic planet was in opposition to the place of the Moon at birth.

On the 23rd of January, 1874, the Royal Duke was married at St. Petersburg, to the Grand Duchess Marie, daughter of the Tsar Alexander II; the arc for the happy event = 29° 28′, and the arc of direction of Midheaven conjunction Moon, mundo, conversely, is 29° 9′, and that of Moon sextile Sun, zodiac, is 29°47′.[2] If we subtract 0°16′, the Sun's semi-diameter, from this arc we shall bring it up, for first contact, closely to the arc of marriage, thus 29° 47′ - 0° 16′ = 29°31′.

The second attack of fever was suffered in April, 1889. The Prince was stricken with Maltese remittent fever—the evil planet Saturn then being in transit over the places of the Sun and Mars in his nativity; and, moreover, Saturn was *stationary* in *Leo* 13° 25′ on the 14th day of that month. The following primary direction was then in force: Ascendant quartile Moon zodiac, conversely, 44° 35′, the arc for the illness being 44° 41′.

The author warned the Prince of this attack of fever, as follows: "April, 1889. Our Sailor Prince will be troubled by Saturn's stationary position so near the places of the Sun and Mars at his birth; he will do well to avoid staying in unhealthy places where fever lurks."[3] Cer-

[1] Lord Mayo, Viceroy of India, who was assassinated by being stabbed in the back, also had Mars in *Leo* at his birth, and in opposition with the Moon. He was born February 21st, 1822, and died on the 8th of February, 1872.

[2] This direction is computed in R.A., as it falls within one degree of the Midheaven of the Prince's nativity. Thus: R.A. of Gemini, 13° 52′, 72° 30′ - 42° 43′, the Moon's R.A. = 29° 47′ the arc of direction.

3 Vide *Zadkiel's Almanac* for 1889, page 11.

tain Press-scribes, anxious to discredit astrology, endeavoured to belittle this warning by saying that "England has more than one Sailor Prince," but this futile boomerang of theirs only recoiled on themselves, for, in their ignorance, they forgot that only one, and that one Prince Alfred, had both the Sun and Mars in the fourteenth degree of the sign *Leo* at his birth, and that the Sun could only be in that degree on the 6th day of August, 1844, and not at the birth of any other Sailor Prince of England.

A train of evil directions brought on a malignant affection of the larynx, at the root of the tongue, and the Royal Duke succumbed to a sudden seizure with failure of the heart on the 30th of July, 1900, at 56 years of age all but eight days. The arc (1° = 1 year of life) measures to 55° 59′. The following directions measure closely thereto: Moon quartile Uranus zodiac, 55° 45′, Moon parallel Uranus, zodiac, conversely, 55° 49′.

It is remarkable that the *Asselli* were close to the Midheaven by primary direction: M.C. ☌ North Assellus, in the zodiac, 55° 51′.

The Moon, being hyleg and in *Taurus*, the sign ruling the throat, and afflicted by Mars and the Sun, at birth, accounts for the fatal illness, and Uranus being the afflicting planet, by direction, accounts for the suddenness of the demise.[4]

The late King Edward VII, was born at 10h 48m a.m. of the 9th day of November, 1841, at Buckingham Palace, London. At that moment of Greenwich mean time and at the birthplace, the sidereal time was 14h 1m 8.76s = 210° 17′ 11″ in arc of R.A. This gives Scorpio 2° 29′ 1″ on the Midheaven, and Sagittarius 27° 42′ 45″ ascending. The *geocentric* latitude of the birthplace is 51° 18′ 36″ N., and the longitude is 0° 36′ W., of the Royal Observatory, Greenwich. The ascending degree is computed for this latitude, and the semi-arcs of the celestial bodies also.

The horoscope of King Edward was cast by Zadkiel I. within three hours of the time of birth being officially stated, and was published in the second edition of his Almanac for 1842. The learned editor remarked that as Mars was in the first house and in mundane quartile with the Sun (hyleg):

We cannot hope that the child's constitution will be free from lia-

---

[4] In *Zadkiel's Almanac* for 1900, p. 23, will be found the following forecast: "Our Royal Family will be involved in some grief, in the first half of July, we regret to foresee."

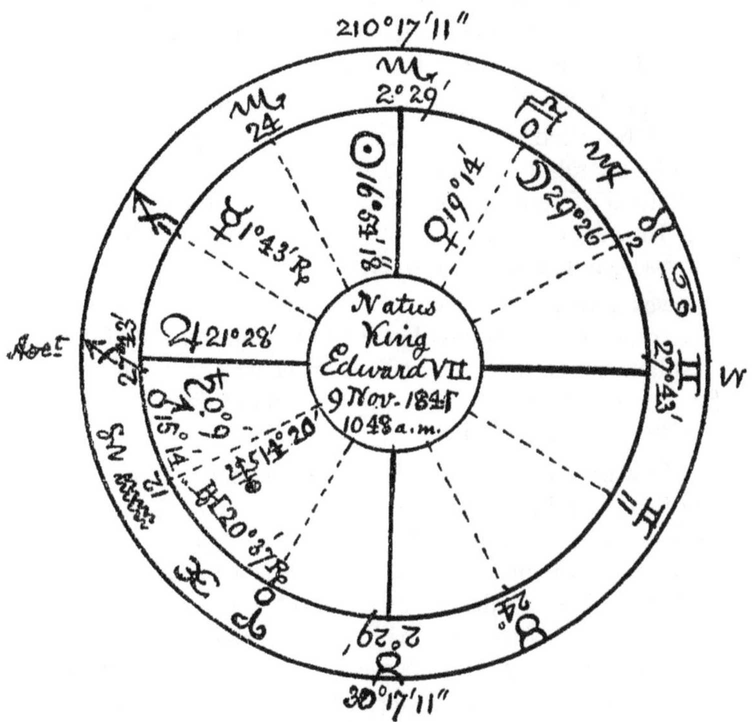

SPECULUM.

	Lat.	Declin.	Rt. Ascn.	Mer. dist.	Semi-Arc.
☉	-	16° 54′ 5″S	224° 6′ 4″	14° 8′ 53″	67° 42′ 13″
☽	4° 11′ S	3 36 38 S	177 49 15	32 27 56	85 28 52
☿	1 46½ S	22 15 39 S	239 12 45	28 55 34	59 15 44
♀	1 42 N	5 57 46 S	198 23 24	11 53 47	82 30 22
♂	1 33 S	24 9 38 S	286 43 17	103 33 54	124 3 53
♃	0 13 N	22 57 56 S	260 43 55	50 26 44	58 03 10
♄	0 44 N	22 43 56 S	270 10 17	120 6 54	121 32 37
♅	0 47 S	4 26 44 S	351 41 17	38 35 54	95 34 15
♆	0 9 S	16 15 S	316 51	73 26	111 21

bility to feverish complaints. This excepted, the hyleg (Sol) is strong, having the mundane parallel of Venus, and we doubt not this scion of our Royal House may live to sway the sceptre of this realm.

The Moon in good aspect (sextile) with Mercury gives him a

shrewd and clever turn of mind with good natural talents, and he has Jupiter so strong that he will become a mild and benevolent sovereign, though firm and positive in opinion."

Again, in *Zadkiel's Legacy* (1842) it was stated "the Prince of Wales shall be called 'The Wise King.' The potent position of Jupiter renders him liberal, frank, brave, benevolent, and calculated for government; fond of sport and exercise; amiable, gracious, noble and brilliant. He will sway the sceptre of this realm in moderation and justice—a gracious and merciful sovereign."

This was a very true forecast of the talents, tact combined with firmness, graciousness, benevolence, of his Majesty; and of that wisdom displayed in his unceasing efforts to secure peace to his Empire, and his wonderful faculty for saying the right thing at the right moment; of his high courage and keen zest for sport.

King Edward VII. incurred a liability to accidents from the proximity of Saturn to the ascendant (only 1° 26′ below the eastern horizon, measured by oblique-ascension), but his Majesty escaped serious injury thereby in most instances, because the benefic planet Jupiter was but 7° 36′ above the ascendant, and strong in his chief dignity the sign Sagittarius. Very early in life he had a narrow escape of being shot; he rolled down the almost perpendicular side of a mountain, owing to a slip of his foot, and escaped with a few severe bruises; he came very near to being crushed by the fall of an enormous chandelier, when at Heidelberg, in September, 1861; he fell into deep water, when touring in Palestine; he nearly fell into the flames, through a floor giving way, while helping the firemen to extinguish the fire at Marlborough House, in July, 1865; he fractured the patella of one knee by slipping on a staircase in July, 1908; he had a fortunate escape from assassination in Belgium, in April, 1900, and injured a foot, while out shooting, in November, 1905.

When Mars arrived at the ascendant, by primary direction—Asct. ☌ ♂ mundo 20° 30′, preceded by M.C. par. ♅ zodiac, conversely 19° 58′—the King suffered the sad bereavement by the death of his talented and affectionate father, in December, 1861, in which fatal month a lunar eclipse took place whereat Mars was exactly in transit over the place of the Sun at his Majesty's birth. Under this martial direction, he went for his tour in the East.

His Majesty's marriage with the charming Princess Alexandra of Denmark, took place on the 10th day of March, 1863, under the happy influence of Moon sextile Venus, zodiac, conversely 21° 2′ and Venus parallel Moon, zodiac, conversely 21° 50′ by primary direction.

As the Sun arrived at the parallel declination of Saturn, by primary direction, his Majesty was attacked with enteric fever, which so nearly proved fatal in December, 1871. The arc for the crisis of this dangerous attack is 30° 4′. That of Sun parallel Saturn, zodiac, first contact is 29° 42′. It is computed in the following manner: Saturn's declination 22° 43′ 56.3″ - 16′ 10.6″ (Sun's semi-diameter) = 22° 27′ 45.7″, which the Sun's limit attains on reaching longitude ♐ 13° 40′ 36″. The R.A. is 252° 17′ 38″, and meridian distance 42° 0′ 37″. The second distance of the Sun (as computed by the rule already given) is 12° 18′ 44″, which is to be subtracted from 42° 0′ 27″, and the quotient is the arc of Sun parallel Saturn, first contact, 29°41′ 43″.

The direction of the Sun's centre to the parallel of Saturn in the zodiac measures 32° 22′ 16″, and its operation coincided with his Majesty's narrow escape, in a collision of his yacht, in 1873 (attended by M.C. ☌ ☽ mundo, conversely, 32° 28′).

At the King's 30th Solar revolution, the configurations of the Moon pre-signified illness, and Zadkiel I. directed attention to this pre-signification in his Almanac for 1871, thus:

"On the 9th of November, 1871, the Moon is afflicted by a square of Mars and Saturn, which bespeaks serious losses and troubles for all persons born that day, be they prince or peasant."

The author, in an annual (1871) which he then edited, wrote that:

"At the Solar eclipse of December 22nd, 1870, Saturn is in transit over his own place at birth of H.R.H. the Prince of Wales. This transit taken into consideration with the fact that the eclipse falls in the place of Saturn at birth, and in square to the Moon's place, indicates trouble and ill-health—further than this we may not say but 'the wise' will understand."

This was written in July, 1870, sixteen months before the serious illness began (November, 1871). The effect of the Solar eclipse of December 22nd, 1870, was retarded until the primary direction of Sun par. Saturn came into operation, when the combination of these evil influences very nearly ended the valuable life of the Prince of Wales. The eclipse lasted for four hours and twenty-eight minutes, and its rule, therefore, continued for nearly four years and a half. It was total, and was visible as a partial eclipse in the United Kingdom.

In the autumn of 1876, his Majesty went to India, and in December of that year met with an accident there, and was on one occasion in some danger from the charge of a tiger. As both Mars and Saturn were in *Capricornus*, and in the ascendant, the author wrote (in July, 1875, when the visit to India was announced by the Prime Minister, in the House of Commons): "But for the generally fortunate character of the directional influences operating during the period of his Royal Highness' projected visit to India, one would be apprehensive for his personal safety in that country. Care will have to be taken to avoid accidents " etc.[5] The primary directions then operating were Ascendt. 45° Mars, zodiac, conversely, 34° 52′ Sun parallel Jupiter, zodiac, 35° 7′, Sun quartile Moon, mundo 35° 9′, and Sun sextile Venus, zodiac, 35° 53′.

In July, 1898, his Majesty's accident to his knee took place under the primary direction of Ascendt. parallel Neptune, zodiac, con. 56° 45′ closely followed by Ascendt. conjunction Uranus, mundo 56° 58′.

Sipido's abominable attempt to assassinate his Majesty at the railway station at Brussels on the 4th April, 1900 (when Saturn was in *Capricornus* 4° 58′ the sign ruling Brussels), was, Providentially, unsuccessful. The arc for this danger is 58° 24′, and that for the death of Prince Leopold is 58° 43′. The primary directions then operating in the royal nativity were: Sun 135° Saturn, zodiac, conversely 58° 18′, Ascendt. sesqui-quadrate Mercury, mundo, 58° 33′, Sun opposition Neptune, zodiac, con, 58° 40′. His Majesty's health was not good at the time.

In 1901, at the age of 59 years and two months (arc = 59° 12′) on the demise of his beloved mother, Queen Victoria, the Prince of Wales acceded to the throne, under the following train of primary directions:

Midheaven quartile Moon, zodiac	59° 06′
Sun parallel Sun. zodiac, conversely	59 12
Midheaven sextile Sun, mundo	59 17
Ascendant opposition Moon, zodiac	59 29
Moon trine Uranus, mundo, con.	59 41
Ascendant quartile Saturn, zodiac	59 47
M.C. conjunction Saturn, zodiac	59 53
M.C. conjunction Saturn, mundo	59 53
Sun rapt parallel Neptune	60 01
Sun parallel Jupiter, zodiac	60 03

[5] Vide *Zadkiel's Almanac* for 1876, pp. 50, 51.

The directions of Saturn to the Midheaven, in the zodiac and in the world, account for the accession to the throne in a time of war and national trouble. As, however, the Sun lay, by direction, in the parallel of Jupiter, an honourable peace in South Africa was soon concluded[6] and a brilliant, although all too short a reign of nine years and four months followed.

The effect of the fourth direction in the preceding list, namely the opposition of the Moon to the ascendant, in the zodiac, 59° 29′ = May, 1901, was also manifest in the very narrow escape which his Majesty had of a dangerous accident, on the 22nd of May, 1901, by the fall of the mast of the yacht Shamrock II., due to a sudden gust of wind. Had the snapping of the mast happened ten seconds later, the boom would have been right aboard, and would have fallen on the deck. At the time of the accident the King was standing in the companion way.[7] This direction is said to presignify "misfortunes at sea," as was stated in the "Grammar of Astrology " (1840), and at p. 235 of the first volume of "The Text-Book of Astrology," first edition (1879).

On the 14th of June, 1902, his Majesty felt indisposed, but insisted that the troops at Aldershot should not be disappointed of his presence, and therefore travelled thither to attend the tattoo that evening, which unfortunately was very rainy. After dinner the King began to suffer much pain. On the 16th his physicians advised his return to Windsor. On the 19th his condition improved, and continued to the 23rd of June, when his Majesty proceeded from Windsor to London; but that evening fever returned, and the swelling in the right iliac fossa rapidly increased. The King received the information that a purulent inflammation had occurred with his usual courage and equanimity, and expressed the greatest distress that his people should be disappointed, for the coronation would, necessarily, have to be postponed. On the 24th of June Sir F. Treves performed the operation for appendicitis. A rapid recovery followed, after the 26th. The Coronation of the King and Queen took place at Westminster Abbey on the 9th of August. This critical and dangerous illness was due, astrologically speaking, to the primary direction of Sun parallel Saturn, first contact, 59° 36′, followed by Ascendant 135° Sun, zodiac, 60° 32′. The arc for the illness and operation is 60° 36′.

It has already been shown that the attack of typhoid fever in December, 1871, was due to the first contact (of the Sun's limb) of Sun

[6] Peace was signed at 10h 30m p.m. of the 31st of May, 1902, at Pretoria.

[7] Vide STAR LORE, June, 1901, and December, 1902.

parallel Saturn in ♐ 13° 40′ 36″. When the Sun again reached the parallel of Saturn, first contact in ♑ 16° 19′ 24″, the King's life was, soon after, again endangered, and this time by appendicitis.[8] At birth the Sun was in Scorpio 16° 54′ 18″ in zodiacal sextile and mundane quartile with Mars, and thereby takes the nature of the ruddy planet; and this accounts for the dangerous purulent inflammation necessitating the surgical operation. The Sun (hyleg) lay in the parallel of Saturn's declination, by direction from June, 1901, to June, 1904. Moreover, another evil direction interposed to increase the suffering and danger to life, namely, that of Midheaven conjunction Regulus, mundo, conversely (which is the meridian distance of that wholly martial star at birth) 60° 18′. At the King's 60th Solar revolution the Moon was in *Scorpio* 2° 45′, exactly on the midheaven of the nativity; and on the 22nd of April, 1902, she was totally eclipsed in Scorpio 1° 42′. At the 60th lunar progress (7h 16m a.m. of the 16th of September, 1846) the Sun was within two degrees of exact conjunction with Mars in the sign *Virgo* (in the eighth house of the nativity), in opposition to the place of Uranus at birth, and in parallel declination with both Mars and Uranus.

The King's grandson, now the Prince of Wales, had the Sun in conjunction with both Mercury and Neptune at his eighth Solar revolution, June 23rd, 1902. Accordingly the author wrote (in July, 1901) that: "The 23rd of June brings a crisis" and his grandfather became alarmingly ill on that day.[9]

The passing of King Edward VII. took place at 11h 45m p.m. of the 6th of May, 1910, to the intense grief and consternation of his loyal subjects throughout the British Empire. His Majesty left England for Paris at 9.30 p.m. of the 6th of March, 1910, and contracted a chill *en route*. The arrival at Biarritz, on the 9th, was soon followed by a state of health which caused anxiety to his physicians—"the bronchitic attack, raised temperature, accelerated pulse and respirations." This attack lasted ten days. The train of adverse primary directions falling due in his Majesty's sixty-ninth year gave rise to serious apprehension, and led the author to issue this solemn warning:

"If the King's physicians would pay attention to astrological sci-

---

[8] The student can readily compute this primary direction as follows: As Sun's semi-arc is to the semi-arc of the parallel 57°59′ 23″ so is the Sun's meridian distance to his second distance 12° 7′ 5″, which subtracted from the meridian distance of the parallel, 71° 43′ 16″ = 59° 36′ 11″ the arc of direction.

[9] Vide ZADKIEL'S ALMANAC, 1902, p. 21.

ence, they would not advise his Majesty to travel abroad either this spring or summer, in view of the first, fourth, and seventh of the primary directions operating in this year [1910], and the meridional [proximate] position of Saturn at the 68th Solar revolution.[10] May they [the favourable influences] entirely neutralise the unfavourable arcs!"

Alas! the King's physicians permitted, if they did not advise, his Majesty to travel abroad at the beginning of March, 1910, and to return to this country on the 27th of April. The first direction was Mercury parallel Sun, zodiac, conversely 68° 22′ = March, 1910. The fourth was Moon parallel Mars, mundo, conversely, 68° 38′; the seventh was Moon quartile Uranus, zodiac, cum lat. 68° 53′. The Sun being hyleg the first direction was a serious one for health; the fourth was one calculated to excite inflammation, threaten failure of the heart, and to render travelling afar very risky, just as the first would.

During his last illness, his Majesty showed as indomitable a courage as on previous occasions. Although he had not shaken off the depressing effects of his dangerous attack of bronchitis at Biarritz, which was so near being fatal, he faced the risk of returning to London and Sandringham ere the cold winds of an English spring had subsided, making a hurried and exhausting journey without breaking it, anxious as to the Constitutional crisis then existing, and working to the last for the good of his subjects.

---

[10] Vide ZADKIEL'S ALMANAC for 1910, p. 79, and for 1911, pp. 81-84.

CHAPTER XXXV.

ON RECTIFYING A NATIVITY.

WHEN the time of birth is only known approximately, no observation of it having been recorded, an attempt to determine the true moment of birth can only be made by means of the Placidian system. An error of four minutes will throw out the primary directions of the Ascendant and Midheaven a whole year, and mundane parallels two years, more or less. An error of eight minutes, or more, will accelerate or retard the directions of the Sun or Moon, according to whether the error is later or sooner than the true moment of birth, by weeks or months.

Before railways were made, local time was kept in all towns remote from London, in England and Wales and Scotland. Since the middle of the nineteenth century "railway time"—that is to say, Greenwich mean time—has been kept throughout the United Kingdom, except in Ireland, where Dublin time is kept. For every degree of longitude west of Greenwich "railway time" is four minutes in advance of local mean (or clock) time; and for every degree east, it is four minutes later. Before the railway era, time was kept in many country places by means of the sun-dial. It is, therefore, important to learn whether the stated time of birth, in a country place, is local or railway time. Abroad, standard time is kept, which differs considerably from local time in places remote from the standard in each country. The following Standard Times, referred to the Meridian of Greenwich, have been adopted for railway and other purposes:

	h.	.	h.
Mid-Europe	1 East.	N. S. Wales	10 East.
East Europe	2 East.	Queensland	10 East.
India	5½ East.	Tasmania	10 East.
Burma	6½ East.	New Zealand	11½ East.
Hong Kong	8 East.	America—	
Japan	9 East.	Atlantic	4 West.
South Africa	2 East.	Eastern	5 West.
West Australia	8 East.	Central	6 West.
South Australia	9½ East.	Mountain	7 West.
Victoria	10 East.	Pacific	8 West.

Before computing the nativity the student should carefully ascertain whether the time of birth furnished is standard (or railway) time, as shown by the clock or watch by which it was noted. Paris time was synchronised with Greenwich time on the 10th of March, 1911.

An additional source of error frequently arises from the excitement in the household wherein the birth takes place. Indeed, except when the first act of respiration, or first cry of the infant is noted by the doctor, or for astrological purposes, a guess is usually made some minutes after the event as to the nearest minute, which may differ from five to ten minutes from the true moment.

When the exact moment has been correctly observed and recorded, the student will find the arcs of primary direction, equated by the Ptolemaic method (1° = year of life) will approximate very closely to the periods of important events in the life of the owner of the horoscope to be computed, especially in the case of directions of the angles to the conjunction, opposition, trine, and quartile of Mars. As already stated, parallels, whether mundane or zodiacal usually begin to operate some weeks in advance; and so do the mutual directions of the Sun and Moon, in the zodiac.

A most misleading and unwarrantable assertion was made about thirty-two years ago, by the writer of an astrological primer, that "the exact moment of birth (always so difficult to get at) is of no vital importance whatever." The same writer also asserted that astrology does not consist of the casting of horoscopes "and the working out of directions, but the judgment of the horoscope and the effects of directions." He also deprecated mathematics as applied to astrological calculations, and exalted the judgment of persons of such imperfect education that they cannot compute horoscopes or planets' places nearer than to degrees! He would be a sorry specimen of an astrologer who cannot compute horoscopes, planets' places, and primary directions correctly.

Several methods have been propounded for rectifying approximate times of birth. The only true process is by computing arcs of primary direction for past events of importance—such as, serious accidents, dangerous illness, death of father or mother, emigration, etc.—and comparing the arcs of such directions as may fall due near the periods of such events and harmonise with the nature of them. For this purpose the speculum must first be computed. If a direction of the ascendant or midheaven, satisfactory as to its nature corresponding to that of the selected event, is found to measure within a degree, more or less, of the arc for such event, it may be taken as the argument and a tentative rectification made by means of it. Thus if it differs one degree of arc *late*, *add* four minutes to the estimated time of birth; if one degree too *early*, *subtract* four minutes[1], and its arc will then be found to measure the same as that of the event.

It is usually found that directions of Mars afford the most reliable means of rectifying an uncertain estimate of the birth-moment; especially in the case of an acute fever, or an accident causing much loss of blood, or necessitating a surgical operation, or the sudden death of a parent.

The date of marriage, if already entered upon, will sometimes be useful to this end, especially in the case of a real love-match, of happy and advantageous nature; in such case a direction of Venus may fall a little earlier than the arc of marriage, thereby accounting for the fascination leading up to the engagement and wedding.

When rectification cannot be made by means of directions of the ascendant or midheaven, those of the Sun and Moon, in the zodiac and in the world, may enable it to be effected. In such case the following rules, given by Oxley and Zadkiel I. (in the first half of last century) must be followed:

RULE 1.—Reduce the meridian distance of Sun or Moon, whichever is directed, into minutes of a degree, and call it the *first* position; then add to this meridian distance one degree, reducing it also to minutes, and call it the *second* position. Then, opposite the second position, place the error of the arc of direction, multiply them together, and call the amount A. Work the same direction with the altered meridian distance (taking care to correct by one degree the meridian distance of the planet employed also); find the error of the arc of direction and place it opposite the first position. Multiply these together, and call the amount B.

RULE 2.—If *both* errors be *greater* or *less* than the arc of the event, find the *difference* between the errors, make it a divisor; find also the difference between A and B, and make it a dividend; the quotient will be the *true meridian distance* of the Sun or Moon at the moment of birth, the difference between which and the amount of the meridian distance which was made the *first* position, is the error of the R.A. of the Midheaven at the estimate moment of birth.

[1] This relates to *direct* directions of the angles. In the case of *converse* directions of the angles, if the arc of direction is one degree *greater* than that of the event *subtract* one degree from the B.A. of the M.C., and if it be *less* add one degree to the R.A. of M.C.

RULE 3.—But if one be *greater* and the other *less* than the arc of the event, take the sum of the errors for a divisor, and the sum of A and B for the dividend; and the quotient will give the true meridian distance as before stated.

The rectification having been effected, the horoscope and the speculum must be re-calculated to the corrected R.A. of the Midheaven, and the directions employed in the process of rectification must be re-calculated also; and all directions for future years must be computed to the rectified R.A. of M.C.

The Nativity of H.R.H. the Late Prince Consort requires a rectification of three minutes and twenty-four seconds later than the hour (6 o'clock a.m.) given in his biography, to bring up the arcs of direction more closely to the following chief events of his lamentably short life of forty-two years:

R.A. of M.C. = 64° 28′ 18″.

EVENTS AND DIRECTIONS.

Death of the mother, Aug. 30, 1831 = 12° 1′: Ascendant □ ♅ zodiac 12° 16′

Accident to a knee, Dec. 1837 = 18° 18′: M.C. ☌ ♂ mundo, 18° 18′, Asc. □ ♂ mundo, 18° 18′

Engagement, Oct. 15, 1839 = 20° 8′: ☽ □ ♀ zodiac, d. 20° 22′

Marriage, Feb. 10, 1840 = 20° 28′: ☽ rapt parallel ♀ 21° 14′, M.C. ⚹ ☉ Mundo, d. 20° 50′

Death of the father, Jan. 29, 1844 = 24° 25′: Asct. ☍ ♄ zodiac, d. 24° 26′, M.C. □ ♄ zodiac, d. 24° 41′

Died, Dec. 14, 1861 = 42° 18′: ☉ quadra-sextile ♅ m. con. 42° 17′, ☽ rapt parallel ☿ 42° 21′, ♄ ☍ ☽ zodiac, d. 42° 23′, ♂ □ ☽ zodiac, d. 42° 52′

Had the malefic planets, Mars, Saturn, and Uranus not been in angles and afflicting Mercury in the ascendant, and had not Mars been elevated above the Sun, Moon, and the benefic planets at the moment of birth, and had the Sun (hyleg) been supported by Jupiter and Venus, the Prince Consort would, probably, not have succumbed to the fever which attacked him in December, 1861, in his forty-third year.

That a dangerous crisis was about to take place in the forty-third year, was foreseen by Zadkiel I., who, in a guarded manner, expressed his anxiety for the health of the Prince, at pages 41 and 45 of his Almanac for 1861. Commenting on the nineteenth Solar revolution of the heir-apparent, Zadkiel said: "1861 is evil for the father of the Prince of Wales." Again, in his judgment on the lunation nearest the Vernal Ingress of 1861, the following remark was made: "The stationary position of Saturn in the third degree of Virgo [the degree held by the Sun at birth] following upon this lunation [whereat Saturn was in the ascendant as at the vernal ingress] will be very evil for all persons born on or near the 26th of August; among the sufferers I regret to see the worthy Prince Consort of these realms."

Alderman Humphrey, of London, in announcing from the magisterial bench the demise of the Prince Consort, mentioned, as a remarkable fact, that Zadkiel [I.] had expressed in his almanac great anxiety as to the state of His Royal Highness's health in the year 1861. This announcement caused a great sensation, and, as a matter of course, the worthy alderman as well as Zadkiel, was roundly abused in the newspapers of the following day, with one or two honourable exceptions. The writers of the disgraceful abuse looked rather foolish when it soon afterwards transpired that the Prince Consort had taken some little interest in scientific astrology.

Well may Tennyson have written of the talented Prince as:

> "Wearing the white flower of a blameless life
> Before a thousand peering littlenesses."

It may be mentioned that the Prince Consort, by falling through the ice when skating, caused Queen Victoria some alarm, under the operation, in his nativity, of a Neptune primary direction.

NATIVITY OF HIS MAJESTY KING GEORGE V.

In the year 1868, the nativity of Prince George of Wales, together with that of his elder brother, the late Prince Albert Victor of Wales, was presented by the author in an annual which he wrote (from 1868 to 1871 inclusive) in 1867. The following judgment was appended to the diagram:

The regal sign *Aries* occupies the eastern horizon, and Mars, the ruling planet of the ascending sign, is in *Leo*, also a regal sign. The benefic Jupiter, strongly posited in his own sign *Sagittarius*, is within six degrees of the upper meridian. Venus is in her chief dignity *Taurus*, and in the ascendant. Saturn is in the seventh house in his exaltation [*Libra*]. So that in this *truly royal nativity* we find three planets dignified, the glorious Jupiter close to the midheaven, the Sun and Moon nearly in mutual trine aspect, a royal sign ascending, and Mars and Jupiter in royal signs. From these positions we may conclude and predict that this Prince *will, if he live, become* King of England under the title of George V.

Let us now consider the question of *vitality*. The Moon is hyleg, being within five degrees of the western horizon [cadent, by oblique descension 4° 13′], within three degrees of the quartile of Uranus, applying to sextile with Mars, and in parallel of declination with Neptune.* There is nothing to indicate either an early death or a delicate constitution. The Prince will suffer occasionally from cough or chest affection, but these may be easily remedied, under God's blessing, by skilful treatment; and may be also troubled with headache at times. If Neptune have benefic influence, as is supposed,* his exact parallel declination with the Moon should strengthen the physical constitution.

The Moon and Mercury are both "disposed" of by Venus. Venus being dignified, according to Claudius Ptolemy, "renders the mind and disposition benignant, good, copious in wit, fond of dancing, abhorring wickedness, delighting in the arts, affectionate, refined in taste, easily reconciled, tractable, and entirely amiable." Venus in par. dec. Mercury will render the Prince "philosophical, of scientific mind and good genius, poetical, delighting in learning and elegance, luxurious, intelligent, emulous of worth, delighting in exercise, judicious, and high-minded."

It will be seen from the foregoing judgment that the Prince will, in mind and taste, greatly resemble his grandfather, the good and great Prince Albert. Indeed, *England will be proud of her fifth King George, and his fame shall descend to posterity as one of the wisest and best of monarchs.*†

Let the student watch the development of character in this Prince, for the nativity is especially interesting from the fact that Neptune, whose influence is little understood, occupies the proud position of the ascending planet. The position of Jupiter pre-signifies a very prosperous and peaceful reign; the good is somewhat marred by the opposition of Uranus, but this cannot seriously interfere with the happy influence of the glorious Jove.

The horoscope was computed for the time stated in the official bulletin, namely, 1h 18m a.m., and it was again given in FUTURE, March,

* The Moon also is in mundane trine with the Sun. the arc = 2° 25′.

* Later experience shows that the influence of Neptune is not benefic.

† The capitals and italics were so printed in the original.

1892, and in ZADKIEL'S ALMANAC for 1911.

However, if the time be rectified to 1h 15m a.m., the arcs of the primary directions operating near the period of the accession to the throne will be brought up much more closely. As it very frequently happens that, astrologically speaking, the true moment of birth—that at which the infant's first breath is drawn—is found to be from two to five minutes earlier than that observed, no objection can be raised to His Majesty's true moment of birth being rectified three minutes earlier. The diagram here presented is drawn for 1h 15m a.m. of the 3rd of June, 1865, Marlborough House, in latitude 51° 30′ 16″ N., and longitude (in time) 37^s W.

	h. m. s.
Sidereal time at Greenwich mean noon	4 43 52.13
Add time elapsed	13 15
Add diff. mean and sidereal time, 13h 15m	2 10.59
	18 1 2.72
Subtract long. of birthplace 37s W	37.00
R.A. of M.C. is 270° 6′ 26″=	18 0 25.72

The arc of accession to the throne, at 44y. and 11m., is 44° 55′. The following train of primary directions will be found to approximate closely thereto:

Sun opposition Moon, mundo, conversely	44° 21′
Midheaven trine Sun, zodiac, direct	44 47
Sun quartile Saturn, zodiac, direct	44 57
Ascendt. parallel Jupiter, zodiac, direct	45 3
Ascendt. parallel Jupiter, zodiac, conversely	45 16
Moon 45° Sun, zodiac, conversely	45 21
Jupiter conjunction Saturn, zodiac, con.	45 27
Sun 135° Mars, zodiac, conversely	45 33

By rectifying the time of birth from 1h 18m a.m. to 1h 15m a.m., the arc of ☉ □ ♄ zod. con. is brought from 45° 36′ to 44° 57′, as close as is necessary to the arc for the demise of the father and his Majesty's accession to the throne, May 6th, 1911. Again, the arc of M.C. △ ☉ zodiac is brought from 44° 2′ to 44° 47′, and that of Ascendant parallel ♃, zodiac, direct, from 44° 18′ to 45° 3′, and that of the same direction conversely, from 46° 1′ to 45° 16′.* These three last named

* See *Zadkiel's Almanac* for 1911, page 80.

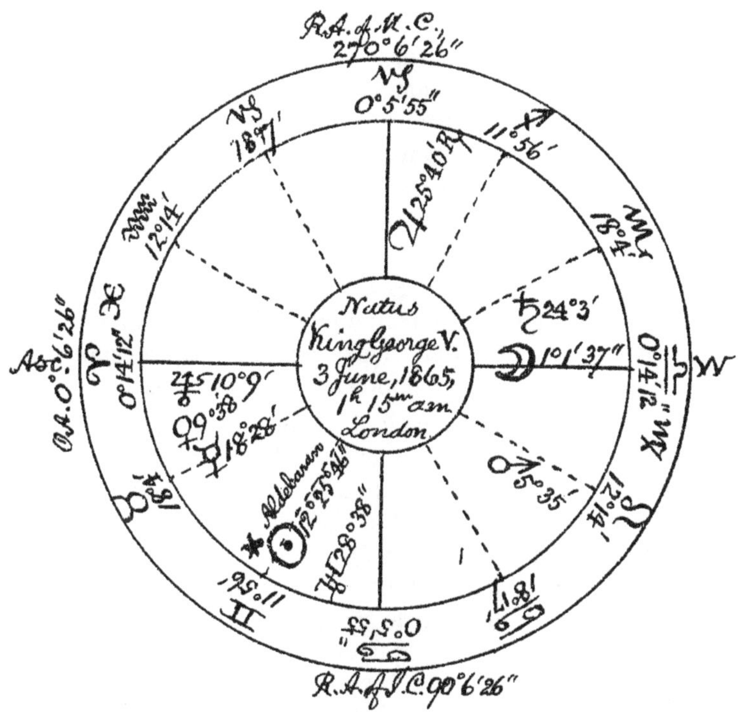

The Speculum.

	Lat.	Declin.	Rt. Asc.	Mer. Dist.	Semi-Arc.
☉		22°17′59″N	70° 57′25″	19°19′1″	58°57′26″
☽	2 27½S	2 39 54 S	179 57 45	89 51 19	93 21 19
☿	3 17½ S	14 10 15 N	46 57 13	43 9 13	71 29 20
♀	1 30 S	13 16 59 N	37 43 27	52 22 29	72 43 56
♂	1 26 N	20 16 34 N	128 19 54	38 13 28	62 19 16
♃	0 26½ N	22 56 30 S	265 17 31	4 48 55	57 50 42
♄	2 40 N	6 51 24 S	203 15 39	66 50 47	81 18 14
♅	0 12 N	23 39 12 N	88 30 3	1 36 23	56 34 59
♆	1 29½ S	2 39 9 N	9 55 1	80 11 25	86 39 38

directions are powerful for good, and pre-signify a fortunate and prosperous reign.

It has been said that as Jupiter was retrograde and in opposition to Uranus, near the lower meridian, at the birth of King George V., the prospects of a long reign are not good, and that loss of inheritance is threatened.† Jupiter is elevated above Uranus and all the other celestial bodies, and very near the upper meridian, and is in Sagittarius his chief dignity. His retrogradation matters not. As far back as 1878, in which year the first edition of this work was published, the author wrote: "Planets retrograde at birth are said to bring poverty and sickness, but this can only apply to the infortunes"—Mars and Saturn. Again, in the first edition of the "Science of the Stars" (1881) this was reiterated as follows:

RETROGRADATION.—An apparent motion of the planets contrary to the order of the signs and to their orbital motion. In nativities it was formerly held that a retrograde planet can do little or no good unless well dignified. It is an absurd notion and is now abandoned.

This royal horoscope is rendered additionally strong by the mundane sextile of the Sun to the ascendant, the position of the benefic Venus in the ascendant and in her chief dignity the sign Taurus, the proximate mutual trine aspect of the Sun and Moon (☉ △ ☽ mundo, con. 2° 48′, and in the zodiac 6° 34′), and the proximate trine of Mars to the ascendant (2° 14′). Neptune, although in the ascendant, is deprived of most of his power to do evil by reason of the sextile aspect of the Sun, and Saturn's evil influence is greatly mitigated by the sextile of Jupiter. In fact, there is no valid reason for qualifying the opinion expressed by the author forty-four years ago, namely that his Majesty's reign would prove to be very prosperous and peaceful.

The rectification adopted is supported by the primary directions measuring to the period of his Majesty's marriage, July 6th, 1898, arc = 28° 5′:

Moon Sextile Sun, zodiac, conversely	27° 42′
Ascendant sextile Venus, mundo, con.	28 8

† This statement was made on a post-card sent, anonymously, to the author on the 5th of January, 1911, by a disloyal Socialist, who disgraced himself by writing very disrespectfully of his gracious Majesty. Evidently the wish was father to the thought. He laid stress on the accession taking place coincidently with the direction of ☉ □ ♄. But he forgot that Queen Victoria acceded to the throne in 1887, under the primary direction, in her Majesty's nativity, of ☉ ☍ ♅ 18° 3′, attended by ♄ par ☉ 18° 37′; and the Victorian reign was a brilliant one, and continued for sixty-three years (1837-1901). He also said that "Neptune's influence is better understood now than in 1865," but did not acknowledge that the author was the first to discover and demonstrate that Neptune's influence is more evil than good.

The Sun directed to the sextile of Venus in the zodiac, 29° 16′ followed, and coincided very closely with the birth of the Prince of Wales, June 23rd, 1894 = 29° 3′.

The longitudes placed on the 11th, 12th, 2nd and 3rd houses were computed by means of the formula *Oblique Ascension given to find ecliptic longitude* given in the appendix. The poles of those houses were first computed, the pole of the 11th and 3rd houses being 28° 39′ 6″, and that of the 12th and 2nd houses being 40° 45′ 4″. The oblique ascension of the 11th house is found by adding 30° to the right ascension of the meridian thus: 270° 6′ 26″ + 30° = 300° 6′ 26″. In like manner, adding 60° to the R.A. of M.C. we have 330° 6′ 26″ as the O.A. of the twelfth house.

With the foregoing examples of rectifying, when necessary, the stated time of birth, the student should soon become expert in the process. It is a difficult task at first, especially when the time of birth is not known nearer than within fifteen or twenty minutes when a sign of short ascension rises, or half an hour or more when a sign of long ascension may occupy the ascendant.

That great astronomer Kepler devoted much time and labour to rectification. One astronomer opposed to astrology did not scruple to insult the memory of that genius by writing that Kepler "though on behalf of the world he worked at astronomy, for his own daily bread he was in the employ of astrology, making almanacks and drawing horoscopes that he might live."*

Max Müller wrote of Kepler that: "The torch of imagination is as necessary to him who looks for truth, as the lamp of study; Kepler held both, and, more than that, he had the star of faith to guide him in all things from darkness to light." "Kepler believed that a man brings the celestial influences on himself by his own deeds, often to acceleration or retardation. In his opinion a marriage and its attendant circumstances depend on our own action. But a dangerous illness, a severe accident, and any unexpected important event, may be due to planetary influence. Such events as these last were only made use of by Kepler for the purpose of rectification of a doubtful or inexact statement of the moment of birth. Here follows his method of rectification in his own words:*

The horoscope of Wallenstein was computed by Kepler; the state-

---

* Vide "Astronomical Myths" based on Flammarion's "History of the Heavens," by John F. Blake. London: Macmillan and Co., 1877.

ment of the great general's birth being "September 14th, 1853, at Prague about 4h 30m p.m." Wallenstein having suffered from illness "aetatis 22, anno 1605, in January"—the Hungarian sickness or plague—the "directionis Ascendentis ad corpus Saturni" probably was the cause, for Nature takes her modos et leges de directionibus. Therefore the Ascensio obliqua Saturnis must be taken sub altitudine poli 51°. [N.B.—The latitude of Prague is 50° 5′ 16″ as lately determined.] Oriente circiter 22° of Pisces est angulus orientis 15° 36′. The latitude of ♄ meridiana est 2° 27′, differentia igitur coorientaria 8° 47′, et ♄ oritur cum 27° 47′ Pisces circitur. Laboriosus igitur luriando hunc coorientem, angulus apud ilium est 15° 29′; differentia coorientaria 8° 50′. Ita ♄ oritur cum 27° 50′ of Pisces.

Et quia Jovi latitude meridiana est 1° 37′ eodum angulo. Ergo differentia coorientaria 5° 50′, et Jupiter oritur cum 28° 33′ ♓. Sic etiam, quia oppositi Mercurio puncti latitude cit 1° 46′ angulo eodem. Differentia ejus coorientaria 6° 28′ quare occidit Mercurius cum 28o 58′ 6.

Jam ascensiones obliqui sunt—

Saturni	350° 3′
Jovis	359 30
Mercurii	359 34

Therefore the three directions fall within half a year, whilst the fourth—Ascendant opposition Sun—will operate the next year. What is very remarkable, while Saturn may have given the Hungarian sickness, Mercury the plague, we find Ascendant conjunction Jupiter as a saving direction after the rules of astrology. Now if we take the middle, 359° 30′, 269° 30′ culminavit, or Sagittarius 29° 22′, and compute the course of the Sun for 21⅓ days = 21° 7′, which must be added to the place of the Sun radix 0° 44½′ ♎ so locus directionis will be 21° 52′ ♎, ascensio recta ejus being 200° 12′. This subtracted from 269° 20′ gives the rectified time of birth 69° 8′ or 4h 36½m p.m.

The true M.C. is 69° 8′ + 180o 44′ = R.A. 249° 52′, or 11° 25′ of Sagittarius, the true ascendant 17° of *Aquarius*.

Kepler predicted serious effects from "the transits and the five oppositions of Saturn and Jupiter from 1632 to 1634, which affect

* Vide Dr. Struve's (of Sulkowa) work on "The Relations of Kepler with Wallenstein," containing interesting letters of that distinguished astronomer. Mr. Albert Kniepf, of Hamburg, quoted from this work in his paper, printed in Zadkiel's Almanac for 1903, pp. 82-84.

first the locus directionis Solis, and will operate in 1634, on the radical places of Saturn, Jupiter, and Mercury; whilst in March, 1634, Mars will oppose the Sun, Venus and Mercury will form a curious cross, for which time it will again come to my prognostication already given [in the horoscope, in 1608] as far as may be expected, terrible entanglements in the country, connected with the fortunes of Wallenstein."

Wallenstein was murdered on the 25th of February, 1634; the political troubles were prognosticated by Kepler exactly by means of the above-named transits.

Dr. Struve writes of Kepler that "thousands of schemes"—or horoscopes—"which must be dated, from the handwriting, prior to 1608, and for which Kepler could not have been adequately remunerated by persons who consulted him, constitute a testimony to his great pains and labour to discover a connexion between the events in the lives of men and the primary directions in their nativities. It is clearly to be recognised that his laborious calculations must have occupied an immense amount of his time."

If there were no truth whatever in astrologia sana, and if the pursuit of it were a delusion, as its enemies, who are utterly ignorant of it, inanely aver, so honest a man as Kepler could never have practised it in any way. His genius would soon have penetrated its falseness, and he would have published the result of his long investigation as proving that it was unreal and unworthy of serious study. But neither Kepler nor Tycho Brahe ever gave such a verdict, nor did the author of the Novum Organum condemn astrology as worthless, for they wrote of it with respect, and, moreover, sought to improve it.

My valued friend Mr. Arthur Mee, of Llanishen, Cardiff, an astronomer who has investigated astrology in an impartial spirit of enquiry, with the result that he is convinced that it is based on truth, and is "a great physical fact capable of rendering unlimited assistance in the social and moral field," states that "Dr. Alfred B. Wallace candidly admits the remarkable correctness of some astrological predictions which have come under his notice, but refers the whole thing to some sort of spirit influence." Dr. Wallace's conclusion is that "the care, attention, labour, and study required to draw out an accurate horoscope and derive from it accurate results, offer the conditions which enable spirits to impress on the astrological student the particular results he gets from the perplexities of the figures."

I have, from time to time, during half a century, protested that *astrologia sana* is not "occult," and has no part nor lot with spiritism. When, in 1867, I wrote my judgment on the import of the horoscope of Prince George, second son (then only two years old) of the Prince of Wales, I gave the astrological reasons for my belief that the horoscope was indeed a royal one, and that the second son of H.R.H. the Prince of Wales would one day be King of England under the title of King George V. I consulted no seer, neither any crystal (or other) clairvoyant, and showed the prediction I had written to no one before it was printed and published—forty-three years before his gracious Majesty succeeded to the throne. I have never sought the impress, nor ever was conscious of the impress, of any spirit, when writing any of my astrological predictions. Daily I humbly pray for Divine guidance in my studies, and in my efforts to discover truths which may be, under the Divine blessing, useful to mankind. This prediction under consideration was read in 1867 and 1868 by quite thirty thousand purchasers (and others) of the annual in which it was printed; and was attested, unsolicited by me, by a scientific gentleman of impartial mind, for he was quite unknown to me until I received the following valuable letter from him, in July, 1910:

"Dear Sir,—Your readers will agree with me, I feel sure, that your prediction made in 1867 was a very remarkable one, to say the least. I have pointed it out to many persons in my copy of your annual for 1868, which I read that year, when a youth of sixteen, and have carefully preserved. I do not dogmatise for or against astrology. As an examiner in English Literature I can testify to the value of a knowledge of astrology for one who reads Chaucer. What is so nauseating is the conceited manner in which those who are absolutely ignorant of both astrology and astronomy condemn the former science, although it won the attention and respect of many of the greatest men who ever lived. In your annual for 1868 you gave the maps of the heavens, specula, and astrological judgments respecting Prince Albert Victor and Prince George of Wales. The inner circle of the horoscope of the former Prince contained the three ostrich plumes, that of Prince George had a *royal crown*. This was very significant. Writing of this nativity, you said that the younger Prince would be King of England, under the title of King George V.

"The universal solvent to get rid of such facts, among sceptics, is *coincidence*, a word which must be as comfortable to them as *Mesopotamia* was to the old lady. People ought to form their own judgment; and ought not to be content to deny the truth of astrology merely because it is the fashion to do so—Edmund S. Payne."

This exactly fulfilled prediction should satisfy even sceptics that *astrologia sana* is true and that, as De Morgan, the great mathematician, admitted, "If astrology be true, it is a useful truth." Dr. Alfred R. Wallace, for whose talents, attainments, and independence of mind, I have the highest admiration and respect, will, I trust, admit that pure astrology is a science and is not dependent on spirit impress.

A sceptic has recently asserted that: "Although when St. Augustine relinquished astrology he was of the opinion that chance was the cause of some of the predictions being fulfilled, he altered his opinion, evidently, because as a theist he could not hold to the idea of chance occurrences." St. Augustine said: "We have good reason to believe that when astrologers give many wonderful answers it is to be attributed to the occult inspiration of spirits not of the best kind, whose care it is to insinuate into the minds of men and to confirm in those false and noxious opinions concerning the fatal influences of the stars, and not to their marking and inspecting of horoscopes, according to some kind of art which has no existence."

This argument can only apply to occultists, who mix up astrology with spiritism, and who never attempt to master the mathematical system of the ancient science. I have repeatedly protested that astrology is not "occult." It should be pursued and practised as a science. In the first edition (1881) of my "Science of the Stars," I stated that *Astrologia sana* has nothing whatever with spirit-rapping, palmistry, card-shuffling, or witchcraft: it does not lead to atheism nor fatalism. As Bacon (Lord Verulam) said: "there is no fatal necessity in the stars, and this the more prudent astrologers have allowed."

St. Augustine took a very erroneous view of pure astrology, and it seems that he forgot that Our Saviour alluded to the "powers"—or virtues—in the celestial bodies—*vide* Matthew xxiv. 29, and Mark xiii. 25.

CHAPTER XXXVI.

ON SOLAR REVOLUTIONS.

THE "Solar Revolution" is a figure of the heavens drawn for the moment of the return of the Sun to the longitude (in degrees, minutes, and seconds), held by the great luminary at the moment of birth. It is, of course, purely symbolical, and its import is not so great when it differs greatly from the nature of the primary directions falling due in the year of life then being entered upon. It should be drawn for the birthplace; but if permanent residence has been taken up at a great distance from the birthplace, then an additional figure should be also computed to the latitude and longitude of such place, and compared with the former one.

Zadkiel I. thought that the chart of birth should be copied (in black ink), and the places of the Moon and planets at the Solar return marked in the various signs and houses (in red ink)—because the signification of the revolutional signification depends on the transits which coincide with the moment of the Sun's return to his place at birth, more or less nearly. The importance of such transits is great by reason of their occurring at or near the time of the earth being in the same part of her orbit as at the moment of birth. This teaching is sound. However, when a planet happens to be culminating, rising, setting, or on the lower meridian, at the moment of the Sun's return, it is found to have some signification by reason of its relative position, and all the more if configurated with the Sun, Moon, or some other celestial body. In all cases it is advisable to compare the revolutional figure with the nativity.

Revolutional figures are much more forceful, as a rule, when the same sign ascends as ascended at birth, and especially if the degree ascending is within a few degrees of the radical ascending degree. Every thirty-three years the ascending degree of the revolution approximates very closely to that rising at birth. For example, at the author's birth the sign Sagittarius 10° 29′ ascended (November 10th, 1840, 9h 20m a.m. London). At the thirty-third Solar return ♐ 11° 30′ ascended, and at the sixty-sixth, ♐ 13° 41′ ascended. In all, nine revolutional figures show the sign Sagittarius rising, down to that of

1910.

The Sun was but 8° 58′ from Jupiter at birth; and at the revolutions of 1851, 1863, 1875, 1887, 1899, and 1911, the same benefic planet will be found to be very near the Sun; the sidereal revolution of Jupiter being 11.9 years.

When the angles of the nativity are reversed at the Solar revolution it is not a promising indication. If, however, Jupiter or Venus be exactly rising or culminating the figure would be a favourable one, nevertheless.

Aspects have not any great power unless they are very close, *i.e.* within five degrees in the case of the Sun and Moon (applying), within two degrees if a major aspect between planets, or within one degree if a minor aspect. Sextiles are weak compared with conjunctions, parallel declinations, trines, and oppositions.

When more than one planet happens to be close to the cusp of the ascendant, descendant, upper or lower meridian, the revolution is a very important one.

The position of the Sun is of the greatest importance. The position of the Moon is very important when she is in the tenth house and in close aspect with the Sun or a planet. Next in importance is the position of the planet (if any) which was close to the ascendant or upper meridian at the moment of birth. Mars rising at birth and again at a Solar revolution "brings a return of an old complaint," so it is said. I have observed many instances wherein the ruddy planet, thus situated, presignified accidents or illness, or strife. Saturn, so situated, indicates accidents or illness, or else misfortune.

If at birth Saturn, Mars, or Uranus, was on the cusp of the sixth or seventh house and the degree of the zodiac held by such planet should ascend at the revolution, illness is pre-signified. If one of these planets was on the cusp of the third or ninth house of the nativity and its place ascends at a revolution, danger in travelling is threatened, in the ensuing year. When Jupiter, or Venus, is on the cusp of the second house of the nativity, the thirty-third and sixty-sixth Solar revolutions bring increase of income, or of wealth. If its place in the zodiac ascends or occupies the upper meridian at any revolution, the ensuing year proves a very successful one.

The Sun in opposition or quadrature with Saturn at a revolution pre-signifies illness or losses to the father; and if the Sun be in an angle and near the cusp, or in the eighth house, the father will be in danger. [The author's forty-second Solar revolution (Nov. 10th, 1882, 1h

40m p.m.) had the Sun in the eighth house, in opposition with Saturn, nearly, in Taurus 23° 4′, applying to conjunction with Mars in Scorpio 26° 45′, and separating from opposition with Neptune in Taurus 17° 24′,—the Sun was eclipsed at 11h 20m1 p.m. that day. His father died on the 9th May, 1883.]

The Moon, if eclipsed near the time of the Solar return, and afflicted by Saturn, Mars, or Uranus, indicates danger to the mother (or if the Moon was in the seventh house at birth, to the wife or husband, as the case may be); and especially if the place of an evil planet at birth ascends or if Saturn ascends at the moment of the Sun's return.

The Moon, if afflicted at birth by quartile, opposition or conjunction with Saturn or Mars, and if she transits the radical place of either of these planets at the moment of Solar return, serious risk of an injury to an eye, is pre-signified.

The Moon, in conjunction, quartile or opposition, with Saturn at the Solar revolution threatens rheumatism, influenza, or an accident. If the ☽ occupied a fixed sign at birth and applied to Saturn, there is grave risk of a malignant chronic disease setting in.

The place of the radical Moon, Mercury, or Uranus, ascending at the Solar return, there is a disposition to travel far, to be restless, or to indulge in some romantic exploit, that year.

The place of Venus—especially if ♀ was in Taurus or Libra, or in the ascendant or seventh house at birth—ascending at a Solar revolution, inclines to courtship and marriage. If the owner of the nativity is already married, an increase of family usually takes place in the course of the ensuing year of life. Anyone engaged in a profession or business under the rule of Venus may realise advancement, promotion, and increase of income.

Venus, or Jupiter, or both, exactly rising at a Solar revolution a good year for health and affairs may be anticipated, whether either of them ascended at birth or not.

THE FIRST HOUSE.—If the celestial body ruling the ascending sign of the nativity be found in the *seventh* house of the revolution, a single person is inclined towards marrying, more especially if a primary direction of Venus coincides. If in the *ninth* house, there is a disposition to travel; but if the significator is with Saturn or Mars it would be best to refrain from voyaging abroad.

SECOND HOUSE.—The ruler of the radical second house in the revolutional *second* and assisted by Jupiter favours the development of business and the acquirement of wealth; if afflicted by Saturn, Mars, or Uranus, precaution is needful against losses and being defrauded. In the *fourth*, some advantage may be gained from property in land or houses; if afflicted by Mars, extra precaution and insurance against fire is advisable, and fresh investments in lands, houses, or mines should be very small indeed. In the *eighth* some advantage may accrue under a will. In the *tenth*, good business will be done; if afflicted by Saturn losses will be suffered.

THIRD HOUSE.—If the ruler of the radical third be in the revolutional *eighth* house, and in conjunction with Saturn or Mars, travelling will not be profitable, and danger therein will be incurred if the ruler had the quartile or opposition of Mars or Saturn at birth. In the *ninth*, profitable journeys and good business are promised, unless the ruler receives the evil influence of ♂, ♄, ♅, or ♆. If the ruler of the radical third be Venus or Jupiter, and in the revolutional *tenth* house, business will be prosperous, and some public honour may be received.

FOURTH HOUSE.—If the ruler of the radical fourth house be a malefic planet, and in the revolutional *fourth*, or radical *eleventh*, and afflicted, the father will be in some serious danger. If in the revolutional *twelfth*, the owner of the nativity must beware of losses by a tenant, if he lets land or houses.

SIXTH HOUSE.—If the ruler of the radical sixth house be Saturn or Mars, and afflicted in the revolutional *third* or *ninth*, there is risk of illness as the result of a journey, or an accident in travelling, especially if the ruler is "hyleg." In the *tenth*, disputes may arise with the landlord, or (if in employment) with a master.

SEVENTH HOUSE.—The Moon or Venus in the revolutional seventh, and in conjunction or opposition with Mars, Saturn, or Uranus threatens a man's wife or *fiancee* with illness. If Saturn or Mars be in the radical seventh, very near the cusp, and in the revolutional *seventh* again, it threatens serious danger to the wife; and in women's nativities, the same to the husband. The ruler of the radical seventh in the revolutional *sixth*, and afflicted, domestic quarrels and misunderstandings ensue, Jupiter or Venus, ruler of the radical seventh and in the revolutional seventh, conjugal happiness is assured; in the case of a single person, the year will be a favourable one for marrying. If Saturn, Mars, or Uranus be ruler of the radical seventh and afflicting the ruler of the radical first in the revolutional tenth there is risk of loss of office, or business losses through an enemy. If the ruler of the radical seventh be in the revolutional *twelfth*, and afflicted, a single person should avoid marrying during the ensuing year; a debtor should beware of imprisonment. Emigration should *not* take place if an evil planet be in the *seventh*.

EIGHTH HOUSE.—If the Sun or Moon, whichever may be hyleg, be ruler of the radical *ascendant*, in the revolutional *eighth* house, and in conjunction, quartile, or opposition with Mars or Saturn, strict precaution must be taken against illness; and the countries and places ruled by the sign containing the hyleg at birth and in the revolutional figure, must be avoided that year. The ruler of the radical *eighth* in the revolutional *fourth*, and afflicted portends accidents, damage to property, and an ill time for buying land and houses. In the revolutional *seventh*, long journeys should not be taken alone, especially abroad, for if the nativity be a violent one, the owner of it may never return home safe and sound. In the *ninth*, if the ruler (of the radical eighth) be Mars, Saturn, Uranus, or Neptune, and afflicted therein, no journey abroad should be taken, for it may too probably prove fatal.* The ruler of the radical eighth a benefic and in the revolutional eighth, well configurated, promises benefits by a legacy, or by the partner in marriage coming into property.

NINTH HOUSE.—The Moon in the revolutional ninth house usually pre-signifies a sea voyage, more especially if at the time in *Cancer*, *Virgo*, *Scorpio* or *Pisces*. If the Moon be afflicted by Saturn or Mars, no sea voyage of long duration should be taken, if avoidable. The ruler of the radical ninth in the revolutional *fourth*, and afflicted, foreign journeys had best be avoided. If the ruler of the radical ninth be Jupiter or Venus, or if Mercury be with ♃ or ♀, in either the revolutional *seventh* or *ninth*, free from affliction and well configurated, emigration may be made with a good prospect of success, especially if a suitable primary direction should fall due about the same time as the Solar revolution under consideration.

Tenth HOUSE.—Saturn in the tenth house of the revolution, or elevated above the other celestial bodies near the upper meridian, threatens misfortunes, troubles, and anxiety of mind. If at the same time Saturn afflicts the Sun or Moon, and Mercury, professional and business men are only too likely to meet with serious reverses, or loss of

* Mr. G., whose nativity had *Scorpio* on the eighth cusp, had ♂ ☌ ♅ in the ninth of his 75th solar revolution. He went abroad to winter, although advised not to do so, and died in a foreign country. His health was delicate but not in any serious state when he left England. The fatal primary direction was ascendant conjunction Saturn.

income and of popularity, especially if an evil primary direction of Saturn be then operating in the nativity. Mars threatens troubles from an official, a magistrate, or a judge, or through being scandalised or libelled. Jupiter elevates and brings some honour or promotion. Venus brings social pleasures, advancement, and the friendship of ladies of wealth or rank. Mercury, well aspected, increases professional or business reputation and success. The Moon exactly on the upper meridian usually causes change of residence or of employment, or else a long journey. Changes will be beneficial or otherwise according to the nature of the celestial bodies with which the Moon may hold a conjunction, trine, or sextile aspect, on the one hand, or conjunction, quartile, or opposition on the other. If the ruler of the radical tenth house be the Sun, Moon, Venus, Jupiter, or Mercury, and located in the revolutional *first*, especially if the radical ascending sign be again ascending, and well configurated, it promises advancement, promotion, honours, and prosperity. In the *second*, good business and increase of substance. In the *third* or *ninth*, a good year for travelling on business. In the *tenth*, honours, promotion, and success. In the *eleventh*, new friends of position, and influential; and success to children.

ELEVENTH HOUSE.—If Jupiter or Venus be located in the revolutional eleventh house and in benefic aspect with the Sun, Moon, or Mercury in the ascendant new friends of good social status or wealth, will be made, in the ensuing year. If a conjunction of two of the infortunes, or of the Sun or Moon with Mars, Saturn, or Uranus, takes place in either the radical or revolutional eleventh house, a friend will be lost by death or some misfortune. A mutual sextile of the Sun and Moon from the ascendant and eleventh of either the radix or revolution would be of valuable help in bringing the influence of good friends to the benefit of the owner of the horoscope. The ruler of the radical eleventh afflicted in the revolutional *sixth* is said to pre-signify danger to a friend.

TWELFTH HOUSE.—If Mars, or Mercury afflicted by Mars, be ruler of the twelfth of the radix, and found on the cusp of the seventh house of either the radix or revolution, there is a great risk of incurring serious losses by the depredations of thieves and knaves, and of personal injury at the hands of highwaymen, in the ensuing year. If the ruler of the ascendant of the radix be more powerful and better aspected than that of the twelfth, there is a good prospect of overcoming such enemies. An evil planet ruler of the radical twelfth located in the revolutional second house pre-signifies loss of money; and loss of cattle to a breeder of them. In the *twelfth* some loss of or injury from cattle, or at the hands of a convict.

The last Solar revolution of King Edward VII. was remarkable for the proximity of the evil Saturn to the upper meridian and its elevation above all the other celestial bodies. Here are the elements of the revolution figure:

Time of the Sun's sixty-eighth return to the longitude held at the moment of birth, 10h 42m 3 p.m. of the 9th of November, 1909. R.A. of M.C. = 28° 53′, Taurus 1° 1′ culminating, and Leo 17° 9′ ascending. Sun in the fourth house, in ♏ 16° 54′ 18″, attended by Mercury in 3° 28′ of the same sign. Moon in the third house, in ♎ 12° 32′ (intercepted) attended by Jupiter in 5° 49′ of the same sign. Venus in the fifth house in ♑ 2° 44′. Mars close to the cusp of the ninth house, in ♓ 27° 11′. Saturn in the ninth house in ♈ 17° 45′, retrograde, receiving the application of the Moon by opposition aspect. Uranus on the cusp of the sixth house, in ♑ 17° 55′, in opposition, nearly, with Neptune in the twelfth house, in ♋ 19° 15′.

Saturn passed the meridian at 9h 56m p.m. (forty-six minutes only before the Sun's return to his place at birth), and was in the ninth, the house ruling long journeys, in quartile aspect with Uranus on the cusp of the sixth, the house of sickness, and receiving the opposition aspect of the Moon from the third, the house ruling short journeys. The indications that a serious risk would be incurred by his late Majesty venturing on a long journey abroad, during the ensuing year of life, were clear and unmistakeable. The primary directions operating in the following March to June (1910) also being serious for health and travelling, the author wrote the guardedly worded warning to the King's physicians, already quoted. At 9h 30m p.m. of March 6th, 1910, when King Edward started on his journey, the Moon was in ♑ 15°, exactly in the place of Mars at birth, close to the place of Uranus at the Solar revolution, and in quartile to the place of Saturn. At the time of his Majesty's demise the Moon was in ♈ 13° 50′, close to the place of Saturn at the Solar revolution!

At King Edward's sixty-fourth Solar revolution, viz. 11h 20.2m p.m. of November 9th, 1905, Leo 23° 36′ ascended, and Saturn was setting in ♒ 26° 17′, retrograde, the Sun had the semi-quartile aspect with Uranus, and the Moon had the quartile with Mars. His Majesty whilst shooting in Windsor Forest, on the 16th of the same month, put his foot into a rabbit burrow, and, slipping, fell to the ground and sprained his ankle. In April, 1906, during his holiday at Biarritz, the automobile in which his Majesty was travelling had the narrowest of escapes from collision with a runaway horse, an accident being avoided only by the dexterity of the driver. Again, while at Corfu, on the thirteenth of the same month the royal carriage came into collision with a cart driven by some drunken peasants, who were thrown out, and one of them was injured. Happily the King and Queen escaped injury. Three accidents thus happened within five months of the revolution under consideration.*

In URANIA, February, 1880, the author gave the horoscope of the Tsar Alexander II., who was born at Moscow, April 29th, 1818, at 10h a.m., *Aries* 7° 16′ on the M.C., and *Leo* 4° 42′ ascending. Mars was in the twelfth house (that ruling secret enemies), in semi-quartile with the Sun (mundo), and in zodiacal sesquiquadrate with the Moon in the eighth. The Sun (hyleg) had the mundane parallel of Saturn; and the ascending degree had the sesquiquadrate of Uranus. At the sixty-second Solar revolution, April 28th, 1880, 9h 40m a.m., Moscow, Mars was again in the twelfth house, in Cancer 9° 37′, in sextile with the Sun. Neptune was in Taurus 11° 38′ only three degrees from conjunction with the Sun. The Moon was in Sagittarius 25° 3′ close to the place of Neptune at birth, and only five degrees past that of Uranus, and her declination (24° 31′ S.) was in contra-parallel with that of Mars (24° 43′ N.) The Tsar was cruelly assassinated, on the 18th of March, 1881, at 62y. and 10m., arc = 62° 52′, under the operation of the primary direction of Sun rapt parallel Mars 63° 10′. If we take the Sun's semi-diameter 0° 16′ from this arc we have 62° 54′, for first contact, exactly coinciding with the awfully tragic death of that well-meaning monarch. The author wrote at p. 46 of URANIA that "the year 1881 indicates personal suffering and misfortunes—the Tsar will find it difficult indeed to weather the storm." The Solar eclipse of December 21st, 1880, fell in opposition to the place of Mars at the Solar return.

---

*At the author's sixty-filth Solar revolution, November 10th, 1905, 3h 40m 22s a.m., *Libra* 10° 16′ ascended, the ascending degree having the sesquiquadrate of Saturn in ♒ 26° 19′, and the quartile of Neptune in ♋ 10° 12′. On the 18th of the same month, a fall when alighting from a vehicle in the city of London, injured his right leg, and imminent risk of being run over the head by a following carriage, was incurred.

CHAPTER XXXVII.

ON SECONDARY DIRECTIONS.

THERE is no reliable evidence of any rational system of Astrology founded on mathematics before the first century, although Sir Isaac Newton, in his CHRONOLOGY, admitted that astrology was in existence nearly nine hundred years earlier than that period. It was about the year 133 that the TETRABIBLOS was compiled by Claudius Ptolemy, it is believed. Not until 1647 and 1657, when the Spanish monk, Placidus de Titus, published his great work, the PRIMUM MOBILE, were the principles enunciated in the TETRABIBLOS clearly understood. This work was translated into English by John Cooper, from the original Latin, and published in the year 1816. And in 1822, Ashmand published his translation of the TETRABIBLOS from the Greek into English. Prior to 1816 and 1822, the various translations of those valuable works, and especially those by Sibly, were wretched and misleading, and led to numerous errors on the part of Lilly, Colley, Sibly, Gadbury, White, and others (when they treated on nativities and the method of directing) who followed the erroneous Arabian system of mixing up the system of divination (horary questions), with the science of genethlialogy. It is lamentable to find that this Arabian folly is still taught and practised in certain publications of the present day.

Placidus most probably would not have regarded secondary directions as of the slightest importance had he not departed from Ptolemy's equation of arcs of primary direction and substituted for it that of adding the arc to the right ascension of the Sun at birth, and then determining in how many days after birth the Sun reached such R.A., and allowing for each day one year of life, and for every two hours one month.

"By some secondary means," wrote Placidus, "the aspects that are made to the luminaries and angles on those days, jointly assist the significators of the primary directions; for this reason, we say, that the days whereon these aspects happen are very powerful in those years which answer to those days and on which they depend. From these motions, in preference to the rest, appears the true, real, and hitherto unknown foundation of the *critical* or *climacterical* years; for the Moon almost every seventh day is placed in the critical place with respect to her place in the nativity. "We call these motions the secondary directions, to distinguish them from the primary and principal, and we are of opinion that Ptolemy, writing of annual places, is to be understood of the places of those motions, and when of the menstrual, hints at the places of the progression."

Yet modern practitioners of the Arabian and Chaldaean astrology regard Secondary Directions as Primary, and pass off the former alone as reliable, and without any arcs of primary direction which may happen to coincide, and without which the secondary directions are of not the slightest importance. I have never found any secondary directions effective in my own nativity.

While Zadkiel I. was investigating and writing on the science, in the first few years of his study of it, he paid some attention to secondary directions. Even then (in 1840) he wrote of their supposed effects as enduring "only for a week or two,"[1] and that "they are far less powerful than primary directions, and if these are opposed to them in nature, at the time, they have little or no effect." In some of his early almanacks Zadkiel I. gave some secondary directions, attending primary, in nativities of eminent persons; but he ceased to do so after 1845 (except in 1868, when he quoted two or three, which proved to be of no effect). When he found that the Ptolemaic *equation* of the arcs of primary direction came much nearer to the truth than the Placidian, he observed that the aid of no secondary direction was needed to ascertain when the influence of the primary one would take effect.

Secondary directions are nothing more than transits in the heavens on the days *after* birth. Whereas primary directions are all formed, as already shown, within a few hours of the moment of birth.

The attempt to galvanise into a semblance of life the dead Arabian system of judging nativities and computing "directions," made by practising astrologers who cannot, or will not take the time and trouble to compute nativities on the Ptolemaic and Placidian system, is to present a very imperfect, unsound, and incorrect description of the grand truths of Astrologia Sana.

In the nativity of his Majesty King George V., the Sun by secondary direction, would arrive at the quartile of the place of Saturn, at 43

[1] Grammar of Astrology, page 107.

years and seven and a half months (4.3 days and fifteen hours) after birth, which measures to January, 1910. The demise of King Edward VII. took place on the 6th of May, 1910. There were no other secondary directions falling due in the same year except Moon conjunction Mercury = November, 1910. This "direction" of the Sun to the square of Saturn did *not* indicate the time when the primary direction of ☉ □ ♄ zodiac, 44° 57′ = May, 1910, would operate, for it measured four months short of the bereavement. The student on comparing this secondary direction with the primary ones falling due at the time of his Majesty's accession to the throne will perceive how high the Placidian towers over the halting and defective Arabian system.

Secondary directions are computed as follows:

RULE.—Find the hour, by proportion, by means of Zadkiel's Ephemeris for the year of birth, at which the Sun, Moon, or planet forms an aspect with the place of one of the celestial bodies, or the degree in the Midheaven or Ascendant, and subtract from it the day and hour of birth, and the difference is the arc of direction. Convert the arc into time by taking the number of the days after birth as that of years, and allowing one month for every two hours.

There is no need to give an example of so simple a calculation.

In conclusion it may be said that the secondary as compared with the primary system of directing is—

"As moonlight is to sunlight,
And as water unto wine."

CHAPTER XXXVIII.

ON LUNATIONS, ECLIPSES, AND PROGRESSES.

"Alack our terrene Moon
Is now eclipsed; and it portends alone
The fall of Antony."—SHAKESPEARE

LUNATIONS are the NEW and FULL MOONS which immediately precede or coincide with the occurrence of dangerous accidents, severe illnesses, or events of great importance to individuals or nations.

When a new or full moon takes place close to the longitude held by the Sun, Venus, or Jupiter at birth, some benefit usually coincides, or follows within the space of a fortnight or so. When the lunation falls in the radical place of Saturn, Mars, Uranus, or Neptune, accidents, illness, or trouble may be experienced, especially if it coincides with the period of operation of an adverse primary direction in the nativity.

ECLIPSES.—An eclipse of the Sun or Moon falling close to the place of either luminary at birth, or in opposition thereto, or near conjunction or opposition with a malefic planet (in the heavens), pre-signifies troubles or ill-health, especially if such eclipse falls in the place of the hyleg, and happens to be visible at the birthplace or the place of residence at the time. If falling within five to eight degrees of the place of the Sun or Moon at birth, some trouble is threatened, but to a less extent than when falling within two degrees. As great eclipses affect the multitude generally, serious results may follow, although no evil primary direction may fall due in the same year of life of the individual whose nativity is affected by them.

A great eclipse falling in, or within two or three degrees of, the place of Jupiter or Venus at birth, pre-signifies some honour, distinction, increase of income, or improvement of health, as the case may be. It may bring marriage to pass, in the case of an unmarried person of full age. The kind of benefit is usually indicated by the accidental position (in the nativity) of the benefic planet and its configurations.

Eclipses taking place within two or three days, if of the Sun, and within two to four hours, if of the Moon, of the time of the Sun's return to his longitude in the nativity, are of the greatest importance, and the effects are of longer endurance than at other times, as a rule.

The annular eclipse of the Sun of the 19th of October, 1865, took place very nearly in the degree of longitude held by the Sun at the birth of Lord Palmerston, and that illustrious statesman passed away ere that eclipse attained its greatest phase. Zadkiel I. foretold the dangerous character of that eclipse as follows: "This eclipse will, I expect, put an end to his (Lord Palmerston's) power, and endanger his life."[1]

Lord Palmerston was born on the 20th of October, 1784, hour not stated. Here are the places of the celestial bodies at Solar noon of that day, at Greenwich:

☉ 27♎44	☽ 12♑27	☿ 11♎40
♀ 16♏57	♂ 20♎34	♃ 28♒6
♄ 18♑10	♅ 16♋21	♆ 14♎10

The Sun was, no doubt, hyleg, and his close trine (120°) aspect with the benefic Jupiter gave Lord Palmerston that vitality, energy, jovialness, and juvenility, for which he was so famous—enabling him to attain the ripe age of eighty-one years. It is remarkable that at his birth seven of the celestial bodies were in cardinal signs.

In the chapter on Equating Arcs of Primary Direction, it has been already shown how the Solar eclipses of 1902 and 1910 affected the health of his late Majesty King Edward VII.

In STAR LORE, December, 1897, the author mentioned that during the illness of her Majesty Queen Alexandra in February and March, 1867, the Sun was eclipsed in Pisces 15° 23′, near the place of Jupiter (♓ 24° 19′) at birth, and that immediately after an improvement set in, and the attack of acute rheumatism gradually passed off. That severe illness was due, astrologically speaking, to the primary direction of Saturn parallel Moon, in the zodiac, direct 22° 20′.

In the same edition of STAR LORE, the author wrote that "the Solar eclipse of the 22nd of January, 1898, falls close to the place of Saturn in this nativity. Happily, no evil effects need be apprehended, beyond suffering and danger to a near relation."

The Queen of Denmark, the mother of Queen Alexandra, died in September, 1898.

---

[1] *Zadkiel's Almanac* for 1865, p. 48.

It is related of Charles D'Escaro, Bishop of Langres, that he always fainted at an eclipse of the Moon, and remained insensible as long as it lasted. When he was very old and infirm an eclipse took place, the venerable prelate fainted, as usual, and he did not revive again.

It was the inconvenient idiosyncracy of the great Lord Verulam always to faint at the commencement of a lunar eclipse.

Progresses consist of the procession of the Moon, by allowing an embolismic or synodical lunation, consisting of twenty-nine and a half days, for a year of life. The Moon at the progress is at exactly the same distance in longitude from the Sun as at the moment of birth.

The Moon finishes twelve lunations and enters the thirteenth eleven days less than one year after birth; finishes twenty-four lunations in twenty-two days less than two years after birth; completes thirty-six lunations (corresponding to the age of thirty-six years) in thirty-three days less than three years after birth, and so on.

In Zadkiel's Almanac, 1908, the author directed attention to the fact that at the sixtieth lunar progress of King Edward VII., September 16th, 1846, 7h 16m a.m., G.M.T., when the Moon was at the same distance, 47° 28′, from the Sun as at the moment of birth, the Sun was within two degrees of exact conjunction with Mars in the sign Virgo (in the eighth house of the royal nativity), in opposition to the place of Uranus, and in parallel declination with both Mars and Uranus—thus accounting for the serious illness, and the surgical operation on that part of the body ruled by the Moon in Virgo at birth. Moreover, on the 4th of October, 1846, at 10h 6m p.m. the Moon formed the opposition with the Sun, and by proportion, this measured to and took effect in the latter half of June, 1902, when the operation was undergone. Here follow the places of the celestial bodies at that critical lunar progress:

☉ 23♍1	☽ 5♌33	☿ 6♍26
♀ 0♍20	♂ 21♍2	♃ 16♊3
♄ 25♒35	♅ 13♈3	♆ 26♒4

The Moon is seen to be in semi-quartile aspect with Mars at the time of the lunation, the Sun, Mars and Mercury are all in the sixth, the house of illness. Between the times of occurrence of the sixtieth and sixty-first progresses there is a space of 714 hours. Then say: As 714h: 447h : : 365¼d : 229 days. Reckoning from the 9th November, 1901, 229 days we find that the Moon opposition Sun (full moon) of October 4th, 1846, measures to June 26th, 1902.

At the author's fourth lunar progress, March 8th, 1841, the Sun was exactly in the place of Uranus at birth, and in opposition to that of Mars, and in quartile to that of Saturn. My father was seized with sciatica of so severe a character that it became chronic, despite the skill of the eminent physician—Sir B. Brodie—who attended him, in 1845. At my fifth lunar progress, April 6th, 1841, the Sun was in trine aspect with Jupiter, and in my sixth year (1846) my father recovered his health.

CHAPTER XXXIX.

ON TRANSITS.

A TRANSIT, astrologically speaking, is the passing of the Sun, Moon, or a planet over the place—degree and minute of longitude—of a celestial body, or the degree in the upper meridian, at the moment of birth.

Those transits which take place on or about the birthday anniversary—and more especially if the celestial body in transit happens to be rising, culminating, setting, or on the lower meridian at the time of Solar return—are the most powerful.

When transits are opposed in nature to that of the primary directions operating at the same time, they can have but little effect.

Transits usually combine the influences of the body in transit and the one whose place is affected. They sometimes hasten or retard the operation of a primary direction about to operate. For example, if by primary direction, the Sun is in conjunction with Saturn, if a transit of Saturn over either the place of the Sun or of Saturn at birth takes place a few weeks before the arc of direction is complete, such transit usually brings to a focus the influence of such direction.

Transits over the ascending and descending degrees of nativities in high latitudes cannot be relied upon, except in the case of one of the three last degrees of Virgo or one of the three first of Libra ascending.

The student is advised to look to the declination of the transiting body at the time of transit, because if it differs widely (by reason of the body having much latitude, or such as is of opposite name to that of the transitted body) from the declination of the body over which the transit takes place such transit is necessarily very weak. If there is a close parallel of declination at the time of transit, the effects are greater.

Transits of the planets Saturn and Jupiter over the place of the Sun or Moon near the birthday anniversary usually continue in force for a few weeks. Transits of Mars and Uranus generally act very suddenly and punctually.

The transit of a superior planet at a time when it is "stationary," is much more forceful than when it is quick in motion.

The second transit of a superior planet after retrogradation is usually much more powerful in its effects than the first.

When the Moon has much latitude at birth, transits over her place are of little effect unless the transiting body has latitude of the same name and nearly as great. In all cases the closer the approximation to the exact parallel of declination, the greater is the effect of the transit. A planet in the ascendant or tenth house, near the cusp, at birth, is more powerful in transit than when it is cadent, or far removed from one of the angles.

At the moment of my birth the Moon was in Taurus 27° 8′, with latitude 4° 59′ N., and declination 24° 23′ N. On the 6th of October, 1879, Mars was stationary in Taurus 28° 48′. My mother, who had been in a debilitated state of health for some months previously, became suddenly seriously worse on the 9th, and died on the 14th of October, 1879. Saturn was retrograde in Aries 11° 41′ on the day of bereavement, in opposition to the degree in the midheaven of my nativity, Libra 10°.

THE GENERAL EFFECTS OF TRANSITS.—The following is a brief sketch of the general effects of transits when not opposed in nature to the coinciding primary directions.

THE MOON'S TRANSITS.

The Moon passing (at the Solar revolution) over her own place at birth, and well aspected by Venus or Jupiter or the Sun, denotes pleasant journeys, good health, and peace of mind. If she be evilly aspected by the infortunes, vexations, fruitless journeys, and annoyance from vulgar people, may probably be experienced.

The Moon passing over the radical place of Mercury, inclines the native to travel, gives him active and profitable employment, and, if he be a literary character, gain and credit by his writings. If, however, the Moon be evilly aspected, the reverse of these benefits may occur.

The Moon passing over the place of Venus is indicative of a pleasurable time and gain through the good offices of ladies and relatives. But if Venus was afflicted at birth, suffering in mind and body may result.

The Moon passing over the place of the Sun (at his revolution) imports troubles and quarrels with employers, or magnates (unless extremely well aspected). The native will be disposed to make changes; and he may suffer in his eyes. If both the luminaries be well aspected by the fortunes, he may gain preferment and comparative wealth.

The Moon passing over the place of Mars predicates trouble and suffering in mind and body. The native will be involved in quarrels and controversies; and will suffer through martial persons and affairs. He must be very wary of thieves, fire, and gunshot wounds. If Mars was in sextile or trine to either luminary at birth, and the employment of the native of a martial character, less serious evils will result. If the Moon be afflicted at the revolution, danger to life is threatened.

The Moon passing over the place of Jupiter brings gain and an improved state of health; also friendship of rich persons, new friends, etc.; in many cases birth of a child.

The Moon passing over the place of Saturn brings sickness, sadness, or danger of an accident (according to the position of ♄ at birth). In some cases danger by water, or of imprisonment. It will be a bad year for engaging in building, mining, or any other kind of speculations. The wife or mother may suffer.

The Moon passing over the place of Uranus brings sudden changes, and generally a family loss. In a man's nativity it frequently causes a serious misunderstanding with his wife or sweetheart.

Mercury's Transits.

Mercury in conjunction with the Sun (at the revolution) and well aspected, especially if stationary, will produce prosperous and active employment, journeys, and literary distinction. If afflicted, no good can result, and the native may suffer through knavery, or through attacks of press writers.

Mercury passing over the place of the Moon (at the Solar revolution) will produce journeys, and a busy year generally.

Mercury passing over his own radical place, and stationary, brings gain by ☿ men and affairs, journeys, trade, etc.

Mercury passing over the place of Venus inclines the native to indulge in pleasure, the society of ladies, music, the drama, etc. He may have a child born.

Mercury passing over the radical place of Mars, and evilly aspected, leads to evil conduct; and produces quarrels, troubles, and libels. If well aspected by the fortunes, less mischief will result, and the native may gain by martial pursuits. In either case he must beware of fraud.

Mercury passing over the radical place of Jupiter gives honour, active business, and some prosperity. A good year for literary pursuits.

Mercury passing over the radical place of Saturn will too often produce vexation, deception, fraud and consequent loss; unless ☿ be well aspected by the fortunes, in such case gain by Saturnine pursuits, lands, buildings, or mines may result.

Mercury passing over the radical place of Uranus will not do any harm unless he be afflicted, when mischief will arise through ☿ or ♅ characters.

TRANSITS OF VENUS.

Venus in conjunction with the Sun, at the revolution, will bring honour, pleasure, and the favour of women and rich persons. But if ☿ be evilly aspected trouble will result.

Venus passing over the radical place of the Moon brings gain, and favour of ladies of quality, and a pleasurable time. If afflicted, however, extravagance and dissipation may result, especially if the ☽ was in ♏ or ♓ at birth.

Venus passing over the radical place of Merciry gives gain through men of science, literary persons, and by trade; the favour of young persons and ladies.

Venus passing over the place of Mars, unless well aspected, inclines to dissipation, and suffering may result therefrom.

Venus passing over the place of Jupiter renders the native jovial, and fortunate during the ensuing year of his life. If ♃ was angular at birth, or with the Moon, this transit will bring great gain.

Venus passing over the place of Saturn, and well aspected, will incline the native to pleasure and bring him gain. But if ♀ be evilly aspected, evil tendencies, and loss or ill-health will result.

Venus passing over the place of Uranus, unless she be well aspected, will bring troubles in love or matrimonial affairs.

TRANSITS OF MARS.

Mars in conjunction with the Sun (at the revolution) denotes affliction, quarrels, and possibly an accident accompanied with loss of blood. The native should act with great caution and prudence in everything. The sextile or trine of Mars to the Sun gives a prosperous year; to a monarch victory over enemies.

Mars passing over the place of the Moon, causes losses, quarrels, ill-health to the native or to a female relative, and sometimes leads him into bad courses. Travelling and active employment are also promised. The good aspects of Mars to the Moon, or to her radical place, promise activity, gain, and travelling; to a sailor or soldier honour and promotion.

Mars passing over the radical place of Mercury, unless evilly aspected, gives an active, busy, and tolerably prosperous year. If he be afflicted, quarrels and loss are threatened.

Mars passing over the place of Venus inclines the native to loose conduct, and involves him. in troubles and discredit, and often ill-health, too, if ♂ was with or in opposition with ♀ at birth.

Mars passing over the place of Jupiter will produce gain and a change for the better, generally, unless he be evilly aspected by Saturn or Uranus—for, in such case, quarrels with the clergy, or magistrates, will result.

Mars passing over the place of Saturn often causes troubles, delay, and difficulty in gaining employment, and ill-health or accidents. The native's father may suffer, also.

Mars passing over the place of Uranus brings sudden and serious mischief, particularly if ♅ was in evil aspect with ☉, ☽, M.C., or ascendant, at birth. The native must beware of accidents.

JUPITER'S TRANSITS.

Jupiter in conjunction or parallel declination with the Sun (at the revolution), gives honours and gain from superiors, according to the social position of the native. To women such a configuration often brings marriage, advancement to the husband, or birth of a son. But if Jupiter be evilly configurated with the malefics, evil will result, such as quarrels with men in power, and a bad state of health if the Sun be hyleg.

Jupiter passing over the radical place of the Moon, or in conjunction with her at the solar revolution, gives health of body, peace of mind, increase of substance, honours, popularity, pleasure, and birth of a child.

Jupiter passing over the place of Mercury shows gain by ☿ men and affairs; augments religious feeling, and inclines to studious habits.

Jupiter passing over the place of Venus gives mirth, pleasure, gain, credit, and the favour of ladies of means.

Jupiter passing over the place of Mars gives new friends of a martial character, journeys, and increase of business. If badly aspected, losses and troubles ensue.

Jupiter passing over his own radical place, when angular, or in good configuration with either of the luminaries, brings honours, new friends, office or employment, advancement of reputation, and general prosperity.

Jupiter passing over the place of Saturn, if well aspected, gives gain, peace of mind, and benefits from ♄ people and affairs. If both ♃ and ♄ were badly situated at birth, no great good can result.

Jupiter passing over the place of Uranus promises unexpected and sudden benefits, success in scientific pursuits, and travelling. But if ♅ afflicted the ☉ or ☽ at birth, this transit may bring loss and trouble.

SATURN'S TRANSITS.

Saturn in conjunction or parallel declination with the Sun (at the revolution) will bring disputes with persons in authority, loss of reputation, pecuniary difficulties, and a bad state of health (if ☉ be hyleg). To a woman, this transit is of very evil import, for loss of her father or her husband, or defamation of character, is threatened, especially if ♄ be *stationary*.

Saturn passing over the radical place of the Moon, or in conjunction with her at the revolution, signifies danger in travelling either by land or water; affliction of mind, body, and estate; and quarrels with ♄ persons. A near relative (female) will suffer and may die.

Saturn passing over the place of Mercury[1], if the latter planet was angular at birth, the native becomes inventive, and prospers generally. If weak, or afflicted, this transit will very probably involve the native in quarrels with ☿ and ♄ people; and illness may also result.

Saturn passing over the place of Venus brings trouble to the native, and often to his wife, mother, or sister, also. He may also become involved in some scandal.

Saturn passing over the place of Mars, and well aspected, gain by martial men and pursuits will result. If badly aspected the native will be in danger from thieves, highwaymen, and quarrelsome persons.

Saturn passing over the place of Jupiter brings the native into favour with rich and powerful persons, merchants, or clergymen, and he will be prosperous—unless ♃ was much afflicted at birth.

---

[1] At the commencement of the fatal illness of the Prince Consort ♄ passed over the place of ☿ in the ascendant of the nativity.

Saturn passing over his own radical place, and well aspected, denotes gain by houses, land, buildings, or mines. In some cases a legacy is promised.

Saturn passing over the place of Uranus, and well aspected, renders the native ingenious, studious of occult sciences, and eccentric. But if badly aspected a family loss is threatened, and other troubles, also, may result.

TRANSITS OF URANUS.

Uranus in conjunction or parallel declination with the Sun (at the revolution), frequently signifies a family loss, pecuniary difficulties, or accidents. If ☉ be hyleg, ill-health of a peculiar character will result.

Uranus passing over the radical place of the Moon, or in conjunction with her at the revolution, brings sudden changes, family losses, journeys, or sudden removals. At the same time, it inclines the native to investigate occult matters.

Uranus passing over the place of Mercury inclines the native to pursue occult science; and if afflicted, brings troubles in connexion with ☿ affairs and employment.

Uranus passing over the place of Venus bring troubles in love or matrimonial affairs; a (female) relative will suffer, and may die.

Uranus passing over the place of Mars brings sudden and serious mischief; in some cases, danger to life (if afflicting the ☉ at the same time).

Uranus passing over the place of Jupiter involves the native in dispute with religious persons; if well aspected pecuniary gain will result.

Uranus passing over the place of Saturn causes sudden troubles, and often danger to the father or a near relative.

Uranus passing over his own radical place, and in good aspect to ☉ or ☽, brings sudden and unexpected benefits. His evil aspects produce troubles, family losses, and pecuniary difficulties.

TRANSITS OF NEPTUNE.

Neptune's chief effects seem to lie in the direction of Crises, as was shown in an article in URANIA (1880).

Personally, the transit of Neptune over the opposition of the Sun in my nativity (Scorpio 18° 5½′), in 1883 coincided with the death of my talented father, on the 9th of May in that year, when that distant planet was in Taurus 18° 31′. An annular eclipse of the Sun, invisible in England, took place on the 10th of November, 1882, ten hours after the Sun had returned (on that day) to his place at my birth, the great luminary being then in opposition to Neptune in Taurus 17° 24′, and applying to the same aspect with Saturn in Taurus 23° 4′, and being attended by Mars in Scorpio 26° 43′. My forty-third year was over-clouded by the long illness of my father, and it was decidedly an unfortunate one.

Neptune in ☌ or par. dec. ☉ at the Solar Revolution pre-signifies a critical time for health, if the Sun was hyleg at birth; otherwise, a crisis in affairs, to advantage if the Sun was in an angle or in trine with ♃ or with ♀ or ♃ at birth. If ☉ was in ♋, ♏, or ♓, a sea voyage soon follows.

Neptune in transit over the place of the Moon at birth inclines to travelling; and if ☽ be hyleg debility of health is threatened.

Neptune over the place of Mercury pre-signifies restlessness, a change of residence or occupation, and financial troubles.

Neptune over Venus indicates for young people a romantic attachment; for others, some advantages attended with much expense and some domestic trouble or anxiety.

Neptune over Mars threatens (in ♋, ♏, or ♓), danger by water, in travelling, and serious disputes.

Neptune over Jupiter is advantageous—unless ♃ was much afflicted by ♄ or ♂ at birth—and promises either advancement or increase of income.

Neptune over Saturn threatens disasters; if in *Libra* falls. Caution will be needed in all new transactions.

Neptune over Uranus pre-signifies accidents more or less serious according to the relative position and aspects of these two planets at birth. Scientific men and inventors will gain kudos under this influence.

CHAPTER XL.

ON THE EFFECTS OF PRIMARY DIRECTIONS.

"Knowledge by favour sent
Down from the empyrean, to forewarn
Us timely."—MILTON.

A NATIVITY having been computed and rectified if necessary, and the primary directions for a series of years having been tabulated an attempt must be made to forecast the probable effects of those directions. The experience of centuries has afforded us some general rules to this end.

Directions may be of a fortunate or an unfortunate character; they may be powerful or feeble. The student has already learnt that certain aspects are fortunate, that certain others are usually unfortunate, and that conjunctions and parallels are convertible. He has also learnt that certain planets and stars possess good influences, that certain others possess evil influences; and that some of their relative positions are more powerful than others. He has now to learn that the strength or weakness of every "direction" depends on the position of the body directed in the radix (horoscope), and that of the planet to which the moderator (Sun, Moon, M.C., or Asc.) is directed. A planet which is angular is more powerfully situated, and much more powerful in direction, than another planet cadent. A planet culminating is elevated above, and is therefore more powerful than the rest of the heavenly bodies. A planet cadent is not so weak if it be in trine with a moderator. The planet receiving the application of the Moon (either by conjunction, parallel, sextile, trine, or opposition) is more powerful than any other planet which is not angularly posited. A benefic which may happen to be in close conjunction, square, opposition, or parallel with Saturn or Mars cannot be very effective for good by direction—unless the benefic be angular and elevated above the malefic. In nativities those aspects from which the more swiftly moving planets are separating are found to be much more powerful than those aspects to which they are applying. The semi-square aspect in directions is often found to be quite as powerful as the square when formed by a planet in one of the angles. One direction operating alone (unless the body directed be angular) cannot effect much unless it should happen to be aided by a transit of a superior planet, or by an eclipse. Events of the greatest importance usually occur under a train of directions. A train of good directions may bring (or indicate), an accession of property; but if an evil direction to the hyleg should fall near the same time, ill-health may prevent the enjoyment of the benefit.

GENERAl RULES FOR JUDGING OF THE PROBABLE EFFECTS OF DIRECTIONS.

A good (primary) direction indicates benefit or gain by or through the kind of persons or things signified by the body directed, varied according to the sign (and house, in some cases) in which it was situated in the radix. An evil direction signifies loss, trouble, or illness. In the case of young children, the directions of the Midheaven, Sun, and Moon in their nativities operate sometimes on their parents. In the case of a married woman, directions of the Sun affect her husband, and *vice versá*.

The SUN'S directions affect the health if it be hyleg, honour, advancement, favour of the great, the father, and, in the case of a married woman, her husband.

The MOON'S directions affect the health (if ☽ be hyleg), sometimes mental as well as physical; the estate, family affairs, the mother, sister, or wife.

The ASCENDANT'S directions affect the personal health, the estate, and employment. Ascendant conjunction Mars often coincides with death of a parent.

The MID-HEAVEN'S directions affect the business, profession, or employment, honour, credit, character; and in children's nativities, the parents.

THE SUN'S DIRECTIONS.

The ☉ ☌ or *par. dec.* ☽.—These directions generally impair the health; the head, eyes, and stomach often being affected. Changes or journeys take place. If the Moon be angular and well aspected at birth, the native may gain preferment. If he should marry, the marriage will be fortunate or unfortunate according to the position of the Moon at birth.

☉ ⚹ or △ ☽.—Favour and friendship of rich and powerful persons; advancement, journeys, change of residence, or a public appointment. If ☽ be strong at birth, the native may marry a well endowed wife, or have a child born.

☉ □ or ☍ ☽.—Troubles and losses, enmity of a person in power and authority, conjugal strife, ill-health, mental anxiety, and discredit are pre-signified. If either luminary be hyleg, an eruptive fever, or ophthalmia may attend.

The ☉ ☌ or *par. dec.* ☿.—A busy period, profitable or unprofitable according to the strength and aspects of ☿ at birth. Travelling, writing, and speculating. The birth of a child will, most probably, take place. If ☿ be fortunate, gain, fame, and prosperity are promised. If unfortunate, a lawsuit may result. If ☉ be hyleg, a dangerous illness is threatened, accompanied by cerebral symptoms of a serious nature.

The ☉ ⚹ or △ ☿.—Much business, travelling, or change of residence, and prosperity. Mercurial persons acquire fame and advancement under the influence of these directions.

The ☉ □ ☿.—Fraud, forgery, false accusations, lawsuits, or ill-health are threatened. The native should be wary in dealing with strangers while this direction is in force.

The ☉ ☌ or *par. dec.* ♀.—A pleasurable and profitable period, some extravagance indulged in. A child may be born to the native. If ♀ was angular and well aspected in the nativity, prosperity, and favours from ladies of wealth and position. Ladies frequently marry under this influence.

The ☉ ⚹ or △ ♀.—A happy and prosperous time; indulgence in music, the drama, courtship, etc.; or birth of a child. Single ladies receive offers of marriage, and (if their nativities promise marriage) often marry under this influence.

The ☉ □ ♀.—This brings losses, extravagance, and in some cases dissipation, and consequent suffering; disappointment in love or matrimony, etc.

The ☉ ☌, *par. dec.*, □ or ☍ ♂.—Danger (if ☉ be hyleg) of acute fever, wounds, accidents, haemorrhage, bites of dogs, burns, scalds, etc., according to the position of ♂. The native should carefully avoid quarrels and disputes, pay particular attention to health, and beware of fire (and gunshot wounds if ♂ be in ♐).

The ☉ ⚹ or △ ♂.—Military preferment, distinction in surgery, travelling, etc., according to the native's position and profession. A monarch may become involved in war, and gain victories. Ladies receive offers from martial men.

The ☉ ☌, *par. dec.*, ✶, or △ ♃.—Health, peace of mind, new friends, increase of estate, honours, and general prosperity. Lawyers, churchmen, and merchants gain under this influence. Birth of a son may take place. In the nativities of single women, this influence often brings marriage about.

The ☉ □ or ☍ ♃.—Losses, affronts, and ill-success in legal proceedings. Unless ♃ be afflicted in the nativity, not much harm will be done. In some cases, pleurisy or plethora results. Some benefit may be experienced eventually.

The ☉ ☌ *par. dec.*, □ or ☍ ♄.—Affliction of mind, body, or estate. The heart often becomes weak, and its action deranged, under this influence. Affairs go wrong. If ♄ be ascending in the horoscope, there is danger of accidents or wounds. It is an evil time for travelling, and in some cases there is a likelihood of shipwreck. Monarchs are likely to suffer from conspirators and assassins. Tradesmen are liable to bankruptcy. The father of the native will suffer.

The ☉ ✶ or △ ♄.—Benefits by ♄ people and affairs; a good time for miners, builders, agriculturists, etc. If the nativity promise a legacy, it may now be obtained.

The ☉ ☌, *par. dec.* □ or ☍ ♅.—Losses, troubles, or ill-health, according to the position of ♅ in the nativity. An unfortunate time for change of residence, journeying, and speculating. A lady may lose her lover or her husband, under this influence. Neurasthenia may result.

The ☉ ✶ or △ ♅.—Travelling, general prosperity, active employment; gain by an invention.

The ☉ ☌ or *par. dec.* Aldebaran.—Soldiers and surgeons gain preferment and distinction; but it is said to be not of long continuance.

☉ ☌, □ or ☍ ♆.—A crisis in affairs. If the Sun be hyleg, ill-health. Not a favourable time to travel.

☉ ✶ or △ ♆.—Benefits in business or profession; travelling.

The ☉ ☌ or *par. dec.* Antares.—Military preferment, accomipanied by danger. Fever, injury to the eyes, and violent assaults are threatened.

The ☉ ☌ or *par. dec.* Arista.—Advancement, wealth (if the nativity promise such), and happiness.

The ☉ ☌ or *par. dec.* Asselli.—Acute fever, danger by fire, disgrace, imprisonment, and calamities.

The ☉ ☌ or *par. dec.* Regulus.—Preferment, gain, ill-health if Sun be hyleg; and the father suffers. [Lilly says he knows most of this to be true from experience.]

THE MOON'S DIRECTIONS.

The ☽ ☌ or *par. dec.* ☉.— Danger of fever, or mortal illness, if ☽ be hyleg and if ☉ was afflicted at birth. Otherwise, mental troubles, reverses, and discredit. But if ☉ be strong and well configurated with Jupiter or Venus at birth, a change for the better will take place.

The ☽ ⚹ or △ ☉.—New friends, preferment, profitable employment, favour of rich ladies, and popularity. This influence often brings marriage, public employment, and travelling. To monarchs it brings renown, honourable peace, victories, and valuable alliances.

The ☽ □ or ☍ ☉.—This is always evil, producing mental and physical suffering, converting the love of some woman to hatred; foreshowing trouble or illness of wife, sister, or mother; and tending to produce dissensions with employers, persons in authority, etc.

The ☽ ☌ or *par. dec.* ☿.[1]—This brings a journey, or voyage by sea, especially if either ☽ or ☿ was in the 3rd or 9th house, at birth. It brings an active, busy, and prosperous period, if ☿ be fortunate; if unfortunate, loss by fraud, theft, libels, etc. If ☽ be hyleg and ☿ afflicted, danger of disease or accident.

The ☽ ⚹ or △ ☿.—Success in literary pursuits, business, accounts, travelling, and litigation. A child may be born.

The ☽ □ or ☍ ☿.—This brings danger to life if ☽ be hyleg and ☿ afflicted, at birth. It always brings either lawsuits or controversies; often loss of employment; troubles by children and young persons, and ill-success in travelling.

The ☽ ☌ or *par. dec.* ♀.—A pleasant, fortunate, and happy period. Marriage frequently occurs under this influence.

The ☽ ⚹ or △ ♀.—This influence brings happiness, pleasure-seeking, courtship, or matrimony, favours of ladies and rich persons, birth of children, or marriage of children. To monarchs it brings peace, new allies, etc.

---

[1] If in directing the Moon with latitude in the zodiac, to the *conjunction* of a planet if she have *latitude* of an opposite nature to that of the planet, at birth, so that the difference shall amount to 5°, such direction is weak. In the case of the ☍, if the latitudes be of the same name, the direction is weak, and *vice versá*.

The ☽ □ or ☍ ♀.—This brings scandal, discredit; illness of wife, sister, or mother; extravagance, and often personal suffering. If the native should marry under this influence, he will not be very happy or fortunate in marriage. To women, this often brings serious internal complaints.

The ☽ ☌, *par. dec.*, □, or ☍ ♂.—This brings either accidents or illness, according to the position of ♂. Loss by theft, fire, violence, or fraud is threatened. If ☽ be hyleg there is danger, and, if ♂ be in a fiery sign, it may be by fire, wounds, bites, or gunshot; if in a watery sign, by drowning; if in an airy sign, by fall from a height; if in an earthy sign, by fever, smallpox, dysentery, diphtheria, etc. The face and eyes are sometimes injured under this influence. Marriage under it is unfortunate. To monarchs, it brings war, and risk of, if not actual defeat.

The ☽ ⚹ or △ ♂.—A desire for active out-door exercise, sports, horse-riding, martial exercises, shooting, and travelling. Men sometimes marry under this influence. Monarchs increase their army or navy, and may gain victories.

The ☽ ☌ *par. dec.*, ⚹, or △ ♃.—Health of body and mind, preferment, advancement, new friends; increase of business, university distinction, the gaining of degrees or diplomas, etc., according to the native's profession and position. This influence assists in producing marriage to either sex.

The ☽ □ or ☍ ♃.—This brings extravagant expenditure, and dissensions with employers. If the ☽ be hyleg, and if afflicted, at birth, pleurisy, etc., may attack the native. Unless ♃ be much afflicted, no material harm will be done in any way, and any present evil may eventually bring recompense.

The ☽ ☌, *par. dec.*, □, or ☍ ♄.—This influence produces chronic maladies, and danger to life if ☽ be hyleg. Sciatica, atonic gout, rheumatic fever, gastric fever, or mental derangement may follow. In any case, either pecuniary loss, or death of a fair relative results. The native should act with extreme caution in all his affairs.

The ☽ ⚹ or △ ♄.—Favour and friendship of old persons; a legacy; or success in building, mining, or farming.

The ☽ ☌ *par. dec.*, □, or ☍ ♅.—Danger of an accident or nervous illness if ☽ be hyleg. Otherwise danger to the mother, wife, or sister; or separation from the wife. Pecuniary loss, and sudden troubles.

The ☽ ⚹ or △ ♅.—A prosperous time for business. Gain in an unexpected manner. A journey if either ☽ or ♅ be cadent. This influence often gives an inclination to study astrology and occult matters.

The ☽ ☌, □, or ☍ ♆.—This brings a crisis, nervous depression, and troubles.

The ☽ ⚹ or △ ♆.—A favourable time, some travelling.

The ☽ ☌ or *par. dec.*, Aldebaran.—Preferment to soldiers and surgeons, attended with danger.

The ☽ ☌ or *par. dec.*, Antares.—Preferment attended with danger and suffering.

The ☽ ☌ or *par. dec.*, Arista.—Pecuniary gain—in some cases, wealth—honour, good fortune in pursuits of the nature of ☿, ♀, or ♃.

The ☽ ☌ or *par. dec.*, North Scale.—Good fortune and preferment.

The ☽ ☌ or *par. dec.*, South Scale.—Misfortune, scandal, or ill-health.

The ☽ ☌ or *par. dec.*, Regulus.—Honour and preferment, but attended with danger if ☽ be hyleg. The mother suffers, and may be in serious danger.

DIRECTIONS OF THE MID-HEAVEN.

The M.C. ☌ or *par. dec.* ☉.—This brings honours, advancement, and increase of substance. To single ladies, it often brings marriage.

But if ☉ be evilly configurated with the malefics, or in conjunction with fixed stars of a violent nature, this conjunction brings disputes and misfortunes, maybe of a public nature; and some danger to the mother.

The M.C. ⚹ or △ ☉.—This influence usually elevates the native's condition, and, when the nativity promises it, brings him renown and great advancement. It may benefit the native's parents. A public office may be gained. To women, it brings either marriage or employment of a public character.

The M.C. □ or ☍ ☉.—This often brings loss of office or employment, bad trading, disgrace; and, sometimes, bankruptcy and imprisonment. One of the parents suffers. Married women may lose their husbands under this influence.

The M.C. ☌ or *par. dec.* ☽.—If ☽ be strong and fortunate at birth, honour, fame, advantageous changes, travelling, and popularity. Men may marry under this influence. But if ☽ be weak and evilly conflgurated, losses, and unproductive journeys or voyages result; and the wife, or mother, suffers.

The M.C. ⚹ or △ ☽.—Increase of substance, popularity, honours, gifts, favours from women, active business, and travelling are promised. To men, it denotes marriage, or birth of children.

The M.C. □ or ☍ ☽.—This brings unpopularity, scandal, quarrels with women, suffering of wife or mother, and family disputes—according to the position of the ☽.

The M.C. ☌ or *par. dec.* ☿.—If ☿ be strong, gain by literary pursuits, by travelling, by teaching, etc. Should ☿ be afflicted, libel, legal difficulties, and unfortunate trading.

The M.C. ⚹ or △ ☿.—Preferment, honour, and increase of business, according to the strength and situation of ☿ at birth. Children are often first sent to school, and young men to college, under this influence. It often produces a change of residence.

The M.C. □ or ☍ ☿.—Troubles and losses are indicated; and, also, danger of lawsuits, unjust sentences, libels, and false accusations. Death of a child frequently happens under this influence.

The M.C. ☌, *par. dec.*, ⚹ or △ ♀.—This brings mirth, gaiety, pleasure-seeking, renewal of furniture, free expenditure, advancement in artistic pursuits, the birth of a child, and general prosperity. Marriage frequently takes place under this influence.

The M.C. □ or ☍ ♀.—Indicates scandal, extravagance, and, in some cases, dissipation. The mother, wife, or sister suffers. To kings this influence brings scandals, and wasteful expenditure.

The M.C. ☌, *par. dec.*, □, or ☍ ♂.—This evil influence brings quarrels, losses, fires, thefts, or fraud. To military men, and to surgeons, the ☌ brings advancement, but it is attended with some danger. The parents suffer. Misfortunes are sure to result if changes and speculations be made while this martial influence lasts.

The M.C. ⚹ or △ ♂.—This signifies an active, a busy, and a prosperous period, especially to martialists. Military and naval men, surgeons, etc., gain preferment. Generally a journey is taken. Monarchs increase their armies, and, if at war, they gain victories.

The M.C. ☌, *par. dec.*, ⚹ or △ ♃.—Preferment, honours, increase of wealth, benefits from persons in power, and general happiness and prosperity. In the nativities of single women marriage comes to pass. To merchants it brings increase of trade; to the clergy, preferment; to lawyers, advancement and high repute. To a Crown Prince it may bring either a regency or elevation to the throne.

The M.C. □ or ☍ ♃.—This usually brings heavy expenses; but nothing very evil. To monarchs its brings disputes about laws and privileges, and trouble with the nobility and clergy.

The M.C. □, *par. dec.*, □ or ☍ ♄.—This indicates family troubles and losses, death of a parent, loss of reputation and credit, theft, fraud, and unpopularity. Merchants and tradesmen lose heavily in speculative transactions. To monarchs it brings tumults, discontent of the people, the spread of Nihilism among their subjects, breach of treaties or defeat in battle.

The M.C. ⚹ or △ ♄.—This gives pecuniary gain by farming, mining, building, legacies, favour and friendship of old persons.

The M.C. ☌, *par. dec.*, □ or ☍ ♅.—This is often attended by a sudden death in the family; pecuniary loss, and troubles of a strange nature; disappointment in love and marriage, or separation.

The M.C. ⚹ or △ ♅.—Unexpected gain; sudden changes, or travelling of an advantageous nature; favour and friendship of scientists. Benefit by an invention or a discovery.

M.C. ☌, □ or ☍ ♆.—Brings family troubles, unfortunate travelling, and losses in business.

M.C. ⚹ or △ ♅.—Good business, advancement.

DIRECTIONS OF THE ASCENDANT.

The *Ascendant* ☌ ☉.—If ☉ be strong and fortunate, gain by public favours from great men, advancement, employment, increase of reputation and credit; at the same time there may be some ill-health. To military men preferment is promised. To monarchs increase of territory or power, and, when at war, brilliant victories. But if ☉ be afflicted by the malefics, danger is threatened, the head and eyes suffering. If ☉ be in ☌ with ♂, danger by fire, or fire-arms; and accidents involving loss of blood.

The Asc. ⚹ or △ ☉.—Health of body, peace of mind, favours from persons in authority, new friends, some elevation of rank, etc., according to the native's social position. Women often marry, or have a son born, under this influence.

The Asc. □ or ☍ ☉.—Diseases according to the sign occupied by ☉. Envy and enmity of persons in power; loss of employment and credit; danger to the father; and, in some cases, danger of imprisonment. Travelling, changes, and speculation should be avoided while this influence lasts.

The Asc. ☌ or *par. dec.* ☽.—Changes of residence, travelling by land or sea, and preferment, if ☽ be fortunate. Otherwise, adversity or accidents, or danger by water.

The Asc. ⚹ or △ ☽.—Active employment, friendship of great ladies, popularity, general prosperity, marriage, birth of a daughter, etc., according to circumstances.

The Asc. □ or ☍ ☽.—Controversies, strife, conjugal misery, divorce, discord, jealousy, unpopularity, ill-health, intemperance, etc., according to the position of ☽ in the horoscope. A bad time for travelling by land or sea.

The Asc. ☌ or *par. dec.* ☿.—Change of residence, a journey, active business, a propensity to study, invention, and writing—the results of which will be fortunate or unfortunate, according to the position of ☿ at birth. If ☿ be much afflicted, a dangerous accident, or serious attack of illness, is threatened.

The Asc. ⚹ or △ ☿.—Prosperity, active employment, travelling; gain by literary work, teaching or travelling; birth of a child or change of residence.

The Asc. □ or ☍ ☿.—This influence gives a disinclination for study, failure to pass examinations at college; mischief by writings, pressmen, and overwork; diseases of the nature of ☿ or the planet with which he may be evilly configurated; anxiety about young persons. To children this influence often brings whooping-cough, bronchitis, or convulsions.

The Asc. ☌ par. dec., ⚹ or △ ♀.—This influence brings pleasure, gain, new friends, courtship, marriage, birth of children; purchase of articles of luxury, furniture, ornaments, etc., according to circumstances.

Asc. □ or ☍ ♀.—Brings trouble in love and conjugal life, heavy expenses, and extravagance; illness of wife or mother.

The Asc. ☌, *par. dec.*, □, or ☍ ♂.—Accidents or diseases, according to the position of ♂. Haemorrhage frequently results. Danger to a parent. If ♂ be in a fiery sign, acute fevers, or accidents by fire; in an earthy sign, danger of suffocation, in ♉, smallpox or diphtheria; in a sign of human form, danger of homicide, or of being killed in a quarrel or battle; in a watery sign, danger of death by drowning; in an airy sign, danger of a fall from a height, or acute fever.

The Asc. ⚹ or △ ♂.—This inclines the native to travel, shoot, hunt, fence, indulge in martial exercises, enter the army or navy; study medicine, surgery, or chemistry; become an engineer, etc., according to the nativity. Women sometimes marry under this influence.

The Asc. ☌ *par. dec.*, ⚹ or △ ♃.—This is fortunate for health and affairs. Prosperity, conviviality, new friends, advancement, favours from the great, marriage, birth of children. If ♃ be afflicted, the ☌ or *par. dec.*, may bring a serious (but not fatal) illness, arising from some affection of the lungs, the liver, or the blood.

The Asc. □ or ☍ ♃.—An indifferent state of health, often due to plethora. If ♃ be afflicted by ♂, danger of measles, scarlatina, smallpox, pleurisy, etc. A bad time to deal with lawyers. Extravagant expenditure, and too much conviviality.

The Asc. ☌, *par dec.*, □, or ☍ ♄.—If ♄ be oriental, a dangerous accident, or a broken limb; if occidental, a dangerous chronic malady. In some cases this is the beginning of some form of consumption; in others, of melancholia. To women, dangerous internal diseases; and disappointment and trouble in love or matrimony, may result if Saturn afflicted the Sun at birth.

The Asc. ⚹ or △ ♄.—Gain by elderly persons, legacies, mining, building, purchase or sale of houses, etc.

The Asc. ☌, *par. dec.*, □, or ☍ ♅.—This brings sudden losses—either in the family or the estate; travelling, removals, and changes of occupation; or else neurasthenia, or an accident.

The Asc. ⚹ or △ ♅.—Gain of an unexpected nature; fortunate journeys, and active business; also, a desire to study astronomy and astrology, chemistry, electricity, etc.

The Asc. ☌, *par. dec.*, □ or ☍ ♆.—Health weak or else an accident. No long journey by sea should be made.

The Asc. ⚹ or △ ♆.—Gains, travelling for pleasure.

DIRECTIONS OF THE SUN AND MOON TO THEIR OWN ASPECTS.

The ☉ to his own ⚹ tends to experience of preferment, honours, fame and general prosperity.

The ☉ to his own *parallel* brings preferment, friends among the great, and success.

The ☉ to his own □, sorrow, sometimes ill-health, and losses; a desire to depart and be at rest.

The ☽ to her own *parallel*, changes and travelling.

The ☽ to her own □ losses and troubles, enmity of the vulgar, and disadvantageous changes.

The student should bear in mind that the *general* nature of an expected event must be estimated, firstly, by the nature of the planets operating by direction; secondly, by the moderator affected by the directional influence; thirdly, by the strength of the moderator and planet directed, in the nativity; fourthly, by the sign and mansion in which the direction falls. The student should remember, also, that it is unsafe to judge of the probable effects of any direction acting *alone* without taking into consideration other directions that may fall within 1° or 2° of its arc, and without attending to the Solar revolution, an eclipse or a lunation, which may coincide and so assist or counteract it to some extent. "It is the neglect of these precautions," wrote Zadkiel I. "that makes so many failures on the part of even otherwise tolerably good astrologers. And it is the labour, the skill, the persevering industry required to accomplish this true and perfect reading of the heavens which renders the doctrine of nativities one of the vastest and most comprehensive undertakings which the mind of man can grasp and understand. Let not the student, therefore play with this mighty matter, but either resolve to abandon the research, or otherwise to approach these portals of the temple of truth with a resolute will to conquer the obstacles that beset his path, and finally to take his seat among the niches that contain the names of a thousand great and glorious lovers of truth, real philosophers, friends of mankind, and earnest servants of the Living God."

In the experience of the author, he has known, in private life, events to correspond very closely both in their nature and in the periods of their occurrence, to prediction. For example: A lady who was born on the 14th of December, 1840, at five minutes past 12 o'clock a.m., in lat. 51° 28′ N. Her nativity was rectified, by the author, by taking Asc. ☌ ♂ zod. 15° 28′ for her sister's death, in May, 1856; and *her marriage took place as predicted* in June, 1874, under the direction of ☉ par. ♀ in 33° 27′. In this case the R.A. of the M.C. was (as rectified) 83° 59′. Here is another example: A lady who was born on the 14th of April, 1843, at 11h 35m p.m., in lat. 52° 58′ N. Her nativity was rectified, and *her marriage took place in the very month foretold*, viz., July, 1874, under Asc. ⚹ ♀ zod. 31° 18′, assisted by other directions.

As Ptolemy said:

"A skilful person, acquainted with the nature of the stars, is enabled to avert many of their [evil] effects, and to prepare himself for those effects before they arrive." Again: "A sagacious mind improves the operation of the heavens, as a skilful farmer, by cultivation, improves nature."

In regard to diseases, Ptolemy says:

"Should a disease begin when the Moon may be in a sign occupied at the birth by some malefic, or in quartile or opposition to any such sign, such disease will be most severe; and if the malefic also behold the said sign it will be dangerous. On the other hand there will be no danger if the Moon be in a place held at the time of birth by some benefic."

People commonly observe that one evil seldom comes alone and this is frequently due to the combined effects of evil directions and eclipses.

In the appendix will be found a rule for computing the *arc of duration* in the cases of certain directions of the luminaries. Rapt parallels and zodiacal parallels often continue in operation for many months, and sometimes for several years. The rule referred to will enable the student to gauge very nearly the period of time over which the direction may expend its force from first to last contact.

As was stated, in the nativity of the late King Edward VII., the Sun again reached the parallel of Saturn, first contact, in ♑ 16° 19′ 24″. This was a clerical error, for the Sun's limb *first* reached the parallel in ♑ 11° 2′ 25″, and the *last* contact was made in ♑ 16° 19′ 24″, the Sun's centre forming the parallel in ♑ 13° 55′ 37″.

The three arcs of direction are, respectively:

☉ par. ♄ zodiac first contact (♑ 11° 2′ 25″), 59° 36′ 11″.

☉ par. ♄ centre (♑ 13° 55′ 37″), 62° 37′ 30″.

☉ par. ♄ last contact (♑ 16° 19′ 24″), 65° 6′ 27″.

Then, 65° 6′ 27″ - 59° 36′ 11″ gives the *arc of duration* of this parallel of the Sun with Saturn as 5° 30′ 16″ = five years and a half.

The working given is quite correct, as regards the first contact of the Sun's limb with the parallel. This was the most powerful of the three arcs in *Capricornus*, and it depressed his Majesty's health, and brought a narrow escape from serious or fatal injury on board a yacht; and the first contact in *Sagittarius*, in 1871, brought enteric fever, which very nearly proved fatal.

CHAPTER XLI.

ON THE PRACTICAL USES OF ASTROLOGY.

"If Astrology be true, it is a useful Truth."—DE MORGAN.

THAT the Universe is a concrete reality, and that we are in direct relationship with every part of it is a truth. Astrologia sana is in principle demonstrably true, or at least based on truth, for there can be nothing extravagant in believing that ethereal vibrations extend from the Sun to the great planets, and from planet to planet. All space is a network of interacting forces.

The central fact of Astrology is the law of Nature that every celestial body in the Solar System operates on the Earth and its inhabitants, and on the atmosphere. This is a direct consequence of the philosophic truth of relativity.

"To belong to a whole is to have all other parts of the whole in essential and potentially effective relation with oneself. And as belonging to a subordinate whole (our Earth) we participate in the influence of other subordinate wholes upon that. In like manner, as a consequence of the same universal truth of relativity, the things of time must be essentially connected with the things of space. Thus Astrology is, in principle, demonstrable *a priori*. One remark as to the unitary double meaning (or the distinctly-one meaning) of the word '*principium*'—'beginning,' and 'principle.' The principle in logic is the beginning in time; therefore the related totality at the beginning of anything (its 'horoscope') will contain and show the 'principle of its course and development.' The principle of genethliacal astrology is that Man is the microcosmic representation and correspondence of the macrocosm. As the latter in its external aspect, is spread out at the moment of birth, so if we have the science, can we read the [general] character, tendencies, and 'accidents' (in the literal and more comprehensive sense of the term) which will become manifest in the life of the newly born. And as time is related to space, so are the larger to the lesser circles of time. It is upon this relation that the possibility of 'directing' depends. The day is the year writ small. The single degree (or approximate diurnal measure of zodiacal progress) represents the circle, or larger day, the year." So wrote the late C. C. Massey.[1]

Science accepts the view that the Earth is an electro-magnet so rendered by the current of electricity emanating from the Sun, which the Earth, in her axial revolution, is continually winding upon herself. Other members of the Solar system cannot differ in this respect. This being the case, when observers find that certain terrestrial and atmospheric disturbances constantly coincide with the combined force of the planets exerted in a line against the Earth—as at a Solar eclipse, and at mutual conjunctions and oppositions of the major planets—there is nothing either unscientific or extravagant in believing that such coincidences may be related as cause and effect.

As Mr. W. Buist Picken has said:

"In constitutional disease a veritable world of forces are in disorder, and the products of disease are all results of morbid motions. The human organism is constituted of twenty-one different systems of forces, arranged into three groups of seven each, interacting *ad infinitum*. . . . The compositions of molecular forces in the organism are incalculable. Instead of representing them by the simple combinations of molecular and atomic motion that may occur in a pool of water, there is reason to believe that they are more justly represented by the molecular and atomic action of all the stars in the heavens. . . . The stability of health is in the ratio of the stability of equilibrium of the complex normal motions of the organism under adverse influences."[2]

Astrology is rejected by the scientific world (without any patient and thorough examination of it) as absurd and superstitious. It is anathema to modern science! No "scientific authority" accepts the suggestion that the proper way of dealing with the problems of astrology is not to theorise about and condemn them, but to investigate, them by the aid of well-attested facts. Such an idea seems to be quite foreign to the habits of thought of our scientific opponents. As the late Dr. Richard Garnett wrote: " The study of facts and the observation of Nature must always be stronger than any abstract reasoning; and the investigation of the arguments brought against astrology will disclose a great reluctance on the part of the objector to resort to the testimony of facts, and a thoroughly unscientific habit of mind."

---

[1] Vide Letter in LIGHT, January 1st, 1898, re-printed in STAR LORE, February, 1898.

[2] "On Physics and Medicine," HOMOEOPATHIC WORLD, July, 1897.

Well might M. Ferdinand Brunetiére[3] have declared not long ago that "Science is bankrupt," and "if not totally bankrupt it is virtually insolvent. The physical or natural sciences promised us to suppress mystery. Now, not only have they not done so, but we see clearly that they have never shed a ray of light upon it. They are powerless to adequately state the only questions which concern us—those which relate to the origin of Man, to the law of his conduct and to his future destiny! The unknowable surrounds us; and we cannot extract from the laws of Physics, or from the results of Physiology, any means of knowing anything about it. . . . Science has lost its prestige, and Religion has conquered a part of its own." In the present year, 1911, M. R. Legendre in the course of his lecture at the National Museum for Natural History, Paris, on "The Physiology of Sleep," admitted that it is impossible to give any exact definition of sleep, which must be distinguished from narcosis, lethargy, and hypnotism.[4]

Astrology also has reconquered part of its own. If anyone doubts this let him ponder over the fact that at the Oxford Congress, September 18th, 1908, M. Saloman Reinach, one of the very first rank of savants and scholars, who presided over the important Section 6—Religions of the Greeks and Romans—insisted that:

"The question, is rife: What is the bearing of primitive Astrology and star-worship on the formation of Oriental and Greek myths? We may, for the moment, answer by a *non liquet*, but it is *certain* that the learned work of Prof. Bouché Leclerq on Greek Astrology, the publication of forgotten astrological treatises by Prof. Cumont, and his admirable lectures at the Collége de France, where the religious importance of Astrology has been so forcibly emphasised, cannot fail to make us once more turn our eyes to the starry heavens, after we have, perhaps, dwelt too exclusively on the earthly and psychological elements of cult and myth."

Yet Science, in this twentieth century, "bankrupt'' or at least "virtually insolvent" as it is, rejects with scorn and contempt Astrologia sana.

It may well be asked "What is Science?" that it is so arrogant and contemptuous. Here is the definition of G. H. Lewes, who in his day was regarded as an authority on Science, presented by him in his "Aristotle":

---

[3] The learned editor of the REVUE DES DEUX MONDES.

[4] This lecture was reported in full in the REVUE SCIENTIFIQUE, June 17th, 1911.

"Science is the systematic co-ordination of the facts of co-existence and succession."

It is the parrot-like cry that astrology is an "exploded " superstition. So that astrology has been "exploded" by "the systematic co-ordination of the facts of co-existence and succession"—which, wrote R. J. Morrison, is about "as clear as mud in a wine-glass." And none can tell who "exploded" astrology neither point to the work which exploded it!

As a distinguished physician and philosopher has written: "There is one word in particular against which it is necessary at the present day to be on our guard, if we would preserve our independence of character and our peace of mind—the word 'scientific.' To be deemed scientific is to have found salvation—from the prize-ring upwards. The first thing about the word 'scientific' is that it has no absolute meaning whatever; it is simply relative. It is rightly used to describe any method or action which is in accordance with the laws of the universe, so far as they have been at present spelled out in the department to which the matter described belongs. But as we are every day learning more and more about these laws, it follows that what is truly scientific to-day may, in the light of some new discovery, be utterly unscientific to-morrow. The next thing to be noted is that the word is apt to be used by each person from the standpoint of his own position in science; and thus the Tower of Babel episode comes to be enacted over again in another sphere. Now, if it could always be borne in mind that the word 'scientific' is a purely question-begging term unless it is (either explicitly or implicitly) qualified by a statement of the precise sense in which it is used, and of the personal equation of him who uses it, the occasion of a vast amount of personal bitterness and misunderstanding would be got rid of."[5]

All things tend to one conclusion—a Great First Cause Who in wisdom rules the Universe. Yet in 1871, the President of the British Association for the Advancement of Science, declared that great masses move through space "without intelligence directed to prevent their collision." This atheistic and absurd idea he borrowed from Laplace.

That Prescience is useful was shown by Claudius Ptolemy in his *Tetrabiblos*, eighteen centuries ago. He declared that "prescience by astronomy is possible under certain adaptation, and that alone it will afford premonition, as far as symptoms in the Ambient enable it to do

[5] Vide STAR LORE, January, 1898.

so, of all such events as happen to men by the influence of the Ambient. . . . Man is subject not only to events applicable to his own private and individual nature, but also to others arising from general causes. He suffers by pestilences, inundations, or conflagrations, produced by certain extensive changes in the Ambient, and destroying multitudes at once; since a greater and more powerful agency must always absorb and overcome one that is minute and weaker."

My forecast (published in October, 1908) of shocks of earthquake in Italy, etc., about the tenth degree of east longitude, about the 25th and 30th of December, 1908, led three heads of families to ask me if I apprehended that such seismic phenomena would be so serious as to render it unwise to spend the winter in Italy or Sicily. I replied that they should avoid both Italy and Sicily—the latter because Messina is related to Scorpio the sign occupied by Mars (at the winter solstice) in semi-quartile (45°) aspect with the Sun, the great luminary being also in quadrature with Saturn. As they had faith in the ancient science, they followed my advice, and took their families elsewhere for that winter (1908-09), and on the occurrence of the awful earthquakes of December 28th, 1908, which destroyed Messina, and shook Italy and vicinity from the eighth to the fifteenth degrees of east longitude, my correspondents wrote warmly thanking me for my forecast and advice.

Dr. S. wrote (in the spring of 1908) a letter to me in which he said: "I am studying your treatise on Medical Astrology in your Text Book, and find it a great help in practice. I firmly believe that planetary action has, besides the magnetism of the earth, all to do with the health and career of terrestrial beings as well as with mundane affairs."

Some years ago, in the course of a long series of lessons in computing arcs of primary direction, four evil ones were found to be about to take effect in my þupil's nativity. They were ♅ ☌ ☿ zodiac 48° 0′, ♅ □ ☽ zodiac 48° 4′, M.C. ☌ ♅ 48° 14′, and ☉ par. ♄ zodiac 48° 26′. It was pointed out to my friend that this train of primary directions presignified danger of losses, and personal danger by a fall or by an explosion. On reflection, my friend said that he would have an old boiler at his works examined. The examination was ordered and promptly made, and a serious defect was discovered and repaired. As my friend's office was directly over a part of the boiler in question, and as he passed several hours in that office daily, for five days per week, he was running considerable risk of his life. The directions had their effect in weakening his health, temporarily, and in a serious loss of money.

A Scottish gentleman who was born when the Moon was in conjunction with Mars in Cancer, in the eighth house, and Jupiter close to the upper meridian, had suffered seriously in health, and had been very unsuccessful in his profession, in Scotland, up to the time when he began the study of the Placidian system of directing. He was advised to leave his native country and come south, to an English town in a direction pointed out. He did so, under the direction, in his nativity, of Sun parallel Jupiter, and recovered his health and prospered well.

On the 24th May, 1888, at 3h 45m p.m., in the City of London, the author was asked by a scientific friend (who had studied astrology under his tuition) whether he might win an action in the Court of Appeal, if he decided to proceed against the directors of a firm for infringing his patent rights. After careful consideration of the primary directions then operating (in the nativity of my pupil)—that of ☽ ✶ ♂ mundo, the Moon occupying the tenth house at birth, being the chief one—, and finding the figure of the heavens drawn for the moment of consultation also very favourable to success, I gave my opinion that my good friend would win on the appeal. The action was tried by three judges, in July, 1888, who allowed the appeal, and awarded to the plaintiff costs on the higher scale. The plaintiff's solicitor was very doubtful indeed of success in the Court of Appeal, in view of having lost the first trial. It may be mentioned that my friend had telegraphed for me to come to his office, but I had started for the city more than half-an-hour before his telegram was delivered at my house. I called at his office only on intuitive perception that he wished to see me; and I had neither heard nor read of the first trial, and was unaware that he was in so anxious a state of mind—this was a pretty clear case of telepathy.

With regard to surgical operations, Claudius Ptolemy wrote, "Pierce not with iron that part of the body which may be governed by the sign [of the zodiac] actually occupied by the Moon" [at the time of the operation]—to which may be added, specially if the Moon be in conjunction, quadrature or opposition with Mars, Saturn, Uranus, or Neptune at the time.

This precept can be followed in major operations which admit of a few hours' delay, when evil planets are predominant and afflicting the Sun and Moon.

When a student of surgery and medicine, I well remember a case of ovariotomy performed by a skilful surgeon at one of the great hospitals of London, in the afternoon of the 13th of December, 1865, when the Moon was in the sign *Scorpio* 2° and applying to conjunction with Saturn in 8° 37′ of the same sign. The poor woman died on the following day. Ovariotomy is a very serious operation, and it is often performed with success; nevertheless, it should be delayed when the Moon is afflicted and passing through either *Virgo* or *Scorpio.* It would be better to run the risk of being deemed superstitious than to neglect an astrological consideration which might give the poor sufferer a better prospect of recovery from the shock of a serious surgical operation.

The dominion of the Moon in the human body as she passes through the twelve signs of the zodiac is as follows:

In *Aries* (0° to 30° of longitude) head and face; *Taurus*, neck and throat; *Gemini*, arms and shoulders; *Cancer*, breast and stomach; *Leo*, heart and spine; *Virgo*, abdominal organs; *Libra*, loins and kidneys; Scorpio, reproductive organs and bladder; *Sagittarius*, hips and thighs; *Capricornus*, knees and hams; *Aquarius*, legs and ankles; *Pisces*, feet and toes.

Jerome Cardan, the celebrated physician and astrologer, was sent for in the year 1552 by the Archbishop of St. Andrews, whom he cured of a dangerous disease which the distinguished physicians of his day failed to cure and pronounced incurable. Cardan's astrological skill enabled him to succeed in this inveterate case wherein other physicians less skilled both in astrology and medicine had utterly failed to effect a cure.

In the treatise on Medical Astrology this very important subject will be more elaborated.

Appendix to Book I.

TO REDUCE MEAN TO SIDEREAL TIME.

Hour	*Add* *Min.*	*Sec.*	*Min.*	*Add* *Sec.*	*Min.*	*Add* *Sec.*	*Sec.*	*Add* *Sec.*
1	0	9.86	1	0.16	31	5.09	2	0.01
2	0	19.71	2	0.33	32	5.26	6	0.02
3	0	29.57	3	0.49	33	5.42	9	0.03
4	0	39.43	4	0.66	34	5.59	13	0.04
5	0	49.28	5	0.82	35	5.75	17	0.05
6	0	59.14	6	0.99	36	5.92	19	0.05
7	1	9.00	7	1.15	37	6.08	20	0.06
8	1	18.85	8	1.31	38	6.24	23	0.06
9	1	28.71	9	1.48	39	6.41	24	0.07
10	1	38.56	10	1.64	40	6.57	26	0.07
11	1	48.42	11	1.81	41	6.74	27	0.08
12	1	58.28	12	1.97	42	6.90	30	0.08
13	2	8.13	13	2.14	43	7.07	31	0.08
14	2	17.99	14	2.30	44	7.23	32	0.09
15	2	27.85	15	2.46	45	7.39	34	0.09
16	2	37.70	16	2.63	46	7.56	35	0.10
17	2	47.56	17	2.79	47	7.72	38	0.10
18	2	57.52	19	3.12	48	7.89	39	0.11
19	3	7.27	21	3.45	49	8.05	42	0.12
20	3	17.13	23	3.78	51	8.38	45	0.12
21	3	26.99	25	4.11	53	8.71	48	0.13
22	3	36.84	27	4.44	55	9.04	51	0.14
23	3	46.70	29	4.76	57	9.37	55	0.15
24	3	56.56	30	4.93	59	9.69	59	0.16

ON THE USE OF LOGARITHMS IN ASTRONOMICAL CALCULATIONS.

Logarithms were invented by Baron Napier, of Merchistoun, for the purpose of facilitating his astronomical calculations, and for astrological purposes. By means of logarithms multiplication is performed by addition; division by subtraction; proportion, or the rule of three, by adding three numbers together; and roots are extracted by a very simple process.

[Note.—In working by rule of three, the ternary proportional logarithm of the first term must be taken from 10.00000 to find its arithmetical complement. Where the index (in the sum) exceeds 10, this amount must be rejected.]

The best Tables of Logarithms are those of Callet and Bruhns, the sines, cosines, tangents, and co-tangents being given by them to seconds—Chambers' Tables only give them to deg. and min. By means of the following formulae a map of the heavens may be drawn for any part of the world.

FORMULA 1.

Oblique Ascension given to find Ecliptic Longitude.

1°.—Log. *cosine* Obl. Asc. from the first point of ♈ or ♎ (or log. *sine* Obl. Asc. from ♋ or ♑) + log. *cotang.* lat. or pole of the house[1] = log. *cotang.* ∠ A.

2°.—Then, if Obl. Asc. be less than 90° or above 270° ∠ A + 23° 27′ (the obliquity of the ecliptic)[2] = ∠ B. If Obl. Asc. be more than 90°, and less than 270°, the *difference* of ∠ A and 23° 27′ = ∠ B.

3°.—And log. *cosine* ∠ B (*a.c.*) + log. *cosine* ∠ A + log. tang. Obl. Asc. from ♈ or ♎ (or log. *cotang.* Obl. Asc. ♋ or ♑) = log. *tang.* long. from ♈ or ♎ (or log. *cotang.* long. ♋ or ♑).

[Note.—If ∠ B exceed 90°, take log. *sine* of its excess, instead of log. *cosine*, using the arith. comp. of the log., as usual, in the first term. If ∠ B should exceed 90°, the long. will fall the reverse way from the point from which the Obl. Asc. is taken.]

FORMULA 2.

The Oblique Ascension being exactly 90° from ♈ or ♎, to find the degree ascending.

---

[1] A table of the Poles of the Houses will be found in this volume. The pole of the ascendant (or first house) is always the latitude of the birth-place.

[2] The Obliquity of the Ecliptic is given in the *Nautical Almanac* and Zadkiel's *Ephemeris*. When the birthplace is in a *southern* latitude the obliquity of the ecliptic must be *added* to ∠ A when the Obl. Asc. is greater than 90° and less than 270°; and when the Obl. Asc. is less than 90° or greater than 270o the difference between ∠ A and the obliquity of the ecliptic must be taken to find D B.

Log. *sine* of the obliquity of the ecliptic for the given year + log. *tang*. lat. of the birthplace = log. *tang*. of the ascending degree.

FORMULA 3.

To find Ascensional Difference.

Log. *tang*. lat. of the birthplace + log. *tang*. declin. of the heavenly body = log. *sine* of the ascensional difference.

FORMULA 4.

The Declination and Ascensional Difference being given, to find the Pole.

Log. *cotang*. dec. + log. *sine* asc. diff. = log. *tang*. of the pole.

FORMULA 5.

To find the Circle of Position.[3]

1°.—Say: "As the semi-arc is to 90°, so is the merid. dist. to the circle of position from the meridian."

2°.—Then, the circle of position, taken from the merid. dist. gives the asc. diff. under the pole.

FORMULA 6.

The Sun's Longitude being given, to find his Right-Ascension.

Log. *cosine* of the obliquity of the ecliptic + log. *tang*. long. from ♈ or ♎ (or log. *cotang* long. ♋ or ♑) = log. *tang*. R.A. from ♈ or ♎ (or log. *cotang* R.A. from ♋ or ♑).

FORMULA 7.

The Sun's Longitude being given, to find his Declination.

Log. *sine* of obliquity of ecliptic + log. *sine* long, from ♈ or ♎ (or log. *cosine* long. ♋ or ♑) = log. *sine* declination.

FORMULA 8.

The Sun's Declination being given, to find his Longitude.

Log. *sine* of his declin., - *sine* obliq. of ecliptic = *sine* of longitude.

[3] The circles of position of all bodies between the meridian and horizon are analogous to the circles of latitude, being small circles of the sphere, having their planes parallel with the plane of the meridian.

FORMULA 9.

The Sun's Right-Ascension being given, to find his Longitude.

Log. *cosine* of obliquity of ecliptic + log. *cotang*. R.A. from ♈ or ♎ (or log. *tang*. R.A. ♋ or ♑) = log. *cotang* long. from ♈ or ♎ (or log. *tang*. long, ♋ or ♑).

FORMULA 10.

The Right-Ascension and Declination of a Heavenly Body, being given, to find its Longitude and Latitude.

1° Log *sine* R.A., from ♈ or ♎, or log. *cosine* R.A., from ♋ or ♑ + log. *cotang* dec.= log. *tang*. ∠ A

2° R.A. and dec. same name,[4] ∠ A + obliquity of ecliptic = ∠ B. R.A. and dec. of difierent names, the difference ∠ A and obl. of .eclip. = ∠ B.

Then, for the *Longitude*:

Log. *sine* ∠ A. (a.c.) + log. *sine* ∠ B + log. *tang*. R.A., ♈ or ♎ or log. *cotang*, R.A., ♋ or ♑ = log. *tang*. long. ♈ or ♎, or log. *cotang*. long. ♋ or ♑

For the *Latitude*:

Log. *cosine* ∠ A (a.c.) + log. *cosine* ∠ B + log. *sine* declin. = log. *sine* latitude.[5]

FORMULA 11.

The, Longitude and Latitude of a Heavenly Body being given, to find its Right-Ascension and Declination.

1° Log. *sine* long. ♈ or ♎, or log. cosine long. ♋ or ♑ + log. *tang*. of obliquity of ecliptic = log. *tang*. ∠ A.

2° Long. and lat. same name 90° - lat. = ∠ B.

or long. and lat. different names 90° - lat. = ∠ B.

3° ∠ B - ∠ A = ∠ C.

Then, for the *Declination*:

Log. *cosine* ∠ A (a.c.) + log. *cosine* ∠ C + log. *cosine* obliquity of ecliptic = log. *sine* of the declination.

For the *Right-Ascension*:

log. *cosine* dec. (*a.c.*) +

---

[4] If the R.A. be less than 180°, call it *North*; if greater than 180°, call it *South*.

[5] If ∠ B should exceed 90°, the latitude will be of contrary name to the declination.

log. *cosine* long. from ♈ or ♎, or log. *sine* long. from ♋ or ♑
+ log. *cosine* lat.
= log. *cosine* R.A. from ♈ or ♎, or log. *sine* R.A. from ♋ or ♑

FORMULA 12.

To Find the Longitude of a Heavenly Body from the Ephemeris.

1°.—Find the difference between its longitude at the noon preceding and the noon succeeding the given time.

2°.—Find the diurnal proportional logarithm[6] corresponding to the amount of that difference; find, also, the diurnal proportional logarithm of the time elapsed since the preceding noon; add the logs. together and the sum will be the diurnal proportional logarithm of the motion of the heavenly body in longitude.

3°.—Add the sum obtained in this manner to the longitude at the preceding noon (but subtract it in the case of a retrograde planet), and the sum will be the longitude required.

EXAMPLE.—Let it be required to find the longitude of the Moon at 4h 5m p.m. (G.M.T.) of November 20th, 1877. The moon's motion in the 24h was (according to *Zadkiel's Ephemeris*) 13° 23′.

Diurnal prop. log. of 13° 23′	.25365
Diurnal prop. log. of 4h 5m	.76920
Moon's motion in 4h 5m = 2° 17′	1.02285

Then, the Moon's long. at noon, 23° 2′ of ♉ + 2° 17′ = 25° 19′ of ♉ the Moon's longitude required.

TO FIND THE LATITUDE AND LONGITUDE OF A STAR BY THE CELESTIAL GLOBE.

RULE.—Place the upper end of the quadrant of altitude on the north or south pole of the ecliptic, according to whether the star is on the north or south side of the ecliptic, and move the other end until the star comes to the graduated edge of the quadrant: the number of degrees between the ecliptic and the star is the *latitude*; and the number of degrees on the ecliptic, reckoned eastward from the first point of *Aries* to the quadrant, is the *longitude*.

Or, elevate the north or south pole 66½° above the horizon, according to whether the star is on the north or south side of the ecliptic;

6 A table of diurnal proportional logarithms is given at pages 396, 397, of the latest edition of Chambers' *Mathematical Tables*.

bring the pole of the ecliptic to that part of the brass meridian which is numbered from the equinoctial towards the pole; then the ecliptic will coincide with the horizon; screw the quadrant of latitude upon the brass meridian over the pole of the ecliptic; keep the globe from revolving on its axis, and move the quadrant until its graduated edge comes over the given star; the degree on the quadrant cut by the star is its *latitude*; and the sign and degree on the ecliptic cut by the quadrant shows its *longitude*.

TO FIND THE ARC OF DURATION OF A PRIMARY DIRECTION OF THE SUN OR MOON.

If the Sun be in either ♋, ♌, ♍, ♎, ♏, or ♐, when the parallel is completed, his *south* limb will *first* enter the *parallel declination*, or the *declination of the aspect*, and his *north* limb will be the last to enter it. If the Sun be in ♑, ♒, ♓, ♈, ♉, or ♊, when the parallel is completed, or the declination of the aspect reached, his *north* limb will *first* enter the declination of the parallel or aspect, and his *south* limb will be the *last* immersed in it. To and from the degrees and minutes of declination of the given parallel of declination (or, of the declination that the Sun's centre will have at the place of the aspect) add or subtract 0° 16′, and the sum or difference will be the declination of the Sun's centre when the north or south limb first touches upon the parallel declination (or the declination of the place of the aspect).

This process of adding or subtracting 0° 16′ is also applicable as regards the Moon, only that the Moon's declination, etc., must be found in the *Ephemeris* or *Nautical Almanac* for the year of birth.

Find the longitudes corresponding to the two declinations thus found, and work the two directions by the rule given at page 193. The difference (in arc) between the two values will be the *arc of duration*,[7] which is to be converted into time in the manner described. [Oxley.]

In the case of *mundane* directions 0° 16′ should be added to and also subtracted from the R.A., and the sum or remainder should be worked with in such manner as to direct the east and west limb to the parallels and aspects; and by subtracting the lesser arc from the greater, the *arc of duration*, or of anticipation and retardation, may be determined.

[7] The arc of duration will vary in length according to the sign in which the aspect or parallel of declination falls; the longest will be in ♊, ♋, ♐, and ♑, and in some cases the same limb of the luminary that first entered on the declination *may* be the last to leave it. The longest arc, near the tropics, will be about 17° 20′; the shortest, near the equinoxes, about 1° 20′.

TABLE OF THE POLES OF THE HOUSES.

Lat. Deg.	*11th House.*		*12th House.*		*Lat. Deg.*	*11th House.*		*12th House.*	
1	0	21	0	42	31	11	26	21	56
2	0	41	1	22	32	11	54	22	46
3	1	0	2	0	33	12	23	23	36
4	1	21	2	41	34	12	51	24	25
5	1	41	3	23	35	13	26	25	15
6	2	0	4	0	36	13	51	26	5
7	2	21	4	40	37	14	18	26	55
8	2	41	5	21	38	14	52	27	48
9	3	2	6	2	39	15	24	28	40
10	3	23	6	43	40	15	56	29	32
11	3	43	7	24	41	16	29	30	25
12	4	4	8	5	42	17	5	31	20
13	4	24	8	45	43	17	42	32	18
14	4	45	9	26	44	18	20	33	15
15	5	7	10	10	45	18	58	34	13
16	5	29	10	50	46	19	37	35	10
17	5	49	11	30	47	20	19	36	10
18	6	12	12	14	48	21	3	37	12
19	6	34	12	57	49	21	46	38	12
20	6	57	13	41	50	22	33	39	14
21	7	20	14	24	51	23	21	40	18
22	7	43	15	7	52	24	12	41	24
23	8	5	15	50	53	25	6	42	32
24	8	30	16	36	54	26	1	43	39
25	8	54	17	22	55	26	59	44	48
26	9	17	18	5	56	28	1	45	59
27	9	43	18	52	57	29	6	47	13
28	10	8	19	37	58	30	15	48	27
29	10	32	20	21	59	31	29	49	44
30	10	59	21	9	60	32	48	51	4
					60⅔	33	45	51	59

Note.—The poles of the 3rd, 5th and 9th houses, are the same as the 11th. The poles of the 2nd, 6th and 8th houses, are the same as those of the 12th.

BOOK II.

MUNDANE ASTROLOGY.

CHAPTER I.

INTRODUCTION.

"They saw the stars their constant round maintain,
Perform their course, and then return again;
They on their aspects saw the Fates attend,
Their change on their variety depend,
And thence they fixed unalterable laws,
Settling the same effect on the same cause.—MANILIUS.

MUNDANE (or STATE) ASTROLOGY relates to the prediction of general events, wars, revolutions, the rise and fall of empires, plague, pestilence, famine, etc.

There can be no question that mundane astrology was based upon the results of a long series of observations, as Manilius avers, the inductive method being followed in reducing it to a science.

The belief of the ancients that the planets were gods who had under their special care the affairs of mankind arose, not from mere barbaric superstition, but from observation of calamities accompanying, or immediately following, certain relative positions of the planets Saturn and Mars; and of benefits attending upon similar relative positions of Jupiter and Venus, and the configurations of the Sun with Mercury, Venus, Mars, Jupiter, and Saturn.

It is beyond question that the planets and stars were the gods of the Egyptians. The seven planets were (according to the philosopher Albricus) the first seven gods of the heathen, in the following order: Saturn, Jupiter, Mars, Apollo, Venus, Mercury, and the Moon.

Clemens, of Alexandria, placed the stars and heavenly bodies in the first class of pagan deities. The summary of Egyptian theology given by Diogenes Laertius from Manetho and Hecataeus, is in the same spirit, which considers that matter was the first principle, and the Sun and Moon were the first deities of the Egyptians.[1] This agrees with an expression found in the Cratylus of Plato: "the only gods are the Sun, Moon, and Stars," In the Timaeus he speaks of *revolving* gods: "as many as visibly revolve."

The Platonist Porphyry, also, treats the gods as visible: "which gods you now see." Again: "To the remaining gods, therefore to the world, to the inerratic and erratic stars, who are visible gods." Of these he says: "The Pythagoreans frequently employed their aid in *divination*, and if they were in want of a certain thing for the purpose of some investigation. In order, therefore, to effect this, they make use of the gods within the heavens, both the erratic and non-erratic, of all of whom it is requisite to consider the Sun as the leader, but to rank the Moon in the second place; and we should conjoin with those fire [Mars] in the third place, from its alliance with them, according to the theologist."

The Greek poet and philosopher Aratus in his *Phenomena* (as translated by Dr. Lamb), says:

"Let us begin from Jove, Let every mortal raise
His grateful voice to tune Jove's endless praise,
Jove fills the heaven—the earth—the sea—the air;
We feel his spirit moving here and everywhere.
And we his offspring are[2]. He, ever good,
Daily provides for man his daily food.
Ordains the seasons by his signs on high,
Studding with gems of light the azure canopy.
What time with plough and spade to break the soil,
That plenteous stores may bless the reaper's toil;
What time to plant and prune the vine he shows.
And hangs the purple cluster on its boughs,
To Him—the First—the Last-all homage yield,
Our Father—Wonderful—our Help—our Shield."

The *Phenomena* of Aratus was a poem teaching astrology.

Berosus was a native of Chaldaea. He migrated to Greece and resided for a long period in Athens. He there immortalised himself by writing the history of Chaldaea, and by his, *astrological predictions*,

[1] Wilkinson's "Egypt," vol. iv.

[2] These are the words quoted by St. Paul, *Acts* 17, v. 28.

in recognition of which the Athenians erected a statue, in honour to his memory, having a golden tongue.[3] This fact will serve to show how highly the Athenians prized astrological predictions.

Claudius Ptolemy has handed down to us the method followed by the ancients in formulating their predictions from the configurations of the planets at the *vernal equinox*.

It was an accepted belief of the ancients that the world was created at the vernal equinox. Dante alludes to this belief[4]:

> "Aloft the Sun ascended with those stars,
> That with him rose, when Love divine first mov'd,
> Those its fair works."

The Jewish *mundane* era dates from the vernal equinox, 3761 B.C. Hence arose the astrological observance of each returning vernal equinox as the "revolution of the world." The Hindu god *Balaram*,[5] is the Sun in his chief dignity *Aries*, the *ram*. It is remarkable that the paschal sacrifice was fixed at the vernal equinox (and the lunation nearest thereto), when the Sun entered *Aries* (the sacrificial ram or *lamb*). At the crucifixion the Sun was in *Aries* and near the stars called El Nath and Natik—the wounded, the slain.

The numbers *twelve* and *seven*—the former being the number of the *signs* of the *zodiac*, the latter that of the *planets*—recur again and again in both the Old and the New Testament. When the tribe of Levi was appointed to the office of the priesthood and the service of the Tabernacle, the original number of the tribes was made up by the sub-division of the family of Joseph into the tribes of Ephraim and Manasseh. This full number was likewise required for the symmetrical arrangement of the tribes around the *four* sides of the Tabernacle, just as the *Zodiac* was divided into *four triplicities* of three signs each. The prophet Elijah, at Mount Carmel, "took twelve stones, according to the number of the tribes of the sons of Jacob, unto whom the word of Jehovah came, saying, Israel shall be thy name; and with the stones he built an altar in the name of Jehovah." The number of the Apostles of Christ was *twelve*, to whom He said: "Ye who have followed me . . . shall sit upon twelve thrones, judging the twelve tribes of Israel." In *Revelations* we are informed that the heavenly Jerusalem had twelve gates, and at the twelve gates angels, and names written thereon,

---

[3] Plin. 2, 103; *Id.* 7,37.

[4] *Inferno*, Canto I.

[5] Vide p. 9.

which are the names of the twelve tribes of the children of Israel; on the east, three gates; on the north, three gates; on the south, three gates; and on the west, three gates. The wall of the City had twelve foundations, and in them the names of the twelve Apostles of the Lamb." "I heard," says St. John, "the number of them who were sealed; and there were sealed one hundred and forty-four thousand, of all the tribes of the children of Israel. Of the tribe of Judah were sealed twelve thousand; of the tribe of Reuben were sealed twelve thousand." and so on.[6] Allusion has already been made, in the first book of this work, to the scriptual teaching that however numerous the nations are, they are all in relationship with one or other of the *twelve signs of the Zodiac*. Ptolemy says:

"The peculiarities of all nations are distinguished *according to entire parallels and entire angles*, and by their situation with regard to the Sun and the *Ecliptic*.

"The climate which we inhabit is situated in one of the northern Quadrants; but other nations, which lie under more southern parallels, that is to say, in the space between the equinoctial line and the summer tropic, have the sun in their zenith, and are continually scorched by it. They are consequently black in complexion, and have thick and curled hair. They are, moreover, ugly in person, of contracted stature, hot in disposition, and fierce in manners, in consequence of the incessant heats to which they are exposed; and they are called by the common name of Ethiopians.

"The natives of those countries which lie under the more remote northern parallels (that is to say, under the Arctic circle and beyond it) have their zenith far distant from the zodiac and the Sun's heat. Their constitutions, therefore, abound in cold, and are also highly imbued with moisture, which is in itself a most nutritive quality, and in these latitudes is not exhausted by heat; hence they are fair in complexion, with straight hair, of large bodies and full stature. They are cold in disposition, and wild in manners, owing to the constant cold.

"The nations situated between the summer tropic and the Arctic circle, having the meridian Sun neither in their zenith nor yet far remote from it, enjoy a well temperated atmosphere. This favourable temperature, however, still undergoes variation, and changes alternately from heat to cold; but the variation is neither vast nor violent. The people who enjoy this kindly atmosphere are consequently of

---

[6] *Vide* "Astrology in the Apocalypse," An Essay on Biblical Allusions to Chaldaean Science. By W.G. Collingwood, M.A.

proportionate stature and complexion, and of good natural disposition; they live not in a state of dispersion, but dwell together in societies and are civilized in their habits. Among the nations comprehended in this division, those verging towards the south are more industrious and ingenious than the others, and more adapted to the sciences; and these qualifications are engendered in them by the vicinity of the zodiac to their zenith, and by the familiarity thus subsisting between them and the planets moving in the zodiac, which familiarity gives activity and an intellectual impulse to their minds.

"It has been already stated that there are *four triplicities* distinguishable in the zodiac. The first composed of *Aries*, *Leo*, and *Sagittarius*, is the *north-west triplicity*; and Jupiter has chief dominion over it on behalf of its *northern* proportion, but Mars also rules with him in reference to the west. The second, consisting of *Taurus*, *Virgo*, and *Capricorn*, is the *south-east*; and in this triplicity Venus bears chief rule, in consequence of the *southern* proportion; but Saturn also governs with her in consideration of the east. The third, composed of *Gemini*, *Libra*, and *Aquarius*, is *north-east*; and Saturn is here the principal lord, in consequence of the *eastern* proportion; Jupiter, however, governs with him in reference to the *north*. The fourth triplicity is constituted of *Cancer*, *Scorpio*, and *Pisces* and is south-west; it owns Mars as its principal ruler, in consideration of its western proportion; and on behalf of the *south*, it is also governed by Venus.

"The four triplicities being thus established, the whole inhabited earth is accordingly divided into four parts agreeing with the number of the triplicities. It is divided latitudinally by the line of the Mediterranean Sea, from the Straits of Hercules to the Issican Gulf, continued onwards through the mountainous ridge extending towards the east; and by this latitudinal division its southern and northern parts are defined. Its longitudinal division is made by the line of the Arabian Gulf, the Aegean Sea, Pontus, and the lake Maeotis; and by this line are separated its eastern and western parts.

"Of the four quadrants of the Earth, thus agreeing in number with the four triplicities, one is situated in the north-west of the entire earth, and contains Celto-Galatia; or, as is commonly called Europe. Opposed to this quadrant lies that of the south-east, towards Eastern Aethiopia; it is called the southern part of Asia Magna. Another quadrant of the entire earth is in the north-east, about Scythia, and is called the northern part of Asia Magna. To this is opposed the quadrant of the south-west, which lies about Western Aethiopia, and is known by the general name of Libya.

"Under this arrangement, it follows that the north-western parts of the first quadrant, or that of Europe, are in familiarity with the north-west triplicity, composed of *Aries*, *Leo*, and *Sagittarius*; and they are accordingly governed by the lords of that triplicity, Jupiter and Mars. These parts, as distinguished by their appropriation to entire nations, are Britain, Galatia, Germany, Bastarnia, Italy, Apulia, Sicily, Gaul, Tuscany, Celtica, and Spain. And, since the triplicity itself and the planets connected with it in dominion are adapted to command, the natives of these countries are consequently impatient of restraint, lovers of freedom, warlike, industrious, imperious, cleanly, and high-minded. Among the countries beforenamed, Britain, Galatia, Germany, and Bastarnia have a greater familiarity with *Aries* and Mars, and their inhabitants are accordingly wilder, bolder, and more ferocious. Italy, Apulia, Sicily, and Gaul are in familiarity with *Leo* and the Sun; and the natives of these countries are more imperious, yet kind and benevolent, and careful of the commonwealth. Tuscany, Celtica, and Spain, are connected with *Sagittarius* and Jupiter; and their inhabitants are lovers of freedom, simplicity and elegance."

Ptolemy proceeds to describe, in like manner, the remaining quadrants of the earth and the inhabitants thereof, as known in his day. It is a remarkable fact that Great Britain and Germany are to this day affected by the transits of the superior planets through their ruling sign *Aries* as declared by Ptolemy; that France and Italy are similarly affected by such transits through *Leo*; Lower Egypt by *Gemini*; Persia and the Grecian Archipelago by *Taurus*; Spain by *Sagittarius*; and Africa by *Cancer*. No alteration whatever has been found necessary by the astrologers of the middle ages and those of the nineteenth century; for the constantly recurring coincidences of many centuries have proved the truth of the aphorisms of the ancients. No country ever prospers during the period of Saturn's visitation to its ruling sign; on the other hand, the transits of Jupiter are almost invariably found to coincide with prosperity, or fortunate changes. Countries like America, which have been discovered and populated since Ptolemy's day have (by observation) been found to have familiarity with certain signs of the zodiac. When the independence of America was declared, and the United States established as a separate nation from the mother-country, the sign *Gemini* ascended, and, accordingly transits through that sign are found to affect the welfare of the American nation.[7] Ptolemy says that: "With regard to *metropolitan cities*, it is nec-

[7] Vide "FUTURE," Sept. 1893.

essary to state that those points or degrees of the Zodiac over which the Sun and Moon were in transit at the time when the construction of any such city was first undertaken and commenced, are to be considered as sympathising, with that city in an especial manner; and that, among the angles, the *ascendant is principally in accordance with it.*" It is obviously very difficult to obtain the exact moment when a metropolitan city was first founded, and Ptolemy recommends in such case, that "the midheaven in the nativity of the reigning king, or other chief magistrate" be substituted and considered as "that part of the Zodiac with which it chiefly sympathises." This is frequently, also, very difficult if not impossible to ascertain. Accordingly, modern astrologers note the places of the principal fixed stars and the major planets at the dates of occurrence of the chief events affecting the metropolitan city, the ascendant of which it is desired to ascertain; and when the moment of the laying of the foundation stone of the chief public buildings, or of bridges, can be ascertained, the degree ascending is carefully computed; and when a manifest correlation is found the *ascendant* and *midheaven* of the city are determined.

"In addition to the rules which have been already given," says Ptolemy, "respecting the familiarity of the regions of the earth with the signs and planets, it must be observed that all fixed stars which may be posited on any line drawn from one zodiacal pole to the other, through such parts of the zodiac as may be connected with any particular country, are also in familiarity therewith."

The *ascendant* of the great metropolitan city of London was determined, some centuries since, to be 17° 54′ of the sign *Gemini*. That eminent fixed star, of the second magnitude and of the nature of Mars, the *Bull's North Horn* (*ß Tauri*), attained this longitude (♊ 17° 54′) in 1665-6, when the plague and fire of London took place. William Lilly, the celebrated astrologer, foretold, fifteen years beforehand, those momentous events, *from the transit of that martial star over the ascendant of London*. Lilly had observed the coincidence of the outbreak of plague in London in 1625 (the year of accession of Charles I.), to which no less than 35,417 persons fell victims, with the approach of the *Bull's North Horn* to the ascendant of the metropolis for it had then reached 17° 20′ of *Gemini*. It is worthy of remark that the civil war coincided with this approach of that martial star to the ascendant of the capital; and that in 1649, when it had arrived at 17° 40′ of *Gemini*, the king was beheaded.

The longitude of the *Bull's North Horn* in the year 1665 may be thus determined:

Longitude of *β Tauri*, Jan. 1st, 1879	♊ 20° 53′ 40″
Longitude of the ascendant of London	♊ 17 54 00
	2 59 40

Then, 2° 59′ 40″ = 10, 780 *seconds of longitude*, which divided by 50″ 25 (the annual motion of the fixed stars) = 214, the number of years since the star was in ♊ 17° 54′. From the year 1879 take 214 and the remainder is 1665.

Nostradamus[8] also foretold the fire of London.

This justifies the remark of Whalley on the aphorism of Ptolemy in regard to the pre-signification of the fixed stars: "The gradual progress of the fixed stars from one sign to another is in an especial manner to be regarded in considering the mutations, manners, customs, laws, government, and fortune of a kingdom."

Lilly, in his Almanack for 1666, said: "The eighteenth degree of *Gemini* is London's horoscope; and at the foundation of the City the Sun was in 25° of the same sign. This is certainly true, that when any notable event happens to concern that city, the planets are in those degrees, or those signs and degrees are affected."

The first pile of the present London Bridge was driven at 9h 21m a.m. of March 15th, 1824; at that moment, the ascendant was *Gemini* 16° 11′ and *Aquarius* 10° 43′ culminated—the R.A. of the meridian was 313° 10′ 45″. When the Fenian attempt was made to blow up with dynamite London Bridge, on December 13th, 1884, Saturn was retrograde in Gemini 20° 38′ and in opposition to the Sun.

When the Fenian attempt was made to blow up with dynamite the Houses of Parliament, Westminster Hall, and the Tower of London, on January 24th, 1885, at 2h p.m., Saturn was retrograde in Gemini 17° 47′.

Rome has, from the earliest history, been held to be influenced by the sign *Leo*. The symbol (♌) of this sign is found on many Roman gems.[9] Plutarch ("Romulus") records that L. Tarrutius, a friend of Cicero's, had cast the nativity of Rome according to the rules followed in the case of a human birth; and one cannot help seeing the pictured horoscope of the mistress of the world in a design of which many repetitions are extant, both antique and of Renaissance date: Jupiter is shown enthroned between Mars and Mercury, standing upon

[8] Vide the "Science of the Stars," p. 21.

[9] Vide "Antique Gems and Rings." By C. W. King, M.A.

an arch, under which old Oceanus half emerges from his waves, the whole enclosed within the circle of the Zodiac. The mystical importance of this design is apparent from the fact that it has been kept in view by the sculptor who executed the tomb of Junius Bassus, Prefect of Rome (dec. 359), the earliest, perhaps the most interesting Christian monument in existence, still remaining in situ upon the floor of the ancient basilica of St. Peter, now the crypt of the modern edifice. In this the principal bas-relief represents Christ seated between S.S. Peter and Paul standing, his feet resting upon an aged man emerging from beneath, whose robe flies in a semicircle over his head, here probably representing *Saeculum*, the Genius of the world.

That very brilliant *martial* star *Regulus* or *Cor Leonis*, the Lion's Heart, entered the sign *Leo* (in the manner described by Ptolemy) in the year 293 B.C., and the power of Rome then became very fully established, more especially its religious power or that of the Pontifex Maximus. In 571 A.D., the star entered decanate of Jupiter (the second ten degrees of ♌), whereupon the power of the Popes increase immensely. In 1291, the star left the decanate of Jupiter, and in that same year, on the 18th of May, the Holy Land was entirely lost by the capture of Acre. When, in 1507, the star left the *term* of Jupiter, the Pontifical power in Europe was broken by the efforts of Luther to establish the Reformation. In the year 1868, the star passed the twenty-eighth degree of *Leo* (and, therefore, according to Ptolemy, it must be considered to have entered the sign next in order), and two years later the French troops were withdrawn from Rome and the Italian troops entered it, the Papal (temporal) power being thus completely overthrown[10] (having been already considerably curtailed by the invasion of the Papal States by the troops of Victor Emanuel).

The relationship of the several *signs of the Zodiac* with certain *countries* and *cities* of the world is, as far as at present determined, as follows:

ARIES influences Britain, Germany, Denmark, Lesser Poland, Palestine, Syria, or Judea. Towns: Brunswick, Capua, Cracow, Florence, Marseilles, Naples, Padua, Saragossa, Utrecht, Verona, Leicester, and Birmingham.

TAURUS relates to Asia Minor, Cyprus, Georgia, the Caucasus, Media, Persia, Poland, Ireland, White Russia, and the Archipelago. Towns: Dublin, Leipsic, Mantua, Parma, Palermo, and Rhodes.

[10] Vide *Zadkiel's Almanac* for 1861, pp. 48-49, wherein the "speedy overthrow of the Papal power " was foretold from this circumstance.

GEMINI relates to the West of England, the United States of North America, the north-east coast of Africa, Lower Egypt, Flanders, Lombardy, Brabant, Belgium, and Sardinia. Towns: London, Versailles, Metz, Louraine, Bruges, Cordova, Nuremberg, Plymouth, and Melbourne.

CANCER rules Scotland, Holland, Zealand, and Northern and Western Africa. Towns: Amsterdam, Cadiz, Constantinople, Algiers, Genoa, Berne, Lubeck, Magdeburg, Manchester (the last decanate), Milan, New York, St. Andrews, Stockholm, Tunis, York, Venice, and Vincentia.

LEO relates to France, Italy, Sicily, the Alps, Bohemia, Chaldaea, the ancient Phoenicia, or the northern parts of Roumania. Towns: Rome, Bath, Bristol, Taunton, Damascus, Prague, Philadelphia, Ravenna, and Portsmouth.

VIRGO influences Turkey in Europe and Asia; Babylonia, Assyria; all the country between the Tigris and the Euphrates; Greece, Thessaly, Corinth, the Morea, the island of Candia, Croatia, Switzerland, and the West Indies. Towns: Paris, Lyons, Toulouse, Reading, Heidelberg, Jerusalem, and Cheltenham.

LIBRA relates to the borders of the Caspian; part of Thibet; China, especially the northern provinces; parts of India near China; Japan, Austria, Bactriana, Savoy, Upper Egypt, and ancient Libya. Towns: Antwerp, Charlestown, Frankfort, Fribourg, Gaëta, Lisbon, Placenza, Spires, and Vienna.

SCORPIO rules Algiers, Barbary, Fez, Judea, Syria, Cappadocia, Bavaria, Norway and Jutland, Valentia, Catalonia, and the Transvaal. Towns: Dover, Liverpool, Frankfort-on-the-Oder, and Messina.

SAGITTARIUS influences Spain, Hungary, Tuscany, lower Italy, (especially Tarento), that part of France between La Seine and La Garonne to Cape Finisterre, Arabia Felix, Dalmatia, Sclavonia, and Moravia. Towns: Avignon, Cologne, Buda, Narbonne, Rotenburg, Toledo, Stutgardt, Nottingham, Sheffield, Sunderland-on-Sea, and Northampton.

CAPRICORNUs relates to India, Afghanistan, the modern Punjaub, parts of Persia about Circan and Maracan, Chorassan, Thrace, Macedonia., the Morea, and Illyria, Albania, Bosnia, Bulgaria, Styria, Romandiola in Italy, the south-west of Saxony Hesse, Mecklenburg, the Orkney Islands, and Mexico. Towns: Oxford, Salisbury, Brandenburg, Prato in Tuscany, Canstanz, Tortona, Brussels, and Port Said.

AQUARIUS relates to Arabia the Stony, Red Russia, Prussia, part of Poland, Lithuania, Tartary, part of Muscovy, Circassia, Wallachia, Westphalia, Lower Sweden, Piedmont, Azania, and Abyssinia. Towns: Bremen, Hamburg, Ingoldstadt, Saltzburg, Trent, and Brighton.

PISCES relates to Portugal, Calabria, Normandy, Galicia in Spain, Upper Egypt, Nubia, and the southern parts of Asia Minor. Towns: Alexandria, Ratisbon, Seville, Tiverton, Worms, Compostella, Bournemouth, and Farnham.

The ancients observed that Saturn in Libra and Jupiter in Cancer, in mutual quadrature, brought great changes and alterations in "the balance of Power" in the world.

The author has observed that those distant planets Uranus and Neptune also effect great changes when their mutual configurations are formed from tropical and equinoctial signs. Such relative positions only take place very rarely.

In the year 1615, Uranus was in the third degree of the tropical sign *Cancer* and in quartile with Neptune in the third degree of *Libra*. In that year Captain Best, with four English ships, won a great victory over the Portuguese squadron off Surat. In that year the foundation of the British Empire in India may be said to have been laid.

In the year 1698, Uranus in the sixth degree of *Cancer* formed the quartile with Neptune in the sixth degree of *Aries*, a rival company was formed called "the English East India Company," to distinguish it from the old "London Company." The competition resulted in over-trading. In 1702, when Jupiter and Saturn were also in *Aries*, Uranus being still in *Cancer*, the two companies were united.

In 1744, when Neptune was in *Cancer*, Uranus in *Capricornus*, and Saturn in *Libra*, England engaged in the war of the Austrian succession, which brought the rival companies of England and France into collision, the result being the capture of Madras in 1746. In 1760 and 1761, when ♅, ♄, and ♃ were in *Aries*, the French were completely defeated at Wandewash and Pondicherry.

In 1909 and 1910, Uranus in *Capricornus* in opposition to Neptune in *Cancer*, India passed through a great crisis, as foretold by the author; and N. Africa, in 1911, was in a critical state.

The following table showing all the countries relating to each sign of the Zodiac respectively, is given as found in Ptolemy's *Tetrabiblos*, Book II, Chap. 3.

Signs	*Aries*	*Taurus*	*Gemini*	*Cancer*	*Leo*	*Virgo*
Triplicity	North-West	South-East	North-East	South-West	North-West	South-East
Quadrant of the Countries	North-West	South-East	North-East	South-West	North-West	South-East
Countries remote from the middle of the Earth	Britain Galatia Germany Barsania	Parthia Media Persia	Hyrcania Armenia Mantiana	Numidia Carthage Africa	Italy Apudia Sicily Gaul	Mesopotamia Babylonia Assyria
Quadrant of the Countries	South-East	North-West	South-West	North-East	South-East	North-West
Countries near the midde of the Earth	Caelesyria Idumea Judaea	Cyclades Cyprus Asia Minor	Cyrenaica Marmarica Lower Egypt	Bithynia Phrygia Colchis	Phoenicia Chaldaea Orchynia	Hellas Achain Crete
Signs	*Libra*	*Scorpio*	*Sagittarius*	*Capricornus*	*Aquarius*	*Pisces*
Triplicity	North-East	South-West	North-West	South-East	North-East	South-West
Quadrant of the Countries	North-East	South-West	North-West	South-East	North-East	South-West
Countries remote from the middle o f the Earth	Bactriana Casperia Serica	Metagonitis Mauritania Getulia	Tuscany Celtica Spain	India Arriana Gedrosia	Sauromatica Oxiana Sogdiana	Phazania Nasamonitis Garamantica
Quadrant of the Countries	South-West	North-East	South-East	North-West	South-West	North-East
Countries near the middle of the Earth	Thebais Oasis Troglodytica	Syria Connuagene Cappadocia	Arabia Felix	Thrace Macedonia Illyria	Arabia Azania Middle Ethio- pia	Lydia Cilicia Pamphyli

By observing eclipses of the Sun and Moon, and transits of the major planets and fixed stars, the ancient astrologers foretold the nature of the benefits or calamities about to happen, and named the countries likely to be affected by them. Modern astrologers follow the same rules. Mundane astrology takes precedence of all other branches because It deals wIth what Ptolemy described as "the superior cause." He wrote that:

"It must not be imagined that all things happen to mankind as though every individual circumstance were ordained by divine decree and some indissoluble supernal cause; nor is it to be thought that all events are shown to proceed from one single inevitable fate, without being influenced by the interposition of any other agency. Such an opinion is entirely inadmissible; for it is on the contrary most essential to observe, not only the heavenly motion which, perfect in its divine institution and order, is eternally regular and undeviating; but also the variety which exists in earthly affairs, subjected to and diversified by the institutions and courses of nature, and in connexion with which the superior cause operates in respect to the accidents produced.

"It is further to be remarked that man is subject not only to events applicable to his own private and individual nature, but also to others arising from general causes. He suffers for instance, by pestilence, inundations, or conflagrations produced by certain extensive changes in the Ambient and destroying multitudes at once; since a greater and more powerful agency must of course always absorb and overcome one that is more minute and weaker.

"In exercising prognostication, strict care must be taken to foretell future events by that natural process only which is admitted in the doctrine here delivered. In this manner experienced physicians, accustomed to the observation of diseases, foresee that some will be inevitably mortal, and that others are susceptible of cure. . . . The defect of not sufficiently considering the opposing influence has naturally induced an opinion that all future events are entirely unalterable and inevitable. But, since the foreknowledge of particular circumstances, although it may not wholly claim infallibility, seems yet so far practicable as to merit consideration, so the precaution it affords, in particular circumstances, deserves in like manner to be attended to; and if it be not of universal advantage, but useful in few instances only, it is still most worthy of estimation, and to be considered of no moderate value. Of this the Egyptians seem to have been well aware; their discoveries of the great faculties of this science have exceeded those of other nations, and *they have in all cases combined the medical art with astronomical prognostication.* And, had they been of opinion that all expected events are unalterable and not to be averted, they never would have instituted any propitiations, remedies, and preservatives against the influence of the Ambient, whether present or approaching, general or particular. But, by means of the science called by them Medical Mathematics they combined with power of prognostication the concurrent secondary influence arising out of the institutions and courses of nature, as well as the contrary influence which might be procured out of nature's variety; and by means of these they rendered the indicated agency useful and advantageous; since their astronomy pointed out to them the kind of temperament liable to be acted upon, as well as the events about to proceed from the Ambient, and the peculiar influence of those events, while their medical skill made them acquainted with everything suitable or unsuitable to each of the effects to be produced. And it is by this process that remedies for present and preservatives against future disorders are to be acquired; for, without astronomical knowledge, medical aid would be most frequently unvailing, since the same identical remedies are not better calculated for all persons whatsoever than they are for all diseases whatsoever."[11]

[11] Ashmand remarks that "this explains the origin of the old alliance between medicine and astrology, so universally preserved until almost within the last century."

CHAPTER II.

ON THE EQUINOXES AND SOLSTICES.

"First Aries, glorious in his golden wool."—MANILIUS.

THE VERNAL EQUINOX—the exact moment of the ingress of the Sun into *Aries*—is the commencement of the astrological year.

From the remotest antiquity there existed a belief that the world was created at the vernal equinox. It is a remarkable fact that the Christian era is connected with the epoch of the vernal equinox in *Aries*—the sacrificial *ram* or *lamb*.

Astrologers regarded every successive ingress of the Sun into *Aries* as the "revolution" of the world. A map of the Heavens was drawn for the moment of ingress, at the seat of government. If a *fixed* sign (either *Taurus*, *Leo*, *Scorpio*, or *Aquarius*) ascended, the pre-signification of the relative positions of the planets thereat was held to bear rule for the whole year. If a common sign (*Gemini*, *Virgo*, *Sagittarius*, or *Pisces*) ascended, the figure was held to bear rule for six months only, and another was drawn for the autumnal equinox. If a *moveable* sign *Aries*, *Cancer*, *Libra*, or *Capricornus*) ascended, the figure was held to retain influence for *three* months only, and figures were drawn for the summer solstice, autumnal equinox, and winter solstice. Modern experience appears to warrant a belief that the figure for the vernal equinox always bears chief rule for the ensuing year, that the succeeding ingresses into the other cardinal points have also a pre-signification, but subsidiary to the first-named.

The approved method of dividing the heavens and casting the figure has already been described in the first book. The order of importance of the twelve mansions or "houses" was formerly stated as follows: 1st, 10th, 7th, 4th, 11th, 9th, 5th, 2nd, 3rd, 8th, 6th and 12th. Experience shows the ascendant (1st) to be the most important, then the upper meridian (10th), next the descendant (7th), and lower meridian (4th). Next, after these angles, come the diurnal houses, 11th, 9th, 8th, and 12th; the nocturnal 2nd, 3rd, 5th, and 6th.

In mundane astrology, the twelve houses have a somewhat different signification to that described in genethlialogy. The annexed diagram will demonstrate this at a glance:

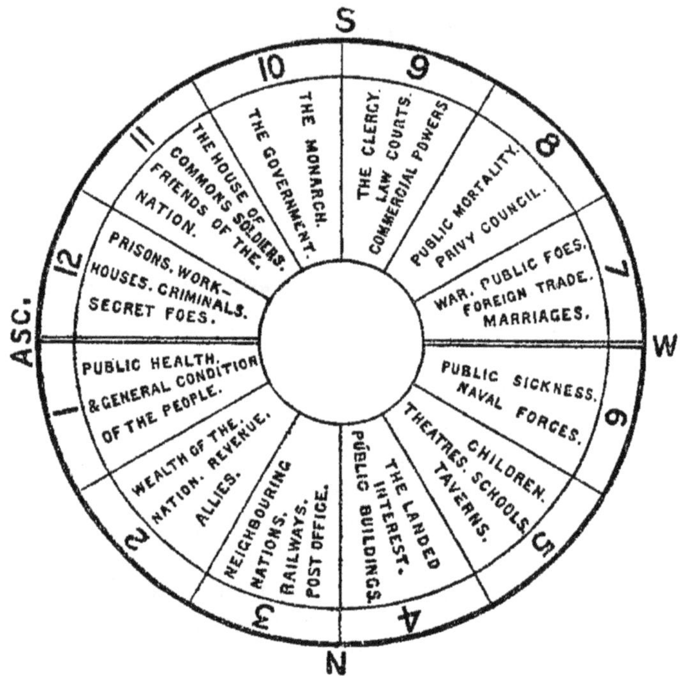

This traditional signification of the various houses has been fairly borne out by experience, *e.g.*, the success of the predictions given in *Zadkiel's Almanac* extending over the last eighty years. It is no wonder that judgment has been occasionally at fault and that some predictions have failed when we find that each house has several significations. With even a thorough knowledge of politics, and good judgment, it becomes occasionally difficult to forecast whether the presence of a benefic or malefic planet, as the case may be, in a certain house presignifies gain or loss to one or more of the public interests involved. Mars on the cusp of the lower meridian (4th house), at the vernal ingress of 1880,[1] clearly presignified the powerful enemies of Lord Beaconsfield's Government, and that, in the event of a dissolution, the Government would be beaten. [Had the Conservative leader

[1] Vide *Urania* for March, 1880, p. 86.

understood and relied upon astrology, he might have avoided defeat by postponing the dissolution until after the spring quarter had elapsed.] Thus the effects, in this instance, fell on the Government and not so much on the landed interest and public buildings. In like manner, the presence of Mars in the seventh house, at an ingress, does not always presignify actual warfare, but it usually causes strained relations and danger of war with a foreign Power. Saturn in the twelfth house may presignify trouble in connection with either workhouses, prisons, criminals, or seditious persons. The presence of Jupiter in the ninth house may benefit either the clergy or the gentlemen of the long robe, or may presignify commercial prosperity, for it does not follow that all will equally benefit thereby. Hence the true reading of a figure is often rendered difficult to accomplish beforehand. Moreover, before giving judgment on the figure of the vernal ingress it is imperative to examine that of the new Moon nearest thereto. If both figures coincide in their pre-signification, judgment may be given with confidence; when they differ greatly, very careful discrimination will be required to determine which to prefer. As a general rule, we should regard the ingress as having the more important signification, *unless the new or full Moon nearest thereto happen to be an Eclipse*. Ptolemy regarded the new Moon nearest the vernal equinox as having the most important pre-signification, and Zadkiel I. followed Ptolemy's injunction to this effect in the first few annual editions of his *Almanac*, but afterwards relied more on the figures for the Solar ingresses, so we may take it that his experience was in favour of the latter. The present editor (since 1876) of *Zadkiel's Almanac* relies chiefly on the Solar ingresses when no eclipse visible in England happens to nearly coincide.

CHAPTER III.

ON THE NEW MOON OF THE YEAR

> "Let no man, therefore, judge you in meat, or in drink, or in respect of a holiday, or of the New Moon, or of the Sabbath days: which are a shadow of things to come."—ST. PAUL.

THE NEOMENIA, or New Moon of the Year, is that nearest to the Sun's ingress into Aries (the vernal equinox). It was observed as a festival, with great solemnity, in the earliest ages of the world and by the most ancient nations. The Israelites as well as the Pagans celebrated it. The 5th and 6th verses of the 20th chapter of the first book of Samuel show that it was kept with greater solemnity than the ordinary new moons, all of which were celebrated by the Israelites. Had it not been found, by observation, that the new moon was really "a shadow of things to come"—especially when it happened to be an eclipse—no celebration of it would have continued to be observed by either the Israelites or by the Pagans.

Ptolemy says (Ashmand's translation):

"In the ecliptic, which, as a circle, has in fact no actual or definite beginning, the two equinoctial and the two tropical points, marked by the equator and the tropical circles, are reasonably assumed as beginnings.

"Although the foregoing arrangement has been adopted by men of science to denote the commencement of the several seasons of the year, it yet seems to be more consonant to nature, and more consistent with the facts, that the combined positions of the Sun and the new or full Moon which happens when the Sun is nearest to the points above mentioned, should mark the four beginnings; and more especially if such combined positions should produce eclipses; thus, from the new or full Moon taking place when the Sun is nearest to the first point of Aries, the spring should be dated; from that, when the Sun is nearest to the first point of Cancer, the summer; from that when he is nearest to the first point of Libra, the autumn; and from that when he is nearest to the first point of Capricornus, the winter. The Sun not only produces the general qualities of the seasons, but regulates the significations with regard to the excitations of the winds, as well as other general occurrences more or less subjected to occasional variation. All these general effects are usually brought about by the new or full Moon which takes place at the aforesaid points, and by the configurations then existing between the luminaries and the planets; but there are certain particular consequences which result from the new and full Moon in every sign, and from the transits of the planets, which require monthly investigation."

Although not giving the New Moon of the Year precedence over the vernal equinox, our experience teaches that it must not be overlooked. There is no doubt that germination is regulated by the combined influences of the Sun and Moon, and that unless they be taken advantage of for sowing (just *before* the new moon), good crops do not follow.[1] As Solomon said, "there is a time to sow and a time to reap." The ancients recognised the fact that the Moon had great influence on germination, etc., hence the myth of Isis. The neglect of this fact has led to the failure of crops, the loss of cattle, the dry rot in timber, etc.

Haly insisted that "we are to judge the alteration of the weather from the various configurations and positions of the planets at certain times, especially at the *conjunction* and prevention *of the luminaries* before the Sun's entrance into Aries." In this he followed Ptolemy's injunctions. Haly said that if Saturn be in one of the angles at the new moon, essentially dignified, especially in the midheaven, it presignifies "a various and diverse temper of air, thick and dark clouds; in hot weather lessening of heat; in winter, the cold augmented."

If Mars be so placed, "the heat in summer shall be increased; the cold in winter diminished; the spring or autumn shall incline to heat rather than cold."

If Jupiter, Venus, or the Moon be so placed, "a temperate, good, and wholesome air; and everything that is sown or planted in the earth shall increase and fructify well."

Again, if Mercury be so placed, or in one of the signs of the airy triplicity, at any new or full moon, "it denotes much change of air, great and high winds and very hurtful."

At the same time, Haly enjoined particular attention to the planetary positions at the ingress of the Sun into the cardinal signs. The student is advised to give precedence to the figure for the vernal equinox.

---

[1] Vide *Urania*, April, 1880, pp. 117-119.

CHAPTER IV.

NECESSARY CONSIDERATIONS BEFORE JUDGMENT.

"Celestial and immortal Powers!
O! aid my pen. What in me is dark
Illumine: while I presume to treat
Of fate and chance and change in sublunary
Things."—MILTON.

THE MAP OF THE HEAVENS for the moment of ingress of the Sun into the sign Aries being carefully drawn, for the seat of government, there are certain considerations to be entertained before proceeding to give judgment thereon.

In the diagram given in Chapter II, it is seen that the first house or ascendant bears relation to the people, their condition and general state of health; and the tenth house (upper meridian) to the Monarch and the Government. The planet ascending and the Moon (unless Cancer be in the meridian) are the significators of the people, the planet culminating is the significator of the Government.

If the planet ascending be in benefic aspect with one or both of the fortunes (Jupiter and Venus), swift in motion and more than 17° distant from the sun; or, if the Moon be so placed, then judge that the people will be prosperous, healthy, and safe in their possessions during the rule of that ingress. On the other hand, if the planet ascending, or the Moon, be under the Sun's beams, and afflicted by one or more of the infortunes (Mars Saturn, and Uranus), then judge that the people will be unfortunate, sickly, and insecure in their possessions.

Again, if there be an evil planet in the ascendant (Mars is not so evil for England, when rising, for he is the ruling planet of this country), judge that the season will be unhealthy, and that some misfortune will fall on the people. But, if a fortune ascend, free from the evil rays of the infortunes, and receive the application of the Moon by conjunction, sextile or trine aspect, then judge that the people will be very prosperous, successful, and secure.

If an evil planet in the eighth house afflict either the Moon or the planet ascending, judge that there will be great mortality during the rule of such ingress. If the afflicting planet be Saturn, rheumatism, consumption, catarrh, and paralysis will be very fatal (according to the nature of the sign occupied by ♄); if Mars, then acute fever, small-pox, and murderous outrages will cause great mortality; if Mercury (afflicted), mania or epilepsy will be very prevalent; if Uranus, peculiar accidents, cholera (if in ♍), or diphtheria (if in ♉) will prove fatal.

If the Moon or planet ascending be afflicted by Mars in the seventh house, there will be great danger of war, and the people will be much annoyed by their enemies. If by Saturn and Mars conjoined in *Taurus*, *Gemini*, *Leo*, or *Scorpio*, in the lower meridian, there will be great danger of earthquakes, and of deaths by accidents in mines and fall of houses and buildings.

The ancients said that, "If the ascending sign be *Aries* and Mars afflicted, the people of countries and towns ruled by ♈ will be afflicted with misfortunes, by heat or drought, and brain-fever; if *Scorpio* ascend, they will be afflicted by water (floods ?), venemous creatures, etc.

"If the ascending sign be *Taurus*, and Venus afflicted, there will be extremity of cold and snow, the fruits destroyed, etc.; if Libra, the people will suffer by storms of wind, pestilential air, etc.

"If the ascending sign be *Gemini*, and Mercury afflicted, the people under ♊ will suffer through corrupt air, and high winds, also obstruction of the lungs and bronchial tubes; if *Virgo*, the people under ♍ will suffer through great cold and dryness, scarcity of the fruits of the earth, affections of the heart and abdominal organs.

"If *Cancer* ascend, and the Moon be afflicted and weak, the people under the jurisdiction of ♋ shall be molested with pains in the head and breast; and there shall be much damage by excessive rain.

"If *Leo* ascend, and the Sun be afflicted, people under ♌ shall be subject to damage through extreme heat and drought, warm pestilential air; and diseases of the heart and brain shall be very prevalent.

"If *Sagittarius* ascend, and Jupiter be afflicted, people under ♐ will be afflicted with infirmities in the head and legs, and fevers; if *Pisces* ascend, the places ruled by it shall suffer from inundations, and grievous infirmities in the head and feet, gout and dropsy.

"If *Capricornus* ascend and Saturn be afflicted, the places subject to ♑ shall be visited with extreme cold and dry weather, and sterility, and the people with grief and diseases of the joints; if *Aquarius*, the places subject thereunto shall suffer by over moist air and high winds; and the people shall have many infirmities in their legs and heads."

Since the limitation of the power of the reigning Monarch and the exaltation of that of the Government, in a free country, the determination of the significator of the monarch has become rather difficult. In the case of an absolute monarch, we should undoubtedly take the planet in the midheaven, as his significator. The tenth house may be taken as signifying the Government in a general sense.

The ancients took the Sun to represent the reigning monarch; Jupiter, the rich and noble; Mars, the military; Saturn, the priests; Venus, women; Mercury, scribes, lawyers, students, merchants, and artists; and the Moon, the common people.

The Arabian astrologers had an aphorism to the effect that "if the significator of the king be under the Sun's beams, there is much danger of his decease during that revolution"; whereupon Ramesey remarked that he should rather "judge his kingly power to be then near its end, or likely to be much eclipsed, for there are many significators to be considered before judging as to the death of the king which ought never to be pronounced on bare testimony; besides, were this admitted, we should consequently conclude by the same rule, the death of a whole senate where there is no king." If the Sun alone had been taken as the significator of the king, it could not be under its own beams, hence the Arabian astrology must have taken the ruler of the sign in the meridian as the significator of the monarch. Be it remembered that we are writing of Solar *ingresses*, and not of Solar eclipses.

Ramesey says: "When the sign in the tenth house is Leo and the Sun happens to be at the same time afflicted by the conjunction, square, or opposition of Mars, especially if ♂ be ruler of the eighth house or therein located, or conjoined with or opposed by Saturn, danger of death of the reigning monarch is presignified." An instance of this is to be found in the figure for the moment of the Sun's ingress into *Libra* at Cabul, 1878. The sign *Leo* 15° culminated, and the Sun was in opposition to Saturn and in conjunction with Mars. Shere Ali, the Ameer of Afghanistan, having frittered away the weeks of grace generously allowed him by the British, found his country invaded, fled from his capital in December, 1878, and died in February, 1879.

To ascertain which planet is "lord of the year" or chief significator, say the ancients, "first see if there be any planet in an angle, if so, it is lord of the year (or the quarter, as the case may be). If there be more than one of the planets in angles, take that which is strongest as lord of the year. If there be none of the heavenly bodies in either of the angles, see if there be one in the eleventh, ninth, fifth, or third house (in the order named). If there be none in either of the last named houses, take the Sun if in an angle by day, or the Moon by night, to be chief ruler of the year—unless (says Haly) the lord of the ascendant be also lord of the sign containing the Sun, or the Moon by night, if so, then the lord of the ascendant shall be lord of the year.

"If the lord of the year be free from impediment, well dignified and well aspected, the year shall be plentiful, temperate and healthy, the people in good condition, fortunate and successful. If the lord of the year be impedited, afflicted and unfortunate, judge the contrary, especially if the Moon concur in the signification."

Bonatus gave more than fifty rules for ascertaining which planet is lord of the year. Ramesey's opinion was that either the planet ruling the ascending sign or the one having dignities therein, whichever may be the stronger, is lord of the year.

In my opinion, founded on over forty years' study of this branch of astrology, *the planet ascending or in the midheaven; and if one in the forth or second house and receiving the application of the Moon, or the sextile, square or trine, of the Sun,* is lord of the year. If there be no planet in either the ascendant or midheaven, take the one in the descendant or lower meridian.

If there be no planet in an angle, no planet must be taken as lord of the year, however essentially dignified, unless it be configurated with either the Sun or Moon. A planet in the lower meridian has chief signification as to the *general character of the weather* of the ensuing quarter, unless there be a planet in one of the other angles configurated with both the sun and moon.

My forecasts have been based on these last-named rules, for many years past.

In diurnal figures chief attention must be paid to the position and configurations of the Sun; in nocturnal, to those of the Moon—so say the ancients.

When Libra ascends and Venus happens to be afflicted and weak, trouble will fall especially on women during the ensuing quarter, and places ruled by Libra will have many misfortunes.

When Mars and Saturn happen to be in conjunction or in mutual square or opposition, especially if from angles, trouble will fall on the places ruled by the sign or signs occupied by them, however fortunate the figure may be in other respects. If they be in signs of human form, much mortality and many troubles will fall on mankind. If in conjunction in *Virgo*, or if one of these planets be located in ♍ and in square or opposition with the other, great mortality from intestinal diseases, or in warfare, will most probably follow. If at the same time one of these planets afflict the Sun in the tenth house (or if *Leo* be in the tenth house and the Sun be afflicted by ♂ or ♄) danger to the chief ruler (king, queen, or president) is presignified.

The foregoing instructions being carefully studied, it will render them easier to comprehend and remember if we take a Solar Ingress as an example. A better one for the purpose could not well be found than that of 1884, from which the predictions published in *Zadkiel's Almanac* and so strikingly fulfilled, were made.

To find the time at which the Sun enters Aries, in 1884, this is the process:

Sun's longitude, March 20	0° 18′ 0.8″	♈ 0° 0′ 0.0″
Sun's longitude, March 19	359 18 27.8	☉ 359 18 27.8
Motion in 24h	59 33.0	41 32.2

Then, by proportional logarithms:

As 59′ 33″ (*a.c.*)	9.51961
To 41 32.2	.63684
So 24h	.87506
To 16h 44m 25.12s =	1.03151

This is equivalent to 4h 44.4m a.m. of March 20th, 1884.

To find the right-ascension of the meridian:

	h. m. s.
Sidereal Time, March 19th	23 49 44.67
Add	16 44 25.12
Diff. mean and sidl. time for 16h 44m 25s	2 45.00
R. A. of Meridian = 249° 13′ 42″ or	16 36 54.79

This is the right ascension of the meridian at Greenwich Observatory, which is near enough for our purpose, there being only 23s difference of time between the Royal Observatory and the City of London (St. Paul's).

With a "Table of Houses" for London the figure can now be readily cast; the planets' geocentric longitudes can be reduced to the moment of Ingress by the aid of Zadkiel's *Ephemeris* for 1884.

The long. of the Moon is ♑ 2° 35′, of Mercury ♓ 20° 20′, of Venus ♉ 11° 9′, of Mars ♌ 2° 50′, of Jupiter ♋ 24° 40′ R., of Saturn ♊ 5° 4′ 21″, of Uranus ♍ 25° 56′ R., and of Neptune ♉ 19°1′.

The *declinations* of the heavenly bodies were: ☽ 18° 30′ 37″ S., ☿ 5° 43′ 27″ S., ♀ 16° 20′ 15″ N., ♂ 22° 45′ 50″ N., ♃ 21° 50′ 11″ N., ♄ 19° 35′ 3″ N., ♅ 2° 20′ 45″ N., and ♆ 15° 49′ 50″ N.

The first thing to determine is the distance of the planet Saturn from the cusp of the fourth house (lower meridian), as it is of great importance whether ♄ is within 5° of it or not. If we compute the longitude of the midheaven and of Saturn to seconds, we shall find that (♊ 10° 48′ 50″ being in the lower meridian) the distance of ♄ is 5° 44′ 29″ in *longitude*. But distances from either meridian are always reckoned by *right ascension*; the R.A. of ♄ being 63° 25′ 58″ it follows that its meridian distance is 5° 47′ 44″, Saturn is, therefore, *cadent* from the lower meridian and in the third house. Still, inasmuch as Saturn would in the course of a few weeks transit the degree of longitude in the lower meridian, it might be expected that it would then embarrass the Government (by reason of its opposition to the upper meridian) and bring trouble on London (being in *Gemini*). Hence this effect was foretold at p. 113 of *Zadkiel's Almanac* for 1884, in the following words:

"On the 13th inst. (May), Saturn enters the longitude (♊ 10° 49′) in the lower meridian at the vernal ingress; this presignifies trouble to the Government and an attempt to overthrow it, which will go very near to succeed. What with home and foreign questions, the Government will be in a great strait this month. In London some turbulence or acts of violence will be perpetrated, and Fenian machinations must be carefully guarded against."

It is now a matter of history that the division in the House of Commons on the Vote of Censure took place at 1h 40m a.m. of the 13th of May, 1884, 275 members voting for the motion and only 303 against it, the Government being saved by a majority of 28. The deplorable muddle in Egypt aroused public indignation against the Government, and nothing but a "mechanical majority" saved it from dissolution. On the 30th of May the Fenian explosions took place at Scotland Yard and St. James's Square, London. We venture to say that this is something like scientific precision in the way of forecasts, and that it demonstrates the fact that the heavenly bodies are "for signs of the future," or, literally, "future events." Let it be remembered that we wrote these forecasts in the summer of 1883 and that they were in the hands of the public early in October of that year. At p. 46 of *Zadkiel's Almanac*, it was stated that:

"This would be a very fortunate figure but for the proximity of Saturn to the cusp of the fourth house, which presignifies, says Ramesey, 'many great and high western winds; the birds of the air shall suffer detriment; also, men shall be afflicted with diseases; there shall be earthquakes in the western parts. In the fourth house, and in *Gemini* there shall be many controversies about rule and government; (having south latitude) a hot and dry air, little rain, and great mortality.' These effects of Saturn may be expected about the middle of May, when ♄ arrives at ♊ 10° 49′, and at the beginning of June, when the Sun conjoins with Saturn.

"The Sun being in trine aspect with Mars promises a fine and dry season; a fortunate and victorious year for Old England, with the exception of the periods before-named. Mercury in the ascendant and in trine aspect with Jupiter, presignifies good trade and extension of commerce; as, however, ☿ is applying to the opposition of ♅, there will be some loss to merchants through strange events, possibly through the disturbed state of the East."

An earthquake shock was felt in the Strand and north of London, Colchester, the Midlands, etc., on the 22nd of April, 1884, at 9h 20m a.m. In Essex great damage was done to houses, etc. The weather of the spring and summer was very dry, and, after the l0th of May, exceedingly hot, indeed the heat and drought of 1884 will be long remembered. Controversies about rule and government were waged with great spirit and determination. Trade and commerce suffered through the disturbed state of the East, in Egypt, and in China.

As a *fixed* sign (*Aquarius*), ascended, the vernal ingress bears chief rule for the whole year. The Sun is "lord of the year" being in an angle and in the sign of his exaltation (*Aries*). The ruler of the ascendant (Saturn) being cadent, and the Moon in square aspect with the Sun, presignified the unfortunate condition, generally speaking, of the common people, especially in the north where thousands of workmen and their families were in a state of semi-starvation.

The foregoing example will serve to prove that there is a great deal of truth in Mundane Astrology, and that its great usefulness to mankind cannot be overrated. Indeed we may say that in the wide range of physical science there is no question of higher national importance than this. So far from a belief in astrology leading to fatality, it is the *neglect* of astrology that tends to fatality; for the laws of nature go on working until the catastrophe arrives which might have been foreseen, and its effects mitigated, had the warning of the heavens been attended to by statesmen and philosophers. Consider for a moment the folly of the Government in 1854 in declaring war against Russia, and commencing it at the time when evil influences obtained, in sending a fine army to the Crimea to perish in the frightful winter of 1854-55. The planetary warnings were plain enough; Zadkiel I. expressed his opinion, from the vernal ingress, 1854, that, "War may be expected," that "*extensive warfare and much shedding of blood in the dominions of the Great Turk*" would result from the position of Mars in Virgo; that the nativity of our good Queen and that of Napoleon III were both afflicted. Yet the Government drifted into war, and began it at the wrong time!

To return to our aphorisms:

If the lord of the year be harmoniously configurated with the planet ruling the sign in which it is located, and free from impediment, *i.e.*, from affliction by the infortunes, the people will be "in a good condition, quiet, secure, at peace, and joyful."

If it be afflicted and have no configuration with its dispositor, the people will be "sad, fearful, molested with war, trouble, and anxiety."

According to the "house" in which the lord of the year happens to be located will the good or evil condition of the people be shown.

If SATURN be lord of the year and well configurated, great impetus will be given to building; the earth will be fruitful; the people held in esteem by neighbouring nations; and husbandmen will be successful. If Saturn be afflicted, there will be much cold weather; grievous infirmities, losses, crosses, and sorrows; great damage by winds, storms, and rain (if other testimonies concur); much mortality among the aged; and these evils will be most apparent in the places under the dominion of ♑, ♒, and the sign in which ♄ is located.

If JUPITER be lord of the year and happily configurated, the rulers shall do justice, measures of reform will be enacted; religious orders will prosper and do well; the people will be prosperous, happy and contented, and well affected towards their rulers. But if Jupiter be afflicted, little benefit will accrue, and indeed some misfortunes are likely to happen.

If MARS be lord of the year and harmoniously aspected, soldiers and all who bear arms will be fortunate and victorious over their foes; the people will be prosperous (especially those under *Aries* or *Scorpio*). But if Mars be afflicted, the contrary will happen.

If the SUN be lord of the year and free from affliction, the monarch and nobles will be in good condition and may increase their renown; corn, cattle and birds will be plentiful; the people generally prosperous and successful. If the Sun be afflicted by the infortunes, the nobles will probably suffer diminution of power and of privilege.

If VENUS be lady of the year and well configurated, women will be advantaged; the people generally will thrive and be much given to sport, recreation, and mirth; and marriages will be numerous. If Venus be afflicted by Saturn or Uranus, women will be unforturnate, cases of cruelty to them will be numerous, the marriage-rate will be below the average; there will be little of feasting and of merry-making, and the people generally will not be fortunate.

If MERCURY be lord of the year and happily configurated, scientific men, artists, students, school-teachers, merchants and tradesmen will have a successful year. If Mercury be affiicted, judge the contrary.

If the MOON be lady of the year, well configurated, and free from affliction by the Sun or the infortunes, the people will be, generally speaking, healthy and fortunate. But if afflicted, judge the contrary.

An example of the power of Mars as the significator of violence and murder when situated in the seventh house at the solstice may be mentioned in the summer solstice, 1888. The Sun's ingress into the first point of *Cancer* took place at 0h 14m 12s a.m., G.M.T., of June 21st. The R.A. of the M.C. is 18h 12m 43s.16 or 273° 10′ 47″ in arc, *Capricornus* 2° 55′ culminating, and *Aries* 7° 29′ ascending at Greenwich. The planet Mars is found in the seventh house, in *Libra* 17° 0′, near Uranus in ♎ 13° 7 ′. The Moon is in *Scorpio* 20° 8′, on the cusp of the eighth house (that of death). The appalling murders in Whitechapel took place during the ensuing quarter; one woman was murdered on the 7th of August; another on the 1st of September, and two in the early morning of the 30th of the same month; all four women having their throats cut, and three of them were mutilated, presumably by the same expert hand. The excitement and horror caused by those murders were unparalleled in London. In *Zadkiel's Almanac* for 1888, page 50, will be found the following forecast:

"Criminals will give a good deal of trouble, and robberies with violence will be very numerous; in fact, murderous outrages will be appalling."

Robberies with violence were unusally numerous in that summer quarter. The Whitehall murder and mutilation took place in the same period.

CHAPTER V

ON THE PRESIGNIFICATION OF THE PLANET SATURN WHEN LORD OF THE YEAR.

> "The evidence with which we see the future portrayed in the source of all truth, no more necessitates that future than does the image reflected in the sight by a ship sailing down a stream, necessitate the motion of the vessel."—DANTE.

SATURN, according to Albumasar, is in nature, "cold, dry, melancholy, sombre, of grave asperity, and may be cold and moist."

When SATURN is lord of the year and in the sign *Aries*, it causes many great easterly winds, and scarcity of provisions. If afflicted, it presignifies many thefts, highway-robberies, much anxiety, sadness, and tribulation. If in evil aspect with Mars, very cold weather, epidemic diseases among sheep and cattle. If Saturn be *direct* in motion and in one of the angles, much rain or cold; and discord between the various classes of society; if *retrograde*, the state and condition of the people will be grievous; and if both Mars and the Moon be in evil aspect with Saturn, there will be terribly cold weather, dissensions and perhaps wars, and cattle will die. If Saturn have *north* latitude, it presignifies a dense atmosphere and many dark clouds; if the latitude be *south*, cold weather and frost. If *occidental* (in regard to the Sun), there will be earthquakes in the eastern parts.

SATURN in *Taurus*, in an angle and *direct* in motion, presignifies war or discord, chiefly in the places subject to ♉ and in the southern parts of the country for which the figure is cast; destruction of seeds and plants—unless the benefic aspects of the fortunes prevent it—a great prevalence of caterpillars and worms; destruction of houses in the southern parts and those ruled by ♉. If afflicted, much mortality, especially among the great. If afflicted by Mars and the Moon by aspect, scarcity and mortality; if by *conjunction*, trouble and vexation to the rulers, and danger of war, especially if in the tenth house. If *retrograde*, destruction and violence.

SATURN in *Gemini* and direct in motion in an angle, presignifies many great westerly winds, very sharp cold weather in winter; the birds of the air will suffer detriment; men shall be afflicted with diseases; in summer corruption of air, thunder, lightning and rain. If *retrograde*, discord is presignified; earthquakes in the western parts. If in the fourth and in *Gemini*, earthquakes in the western parts; if he be in aspect with the ruler of the tenth house, there shall be many controversies and dissensions about rule and government, and inundations by which the fruits of the earth will be injured. If Saturn have *north* latitude, there will be a foggy dark atmosphere, and earthquakes chiefly in the western parts and places subject to *Gemini*. If the latitude of ♄ be *south*, there will be a hot and dry air, and little or no rain. If *oriental*, infirmities and sickness and trouble to the nobles; if *occidental*, very dry air and little rain.

SATURN in Cancer, there shall be an increase of water, fish, locusts (or caterpillars in our country), and worms. If Mars be not in any aspect with Saturn, the weather will be very cold. If Saturn be *retrograde*, let the monarch beware of an attempt on his life; and if in aspect with Mars, there will be abundance of rain or cold weather, and many shipwrecks, also death to fish in the seas and rivers. If Saturn have *north* latitude, it presignifies a scarcity of waters, a drought of fountains, and but little rain; if south, trade will be unprofitable. If *oriental*, dark and unhealthy air; great cold ill winter; damage to fruit by northern winds; if *occidental*, much rain.

SATURN in *Leo* and having *north* latitude, presignifies much rain and corruption of fruit, and trouble to rulers and people. If *oriental*, much sickness; if *occidental*, great mortality, the more if ♄ be retrograde.

SATURN in *Virgo* and in *north* latitude, presignifies a pleasant and healthy air; in *south* latitude, scarcity of rain and a drought of fountains. If *oriental*, women will suffer; if *occidental*, acute and sharp fevers will follow.

SATURN in *Libra* in *north* latitude, presignifies a hot and dry air, little or no rain, and a scarcity of waters; in *south* latitude, a pleasant and healthy air. If *retrograde*, infirmities to servants and the common people; if *direct*, the fruits of the earth will be plentiful.

SATURN in *Scorpio* with *north* latitude, presignifies abundance of rain and increase of water in rivers and fountains; with *south* latitude, a scarcity of provisions, especially fruits of the earth. If *oriental*, there will be many dissensions and quarrels among great men; if *occiden-*

tal, destruction of ships and loss of life to sailors. If *retrograde*, epidemic diseases; if direct in motion, said some of the ancients, "Babylon shall be safe."

If SATURN be in *Sagittarius* and in *north* latitude, it presignifies increase of fountains and much cold in winter; if in *south* latitude, less cold and rain. If *oriental*, noble and rich men will be expatriated and have their estates confiscated; if *occidental*, there will be many dissensions, quarrels, and war between kings and great men. If *retrograde*, it will go ill with all kinds of men and their affairs; if *direct*, travellers by sea and land shall be prosperous, safe, and successful.

When SATURN is in *Capricornus* and in *north* latitude, the air will be temperate and healthy, with moderate and seasonable rains; in *south* latitude, there will be dark, cloudy, cold weather. If *oriental*, there will be dissensions between the nobles and the common people; if *occidental*, the fruits of the earth shall be wasted and consumed by and through extremity of heat (in summer) and creeping things, such as caterpillars and the like. If *retrograde*, the common people will be angry and quarrelsome one with another; if *direct*, it presignifies the good condition of the great, and that they shall bear themselves well towards all men and observe the law.

SATURN when in *Aquarius* and in *north* latitude presignifies much rain, frost, or cold weather according to the season; in *south* latitude, a scarcity of water in fountains and rivers. If *oriental*, the common people will not thrive well; if *occidental*, there will be many great fires. If *retrograde*, the evil will be increased; if *direct*, it presignifies the death of cattle breeders and large cattle.

SATURN in *Pisces* and in *north* latitude, presignifies many tempestuous winds chiefly from the north, and very great cold in winter; in *south* latitude, storms and tempests at sea and many shipwrecks, injury to sailors and maritime people generally. When *oriental*, dissensions and discords among the great, also mortality amongst them; *occidental*, the common people will exalt themselves above their superiors. If *retrograde*, there shall be many dissensions amongst religious men and theologians; if *direct*, men will be devout in their worship of the Almighty.

Cardan said: "When Saturn is in *Libra* and Jupiter is in *Cancer*, great changes and alterations will happen in the world."

A conjunction of Mars and Saturn in the sixth or eighth house, especially in a humane sign (♊, ♍, first half of ♐, or ♒), presignifies a great pestilence."

CHAPTER VI.

ON THE PRESIGNIFICATION OF JUPITER.

"We behold the things that we predict in the mirrors of eternal truth."—DANTE.

JUPITER—the largest planet of the Solar system, more than eleven times the diameter of the Earth and nearly one-tenth part of that of the Sun, the mass of ♃ exceeding that of the earth 1,428 times, its magnitude so vast that if the Earth, the Moon, Mercury, Venus, Mars, Saturn, Uranus and four of the largest planetoids could be combined they would hardly equal it—"with mighty state the rival of the Sun"—comes next in order to Saturn in the aphorisms of the ancients as to presignification. Jupiter is described as the *greater fortune*, as Saturn is the *greater infortune*.

When JUPITER happens to be lord of the year, in the sign *Aries*, it presignifies that a new form of religion will arise in the East; men shall observe religion and the law, be given to good works; the weather will be windy, seasonable, and favourable to health; the fruits of the earth shall be plenteously produced. If well aspected, it presignifies the prosperity of places subject to ♈. If afflicted, little benefit will accrue.

JUPITER in *Taurus*, it presignifies fertility of the earth, a temperate and good air, prevalence of southerly winds; prosperity for the people and good feeling between them and the nobles. If afflicted, little good will result.

JUPITER in *Gemini*, well configurated, there will be extremely warm air and much wind; if in aspect with Mars, many casualties by lightning; if in aspect with Saturn, corrupt air and epidemic disease. If afflicted, no good will result.

JUPITER in *Cancer*, the people and nobles shall be in a very prosperous condition; the air shall be pleasant and healthy, the earth fruitful, the fruit good and wholesome; voyages shall be pleasant and successful, generally. If afflicted, the good resulting will be much less.

JUPITER in *Leo* presignifies fine and warm weather, a good harvest, and a dry season. If afflicted by Saturn or Uranus, there will be tempests, and great thunderstorms; and earthquakes in places under ♌. If in aspect with Mars, a drought of fountains and great heat in summer.

JUPITER in *Virgo*, men shall be sociable and delight in agriculture; the fruits of the earth shall be plentiful; southerly winds will prevail. If afflicted, fruit will soon rot; and little benefit to mankind will result.

JUPITER in *Libra* presignifies a temperate and healthy air, warm winds, pleasant showers for the fruits of the earth. If afflicted by Mars. there shall be much thunder and lightning in summer, and casualties therefrom in the western parts.

JUPITER in *Scorpio* presignifies a good clear air; the season shall be plentiful; heat in summer, cold in winter; a prevalence of northerly wind. If *retrograde* or afflicted, the good will be lessened, and perchance there will be shipwrecks through tempests, and some danger of war.

JUPITER in *Sagittarius* presignifies a temperate air in the beginning of winter, but at the end thereof great cold; but few high winds. If in *north* latitude, little rain and pleasant air; if *south*, gusts of wind. If *oriental*, the nobles and rich men shall be in good and joyful condition; if *occidental*, their dignity and renown shall be increased. If *retrograde*, travelling will hardly be safe or successful; if *direct* in motion, travelling by sea and land shall be safe; fish shall be plentiful. If afflicted by ♄ or ♅ there will be snow and frost in the spring doing great damage to fruit.

JUPITER in *Capricornus* presignifies a plentiful year, pleasant air, and many great southerly winds; success and profit to the common people. If afflicted or *retrograde*, no good will result; and storms will do great damage.

JUPITER in *Aquarius* presignifies a temperate, pleasant air, and pleasant showers; a prosperous year. If afflicted, damage by high winds, storms, rain, or snow, according to the season.

JUPITER in *Pisces*, the year shall be plentiful; the people successful, sailors and merchants fortunate and prosperous; the air temperate and pleasant, with seasonable fructifying showers; abundance of fish. If afflicted, there will be much thunder and rain, and possibly destruction of fish.

JUPITER in the *ascendant*—whether or not lord of the year—free from affliction, presignifies that the people will be prosperous, healthy, jovial, honoured and at peace. If afflicted, the condition of the people will not be so good as when ♃ happens to be strong, and well configurated.

CHAPTER VII.

ON THE PRESIGNIFICATION OF MARS.

"Mars, the fierce god of war,
Of discord dire and slaughter;
Bellona's aid, the scourge of Providence."—CONGREVE.

THE RED PLANET—so-called from the red appearance of its disc, being in fact the ruddiest star in the heavens—*Mars*, "the god of war," "the star of strength," "the star of the unconquered will," the Hercules of the Chaldaeans, has very potent influence over the affairs of this world, when in certain positions. Evidence of its influence when in perigree will be found in the first volume of this work.

Of its symbolism, Dante[1] says:

"Mars dries up and burns things, because its heat is like to that of the fire; and this is the reason why it appears fiery in colour, sometimes more and sometimes less, according to the density and rarity of the vapours which follow it, which sometimes take fire of themselves as is declared in the first book of *Meteors*. [And, therefore, Albumasar says, that the ignition of these vapours signifies death of kings, and change of Empires, being effects of the dominion of Mars. And accordingly Seneca says that at the death of the Emperor Augustus a ball of fire was seen in the heavens. And in Florence, at the beginning of its downfall, a great quantity of these vapours, which follow Mars, were seen in the air in the form of a cross.]"

There is no doubt about the combativeness of Mars-men; and the most destructive and dangerous lunatics are those under Mars's influence.

Dante describes the Heaven of Mars as the abode of martyrs and crusaders who died fighting for the faith, in harmony with Plato's idea that the soul returned to its proper planet: "The Creator, when he had framed the universe, distributed to the stars an equal number of souls, appointing to each soul its several stars."

---

[1] *Convito*, II., 14.

It has been already stated that Mars is the ruling planet and Aries the ruling sign of Britain, hence to this day the British are, as Claudius Ptolemy declared, "impatient of restraint, lovers of freedom, warlike, industrious, imperious, cleanly, and high-minded." It is to this that England owes her naval supremacy, to the native courage of her sailors and their wandering propensities that lead them to "plough the ocean and to tempt the winds." Had Manilius, the Augustan poet, lived after the days of Nelson (who was born with ♂ rising in ♏). Blake, Boscawen, Brenton, Lord Cochrane, and Drake, he could not have better described the attributes of our naval heroes than when writing of the ship in *Aries*, in his fifth book. It is probable that Cromwell was born when Mars was rising in *Aries*. When Mars is passing through either *Aries*, *Leo*, *Scorpio*, or *Capricornus*, or in the ascendant at a Solar ingress or eclipse (at London), the arms of England are victorious.

The following are the aphorisms of the ancients (revised, rewritten, and condensed) as to the presignification of Mars when lord of the year:

When MARS is lord of the year and in *Aries*, free from the evil rays of Saturn and Uranus, free from combustion, and *direct* in motion, it presignifies that the people shall be in a secure condition, victorious over their enemies; the air temperate and the earth fruitful. If in *north* latitude, there will be little or no rain and a hot air; if in *south* latitude, much thunder and lightning. If *oriental*, war is likely, and discord among the nobles; if *occidental*, troubles and quarrels. If afflicted by Saturn, there will be many great winds, chiefly from the east, little or no rain; quarrels among men; inflammation of the eyes, smallpox, scarlet-fever, or measles. If *retrograde*, there will be much sickness.

MARS in *Taurus* presignifies many great southerly winds, much rain, thunder and lightning; the fruits of the earth injured; the cattle unhealthy. If in *north* latitude, much rain, but less harm to the fruits of the earth; if in *south* latitude, many gusts of wind, and destruction of fruit. If *oriental*, there shall be paace in the southern and western parts; if *occidental*, much mortality and sickness, especially to women. If *retrograde*, many children and young people will die (probably from smallpox or scarlatina).

MARS in *Gemini* presignifies many casualties from thunderstorms, and excessive heat; quarrels, thefts and robberies in the northern and western parts; the monarch and rulers shall overcome their enemies; inflammation of the ears and pustules. If in *north* latitude, much rain; if in *south* latitude, a drought of fountains and scarcity of water. If *ori-*

ental, skin diseases will be prevalent; if *occidental*, trouble to lawyers, writers, judges and merchants. If *direct*, much slandering; if *retrograde*, dissensions and quarrels amongst professors of religion.

MARS in *Cancer* presignifies many shipwrecks; dissensions and quarrels in the western parts; heavy taxation; fevers, throat-diseases, chest affections, etc.; the air unhealthy; rain scarce; many cattle and horses will die; and scarcity of the fruits of the earth. If in *north* latitude, the weather will be cold and dry; in *south* latitude, many gusts of wind destructive to trees. If *oriental*, mortality amongst cattle. If *direct*, the air will be healthier and pleasanter; if *retrograde*, there will be much crime.

MARS in *Leo* presignifies war and effusion of blood, chiefly in places under ♌; scarcity of provisions, especially in the eastern parts; mortality amongst young men. If in *north* latitude, a scarcity of water; if in *south* latitude, there will be no want of water. If *oriental*, damage to cattle; if *occidental*, fish will die. If *retrograde*, loss and detriment to great and rich men; if *direct*, much wind from the west.

MARS in *Virgo* presignifies war and effusion of blood in the northern parts and in places subject to ♍; plenty of provisions; also diseases of the eyes, and much mortality amongst women. If in *north* latitude, damage to fruits and seeds; much sickness; if south, profusion of fruit. If *oriental*, mortality among the aged; if *occidental*, great and tempestuous winds. If *direct* in motion, prosperity of the great and rich; if *retrograde*, war will quickly follow.

MARS in *Libra* presignifies much wind, rain, and mist, southerly winds prevalent; mortality amongst men; scarcity of the fruits of the earth, of corn and wine; danger of war, quarrels and discord amongst men, and tribulation. If in *north* latitude, much thunder and lightning; if in *south* latitude, much sickness. If *oriental*, war, and dissension amongst noble and rich men; if *occidental*, the rich aud noble will be safe and secure. If *direct* in motion, the rich will do well; if *retrograde*, there will be much sickness among the great.

MARS in *Scorpio* presignifies misty or cloudy weather, much cold in winter, excessive heat in summer, and injury to seeds and herbs; men will suffer in their eyes; thefts, robberies, quarrels and murders will be numerous. If in *north* latitude, a scarcity of water; in *south* abundance of water. If *oriental*, much sickness and a prevalence of complaints under ♏; if *occidental*, little piety among men. If *retrograde*, many troubles; if *direct* in motion, affairs will be better.

MARS in Sagittarius presignifies war in the eastern parts; mischief to places under ♐; a good deal of sickness; little rain, extreme cold in winter and spring; injury to fruit-trees, plants and herbs; the year generally will be marked by scarcity; bees will be destroyed and honey scarce. If well aspected, such as bear arms shall be in good condition, fortunate, and successful. Albumasar said that if Mars be in one of the first fifteen degrees of ♐, and lord of the year (or in ♊, ♍, or ♒), it presignifies war, tumult, and mischief to kings and nobles—unless in benefic aspect with ♃. If the latitude of ♂ be *north*, it presignifies a good, pleasant, and temperate air; if *south*, merchants and tradesmen will gain. If *oriental*, peace and security; if *occidental*, abundance of fruit. If *direct*, mortality amongst horses and oxen; if *retrograde*, men will suffer with affections of the head, neck, and thighs.

MARS in *Capricornus* presignifies danger of war, trouble, and much mortality in the eastern parts; rain in due season, plenty of provisions and fruit. If in *north* latitude, much snow in winter; in *south*, a close, hot air. If *oriental*, "let the Roman Emperor have a care of a stab, and so much the more certain will this be if ☽ be in the 8th house or with the lord thereof, or with ♂ in an angle, and ♃ prevent it not, unless the Almighty miraculously show His infinite mercy unto him"; if *occidental*, boils and carbuncles will be prevalent. If *direct* in motion, plenty; if *retrograde*, want.

MARS in *Aquarius* presignifies trouble; abundance of rain, snow and cold in winter; a probability of dethroning of kings and great men, chiefly in places under ♒; a scarcity of provisions, especially in the western parts, unless ♂ be in aspect with ♀. If in *north* latitude, much snow and cold winter; if *south*, much heat, but a thick atmosphere. If *oriental*, the great will be prosperous and jovial; if *occidental*, not so well. If *direct*, there shall be many caterpillars, and such like creatures shall destroy trees; if *retrograde*, very hot summer, and some detriment to fruit.

MARS in *Pisces* presignifies much snow and rain in winter and spring, rain in summer and autumn; destruction of fish, of which men shall catch many; danger of assassination to kings and great men; scarcity of the fruits of the earth; and generally it will be a turbulent and hard period for man and beast. If in *north* latitude, the air will be good, pleasant and healthy; if *south*, there will be many caterpillars, and locusts in some places. If *oriental*, it presignifies the slaughter of great men; if *occidental*, many troubles will fall on servants. If *direct* in motion, the people will be safe and healthy; if *retrograde*, traders will profit.

MARS in the *ascendant* presignifies that the people of that country will gain by war and overcome their enemies during that revolution. If Mars be weak or afflicted, there will be danger of riot, bloodshed, and even of civil war if other testimonies concur.

Guido Bonatus said: "I have experienced that a planet is in an angle to the space of 5° beyond the cusp; for as once I sought the revolution of a year, I found Mars in the 5th deg. beyond the cusp of the angle of the earth in *Capricornus*, south latitude, which presignifies the killing of the Roman Emperor; and acquainted him with it, for his court was at Grossietti and I at Folirii; and it was found that Pandulfus de Farsenella and Theobaldus Franciscus, and divers others of the secretaries had conspired to slay him, and none of his own astrologers had observed it, because they did not believe that Mars was in an angle, for he was 4° 58′ beyond the cusp in their opinion; however, after a planet shall be removed from the cusp or line of any angle full 5° or more, he is to be accounted cadent from that angle."—Aphorism 58, translation published in 1676.

Cardan wrote: "If wars be presignified, note the angle of the figure wherein Mars is posited, for from that part the enemies will come."

CHAPTER VIII.

ON THE PRESIGNIFICATION OF THE SUN.

"Through divers passages, the world's bright lamp
Rises to mortals, but through that which joins
Four circles with the threefold cross,[1] in best
Course, and in happiest constellation set
He comes, and to the worldly wax best gives
Its temper and impression."—DANTE.

"THE SUN that giveth light looketh upon all things, and the work thereof is full of the glory of Jehovah."[2]

The ancients gave precedence to Saturn, Jupiter, and Mars, before the Sun; Venus, Mercury, and the Moon, following the "greater light"—*i.e.*, in *the order of their motion*. This explains the meaning of the fourth verse of the nineteenth psalm, which, after declaring that the "rule" of the planets has gone forth through all the earth, says: "In the midst of them a dwelling-place is established for the Sun. The word translated in the authorised version "the heavens" really means "the planets." It is not true of the heavens that the Sun is in the midst of them, but as regards motion the Sun is in the midst of the planets (as known to the ancients), having Saturn, Jupiter, and Mars, on one side, and Venus, Mercury, and the Moon on the other.[3]

Claudius Ptolemy declared that "the power of the Sun predominates, the others either co-operate with his power or diminish its effect."

If the SUN be lord of the year in *Aries* (at the vernal equinox), said the ancients, free from the malefic aspect of the infortunes, it shall be well with the common people; the year shall be fruitful; kings and

[1] "Where the four circles, the horizon, the zodiac, the equator, and the equinoctial colure, join; the last three intersecting each other so as to form three crosses, as may be seen in the armillary sphere."—Cary's translation.

[2] *Ecclesiasticus*, xliii., 16.

[3] *Vide Zadkiel's Almanac* for 1861, art. "The 19th Psalm newly rendered."

grandees shall prosper, and shall overcome their enemies, and do justice. If the Sun be afflicted, judge the contrary. Places under the rule of ♈ will be chiefly affected.

If the SUN be lord of the summer quarter (in *Cancer*), seafaring men, and the inhabitants of places ruled by ♋ will be prosperous. If afflicted, judge the contrary.

If the SUN be lord of the autumn quarter (in *Libra*) and free from affliction, people under ♑ will prosper. If afflicted, judge the contrary.

If the SUN be lord of the winter quarter (in *Capricornus*) and free from affliction), the people under ♑ will be prosperous and secure. Farmers and cattle-dealers will do well. If afflicted, judge the contrary.

The SUN can never be *oriental* or *occidental* in the same sense as the planets, for they are thus reckoned according to their position in regard to the Sun. Nor can the Sun be either *retrograde* or *stationary*.

The SUN when in the *ascendant* presignifies (if free from affliction) a fortunate year and advancement for the nation; if afflicted, the great will suffer in health and power.

The SUN in the *second* house presignifies waste of the public revenue, and that the monarch or rulers will lead a retired and miserly life.

The SUN in the *third* house presignifies social pleasures and harmony among the people.

The SUN in the *fourth* house presignifies (if afflicted or in ♈) detriment to vegetables; degradation of some great men, or lessening of the power of the nobles; and a deficiency of rainfall.

The SUN in the *fifth* house presignifies detriment to women and children, unless the ☉ be extremely well configurated.

The SUN in the *sixth* house presignifies a prevalence of affections of the head and eyes; sadness to the monarch and rulers; losses through servants; and a lessening of the privileges of the nobles—especially if ☉ be afflicted.

The SUN in the *seventh* house is not of good omen of good feeling between the monarch or government and the people; and presignifies that the monarch will live retired.

The SUN in the *eighth* house presignifies mortality among the great, and a lessening of their privileges, especially if ☉ be in evil aspect with the ruler of the eighth.

The SUN in the *ninth* house presignifies an increase of travelling, and (if free from affliction) prosperity for churchmen, lawyers, and scientific men.

The SUN in the *tenth* house (especially when in ♈ and harmoniously configurated with the fortunes) presignifies the glory, honour, renown, and prosperity of the monarch and chief rulers, and a fortunate year.

The SUN in the *eleventh* house, free from affliction, presignifies that the people shall be merry and friendly, shall achieve their desires, and that there shall be an excellent understanding between them and their rulers. If ☉ be in ♈ and happily configurated with ♂, soldiers, surgeons and engineers will receive honours and do well.

The SUN in the *twelfth* house (unless extremely well aspected) presignifies losses, crosses, and perchance lessening of privileges to the great, and an ill-feeling between them and the people.

CHAPTER IX.

ON THE PRESIGNIFICATION OF VENUS.

"That star which views
Now obvious, now averse, the Sun."—DANTE.

VENUS, according to Dante, plays with or caresses the Sun, "now behind and now in front." When it follows it is Hesperus, the evening star; when it precedes it is Phosphor, the morning star.

Brunetto Latini[1] says that Venus "always follows the Sun, and is beautiful and gentle, and is called the Goddess of Love."

Albumasar says: "Venus is cold and moist, and of phlegmatic temperament, and signifies beauty, liberality, patience, sweetness, dignity of manners, love of dress and ornaments of gold and silver; delectation and delight in singing, gladness, and dancing; skill in the game of chess; love of pleasure, of wine, and of children; observance of faith and justice," etc. Venus when afflicted and weak inclines to excesses. Albumasar says: "All [these qualities] are not found in one man, but a part in one and part in another, according to Divine Providence; and the wise man adheres to the good and overcomes the others."

In mundane astrology Venus is the harbinger of mirth, love, feasting, pleasure-seeking, and prosperity.

VENUS lady of the year in *Aries*, happily configurated and free from affliction, presignifies a temperate air, showers, and a fruitful season; general prosperity, public merrymaking, and national good fortune. If afflicted, not much good can be expected.

VENUS in *Taurus* presignifies general prosperity, health and gladness; plenty of provisions and of fruits of the earth; pleasant air with moderate showers; gain and security for women. If afflicted or *retrograde*, little good will result.

VENUS in *Gemini* presignifies health, happiness, and prosperity;

[1] *Tresor*, I, ch. 3.

fruit pleasant and plentiful; the air temperate. If afflicted, no good will result.

VENUS in *Cancer* presignifies plenty of rain, and a plentiful year. If afflicted by Mars, Saturn, or Uranus, floods are to be feared.

VENUS in *Leo* presignifies a good time generally. If afflicted, a good deal of sickness is to be apprehended.

VENUS in *Virgo* presignifies plenty, and a pleasant season. If afflicted, no good can be expected.

VENUS in *Libra* presignifies a prosperous season, especially for places under ♎; good health for the people and much merrymaking. If afflicted, little good will result.

VENUS in *Scorpio* presignifies a temperate air, but plenty of rain. If afflicted there may be floods and detriment to the fruits of the earth.

VENUS in *Sagittarius* promises peace and prosperity, especially for the western parts. If afflicted, evil may result.

VENUS in *Capricornus* presignifies prosperity; little rain in the eastern parts, earth generally fruitful. If afflicted, little benefit must be expected.

VENUS in *Aquarius* presignifies happiness, peace, and prosperity; a temperate air, and sufficient rain. If afflicted, high winds and much rain may be expected.

VENUS in *Pisces* presignifies a plentiful season, sufficient rain and a temperate air. If afflicted, thunderstorms, heavy rains, perchance floods, may follow, mortality amongst men and women, and affections of the eyes.

VENUS in the *ascendant*, whether she be lady of the year or not, well configurated, direct in motion, and free from the rays of the malefics, presignifies a happy, prosperous, and healthy season for the people; advantage and benefits for women; and abundance of food.

CHAPTER X.

ON THE PRESIGNIFICATION OF MERCURY.

"Tis Jove's world-wandering herald,
Mercury."—SHELLEY.

MERCURY—says Albumasar, in the introduction to his seventh treatise, ninth division, wherein he treats of the natures of the planets and their properties,—"signifies desire of knowledge and of seeing secret things; foreknowledge of things future; knowledge and profundity of knowledge; in profound books; study of wisdom; eloquence with polish of language; subtlety of genius; appetite for praise and fame; desire of perfection; cunning of hand in all arts; practice of trade; concealing thoughts; change of habits," etc.

In the heaven of MERCURY, Dante places the spirit of those who for the love of fame achieved great deeds; he discriminates between the direct or immediate inspirations of the Almighty, and those influences that come indirectly through the stars.

In mundane astrology MERCURY is the herald of busy times, advancement of science, literature, art, and inventions—when strong and free from affliction, for ☿ is convertible, being good when with Jupiter, and evil with Mars and Saturn.

If MERCURY be in conjunction with the Sun in *Aries*, it presignifies plenty of wine; and if with Venus also, safety and prosperity to women; if with the Moon, plenty of fish; if with Mars, inflammation of the eyes, war, and bloodshed; and if with Saturn, much rain and abundance of waters. Generally speaking, ☿ in ♈ and lord of the year, presignifies a temperate or warm air, high winds, rather dearth than plenty; if *retrograde*, much rain.

MERCURY in *Gemini* and supported by Jupiter, presignifies a temperate air, pleasant breezes; plenty and prosperity. If with Venus, much rain or mist; a merry time, advancement of art and sciences. If with Mars, a stormy and warm season, damage by lightning and incendiary fires; an unhealthy time, fever prevalent; murders, outrages, and danger of war. If with Saturn, much snow in winter and spring. If *retrograde*, many troubles and changes.

MERCURY in *Cancer* presignifies, if afflicted by Mars, war and bloodshed in the north-western parts, scarcity of provisions and of fruits of the earth; many shipwrecks; great storms; a prevalence of chest affection with expectoration of blood. If with Mars and Venus, murders of noblemen and women. If supported by Jupiter, a pleasant, healthy and prosperous season.

MERCURY in *Virgo* presignifies sufficient rain, a temperate air, plenty of corn and of fruits of the earth. If afflicted, places under ♍ will suffer many evils (according to the nature of the evil planet); cholera and diarrhoea.

MERCURY in *Libra* presignifies much wind, a temperate air, and many changes. If *retrograde*, much rain. If afflicted, an evil period, much sickness, especially low fever and abdominal complaints.

MERCURY in *Sagittarius* and configurated with Saturn, presignifies much snow and frost, a turbulent, unhealthy air. If with Mars, high winds, and lightning (or meteors). If with Venus, much rain. If with Jupiter, fine weather, mild air, and a healthy and prosperous quarter.

MERCURY in *Capricornus* is evil for places under this sign, wherein war, trouble, and sorrow will prevail, unless ☿ be well configurated. If afflicted, bad weather will be general.

MERCURY in *Pisces* presignifies much wind and rain in the northern parts; abundance of fish and of the fruits of the earth; much sickness; many shipwrecks.

MERCURY in the *ascendant* (whether lord of the year or not), presignifies a good and prosperous year for merchants, scientific and literary men, tradesmen, travellers and youths, and advancement of art and science. If afflicted, judge the contrary.

CHAPTER XI.

ON THE PRESIGNIFICATION OF THE MOON.

"The queen of night unclouded now appears;
In ambient azure she her sceptre rears;
Around her throne the beauteous planets rove,
And on their poles through heaven's expansion move."

THE MOON, according to Albumasar, "is cold, moist, and phlegmatic, sometimes warm; and gives lightness, aptitude in all things, a multitude of infirmities," etc. Shakespeare writes of the earth's satelite as "the inconstant Moon, that nightly changes in her circled orb."

Ramesey curtails the aphorisms of the ancients respecting the presignification of the Moon when lady of the year:

"The Moon doth denote all the good that can possibly be desired by the people when she is lady of the year and strong and well configurated; if she be weak and evil aspected, the contrary.

"When you see in your figure the Moon strong, look to the nature of the sign of the Zodiac in which she is located, and judge good to such places as are subject to such sign; if weak, judge the contrary.

"For you must remember that the Moon in *signs* of *human* form shows events affecting mankind; in *airy* signs, the air; in *watery* signs, the waters; in *earthy* signs, the earth and its fruits; in *quadrupedal* signs, cattle.

"Neither ought you to forget to make commixture according to the planet or planets in *conjunction* or configuration with the Moon at the revolution."

As to the position of the Moon in various houses:

The MOON in the *first* house, whether lady of the year or not, presignifies that the people will be fickle, shifting about; prosperous if ☽ be well configurated, unfortunate if afflicted.

The MOON in the *second* house presignifies increase of wealth and plenty of all things. If afflicted, the contrary.

The MOON in the *third* house, fortunate, presignifies sociality and much travelling. If afflicted, enmity among the people, and accidents in travelling.

The MOON in the *fourth* house, fortunate, shows prosperity. If afflicted and especially if the revolution be nocturnal, public losses, quarrels, changes, and misfortunes.

The MOON in the *fifth* house, fortunate, presignifies gain to place of amusement; increase of schools, and of the birth rate. If afflicted, the contrary.

The MOON in the *sixth* house, unless well configurated, presignifies much sickness, loss of cattle, etc.

The MOON in the *seventh* house, fortunate, presignifies an increase in the marriage rate, and gain to women. If afflicted, damage from public enemies, conjugal squabbles, and public misfortunes.

The MOON in the *eighth* house presignifies much mortality, and murder, especially if ☽ be afflicted in ♈, ♏ or ♑.

The MOON in the *ninth* house presignifies much travelling and advancement of art and science. If afflicted, loss of life by shipwreck or disasters on railways (according to the *sign*).

The MOON fortunate in the *tenth* house presignifies the good condition of the monarch and government, especially if the revolution be nocturnal. If afflicted, the contrary.

The MOON fortunate in the *eleventh* house, presignifies the good condition of the army; useful measures carried through Parliament; and a good time generally. If afflicted, the nation's hopes will be blighted.

The MOON in the *twelfth* house and unsupported by the fortunes, presignifies the instability and uncertainty of everything, discord, damage from secret foes, and (if afflicted by ♂) danger of war.

CHAPTER XII.

ON THE PRESIGNIFICATION OF PLANETS WHEN IN MUTUAL CONFIGURATION, ONE BEING ELEVATED ABOVE THE OTHER, AT A SOLAR INGRESS OR AN ECLIPSE.

"To the other five
Their planetary motions, and aspects
In sextile, square, and trine, and opposite
Of noxious efficacy, and when to join
In synod unbenign."—MILTON.

THAT PLANET which is nearest to the midheaven is the most elevated or exalted. When two planets happen to be in mutual configuration *at a Solar Ingress, or Solar or Lunar Eclipse*, and one of the two happens to be near the midheaven, it has the greater power. When *both* are equally near the midheaven, then the one which has the greater *essential* dignity must be taken to be the stronger. The following aphorisms will also be applicable to *great conjunctions* happening near the midheaven.

SATURN in *conjunction*, *square*, or *opposition* with JUPITER, and *elevated above* ♃, presignifies that great and noble men shall be slain. In aspect with and elevated above MARS, it presignifies good. In aspect with and elevated above the SUN, trouble and misfortune to either kings or chief rulers of places subject to the sign in which the SUN is located. Above VENUS, the advancement of art and science. Above MERCURY, the same as VENUS. Above the MOON, the people will be ill behaved and unfortunate.

JUPITER in aspect with and elevated above SATURN, presignifies lamentations, trouble and misfortune. Above MARS, many troubles. Above the SUN, heavy expenditure, and losses. Aboye VENUS, benefits to women. Above MERCURY, public servants will be advantaged. Above the MOON, the nobles and the rich will benefit.

MARS elevated above and configurated with SATURN, presignifies but little harm. Above JUPITER, strife among great men. Above the SUN, kings and rulers will be in danger of assassination. Above VENUS, little merrymaking. Above MERCURY, quarrels, slaughter, and discord. Above the MOON, earthquake shocks.

VENUS elevated above and configurated with SATURN, presignifies public grief and troubles. Above JUPITER, prosperity to the great. Above MARS, much pleasure-seeking. Above the SUN, lavish expenditure. Above MERCURY, advancement of art and science. Above the MOON, much pleasure-seeking.

MERCURY elevated above and configurated with SATURN, presignifies much cheating and treachery. Above JUPITER, prosperity to the great. Above MARS, fear of enemies. Above the SUN, kings and rulers will advance art and science. Above VENUS, great devotion to sport and science. Above the MOON, extension of science, wonderful inventions.

The MOON elevated above and configurated with SATURN, presignifies public misfortunes, and discord. Above JUPITER, general prosperity. Above MARS, houses and buildings will be destroyed by fire; earthquake shocks; and much bloodshed. Above the SUN, mischief and misfortune. Above VENUS, benefits to and advancement of women. Above MERCURY, good laws, spread of education, and new inventions.

The worst evils are said to occur under the following positions: Saturn in *Libra*, retrograde and in opposition with the Sun, and the Sun at the same time in evil configuration with Mars retrograde. Saturn in *Virgo* in square aspect with Mars in *Gemini*, and the Moon in *Sagittarius* in aspect with both Mars and Saturn. Such positions are said to cause misery upon misery, the destruction of kingdoms, and revolutions; especially if the new or full Moon either preceding or following them should happen to be an eclipse. The evils will fall chiefly on those countries subject to the signs containing the malefics and the darkened luminary; and in the case of a Solar eclipse, on the country or countries through which the line of central eclipse passes.

CHAPTER XIII.

ON ECLIPSES OF THE SUN AND MOON.

"The Sun shall be darkened in his going forth, and the Moon shall not cause her light to shine."—ISAIAH, xiii., 10.

"The Sun shall be darkened and the Moon shall not give her light, and the stars shall fall from heaven, and the powers of the heavens shall be shaken."—MATTHEW, xviv., 29.

"There shall be signs in the Sun and in the Moon, and in the Stars,"—LUKE, xxi., 25.

ECLIPSES of the Sun and Moon have from the remotest ages been regarded as constituting a veritable "shadow of things to come."

The opponents of astrology, in their ignorance of it, are very fond of charging us with superstition in believing that great eclipses of the Sun and Moon do really presignify coming events. They look upon it as a relic of the superstitious dread of barbarians who feared that "the dragon" was about to swallow the darkened luminary, and accordingly beat drums and made horrible noises in order to frighten away the adversary. We do not believe that the mere eclipse portends anything, but that the *relative planetary positions at the moment of ecliptic conjunction or opposition of the Sun and Moon* are the indices of coming events; hence some eclipses are considered to portend evil and others good. It is to the *combined action* of the SUN and MOON (together with the planetary configurations) being greater than at other times, the luminaries being in a direct line, the great effects are attributed. Our opponents talk and write as if we were unacquainted with the causes of eclipses, as if none but modern astronomers were aware of their true cause and could predict them, and as if the barbarians who were frightened at the appearance of eclipses were the authors of the aphorisms on which our predictions are based. Really the ignorance of our opponents on this subject would be amusing if it were not so lamentable in these days of widespread education! The

Chaldaean astronomers foretold eclipses correctly, and formulated, from long-continued observations, the rules for judging of their probable effects. The luni-solar period of the Chaldaeans must have been based upon an immense number of accurate observations. Their period of eclipses, which they called saros, consisted of 223 lunations, or 6,585 days 8 hours, at the end of which the MOON returns to the same position in regard to the SUN, and her own node and perigee. The tables of Delambre and Mason make this period 6,585 days 7 hours 42 minutes and 31 seconds; so that the error of the Chaldaeans amounted to only 17 minutes and 29 seconds. Modern astronomers are fairly puzzled to account for the wonderful astronomical knowledge of the Chaldaeans. It is, then, a perversion of the truth, and an insult to the memory of such great men as Thales and Democritus, who verified the astronomical and astrological knowledge of the Chaldaeans, and who perfectly well understood the cause of eclipses and foretold accurately their occurrence[1] to charge them with superstitions.

Let us refer to the words of the celebrated French astronomer Arago (whose arguments against the possible influence of comets are considered so conclusive), in regard to the *influence of the Moon on diseases*:

"With regard to the theory of lunar influence on diseases it still counts a good number of partisans. In truth I know not if the circumstance ought to astonish us. Is it not something to have on our side the authority of the two great physicians of antiquity, and among the moderns that of Mead, Hoffman, and Sauvage? Authorities, I admit, are of little weight in matters of science, in the face of positive facts; but it is necessary that these facts exist, that they have been subjected to severe examinations, that they have been skilfully grouped, with the view to extract the truth they conceal. Now, has this procedure been adopted with regard to the lunar influence? Where do we find them refuted with such arguments as science would acknowledge? He who ventures to treat *a priori* a fact as absurd, wants prudence. He has not reflected on the numerous errors he would have committed with regard to modern discoveries. I address these short reflections to those who may think that the subject of lunar influence is unworthy of any notice."

I commend these words of Arago to opponents, for they will exactly apply to the case of eclipses. The *fact* that eclipses are followed

[1] Vide *Urania* for September, 1880, p. 281.

by striking events in conformity with the aphorisms of the ancients, and in several instances, with predictions made on the basis of those aphorisms, is treated "*a priori* as absurd" by our opponents, who never deign to *examine* this fact. It cannot be "mere coincidence" that Zadkiel I. foretold, from the planetary positions at the annular eclipse of the Sun in *Taurus* 5° 4′, of April 25th, 1846, "drought, failure of the fruits of the earth, and some peculiar disease in potatoes," and that Ireland and Scotland then suffered from these evils to such an extent that thousands were starved.[2] That Zadkiel predicted the termination of the American Civil War from the position of Jupiter at the partial eclipse of the Moon, visible at Washington, April 10th, 1865.[3] That Zadkiel I. foretold the terrible earthquake at Cumana of July 15th, 1853, naming the exact date and place, from the total eclipse of the Sun visible there on the 6th of June, 1853.[4] That Zadkiel II. foretold hostile acts in South Africa, from the annular eclipse of the Sun of January 22nd, 1879, and the disastrous battle of Isandhlwana taking place on that very day. That Zadkiel II. foretold that there would be "great expenditure on munitions of war about midsummer, 1882," and that the effects of the position of Mars at the total eclipse of the Sun of May 17th, 1882, would then be felt in Egypt, which was verified by the British expedition to Egypt. That Zadkiel predicted yet another military expedition to Egypt in the autumn of 1884, from the total eclipse of the Moon of October 4th, 1884. These are facts which cannot be denied, and, in our opinion, they deserve *examination*, and not contempt, at the hands of statesmen, astronomers, philosophers, and the educated portion of the community.

Plutarch relates that in the days of Nicias a man dared not open his mind except to his best friend, and even then with the utmost caution, about the causes of the eclipses of the Sun and Moon which had been recently taught by Anaxagoras. For pointing out the natural causes of phenomena Protagoras was banished from Athens and Anaxagoras was cast into prison. At the present day, the astrologer is ridiculed as a superstitious enthusiast; but many who laugh in public, resort to astrology in private. Many who claim freedom of inquiry and the right of private judgment for themselves in other matters, will not accord the same to the inquirer into astrology; but class the patient student of this ancient science with vagrant fortune-tellers whom magistrates

[2] Vide *Zadkiel's Almanac*, 1846, pp. 15, 34.

[3] *Almanac*, 1865, p. 44.

[4] *Almanac*, 1853, p. 42.

send to the treadmill when brought before them for contravening the Vagrant Act. To boast of this age as the era of "true liberty" is a mockery while such an intolerant, exclusive, and a bigoted spirit animates so many Britons. For atheistical philosophers to declare that astrology is superstition, is not so surprising as for religious persons to do so, who should remember that the Almighty declared that the Sun, Moon, and planets are "for signs of the future."

Let those who are sceptical refer to the great Solar eclipse of September 7th, 1820, which was visible in England. This eclipse fell in the 15th degree of the sign *Virgo*; Mars at the moment of ecliptic conjunction being in the tenth house and nearly in opposition to Saturn in *Aries* (the ruling sign of England). Within a few months England was on the verge of revolution, through the abominable proceedings against the ill-starred Queen, whose sudden death closed the disgraceful drama. The eclipse fell in the place of Mars at the birth of Napoleon I., and he died in May of the following year (1821). Turkey (ruled by *Virgo*) became a dungeon filled with weeping widows and wailing infants of murdered Christians; Greece a slaughter-house reeking with Christian and Mahommedan blood. Asiatic cholera appeared suddenly in June and July, 1821, in the three principal ports of the Persian Gulf, and thence spread up the Tigris to Bagdad, to Aleppo, and the Mediterranean; through Persia to the Caspian, and thence to Astrakan, which it reached in the summer of 1823, but then ceased for a long time to make any further progress. The very places ruled by the sign in which the eclipse took place, and those whereat Mars culminated at the eclipse, were those to suffer. Moreover, the cholera ceased after *three years*, the eclipse having lasted *three hours*, which Ptolemy declared as equivalent to as many revolutions of the Sun. The ancients averred that a Solar eclipse happening in the second decanate of *Virgo* presignifies "famine, *pestilence*, and deadly sedition."

I pass on to the consideration of the aphorisms of the ancients, relating to eclipses.

Hermes said that: "There shall be much inconvenience and trouble happen in the world when both the luminaries shall be eclipsed within one month, and chiefly in those places in which they [the eclipses] arc visible."

Ptolemy said[5]:

"After having gone through the necessary preliminary topics, it is

[5] *Tetrabiblos*, Book II., chap. 5, Ashmand's translation.

now proper to speak of the manner in which predictions are to be formed and considered; beginning with those which relate to general events affecting either certain cities, or districts, or entire countries.

"The strongest and principal cause of all these events exists in the ecliptical conjunctions of the Sun and Moon, and in the several transits made by the planets during those conjunctions.

"One part of the observations required in forming prediction in cases of this nature relates to the locality of the event, and points out the cities or countries liable to be influenced by particular eclipses, or by occasional continued stations of certain planets which at times remain for a certain period in one situation. These planets are Saturn, Jupiter, and Mars; and they furnish portentous indications when they are stationary.

"Another branch relates to time, and gives pre-information of the period at which the event will occur, and how long it will continue to operate.

"The third branch is generic; and points out the classes or kinds which the event will affect.

"The last part is specific; and foreshows the actual quality and character of the coming event."

Ptolemy then proceeds to give instruction as to the several branches:

"In all eclipses of the Sun and Moon, and especially in such as are *fully visible, the place in the zodiac* where the eclipse falls is to be noted; and it must be seen what countries are in familiarity with that place, according to the rules regarding the quadrants and triplicities; and in like manner it must be observed what cities are under the influence of the sign in which the eclipse happens; either by means of the *ascendant* and the situation of the luminaries at the time of their foundation, or by means of the midheaven of their kings or governors; although such time may be subsequent to the building of such cities. Whatever countries and cities shall be thus found in familiarity with the ecliptical place will all be comprehended in the event; which will, however, principally attach to all those parts which may be connected with the identical sign of the eclipse, and in which it was visible while above the earth.

"The second point relates to time, and indicates the date when the event will take place, and the period during which its effect will continue; these are to be ascertained in the following manner:

"It must, however, be premised that as an eclipse occurring at any particular season cannot happen in all climates at the same temporal or solar hour, so neither will the magnitude of the obscuration nor the time of its continuance be equal in all parts of the world. First, therefore (as in a nativity), the angles are to be arranged in every country connected with the eclipse according to the hour at which it takes place and the elevation of the pole of the country. The time during which the obscuration may continue in each country is then to be noted in equatorial hours. And after those particulars have been carefully observed, it is to be understood that *the effect will endure as many years as the obscuration lasted hours, provided the eclipse was solar*; but if *lunar, a like number of months is to be reckoned instead of years*.

"The *commencement* of the effect and the period of its general intensity of strength are to be inferred from the situation of the place of the eclipse with respect to the angles," etc.

No doubt periods of *intensity* may vary according to the "transits of such planets as co-operate in producing the effect," as Ptolemy stated.

"The third division relates to the mode of distinguishing, the genus or species of animals or things about to sustain the expected effects. This distinction is made by means of those signs in which the place of the eclipse, and the places of such fixed stars and planets as are in dominion, according to the actual sign of the eclipse and that of the angle before it may be found. A planet or fixed star is to be considered as holding dominion when circumstanced as follows:

"If there be found one planet having more numerous claims than any other to the place of the eclipse as well as that of the angle, being also in the immediate vicinity of those places and visibly applying to or receding from them, and having likewise more rights over other places connected with them by configuration; the said planet being at the same time lord by house, triplicity, exaltation, and terms; in such a case only that single planet is entitled to dominion. But if the lord of the eclipse and the lord of the angle be not identical, then those two planets which have most connections with each place are to be noted; and of these two, the lord of the eclipse is to be preferred to the chief dominion although the other is to be considered as bearing rule conjointly. And if more than two should be found, having equal pretensions to each place, that particular one among them which may be nearest to an angle, or most concerned with the places in question, by the nature of its condition, is to be selected for dominion."

A planet exactly *rising* or culminating—if there be one—at an eclipse, if none then one setting, or in the lower meridian, as the case may be, holds chief dominion, especially if it be configurated with Sun or Moon.

"Among the fixed stars, the chief bright one (which during the time of the eclipse may hold connection with the angles then actually in passage) is to be admitted to dominion; as also that one which at the ecliptical hour may be in an eminent situation, either having risen or having culminated with the angle following the place of the eclipse.

"Having considered according to the foregoing rules what stars co-operate in regulating the coming event, the conformation and figure of the signs in which the eclipse takes place and the said ruling stars may be posited are also to be observed; and from the properties and characteristics of those signs, the genus or species to be comprehended in the event is chiefly to be inferred.

"For instance, should the zodiacal constellations and those of the ruling fixed stars out of the zodiac be of *human shape the effect will fall upon the human race.* If terrestrial or quadrupedal, upon *animals* of similar form. In addition, the terrestrial signs, situated in the north, about the Arctic circle, indicate sudden *earthquakes*; and those in the south, deluges of rain.

"Again, should the ruling places be situated in *tropical* or *equinoctial* signs, in either case alike they presignify changes in the state of the atmosphere at the respective season to which each sign is appropriated. For example, with regard to the season of spring and the productions of the earth, if the said places should be in the *sign of the vernal equinox*, they will produce an effect on the buds of the vine and fig and of such other trees as sprout forth at that season. Should they be in the *sign of the summer tropic*, the event will affect the gathering and depositing of fruits; and with respect to Egypt in particular, it will impede the rising of the Nile. If they should be in the *sign of the autumnal equinox*, they foreshow that it will operate on grain and on various herbs; if in the *sign of the winter tropic*, on potherbs, esculent vegetables, and such birds and fishes as arrive in that season.

"The *equinoctial signs* further indicate the circumstances liable to happen in ecclesiastical concerns, and in religious matters; the *tropical signs* give warning of changes in the atmosphere and in political affairs; the *fixed signs*, of changes in institutions; and the *bicorporal signs* show that the future event will fall alike, on princes and their subjects.

"Again, the ruling places situated in the past during the time of the eclipse, presignify that fruits and seeds, insipient institutions, and youth will be affected; those in the mid-heaven above the earth announce that the coming event will relate to ecclesiastical affairs, to kings and princes, and to the middle-aged; those in the west, that it will influence the laws, old age, and persons about to die."

Junctinus said that:

"An eclipse either of the Sun or Moon in the *fiery* triplicity (♈, ♌, ♐) presignifies the motion of armies, the death of kings, great men, and cattle; enmity between the nobles and common people, discord, war, murder and theft; sharp fevers and epidemic diseases through excess of heat; apparitions in the air, and scarcity of rain; especially in those places subject to the sign in which the eclipse happens.

"In the *earthly* triplicity (♉, ♍, and ♑), scarcity of the fruits of the earth, chiefly of corn and such things as are sown annually.

"In the *airy* triplicity (♊, ♎, and ♒), scarcity, pestilence, and tempests.

"In the *watery* triplicity (♋, ♏, and ♓), the death of common people, sedition, rumours of war, and irruptions and overflowing of the sea-banks.

"In *Aries*, alteration in fruits; vines and fig trees corrupted.

"In *Libra*, rottenness of seeds and herbs; schisms among ecclesiastics.

"In *Cancer*, corruption of fruit when gathered, causing sickness to those who partake of it.

"In *Capricornus*, olives will be devoured by locusts or caterpillars; shipwrecks and submersion of ships, especially under the dominion of ♑.

"In *Gemini* and *Sagittarius*, destruction of flying fowl, especially such as men eat, whereby many even may come to sudden death.

"In *Virgo* and *Pisces*, harm and destruction to vegetables and creatures living in the waters, corruption of rivers.

"In *Taurus*, *Scorpio*, *Leo*, and *Aquarius*, ruin of houses and ancient buildings, division and hatred among the clergy, and tumults."

CHAPTER XIV.

ON THE PRESIGNIFICATION OF THE PLANETS, ACCORDING TO THEIR POSITIONS AT ECLIPSES OF THE SUN AND MOON.

"All of us have cause
To wail the dimming of our shining star;
But none can help our harms by wailing
them."—SHAKESPEARE.

THE presignification of the five planets—SATURN, JUPITER, MARS, VENUS, and MERCURY—according to their relative positions and configurations at eclipses of the SUN and MOON, now comes under consideration, for it is this which enables us to foretell the good or evil nature of the events about to happen.

Ptolemy says in reference to this point:

"The description of the peculiar properties and character of the effect about to be produced, and of its good or evil nature, occupies the fourth and last division of this part of the subject.

"These properties must be gathered from the power of the stars which control the ruling places, and from the contemperament created by their relative admixture with each other and with the places which they control. For, although the Sun and Moon are the acknowledged sources of all the efficacy and dominion of the stars, and of their strength, or weakness, and in a certain manner regulate and command them, still it is by the theory of the contemperament, produced by the stars in dominion, that the effect is indicated."

Each of the planets, when fully exercising its own separate and distinct influence, will properly produce the peculiar effects above ascribed to it; but should it be combined with others, whether by configuration, by familiarity arising from the *sign* in which it may be posited, or by its position towards the Sun, the coming event will then happen agreeably to the admixture and compound temperament which arise from the whole communion actually subsisting among the influencing powers. It would, however, be a business of infinite labour and innumerable combinations quite beyond the limits of this treatise, to set forth fully every contemperament and all configurations in every mode in which they can possibly exist; and the knowledge of them, must therefore be acquired by particular discrimination in every instance under the guidance of the precepts of science.

Cardan has transmitted to posterity some aphorisms relating to eclipses, some of which are here appended:

"In an eclipse, consider the strength of the ruling planet, for its significations will chiefly appear.

"If eclipses of the Sun fall upon a flourishing and promising crop they generally damnify it, so that it scarcely comes near what might have been expected.

"In general, some eclipses of the luminaries, at the time or even before they happen, raise showers and rain, others great droughts, some violent winds, others earthquakes, some scarcity of the fruits of the earth, and others terrible fires.

"No eclipse whatsoever can threaten a plague or scarcity to the whole earth, nor can the pestilence continue above four years in one place.

"Eclipses operate more powerfully on cities, provinces, or kingdoms than on particular persons, or even upon kings and princes; for their effects rather respect the multitude.

"When eclipses happen in *earthy* signs (♉, ♍, ♑), they portend barrenness and scarcity by reason of excessive drought; when in *watery* signs (♋, ♏, ♓), by reason of too much rain. In *airy* signs (♊, ♎, ♒), they presignify mighty winds, seditions, and pestilence; and in *fiery* signs (♈, ♌, ♐), terrible wars and slaughters. The same observation applies to comets."

The aphorisms of Ptolemy relating to the eclipses of the Sun and Moon will, if borne out by observation, go far to account for countries being at some periods blest with good seasons, peace, and plenty, and at others afflicted with bad seasons, war, and scarcity. Ptolemy speaks of animals and even fish suffering in common with mankind, and history records that: "In all the great plagues which have affected the human race, other animals as horses, cats, dogs, and fowls, together with fish in rivers and the ocean, and even vegetables, have borne their share in the calamity; the pestilential virus has extended to every principle of life."[1]

[1] *Rees's Cyclopaedia.*

When will the lauded science of the Royal Society, of the Royal Astronomical Society, and of kindred associations, enable its votaries to foretell the advent of plenty or scarcity, of good or bad seasons, of great earthquakes, of flood or drought, of war or peace? Not until they examine and adopt the teachings of Claudius Ptolemy—not until they recognise the power of the heavenly bodies, and so follow in the footsteps of Plato, Pliny, Herodotus, Anaxagoras, Hipocrates, Kepler, and the many other great men who perceived that "the heavens do rule."

It will be observed that Cardan said that eclipses sometimes produce effects "even *before* they happen." Some of our opponents will probably say "this is impossible, because it makes the effect precede the cause"; but it does not, for the operating *causes*, at an eclipse are the combined influences of the planets holding certain relative positions at the time, as before stated; and this is not limited to a few honors, for the superior planets move slowly into configurations. Lord Verulam said that: "All the celestial operations produce not their effects instantaneously and in a narrow compass, but exert them in large portions of time and space."

Before concluding this chapter, it will be interesting to quote the following aphorisms relating to the particular *sign* of the zodiac in which a solar or lunar eclipse may fall, given by Junctinus, as gathered from the writings of Proclus:

"When the SUN is eclipsed in the sign *Aries*, it portends the sudden and frequent motion of armies, continual expeditions, assaults and batteries, with many tumults, seditions and controversies; and an inclination of the air to intemperate heat and drought.[2]

"In *Taurus*, it afflicts negotiators, agents, and solicitors, and business generally; and destroys corn and affects cattle.

"In *Gemini*, it causes dissension amongst priests of all orders; sedition and law-breaking.

"In *Cancer*, it disturbs the air and causes various winds and alterations of weather, and dries up rivers.

"In *Leo*, it presignifies the death of some eminent prince, and scarcity of wheat.

"In *Virgo*, it presignifies the grievous calamity or death of some king under Virgo, and trouble to merchants.

---

[2] The Sun was eclipsed in *Aries* 5° 15′, March 25th, 1857; the Indian Mutiny immediately followed, as foretold by Zadkiel I.

"In *Libra*, it corrupts the air, causes pestilence, and scarcity of corn, and death of a king under Libra.

"In *Scorpio*, it presignifies wars and tumults, slaughter, hatred, captivity, and treachery.

"In *Sagittarius*, it presignifies grievous dissensions and deadly feuds, and injury to horses and cattle.

"In *Capricornus*, it presignifies the transmigration of some king, rebellion of nobles and peasants, and mischances to the great, and scarcity of corn.

"In *Aquarius*, it causes public sorrow and sadness, and earthquakes.

"In *Pisces*, it dries up rivers, and presignifies calamities at sea and earthquakes.

"When the MOON is eclipsed in *Aries*, it presignifies fever, destruction of woods by fire, and dryness of the air.

"In *Taurus*, it presignifies destruction of great cattle, death of the queen of some country under ♉, and a scarcity of the fruits of the earth.

"In *Gemini*, it threatens incursion and rapine of armies, and the death of some illustrious and famous man.

"In *Cancer*, it excites wars, grievous exactions, taxations, etc.

"In *Leo*, it presignifies the death of some illustrious king or famous man. It excites the people and armies to new attempts and actions.

"In *Virgo*, it causes diseases to kings, and sedition and discord amongst men.[3]

"In *Libra*, it produces furious and tempestuous hailstorms, and death to some famous and illustrious man.

"In *Scorpio*, it causes great thunderstorms, and sometimes earthquakes; it dries olives, and causes a dry air and burning fevers; sedition, quarrels, and troubles.

"In *Sagittarius*, it presignifies thefts and rapine, pestilence and many evils.

"In *Capricornus*, it presignifies plots and untimely death of some king under ♑, also sedition.

"In *Aquarius*, it presignifies the misfortune of some king under ♒;

[3] There was a lunar eclipse in ♍ 8° on the 26th February, 1831; Paris and Turkey were full of tumult and insurrection, as foretold by Zadkiel.

it injures seeds.

"In *Pisces*, it presignifies sadness and anxiety to priests and churches; the death of some great and illustrious person; and piracy and troubles by sea."

To verify the truth of all these aphorisms would require great research and a long life. Even if this were done, our opponents would attempt to discount the value of such testimony as merely being "wise after the event." What impresses them most is the success of predictions made upon the basis of the foregoing aphorisms, but even such success they endeavour to explain away by asserting that it is but "a lucky hit." Some would not be convinced even "though one rose from the dead," for "a man convinced against his will, is of the same opinion still." The student should disregard the sneers of such captious critics, and follow the example of Lord Byron:

> "But now, so callous grown, so changed since youth,
> I've learned to think and sternly speak the truth;
> Learned to deride the critic's starch decree,
> And break him on the wheel he meant for me;
> To spurn the rod a scribbler bids me kiss,
> Nor care if courts and crowds applause or hiss."

CHAPTER XV.

EXAMPLES OF PREDICTIONS MADE FROM RECENT ECLIPSES OF THE SUN AND MOON, SOLAR INGRESSES, AND TRANSITS OF THE PLANETS.

"Events foretold fulfil the prophecy;
What fortune seconds how can man deny?
The proofs are sacred, and to doubt would be
Not reason's action, but impiety."—MANILIUS.

MANILIUS—the renowned Augustan poet—thus proclaimed his appreciation of the great value of astrology as a predictive science; and he stigmatised those who scoffed at it as stupid. There can be no doubt that the neglect of astrology has brought countless troubles and catastrophes upon nations, which might have been either prevented or greatly mitigated, had the warnings of the heavens been heeded by statesmen. A more striking instance and proof of this could not well be adduced than the total eclipse of the Sun at Cairo, on the 17th of May, 1882, when the planet Mars was exactly rising in "his own lion." The astronomers who went to Cairo, to observe the eclipse, took no heed of the ascending position of Mars; and, neglecting the astrology of Pythagoras, Ptolemy, Proclus, and Kepler, gave no warning to our Government of the impending catastrophe. The British Government drifted into war; gave instructions to Admiral Seymour to bombard the forts of Alexandria, without first providing a landing force to protect the town from incendiaries; so that when the forts were silenced and Arabi fled, the town was at the mercy of the rabble, and in a few hours one of the greatest and most thriving cities of the East was in ruins. The expedition, under General Sir Garnet Wolseley, was then sent out, and our victorious troops marched to Cairo.

The following is the Map of the Heavens for the moment of ecliptic conjunction of the Sun and Moon at Cairo, lat. 30° 2′ N., long.

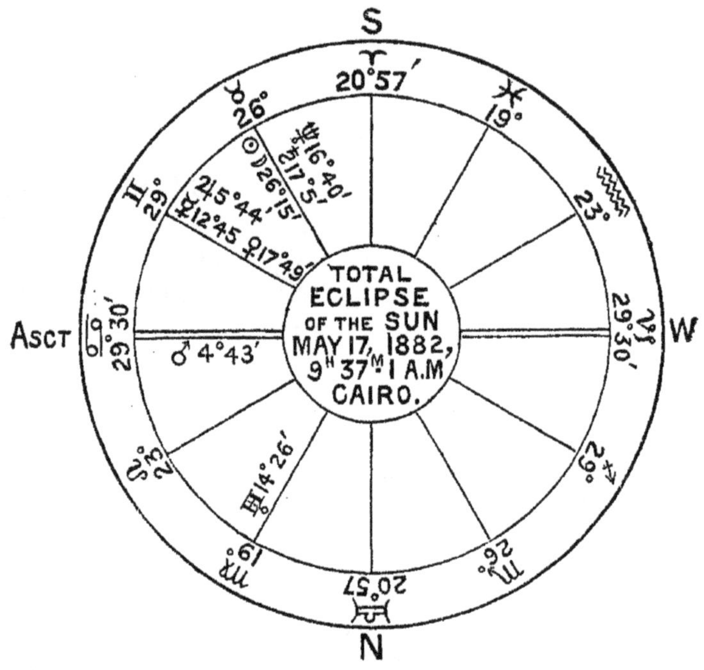

Declinations.

☉	19 20 N	♀	23 45 N	♄	14 58 N
☽	19 38 N	♂	20 42 N	♅	6 51 N
☿	24 22 N	♃	20 43 N	♆	15 11 N

31°18′ E. of Greenwich, R.A. of M.C., 19° 20′ 59″:

It will be observed that the Sun and Moon have the proximate parallel of declination with Mars (and Jupiter); the ascending degree has the parallel with Mars: the planet of war is within five degrees of the Eastern horizon, and in 4° 43′ of the sign *Leo*. Mars is the planet most strongly placed in the figure. Reference to what Ptolemy declared to be the effect of Mars having sole dominion at a Solar eclipse, as quoted in the previous chapter, affords a true description of the state of Alexandria and of Upper Egypt within a few weeks of the occurrence of this great eclipse. As the eclipse lasted three hours and twenty-five minutes, its influence was not entirely exhausted under three years and five months. Cholera broke out in 1883, so that "painful death" quickly followed from disease, as Ptolemy declared; moreover, "haemorrhages" in the shape of dysentery were prevalent, to which many of our brave soldiers succumbed. When the *conjunction* of Mars and Jupiter in *Leo* 2° 56′ 8″ took place, on the 20th of October, 1883, *i.e.*, in the ascendant and place of Mars at this eclipse, a religious insurrection in the Soudan broke out; and the Egyptian Army of General Hicks was annihilated by the Mahdi's hordes. Then a British expedition was sent to defeat Osman Digna's army, in February, 1884; General Gordon was sent to defend Khartoum and abandoned for months; and yet another British expedition had to be sent out in September, under Lord Wolseley, to attempt to rescue Gordon and Stewart.

The following predictions will be found in *Zadkiel's Almanac* for the years 1881, 1882, 1883, and 1884:

From the *conjunction* of Saturn and Jupiter in ♉ 1° 36′ 41″, April 18th, 1881: "But what of the position of Mars in the seventh house and in opposition to Uranus rising? will be the question of students. Would that such a position could be blotted out! For it presignifies many wars during the rule of this conjunction (twenty years), and, as Mars is in Pisces, the navy of Old England will be engaged in many a battle. I trust that the Government will not only man the fleet, but see to it that our ships shall be equipped with the best and most powerful guns. Dark days are in store for Great Britain, and woe be to those who, heedless of the warnings plainly written on the face of the heavens, shall neglect to prepare for the mighty struggle. The Eastern Question will write the future history of Europe in letters of blood and flame. Happily the sign in the midheaven at this conjunction is the ascendant of our good Queen. The valour of Britain's sons will again be rewarded with victory, and if England be but true to herself, her mighty Empire will be made secure and will also be extended. The periods at which the evils foreshadowed by this great conjunction may be expected, will be when eclipses shall fall either in the place of this conjunction or in that of Mars; also when Mars shall transit the ascendant of this figure (♍ 7° 31′)."[1]—*Almanac*, for 1881, pp. 50, 51.

From the *Solar Eclipse*, May 17th, 1882:

"The effects of the recent eclipse of the Sun will now [June, 1882] be manifest in the countries through which the line of central eclipse passed, viz., Northern Africa, Egypt, etc.—*Almanac*, 1882, p. 15.

"About midsummer there will be great expenditure on munitions of war (when Mars forms the square aspect with this eclipse)"—*Ibid*,

[1] The first Transit of Mars over this ascendant took place on the 11th and 12th of July, 1882, the very time of the destruction of Alexandria.

p. 46.

From the *transit of Saturn through the sign Gemini*:

"Unfortunately for Egypt, Saturn enters its ruling sign (*Gemini*) on the 24th of May (1883) bringing sorrow and misfortune on the land of the Pharaohs."—*Almanac*, 1883, p. 13.

"Old Saturn drags his slow length along through *Gemini*, bringing trouble on Egypt."—*Ibid*, p. 15.

"Portsmouth will be the scene of busy preparation, for England will still find it necessary to assert herself in order to safeguard her Empire. There is every probability that our ironclads will be on active service. Saturn retrograding in *Gemini* brings serious troubles and misfortunes on Lower Egypt."—*Ibid*, p. 25 (November).

"The Government will be perplexed with the state of home and foreign affairs."—*Ibid*, p. 27.

"Saturn halts in the fourth degree, *Gemini*, bringing troubles on London, Egypt, and the United States."—*Almanac*, 1884, p. 4 (February).

"Europe must prepare for startling events in the East. At the new Moon of the 19th of September, Mars will be rising, hence the ensuing four weeks will be favourable for the arms of Old England, and she shall beat her enemies under her feet. The navy will gain prestige and renown."—*Ibid*, p. 21.

From the *Solar ingress into Libra*, September 22nd, 1884:

"At Cairo, Saturn is exactly on the cusp of the fourth house in the ruling sign of Lower Egypt. The Moon and Mars are together in the eighth house. Further misfortunes will fall on Egypt. There is danger of revolt and of war. Let the British be on their guard. Treachery is strongly indicated. Many deaths from violence and from martial acts will occur," etc.—*Ibid*, p. 50.

When the author wrote the first of the foregoing predictions (viz., in July 1880) the Liberal Government of the Rt. Ron. W. E. Gladstone had just come into power pledged to the maintenance of peace. Who among politicians then foresaw that England would soon be engaged in war in the East? Did any statesman foretell in 1883 another crisis in Egypt? Not one. Even at the opening of the session of Parliament in February 1884, the Government declared that there was *no cause for alarm*, as to the state of Egypt, and insisted that affairs were progressing well! In *Zadkiel's Almanac* for 1883, 1884 and 1885, repeated warnings were given of misfortune, of revolt, and of war in Egypt.

The British people had to pay many millions sterling for the want of foresight of their Government and for their want of attention to those predictions. There is an old proverb to the effect that "Forewarned is fore-armed." Had the Government heeded those predictions they might have prevented by timely action the sacrifice of Gordon's life, of other valuable lives and much treasure. In face of these astrological predictions we are told, forsooth, that "Astrology leads to fatality." We have seen that *it is the neglect of astrology which leads to fatalities*. Disaster followed disaster! Naught but the heroism of British soldiers and sailors saved us from worse calamities.

CHAPTER XVI.

MUTUAL CONJUNCTIONS OF THE MAJOR PLANETS.

> "Oh! Sir," replied the innkeeper, "there was a red spot on thy very cheekbone, which boded of a late brawl as sure as the conjunction of Mars and Saturn threatens misfortune."—KENILWORTH.

CLAUDIUS PTOLEMY urged his disciples to "overlook none of the hundred and nineteen conjunctions; for on them depends the knowledge of worldly operations, whether of generation or corruption."

Ramesey stated that "there are seven sorts of conjunctions considerable:

"1. The *first* and greatest of all the rest is the conjunction of the two superior planets SATURN and JUPITER in the first term or degree of *Aries*, which happens but once in 960 years.

"2. The *second* is the conjunction of SATURN and JUPITER in the first term or degree of every triplicity, and this is accomplished once in 240 years; yet once in 20 years they come in conjunction in one part or other of the Zodiac.

"3. The conjunction of SATURN and MARS in the first term or degree of *Cancer*, and is once in 30 years.

"4. The conjunction of the three superiors, SATURN, JUPITER and MARS, in one term or face of any sign.

"5. The conjunction of JUPITER and MARS, which is a mean and the least conjunction of the superiors, and therefore is not the forerunner of such great mischiefs.

"6. The conjunction of the SUN with any planet at the time of his entrance into the first point of *Aries*.

"7. The conjunction of the SUN and MOON, which happeneth once in every month."

The discovery of the planets URANUS and NEPTUNE necessitates a re-arrangement of "great conjunctions." The influence of Neptune is not nearly so potent as that of Uranus, therefore we may regard the conjunction of the former with any planet as of much less importance than any of the seven "considerable conjunctions" mentioned by Ramesey. The conjunction of URANUS with either JUPITER or SATURN is very important. We may consider the following as the most important conjunctions.

1. The conjunction of Jupiter and Saturn.
2. The conjunction of Mars and Saturn.
3. The conjunction of Jupiter and Uranus.
4. The conjunction of Saturn and Uranus.
5. The conjunction of Mars and Jupiter.
6. The conjunction of Mars and Uranus.
7. The conjunction of either of the above named planets with the SUN at the moment of Solar eclipse or of the Sun's ingress into *Aries*.

The effects of a conjunction are greatly augmented when one of the conjoined planets happens to be in *perigree*. When the conjoined planets differ greatly in latitude the importance of the conjunction is greatly lessened. The approximate conjunction or opposition of the Moon with the conjoined planets adds greatly to its importance.

It has been asserted that when conjunctions happen in either of the "fixed" signs (♉, ♌, ♏, and ♒) their effects are much more lasting than in any other signs; this is, in the author's opinion, very doubtful, and it is more probable that the *cardinal* signs (♈, ♋, ♎, and ♑) take precedence of all the rest.

Ramesey asserts that the conjunction of Saturn and Jupiter in the first point, or first six degrees of *Aries*, is the greatest and most notable of all; and is accompanied or quickly followed by "commotions, wars, seditions, revolutions, alteration of laws, plagues, the death of kings," etc. In like manner "the conjunction of MARS and SATURN in the first three degrees of *Cancer* is the forerunner of much evil, *viz.*, terrible wars, slaughter, depopulation, alteration of government," etc.

SATURN and URANUS were in conjunction, in the sign *Taurus*, on March 16th, 1852. *Taurus* rules the Crimea—formerly called Taurica Chersonesus—and shortly after this very rare conjunction in ♉, the Crimea was invaded by the allied armies and a terrible and protracted war ensued. Earthquakes in Persia (ruled by *Taurus*) followed—notably that of May 14th, 1853, by which Shiraz was overthrown and 12,000 people killed—as foretold by Zadkiel; and the Persian Gulf was the scene of sanguinary naval warfare, as also predicted by

Zadkiel.

The conjunctions of JUPITER and URANUS (and likewise their oppositions) have been almost invariably attended by epidemics[1]; in the middle ages the visitations of plague, etc., coincided most frequently with ♃ ☌ or ☍ ♅.

The conjunctions of the two malefic planets, MARS and SATURN, are always attended by misfortunes—either great and destructive storms, inundations, wars, or earthquakes, according to the signs. The conjunctions of November 3rd, 1877, June 30th, 1879, July 6th, 1881, and July 20th, 1883, gave strong evidence of their malefic influence. The conjunction due on August 6th, 1885, in ♋ 3° 49′ 29.5″ did not fail to afford additional proof.[2]

The conjunctions of MARS and JUPITER are often attended by earthquakes (when happening in ♉, ♏, ♌ or ♑); at other times by the outbreak of religious warfare, as in 1877 and 1883; in summer by thunderstorms or intense heat, and in winter by gales and lightning.

The following are the aphorisms of Hermes as to the effects of the most important conjunctions, as stated by Ramesey:

"When JUPITER, VENUS, MERCURY, and the MOON are conjoined in *Aries*, they promise benefits and success to mankind; fertile showers; honour to women and Secretaries of State.

"When JUPITER, VENUS, MARS, and the MOON are conjoined in *Taurus*, they presignify injury to kings and nobles; and earthquakes.

"When SATURN, JUPITER, and MARS are conjoined in *Taurus*, they presignify mortality among cattle; migration of kings; and epidemics among men.

"SATURN, JUPITER, MARS, and the SUN; or VENUS, MERCURY, and the MOON, conjoined in *Cancer*, presignify detriment to everything, earthquakes and inundations.

"SATURN, JUPITER, MARS, and the MOON conjoined in *Leo*, kings shall go to war and kill one another, and many evils will fall upon men.

SATURN, MARS, and MERCURY conjoined in *Virgo*, kings shall be deceived; women will suffer detriment. And if the Sun be eclipsed in *Virgo* and in conjunction with MARS, there will be civil war. Also, when SATURN and VENUS are conjoined in *Virgo*, it denotes an increase of waters.

[1] See *Urunia* for May, 1880, art. Epidemics and Planetary Influence.

[2] See *Zadkiel's Almanac* for 1885, pp. 50-52.

"MARS and JUPITER conjoined in *Libra*, noblemen and their associates will suffer. When JUPITER, the SUN, and MOON are conjoined in ♎, there will be mortality among women and just men; much rain, cloudy and malignant air.

"When SATURN, MARS, and VENUS are conjoined in *Scorpio*, it presignifies that the king will be wounded, or bitten by some beast, or stung by an adder or obnoxious creature; kings shall quarrel with one another and break leagues and promises; and when the MOON is joined with those planets, much rain and increase of waters.

"Moreover, if *Scorpio* be the sign ascending at the vernal ingress, and SATURN be therein conjoined with MARS, or in any participation with ♂ in the ascendant, and VENUS be then combust, and JUPITER retrograde, judge evil in everything, wars and quarrels, sackings of cities and towns, earthquakes, terrors, and bloodshed, and destructive epidemics—for *Scorpio* is the most evil of all the signs. Judge, also that kings will quarrel and fight with one another, and noble and great men die. And if both fortunes (♃ and ♀) be conjoined in this sign, there will be many men come forth to draw people away from true religion.

"When SATURN, JUPITER, MERCURY, and the MOON, are conjoined in *Sagittarius* it presignifies that there shall be floods; that kings shall exalt themselves; and that noblemen, scribes, astrologers, and ingenious men shall be held in great esteem.

"When the SUN, MARS, and MERCURY are conjoined in *Capricornus* it presignifies death of kings; epidemic fevers, configurations; apparitions in the air; high winds; a scarcity of vegetables; and many thefts and robberies.

"When MARS, SATURN, and the MOON are conjoined in *Aquarius*, it presignifies scarcity of water and rain; injury to travellers; and many snakes and serpents.

"When SATURN, JUPITER and MARS are conjoined in *Pisces*, it presignifies the death of kings, noblemen, and grandees; and if the SUN be with MARS and SATURN, the king shall be slain; there shall be little or no rain; and many fish will be taken in the sea."

Ramesey lays stress on the necessity for casting a figure of the heavens "for the punctual time of partile conjunction—*viz*., in the very same sign, degree. and minute of the zodiac." He should have added, " to the same *second*," but in his day the English astrologers appear to have been unequal (like many of the self-styled "professors" of astrology at the present day) to such a task. For unless the conjunction of Saturn and Jupiter, for example, be computed to *seconds*, the figure of the heavens would be entirely erroneous: the ordinary astrological *Ephemerides* giving the longitudes of the planets to degrees and minutes only do not permit of such accuracy. There can be no wonder that some of the predictions failed when the time of conjunction could not be determined within hours, or even days. Astrologers base their predictions on the features of figures drawn for the moment of conjunction in longitude (*i.e.*, in the *ecliptic*); whereas astronomers now-a-days compute conjunction in *right ascension*; hence there is an apparent discrepancy frequently found between the time of conjunction of any two of the heavenly bodies, as stated in the *Nautical Almanac* and *Zadkiel's Almanac*. The last conjunction of Saturn and Jupiter, in 1881, is given in the latter publication as occurring at 2h 4m 56s p.m. of April 18th in ♉ 1° 36′ 41″; in the *Nautical Almanac*, at 1h p.m. of April 22nd (in R.A.). Although the author published the process of calculation in *Urania* for July, 1880, several persons wrote charging him with having made a mistake, as the *Nautical Almanac* gave a different time. There can be no doubt that astrologers are right in taking the *ecliptic* conjunction of planets as the *true* one for astrological judgment, in the same manner as the conjunction of the Sun and Moon (New Moon) is taken. The success of predictions made on this basis, and published in *Zadkiel's Almanac*, give evidence of its reliability. Geocentric *longitude* of a heavenly body is its angular distance from the first point of *Aries* measured upon the *ecliptic*, as viewed from the Earth; its right ascension is its distance from Aries measured upon the *Equator*.

After computing the exact moment of conjunction in longitude, it becomes important to ascertain where the conjoined planets will be *rising* at that moment, for the chief effects are usually felt in such a place; next, where they will be *southing*, *setting*, or in the *lower meridian*. This may be readily done by means of the globe. The countries ruled by the *sign* in which the conjunction falls will also be affected.

Generally speaking, conjunctions of evil planets in *fiery* signs (♈, ♌ and ♐) presignify "impediment in the air; corruption, and much damage thereby both to men and fruits of the earth. In *fixed* signs (♉, ♌, ♏ and ♒), whether the conjoined planets be benevolents or malevolents, what they portend is of continuance; in *movable* signs (♈, ♋, ♎, and ♑), of little or no continuance; in *common* signs (♊, ♍, ♐, ♓), a mean between these, neither of long nor short continuance." The last-named distinctions are arbitrary and fanciful.

It has already been stated that the ancients considered the

conjunction of Saturn and Jupiter in the first term of *Aries* as the greatest of all. The next in importance is their conjunction in the first term of *Taurus*, *Gemini* and *Cancer*, because these are held to be the first terms of the various trigons or triplicities. When Saturn is in the stronger (as in ♎, ♑, and ♒) the evils resulting will be very terrible; when Jupiter is the stronger planet (as in ♋, ♐, and ♓) the evil will be abated. In fiery, earthy, and airy signs the conjunctions of Saturn and Jupiter were held to presignify drought, barrenness of the earth, and scarcity of provisions; in watery signs, detriment by super-abundance of water.

The conjunction of Saturn, Jupiter, and Mars in any term or face and configurated with the Sun, presignifies "the destruction of kingdoms, sects, and schisms, according to the strength and nature of the planet which is strongest in the sign" in which the conjunction takes place. "Note that when these planets are conjoined in their exaltations (♋, ♎, or ♑), they denote good, to their power; yet there shall be much war and many miracles; if in their falls, they denote mischief, famine, pestilence, etc."—says Ramesey.

The conjunction of Mars and Saturn in human signs (♊, ♍, the first half of ♐, and ♒) presignifies "many infirmities shall be incident to men, according to the nature of the stronger planet. In earthy signs, frost, snow, and cold shall molest and prove hurtful and destructive to the fruits and seeds of the earth. In fiery signs, the earth shall be barren through extremity of heat and drought. In airy signs, there shall be many high and tempestuous winds. In watery signs, abundance of water and many inundations. In either ♈, ♉, ♌, the latter half of ♐, or ♑, the evil will fall on animals, chiefly those of the nature and form of the sign. In this manner thou mayest enlarge upon all the important conjunctions. If Mars and Saturn be conjoined in an angle, they declare *war*[3] amongst the great, many tribulations and discussions which shall continue until they are otherwise conjoined."

The conjunction of Mars and Jupiter presignifies mischief "by rain, snow, corruption of the air, war, and bloodshed. If Jupiter be the stronger, the effects will not be so bad. If they be conjoined in the ascendant of the vernal equinox, mischief and misfortune will assuredly happen to the people in general. The nature of the evil may be judged from the nature of the sign and the planet which is the stronger of the two."

In judging which is the stronger of two conjoined planets, the author believes from experience that the planet which has the more *northerly* declination, especially if in *perigee*, should be considered

[3] As in 1879, at Cabul. See Urania for January, 1880.

as the stronger. In the southern hemisphere, the one having the more southern declination should be taken to be the stronger. The chief dignities may be next considered, but they ought not to be preferred before *perigree* and declination. At the conjunction of MARS and SATURN in the year 1877, Mars was in *perigee*, and the fearful slaughter of Russians and Turks attested the power of the planet of war.[4] In that year, Mars was retrograde (and therefore very near the earth) from August 7th to October 7th.

Sir George Wharton, a clever astronomer of the seventeenth century, averred his belief that a great (fourth) cause of the mutations of empires, kingdoms, etc., is "the conjunction of the two superior planets, SATURN and JUPITER." He recognised that "the FIRST CAUSE IS ALMIGHTY GOD, the Creator and Governor of all things. Forasmuch," wrote Wharton, "as God performs his greatest works in the world by angels, it is not impossible or strange, if I say and aver, that every empire, kingdom, and republic, hath some certain angel and genius peculiarly appropriated thereunto as a governor ordained by God. For this is the constant opinion of the Jews, who believe that every person and place hath a certain guardian angel set over it; nor do a few doctors of the Catholic Church believe otherwise, whilst in *Daniel* 10, 11, there is mention made of an angel governor of Persia, and Greece; and the apostle (*Ephesians* 3) expressly constitutes a certain order of angels which he calls *potestates* (rulers or potentates, as our English translation hath it, principalities and powers)."

The conjunctions of Mercury and Mars near the Equator or tropics, especially when they are at the same time in parallel declination, cause much public excitement; a prevalence of robberies with violence, and of murders; and often help to cause war. On the atmosphere, these conjunctions exercise a most potent and disturbing influence, as Kepler records. In August, 1831, Mercury, Mars, and Saturn were conjoined; tempests in England and the West Indies destroyed over 5,000 lives.

The student should always bear in mind Ptolemy's injunctions: "In the conjunction of SATURN and JUPITER, pronounce according to the nature of that one which may be higher in elevation. Follow the same rule with other stars. Judgment is not to be drawn from any figure until the next conjunction shall have been considered; for principles are varied by every conjunction; and, therefore, to avoid error, both the last and the next should be combined."

---

[4] See page 21.

CHAPTER XVII.

COMETS.

> "Like a comet burn'd,
> That fires the length of Ophiuchus huge
> In the arctic sky and from his horrid hair
> Shakes pestilence and war."—MILTON.

THE WORD comet is derived from κομή, hair; the nebulous matter of which the *coma* and tail are composed being supposed to resemble hair, the object being called κομήιη, (kometes), a hairy star.

The tails of comets usually incline towards the region last quitted; they are sometimes curved. Many comets have appeared without tails, some with several separate tails; some (like Donati's comet in 1859) have a tail extending over a very considerable part of the heavens.

Lexell's comet was supposed to have passed among the satellites of Jupiter; if so, their motions were not in the least affected by it. The nearest approaches to the earth ever made by comets, were in 1684 and 1861. In the former year, the comet (which passed its perihelion on June 8th) came within 216 semi-diameters of the earth. In 1861, the earth passed through the tail of a great comet; the world was greatly alarmed by the speculations of astronomers as to the effects of this passage, but the event proved to be perfectly harmless. In 1856, far greater alarm was excited by the prediction of a learned astronomer that the comet of 1556 would then reappear and come into collision with the earth. Many persons went foolishly mad about the comet, which, after all, never appeared. Had an astrologer foretold such a calamity, the newspapers would have teemed with virtuous indignation and denouncement when the scare was found to be groundless. The learned astronomer was flatly contradicted by the learned astrologer Zadkiel I. (Morrison) who told his readers that there was nothing to be alarmed at, and that astronomers knew very little about comets. This fiasco is not remembered against astronomers; and this marks the difference between orthodox and heterodox science! Astronomers claim to have discovered a singular bond of relationship between comets and shooting-stars (this may account for the frequent failure to predict the return of comets and of meteoric displays). But, hitherto, they have failed to determine either the origin, the real structure, or the causes of the wonderful changes of shape of comets.

Hevelius and Kepler believed that comets proceed from some gross exhalations from the Sun. Halley and Hamilton were of opinion that their tails are composed of electric fluid. Newton's erroneous ideas respecting comets were formed in ignorance of many physical facts and laws subsequently determined.

Sir John Herschel characterised the assertion that "comets cause warm summers, epidemics, potato blights, and so forth" as "all wild talking." History, however, abounds with coincidences of epidemics, wars, overthrow of kingdoms, pestilence, famine, and earthquakes, with the appearance of great comets. Hence, by an empirical law, we may venture to say that when a great comet, or several shall appear, certain great events (according to the nature of the sign of the zodiac in which they may appear) will immediately follow; but this would by no means necessarily involve a belief that the comets were the cause of such events, for all these phenomena might be the result of *a common natural cause.*

We can hardly wonder at the widespread belief in ancient and mediaeval times that comets are portents, considering the before-mentioned coincidences, and that it is stated in Holy Writ that changes or new appearances in the heavens were signs of approaching calamities. Professors of every kind of religion offered up prayers against the evil influences of comets and stars.

The great Kepler declared that comets heralded the overthrow of kingdoms, and various calamities.

In the year 1881 three comets appeared. The tropical heat in England in July, 1881, also in Europe and North America, will long be remembered. In 1882, during the total eclipse of the Sun at Cairo, May 17th, the astronomers observed a great comet in the form of a scimitar close to the Sun. The great comet (β) of 1881, was first seen in R.A. 74° 45′, which is the line of the 16th degree of the sign *Gemini* (which rules Egypt). The war in Egypt in 1882, and that in the Soudan in 1883, '84 and '85, quickly followed, notwithstanding that Mr. Gladstone's Government came into power (in 1880) pledged to maintain peace. The tropical summer of 1884 was one of the most extraordinary seasons ever witnessed in these islands. The volcanic eruption at Java, destroying at least 65,000 lives, took place on August 26th and

27th, 1883.

R. A. Proctor, in his remarks on comets as portents, called attention to the "noteworthy circumstance" that the terrible war of 1870 was "begun and carried on to its termination without the appearance of any great comet"; and that it occurred "near the middle of one of the longest intervals recorded in astronomical annals as unmarked by a single conspicuous comet—the interval between the years 1862 and 1874."

We should certainly never assert that because a great war or the death of a great man occurred a comet must forthwith appear. However, on the night of May 29th, 1870, Dr. Winnecke, of Carlsruhe, discovered a comet "resembling a pretty bright nebula of about 2½ minutes in diameter." He observed it again on the 30th, when its R.A. was 0h 50m 9.55s, and its declination 28° 52′ 18″ north. Hence it was first seen in the second decanate of the sign *Aries*. Now, the ancients averred that a comet appearing in *Aries* presignifies a very extensive drought, drying up of fountains, etc.; and such a drought was experienced in most parts of Europe in 1870. Again, the comet appeared in the north and was vertical to nearly the whole of Germany (ruled by *Aries*); and the terrible war was waged by Germany against France that same year. Moreover, the comet appeared very near the longitudes of the Sun and Mars at the birth of Louis Napoleon, and his armies were beaten and himself taken prisoner. We are not aware that the ancients attributed effects in proportion to the apparent dimensions of comets, but rather to the parts of the zodiac in which they are first seen.

The comet of 1861, which appeared at the end of June, was first seen in the sign *Gemini*. When it passed through the 77th degree of R.A. (the line of ascendant of London) it was not visible, but the great conflagration in London, which lasted for six weeks, and had not been equalled for 200 years, commenced on June 22nd, 1861. In the following September the first shot was fired in the terrible civil war in the United States (ruled by *Gemini*). The Sultan of Turkey, and the Lord High Chancellor of England, died within a week of the appearance of this comet; and the lamented Prince Consort (in the midheaven of whose nativity the comet appeared) died on December 14th, 1861.

The comet of 1858 (Donati's) was followed by the Italian war of 1859 (as foretold by Zadkiel). That of 1853, by the Crimean War. That of 1811, by the Napoleonic Wars.

Proctor thought that the "star" seen by the wise men in the East may have been Halley's comet.[1] "It appeared in the year 66, or seventy years after the Nativity, and as the period of the comet varies, according to the perturbing influences affecting its motion, from 69 to 80 years, it may have appeared at our Saviour's birth, travelling southwards."

Whether the Star of Bethlehem was Halley's comet or the "lost star" of 1572-74 which appeared in *Cassiopeia*, supposed to have a period of 315 years, it is certain that it appeared in the second decanate of *Aries*. Now *Aries* is an *eastern* sign, and rules *Judea*, hence the Magi, or "wise men," went to Jerusalem the capital. This affords a complete answer to the sceptical objection of the celebrated Deist, Thomas Paine, viz.: "If the wise men saw the star in the *east* (or towards the east as it may be rendered) why did they go to the *west*? why did they not go *to* the east instead of from the east? why go to Jerusalem? The true meaning of the term *east* is that the Magi had seen the star or comet in the eastern part of the zodiac in regard to the position of the Sun. If the comet became *stationary* in the meridian of Bethlehem, as seems very probable, it would explain the meaning of another verse—"The star came and stood over where the young child was." No theological writer has ever been able to answer Paine's objection, because of the neglect of astrology to which so many allusions are made in the Bible. Ptolemy declared that *Aries* influenced Judea.

It was Halley's comet, wrote Proctor, which in the year 1456 created such alarm throughout Europe. At that time the Turks had in their victorious career crossed the Hellespont aud seemed likely to overrun Europe. Millions of people believed that the comet portended the doom of the world. It passed its perihelion on June 18th, 1456, and in the following winter the Baltic was frozen from Mecklenburg to Denmark; the Danube was frozen for two months; and many vineyards in Germany were totally destroyed. An earthquake occurred in Naples, followed by violent rains and great inundations, 40,000 lives being lost.

The next appearance of Halley's comet was in 1531. Religious houses were suppressed by Henry VIII. The Cabaqua Sea rose four feet above its usual height. Spotted fever raged throughout Europe, and was followed by the plague. Aetna was in eruption: great inunda-

---

[1] See *Zadkiel's Almanac* for 1879, p. 67. art. "The Star of Bethlehem, and Z.A. for 1911, pp. 86-89.

tions took place in Switzerland, Rome, and Antwerp; in England, from Somersetshire to Norfolk, the country had the appearance of a great sea. At Lisbon, the same year, an earthquake continued for eight days, overthrowing 1,500 houses and killing 30,000 people; and several neighbouring towns were swallowed up.

The next return of Halley's comet took place in 1606, the year memorable for the gunpowder plot. In the following year it appeared of a dark livid colour (*i.e.* of the character of SATURN); the plague raged in London, 850 dying of it per week. On June 12th (the day of the summer solstice, before the alteration of the calendar), there occurred a severe frost, and the following winter was intensely cold all over the world; the sea overflowed its banks and inundated a great part of England, so that "hay and corn stacks floated about like ships on the sea; pigeons were seen upon the stacks, which were carried away by the floods." The coasts of America were visited by storms of fearful violence.

In the year 1682, Halley's comet reappeared and passed its perihelion on September 4th. The heat on its approach was most intense throughout England and Europe; the thermometer in England stood at 96° in the shade. Disease and pestilence followed over all Europe, especially in Spain and Algiers; at Halle 300 per day died of plague. The City of Catana was destroyed by an earthquake, and 60,000 of its inhabitants perished. Aetna and Vesuvius were both in eruption. Earthquakes were felt in various parts of England. On the departure of the comet, severe frosts ensued, a fair being held on the Thames.

In 1759 Halley's comet re-appeared, and was visible in the following year. In 1759 earthquakes were felt in Tripoli, Syria, etc., spreading over an area of 10,000 square miles.

Halley's comet re-appeared in 1909. It was first seen as a telescopic object at 1h 30m a.m. of September 12th, and was photographed by Dr. Wolf, of Heidelberg, in R.A. 94° 33′ (the line of R.A. of Cancer 4° 11′) and declin. 17° 11′ N. It first became visible to the unaided eye at 3h 30m a.m. of April 25th, 1910, like a star of the second magnitude, in R.A. 358°, which is that of the sign Pisces 27° 49′ on the threshold of Aries. Within twelve days King Edward VII. expired, to the great grief of the British Empire. On October 3rd, 1910, a revolution broke out in Portugal and King Manoel fled to England. Heavy rains and great floods in Europe coincided with the approach of the comet in January, 1910. Great heat and severe prolonged drought in Europe and Asia followed in the wonderful summer of

1911, as the comet receded from the Solar system.

Three hundred and seventy-one years before the Christian era a comet appeared and was described by Aristotle. Diodonus Siculus, writing of it says: "In the first year of the 102nd Olympiad, Alcisthenes being Archon of Athens, several prodigies announced the approaching humiliation of the Lacedaemonians; a blazing torch of extraordinary size, which was compared to flaming beam, was seen during several nights." Guillemen remarks that this same comet was considered by the ancients merely to have presaged but produced the earthquakes which caused the towns of Helice and Bura to be submerged. Seneca said that as soon as it appeared it brought about the submergence of those towns.

The comets of 134 B.C. and 118 B.C. were not regarded portents of death, but as signalising, the former the birth, latter the accession, of Mithridates.

A comet of an alarming nature appeared and was seen in daytime with the naked eye 43 B.C., and just after the death of Julius Caesar; the Romans thought that it was Caesar's metamorphosed soul armed with fire and seeking vengeance for his death.

Pliny says: "A fearful star is the comet, and not easily appeased, as appeared in the late civil troubles when Octavius was consul; a second time by the intestine war of Pompey and Caesar; and in our own time, when Claudius Caesar having been poisoned, the Empire was left to Domitian, in whose reign there appeared a blazing comet."

Lurcan records that during the war, "the darkest nights were lit up by unknown stars, the heavens appeared on fire, flaming torches traversed in all directions the depths of space; a comet, that fearful star which overthrows the powers of earth, showed its horrid hair."

Seneca also expressed an opinion that some comets portend evil. He says: "Some comets are very cruel, and portend the worst misfortunes; they bring with them and leave behind them the seeds of blood and slaughter."

Socrates, the historian, says that when Gainas besieged Constantinople, "so great was the danger which hung over the city, that it was presignified and portended by a huge blazing comet which reached from heaven to the earth, the like whereof no man had ever seen before."

Cedrenus, in his "Compendium of History," states that a comet appeared before the death of Johannes Tzimicas, the Emperor of the East, which foreshadowed not alone his death, but the great calamities which were to befall the Roman Empire by reason of their civil wars. In like manner, the comet of 451 is said to have announced the death of Attila, and that of 455 the death of Valentinian. The death of Merovingius was announced by the comet of 577; that of Chilperic by the comet of 584; that of the Emperor Maurice by the comet of 602; that of Mahomet by the comet of 632; that of Louis Debonair by the comet of 837. Shakespeare has reflected this universal belief that comets often indicated the approaching death of great men, in the following lines:

> "When beggars die there are no comets seen;
> The heavens themselves blaze forth the death of princes."

The comet of 1528 seems to have been *par excellence* a horrible and portentous one. Of this, Andrew Pare writes: "This comet was so horrible and dreadful, and engendered such terror in the minds of men that they died, some from fear alone, others from illness engendered by fear. It was of immense length and blood-red colour, at its head was seen the figure of a curved arm, holding a large sword in the hand as if preparing to strike. At the point of this sword were three stars; and on either side a number of axes, knives, and swords covered with blood, amongst which were many hideous faces with bristling beards and hair."

Tennyson, in his drama "Harold" alludes to the popular dread of comets:

> "*Aldwyth*: What thinkest thou this means ?
> *Gamel*: War, my dear lady!"

Proctor evidently took a great deal of trouble to reproduce authentic records of the appearance of comets and of dire calamities following. In this way, he, unconsciously perhaps, makes out a very strong case in favour of comets as portents. He made two great mistakes: (1) in confounding the superstitious fears of the vulgar with the speculations of ancient learned astrologers, whose astrology was deduced from the most patient and careful examination of Nature; and (2) in overlooking the fact that astrologers ascribed various significations according to the appearance of comets in the various signs of the zodiac and the several divisions of the heavens. Even if the premature assertion of Proctor that "the movements of comets are as well understood as those of the most orderly planets" were strictly true—and it is considerably discounted by the fact that the great comets of 1811 and 1861, *never drew nearer to the Sun* (greatly to the astonishment of the Newtonian astronomers), and the non-re-appearance of the comet of

1556 in 1856, as foretold—it would not controvert the fact that the appearance of comets followed by great convulsions, etc. Leverrier acknowledged that the comet of 1861 "resembled none of those already observed" and he added that "this circumstance will contribute not a little to throw confusion upon the little we know of those erratic bodies; moreover, the comet has not drawn nearer to the Sun; these are all circumstances calculated to introduce great complications into the theory of comets." It would seem that Proctor either never read these comments of that great French astronomer or chose to ignore them. If the Sun attracts other comets why did it fail to attract those of 1811 and 1861. Which of our distinguished astronomers will answer this question clearly and satisfactorily?

The conjunctions of SATURN and JUPITER—which can always be accurately foretold—are still regarded, as we have seen, portents of great changes, etc. It may seem clever, to the superficial and the frivolous, to laugh at the science of the ancients; but philosophers should show more respect for it, especially when they remember that the founders of modern astronomy, Pythagoras, Democritus, and Kepler, believed in Astrology. There has been nothing advanced by astrologers in reference to the portentous appearance of comets more absurd than the vagaries of Newton, Whiston, and others, concerning the movements of those bodies.

In a catalogue of pestilences which have occurred since the Christian era, it was shown by Dr. Forster[2] that on 262 occasions appearances of comets coincided very closely therewith.

Comet years are invariably and proverbially good wine years.

The great comet of 1811, which appeared near the constellation of Ursa Major, and continued to be visible for 510 days (the longest appearance on record), was the forerunner of the Russian war, and of that great convulsion which separated some of those vast continents of ice near the North Pole, which had existed for ages. Some idea of their age may be formed from the observations of Kotzebue, who found icebergs covered with land, vegetables, and even trees; and one of them contained the body of a mammoth in a state of putrefaction, due to exposure to a warmer climate after its separation.

The comet which heralded the birth of Christ is the only one recorded as the messenger of "glad tidings" and "peace on earth." It is a remarkable fact that whereas all ancient writers have represented all

[2] "Illustrations of the Atmospherical Origin of Epidemic Diseases." By T. Foster, M.B. Chelmsford, 1829.

other comets as portents of evil or as scourges, not one ascribed such a character to the "Star of Bethlehem." What a contrast to that comet which Josephus says appeared "in the form of a sword," and "hung over Jerusalem for a whole year," and thus foreshadowed the destruction of that ancient city!

The following are the aphorisms of the ancients in regard to the appearance of comets, as collated by Ramesey:

"Comets appearing in the sign *Aries* presignify evil and detriment to noblemen and grandees in the Eastern parts; sorrow to the peoples under ♈; the clash of arms and bloodshed; death or dethroning of some king; also great drought, disease among small cattle, especially sheep.

"In *Taurus*, mischief to men under ♉; death of some great man; detriment to the greater sort of cattle, especially oxen; corruption of fruit, destruction of corn; in winter much cold and great winds; also grievous earthquakes, vehement sicknesses, etc.

"In *Gemini*, quarrels, wars, and dissensions amongst men; sickness and death of children and young men especially; the slaughter of birds; scarcity of food; thunderstorms, and hurricanes.

"In *Cancer*, abundance of locusts (in the countries subject to their invasions; in our climate, caterpillars, and pernicious worms); a scarcity of fruit; wars, discord; death of some great man; and pestilence.

"In *Leo*, wild beasts shall attack mankind (in regions infested by feral creatures); worms and vermin will be destructive to corn; the nobility and gentry will suffer detriment, and many of them death; war amongst kings, much bloodshed in Eastern parts; prevalence of affections of the eyes.

"In *Virgo*, banishment of servants of kings; damage to merchants; troubles, sadness, fevers; a noise of arms, etc.

"In *Libra*, highway robberies; poverty; great cold; death of some eminent man, plots, treachery, and slaughter; scarcity of rain, impetuous winds; a drought of fountains; scarcity of the fruits of the earth; earthquakes, etc.

"In *Scorpio*, great wars or rebellions, changes of kingdoms; great perils; the death of some eminent man; scarcity of waters; dangers to women; scarcity of corn and fruits of the earth; and prevalence of diseases of the urinary and reproductive organs.

"In *Sagittarius*, decay of the nobility and of wise and learned men; captivity of some prince; war, and such like.

"In *Capricornus*, increase of crime; war amongst kings and nobles; many calamities, death of princes; contempt of religion; highway robberies; abundance of hail, snow, and frost, to the detriment of the seeds of the earth; also it threateneth famine, pestilence, and the like.

"In *Aquarius*, war and bloodshed; death of some eminent prince or lady; epidemics; obscuration of the air, with thunder and lightning; pestilence, etc.

"In *Pisces*, war amongst kindred and allies, much slaughter contentions about religion and ancient tradition; apparitions in the air; destruction of fish; and dangers in navigation.

"Comets appearing in the eastern quarter of the heavens generally bring their effects quickly to pass, the effect on the atmosphere being drier; in the western, the effects manifest themselves more slowly and often extend over three years, and the effect on the atmosphere is to condense the aqueous vapours. The quarter of the heavens in which comets appear shows the part of the globe on which their effects will mostly fall; the sign of the zodiac, the particular kingdoms or countries. The effects are usually most manifest when the Sun arrives at the degree of the ecliptic affected by the appearance of the comet."

The *Times* of October 12th, 1832, published a letter "On Comets," from Mr. John Herapath, from which the following paragraphs are extracted:

"On this point—namely, the influence of comets to affect the temperature—M. Arago has made some researches, the result of which is, that comets have no effect in altering the mean annual temperature of the earth. Granting to M. Arago the full benefit of his inference, it by no means follows that they may not have a powerful influence on the season, separately considered, although they may have none on the mean temperature of the year. For example, let us suppose that one was by any means rendered either uncommonly clear or uncommonly cloudy, for a whole year, what would be the consequence? Would not the summer temperature in the former case be considerably elevated, and the winter as much depressed, and the contrary in the latter case; yet the mean temperature in both instances might be the same?

"History furnishes us with numberless instances of the great atmospheric changes which have accompanied or succeeded the apparition of large and notorious comets; and unless we reject altogether its often iterated testimonies, I do not see how we can refuse our assent to influences so manifest, and yet so simple and perfectly philosophical."

Mr.Maunder writes: "The suggestion has been made—following the closing lines of Paradise Lost (for Milton is responsible for many of our interpretations of Scripture):

'High in front advanced
The brandished sword of God before them blazed,
Fierce as a comet,'

—that a comet was indeed the "flaming sword which turned every way, to keep the way of the tree of life."[3]

It may be mentioned that the appearance of Halley's comet in 1759 was followed by the death of King George II. in 1760.

Its appearance in 1066 was immediately followed by the death of King Harold and the Norman Conquest of England. William of Normandy is said to have remarked to his courtiers that: "A comet like this is only seen when a kingdom wants a king."

Sceptics advanced the argument that as the appearance of Halley's comet in 1835 was not attended by any great catastrophes it was vain and superstitious to apprehend any disasters as likely to attend and follow its reappearance in 1910. Zadkiel I. declared, in his "Herald" for 1833, his opinion that there would be no very great evil of a physical nature attending the return in 1835, because the years 1834, 1835, and 1836 would be free from important conjunctions or oppositions of the major planets. How different was the case in 1909 and 1910 (when ♃, ♄, ♆, and ♅ were in the cardinal signs Libra, Aries, Cancer, and Capricornus) has been already recorded on previous pages.

As Evelyn wrote in 1682, "Comets may be warnings from God, as they commonly are forerunners of His animadversions."

---

[3] "The Astronomy of the Bible," by E. Walter Maunder, F.R.A.S., second edition, p. 107.

BOOK III.

ASTRO-METEOROLOGY.

CHAPTER I.

INTRODUCTION.

> "The love of truth is of equal importance in the reception of facts and in the formation of opinions; and it includes, also, a readiness to relinquish our own opinions when new facts or arguments are presented to us which are calculated to overturn them."—ABERCROMBIE.

THE study of Meteorology is of the highest antiquity, being co-eval with that of Astrology the foster-mother of Astronomy. "The disclosures of the cuneiform inscriptions prove that the phenomena of the weather were observed and recorded together with the configurations of the heavenly bodies."[1]

In the earliest ages of the world, the shepherds, agriculturists, and seamen watched for indications, of approaching changes of weather, in the appearance of the sky, clouds, changes of the direction of the wind, etc.; also, by observing the habits of animals, birds, insects, and the indications of sensitive plants.

Aristotle, in his Μετεωρολογυκά, published about 300 years B.C., wrote of τὰ μετέωρᾳ, the things above the earth—meteors, air; also of water and *earthquakes*.

The poets Aratus, Lucretius, Virgil, and Manilius wrote largely concerning weather and the prognostics of the ancients.

Pliny records aphorisms relating to the forecasting of weather, and, moreover, relates of Anaximander that "he foretold the earthquakes which overthrew Lacedaemon."

[1] "Lectures on Babylonian Literature." By the Rev. A. H. Sayce.

In the *Geoponica*, a work compiled, by direction of one of the later Greek emperors, by various authors, on agricultural pursuits, there are aphorisms relating to weather, seasons, etc., taken from the writings of Aratus, Democritus, Didymus, and Diophanes, based on the observation of coincidences between the phenomena of the weather with certain relative positions of the heavenly bodies.

The ancient mythology related in great part to the atmosphere and variations of weather. Jupiter was a personification of various atmospherical phenomena, and in turn, Jupiter Ammon, Jupiter Tonans, Jupiter Pluvius.

Some of the ancient Christian hymns and orations, used in times of epidemic pestilence, were prayers that the *sidereal influences* might be repressed. Thus, in the petition to Mary, the mother of Our Lord and Saviour, beginning "*Stella caeli extirpavit, que lactavit dominum*, etc.", we have the prayer, "*Sidera compescere.*"

Mr. Kendrick tells us that: "By their science the Egyptian astrologers could foretell years of scarcity and plenty, pestilences, earthquakes, inundations, and the appearance of comets, and do many other things surpassing the sagacity of the vulgar."[2]

Sir John Herschel observed that: "The discovery of natural truth has been remarkably slow. When the discovery is a single fact, many years commonly elapse before the next fact in connection with it is brought to light. When it is of a more general kind, and partakes of the nature of a law, it more commonly suggests other truths and valuable circumstances in connection with it, by which means a more rapid progress is, for a time, made."

As an illustration of this, Dr. Sharp[3] refers to the *attraction* of magnetic iron, which was known to the ancients; but this was all; its *polarity* was not known in Europe until the year 1180, when it was first described by Guyot; the practical application of this property to navigation was not made until about 1260; the *variation* in the direction of the magnetic needle in different parts of the earth was not known until 1500, when it was discovered by Sebastian Cabot; the *dip* of the needle remained undiscovered until 1576; two hundred and fifty years elapsed before the *changed direction* of the needle by a current of electricity was discovered by Oersted in 1819, which property has since been applied practically in the electric telegraph.

---

[2] "Ancient Egypt under the Pharaohs." By John Kendrick, M,A.

[3] "Essays on Medicine."

Pythagoras, Democritus, Thales, Anaximander, Anaxagoras, Eudoxus, Hippocrates, and Galen recognised the *fact of planetary action* on the atmosphere; Tycho Brahe, Kepler, Bacon, Baron Napier, Flamstead, Dr. Goad, Boerhave, and Mesmer, were convinced of the same *fact*; yet at the close of the nineteenth century the observation of these great men is ignored by astronomers and meteorologists. It may be well asked: "What has meteorology gained by ignoring the experience and observation of the ancients? Can the nineteenth century meteorologists emulate the achievements of the Chaldaeans and ancient Egyptians—can they foretell years of plenty, pestilence, earthquakes, and inundations? "The answer is obvious. Despite the improvement of meteorological instruments and the refinement of observation of temperature, etc., *predictive* meteorology has *retrograded* rather than advanced; for the State-endowed Meteorologic Office frequently fails to foretell the general character of the weather only twenty-four hours in advance, and dare not attempt to forecast the general character of a coming season!

Kepler gave the key to the discovery of the laws which regulate the weather, for he averred that "A Most Unfailing Experience of the Excitement of Sublunary Natures by the Conjunctions and Aspects of the Planets, has instructed and compelled my Unwilling Belief."[4]

It may be truly said that there is not a department in nature which has hitherto been so successfully studied as to constitute a science, which has not been founded upon one or more of such general facts or laws of nature. For example, the law of *specific gravity* was discovered by Archimedes; and the law which is the basis of mechanics was discovered by Galileo. The laws of Kepler, as they are called from their discoverer, are three important general facts in astronomy. "1°.—*The orbits of the planets are ellipses, with the Sun in one of the foci*. 2°.—*The planets move over equal areas in equal times*. 3°.—*The squares of the times of revolution of any two planets are to each other in the same proportion as the cubes of their mean distances from the Sun*."

"Of all the laws," says Sir John Herschel, "to which the induction from pure observation has ever conducted man, this third law of Kepler may justly be regarded as the most remarkable and the most pregnant with important consequences."

Sir Isaac Newton was indebted to Kepler for many of his discoveries.

[4] Extract from a work of Kepler's, quoted in Observations on the Life of Kepler, published by the Society for the Promotion of Useful Knowledge, 1830.

If the meteorologists of the present day will but follow the lead of Kepler in meteorology as Newton did in astronomy, they will constitute meteorology a predictive science. No other guide can lead them from darkness to light. Kepler found "from pure observation," that the ancients were right when they averred that "sublunary natures are excited by the conjunctions and aspects of the planets."

The "aspects" of the planets are certain relative positions. Kepler's definition of the term is as follows: "*Aspectus est angulas a radiis luminosis binorum planetarum in terra formatus, efficax ad stimulandum naturam sublunarem;*"—An aspect is an angle formed on the earth by the luminous beams of two planets, of strength to stir up the virtue of sublunary things. Thus, when the great planet Jupiter is 90° distant in (geocentric) longitude from the Sun, it is said to be in *square aspect* with Sun, as on August 30th, 1911, marked in the *Nautical Almanac* as ♃ □ ☉, in the table of *Phenomena*. When two of the heavenly bodies are in conjunction or opposition, they have nearly the same declination, and act powerfully on the earth and its atmosphere, because they attract in the same line; they rise, culminate, and set nearly together, when in conjunction; when in opposition, one rises as the other sets, one is in the upper when the other is in the lower meridian.

Observation shows that certain of the celestial bodies are in certain relative positions when *excess of heat or drought* prevails, and that certain others are in similar relative positions when *excess of cold or moisture* prevails. Hence it is inferred:

1°.—*That the said position of those celestial bodies are the original, though not the proximate, causes of such atmospheric phenomena.* 2°—*That, since the periods at which such celestial positions shall recur can always be accurately computed, it is possible to foretell the periods concurrent therewith, at which such atmospheric phenomena will also recur.*

Astronomers inform us that the great planets Jupiter and Saturn attract the earth very powerfully indeed, and that Venus and Mars do the same; that each planet is always attracting its fellows away from the average path round the Sun.

Sir John Herschel said that: "Meteorology included in its ancient and etymological sense all the appearances of the heavens, as well astronomical as atmospheric, but is at present restricted in its meaning to the description and explanation of those phenomena which group themselves under the heads of the weather, of the seasons, and of climate—phenomena which, scientifically regarded, are referable almost entirely to the agencies of those laws which govern the ever-varying affections of the atmosphere of our globe in its relations to heat, moisture, and electricity, and the movements which the changes of those relations, brought about by astronomical or other causes, impress upon its parts." Nevertheless, we search in vain for any inquiry into, any recognition of "*astronomical causes*" in Herschel's valuable work on Meteorology, beyond a mere allusion to planetary action on the photosphere of the Sun. It is this neglect of *astronomical causes* which bars the way to any real progress in predictive meteorology.

The late Commander Morrison, R.N., who was a member of the original Meteorological Society of Great Britain, and the late Mr. W. H. White, who was the Secretary of that Society, averred their belief in planetary action on the weather and did good service in directing public attention to it. The author published in the year 1864, "The Weather Guide-Book," in which he appealed to the scientific world to investigate astro-meteorology; and corresponded with the late Admiral Fitz-Roy on the subject. But my appeal was made in vain.

Mr. Jenkins considers it "surprising to learn that Mercury is most powerful in its disturbing effect on our atmosphere." If he will re£er to Dr. Goad's work, "Astro-Meteorologica," published in 1686, he will find that this fact was known to Kepler and Goad. Kepler wrote: "*Conjunctio ☿ ad ⊙ quorum in Meteoris magna vis est,*" etc.; and again, "*in commovendis tempestatibus multum valet, de stella nova.*"

In Chap. viii. of "The Weather Guide-Book," the author stated that: "It is observed that when Mercury is in conjunction with the Sun, the atmosphere is greatly disturbed, and the wind is strong; in winter, hurricanes sometimes happen, as in December, 1863." And in Chap. xii. of the same work, the author showed that to Mercury's action the greater number of storms were traceable.

CHAPTER II.

THE SUN.

> "The seven strings of Apollo's harp were the symbolical representation of the seven planets."

IT is unnecessary to explain in these pages the general dependence of climate on geographical situation; the high temperature at the equator and the extreme cold at the poles; the annual variations of temperature which accompany the changes of season and the diurnal alterations of heat and cold; all being such obvious consequences of the Sun attaining a greater or less meridian altitude and continuing for a longer or shorter period above the horizon; and already explained in the text-books of astronomy and meteorology.

Our task is to search for the *causes* of *variations* in the seasons—of a *hot* or a *cool* summer, of a *severe* or a *mild* winter—and of the visitations of drought, floods, storms, etc.

As we have already stated, from the remotest ages the causes of these atmospheric phenomena have been sought among the phenomena of the heavens. We propose to continue this research, being convinced, from observation, that to abandon it is to render the discovery of the laws which regulate the weather, hopeless.

To do this, we must watch for *coincidences between astronomic and atmospheric phenomena.*

Pouillet, whose observations (in 1837-38) at Paris were quoted by Sir John Herschel in his work on Meteorology, found that: "The Solar heat alone constitutes only two-thirds of the entire quantity of heat supplied to the earth to repair its thermal losses by terrestrial radiation; and that without the heat supplied by stellar radiation, the temperature of the earth would fall to a point which would be incompatible with organic life."

Observation shows that when the SUN is in *conjunction, parallel declination, opposition, sextile, quartile*, or *trine* aspect with Jupiter, the weather is warm and is usually fine, often both (the exceptions being when the Sun happens to be at the same time in aspect with Saturn or Uranus). This is a *fact* in nature, and, being constantly repeated, there can be no superstition attaching to a belief that the planet Jupiter (when in such relative position) is the cause of it. The *sextile* aspect is the angle of 60°, and this is the angle at which water crystallizes. When the Sun and Jupiter are 60° distant in longitude, the temperature of the air *rises*, but when those bodies are 65° apart no such effect is found. In like manner, water crystallizes at 60° but does not crystallize at 65°. In both cases the *fact* is known, but in neither can the reason (in the present state of our knowledge) be given. The "rule of six" is carried out by Nature in both operations.

The hexagonal formation of snow crystals, which always retain the hexagonal in outline on the six sides, is a law which governs Nature alike in these "ice-jewels" and in the "sextile aspect"—the angle of 60° which is one-sixth of the circle (360°)—the effects of this angle or aspect being well-known to astro-meteorologists.

In the first edition of this work (in 1889) the author declared that observations of Sun-spots alone will never lead to the discovery of the laws regulating the weather. The atmosphere is often liable to continuing impressions, sometimes unusual, and these are apparently produced by Solar configurations with the major planets, chiefly at or near the equinoxes and solstices.

Mr. Maunder's examination of the Greenwich Observatory records in his, the Solar Department, proves that seasons like that "wonderful summer" of heat and drought in 1911, "are quite independent of Sun-spots," for they have occurred at maxima and minima, or intermediate periods so that the cause must be looked for elsewhere."

When will Mr. Maunder and his colleagues cast aside their prejudices and investigate planetary action on the Sun?

CHAPTER III.

THE MOON.

"Therefore the Moon, the governess of floods,
Pale in her anger, washes all the air."—SHAKESPEARE.

"FAIR Cynthia's ever-changing face," has been ever regarded as more or less symbolical of weather changes. Aratus and Virgil allude to this, in their poems.

Pliny says: "In Africa, the south wind is serene, the northeast cloudy. All the winds have their turns. To judge rationally of their changes, the *fourth* day of the Moon is to be regarded." This probably gave rise to the vulgar Latin proverb: "Primus, secundus, tertius, nullus. Quartus, aliquis, quintus, sextus, qualis, tota luna talis." "As is the fourth and fifth days' weather, so's that lunation altogether"; when the Moon forms her first *semi-quartile aspect* (45°) with the Sun, after conjunction.

Arago endeavoured to prove that the Moon has no connection with the state of the weather. The publication of his paper on this subject led the Society for the Diffusion of Useful Knowledge to publish the results of their observations, some fifty years since, in the *Penny Magazine*, which showed that: "There are more *rainy days* in the *second quarter* of the Moon than any other, and *fewer* in the *fourth*. Also, that the *first* half of the lunar month is *more rainy* than the second." These conclusions are in harmony with those of Dr. Goad, as published in his work, "Astro-Meteorologica," two centuries since. Dr. Goad found that, in London, during the seven years 1671-77, during the increase of the Moon (when in *sextile* and *square aspect* with the Sun), the *excess* of days of rain (or snow) over those during her decrease (when in the same *aspects* with the Sun) was 61 in 795 days, or 1 in 13.

It is the disturbing action of the larger planets which renders the problem most complex and difficult of solution; in fact great changes of weather are often found to occur, *when the Moon is in major anpect with the Sun and one or more of the larger planets simultaneously*. Hence the following aphorisms were compiled two centuries since:

"If the Moon after *conjunction* or *opposition* with the SUN, immediately apply to SATURN (especially in either of the *signs Cancer, Scorpio or Pisces*), rain shall follow.

"If the Moon apply to *Jupiter, fine weather*, with hardly any rain (for seldom is any rain or weather produced by Jupiter destructive or unseasonable) will follow.

"If the Moon apply to *Mars, rain* will follow, unless Mars be in *Aries, Leo*, or *Sagittarius*, or in aspect with Jupiter. If Mars be in aspect with Venus or Saturn, *much rain* will follow.

"If the *new* Moon apply to *Venus*, without doubt *rain* will follow (unless Venus be in aspect with Jupiter). If Venus be in aspect with Saturn [to which we may now add Uranus], cold, rain, or snow (according to the season) will follow.

"If the *new* Moon apply to *Mercury* retrograde, *rain* will follow. If Mercury be with Venus or Saturn, *much rain*. If with Mars or Jupiter, warm or dry weather may be expected. In any case, brisk winds will follow." (Haly.)

Dr. Goad wrote: "'Tis confessed by the experience of Eichstad, that the aspect [☌ of ☉ and ☽ or new-moon] happening in the *angles i.e.*, the oriental, occidental, or meridional, is wont to bring rain. But the course of the Moon is the same in those angles as elsewhere, and seeing platic aspects are also operative, what conjunction is there that doth not visit those angles at distance, more or less. The fault, therefore, lies in the principles of those who discern not, or overlook the other causes, which are of the secret committee, as I may call it, where this aspect seems to preside."[1]

From some observations made at Montpellier, in the year 1774, it was found that out of 760 rains, 646 began when the Moon was very near the upper or lower meridian, or very near rising or setting.

Thunderstorms rarely begin when the Moon is *above* the horizon.

It is a well-known fact that changes of weather take place more frequently about twelve o'clock in the day, when the Sun arrives at the upper meridian, than at any other hour of the twenty-four.

The fact that more rain usually falls during the *increase* than during the *decrease* of the Moon, is demonstrated in the case of the 172 consecutive lunations during the fourteen years 1868-1881, the ex-

---

[1] "Astro-Meteorologica, or Aphorisms and Discourses of the Bodies Caelestial, founded on the Observations of Thirty Years." By J. Goad, London, 1686. Book I, chap. 12.

cess being more than seven-and-a-half inches (during the increase) or as 24 to 23.

Changes of weather take place more frequently at the *first quarter* and the *last sextile* than at any other period of the lunations—but the *nature* of the change depends on the *planet* with which the Sun and Moon may be configurated at such periods.

In regard to the *direction of the wind*, Dr. Goad found that the *first* quartile, the *last* trine, and the *second* sextile aspect formed by the Moon with the Sun raised *easterly* winds more frequently than other aspects; and that the *full* moon brought more *south* winds than the change.

That variations of weather are not attributable, however, solely to the Sun and Moon, Dr. Goad considered as proved by his observations of the coincidences of weather-changes with certain relative positions of the planets Mercury, Venus, Mars, Jupiter, and Saturn; and Kepler was of opinion that planetary as well as luni-solar action must be taken into account. Goad wrote: "We say that the depression of the Sun makes winter, but how come winters to be warm? often for a month or more, when the daisy, anemone, and the strawberry shall blow and proclaim a favourable season ; the Moon for half the time is in winter signs, as low and humble as the Sun."

Let us then pass to the examination of that planetary action on the weather, which has been derided by so many unphilosophical philosophers of the present day, who refuse to inquire into it!

CHAPTER IV.

THE PLANET JUPITER.

"Through silvery whiteness of that temperate star."—DANTE.

THE ancients described JUPITER as a planet of "a temperate complexion, midway between the coldness of Saturn and the heat of Mars."

Albumasar said that this planet is of "a temperate nature."

Claudius Ptolemy taught that: "Jupiter is fruitful and airy, and expressly connected with winds proceeding from the north."

In the book of *Job* we read that "fair weather cometh from the north." In *Proverbs* it is recorded that "the north wind driveth away rain."

Under the action of Jupiter, in our climate, the north wind brings fair weather and a rising barometer.

When we find constantly recurring incidences of the configurations of Jupiter with the Sun, Moon and Mars, coinciding with *fine* weather, we are justified in looking upon these coincidences as *cause and effect*. It is no reason why we should be deterred from such a conclusion that we cannot, in the present state of our knowledge, explain the *modus operandi*. "Till very lately," says Max Müller, "*caloric* was a term in constant use, and it was supposed to express some real matter, something that produced heat. That idea is now exploded, and heat is understood to be the result of molecular and ethereal vibrations."

Yes, and planetary action, that of Mars and Jupiter, chiefly is the cause of such vibrations as produce elevation of temperature.

The maximum generation of ozone is generally observed to coincide with northerly winds under Jupiter's action.

It has been demonstrated that there is a connection between the fluctuations of the annual death-rate and the position of Jupiter in his orbit.[1]

[1] *Vide* the *Journal of the Statistical Society*, March, 1869, article communicated by Mr. B. G. Jenkins, F.R.A.S.

Under Jupiter's action, frequently has summer heat been experienced even in the early spring. An instance of this is afforded in the extraordinary heat of May, 1864. Similar instances may be adduced in May, 1848; May, 1883; and April, 1840.

Numerous instances could be narrated of extreme heat in summer and autumn coinciding with Jupiter's "aspects," but these remarkable instances of *summer heat in spring time* are the most forcible. The extraordinary heat of July, 1881, when the shade temperature at Greenwich Royal Observatory reached 97°, coincided with the Sun in sextile with Jupiter—the "rule of six," again.

The position of Jupiter in the western angle at the vernal equinox of 1864, was followed by a remarkably fine, warm, and dry season. It is remarkable that while Europe was visited in 1864 with drought, Australia suffered from inundations; at the vernal equinox at Melbourne, however, Uranus was southing and Saturn (retrograde) was in the ascendant.

At the autumnal equinox of 1866, Jupiter was in the lower meridian, and a fine autumn followed. Although the total rainfall of the year (in London) was 4 inches in excess, the rainfall of the last three months was much below the average.

When Jupiter's action is unimpeded the effect is unmistakable. Thus do we find the aphorism of Haly, written several centuries since, strictly verified, viz.: "If Jupiter be in an angle at a solstice or an equinox, or receive the application of the Moon at new-moon (especially that nearest the equinox) *a temperate, good, and wholesome air*, and a season favourable to the increase and fructifying of that which is sown and planted in the earth, will follow."

The ancients held that the action of Jupiter was varied in his passage through the various signs of the zodiac, so that when in either *Cancer*, *Aquarius*, or *Pisces*, more rain falls under Jupiter's *aspects* than when in other signs.

In the "Geoponica,"[2] an ancient work on agricultural pursuits, there are several chapters on prognostics of weather and aphorisms by Aratus, Democritus, Didymus, Diophanes, and Zoroastres.

[2] Translated from the Greek by the Rev. T. Owen, M.A., and published in London in the year 1805.

CHAPTER V.

THE PLANET SATURN.

"Then comes the father of the tempest forth,
Wrapt in black glooms."

THE PLANET next in order of importance to Jupiter, is Saturn. Saturn's action, when configurated with the Sun, is to *condense aqueous vapour*, to *lower the temperature* of the air, and to excite tempests. When the atmosphere happens to be quiescent under Saturn's ascendancy, it is often dark or foggy. In contrast to the health-giving breezes of Jupiter, we have either bleak, bronchitis-producing easterly winds, or a stagnant, mephitic atmosphere favouring the spread of fevers; in the spring, blossoms are blighted, in the summer the crops are injured.

When Saturn crosses the equator, the atmosphere is greatly disturbed. A notable instance of this was the month of January, 1863. From the 25th of December, 1862, to the 24th of January, 1863, Saturn had less than five minutes of arc in declination, and being so nearly *stationary*, his rays fell perpendicularly upon the earth for a month.[1] The extraordinarily prolonged disturbance resulting cannot be accounted for in any other manner, for it did not begin until ten days after the winter solstice, and the lunar positions were of far less importance than those of January, 1864, in which month the disturbance was most trifling in comparsion with that of January, 1863.

Saturn only crosses the equator once in fifteen years, were he to cross it more frequently his influence on the atmosphere would be more readily recognised and not so soon forgotten. Saturn again crossed the equator on the 20th of March, 1879, and on the 26th of the same month the Sun was in conjunction with Saturn (having been in parallel declination on the 21st). A cold and stormy period set in on the 20th of March, 1879, and lasted until the 27th (when the Sun formed the sextile aspect with Mars).

The singular coincidence of Saturn *stationary in equator* (in Janu-

---

[1] *Vide* "The Weather Guide Book," pp. 56, 57, and 99.

ary, 1863) is extremely rare and may not occur again for a century. The scientific world ridicules the idea of planets so distant affecting the atmosphere of the earth. Plutarch informs us that in the days of Nicias a man dared not open his mind, except to his best and most intimate friend, and then only with the utmost caution, about the true causes of the eclipses of the Moon, which had then been recently taught by Anaxagoras, who was cast into prison for daring to make public avowal of his discoveries. A similar spirit of prejudice is extant at the present day against the belief in planetary action on the atmosphere. To talk of the *distance* of the great planets being an insuperable barrier to such action is puerile, since the same astronomers who make this assertion teach that Jupiter and Saturn draw the earth many hundreds of miles out of her orbit!

Saturn crossed the equator on the 20th of March, 1879, at the vernal equinox, nearly in conjunction with the Sun in the lower meridian. The effects on the weather of the ensuing severe season were most disastrous. The barometer and thermometer fell rapidly, and a cold, sun-less, rainy season immediately set in.

At the summer solstice of 1875, viz., at 8h 46m 38s p.m. of June 21st at Greenwich, the Moon was in the ascendant in the sign *Aquarius* and applying to conjunction with Saturn; and Mercury was in the descendant in the sign *Cancer* about to fall retrograde. The heavy rain that soon followed, 0.34 in. on the 28th. 0.73 in. on the 1st of July, 0.50 in. on the 14th, 1.28 in. on the 15th, and 0.76 in. on the 16th, as registered at the Royal Observatory, the rainfall of the month of July, 1875, being 2.74 in. greater than the average of 60 years; the floods in Wales and in France—all this was in accordance with the aphorism of the ancients to the effect that "If the Moon apply to Saturn, rain shall abundantly follow."

Dr. Goad wrote of the "horrid frost" coinciding with the Solar conjunction with Saturn in *Capricornus* (a sign in which Saturn "has dominion") in January, 1667; of the "bitter frost" of January, 1668, when the Solar conjunction with Saturn took place in Aquarius (in which Saturn "has dominion" also); and similar severe weather in January, 1669, and February, 1670, under Solar conjunctions with Saturn (in ♒).

Again, the severe winter of 1870-71, followed on Saturn being in conjunction with the Sun at the winter solstice, in *Capricornus*. The following Solar conjunction with Saturn, viz., on January 3rd, 1872, was not attended with severe weather, but the rainfall at Greenwich Observatory, registered that month amounted to 3.63 in., "being 1.76

in. *greater* than the average fall of the preceding 57 years," and it was a very stormy month—the Sun being in opposition with Jupiter on the 15th, so that opposing influences were in operation. The Sun was again in conjunction with Saturn on the 13th of January, 1873; that month was mild, but the rainfall was "0.55 in. *greater* than the average of the preceding 58 years." Severe frost attended the ☉ ☌ ♄ of February 5th, 1875, when no opposing influence obtained. [The conjunctions of the Sun with Saturn take place about eleven days later every year.]

CHAPTER VI.

THE PLANET MARS.

"The good wit finds the law from a single observation,
—the law, its limitations, and its correspondence."—EMERSON.

MARS when in an angle at the equinox or solstice promotes evaporation and raises the temperature, causing a drier state of the weather than Jupiter, particularly when in *Aries*, *Leo*, or *Cancer*, with north latitude.

When Mars is in conjunction or opposition with the Sun, calorific influence is usually observed to extend over a period of from two to five days before the completion of the aspect, and a reaction frequently takes place immediately after.

Cicero in his work *de Nat. Deorum*, says of Mars: "*Media Martis incendit Igneae ardentisque naturae.*" Tully writes of Mars: "His hot, rampant character, long and persistent droughts whereby all verdure is parched and burnt; fevers and pestilence," that is to say when the influence of Mars is predominant. Claudius Ptolemy avers that Mars when in power: "Generally causes such mischief and destruction as are concomitant with dryness. The atmosphere parched by hot, pestilential, and blasting winds, accompanied by drought, lightnings, and fires emitted from the sky. At sea, ships suddenly wrecked by the turbulence of the wind and strokes of lightning. Rivers fail, and springs are dried up."

In our more temperate climate and insular situation, the action of Mars is not often so strongly marked, although tending to dryness. Dr. Goad believed that the conjunction and opposition of Mars with the Sun disturbed the ocean currents, and he mentions that on December 18th, 1550 (O.S.), when Mars was in opposition with the Sun, the River Thames flowed thrice in nine hours, as recorded by Fromond.

The winter of 1881-2 was extraordinarily mild, fine, and dry. Mars made a prolonged stay in the sign *Cancer*—viz., from September 24th, 1881, to May 4th, 1882—having north latitude, his declination extended to 27° 10′ 30″ north on the 11th of January, 1882; at the winter solstice, December 21st, 1881, 4h p.m., Mars was in the ascendant, and nearly in opposition with both the Sun and Moon; and the planet was retrograde from the 18th November, 1881, to the 2nd of February, 1882. On the 18th January, 1882, the barometer rose to 30.95 in., the highest point recorded at the Royal Observatory, Greenwich, for thirty years. It would be interesting to learn whether the stay of Mars in the *South* tropic from March 19th, 1860, to October 1st, and from December 14th, 1866, to April 13th, 1867, had a calorific effect in the Southern Hemisphere.

The power of Mars in *Leo* was exemplified in the winter of 1883-4. At the winter solstice, December 22nd, 1883, 3h 51.9m a.m., Mars close to the meridian and in ♌ 21° 56′, stationary. The ensuing winter quarter was fair and mild, and the driest of the century, in England. This exactly corresponded with the author's forecast—viz.: "The general character of the weather of the winter quarter will be fair, mild, and drier than usual. In the south of England drought may be experienced."

CHAPTER VII.

THE PLANET VENUS.

> "Astronomy is excellent; but it must come up into life to have its full value, and not remain there in globes and spaces."—EMERSON.

VENUS exerts a temperate and moist influence when in one of the angles at the equinox or solstice, when in conjunction and parallel declination with the Sun, and when in the equator.

This explains why it is so difficult to see a transit of Venus across the Sun's disc—a very rare phenomenon. The last transits of Venus took place December 6th, 1882, December 9th, 1874, in 1769 and 1761. Writing in 1881, the author ventured to say that: "The rainy weather likely to coincide with the phenomenon of the transit of Venus on the 6th of December 1882, will prevent it from being seen to advantage in these islands." From the 5th to the 7th rain and snow prevailed generally over Great Britain; and the transit was observed "with varying success" in other quarters of the globe.

Venus's arc of greatest elongation from the Sun never exceeding 48°, it follows that besides the conjunction and parallel declination the only aspect of any force which she can form with the Sun is the angle of 45°. Venus approaches nearer to the earth in the inferior part of her orbit in the ratio of 13 to 30.

I have ascertained from the published records of meteorological observations made at the Royal Observatory, Greenwich, the amount of rainfall coincident with the crossing of the equator by Venus in the years 1862 to 1881, both inclusive, allowing three days (one before and one after in addition to the actual day of crossing) to each occasion.

I find that Venus was in the equator on 42 occasions, in that space of time. We have, therefore, 126 days allotted to her action, and the rainfall for those 126 days amounts to 9.27 in., which is considerably above the average. In some instances the fall was very heavy, as on the 9th of May, 1862 (0.77 in.); October 11th, 1862 (0.72 in.) and the following day (0.36); October 26th, 1865 (0.72 in.); September 25th,

1875 (0.70 in.); and August 25th, 1877 (0.54 in.). The rainfall when Venus was in *Libra* and in the equator amounted to 4.71 in., and when in *Aries* 3.86 in. On every occasion but two, the sky was cloudy, the exceptions being March 3rd, 1863, and August 26th, 1869, when the weather was fine. On 27 occasions there was a falling barometer and on 15 a rising one. The barometer was very low on the 1st of February, 1865, 28.718 in., the Sun being then in 45° aspect with Venus and the planet about to cross the equator; and again on the 17th March, 1866, 28.945 in. No distinct effects on temperature are traceable, for it rose on 19 and fell on 16 occasions.

Kepler recorded inundations coinciding with Venus being at her greatest elongation: "1622, February 13th, *Inundatio, pous ruptus*; ♀ *elong. a.* ☉ 47°. 1622, March 17th, *Fluvius crevit*; ♀ 43°. 1623, June 11th, *Exundabat Danub. admodum*, ♀ 30°: December 26th, *Auctus Danub.*, ♀ 30°. 1624, February 18th, *Auctus fluv.*, ♀ 47°. 1625, January 15th, *Danub. crevit*, ♀ 30°; May 3rd, *Aucti amnes*, ♀ 38°; May 5th, *Auctus Danub.*; August 20th, *Danub. crevit*, ♀ 43°.

CHAPTER VIII.

THE PLANET MERCURY.

"Go, speed the stars of Thought,
On to their shining goals."

MERCURY—the electric planet as it is designated by some authors—produces rapid changes of weather, "sometimes dryness and at other times moisture, and each with equal vigour," as Ptolemy observed. The ancient astronomer also averred that: "In consequence of the dryness of its nature, arising from its proximity to the Sun, and the rapidity of its motion, it generates in the atmosphere turbulent, sharp, and variable winds"; and at times "thunders, meteors, and lightnings, accompanied by sudden chasms in the earth and earthquakes." The last-named are only produced when Mercury is in conjunction or opposition with Mars, Jupiter, or Saturn, especially if at the same time in or near the equator or the tropics, or in the sign *Scorpio* or *Leo*, or with the Sun and Moon at an eclipse.

Dr. Goad observed that "the Sun in conjunction with Mercury is more prone to send us a hurricane than the Sun with Venus, hence the ancient character of Mercury is justified."

The conjunction of the Sun with both Mercury and Venus, especially if one or both of them be retrograde, as at the new moon of July 9th, 1888 (when their longitudes were ☉ and ☽ ♋ 17° 24′, ☿ ♋ 17° 21′ retrograde, and ♀ ♋ 16° 43′), produces storms and floods. Happily, such a phenomenon rarely occurs, and most people will wish that there may be no recurrence of similar weather in future summers.

As Mercury is never more than 28° distant from the Sun, only the conjunction and parallel declination can be formed between them.

At the vernal equinox, 1878, March 20th, 5h 42.5m p.m. G.M.T., Mercury was setting in ♓ 29° 32′, separating from conjunction with Saturn and applying to conjunction with the Sun. The weather of the spring quarter of 1878 was very rainy and boisterous. That this was predicted can be proved by the following forecast published by the author in September, 1877: "The weather of the apring quarter of

1878 will be remarkable for wind and rain, and many disastrous shipwrecks will result." The sinking of the *Eurydice*, with a crew of 330, took place on the 26th of March, 1878, during a heavy squall; and numerous disasters to shipping in that spring quarter will be fresh in the memory of some of my readers.

At Greenwich Observatory no less than 12½ inches of rain will be found to have been registered between the 20th of March and the 21st of June, 1878. The rainfall of April was 2.74 in. *greater* than the average; that of May, 2.32 in. greater, and that of June, 2.66 in. greater. The first twenty days of March were unusually dry; and the rainfall of the month of July, 1878, was 2.12 in. *less* than the average. In the *Times' Register of Events* for 1878, it is stated that: "The storms of the spring were most formidable."

An instance of the influence of Mercury when in an angle at the solstice or equinox may be cited. At Washington, 21st of December, 1887, at 9h 56.4m p.m., Mercury was in the fourth angle (lower meridian) and nearly in sextile aspect with Uranus. The fearfully severe winter that followed and the terrible blizzards resulting in appalling loss of life, will long be remembered. The following forecast was made by the author: "Mercury being in the fourth angle and in aspect with Uranus, the American winter will be a very cold one, marked by unusually heavy falls of snow in the Northern States, and several great and destructive storms."

Kepler wrote of Mercury's influence thus: "*Conjunctio ☿ ad ☉, quorum in Meteoris magna ris est.*" Again: "*In commovendis tempestatibus multum valet.*" As that great astronomer kept a diary of the weather for many years, his opinion is entitled to the greatest respect.

CHAPTER IX.

THE PLANET URANUS.

" For when the world was framed, the mighty cause,
These powers bestowed, and did enact these
laws."—MANILIUS.

URANUS although so distant is found to exert an influence on the weather, when in certain relative positions. Disturbance caused by Uranus usually sets in very suddenly, and frequently takes the shape of hailstorms. Its action tends to condense aqueous vapours and to lower the temperature of the air.

An instance of the force of the influence exerted by Uranus, when in an angle at a solstice, may be found in the winter solstice of 1868, December 21st, 0h 28m p.m., G.M.T., whereat Uranus was in the fourth angle, and in the sign *Cancer* 16° 5′, retrograde. On the same night, the north of Scotland was visited with a fearful storm, the whole of the seaward staging and the stonework executed in the Wick new harbour during the year being carried away. On the 27th and the 28th of the same month severe gales visited all parts of the United Kingdom; in London houses were blown down; at Rochdale a school-house was shattered. The author's forecast, published three months beforehand, was to this effect: "Uranus in the fourth angle seems to threaten much damage by storms, more particularly in Scotland." Storms were very frequent and violent in the ensuing winter quarer and the rainfall of January and February, 1869, was much above the average, as registered at the Royal Observatory, Greenwich.

At the winter solstice of 1860, *viz.* at 1h 51m p.m. of December 21st, Uranus was in the ascendant in ♊ 9° 15′ retrograde, in square (90°) aspect with Saturn stationary in ♍ 9° 32′, and in opposition with Mercury in ♐ 9° 10′; and Venus was setting. The frost which set in on the 18th December, 1860, the day on which Saturn became stationary, and continued until the 20th January, 1861, was the severest of the century. As the influence of Uranus was not then well understood, this severe weather was not foretold by astro-meteorologists, although the late Commander Morrison, R.N.,. did foretell frost and snow during the last five days of December, 1860.

Tracing still further back, we find that at the winter solstice of 1854, December 22nd, 3h a.m., Uranus was the only planet in an angle; a severe and prolonged winter followed.

Uranus was in the equator on the 11th of March, 1844, and was within 5′ of arc of declination from the equator from the 7th to 15th of that month; and on the 22nd, was in conjunction with the Sun. On the 19th of March, 1844, the new Moon took place at 0h 17m a.m., G.M.T., the Moon hastening to conjunction with Uranus.

From the 8th to the 12th of March, 1844, the sky was overcast, and there was occasional rain; and a "gale, and squalls of rain" were registered at Greenwich on the 11th. Gusty and showery weather prevailed on the 20th. The sky was overcast on the 22nd and 23rd, occasional thin rain falling; and squally weather was recorded on the 24th.

Uranus did not again cross the equator until the 14th of November, 1884, when very cold weather prevailed. In 1885, on the 28th of February, and on the 29th of August, Uranus was again in the equator, when cold weather again prevailed.

CHAPTER X.

THE PLANET NEPTUNE.

> " Science is the explanation of Nature . . . . .
> Verification is the Alpha and Omega of philosophy."
> —G. H. LEWES.

NEPTUNE is the most distant planet of the Solar system, yet its immense distance does not prevent it from disturbing the weather when configurated with the Sun.

Neptune was in the equator on the 15th of May and the 22nd of August, 1862; again on the 15th of March, the 25th of November and the 28th of December, 1863.

On the 15th and 16th of May, 1862, the sky was overclouded; there was rain in the morning, afternoon, and night of the 15th, and occasional rain at night of the 16th. On the 22nd of August, 1862, heavy rain in the forenoon; a partially clouded sky in the afternoon, and a fine evening; on the 23rd the sky was half-clouded. On the 15th of March, 1863, there was heavy rain in the early morning and in the afternoon; on the 16th an overcast sky, and strong wind in the afternoon. On the 25th and 26th of November, an almost completely clouded sky. On the 28th of December, an overcast sky, and snow in the afternoon; on the 29th, an overcast sky, and a light rain in the afternoon.

There is evidence, therefore, that Neptune in the equator disturbed the weather, for there was rain on the first three occasions, and snow and slight rain on the fifth, the fourth being the only occasion on which no rain fell; on four occasions the sky was completely overcast the whole day, and on the other the sky was so for the first half of the day. The barometer rose on three and fell on two occasions; on the 15th of March, 1863, it fell to 29.08 in., which was very near the absolute minimum of the year. The temperature rose on the first and last, and fell on the three other occasions. On two occasions—March 16th and December 29th, 1863—there was a very strong wind.

At the summer solstice of 1879, Neptune was in the fourth angle (lower meridian), the Sun (in sextile aspect with Uranus) and Mercury were setting, and neither Mars nor Jupiter was in an angle. The cold and wet summer, so disastrous for agriculturists, of 1879, will be fresh in the memory of most farmers. At the Royal Observatory, the rainfall of July was 3.72 in., being 1.35 in. greater than the average of 38 years; that of August was 5.19 in., being 2.77 in. greater than the average.

CHAPTER XI.

THE MUTUAL CONJUNCTIONS AND OPPOSITIONS OF THE PLANETS.

> "But yet, amid this elemental war
> That scatters desolation from afar,
> Health is engendered, and mankind are blessed."

MARS and SATURN when in *conjunction*, more particularly when their declinations are the same, or nearly so, at the same time, and when the Moon happens to be either in conjunction or opposition with them, cause a turbulent state of the atmosphere. The ancients considered that the conjunction of Mars and Saturn brought "great winds and sometimes rain," at any season of the year; and when in either *Cancer*, *Scorpio*, or *Pisces*, "rain in winter, autumn, and summer, and oft-times thunder and lightning, also inundations." Cardan said that this conjunction "inclines to hail and rain, *si caetera juvent*." Dr. Goad found that it induced "excess of rain"; and "the air to clear and cloud interchangeably for several days"; also that "the sudden mists put on an extraordinary hue, noted for their deep blue as well under the opposition as under the conjunction"; and observed the effects of tho conjunction to "help to qualify the air for a month at least." Dr. Goad records "a dreadful tempest, wind, rain, and hail," on the 18th of November, 1664, in England, following the conjunction of Mars and Saturn in Sagittarius 27° on the 12th.

The author finds that all but one of the conjunctions of Mars and Saturn from September 11th, 1861, to August 16th, 1911, produced storms and great disturbance of weather; moreover, every one of the storms was foretold by him many months beforehand; whereas the official meteorologists failed in several instances to foretell those storms even a few hours in advance!

When due consideration is given to the instances here recounted, planetary action on the atmosphere must be recognised; to dismiss them as mere coincidences would be unphilosophical and culpable. Astronomers would find it more useful and more instructive to watch for and study such coincidences than to confine their observations of conjunctions of Mars and Saturn to the delightful amusement of "testing photometrically and also photographically the lustre of the conjoined planets."

In like manner, it can be shown that the mutual opposition of Mars and Saturn disturbs the weather, although not usually so greatly as the conjunction.

JUPITER and SATURN when in mutual conjunction or opposition disturb the weather very greatly. Their conjunction happens but once in twenty years, and it is worthy of assiduous study.

Kepler wrote that: "*Saturnus cum Jove rapidum ex calentibus terra latebris educit aerum, qui in producendis meteoris, ingentes habet vires.*"

Dr. Goad placed on record instances of the conjunction of Jupiter and Saturn producing *cold* and *dry* weather, and occasionally fogs.

MARS and JUPITER when in mutual conjunction do not always raise the temperature and promote evaporation, but frequently exert so disturbing an influence on the weather that storms of rain and hail attend; in winter and spring, frosty and fine weather often coincides Dr. Goad quotes an Arabian saying that the conjunction of Mars and Jupiter taking place in the sign *Aries* produces great cold; in *Taurus*, snow; and in *Leo*, great cold. Maginus said that when Mars and Jupiter are in conjunction in the same sign as the Sun occupies, "sultry heat and thunder" prevail. Dr. Goad also observed that "a conjunction of Jupiter with any planet will ordinarily make a mist anywhere, except under the line." And that the opposition of Mars and Jupiter, "in ordinary circumstances, produces cold, frosty mornings in winter, and not seldom in spring time, often turbulence in winter, lightning not excepted; in summer ofttimes thunder with violence, wind, rain and hail."

The conjunction of VENUS with SATURN produces either cold weather or much downfall; frequently fog, and sometimes strong gales.

The conjunction of MERCURY with MARS is productive, as Cardan observed, of "vehement winds." Maginus and Eichstad observed that it also sometimes brought rain or snow, hail and thunder; Kyriander supported their view, and held that it is the most turbulent of all conjunctions; Regiomontanus asserted that it brought heat and drought or wind and rain, according to the sign of the zodiac in which it took place; and, to go still further back, Ptolemy averred that it excited "heated and turbulent dispositions in the atmosphere." Dr. Goad's observations led him to support these views, and he quoted Kepler's testimony as to the violent winds raised by this conjunction.

The conjunction of Mercury with Jupiter frequently produces strong winds, and usually raises the temperature; sometimes it brings thunderstorms. Columbus when in America delayed sailing again on account of an opposition of Jupiter with the Sun, Moon, and Mercury. The conjunction of these planets in Aquarius 16° on the 7th of February, 1867, was attended with heavy squally, rain, and lightning; at Greenwich Observatory the greatest pressure of wind on the square foot was 41 lbs. on the 8th.

The conjunction of Venus with Mars, which occurs at irregular intervals, disturbs the weather, when their respective latitudes do not greatly differ, bringing rain and mild temperature usually; in winter months, mist or fog, and sometimes snow; on the whole inclining more to warmth than cold. The following dates of some past conjunctions of these planets will be useful for comparison: July 9th, 1861; June 3rd, 1863; September 27th, 1863; February 5th, 1864; December 29th, 1865; November 15th, 1867; October 6th, 1869; February 21st and July 29th, 1870; June 17th, 1872; May 4th, 1874; March 29th, July 6th, and November 29th, 1876; October 21st, 1878; September 8th, 1880; August 2nd and December 5th, 1882; May 11th, 1883; March 28th, 1885; February 10th, 1887; January 3rd, April 20th, and October 1st, 1889.

The pluvial influence is usually in force from the day before to the day after the day of their conjunction. Dr. Goad considered it continued until Venus had separated two degrees from Mars—if no other major configuration of another celestial body of an opposite nature intervened.

The student will recognise the force of Ptolemy's advice to "overlook none of the conjunctions;" if space would permit, the effects of all of them would be stated. When three or more planets are near together in longitude, great disturbance of the atmosphere is found to result.

CHAPTER XII.

EARTHQUAKES AND VOLCANIC ERUPTIONS.

"And the old
And crazy earth has had her shaking fits
More frequent, and foregone her usual rest—
The rocks falling headlong and the valleys rise."—COWPER.

IN the Μετεωρολογικά of Aristotle, published more than 300 years B.C., we find that that ancient philosopher treated of meteors, water, air, and earthquakes; and he observed that earthquakes chiefly occur "about the Hellespont, Achaia, Sicily, and Euboea." No treatise on meteorology can be complete if the subject of earthquakes be altogether left out of consideration.

Great earthquakes are very irregular in their occurrence, and they affect different localities in an apparently arbitrary and generally unexpected manner. A period of convulsion in Syria corresponds to a period of quiescence in Southern Italy, and *vice versa.*

The most convulsive earthquakes originate under the sea, as for instance the earthquake which overthrew Lisbon. On the American and Japanese coasts this has been observed.

Steam is thought by seismologists to play an important part in the production of earthquakes. The sudden generation of steam in the interior of the earth probably produces electricity, which becomes the proximate cause of shocks of earthquake. This is the view of a scientific friend of the author who was an eye-witness of the earthquake at Menton, in the Riviera, on the 23rd of February, 1887. In his letter to the author, he wrote:

"Great electric action was sensibly felt all the time (23rd to 27th); and my watch stopped twice during the shocks.

"My opinion is that the active agent was, primarily, steam, the force of which generated electricity. At Nice, the sea was observed to boil, and large fish were seen floating about dead."

Some earthquakes have been accompanied by remarkable atmospherical phenomena, such as great hurricanes, thunderstorms, lightning, hail, and rain; others, by calm weather and serene sky. In some instances the magnetic needle has been much affected, in others not so. The electrical condition of the air has indicated great tension in one class of earthquakes. The aurora borealis has frequently coincided with earthquakes.

The shock is most destructive to buildings after its direction has become greatly inclined to the perpendicular, and before its strength has been much diminished by diffuson over a great tract of country. Shocks which are nearly horizontal, if sufficiently powerful, are very destructive to buildings.

Humboldt and others recognize, in addition to the vertical and horizontal shocks, a kind of whirling shock, to which they attribute the twisting of buildings and the displacement of portions of the surface; but some seismologists demur to this mode of explaining such effects.

It seems practically certain that earthquakes are governed by some cosmical influence away from the earth. Seeing that the tides of the ocean are affected by the Sun and Moon, there is nothing extravagant in the theory that the same attracting bodies occasion paroxysmal action, when in a line with the earth, and when the Moon is in *perigee.* But, inasmuch as earthquakes do not always coincide with such relative positions of the Sun and Moon, we should enquire whether planetary action plays an important part.

LUNAR ACTION.—Aristotle placed on record the fact that "it sometimes happen that there is an earthquake about the eclipses of the Moon."[1] M. Barthélémy St. Hilaire, commenting on this statement, says: "'Pendant les eclipses de lune,' c'est là une coincidence toute fortuite; mais les deux phénomènes n'ont aucun rapport." The clever French author here asserts more than he knows, for comparison of the dates of many great earthquakes with the occurrence of eclipses of the Sun and Moon, would lead to the conclusion that the coincidences are not fortuitous, and tend rather to show that they are *en rapport.*

Claudius Ptolemy said:

"The Moon, being of all the heavenly bodies the nearest to the earth, also dispenses much influence; and things animate and inanimate sympathise and vary with her. By the changes of her illumination, rivers swell and are reduced; the tides of the sea are ruled by her

[1] "The Works of Aristotle," translated from the Greek, by Thomas Taylor. Vol. v. "On the Heavens, Meteors," &c. Book ii., p. 528.

risings and settings; and plants and animals are expanded or collapsed, if not entirely at least partially, as she waxes or wanes."[2]

Some modern scientific men who have observed that great earthquakes frequently take place when the Sun and Moon are in a line with the earth (as at an eclipse), and when the Moon is in perigee, are puzzled to account for some eclipses passing away without causing any such effect; and they will never solve the problem until they take notice of planetary positions at eclipses.

The great earthquake of the 23rd of February, 1887, which caused so much destruction in the Riviera, closely followed the *annular eclipse of the* SUN of the 22nd of that month. At this eclipse (invisible in Europe) the Moon was not in perigee, for she was in apogee on the 24th.

The fearful earthquake of the 31st of August, 1886, which overthrew Charleston, quickly followed the total eclipse of the Sun on the 29th, the Moon being in *perigee.* On the 1st of June, 1863, there was a total eclipse of the Moon (nearly in *perigee*), and on the 3rd inst. a terrible earthquake overthrew the City of Manilla, and destroyed 10,000 lives.

PLANETARY ACTION.—This has been recognised in all ages of the world by men of the highest attainments in science and philosophy. In fact planetary action as an exciting cause of earthquakes is only doubted by those modern philosophers who have never made any fair and complete inquiry into it, and yet presume to deny it. It has already been mentioned that Pliny relates of Anaximander that "he foretold the earthquakes which overthrew Lacedaemon." Anaximander was born in the year 610 B.C.; he was the disciple of Thales, and taught that the fixed stars were centres of other systems, perhaps more extensive and more glorious than our own; that the earth moved round the centre of the world; and he erected at Lacedaemon a gnomon for celestial observations. He was an able and renowned astrologer (a fact concealed by the late "Sir David Brewster in his prejudiced philippic against astrology), and he foretold the earthquakes, as Pliny relates, by means of his astrological skill.

Dr. Goad presents a list of twenty earthquakes which happened while the planet Jupiter was passing through the sign *Taurus*; and he remarks: "I am sure as I write that this phenomenon, as great and stupendous as it is, depends upon this celestial appearance—Venus or Mercury with Jupiter."

---

[2] *Tetrabiblos*, book i., chap. 2.

In *Urania* for February, 1880, the author foretold that the entry of Jupiter and Saturn into the sign *Taurus* in 1881 would produce great earthquakes. The earthquake at Chios (Scio), in the Archipelago, on the 3rd of April, 1881, which destroyed 4,000 lives and injured 1,500 persons, took place just as Saturn and Jupiter entered *Taurus* (in the manner described by Ptolemy), the sign relating to the Archipelago. On the 12th of June, 1881, thirty-four villages and 100 lives were destroyed by an earthquake in Armenia; Venus, Jupiter, Saturn, and Neptune were then assembled in *Taurus* (which sign relates also to Armenia), within the space of eight degrees. On the 22nd of July, 1881, when Mars was in conjuction with Jupiter in *Taurus*, violent shocks of earthquake were felt in Switzerland (the sharpest since 1834), at Lyons, and at Grenoble.

Pliny related that the Babylonians held that earthquakes are caused by planetary action, especially of the three superior planets, Saturn, Jupiter, and Mars, which are the causes of thunder. And, says Pliny, earthquakes are caused by the congress of the aforesaid planets with the Sun, or with each other; and this chiefly happens "*circa quadrata mundi*"—meaning the *equinoxes* and *tropics*. Hippocrates observed a similar action in the outbreak of epidemics. Moreover, Pliny states that earthquakes happen frequently about the time of eclipses.

Dr. Goad gives a list of earthquakes from 1516 to 1681 happening in coincidence with mutual conjunctions and oppositions of Jupiter and Saturn.

When the fearful earthquake took place at Lisbon, on the 1st of November, 1755, the geocentric longitude of Jupiter was 187° 31′, and that of Saturn 293° 3′; Mars was in opposition with Saturn (from tropical signs); Venus and the Sun were nearly in conjunction in Scorpio; and Jupiter was in opposition to the longitude (♈ 7°) in which the Moon was eclipsed on the 27th of March, that year.

A terrific earthquake, on the 17th of March, 1818, engulfed Philipoli, in Roumania, with 70,000 lives; and the shock was felt the same day at Bencoolen, India, the sea receding leaving vessels dry, throwing down walls, etc. The following were the relative positions of the heavenly bodies:

March 17th, 1818, Greenwich Noon.

☉	☽	☿	♀	♂	♃	♄	♅
26♓20	23♋37	11♓1	27♓28	25♊58	10♑5	10♓45	20♐7
1S28	26N17	9S25	2S17	25N38	22S53	9S5	28S9

Mercury was in conjunction and par. dec. with Saturn in *Pisces*; and the Sun was nearly in conjunction with Venus in the same sign, and in square aspect with Mars; while Jupiter was in the tropical sign *Capricornus* and in sextile with both Mercury and Saturn, and very nearly in exact par. dec. with Uranus.

On the 15th of July, 1853, the fearful earthquake took place at Cumana, by which 4,000 lives were destroyed; the ancient city disappeared in an instant; several deep fissures were formed from which boiling water ascended. The first shock was felt at a quarter past two o'clock in the afternoon, and in a few seconds the dreadful convulsion took place. *An annular eclipse of the* SUN took place on the 6th of June, 1853, visible in South America. The ecliptic conjunction of the Sun and Moon took place in the sign *Gemini* 15° 56′, and at 3h 47m p.m., local mean time, at Cumana; Mercury was in ♊ 7° 42′; the sign *Scorpio* 11° 23′ ascended at that moment at Cumana; Uranus was setting in *Taurus* 10° 37′, Mars and Saturn, also in *Taurus*, were in the western angle. At the moment of the earthquake at Cumana, the sign *Scorpio* 27° ascended, and the following were the positions of the heavenly bodies:

July 15th, 1883, 2h 15m p.m., Cumana.

☉	☽	☿	♀	♂	♃	♄	♅
23♋5	17♏25	19♌20	10♌9	15♊26	15♐43℞	27♉48	12♉9
21N29	14S24	15N7	19N8	22N43	22S15	17N57	15N5

At the moment of the destruction of Cumana, Saturn was exactly setting there, and in *Taurus*; Mars had reached the degree in which the Sun was eclipsed, and the exact declination of the Sun, and opposition with Jupiter; and the Sun had reached the declination of Mercury at the eclipse.

Commander Morrison, R.N., writing on that eclipse, in the summer of 1852, twelve months before the earthquake, quoted the words of Ptolemy in reference to Mercury being with the Sun and Moon, viz., that there would be "sudden chasms in the earth and earthquakes," in July, 1853, about the 16th day, along the northern coast of South America—thus naming the part of the world affected and the time, within a few hours, of the awful catastrophe. Again do we find undeniable evidence of *planetary* action. It is a remarkable fact, that at the moment of many great earthquakes the sign *Scorpio* is found in the ascendant.

Another *eclipse* (annular) of the SUN in the sign *Pisces* took place on the 23rd of February, 1868. The positions of the heavenly bodies thereat were as follows:

February 23rd, 1868, 2h 20.4m p.m. (G.M.T.)

☉	☽	☿	♀	♂	♃	♄	♅
4♓18	4♓18	22♓4	9♈46	22♒0	16♓31	5♐22	9♋4℞
9S56	9S53	1S28	3N28	15S13	6S16	19S15	23N31

The line of central eclipse passed across South America. The author writing in the summer of 1867, said: "The eclipse passes over Pernambuco, and Upper Peru; it falls in the 5th deg. of *Pisces*, within 1° of the square aspect of Saturn, hence it will injuriously affect those countries, which will suffer physical evils in the form of earthquakes, waterspouts, and floods." The late Commander Morrison said that: "Its effects will fall chiefly on South America. It will dry up rivers and do much detriment to ships and sailors"—as Proclus said. By a succession of earthquakes which lasted from the 13th to the 16th of August, Arica, Araquipa, Yslay, Iquique, Pasco, Juan, Cavelica, Ibarra, and numerous other towns of Peru and Ecuador were totally destroyed. The loss of life in Peru was estimated at 2,000, and in Ecuador at 20,000. Great damage was done to shipping on the coast and the Chincha islands. The British consul at Iquique and his family perished. One of the worst consequences of that fearful calamity was the disappearance of the streams which followed their overthrow; thousands of houseless creatures suffered cruelly from hunger and thirst. At the eclipse, it is seen, that the Sun, Moon, Jupiter, and Mercury were all in *Pisces*, the Sun and Moon were in square (90°) aspect with Saturn, and Venus was in square with Uranus from *Aries* and *Cancer*. At the period of the earthquakes, the Sun had reached the opposite place to that of Mars in the zodiac, and the Moon was in conjunction with Mars in *Cancer* 0° 4′.

Nineteen years after there happened another *annular eclipse* of the SUN in *Pisces*, on the 22nd of February, 1887. The following were the positions of the heavenly bodies.

February 22nd, 1887, 9h 40.2m p.m. (G.M.T.)

☉	☽	☿	♀	♂	♃	♄	♅
3♓59	3♓59	17♓10	23♓27	17♓44	5♏52℞	16♋3℞	11♎53℞
10S3	10S34	5S33	3S47	5S39	12S10	22N24	4S2

Here again we find Mercury receiving the application of the Moon. Moreover, Mercury is in par. dec. and nearly in conjunction with Mars. Five of the heavenly bodies are in *Pisces*; Jupiter is in *Scorpio* and in trine (120°) with the Sun and Moon. At about ten minutes before 6 a.m. of the following day the first shock was felt, and as the Sun, Moon, Mercury, Mars, and Venus ascended, successive shocks of earthquake destroyed one-third of Porto Maurizio and over 1,000 lives, and did great damage at Diano Marino and Menton. The earthquake extended along the Riviera from east to west. The conjunction of Mercury and Mars took place at 11h p.m. of the 23rd of February, 1887, in *Pisces* 18° 9′ 24″; and several minor shocks took place during that night, and the two following mornings, just before sunrise.

On the 10th November, 1882, *an annular eclipse of the* SUN took place (at sunrise at Java) in the second decanate of the sign *Scorpio*. The positions of the heavenly bodies were as follow:

November 10th, 1882, 11h 19.6 p.m. (G.M.T.)

☉	☽	☿	♀	♂	♃	♄	♅	♆
18♏30	18♏30	29♎57	21♐39	27♏2	0♋36	23♉2	22♍19	17♉23
17S20	17S31	9S22	27S55	19S46	23N1	16N12	3N44	15N17

No fewer than seven of the heavenly bodies were in signs which are closely related to earthquakes. The Sun and Moon were in opposition with Neptune and within 5° of opposition with Saturn, and within 9° of conjuction with Mars. Mercury was on the threshold of the sign *Scorpio* and in trine with Jupiter in the northern tropic. At Java, the Sun, Moon and Mars were rising in *Scorpio*, and Saturn was setting in *Taurus*. On the 13th of November, 1882, began that series of earthquakes which continued at short intervals throughout the year 1883, rendering that period memorable for frequency of earthquake shocks and volcanic eruptions, also for the enormous loss of life resulting therefrom. Panama and Colon were the first places to suffer, one shock (in November, 1882) causing a rupture of the telegraph cable about thirty miles from Colon. On the 8th of December (when the Moon was in transit over the place of the eclipse) a very severe shock was felt in Roumania; and about the same time fresh volcanic activity was noticed in the island of Santorin and in a submarine volcano formed near Missolonghi. On the 1st of February, 1883 (when the Moon again passed over the place of the eclipse), Iquique and other places in South America experienced severe shocks, which extended to Panama and Colon on the 4th and 5th, when the cable was again broken there. In the middle of February, when the Sun was in square (90°) aspect with Saturn, Etna and Vesuvius were very active; on the 21st, a very distinct shock of earthquake was felt in South Australia. On the 5th March, when Mars was in square aspect with Saturn, a fearful shock was felt in Cyprus, lasting nearly one minute, the severest recorded in that island for many years. Etna became more active still. About the 12th of May (when the Sun arrived at the opposition of the place of the eclipse, and at that of Saturn), the volcano of Karang in the island of Krakatoa, in the Straits of Sunda, after having been quiescent for the space of 200 years, broke into eruption, the violence of which was distinctly felt at Anjer and Batavia on the 20th to 22nd, and the atmosphere was filled with smoke and fine ashes. On the 28th of July (eight days after the conjunction of Mars and Saturn in *Gemini* 6° 42′, Venus, Mars, and Jupiter being in mutual parallel of declination, and the Sun in conjunction with Mercury in *Leo*), the great earthquake took place at Casamicciola in Ischia, destroying 5,000 lives. On the 26th and 27th of August (when Mars reached the place of Jupiter at the eclipse, and was in conjunction with the Moon), the climax was reached in the awful eruption of Krakatoa, by which at least 100,000 lives were lost, three towns on the coast of Java completely destroyed, and an island 3,000 feet in height was submerged. The volcanic products were thrown up to an inconceivable height, and for many miles around noon was rendered as dark as midnight, darkness lasting for from 36 to 40 hours. The reverberation was heard at a distance of 2,000 miles. A wave of water 100 feet in height was produced by the vibration of the island, which destroyed everything over which it washed and made its mark on tidal registers in many parts of the world. It must not be forgotten that a *total eclipse of the* SUN took place on the 6th of May, 1883, in *Taurus* 15° 59′, Saturn being in *Taurus* 27° 44′, and Jupiter in *Cancer* 0° 22′; and the Moon having been in *perigee* at 8h p.m. of the 5th. This was quickly followed by a severe earthquake in Central America, on the 8th, as foretold by the author. It is remarkable that at both these eclipses of the Sun, the one in November, 1882, and the other in May, 1883, Jupiter was in the 1st degree of the sign *Cancer*, and that when the dreadful eruption of Krakatoa took place, Mars was in transit over the place of Jupiter at both eclipses.

A study of the planetary positions about the time of the terrible earthquake at Charleston will prove interesting. On the 29th of August, 1886, there was a *total eclipse of the* SUN. The following were the positions of the heavenly bodies thereat:

☉	☽	☿	♀	♂	♃	♄	♅	♆
6♍4	6♍4	18♌58	11♌49	4♏45	7♎40	18♋48	6♎7	27♉51
9N17	9N11	14N5	17N49	13S39	2S0	21N47	1S49	18N0

At Charleston, the ecliptic conjunction took place at 7h 34.7m a.m., when the R.A. of the midheaven was 91° 19′ 11″, *Cancer* 1° 13′ culminating, and *Libra* 1° 7′ 28″ ascending, Jupiter and Uranus being just below the eastern horizon.

The Sun and Moon are seen to be in sextile (60°) aspect with Mars in *Scorpio*; and Jupiter but 1° 33′ past conjunction with Uranus near the equator.

Jupiter was in exact conjunction with Uranus in *Libra* 5° 30′ 30″, on the 18th of August, 1886, at 7h 45m a.m., G.M.T. At Charleston, the local mean time of this conjunction was 2h 34m 36s a.m., at which moment the R.A. of the midheaven was 5° 10′ 20″, *Aries* 4° 38′ culminating, the Moon in *Aries* 3° 58′ having just passed the meridian, and *hastening to opposition with Jupiter and Uranus, which planets were within 1° of the lower meridian*. Moreover, Saturn was just rising in *Cancer* 17° 36′.

Tracing still farther back, we find that Mars was in conjunction with Jupiter in *Virgo* 27° 49′ 57″, on the 27th of June, 1886, at 10h 38m 38s a.m., G.M.T., very near the equator, Jupiter's declination being 2° 8′ 20″ N. and that of Mars 1° 14′ 41″ N. At Washington, the local mean time of this conjunction was 5h 30m 25s a.m., at which moment the conjoined planets were exactly in the lower meridian. This led the author to foretell earthquakes in America soon after this conjunction, seeing that it would be so quickly followed by the conjunction of Jupiter and Uranus, and a total eclipse of the Sun, thus in the year 1884: "In 1886, Jupiter and Uranus, will be in *Libra* and in square aspect with Saturn in *Cancer*, hence that year will be signalized by a series of great earthquakes." And in 1885: "As the conjoined planets—Mars and Jupiter—are but 5° 52′ from Uranus, and are near the equator—this conjunction of the 27th of June, 1886, cannot fail to cause serious evils in the shape of earthquakes. At Washington, this conjunction takes place in the lower meridian. Shocks of earthquake in the 77th degree of west longitude may, therefore, be looked for; great thunderstorms and waves of intense heat will pass over the States. There will be great excitement in America, and a religious movement of an enthusiastic nature."

This forecast was exactly verified in every particular. Charleston is situated in 79° 56′ west longitude, reckoned from Greenwich. Severe shocks of earthquake were felt between 76° and 82° of west longitude—in Washington, Richmond, Raleigh, Augusta, Omaha, Mobile, Detroit, Atlanta, Louisville, Indianapolis, Cleveland, Pittsburg, Chicago, Memphis, and New York. In the vicinity of Charleston, great quantities of sand and mud were thrown up from deep fissures in the earth; 200 lives were lost, and 40,000 persons rendered homeless. There was great excitement throughout America, and a religious revival was witnessed in Charleston, especially among the negroes, who thought that the Last Great Day of the world had arrived.

It is thus seen that the planetary positions gradually led up to the fearful catastrophe; for we have: (1°) The conjunction of Mars and Jupiter near the equator, on the 27th of June, 1886; (2°) the conjunction of Jupiter and Uranus, near the equator, on the 18th of August; and (3°) the total eclipse of the Sun, the Moon being in perigee, on the 29th of August. On the 25th of August, a sharp earthquake was felt at Srinagar. Then followed the terrible series of earthquakes in two different parts of the world—of one of which the Peloponnesus, and of the other, South Carolina, were the centres. On the night of the 27th of August, Philitria, Gargaliano, Pyrgo, Caroni, Catacolo, and several other Greek towns were laid in ruins, and over 500 people killed, twice that number injured, and thousands rendered homeless. Simultaneously, Vesuvius exhibited renewed activity. On the 30th of August, the eastern and highest peak of Galita was in eruption. On the 27th of August, in the United States commenced a series of destructive earthquakes, which were continued almost without intermission throughout September, and afterwards, at longer intervals, until the 5th of November, the greater part of Charleston being wrecked on the 31st of August, 1886.

Whenever there has been a maximum of planetary influence, earthquakes, volcanic eruptions, and epidemics, have either coincided or very quickly followed. The "spasmodic convulsions of the sickened earth" have repeatedly been found to synchronize with the outbreak of epidemics; and the wise physicians of antiquity, who were close students of physical science, attributed such phenomena to planetary action.

In the year 1783, the earthquakes in Calabria, destroyed 40,000 lives; Saturn was then in *Capricornus*, Jupiter in the same sign, Uranus in *Cancer*, and Neptune in *Libra*, the maximum of planetary action.

The author clearly foretold the following great earthquakes: Kuchan, 1893; San Francisco, 1906; India, 1905; Valparaiso, 1906; Italy and Messina, 1908-1909. Moreover, these forecasts saved many readers of *Zadkiel's Almanac* for 1905, 1906, 1908 and 1909, from being involved in the horrors of those awful catastrophes.

Captain A. T. Banon, of Kulu-Kangra, Punjab, who was an eye-witness of the great earthquake in India, in 1905, wrote to the author on the 28th of April, 1905, as follows:

"I suppose our earthquake, which you so successfully predicted, exactly as to time and place, has been reported in the English newspapers. I don't know about the English Press, but I believe the Indian Press has done you justice. . . . I have come to the conclusion that your theory, electric telluric currents, as to the cause of earthquakes is correct; and that the scientific orthodox theory is incorrect," etc.[3]

The "New York Herald," European edition, April 2nd, 1907, printed a letter from the author on Earthquakes and the Celestial Bodies.[4]

[3] Vide *Zadkiel's Almanac* for 1906, p. 77, art. " The Great Earthquake in India 1905."

[4] Vide *Zadkiel's Almanac* for 1908, pp. 84-88.

BOOK IV.

MEDICAL ASTROLOGY.

CHAPTER I.

EPIDEMICS AND PLANETARY INFLUENCE.

"Every form of death, and every woe,
Shot from malignant stars to earth below."—CAMPBELL.

THE germ theory, as Beckingham says, "is an assumption of causes of the existence of which we have no evidence to account for effects they do not explain." What is the *contagium vivum*, and what is its origin?

Dr. Maudesley says: "Disease is not a specific morbid entity, that like some evil spirit takes possession of the body, but a condition of degeneration from healthy life." Mr. Wolfe says: "Perhaps minute animalculae may be present, in different stages of decay of tissue, and are assumed to be the cause instead of the consequence."

What of the *change of type* of disease? This is at utter variance with the germ-theory. It is beyond dispute that diseases do, from time to time, undergo great changes in their types and characters. Sydenham records this fact. He says: "Nothing in my opinion strikes the mind that contemplates the whole domain of medicine with greater wonder than the well-known varied and inconsistent character of those diseases which we call epidemic. It is not so much that they reflect and *depend upon different conditions of climate in one and the same year*, as that they represent *different* and *dissimilar* constitutions of different and dissimilar years."

What has become of black death? Has there been a "survival of the fittest" among the "specific morbid entities," and is that of the black death crushed out by its more vigorous rivals? To judge by results, black death having been more fatal than the epidemics of the present century, its specific morbid entity would be presumably more vigorous and more likely to survive; but it is gone. What destroyed its specific germ?

Why is scarlatina at one time malignant and at another mild? Why does one epidemic of small-pox prove to be most virulent—as in 1871, after many years of compulsory vaccination—while another epidemic of the same disease—as in 1791, *before* vaccination—was *so mild* that a fatal instance was scarcely heard of? Why is the comparatively harmless disease called measles in some years so malignant that the mortality runs up to high figures? The germ-theory cannot afford any sufficient answer to these questions. Astrology alone can answer them; for in one year we find three or four of the superior planets in mutual conjunction, or opposition, and a severe epidemic coinciding; in another year, only two of the superior planets in conjunction, or opposition, and a mild form of epidemic disease coinciding. The *periodicity* of the conjunctions and oppositions of the superior planets corresponds to that of great epidemics. When the influence of Mars predominates, one of the martial diseases—scarlatina, small-pox, or measles—prevails. When Jupiter is near his perihelion and free from affliction by Saturn, Mars, or Uranus, the public health is good.

Influenza was defined by the late Dr. Edmund Parkes, F.R.S., whose memory is held in the highest esteem, as:

"An epidemic specific fever, with special and early implication of the naso-laryngo-bronchial mucous membrane; duration definite of from four to eight days; one attack not preservative in future epidemics.

"In the seventeenth century it was first called Influenza, in Italy, because it was attributed to the 'influence' of the stars, and this term has passed into medical use.

"History.—Supposed to be referred to by Hippocrates, who yet gives no perfect description. . . . . . It is not until the fourteenth century that the records became numerous and precise: In the 14th century, 6 epidemics are recorded; in the 15th, 7 epidemics; in the 16th, 11; in the 17th, 16; in the 18th, 18; in the 19th century (first half), 10 epidemics. There is little doubt that the apparent increase of prevalence in the last centuries is merely due to more accurate recording of minor epidemics.

"Of these epidemics, some have been very widely spread over a great part of the known world, as in 1311, 1557, 1580, 1590, 1729, 1762, 1775, 1780-2, 1830-2, 1847. It has prevailed in most places of the habitable globe; in the whole of Europe; in China, Tartary, Egypt, India, and other parts of Asia; in Australia, Polynesia; in North and South America, and in the West Indies; that is to say, in both hemispheres and in all latitudes."[1]

Dr. Parkes remarked:

"So enigmatical are the phenomena connected with Influenza, that caution is necessary in attempting to form some idea of what the nature of the exciting cause may be. It must be a specific agent of some kind. From the earliest times authors have come to this conclusion; the similarity of the symptoms in different epidemics show that this agent is the same in its successive invasions. If it be connected with any unusual meteorological or atmospheric condition, this has not been detected, and cannot be at present even guessed at. It seems to me to be impossible at present to come to any conclusion as to the nature of the cause.

"*Volcanic Eruptions.—Telluric Emanations.*—Noah Webster and Schnurrer have collected the available evidence on this point, but it is entirely negative. There have been constant volcanic eruptions without Influenza, and epidemics of Influenza without great volcanic eruptions. It has been thought that emanations of seleniuretted hydrogen from volcanoes might excite Influenza, but no proof has ever been given of the existence of this substance in the atmosphere.

"*Electrical Conditions.*—No evidence has been collected which shows any connexion with conditions of telluric magnetism or atmospheric electricity; and indeed the peculiar spread and frequent localization of Influenza seem inconsistent with general magnetic conditions.

"*Seasons.*—The disease appears, at all times of the year; nor is there any reason for considering it an affection of the late summer, autumn, and winter, as has been stated.

"*Temperature of the Air.*—Owing to the confusion in the popular mind between Influenza and common catarrhs or catarrhal fevers, it has always been a common opinion that Influenza depends either on a low or a sudden variation of temperature. This error has taken a long time to kill; but almost every writer, since the epidemic of 1580, has examined this point, and has decided that there is no such connexion.

[1] See Dr. Reynolds's "System of Medicine," vol. i.

There is abundant evidence to show that the changes of weather, which may appear to have accompanied or preceded its outbreak were mere coincidences."

Seitz attributed great influence to the effect of vicissitudes of weather in causing epidemic Influenza.[2]

In order to discover the true cause of Influenza we must look beyond the *changes of weather* which have so frequently preceded or accompanied its outbreak.

Sudden variations of temperature and unusual weather (for the season) are, in the opinion of astro-meteorologists, due to the rare conjunctions and oppositions of the superior planets, more especially when such phenomena happen at or near the period of the new moon or solar ingress into one of the cardinal points of the ecliptic. The *modus operandi* is unknown—it may probably be *electrical.* Dr. Pickford says:[3]

"The prevalence of epidemic or pestilential disease has been associated with the absency or deficiency of *positive* electricity in the atmosphere; and the mortality has been found to be in the inverse ratio of the amount of *positive* electricity with which the air is charged.

"In the 'non-electric' states of the air, or when the electricity is 'weak' or 'nothing,' diseases of a low type prevail, and the mortality increases. On the contrary, when the electricity is 'positive,' 'strongly positive,' and 'active throughout the day,' the number of deaths decreases."

Dr. Prout expressed his opinion that the derangement of the atmosphere coincident with pestilence is due to a deranged state of the electric fluid; and there is reason to believe, from his experiments, "it immediately affects that all-important function, the change of the blood in the lungs." Dr. Prout found an increase of the carbonic acid expired during a thunderstorm.

That the atmosphere is affected in some way is proved by Influenza breaking out among horses—in the year 1872, about 16,000 horses in New York alone were attacked with Influenza—although "it has not yet been decided," says Zuelzer, "whether the epizootics prevail simultaneously with Influenza among men." Virgil (*Georg.* lib. iii, 478) observed that the pestilential influence is exerted on animals as well as man. Homer and early writers on medicine record in-

[2] "Catarrh and Influenza," 1865.

[3] "Hygiene." London; 1858, p. 55.

stances of the epizootic attacking animals first and mankind afterwards. Many cases of the kind are given in "*Electricite des Meteors*" published at Lyons, in the year 1787, by the Abbé Bertholon.

The frequency of the coincidence of volcanic eruptions and earthquakes with the outbreaks of epidemics, tends to support the hypothesis of planetary action being the exciting cause of all these phenomena; and electricity may be the agent. Noah Webster relates a very large number of such coincidences.

The fact that specific sources of excitement often prevail for several months in succession and then disappear, giving place either to other specific sources producing other diseases or to a healthy period, points strongly to planetary action; for the larger planets often remain near together (before and after their conjunction) for months, on account of their slow motion, and one of the conjoined planets may then form conjunction with a third.

Hippocrates held that all epidemics came from the atmosphere; the Indian, Arabian, and Turkish physicians held the same opinion.

Professor Zuelzer denied that there is any connection established between atmospheric conditions and Influenza; Drs. Forster and Sietz assert that there is. The fact lost sight of by these disputants is that the atmosphere is the medium through which the influence is spread, and that the atmosphere is variously affected according to the several natures of the planets in mutual configuration. Dr. Parkes said: "Surely no one can doubt the connection of the various attacks in the great epidemics of Influenza with some general and pandemic influence." But the learned doctor did not turn his attention to planetary influence, or he might possibly have come to the same conclusion as the writer, viz., that the "general and pandemic influence" is referable to certain relative positions of the heavenly bodies. The frequent coincidence of sudden variations of temperature and of abnormal seasons, with the outbreak of Influenza and other epidemics, lends force to this conclusion. When the maximum of planetary influence obtains, the maximum of epidemic disease attends or immediately follows.

On the 23rd of February, 1830, there happened an eclipse of the Sun, visible in Tartary, Siberia, etc. At this eclipse, URANUS was in the meridian (in Asia), in the sign *Aquarius*, and within 5° of the opposition of SATURN. On the 9th of March following, there happened an eclipse of the Moon which was total to the greater part of Asia and the Asiatic Isles. There were no fewer than *six* eclipses in 1830, four of the Sun. Zuelzer records that the Influenza first appeared in that part of the world wherein these eclipses were visible. In February, 1831, there happened an annular eclipse of the Sun in *Aquarius* 24°, the luminaries being in *opposition* to SATURN, and the eclipse being visible in North America—which soon after was visited with the epidemic. In the spring of 1831, Jupiter was in conjunction with URANUS in *Aquarius*. Zadkiel foretold, in his *Herald of Astrology* for 1831, "tumult, *sickness*, and destruction" in the East, all of which occurred there; also, "epidemic disease in England in June and July," the Influenza then visited England, and "two hundred excuses were sent to the Queen's ball." In 1832, JUPITER was still nearly in *conjunction* with URANUS; and was in *opposition* to SATURN in March. Again, three great planets in mutual configuration, the maximum of planetary influence and the maximum of epidemic disease!

As to the specific agent, Dr. Parkes concluded that:

"This agent must be in the air; the diffusion is too rapid to suppose it to be conveyed by water; besides water-poisoning is usually localised. It cannot be attributable to food. There remains only the air as a medium of communication, and that this is so seems also shown by the way in which it can attack vessels at some distance at sea. . . . It seems to me to be impossible at present to come to any conclusion as to the nature of the cause."

The rapid and extreme prostration of muscular strength, a very early symptom, together with excruciating headache, seems to point to electrical changes being intimately associated with Influenza—and these changes in the electrical condition of the atmosphere are due to planetary action.

EPIDEMIC CHOLERA in the sporadic form (Cholera Nostras, Europoea) is not nearly so severe as the Asiatic or Oriental.

Lebert says that: Hippocrates, Celsus, and Caelius Aurelianus wrote of it, and Aretaeus described it excellently. Diogenes the cynic is said to have died of it after a fit of indigestion produced by eating cow's feet raw, a melancholy end to the philosophical dweller in a tub. It is only as late as the sixteenth century, however, that we begin to find mention of this disease. Sydenham recorded the London epidemic in 1669-1672.

Dr. Goodene, in writing of Epidemic Cholera, states:[4]

"Most extended observations as to *electricity*, *ozone*, and *baromet-*

---

[4] "A System of Medicine," edited by Dr. Russell Reynolds, vol. i., pp. 671-688.

ric pressure, by Mr. Glaisher are to be found in the Appendix to the Cholera Report for 1853-54; and in the Report of the Indian Sanitary Commission of 1862; but these have not been found to exercise any decided influence, or to have existed in different conditions during different epidemics.

"Some connection between atmospheric states and the epidemics does exist, but it is not that of cause and effect. Mr. Glaisher says: 'The three epidemics of 1832, 1848-49, and 1853-54, were attended with a particular state of the atmosphere (in London), characterised by a prevalent *mist*, thin in high places, dense in low—during the height of the epidemic; in all cases the reading of the barometer was remarkably high and the atmosphere thick.'

"*Departure of Cholera Epidemics.*—These often leave a place rapidly, sometimes after sudden atmospheric changes, and after high winds and storms. . . . Chemical analysis of the air has thrown no light on the cause of Cholera. It is possible, however, that prolonged microscopic examination of strained air, as in the method of Pasteur, might be more successful. . . . It must be confessed that we do not know what is the exciting cause of Cholera."

Dr. Kelsall in his "Remarks on Asiatic Cholera," states his opinion that "the origin of Cholera is in some mysterious and unusual telluric influence," and whenever it occurs, he believes "there is always an unusual and temporary influence which so modifies or changes the condition of the exhalations, that a specific miasm is engendered by chemical union of these gases, and Cholera prevails." This unusual influence he believes "to be some perturbation of the electricity of the earth, either atmospheric or telluric; and some such influence seems to have been mysteriously and intimately connected with all the different pestilences which have periodically passed over the earth." In Dr. Kelsall's opinion:

"The Cholera miasm rises from the earth and floats in the air, sometimes assuming a *visible* appearance *e.g.*, a mass of reddish vapour was seen, in 1820, on the surface of the Yellow Sea; the vapours were at first light, gradually increased, became condensed, and rising from the surface of the water, formed an immense red cloud, which remained for several hours floating in the air. A violent wind suddenly arose, divided the cloud into several columns, and drove them towards the land. Those red vapours spread in a winding course along the hills and valleys, and swept over the towns and villages, and wherever they passed, the people were attacked with Cholera. During the Crimean War, H.M.S. *Britannia* was cruising in the Black Sea, in

1854; an outbreak of Cholera occurred immediately after a remarkable cloud was observed to hover over the ship."

In "Travels and Adventures of an Officer's Widow," it is related that a column of mist enveloped a sanitary station on a hill at Murree, in the Himalaya mountains, more than 7,000 feet above the sea-level, in 1858; and a frightful outbreak of Cholera immediately followed, more than one-sixth of the European soldiers stationed there being buried before the pestilence ceased.

In 1848, Cholera prevailed in Germany. It broke out in Paris, March 11th, 1849; at first it spread slowly; during the first eight days of June it reached a hitherto unheard of intensity. On June 9th, a severe storm occurred, and from this day it markedly diminished, says Lebert. In 1849, Cholera was very fatal in Great Britain. Zadkiel I. foretold this outbreak in these words:[5] "The presence of Uranus in the house of death [at the *conjunction* of MARS and SATURN in ♈, May 25th, 1849,] denotes, I fear, much fatality by the CHOLERA! which fatal disease seems to travel like a thunder-cloud, over the coasts of Britain."

From the great eclipse of the Sun in ♎ 15° 27′, in *opposition* to URANUS in ♈ 16° 20′, retrograde, and in square with JUPITER in ♋ 19° 10′, of October 9th, 1847; at which SATURN was in the fourth angle in ♓ 7° 2′, retrograde, and MARS was just setting; Zadkiel I. foretold "fierce and violent maladies and pestilential diseases."[6] On October 24th, says Lebert, Cholera broke out in Constantinople, which became a chief centre of radiation. From Constantinople all Syria and a large part of the countries about the Mediterranean Sea were attacked.

When, in Paris, the Cholera was at its height, in the first eight days of June, MARS was in *opposition* to the place of the Solar eclipse of October 9th, 1847. The great storm of June 9th, took place under the combined influences of MARS and JUPITER in aspect with the Sun, as reference to the *Ephemeris* will show.

England and France were again attacked with Cholera in 1853, but it was not until 1854, says Lebert, that it prevailed to a wide extent in England, Scotland, and Ireland. In 1853 and 1854 it extended over a considerable portion of the United States of America, and the Antilles. In 1854 and 1855 it showed itself in Switzerland. Its spread and desolation during the Crimean War are well remembered. From the

[5] *Zadkiel's Almanac* for 1849, p. 38.

[6] *Zadkiel's Almanac* for 1848, pp. 43, 44.

planetary positions at the Solar eclipse of June 6th, 1853, Zadkiel I. foretold that "fierce and violent maladies and pestilential diseases will destroy vast numbers of the human race." MARS was separating from *conjunction* with Uranus and about to form the *conjunction* with SATURN. The eclipse took place in ♊ 15° 56′ in *opposition* to Jupiter in ♐ 20° 6′, retrograde. In fact, Zadkiel I. foretold the Cholera year of 1854, and the healthy summer (for England) of 1855.

THE PLAGUE.—The name Pest (Pestis, Pestilentia), says Liebermeister,[7] was given during antiquity and the middle ages to every epidemic disease, in which the mortality was very large. Gradually, however, the term came to be used almost altogether to designate a certain disease, distinguished above all others by its epidemical appearance and by its heavy mortality. At present the term Pest, or Plague is understood exclusively to mean the bubo plague.

"According to the testimony of Rufus of Ephesus, as given by Oribasius, the bubo plague occurred in Egypt, Libya, and Syria, already before the beginning of the present era. The first extensive epidemic of the bubo plague in Europe occurred in the middle of the sixth century, and is known under the name of the *Plague of Justinian*. Since then Plague epidemics have very often occurred on European soil, and during the middle ages and the first years of modern times, it was the worst of the epidemic diseases that visited the people of Europe. Since the middle of the seventeenth century the Plague epidemics have begun, gradually, to be less frequent in Europe, and the western European continent has not been visited by the disease since the serious epidemic which occurred in Provence in the years 1720 and 1721. . . . It seemed for a long time as if the Plague had entirely disappeared from the earth; during the last decades, however, unmistakable epidemics of the disease, though of comparatively limited extent, have appeared in isolated regions of Africa and Asia."

It is universally acknowledged in modern times that the Plague never originated autochthonously in Europe, but that it was always introduced. The doctrine of the contagiousness of the plague is often assailed, and the statement is often made that it arises solely from impurities in the atmosphere or other telluric or cosmical influences. The question as to the manner in which the plague is disseminated cannot yet be decided with certainty.

"The *season of the year* and *the climate* have only a very slight influence, and yet moderate warmth in connection with dampness

[7] Ziemssen's "Cyclopaedia of Medicine," vol. i, p. 465.

seems to be quite favourable to the propagation of the plague.

"The second point of interest in the annihilation of the plague is *the improvement of the sanitary condition* of Europe as well as that part of the Orient which was formerly the chief source of the disease."

The "BLACK DEATH" devastated almost all the known countries of the earth, about the middle of the fourteenth century, and was so-called because it was more fatal than all previous or succeeding epidemics. It presented all the essential characteristics, says Liebermeister, "of the ordinary bubo Plague, but in addition there was always a lung complication; in numerous cases, blood was expectorated, a symptom which seldom occurred in the bubo Plague, properly so-called; death followed more quickly, generally within three days."

The statement of Hecker is that *the atmosphere was really poisoned*. The Black Death first appeared in Europe, Asia, and Africa, in the year 1345, and it prevailed for seven years. The ancients averred that great conjunctions of planets in one of the signs of the "airy triplicity" (♊, ♎, and ♒), caused or presignified "famine, fierce and violent maladies, and *pestilential* diseases."

Guy de Chauliac, a surgeon of Avignon, attributed this outbreak to the grand conjunction of the Planets SATURN, JUPITER, and MARS in *Aquarius*, on the 24th of March, 1345—Neptune was also in the same sign. Here, again, is found the *maximum* of planetary influence, attended by the *maximum* of murderous pandemics. In 1846, JUPITER overtook URANUS in *Aries*. In 1852, SATURN joined URANUS in *Aries*. Guy de Chauliac was right and his narrow minded critic in the *Evening Standard* of March 4th, 1911, was wrong in sneering at "his fatuous belief." The author wrote a letter, which appeared in the same journal of March 6th, protesting again Mr. James McWhir's condemnation of Chauliac, and reminding him of Dr. Parkes' conclusion already quoted in this chapter.

At the summer solstice of the year 1665, SATURN was in the eighth "house" (that of death) of the heavens, *retrograde* in ♑ 6°, and nearly in *opposition* to the Sun and Mars. The Moon was in the sixth house (that of sickness), in ♎ 10° and in square aspect with Saturn, Mercury and Venus. The Map of the Heavens at this ingress will be found in Lilly's *Almanac* for 1665. Lilly foretold "a sickly summer," and said that: "The diseases likely to afflict mankind are fluxes, colic, pestilence and plague"—although, of course, he did not know that there was a *conjunction* of JUPITER and URANUS to increase the mischief.

TYPHOID FEVER (abdominal typhus) is supposed to be described by Hippocrates in his first and third books on the Epidemics. In the seventeenth century and in the eighteenth, there can be no doubt that it occasionally became epidemic. *Typhoid* fever is never directly transmitted from person to person; it is therefore classed by Liebermeister as a "miasmatic-contagious" disease. *Typhus* (derived from Τυφος, smoke or vapour) fever "is certainly a disease which can serve as a prototype of those diseases which are transmitted from person to person. Whoever touches, or even comes near to a case of typhus fever is in danger of contagion. For this reason the greater number of the physicians and attendants who take care of such invalids are themselves attacked with the disease." Liebermister proceeds:

"How then does *typhoid* fever originate? How is the poison elaborated, and how is it transmitted to man? These questions are answered with great unanimity by most persons, even those who believe in direct contagion. They hold that the poison of typhoid fever originates in the decomposition of organic substances. The name pythogenic (produced by putrefaction) fever, proposed by Murchison, is based on this generally received opinion. Yet, if we look more closely at the facts on which this pythogenic theory rests, we can find grounds for doubt."

"It is a fact that typhoid, in contrast with many other diseases, and especially with cholera, attacks, by preference, strong and healthy persons, while it avoids those already suffering with chronic ailments."

As is the case with Influenza, Cholera, and Plague, so it is with Enteric or Typhoid fever—the years of greatest prevalence of the epidemic are those in which the maximum of combined planetary influence obtains. A stagnant atmosphere favours the spread of the specific poison. It is remarkable that typhoid fever attacks young persons chiefly, and those between fifteen and twenty-five years of age furnish one-half of the number of victims—just as in the case of pulmonary phthisis. It seems to be nearly related to intermittent and remittent fevers, and to dysentery; and in some epidemics, typhoid fever appears to undergo a change of type. Dr. Harley writes of three *varieties*, viz., the simple inflammatory, the contagious, and the paludal onteric fever.

MEASLES, SCARLATINA, and SMALL-POX are classed as contagious diseases. They were all known to the ancients, but were frequently grouped together instead of being separately described in ancient and mediaeval times. They are all *martial* diseases; each appears at one time in a mild epidemic form, at another time in a severe or even malignant form.

Dr. Louis Thomas says:[8] "Where measles originated, where and how it spread, and to what extent it has prevailed of old in the inhabited portions of the earth, are questions which do not admit of even a tolerably grounded hypothesis. Probably it is of exotic origin. Dr. Thomas proceeds to say:

"Susceptibility to the contagion of measles is almost universal, except where one attack has already occurred. Second attacks are exceedingly rare, as much so as second attacks of small-pox and scarlet fever. . . . Like all acute infectious diseases, and *especially small-pox*, measles may appear at times with a general, almost pandemic spread, to *then disappear* again more or less completely for a longer or shorter time.

"True *haemorrhagic* measles is much rarer than the same form in small-pox. It occurs even in little children. The oldest accounts of the malignant form are of little value, though by far the most numerous, for the ' black measles' played formerly a great ro l e. Doubtless its ostensible frequence is somewhat explained by the preposterous treatment of old times, but more particularly by the fact that measles and scarlet-fever were included in one category, and malignant forms of scarlet-fever were described as measles."

SCARLATINA was not deemed of sufficient importance, in ancient times, to require an exact description of it. Even in the beginning of the seventeenth century, Sennert refers to scarlatina as only another form of measles; and Morton, at the close of the same century, maintained that both are one and the same disease, differing only in the character of the rash. Sydenham established the specific nature of scarlatina by observations made during the epidemics which occurred in London from 1661 to 1675. It was soon recognised that the character of the scarlatina epidemic was liable to great variation; a series of years of the mild form being followed by others of unprecedented malignancy and danger. Epidemics of scarlatina have maintained this peculiarity down to the latest times, especially in England and Ireland. According to Dr. Farr's statistics, the annual mortality from scarlatina in England and Wales from 1848 to 1855 comprised 1/25th, and in some years 1/20th of the entire death-rate. From Europe it has extended over the rest of the world. Dr. Thomas says:

[8] Ziemssen's "Cyclopaedia of Medicine," vol. i). Art. Measles

"It is indisputable that the *cause* of scarlatina is a peculiar substance which is transferable from the patient to the unaffected individual. Isolation of scarlatinous patients has prevented the further spread of the disease. An intense family predisposition is frequent; the cause of this is as obscure as the nature of the predisposition. On the other hand, there are families in which the susceptibility to scarlatina seems to be entirely absent. The predisposition to scarlatina seems to be extraordinary in those patients who are affected so intensely that death ensues in a short time."

Now this extraordinary predisposition to scarlatina is capable of explanation astrologically. In regard to *measles*, it is found that a "direction" of the Ascendant, Sun, or Moon, to the conjunction, square, semi-square, sesqui-square, opposition, or par. dec. of MARS, or of Jupiter, or the Sun (if either be affected by ♂ at birth), will coincide with and account for the attack. But in regard to *scarlatina*, Mars alone is the cause of it. Those who become so affected as to die in a short time, have Mars afflicting the hyleg at birth,[9] and therefore the *anareta*. Those whose horoscopes are free from the affliction of Mars are insusceptible of scarlatina. Points such as these are likely to remain "obscure" to the wisest physicians while they neglect to be instructed in astrology.

Dr. Thomas proceeds:

"Cases of scarlet fever occur either in *sporadic* or *epidemic* form. The most complete reports concerning the influence of the seasons on the prevalence of scarlatina have emanated from England. The greater prevalence of the disease in the *autumn* has been recognised since Sydenham's time—the largest number of deaths out of 55,956 cases in London, within 24 years, occurred between the middle of September and the middle of November, the smallest number towards the end of March and beginning of April. Scarlatina lacks the regular *periodicity* of measles.

"Occasionally scarlatina, like small-pox and measles, assumes a *pandemic* character, or at least spreads over large tracts of land, as for instance in Germany in 1818; in Denmark, England, Germany, and France in 1825 and 1826; in Ireland, Russia, and Germany in 1832-35; in Germany, Denmark, and England in 1846-49; in the United States in 1821; and over the whole of South America from 1831 to 1837. It may be said that the *pathogenesis of scarlatina* is still a mystery."

---

[9] See case 8, p. 128; also case 14, p. 129 of this work.

In 1818, at the vernal equinox, the Sun was in *square* aspect with MARS. At the Solar eclipse of May 5th, Mars was rising (in ♋ 21°). At the Solar eclipse of October 29th, MARS was within 6° of the luminaries.

In 1821, there was a *conjunction* of MARS with both SATURN and JUPITER in *Aries*.

In 1825, at the vernal equinox, the MOON was separating from the SUN and applying to *conjunction* with MARS in *Aries*. At the lunar eclipse of May 31st, the SUN was in *conjunction* with MARS and SATURN—the two infortunes forming their mutual *conjunction* on the 5th of June. In 1826, Mars was *retrograde* from the 29th of March to the 13th of June.

In 1832, at the Solar eclipse of July 27th, the luminaries were in *square* with MARS (♉ 7°), and MARS was *retrograde* from the 13th of October to the 25th of December. In 1834, at the autumnal equinox, the SUN was in square aspect with MARS; and the red planet was *retrograde* from November, 1834, to February (inclusive), 1835. In 1836, at the solar eclipse of November 9th the luminaries were in *square* with MARS.

SMALL-POX.—Some remarks on this *martial* disease will be found at p.175 of this work.

The advocates for compulsory vaccination assert that the comparative diminution of small-pox nowadays is entirely due to vaccination! This cannot be true, for in the eighteenth century small-pox was artificially maintained and spread by the practice of inoculation; and, moreover, sanitation and isolation of cases have reduced the mortality of all epidemics. Prior to the introduction of vaccination there were mild epidemics of small-pox, as Jenner himself records; and, occasionally, for a series of years there was no epidemic of it. When in the year 1871 a virulent epidemic of small-pox broke out, it caused a high rate of mortality in the very countries (Prussia, for example) the people of which were most efficiently vaccinated and re-vaccinated. When the epidemic declined, as all epidemic diseases do after a time, its decline was attributed to vaccination.

Perusal of "Vital Statistics" (by my father, Dr. C. T. Pearce), and of "Registration Statistics" (by Dr. Wallace), will show that there is very grave reason to doubt whether vaccination has ever effected any diminution of small-pox; at any rate no such effect can be proved by the statistics of the Registrar-General. The contrast afforded between unvaccinated Leicester and vaccinated Sheffield, in 1887, is dead against the theory of the protective power of vaccination. Dr. Creighton's article on Vaccination, in a former edition of the "Encyclopaedia Britannica," is an unanswerable argument against the practice.

Curschmann says:

"The truth is that from an early date down to the present time, fluctuations have occurred in the recurrence of epidemics, so that periods of rest have alternated, with some uniformity, with years of intense prevalence. A recurrence of the disease every 12 or 15 years has been stated.

"Some epidemics are severe, others are mild. The season of the year has some influence on the course of epidemics; they are generally more dangerous in summer than in winter."

Official advocates for vaccination publish statistics of the comparative mortality of the vaccinated and the unvaccinated, from small-pox, but they do not give the *ages* of the victims, so that no fair conclusion can be drawn in favour of vaccination from their statistics. As a rule, the unvaccinated class consists chiefly of children certified to be unfit for vaccination.

Generally speaking, children born when the planet Mars is exactly rising or setting are particularly liable to the small-pox, measles, and scarlatina; if Mars be in either *Aries*, *Taurus*, or *Virgo*, the small-pox more especially. If, at the time of an epidemic, in such a nativity there be a direction of the Ascendant, Sun, or Moon, whichever may be hyleg, to the conjunction, square, opposition, or parallel declination of Mars, the owner of such nativity may not escape being attacked.

In years of epidemic small-pox, the influence of MARS is found supreme. The great epidemic of 1871 took place when Mars became *retrograde* (in the sign *Virgo*); and at the vernal ingress of that year Mars was in opposition to the Sun.

When MARS has little power—that is to say when ♂ is neither in elevation nor configuration with either the Sun or Moon at an eclipse, or at the equinox or solstice, and neither retrograde nor in perigee—martial diseases are almost entirely absent and are not epidemic. The low death-rate and absence of epidemics when Jupiter is in perihelion and supreme at the equinoxes, solstices, and eclipses, contrasted with the high death-rate and prevalence of epidemics coinciding with the planet Mars being in the same relative positions, is very remarkable, and forms a very strong argument in favour of planetary influence, which is, to say the least, deserving of impartial and thorough investigation at the hands of the Medical Profession.

The late Professor Max Muller, M.A., wrote of the ancient science as follows:[10]

"Astrology was not such mere imposition as it is generally supposed to have been. It is counted a science by so sound and sober a scholar as Melancthon; and even Bacon allows it a place among the sciences, though admitting that 'it had better intelligence and confederacy with the imagination of man than with his reason.' In spite of the strong condemnation Luther prononnced against it, astrology continued to sway the destinies of Europe; and a hundred years after Luther, the astrologer was the counsellor of princes and generals, while the founder of modern astronomy died in poverty and despair. In our time the very rudiments of astrology are lost and forgotten.

"According to a writer in *Notes and Queries* (2nd series, vol. x., p. 500), astrology is not so entirely extinct as we suppose. One of our principal writers, he states, one of our leading barristers, and several members of the various antiquarian societies, are practised astrologers at this hour. But no one cares to let his studies be known, so great is the prejudice that confounds an art requiring the highest education with the jargon of the gipsy fortune-teller!" See also a paper on *Medicine and Astrology* read before the Numismatic and Antiquarian Society of Philadelphia, June 7th, 1866.

[10] "Lectures on the Science of Language," 9th edit,, vol. 1, pp. 10, 11. Longmans, 1877.

CHAPTER II.

CRISES IN DISEASE.

"I consider as superstition the imagined knowledge and certainty which men suppose they have of the laws of Nature."—DR. ARNOLD.

GALEN defined crises thus: "*Est velox et repentina morbi mutatio, qua infirmus vel ad salutem vel ad mortem deducitur*"—because the crisis seems to determine the issue, whether for life or death. At the critical day, the issue may usually be correctly discerned if the configurations of the heavenly bodies be attended to. For this purpose, the nativity of the patient and the hour at which he fell ill, or took to his bed, are required. Now-a-days, these data can seldom be obtained.

The ancients held that: "There are two principal sorts of crises; the one is in *acute* diseases, and *lunar*; the other in chronic diseases, and *solar*." They said:

"In acute diseases, the aspects or configurations of the Moon, viz., her quartile and opposition, are not her phases with the Sun, but are reckoned from the degree and minute of the zodiac occupied by her at the beginning of the patient's seizure, until her return to the same point, which is effected in 27 days, 8 hours, or thereabouts. Some acute diseases run from the 8th to the 10th, 11th, 14th, 20th, or 21st day; others to the lunar month. The remittent, increase when the Moon forms evil aspects with the infortunes. Some other acute diseases are terminated in 3, 4, 5, 6, 7, or 8 days, such as pestilential fevers, pleurisy, &c.

"Chronic diseases follow the motion of the Sun, acquiring a crisis after the 40th day; and judgment may be made when the Sun arrives at the square to his own place, as is evident in hectics, dropsies, and quaternaries. When the Sun attains the sextile and trine of his own place, there are only some indicative motions made of such effects as follow in the opposition. Nevertheless, they are oftentimes anticipated or protracted, according to the nature of the planets the Sun becomes configurated with—if benevolent, for the better; if malevolent, for the worse.

"Crises are also distinguished as safe, doubtful, hazardous, and not judged. The *safe* crisis is that which happens without any great and pernicious accident. The *doubtful* crisis is that which appears with great and pernicious accidents, and is the most dangerous. The *hazardous* crisis is when, on the 4th day, the signs of concoction appear, and therefore presage the crisis to be judged on the 7th day. The crisis *not judged* is when the crisis is absolved on the 7th day, yet was not to be judged on the 4th day by any sign of concoction. Hence the days themselves are divided into three classes. For—

"1. Some are called CRITICAL (*nomine generico*).

"2. Others JUDICATIVE, on which judgment is pronounced.

"3. Others INTERCEDENT (which happen between the judicative and critical), whereon the disease is remitted.

"Seeing, therefore, that by these critical days some notable alteration would be foreseen, tending either to the health or death of the patient, it becomes important to define the *beginning* of a disease, which, Galen confessed, is a difficult task. The time when the patient takes to his bed (decumbiture) is not the beginning of the disease, for a robust and strong man resists the onset of a disease for a longer time than one who is weak and nervous. Nevertheless, in some diseases—as in apoplexy, epilepsy, paralysis, haemorrhage, and pleurisy—it is easy to discover the precise beginning or seizure. The same in the case of an *accident*.

"Hippocrates observed his indications from the hour at which a man sickened of a fever, but not from the day whereon he perceived a heaviness of the body merely, or suffered with headache. For by how much sharper and more violent the fever is, by so much is it the more manifest to sense, and impossible that the first assault or invasion thereof should be hidden from the patient."

RULES.—1. Find the places of the Sun, Moon, and planets at the decumbiture or first seizure. If the time was recorded, a map of the heavens should be drawn.

2. In diseases which run a *short* course, the crisis will take place when the Moon shall arrive at 45° distance from her longitude at the first seizure or decumbiture, in from 3 to 4 days, according to her motion.

3. In diseases which ran a longer course the crisis will happen when the Moon shall arrive at 90° distance from her longitude at the decumbiture, in from 6 to 8 days. This is called *criticus primus*, because it is of the utmost importance.

4. In diseases which run a longer course than 8 days, the great crisis will be when the Moon shall arrive at the *opposite* point of the zodiac to that held by her at the decumbiture, which will be from the 13th to the 15th day. This is the second crisis.

5. In diseases which run a longer course than 15 days, the third crisis will take place when the Moon shall arrive at the distance of 270°, the second square to her place at the decumbiture, which will be between the 20th and 22nd days.

6. In diseases which run a longer course than 21 days, the fourth and last crisis will happen when the Moon returns to her place in the zodiac at the decumbiture. For then the disease will either end or degenerate into a chronic or long standing one.

7. The *indicative* crises are those which take place at the 45°, 135°, 225°, and 315° distance of the Moon from her place at the decumbiture, or the half of every quadrate.

While on the subject of Lunar Influence, the following excerpt from *Zadkiel's Almanac* for 1844 will be found very interesting.

Action of the Moon's Rays.—It has been the fashion with savants to deny that any kind of action is traceable to the rays of the Moon. Yet we learn that "the calotype paper will take an impression from simple moonlight, not concentrated by a lens. If a leaf be laid upon a sheet of paper, an image of it may be obtained in this way in from a quarter to half an hour."

As M. Becquerel has arrived at the conclusion that the rays of light which act on the salts of silver are *electrical*, it follows that the rays of the Moon are also *electrical*; and this supports the theory propounded for many years in this work that the Moon acts on our atmosphere by exciting its electricity. If the Moon does this, why not Mars and Venus, which planets reflect the Solar light to us in from two to four minutes after those rays impinge on their respective surfaces?

The photographic action of light may merely crystallise the fine particles of the salts of silver, and so render them unfit to reflect the light—hence the dark hue the surface of calotype, etc., papers attain. All crystallisation is an effect of electric action; and electric action absolutely does fall upon the Earth by the action of the Sun and Moon.

CHAPTER III.

DIAGNOSIS AND PROGNOSIS OF DISEASE.

> "A man is not permitted without censure to follow his own thoughts in the search of truth when they lead him ever so little out of the common road."—LOCKE.

CAN astrology afford any help to the physician in the diagnosis of disease?

If we might trust the confident statements of the *horary* astrologers of the middle ages, we should answer this important question in the affirmative. Unfortunately, little reliance can be placed on either their statements or their common sense. They boasted that their judgment as to the nature of a disease was *infallible* when the planetary testimonies were in harmony. This confident boast was made by Lilly in his "Introduction to Astrology,"[1] published in the year 1647, and most unfortunately allowed to stand by Zadkiel I. in his revised and annotated edition of Lilly's book. The *horary* astrologer—Lilly, for example—took upon himself to decide where doctors disagreed, and to diagnose the nature of an obscure disease which had baffled the wisest physicians, although he never had any medical training, and was evidently ignorant alike of anatomy, physiology, and pathology. The aphorisms given by Lilly relating to disease are too hopeless a jumble to afford much help to the physician. There can be little wonder that these vagaries of *horary* astrologers brought contempt upon the science; but, of course, it is very unjust to condemn astrology because one branch of it (which is not believed in by most scientific astrologers) as applied to questions has been so abused.

Jerome Cardan was sent for, in 1552, by the Archbishop of St. Andrews, whom he cured of a dangerous disease considered incurable by the physicians. But this success of that renowned astrologer—celebrated equally for his genius, his learning, and his mathematical attainments—does not justify any ignorant fellow who chooses to set

[1] "An Introduction to Astrology," by W. Lilly, chapter xxix., p. 158.

himself up as a "professor" of astrology in claiming infallibility of judgment. Cardan was a great physician, and combining medical with astrological skill he succeeded where other physicians had failed.

Figures drawn for the decumbiture or first seizure of the patient may afford—when they agree with the nativity—some aid in the diagnosis of obscure organic diseases; and they do afford reliable foreknowledge of the critical days, as Hippocrates and Galen observed.

Reference to the nativity (when procurable) of the sufferer may be of some assistance, for illness or accident usually happens when the Moon, or the Sun, is in the place of either ♄ or ♂ at birth, or when either of these planets is in the place (or in square or opposition thereto) of the Sun, Moon, or ascendant. It is at all times advisable to take special precaution against illness and accident when any such transits happen, and more particularly when the hyleg is afflicted at the period of new or full Moon.

The sad death of the Princess Alice of Great Britain took place on December 14th, 1878, from diphtheria. The benzoate of soda was administered to her, as a prophylactic, in doses of one drachm per diem, from November 12th, 1878. It was on December 7th, that her actual illness began.[2] A very evil train of directions was operating in her nativity, and the Princess became infected through kissing her children while they were suffering with diphtheria. On the day her illness began, the Moon was (at noon) in *Taurus* 19°, and in *opposition* to Mars in *Scorpio* 19°. Mars had lately passed through the opposite point of the zodiac to that held by the Sun (hyleg) at her birth. The first crisis took place on the 14th of December, when the Moon (at noon) reached *Leo* 19°, and on that day the Princess died. In this case, the part affected and the nature (martial) of the disease are indicated by the directions and transits.

The late King Victor Emanuel, of Italy, was seized with pleurisy at noon of the 6th of January, 1878, when the Moon was in *Aquarius* 19° and not afflicted. On the previous day, Saturn was in transit over the Moon's place (♓ 15° 44′) at his birth, and it was then that the king took cold. On the 3rd of January, the new Moon fell in opposition to the place of Mars (♋ 18° 21′ on the cusp of the 8th house) in his nativity. The king died on the 9th January. In this case, no indication of the illness could be discovered by the Moon's position at the time of the attack.

[2] Vide the *British Medical Journal*, February 8th, 1879, p. 187, which contains an official report of the case.

Generally speaking, Ptolemy's remarks as to the dominion of the planets over the human body are fairly reliable. He says:

"Among the chief parts of the human body, Saturn rules the right ear, the spleen, the bladder, the phlegm, and the bones. Jupiter governs the hand, the lungs, and the arteries. Mars rules the left ear, the kidneys, the veins, and the reproductive organs. The Sun rules the eyes, the brain, the heart, the nerves, and all the right side. Venus rules the nostrils, the liver, and the flesh. Mercury governs the speech, the understanding, the bile, and the tongue. The Moon rules the palate, the throat, the stomach, the abdomen, the uterus, and all the left side of the body."

When any particular configuration of the malefic planets causes either disease or accident, the *nativity* must be affected, and it is the only reliable basis for judgment as to the issue. Cholera and influenza have, as we have already seen, occasionally attacked thousands of people in a few days; in such cases the Moon could not be afflicted by the same evil planet at the seizure of every person.

In great and very fatal epidemics, it is quite possible that the nativities of all the victims, if procurable, would not show in every instance fatal "directions" corresponding to the period of death, because they may be due to "general causes," *viz.*, great eclipses at which the malefic planets were exceedingly powerful, as described by Claudius Ptolemy.

The practical test of a true science is the power which it confers of *prevision*, or of knowing now what will follow hereafter—wrote the late Dr. Russell Reynolds in the introduction to his "System of Medicine."

A proper study of the nativity of the patient, and of the solar revolution and lunar progress for the year, and of the transits at the moment of seizure, would enable the physician to discern "why one case of typhoid fever terminates unfavourably, while another to all appearance running a very similar course ends in recovery." As long as astrology shall be neglected, so long will physicians have to lament that "the science of prognosis has advanced little since the time of Hippocrates"—who insisted on a good knowledge of astrology as indispensable to the wise physician. Unfortunately the exact moment of birth is rarely known, and but few practitioners of astrology can cast the horoscope and the primary directions with the mathematical precision required for this purpose. The physician could not, of course, be expected to do this. When the nativity cannot be procured, the figure for the decumbiture will indicate the period of the crisis and afford some guide as to whether it will be favourable or probably fatal. It was in this way that the author's attention was first directed to the science, in the hope of throwing some light on prognosis, in May, 1860.

To fall ill—or to meet with an accident—when the Moon is in *conjunction*, *square*, *opposition*, or *parallel declination* with either Mars or Saturn, or in the place of either at birth, forebodes serious suffering. If Mars be the afflicting planet, fever will run high, if Saturn debility will be the greater. If Uranus also afflict the Moon, there will be very peculiar symptoms, and the disease will run an erratic course. If Mercury also afflict the Moon, delirium (especially if ☿ be in ♈) will probably supervene and be very troublesome to cure. If the Moon be in benefic aspect with Venus or Jupiter, recovery may be expected (unless ♀ or ♃ be greatly afflicted), however severe the illness may be, unless the nativity be very much afflicted.

The following aphorisms of Cardan are worthy of observation:

"When the Moon at a decumbiture shall be under the beams of the Sun, or with Saturn or Mars, if the patient be aged, even her conjunction with Jupiter, Venus, or Mercury is not without peril.

"Saturn causes long diseases; Mercury various ones; the Moon such as return after a time, like vertigo, epilepsy, etc., Jupiter and the Sun cause short diseases, but Mars the acutest of all.

"When the Moon is in a fixed sign, physic works the less; and if she be in ♈, ♉, or ♑, it will be apt to prove nauseous to the patient.

"When at the beginning of a disease the Sun and Moon are both with the infortunes, or in opposition to them, the sick will hardly escape.

"Mars in the ascendant causes the disease to be swift, violent, affecting the upper parts of the body, and disturbing the mind. If, in addition, the Sun and Moon, and their dispositors be afflicted, death will ensue.

"With respect to *fevers*: when the Sun is afflicted in *Leo*, mischievous fevers are threatened.

"Earthy signs (♉, ♍, and ♑) are free from fevers; but watery signs (♋, ♏, and ♓) threaten putrid fevers, if Mars be in one of them.

"Saturn in fiery signs (♈, ♌, and ♐), when the Sun is weak causes *hectic* fevers; Jupiter, sanguinary, and if Mars behold him, putrid fevers. Mars in fiery signs causes burning fevers; Venus, ephemeral; Mercury, mixed fevers; and, if the Moon be joined with them, she causes portentous fevers. Saturn mixing signification with Mars, causes melancholy fevers.

"If Mars be under the Sun's beams, or in the sixth house, and afflicting the significator of the disease, it occasions burning, pernicious fevers, of a venomous character; if the Sun and Mars and the planet signifying the disease be in *Scorpio* or *Leo*, the fever will be pestilential.

"It will be a *fatal* time to suffer *amputation*, or lose any member, when the Moon is under the Sun's beams and opposed by Mars.

"The significator of the disease in either *Gemini*, *Pisces*, or the first half of *Sagittarius*, presignifies a relapse, or that it will change into some other distemper.

"That *sign* in which the significator of a disease is posited, shows the parts of the body principally affected.

"Mercury unfortunate, prejudices the phantasy and inward faculties, and threatens madness if Mars afflict him. If Mercury be in an earthy sign, it threatens that the patient will make away with himself.

"*Fiery* signs in the ascendant and sixth house, at a decumbiture, or containing the Moon, presignify acute fever, burns, or wounds, as the case may be. *Earthy* signs denote diseases of long continuance, such as ague and consumption. *Airy* signs presignify corrupt blood, gout, or cutaneous affections. *Watery* signs denote diseases arising from cold, also weak stomach; Pisces particularly relates to excesses in eating and drinking."

Chronic diseases are so called because they were held by the ancients to be under the dominion of Saturn, whose name was Kronos.

In *surgical operations*, it would be advisable to wait—when possible—for a favourable time rather than to increase the patients' suffering and danger by operating when the Moon is within 17° of the Sun and in opposition to Mars—which Cardan stated to be a fatal configuration. Ptolemy says: "Pierce not with iron that part of the body which may be governed by the sign actually occupied by the Moon." For example, when the Moon is in Taurus, it is advisable not to operate on the neck or throat, especially if the Moon be in evil aspect with Mars.

In "The Science of the Stars,"[3] the author mentioned the case of Dr. Hewett, who was seized with haemoptysis at 6h a.m. of May 16th, 1865, and died of pulmonary phthisis, September 25th following. At

[3] "The Science of the Stars," chapter xxii., p. 145.

the moment of seizure, the Moon was in opposition with Mars and square with Saturn.

Another instance may be cited. At 9h p.m. (G.M.T.) of July 7th, 1861, Mrs. C. ruptured a blood-vessel in the chest, the haemorrhage was very alarming, and for several hours the patient was in the greatest danger. Within a week she was completely restored to health. The latitude of the place in which she resided is 52° 10′ N., and the longitude 3m 40s W. At the moment above stated, the R.A. of the M.C., was 15h 59m 33s, ♑ 29° in the ascendant, Mars setting in ♌ 1° 54′. The Moon in ♋ 13° 1′, hastening to conjunction with the Sun[4] in ♋ 15° 37′, in the sixth house. The nature of the illness, and the extreme danger, are well indicated in these configurations. In this case there was no affliction at the crisis (lunar), and recovery took place. In Dr. Hewett's case, when the Sun arrived at the square of his own place—*i.e.*, in ♌ 25° 21′—August 18th, 1865, the Moon was in the place of Mars and in square to Saturn; and when Saturn arrived at the square (♎ 29° 30′) of the Moon's place, Dr. H. died. Unfortunately, in neither of these cases could the nativity be procured.

On the 10th of March, 1884, a lady was seized with alarming haemorrhage. Mars was then *stationary* in ♌ 2° 30′ in square aspect with the place of the Sun at her birth—*viz.*, ♉ 2° 59′. On the following day, at 4h p.m., the hasmorrhage returned, when the Sun was in the place of Saturn at her birth—*viz.*, ♓ 21° 6′, and the Moon was in opposition thereto. From day to day the haemorrhage continued, at times passive, and at others active, until by the 21st of March, when it came on again violently, the patient became very greatly anemiated and very feeble. After the new Moon of the 26th of March, when the luminaries were very near the place of Venus at birth (♈ 8° 50′), recovery became rapid, to the surprise of the doctor in attendance, who had very faint hope of a favourable issue. In this case the time of birth is known, approximately—*viz.*, very near 1h a.m. of April 23rd, 1848. The direction of ☉ par. ♂ m.d., was then operating in the nativity.

Cases of severe haemorrhage afford good tests of the value of astrology as an aid to medicine, for the first seizure is usually very sudden and alarming. In cases of fever, etc., the first onset of the disease is seldom sharply marked.

[4] The conjunction of the luminaries happened at 2h 12m a.m. of July 8th, it being an annular eclipse of the Sun, invisible in England.

CHAPTER IV.

THERAPEUTICS AND ASTROLOGY.

> "Science which instructs, and physic which cures us, are excellent, certainly; but science which misleads, and physic which destroys, are equally execrable; teach us how to distinguish them."—ROUSSEAU.

ASTRONOMERS tell us that the science of astronomy instructs, and that astrology misleads.

Physicians say that the art of medicine, as taught by the professors, instructs; and that the astrological art of Hippocrates, Galen, and Cardan misleads.

In this manner we are taught to distinguish true from false science.

But when we remember that astronomers and physicians have no real knowledge of astrology, that they "will not inquire"—to use Mr. R. A. Proctor's expression—what truth there may be in it, their opinion becomes valueless; and when we find, as we have already presented in these pages, evidence of truth in astrology, we cannot but think that they themselves mislead.

Even State astronomers and State physicians cannot be allowed to decide by authority alone a question, of deep and great importance, with which they are totally unacquainted. If they will not inquire what there is of truth in astrology, they cannot deter men of independent mind from examining, exploring, and demonstrating it. Willing observers and workers are wanted, and to facilitate their work, the author has laboured, and here presented to his readers the results of a long period of study and of much thought on his part.

It is well known that State appointments, and frequently even membership of learned societies, tend to discourage individual effort and independent action, and likewise to warp the judgment.

Let us not be misunderstood. We have no desire to disparage either the learned professors of astronomy or learned physicians. Quite the contrary. We have the deepest respect for great astronomers, learned physicians, and distinguished surgeons. But this cannot preclude the privilege of promulgating what we have reason to believe to be *truth*; nor prevent due weight being given to the matured, reasonable, and favourable opinion of astrology avowed by such giants in intellect as Pythagoras and Kepler, by Hippocrates, Galen, and Bacon. As Sir George Birdwood, M.D., of the India Office, has said: "Pharmacy literally means 'enchantment'; and Therapeutics 'the worship of the gods,' or cure by faith in the divinities of certain plants. Now that we have distilled off these plants as essences, and precipitated them as alkaloids, and can weigh them with the nicest exactitude, we despise the prayer of faith, and even prosecute those who put their trust in it." The *Medical Press and Circular* of June 4th, 11th and 18th, 1890, printed three articles by the author on Medical Astrology.

Bacon gave as a reason why medicine had not progressed in his day, and kept pace with the sciences, that: "Physicians have reasoned in a circle and not in a line."

The state of therapeutics at the present day is not encouraging. In fact, as Dr. Sharp says, the orthodox system of medicine is still without any law, and is in a condition like that of navigation before the discovery of the mariner's compass. Many physicians of the old school distrust authority, and, rejecting hypotheses of all kinds, rely upon experience. Dr. Stokes once said in the Medical Council of Great Britain: "There can be no doubt that medicine requires to be placed upon a much more scientific basis than it at present possesses. It is now simply empiricism; and that empiricism is only tolerable and useful because it is wielded by thoughtful men."

Liebig said: "Truly one is tempted to adopt the opinion, that among the sciences which have for their object a knowledge of nature and her forces, medicine as an inductive science occupies the lowest place."[1]

Hippocrates advocated *antipathy*—the curing of disease by a contrary agent—now expressed by *contraria contrariis curantur*; yet he observed that diseases were sometimes cured by *similars*. Galen taught that diseases are to be cured by their contraries, and this doctrine was handed down for many centuries. Paracelsus was the first to suggest the therapeutic principle (afterwards demonstrated by Hahnemann), to give those drugs for the cure of disease which in health are capable of producing a train of symptoms *similar* to those of the malady. Hippocrates gave up in despair the difficult search for the curative action of medicines; had he pursued the course followed by Hahnemann, *viz*., the proving of the action of medicines on the

[1] "Chemical Letters." By Baron Liebig. 3rd edit., p 77.

healthy, he would probably have come to the same conclusion—that the law of *similars* is the *true* law of therapeutics.

The success achieved by Hippocrates, Galen, and Paracelsus in the treatment of disease is explained by the fact that they administered medicines on astrological principles.

The astrological selection of remedies was based chiefly on *antipathy* and *sympathy*. For example: Diseases under the dominion of the SUN were treated with *Saturnine* remedies; diseases under JUPITER by *Mercurial* medicaments—this was by *antipathy*. Diseases under SATURN were treated with *Martial* drugs—this was by *sympathy*. Again, every planet was believed to be capable, to a great extent, of curing its own diseases by means of its medicaments; thus, the Sun and Moon by their remedies cured diseases of the eyes, Saturn the spleen, Jupiter the liver, and so on.

This may seem very absurd to physicians who are unacquainted with astrology, but we may ask such: Can you explain the *modus operandi* of drugs? Dr. Sharp, one of the wisest physicians of the new school, says:

"In respect to the manner of action of drugs we are in total darkness, and we are so blind that the darkness is not felt. Knowledge of this kind cannot be attained; it is labour lost and time wasted to go in search of it. True, hypotheses may be easily conceived; so may straws be gathered from the surface of the stream. But what are either of them worth? There is this difference between them: straws may amuse children, hypotheses are sure to mislead physicians."[2]

Dr. Sharp observes that: "As diseases have a local habitation, so drugs have a local action: drugs to be remedies must operate on the same organs as the disease affects."

This is in perfect harmony with the teachings of astrology. For instance : The Sun and Moon rule the eyes, affliction of the Sun and Moon at birth by the malefic planets gives rise to diseases of the eyes, and certain drugs under the rule of the Sun and Moon are found effectual in the cure of diseases of the eyes. The affinity of certain drugs for certain organs of the human body is thus accounted for.

Among the remedies classed as Jovial we find stannum, and in homoeopathic practice it is proved to be a very valuable remedy for certain affections of the lungs, which organs are under the rule of Jupiter. Among the remedies under the rule of Mars we find arsenic, and this

[2] "Essays on Medicine." By William Sharp, M.D , F.R.S. Essay xxv.

remedy is found very useful by homoeopathists in renal dropsy, and the kidneys are under the rule of Mars. Again, among the medicines termed Saturnine we find aconite, and this is the sheet anchor of homoeopathists for acute inflammations of a martial character; Saturn being friendly with Mars, this is curing by sympathy. Many similar instances could be cited of this verisimilitude in the selection of remedies. Those we have given show that in the absence of a definite and reliable *law* of therapeutics, the ancients did well to rely on the astrologic method, and it is on record that they were very successful in curing diseases. So far from being "wholly destitute of proofs" the starry method is thus shown to have been, in the hands of learned physicians, of incomparable value in ancient and mediaeval times. By rejecting it, the dominant school lost its guiding star, and descended to mere empiricism.

For *sunstroke*, belladonna, a Saturnine plant, is a valuable remedy. For contusions (which are Saturnine), arnica (a Martial plant) is an invaluable remedy. When contusions result in injury to the periosteum, ruta (a Solar remedy) is valuable; when to glandular parts, conium (a Saturnine remedy) is very useful. When fractured bones seem disinclined to unite, symphytum (a Saturnine remedy) is highly commended.

No practitioner of homoeopathy can read "Culpeper's Herbal" without being struck with the remedies therein recommended, for they are in many instances the same as those found most useful by homoeopathists for the same diseases as Culpeper found them to be—the starry method of selection indicating the same remedies as the homoeopathic.

Dr. Sharp, in writing of the local action of drugs presents a table[3] in which we find, under the head of "Brain," the following drugs: Belladonna, opium, hellebore, hyoscyamus, and cannabis. Now, *all* these medicines are ruled by Saturn, and we have seen that the ancients applied Saturnine remedies to diseases of the organs ruled by the Sun, the brain being one of those organs, and this was termed by them curing by antipathy.

The local action of iron—which is under Mars—is on the blood; its kind of action is to increase the *red* corpuscles. Mars-men are notoriously sanguine and full-blooded, and generally florid in complexion. The *Lancet* once remarked on the singular fact that engineers have, comparatively, an excessive amount of iron in their blood, and attrib-

[3] Op. cit., p. 687.

uted this to their absorption of fine particles of iron in the exercise of their calling; the medical writer being, of course, unaware that those who naturally take to engineering are Mars-men, and have, therefore, from birth a large amount of iron, and of red corpuscles, in their blood. If the engineers, as a body, were alone distinguished for the redundancy of iron in their blood, it might be attributable solely to their absorption of iron in their occupation, as the Lancet surmised; but the same observation holds good with regard to the great majority of surgeons and soldiers, who are martialists and distinguished alike for their energy, pluck, and endurance.

The majority of *tonic* medicines are under the rule of Mars—"the star of strength"—such as iron, arsenic, cinchona, and lupulus. The narcotics are under the rule of Saturn.

In regard to *temperaments*: According to Teste,[4] arnica, arsenic, bryonia alba, and nux vomica, act best on persons of "sanguine temperament, robust, and irritable"; this is just what an astrologer would expect, for these are *Martial* remedies and, consequently, are best adapted to persons of *Martial* temperament. On the other hand, aconite, belladonna, and veratrum album act particularly well, according to Teste, on "nervous and melancholy" persons; this is explained by the fact that these are *Saturnine* remedies, and, therefore most suitable to *Saturnine* persons. Again, pulsatilla (anemone pratensis) is found to be most suitable "to persons who by the relative predominance of the adipose tissue in their constitution, by the whiteness of their flesh, the roundness of their forms, the mildness of their disposition, and their fitful mood, exhibit all the marked characteristics of the fair sex"; such are of the Venus type, consequently, pulsatilla being ruled by Venus, its particular suitableness to the ailments of such (Venus) persons is accounted for in a manner of which the learned French doctor did not dream.

When due consideration is paid to the temperament of the patient, the most suitable remedy for the disease is easily discovered; and the singular corroboration to be found in the fact that the careful observations of Teste lead to the same results—although arrived at by a totally different process—as the astrology of the ancients (the Martial remedies suiting the Martial temperament, the Saturnine remedies the Saturnine temperament, etc.), leads the unprejudiced, truth-seeking

[4] "The Materia Medica, arranged systematically and practically." By A. Teste, Graduate of the University of Paris. Translated from the French by C. Hempel, M.D. New York: Radde; 1854.

mind to the inevitable conclusion that the starry method of selection of remedies is true, being based on natural affinity and natural law.

Teste observed that it is almost always in the regions where maladies originate that Providence seems to have created the means for their removal.

The ancients recognised the fact that every temperament has its appropriate remedies for the diseases to which it is particularly liable, and it was their astrological knowledge that led to this discovery. Teste has confirmed this by experiment. Thus do we find that the correlation of therapeutics and astrology is a law of nature.

There are still two schools of therapeutics—the old and the new. The old or dominant school comprises physicians who rely either on experience or on the maxim *contraria contrariis curantur*. The new or homoeopathic school consists of physicians who follow what they believe to be the true law of therapeutics—*similia similibus curantur.* The practitioners of both schools are highly educated and legally qualified gentlemen. Hitherto, the few eminent men of the old school who announced their conversion to the belief in the law of similars met with so much abuse and ridicule from their professional brethren, that others have been deterred from testing the value of Hahnemann's law—the case of Professor Henderson and that of Dr. Conquest are examples of this. Homoeopathy has done incalculable good by teaching people to revolt against the old-fashioned heroic practices of bleeding and violent purging. Until the opposing schools sink their differences, the reproach of Moliére will not lose its point: "Call in the doctor, and if you do not like his physic, I will soon find you another to condemn it.''

As Dr. John H. Glarke writes:

"Hahnemann's arrangement of his *Materia Medica Pura*, like most of his practical deductions, is the truly scientific one. The whole life and soul of Homoeopathy resides in it. The Spirit of Homoeopathy is the Spirit of Liberty. The beauty, the grandeur, the glory of homoeopathy is its freedom. . . . It is Hahnemann who first showed us how to study our patients as well as how to study our drugs. . . . Homoeopathy is destined to spiritualise, to civilise medical practice. The medical practice of the old school is *in extremis*; and medicine's extremity is surgery's opportunity. Surgery has reached a degree of perfection which can hardly be bettered; and the ready recourse to surgery in modern times is an irrefutable evidence of the failure of medicine. . . . Yet there are some homoeopaths who are so much under the denomination of established orthodoxy that they think it a slight on the profession to let the public know that homoeopathy is more successful in curing the sick than orthodox medicine."[5]

[5] "The Homoeopathic World," Oct., 1911, pp. 450-456. 12, Warwick Lane, London, E.C.

CHAPTER V.

MEDICINES AND PLANETARY INFLUENCE.

> "God hath created medicines out of the earth; and he that is wise will not abhor them."—ECCLESIASTICUS, XXXVIII. 4.

In the preceding chapter mention has been made of several medicines under the rule of certain planets. A complete list of the minerals and herbs ruled by each planet is now presented. In the first place, it is deemed advisable to give a list of those medicines in ordinary use, under their Latin names, in order that they may be readily found:

The SUN governs aurum, calendula, chamomilla, chelidonium majus, crocus, drosera rotundifolia, euphrasia, helianthus, hypericum, ruta.

The MOON rules argentum, colocynthis, iris versicolor, mercurialis perennis.

MERCURY influences agaricus, dulcamara, filixmas, laurocerasus ledum palustre, mercurius, valerian, petroselinum.

VENUS rules argentum, cuprum, digitalis, millefolium, narcissus, pulsatilla, viola odorata, zincum.

MARS governs aloes, arum, arnica, arsenicum, asafoetida, bryonia, capsicum, cina, cinnabar, cinchona, ferrum, gentian, lactuca virosa, lobelia inflata, lupulus, nux vomica, pinus, sylvestris, sabina, sarsaparilla, squilla, sulphur, urtica urens, xanthoxylum.

JUPITER rules argentum, asclepias, eupatorium, gelsemium, stramonium, stannum, symphytum, taraxacum, tilia.

SATURN rules antimonium, aconitum, agnus castus, belladonna, cannabis sativa, colchicum, conium, daphne mezereum, graphites, helleborus niger, hyoscyamus, plumbum, rhus toxicodendron, sabadilla, veratrum, verbascum.

The various herbs, etc. (with their English names), under the rule of each planet are thus stated:

The SUN rules angelica, the ash, the bay tree, burnet, butterbur, camomile, celandine, small centaury, eye-bright juniper-bush, lovage, marigold, pimpernel, rosemary, sundew, rue, saffron, St. John's wort, St. Peter's wort, tormentil, turnsole, heart-trefoil, vine, viper's buglas, and the walnut tree.

The MOON governs adder's-tongue, arrack, brankursine, colewort, water caltrop, chickweed, clary, cleavers, coralwort, water cress, cucumber, duckmeat, fleur-de-luce or water flag, fluettin, cuckoo-flower, lettuce, water-lily, white lily, loosestrife, moonwort, mouse-ear, orsine, pellitory of Spain, rattle-grass, saxifrage, stonecrop, pearl-trefoil, wallflower, and the willow tree.

MERCURY rules the bitter-sweet, calamint, wild carrot, carraway, dill, elacampane, fern, fennel, germander, hazelnut, horehound, houndstongue, lavender, lily of the valley, liquorice, walrue or white maiden-hair, golden maiden-hair, marjoram, mulberry tree, nailwort, oats, parsley, parsnip, pellitory of the wall, sauce-alone, savory, scabius, smallage, southernwood, honeysuckle, and valerian.

VENUS governs alkanet, alehoof or ground ivy, artichoke, black or common alder tree, wild arrack, archangel bean, bishop's weed, bramble, blites, bugle, burdock, cherry tree, earth chestnuts, chickpease, columbine, coltsfoot, cudweed, cowslip, crab's claw, crosswort, daisy, devil's bit, eringo, feather-few, figwort, dropwort, foxglove, golden-rod, gromel, gooseberry bush, groundsel, herbrobert, true-love, kidneywort, ladies'mantle, marshmallow, French mercury, dog-mercury, mint, moneywort, motherwort, mugwort, nep or catmint, orchis, parsley piert, parsnip, peach tree, pennyroyal, pear tree, periwinkle, plantain, plum tree, poppy, purslane, primrose, privet, queen of the meadows, ragwort, rye, woodsage, sanicle self-heal, sopewort, sorrel, sow-thistle, spignel, strawberry, tansey, teasel, vervain, wheat, and yarrow.

MARS influences all-heal, barberry, bazil, briony, benedictus, cardines, crowfoot, dovesfoot, flax-weed, furze-bush, garlic, gentian, hawthorn, hedge-hyssop, hop, madder, master-wort, nettle, onion, pepperwort, ground pine, horse radish, rhubarb, savine, star-thistle, tobacco, and wormwood.

JUPITER rules agrimony, Alexander, asparagus, balm, white beet, bilberry, borage, chervil, chesnut-tree, cinque-foil, costmary, dandelion, dock, dog's grass, endive, fig-tree, clove, gilliflowers, heart's-tongue, hyssop, house-leek, liverwort, lung-wort, maple-tree, mellilot, oak-tree, roses, sage, samphire, scurvy-grass, and lady's thistle.

SATURN rules amaranthus, barley, corn, red-beet, beech-tree, bifoil, birdsfoot, blue-bottle, buck's horn plantain, comfrey, sciatica-cress, darmel, dodder, elm-tree, wafer-fern, fleawort, flux weed, fumitory, gladurn, goutwort, winter green, heart's-ease, hawkweed, hemlock, hemp, henbane, black hellebore, horsetail, holly, ivy, knapweed, knotgrass, medlar-tree, mosses, mullein, nightshade, polypody of the oak, poplar-tree, quince-tree, service-tree, shepherd's purse, spleen-wort, tamarisk-tree, melancholy-thistle, black thorn, thorough wax, tulsan, woad, Solomon's seal, Saracen's consound, willow tree, and the yew tree.

The foregoing classification may appear arbitrary, at first sight, but it is not entirely so. It is well known that certain plants turn towards the Moon, and increase and decrease as she waxes and wanes. Certain flowers open as the Sun rises and close as he sets. The plants ruled by Mars grow, mostly, in dry, hard or stony places. Teste lays stress, on the fact that plants transplanted to soils foreign to their nature "lose either totally or partially the medicinal properties of which we know they are possessed."

Ancient and mediseval astrologers laid stress on the importance of gathering herbs, for medicinal purposes, in the hour presided over by their ruling planet. More rational are Coley's instructions as to gathering the required herb "when the planet ruling it is ascending or culminating, and when the Moon is in either sextile or trine aspect with it." Also, "let the herb be taken in its prime, full of juice and green, and from such a place as it thrives in."

The sensitive indications of many plants in regard to changes of weather are well known to naturalists. The common chickweed flowers "are upright, and open from 9 in the morning until noon; but if it rains, they remain closed, after rain they become pendant." The purple sandwort's flowers expand only when the Sun shines and close as evening comes on, or before an approaching shower. The pimpernel (the poor man's weather-glass) closes its tiny flowers long before rain falls and before night draws in. The goat's beard will not open its petals in cloudy weather. The dandelion is a true sun-dial, "closing at 5 in the afternoon and opening again at 7 in the morning." If the trefoil contract its leaves, thunder and heavy rain may be expected. The sensitive plants (Mimosa tribe) give evidence of this in a remarkable degree.

Bearing in mind these facts and the various properties of plants and minerals, it cannot fairly be termed superstitious to believe that there is a correlation between the heavenly bodies and medicaments. Observation has shown that certain countries are influenced by certain planets and certain signs of the zodiac; and seeing that certain plants are only found in certain places—and that if plants be transplanted to soil foreign to their nature, they lose their curative virtues—it is reasonable to conclude that the planet which influences such places may influence the plants flourishing therein. Plants whose habitat is in Martial places are influenced by Mars, and experience proves that Martial plants act on the organs of the body ruled by Mars. Hence arose the classification of plants astrologically. Dr. Sharp says:[1]

"It would obviously be unreasonable to ask a botanist to arrange his plants according to their action, nutritive or poisonous, upon animals, which it does not come within his province to observe. To me it appears equally unreasonable for the physician to adopt the method of the botanist, and arrange his drugs according to those characters only which are open to the botanist to observe.

"It may be safely considered that there is no observed connection between either the external form of plants or the internal structure of the organs or their functions, and their action as drugs. Neither the outward appearance, nor the structure of any part, nor its function, nor the mechanical power, nor the chemical composition of vegetables, throw any light upon their therapeutic action."

As the ancient physicians could not judge of the therapeutic action of plants by either of the methods mentioned by Dr. Sharp, it follows that they discovered what they knew of it by astrology, as Hippocrates and Galen averred they did. This should command respect for the starry method.

Pereira said: "It cannot be doubted that had we a more intimate acquaintance with, and precise knowledge of the action of remedies, the therapeutic properties of medicines would no longer appear incomprehensible and mysterious."

This desirable knowledge of the physiological action of drugs can only be attained by (1) considering the planetary order of each drug, and (2) by following Hahnemann's method of proving its action on the healthy. This will also serve to determine antidotes to poisons. Dr. Ackland, in 1865, urged the General Medical Council to prove the action of drugs on the healthy, but his advice was rejected.

Dr. Frazer once wrote:

"An eminent authority in pharmacology has recently published the

[1] "Essays on Medicine." Essay xix.

statement that the only method whereby the injurious action of a poison, absorbed into the blood, can be made to terminate is by the employment of such means as will cause or hasten the elimination of the poison. This statement, fortunately, does not accurately describe our remedial resources. The existence of so undoubted an example of physiological antagonism as that between atropia and physostigma shows that the toxic influence of a morbific agent *may be directly opposed by a physiological antidote*; and that recovery may be produced by influencing the abnormal conditions themselves, in such a manner as to cause their return to a normal state."[2]

Bacon said: "In all our investigations of nature we must observe what quantity or dose of the body is requisite for a given effect; and must guard ourselves from estimating it at too much or too little."

---

[2] See "Report of the British Association for the Advancement of Science," 1872.

CHAPTER VI.

ON THE PRESERVATION OF HEALTH.

Sanitas, sanitas, omnia sanitas."—BEACONSFIELD.

THE noble vocation of the physician is never better exercised than in concerting measures for the preservation of health and prevention of disease.

The ancient physicians and astrologers recognised this duty, and they laid down a proper mode of living and regimen which was, as Hufeland testifies, much better than prescribing purgatives and emetics.

Down to a very recent period, the insanitary state of London and the great towns of the United Kingdom was deplorable. When in 1849 the Cholera visited London, great exertions were made and still greater promises; the metropolis was to be drained afresh, the outfall of sewage was no longer to be beneath the windows, the river was to be embanked, etc.; but in 1851, none of these works had been commenced.[1] What wonder could there be that Cholera, small-pox, typhoid fever, and other epidemics, in turn, committed great ravages when once they broke out? With the improvements effected in recent years, epidemics have declined.

Of late years works on hygiene and sanitation have been published. Sanitary associations have done much good, but much remains yet to be done.

There is an important lesson requiring constant reiteration, namely, that healthy persons should never take physic—except for scientific experiment. A celebrated British Ambassador on being asked why he was accompanied by his physician when abroad, replied: "So that I may *not* take physic."

Physicians, probably, would prescribe much smaller doses of med-

[1] See Mr. Simon's "Annual Report on the Sanitary State of the City of London," 1851.

icine, and in some cases none at all, were they not afraid that their patients would desert them and run to the nearest druggist to purchase physic. It is to be feared that people will not soon learn to look upon drugs as often a cause of disease. Bleeding has gone out of fashion, but not so physicking. At one time, abbeys had a bleeding house wherein the religious inmates were periodically bled to the strains of Psalmody.

Physicking and vaccination must one day go out of fashion just as bleeding and inoculation have gone. With proper sanitation and isolation, there need be no fear of epidemics becoming devastating plagues. In Spain, inoculation of cholera-virus is being practised as a preservative against Cholera! Doctors seem to forget that there are some people so naturally healthy and robust that they are insusceptible to disease. If vaccination (small-pox-virus passed through the cow) and inoculation of cholera-virus must be submitted to every time an epidemic of smallpox or of cholera threatens, there will soon be no absolutely healthy people left.

Dr. John H. Clarke, in his letter printed in the *Daily Mail*, May 18th, 1910, on the vaccine treatment of King Edward VII., wisely wrote:

"The interesting article by your medical correspondent on the vaccine treatment in connection with King Edward's illness deserves a word of comment. The writer describes the vaccine treatment (or the opsonic treatment as it is sometimes called) as the most modern method of combating disease. He says that originally it was thought that a vaccine of this sort, to give the best results, had to be injected under the skin. Work recently done by Dr. Latham and Dr. Spitta at St. George's Hospital, however, has proved that equally good results can be obtained when the vaccine is taken by mouth on an empty stomach. Without wishing to deprive the doctors of Mt. George's Hospital of their claim to originality, I should like to point out that homoeopathists have adopted this method of administering disease-viruses any time these last hundred years. The method of treating patients suffering from a disease by giving the modified virus of the disease itself is essentially *homoeopathic*—*i.e.*, curing like with like—as Professor von Behring, among others, has admitted, and as the man in the street can plainly see, if the votaries of established medicine cannot. If the latter, when they appropriate bits of homoeopathic practice would only adopt the dosage prescribed by the experience of homoeopaths, they would do their patients much more good, and run very much less risk of doing them harm."

Dr. Forster observed that:[2]

"History incontestably proves that not only in less virulent epidemics, but even in the more violent plagues, when the epidemic constitution of the air has been at its acme, certain persons have totally escaped its attacks; and these have been the temperate and regular, who have that sort of secure and tranquil health in store which is called stamina, from its being capable of bearing up against the incursions of disease."

Again, health is injured by errors in diet, and by innutritious food. Children suffer in London and many large towns through the innutritions bread supplied by most of the bakers. Home-made, or whole-meal bread, is the best for everybody.[3] Intemperance in eating and drinking, excessive flesh diet, neglect of out-door exercise, and uncleanliness, together, will soon undermine the soundest constitution. As Dr. Forster says: "Many are willing to be relieved when they are ill, who will not take the trouble to preserve health." Abernethy used to recommend not drinking at all with meals, and he called hunger and thirst incompatible sensations. Without going quite so far as this, it may be asserted that most people drink too much (whether tea, coffee, or alcoholic beverages) with and between meals. Adults who are free from rheumatism and gout may drink a small quantity of good draught beer (made from malt and hops) with dinner; the *diastase* promotes digestion. Mineral waters should never be drunk, except under medical advice. When the digestion is out of order, a wine-glass full of *natural* (German) seltzer water will prove beneficial; and this is better than taking pills. Children have, usually, too much animal food given them; one such meal per diem is quite sufficient for them and for adults who do not take a great deal of exercise. "Coffee," said Hahnemann, "is the substance which, next to mercury and chagrin, contributes most towards spoiling the teeth." The bad quality of bakers' bread is often a cause of bad teeth among children. Persons born when the planet Saturn is rising, have very indifferent teeth; and they are liable to chagrin, and to weak health. On the other hand, persons born when Jupiter is rising have good teeth, a cheerful disposition and generally good health.

When we consider how easily the "silver cord is broken," and what a subtle and incomprehensible thing is LIFE, we must be impressed

[2] "Illustrations of the Atmospherical Origin of Epidemic Diseases," p. 192.

[3] This was written in the year 1889. The cry for Standard Bread arose in 1911. Hovis bread is the best for assimilation and health.

with the importance of attention to health. Fullom said:[4]

"Philosophers have in vain endeavoured to ascertain, by experiments and researches of every kind, what is that mysterious principle of life which so universally prevails, and, after a time of uncertain duration, is infallibly and unreservedly extinguished. So impenetrable and occult is the question that it has hitherto been found impossible to trace out even the distinctions and modifications of *life*, so as to fix the line of demarcation that divides the animal from the vegetable world. Divisions have, indeed, been made, but they are at once arbitrary and unwarrantable."

Frequent change of air is necessary to some persons—especially the mercurial—to maintain health. It matters not whether we call *life* "vitality," "vital principle," or "vital force"; "irritability," "irritable matter," or "germinal matter"; we can only preserve it by attention to health. We cannot preserve health and life by chemical imitations or concentrations of good food; neither can we restore health when lost by lowering the *vis medicatrix naturae* with large doses of physic.

Persons of sanguine temperament benefit by occasional fasts. Before the institution of the Lenten fast, the ancients abstained from animal food and ate fish largely while the Sun was in the sign *Pisces*; when the Sun entered *Aries*, lamb was eaten and the fast came to an end. On the *sixth* day—the day of Venus—of the week, fish was eaten, and animal food was abstained from because Venus has dignity in the sign *Pisces*.

When epidemic diseases threaten, it is imperatively necessary to avoid over fatigue of mind and body, chills, and errors in diet. If, despite these precautions, debility be felt, Hahnemann recommends a few drops of the tincture of cinchona in a small quantity of wine. The moderate smoking of tobacco, if it does not debilitate the smoker, is a good preservative against infection.

Amulets were worn, in ancient times, as preservatives against infection. Although this practice was, to a certain extent, superstitious, it was based originally on the medicinal properties of certain metals. Workers in copper mines have escaped Cholera when their neighbours died of it.[5] Copper is worn by the Hindoos as a charm against Cholera. In Hungary, the wearing of a copper plate next to the skin has been found preservative against the same disease. Copper filings

---

4 "Marvels of Science," p. 252.

5 See the *Zoist*, July, 1853 ; art. on Cholera by Dr. Burq, translated by Dr. Elliotson.

taken in health to excess have produced symptoms very *similar* to Cholera. A remarkable fact, during the epidemics of 1849 and 1853 was observed at Paris, viz., that steel springs broke and could not be made to perfection during the violence of the epidemic. The practice of wearing coral necklaces was due to coral being considered a charm against whooping cough; and *corallium rubrum* is found useful in the cure thereof.

BOOK 5.

ELECTIONS.

CHAPTER I.

INTRODUCTION.

> "To everything there is a season, and a time to every purpose under the heavens."—SOLOMON.

DRYDEN, the poet, recognised the truth of astrology and the advisability of electing propitious moments for the commencement of new and important works; he wrote:

> "Fortune at some hours to all is kind;
> The lucky have whole days, which still they choose;
> The unlucky have but hours, and those they lose."

To make the election of real service, the nativity must be studied. In affairs of partnership, the nativity of each partner must be compared; otherwise, no safe election can be made. The figure for the revolution of the year, *i.e.*, the Sun's ingress into *Aries*, must also be compared, if the business be of a public *company*. Thus, when the same sign ascends at the vernal equinox as at birth, with the planetary ruler of that sign well situated, or Jupiter in the ascendant, the affair will be likely to succeed well if commenced when the same sign shall ascend and the ruling planet be well placed. "Directions" and transits will, also, need to be studied before the election be made. It is never advisable to begin any new business when the Moon is afflicted, however good other testimonies may be. *Zadkiel's Almanac* gives the days on which the Moon forms benefic aspects with the Sun and planets, under the head of "Lunar Influences." If the business require to be quickly brought about it should be commenced, if possible, when the Moon is quick in motion, and increasing in light. The Moon should not be in a cadent house at the commencement of any business.

The planet ruling the business should be free from the rays of the infortunes, and, if possible, in its chief dignity; or in either the midheaven or ascendant, according to circumstances. No evil planet should be in either of the angles, nor in the "house" ruling the business, unless it (Mars or Saturn) happen to be the planet influencing the affair. It is advisable to place the Sun and Moon, if possible, in trine with the place of the Sun in the nativity.

These precepts may be considered ridiculous and unnecessary by persons who are unacquainted with astrology; but there can be no harm in observing them. We should prefer observing them, when possible, to running the risk of failure by beginning an important transaction at an unfortunate moment. Apart from astrology it is difficult to understand why some businesses fail notwithstanding that capital, energy, and industry have been brought into them; or why one ship, whose keel was laid at one hour proves a fortunate investment, while another, whose keel was laid at another hour, proves a most unlucky one. Some transactions seem doomed to failure from their inception, and even the enemies of astrology speak of such as "ill-starred" affairs, although unaware of the meaning of this expression.

At page 18 of this work, Flamstead's election-figure for the laying of the foundation stone of Greenwich Observatory is given; the great success attending the Royal Observatory and its freedom from misfortune make for astrology. Possibly, had Flamstead not understood and believed in the science, an unlucky moment might have been chosen. Many proud buildings have been destroyed very soon after their completion, the founders of such being of course too "really scientific" to give heed to astrological precepts.

The Moon, on account of her proximity to the earth, her reflection of the Solar light, and the swiftness of her motion, is considered to be the most powerful significator in astrology.

It is, therefore, of the utmost importance that the Moon be free from affliction and in close aspect with either one of the fortunes, or the Sun, or the planet ruling the business in hand, when election of an opportune moment for the commencement of such business is desired.

In many cases, there is not time either to elect the best possible moment for commencement of a new undertaking, or even to wait for such a favourable moment if determined upon. Many persons have not a sufficient knowledge of astrology to enable them to elect a suitable moment and to accurately cast the figure of the heavens. In such cases as these, the most that can be done is to see that the Moon's aspects are of the right kind; or to consult Zadkiel. It must be borne in mind that the *parallel declination* acts like the *conjunction* and that the ☌, p.d., and △ are the most powerful aspects for good, the sextile being much weaker; the opposition is the most powerful evil aspect.

As to the signs of the zodiac, the ancients said that it is best to have the Moon in an *earthy* sign (♉, ♍, or ♑), when sowing or planting; or repairing buildings; in *Cancer* for travelling by sea; in *Sagittarius* for buying horses and cattle.

In commencing any work or business which it is desired to be durable, either the Moon should be in a *fixed* sign (♉, ♌, ♏, or ♒), or a fixed sign should ascend.

In any case, the moon should be more than 12° distant in longitude from the Sun, or the business will be hindered.

Uranus and Neptune, being unknown to the ancients, had no influences assigned to them. Observation has shown that Uranus influences pecuniary affairs to some extent, inventions, and all extraordinary occurrences. It is not advisable to begin any business of great importance when the Moon is in conjunction, square, opposition, or parallel declination with Uranus; neither to marry under such aspects. Neptune's influence is more evil than good, and seems to bring crises rather than to affect the ordinary daily business of life. It is better not to begin any affair of importance when the Sun or Moon happens to be in conjunction, quartile, or opposition with Neptune.

CHAPTER II.

ELECTIONS FOR AFFAIRS APPERTAINING TO THE FIRST SIX HOUSES.

"A time to plant, and a time to pluck up that which is planted; a time to kill, and a time to heal."—SOLOMON.

THE FIRST HOUSE or MANSION of the HEAVENS relates to health, and affairs generally. It is, therefore, most important to have the ascendant free from the presence of the infortunes at the commencement of any new work, business, or journey.

In the sailing of ships, the ascendant and the Moon should be free from affliction. If an evil planet be in the ascendant at the moment of a ship leaving port, it is likely to be fortunate; if Saturn be ascending, the ship will be very likely to run aground; if Mars be ascending, there will be danger of fire or of shipwreck. If Uranus and Mars be ascending, explosion may take place. If the ship be a trading one, Jupiter or Venus should be either in the midheaven, ascendant, second or ninth house.

ELECTIONS APPERTAINING TO THE SECOND HOUSE.

THE SECOND HOUSE OF THE HEAVENS relates to the receiving, lending, and borrowing of money; to buying and selling; and to removing from one place to another. The following are the precepts of the ancients:

1. *Buying for Profit.* Fortify the Moon especially, also Mercury, and the lord of the second house; and, if possible, the lord of the ascendant; let the Moon be either in conjunction or benefic aspect with Mercury free from impediment. Particularly avoid buying when the Moon and Mercury are afflicted by Mars. If possible, let Mercury be in conjunction or benefic aspect with either Venus or Jupiter.

2. *Selling to Advantage.* Let the Moon be in either *Taurus*, *Cancer*, *Virgo*, or *Pisces*, free from affliction, and separating from conjunction or benefic aspect with Jupiter or Venus.

3. *Removing from Place to Place.* If you desire to gain pecuniarily by removal, and the house to which you would remove be your own, let the Moon be in a fixed sign, and a fixed sign ascending; but if the house be hired, let the ascendant be a common sign and the Moon in a common sign. If possible, have ♃ or ♀ in the tenth or first, or fourth angle.

In any case, fortify the Moon and the lords of the ascendant, second and fourth houses; and let Jupiter be in the second house, if possible. Either *Taurus* or *Leo* should be on the cusp of the fourth house, if it can be so arranged; never *Scorpio*.

ELECTIONS RELATING TO THE THIRD HOUSE.

THE THIRD HOUSE relates to short journeys, *i.e.* to such as can be completed within twenty-four hours and within one's native country.

The following is the ancient precept relating thereto:

Short Journeys. Fortify the ascendant, the third house, and the Moon. Start not on thy journey at the moment at which an evil planet ascends or is on the cusp of the third house, and when the Moon is afflicted. If possible, begin the journey when ♃ or ♀ ascends or occupies the third house or ascendant.

Persons who are constantly travelling would, of course, find it impossible to follow this precept always. I recommend the following injunction as of far greater importance: Avoid setting out on a journey, if possible, at or very near the time when the Moon (near the new or full) is in transit over the place of a malefic planet in the *nativity*, and at the same time afflicted; especially if such transit happen near the birthday anniversary.

ELECTIONS RELATING TO THE FOURTH HOUSE.

THE FOURTH HOUSE relates to building houses, etc., buying or renting land or houses, planting trees and sowing seed. The ancients hand down the following rules:

1. *Building Houses, etc.* Endeavour at the beginning of thy work to fortify the ascendant, the lord thereof, the Moon and her dispositor, and the planet to which she is joined either by conjunction or aspect; fortify also the fourth house and its lord, and the tenth house and its lord. Be sure that the significators be not under the earth, for that causeth slow progress, and it may never be brought to perfection. Fortify also Mercury and its dispositor. Let not any of the significators behold Mars. Let the Moon be increasing in light and motion and

configurated with Jupiter, and have a special care that the Moon be not with Saturn or her south node; and that Saturn be not in the fourth house or ascendant, for this would delay the work, or cause vexation, trouble, or early decay. If Mars afflict the significators or be in the fourth house, or ascendant, there will be danger of fire.

Should the building be designed for divine worship let Jupiter be either in the ninth house or ascendant, and in either *Sagittarius* or *Pisces*. If Mars be in the ascendant or ninth house, there will be dissension, wrangling, and discord, in addition to danger by fire; if Saturn, asceticism and strange practices are likely to ensue.

2. *Buying Land or Houses.*—The ascendant, its lord, and the planet from which the Moon last separated, are significators of the buyer; the seventh house, its lord, and the planet to which the Moon applies, are the significators of the seller. The fourth house relates to the land or house, as the case may be.

The buyer should be careful, at the time of signing the covenant, to fortify the fourth house and its lord, the Moon, and her dispositor, and the Sun if possible; and let none of these significators be in any aspect with Mars, for this might cause the land or house then purchased to be soon lost and to be of no continuance to posterity.

To make the bargain good, fortify also the ascendant, its lord, and the planet from which the Moon last separated. If possible, let the Moon be in either *Cancer* or *Taurus*, and in benefic aspect with the lord of the ascendant or planet ascending. Let the fourth house have either *Taurus*, *Leo*, or *Aquarius* on its cusp. Let the fortunes have chief power in the angles, at any rate in the first and fourth. See that the lords of these angles be not retrograde; that no retrograde planet be in either of the angles, the ninth or eleventh houses.

3. *Buying Land, for Agricultural Purposes.*—In this case, fortify the ascendant and its lord, the Moon and her dispositor, the Sun, Jupiter, and Saturn; and let Saturn have the sextile or trine aspect of Jupiter—let Saturn be in *Libra* and Jupiter in *Sagittarius*, or vice versa, if possible—and by all means let not Mars have any familiarity with either Saturn or Jupiter. Let the Moon be in her increase, and in sextile or trine with Saturn; her first quarter is best.

Let the Moon be in the tenth house in *Taurus*, and the ascendant free from affliction.

At the commencement of tilling or manuring the ground, let the Moon be increasing in light and harmoniously configurated with one of the fortunes and Saturn.

4. *Planting or Grafting Trees.* The Moon should be in either *Taurus*, *Leo*, *Virgo*, *Aquarius* or *Pisces*—*Taurus* is the best—and in sextile or trine aspect with Venus. Let Saturn be direct in motion, and either in the ascendant, 11th, 5th, or 2nd house, dignified. If this cannot be done, let Jupiter be in one of these houses and in benefic aspect with Saturn. If neither, then let the Moon be in one of them, or in the 10th free from impediment.

In all plantings and sowings, see that Mars be debilitated, and in no configuration with the Moon.

Let the dispositor of the Moon (wrote Alchaiat) behold her from a watery sign; and if the ascendant be not a fixed sign, let the Moon and the lord of the ascendant be oriental of the Sun and ascending, or at least one of them; for this causeth trees then planted or grafted to grow quickly and be fruitful; if they be ascending and not oriental, the trees shall soon grow but not so soon fructify.

If the ascendant cannot be a fixed sign, let it be a common one, and the significators in common signs.

If it be impossible to fulfil all these conditions, see that the Moon is either in *Taurus* or the latter half of *Sagittarius*, free from affliction and in benefic aspect with Jupiter in the ascendant, 10th, 11th, 5th, or 4th house.

5. *Sowing Seed.* The ascending sign should be movable, and its lord should be in a movable sign, and the Moon beholding it from a movable sign; if this cannot be done, common signs are next best, fixed signs must be avoided.

Let the Moon be in either *Cancer* or *Capricornus*; if she be in *Aries*, let some planet behold her from a watery sign, *Cancer* for choice, lest the seed wither.

Let the Moon be separating from the Sun,[1] and increasing in light and motion—except in the case of sowing peas.

Let the ascendant be free from the presence or affliction of the malefic planets.

ELECTIONS APPERTAINING TO THE FIFTH HOUSE.

THE FIFTH HOUSE relates to the giving or receiving presents, feasting, writing letters, and sending messengers.

1. *Writing Letters or Books.* Fortify the ascendant and the ninth,

[1] See "*Urania*" for April, 1880, art. "The Failure of the Crops."

and let Mercury behold them either with a sextile or trine; and let ☿ be well dignified and no wise afflicted, and not retrograde. Let the Moon be in good aspect with Mercury, and both the ☽ and ascendant free from affliction.

ELECTIONS RELATING TO THE SIXTH HOUSE.

THE SIXTH HOUSE relates to sickness, servants and cattle.

The following rules may be interesting to medical men:

1. *For Surgical Operations*. For such operations that can be safely deferred to a fortunate moment, let the Moon *be increasing* in light and motion, and in sextile or trine aspect with Jupiter or Venus, and let not Mars be in any aspect with the Moon. The Chaldaeans held that the Moon is more afflicted by Mars during her increase, and by Saturn during her decrease.

Let the Moon be in a fixed sign—but not in the sign ruling the member or part of the body to be operated on, and let not such sign ascend.

Fortify the sign ruling the part of the body to be operated on; and let the ruler of the ascending sign, or Venus or Jupiter be in the ascendant or midheaven, and free from the configurations of Mars.

Let the Moon be free from all manner of impediment.

2. *Buying four-footed beasts*. See that thou fortifiest that sign which doth represent the beast to be bought, or that which is nearest to its nature; the Moon, the lord of the ascendant, and that of the 6th house; and see that the Moon have the sextile or trine of the planet ruling the sign signifying the beast, or in reception therewith.

In buying oxen or horses, let the Moon be in either *Taurus* or the last 15° of *Sagittarius*. In buying sheep, let the ☽ be in ♈; goats, ♑ or ♉; dogs ♐ or the last 15° of ♌.

In buying *race-horses*, let the Moon be in *Sagittarius* or the last fifteen degrees of *Leo*; and fortify the ascendant, the 6th house, and their lords; also let the Moon be free from the evil aspects of the infortunes and in sextile or trine with Jupiter or Venus.

To the last precept may be added: Ascertain the day on which the race-horse it is intended to purchase was foaled, and see that the Sun and Moon were free from the evil aspects of Saturn and Uranus, and were in good aspect with Mars. It will be best for ☉ to be in ♈ in △ with ♂ in ♌; or ☉ or ☽ in △ with ♂ in ♑; the ☉ attended by ♀, or ☽ in aspect with ♀ or ♃ or ☉; ☿ in ⚹ or △ with ♂ and ☽—for courage, stoutness, and speed are pretty certain to be possessed by horses foaled under such configurations. Some race-horses are notoriously unlucky, others are soft-hearted, and many turn out worthless for racing purposes, having neither speed nor stamina. Isonomy, one of the stoutest and speediest horses of the last century, was foaled on the 28th of April, 1875, when the ☉ was in △ with ♂ in ♑, ☽ in ⚹ with ♀, and ☿ in ☍ with ♃, Bend Or, a Derby winner, was foaled on the 13th of February, 1877, when the ☉ and ☽ were in ⚹ with both ♂ and ♃ in ♐.

Ormonde, the winner of the Derby, in 1886, was foaled at 6h 30m p.m. of the 18th of March, 1883; Cancer 0° 32′ culminating, and Libra 0° 24′ ascending. The Moon was in trine (separating) with the Sun, the latter separating from quartile with Jupiter and sextile with Saturn. Mercury was in conjunction with Mars in Aries. Jupiter was in the ninth house.

Minoru bred by Colonel W. Hall Walker, M.P., won the Derby, on the 26th of May, 1909, for the late King Edward VII. This colt was foaled at 9h 15m p.m. of the 16th of March, 1906, Kildare. Leo 9° 52′ occupied the midheaven and Libra 29° 6′ the ascendant, Mars setting in Aries 29° 35′ in sextile with the Sun, the Moon in Sagittarius 17° 41′ in trine with Mercury in 13° 37′ of Aries; the Sun applying to sextile with Jupiter.

Prince Palatine, winner of the St. Leger, 1911, was also bred by Colonel W. Hall Walker. This colt was foaled on the 2nd of April, 1908, at 0h 25m a.m., Kildare. Sun in Aries 11° 53′, Moon also in the same sign 22° 53′ in parallel with the Sun. The ascending degree ♐ 14° 2′ had the trinal ray of the Sun and the sextile of Mercury.

CHAPTER III.

ELECTIONS RELATING TO THE LAST SIX HOUSES.

"A time to love, and a time to hate; a time for war and a time for peace."—SOLOMON.

THE SEVENTH HOUSE relates to marriage, partnership, war, lawsuits, etc. The ancients hand down to posterity precepts concerning all these important affairs.

In electing a propitious moment for the putting on of the wedding ring, see that the Moon is increasing in light and motion, and free from affliction. Let not the Moon be in conjunction with an infortune in the ascendant, for this would presignify strife and discord. Neither let the Moon be in conjunction with an infortnne in the ascendant of the nativity of either the bride or bridegroom.

If possible, celebrate the marriage before the Moon shall pass her first quarter.

Know that it is a favourable time for marriage when the ascendant is assisted by the presence or benevolent configurations of the fortunes; and unfavourable when the ascendant and the descendant are afflicted.

Be sure to place the Moon, the ascendant and its lord, at the time of making the partnership or agreement, in *Gemini*, *Virgo*, *Sagittarius*, or *Pisces*. If the affair is to be a public company, let the Moon be in *Leo* in conjunction or benefit aspect with Jupiter, and well configurated with the Sun.

Let the Moon be increasing in light and motion; let the ruler of the 10th house, or a fortune in the 10th house, be in good aspect with the Moon or ruler of the ascendant; and let the rulers of the ascendant and seventh house be in mutual benefic aspect.

3. *Of Declaring War, Commencing Lawsuits, etc.* The ascendant is for the attacking party, and the 7th house for the adversary.

Let, therefore, the ascendant be fortunate, and let the ascending sign be one of those under the dominion of Mars, Jupiter, or Saturn;

Scorpio is best, and *Aries* next best, for this purpose, because they are *martial* signs. Let the lord of the ascendant dispose of the lord of the 7th house, if possible, or, otherwise, more essentially and accidentally dignified; and let the lord of the ascendant be in sextile or trine with Mars and with the ascending degree or that culminating. Have a care that the lord of the ascendant be not in the 7th, 4th, 8th, 6th, or 3rd house, and neither retrograde, debilitated, nor afflicted.

In lawsuits, have regard to the horoscopes, if procurable, of the disputants; and judge that he who hath Mars most essentially fortified in his nativity will overcome, especially if he was born at night.

Begin no quarrel, war, or controversy, neither invade the enemy's country when the Moon is in *Virgo* nor *Capricornus*; but when the Moon is assisted by the fortunes and by Mars, and when Mars is in the eastern part of the heavens. If possible, let Mars be between the 10th degree of *Taurus* and the 10th degree of *Leo*, or between the 10th degree of *Scorpio* and that of *Aquarius*. But if the enemy be to the west of the country, begin the invasion when Mars is in the western part of the heavens, and between the 10th degree of *Leo* and that of *Scorpio*, or between the 10th degree of *Aquarius* and that of *Taurus*.

Begin no invasion when the Moon is combust, or within twelve hours after her conjunction with the Sun. If any war be begun in these combust hours, the beginner will be defeated, or much evil will befall his person and his soldiers and assistants, especially if he begin the war in one of the first four combust hours.

It is a remarkable fact that the battle of Isandhlwana was fought during an eclipse of the Sun, visible in Zululand—viz., on the 22nd of January, 1879, at 1h 5m p.m. (Cape Mean Time). Now, the native accounts of that disastrous battle stated that the Zulus did not intend to deliver their onset until the night of the 22nd or dawn of the 23rd, because "the moon was unfavourable." The Zulus, it is thus demonstrated, understood astrology, and valued its precepts, and therefore would not attack during the combust hours of the Moon. By dawn of the 23rd, more than twelve hours would have elapsed since the time of new Moon. Unfortunately for the British, Colonel Durnford's Basutos discovered and fired on a Zulu regiment; and thus began the battle which ended so disastrously for our soldiers, the British force being annihilated. The map of the heavens for this eclipse is given in "The Science of the Stars," chap. V.

ELECTIONS RELATING TO THE EIGHTH HOUSE.

THE EIGHTH HOUSE of the heavens relates to the making of wills and to inheritance. One might think that no election would be required for making wills, but the ancients considered that there is a time for this purpose; that is to say, when a will is made by a person in health, and not left to dying moments.

1. *Of Making Wills*. "When thou makest thy will let not the Moon be in a movable sign nor in the ascendant, but let her be in a fixed sign, and a fixed sign rising, and if possible the lord of the ascendant in a fixed sign. If the Moon be in conjunction with Mars rising, at the time of making a will, there is danger of it being stolen, lost, or destroyed.

"Let the Moon be in benefic aspect with Saturn, if thou desirest that the will shall not be revoked."

2. *Of Inheritance*. In entering upon possession of inheritance, fortify the eighth house; if possible, let one of the signs of Jupiter or Venus be on the cusp thereof, and make the second house and its lord strong and free from all manner of impediment, and in good aspect with the fortunes. Fortify also the Moon, and let her behold the degree on the cusp of the eighth house or planet therein; and let there be reception between the lords of the second and eighth houses. If possible, let the lord of the ascendant be in the second house, and the lord of the second in the eighth house.

ELECTIONS RELATING TO THE NINTH HOUSE.

THE NINTH HOUSE of the Heavens relates to embarking on foreign travel; to learning, science, art, etc.

1. *Of Foreign Travel*. Fortify the 9th house at the time of setting forth, also the lord thereof, the Moon, and the ascendant. Let one or both of the fortunes be in the ninth house, if possible. Let not an infortune be in the eighth house at the moment of departure, nor in the second at the moment of embarking on the return journey.

As the descendant relates to the place to which the journey is to be made, fortify the seventh house at thy departure, and let no evil planet be in either this or the tenth house. In returning let no evil planet be in either the ascendant or fourth house.

If possible, let the Moon be increasing in light and motion at the time of beginning the journey, also let her be free from impediment and receive some support from the fortunes. Let Mercury be free from combustion and affliction, and in a good house. Let not the Moon be in the place of Saturn, Mars, or Uranus at birth.

If the Moon, or Saturn, or both, be in the ascendant or seventh house, or Saturn in the first and the Moon in the seventh house, there will be danger or loss attending the journey then begun.

2. *Of Building and Launching Ships, and Voyages by Sea.* In *building* ships for war or *swift sailing*, fortify the ascendant and its lord, the Moon and her dispositor; place the lord of the ascendant and Moon in either the first, eleventh, or ninth house; and let the sign ascending be fixed. If possible, let all the angles be fixed, and in any case be sure to have the Moon and lord of the ascendant swift in motion.

Let the planet from which the Moon last separated be strong and well disposed, also swift in motion. Place the Moon's dispositor in a watery sign, free from impediment or affliction. Place one of the fortunes in either the first, tenth, or seventh house. Let the lord of the seventh house be weak and slow in motion.

In building merchant and passenger ships, in addition to following the foregoing instructions, see that Mercury be fortified and assisted by Venus or Jupiter, and in the tenth house. Fortify also the second house.

Let the Moon be in *Taurus*, *Gemini*, or the beginning of *Cancer*, *Virgo*, or *Sagittarius*, or one of the last degrees of *Capricornus*. It is good to have the Moon or the ascendant in *Pisces*.

Let the Sun be in *trine* aspect with Jupiter, and attended by Venus. Let not Mars be in any aspect with the Moon or ascending degree, for this is apt to cause casualties by fire. Let not the Moon be in *Aquarius* and in aspect with the Sun and Mars, for danger of shipwreck will ensue. Let not the Moon be afflicted by Mars from signs of human form, or pirates may probably sink the ship and kill the crew and passengers.

In *launching* ships, and in setting forth on a sea voyage, see that the Moon be strong essentially and accidentally, assisted by Venus or Jupiter, and free from affliction; as likewise the ascendant.

ELECTIONS RELATING TO THE TENTH HOUSE.

THE TENTH HOUSE relates to profession, trade, employment, etc. Ramesey says that he believes the ancients placed occupation under the dominion of the tenth house of the heavens, "because it is the highest dignity such can look for that are bound thereunto."

"Wherefore in this matter thou art to distinguish the planet ruling the profession, trade, or mystery thou wouldst learn; then let the ascendant or tenth house be a sign wherein such planet hath dominion by house; as, for example, if thou desirest to be a merchant, place *Gemini* or *Virgo* in the ascendant or tenth house, or else *Libra*, *Sagittarius* or *Aquarius*.

"Fortify the lord of the ascendant, that of the tenth house, the Moon, and Mercury."

The Western nations do not now-a-days consult astrologers before appointing a Prime Minister or a President; neither do European monarchs elect a fortunate hour for their coronation. The ancients, however, gave rules for these proceedings, and laid stress on the necessity for not making such appointments and ceremonies within fifteen days of an unfortunate new Moon. In the East the precepts of the ancients are still followed.

ELECTIONS RELATING TO THE TWELFTH HOUSE.

THE TWELFTH HOUSE relates to prisoners, captives, and horses. The ancients wrote precepts as to electing suitable moments for freeing prisoners and captives, and buying horses. Those relating to prisoners need not be reproduced in this work, for no Government and no governor of a prison would pay any regard to them, among Western nations, at the present day. In regard to horses, rules have already been given in the seventh chapter, as to purchasing them. Trainers of race-horses would hardly be likely to await a favourable moment for sending a race-horse to a race meeting at which he was engaged to run. The following is the injunction handed down by Ramesey in this connection:

"Let *Sagittarius* ascend, or contain the Moon, if possible, at the time of the race-horse setting forth on his journey to the race meeting; otherwise let the Moon or ascendant be in the first half of *Libra*."

"Fortify the ascendant, its lord, the Moon and her dispositor, and the planet with which either may be joined."

CHAPTER IV.

THE PLANETARY DIGNITIES.

IN ELECTIONS stress was laid by the ancients on the planetary dignities. These dignities are of two kinds—essential and accidental. A planet was said to be *essentially* dignified when in its own sign, exaltation, triplicity, term or face; and was said to be *accidentally* dignified when in the midheaven, ascendant, 7th, 4th, 11th, 9th, 2nd, or 5th house. A planet is *accidentally strong* when swift and direct in motion, and near its greatest distance from the Sun; a superior planet, when oriental of the Sun; an inferior planet, when occidental.

A planet is *essentially weak*, when it is in its fall or detriment. It is *accidentally weak* when in the 12th, 8th, or 6th house, retrograde or very slow in motion, within 8° 30′ of the Sun; a superior planet, when occidental of the Sun; an inferior, when oriental.

Although a planet was held to be weak when within 8° 30′ of the Sun, it was said to be strong when within 17′ of, or in exact conjunction with the Sun—"in cazimi" as the ancients term it.

The following table of the essential dignities of the planets is taken from Ptolemy's *Tetrabiblos*. Experience proves that *Aries* and *Scorpio* are Martial signs; *Sagittarius* and *Pisces* Jovial signs; Gemini and *Virgo*, Mercurial, etc. Hence the chief (essential) dignities of the planets are correctly stated; but it by no means follows that the planets are weak in nativities, when in the signs opposite to their chief dignities. The student may, therefore, safely reject the "detriment" and "fall" of the planets. The exaltations, the rule over the triplicities, and terms may be regarded as purely arbitrary. The "faces" of the planets ought, perhaps, to come under the same category, but there may appear to be a better foundation for these, inasmuch as the influences of certain parts of the same sign are observed to differ; at the same time, although the first 10° of *Aries* may be reasonably ascribed to the rule of Mars, there is no reason why the other planets should follow in the Ptolemaic order—Sun, Venus, Mercury, Moon, Saturn, Jupiter, Mars—through the decanates of the various signs. This is the order of the "hours" of the planets through the day and night, which gave ori-

Signs.	Houses.	Exaltations.	Triplicities Day & Night.		Terms of the Planets.					Faces of the Planets.			Detriment.	Fall.
		°	D.	N.	°	°	°	°	°	°	°	°		
♈	♂ D.	☉ 19	☉	♃	♃ 6	♀ 14	☿ 21	♂ 26	30	♂ 10	☉ 10	♀ 10	♀	♄
♉	♀ N.	☽ 3	♀	☽	♀ 8	☿ 15	♃ 22	♄ 26	♂ 30	☿ 10	☽ 10	♄ 10	♂	
♊	☿ D.		♄	☿	7	♃ 14	♀ 21	♄ 25	♂ 30	♃ 10	♂ 10	☉ 10	♃	☋
♋	☽ D. N.	♃ 15	♂	♂	♂ 6	♃ 13	☿ 20	♀ 27	♄ 30	♀ 10	☿ 10	☽ 10	♄	♂
♌	☉ D. N.		☉	♃	♄ 6	☿ 13	♀ 19	♃ 25	♂ 30	♄ 10	♃ 10	♂ 10	♄	
♍	☿ N.	☿ 15	♀	☽	☿ 7	♀ 13	♃ 18	♄ 24	♂ 30	☉ 10	♀ 10	☿ 10	♃	♀
♎	♀ D.	♄ 21	♄	☿	♄ 6	♀ 11	♃ 19	☿ 24	♂ 30	☽ 10	♄ 10	♃ 10	♂	☉
♏	♂ N.		♂	♂	♂ 6	♃ 14	♀ 21	☿ 27	♄ 30	♂ 10	☉ 10	♀ 10	♀	☽
♐	♃ D.		☉	♃	♃ 8	♀ 14	☿ 19	♄ 25	♂ 30	☿ 10	☽ 10	♄ 10	☿	☊
♑	♄ N.	♂ 28	♀	☽	♀ 6	☿ 12	♃ 19	♂ 25	♄ 30	♃ 10	♂ 10	☉ 10	☽	♃
♒	♄ D.		♄	☿	♄ 6	☿ 12	♀ 20	♃ 25	♂ 30	♀ 10	☿ 10	☽ 10	☉	
♓	♃ N.	♀ 27	♂	♂	♀ 8	♃ 14	☿ 20	♂ 26	♄ 30	♄ 10	♃ 10	♂ 10	☿	

The Essential Dignities of the Planets According to Ptolemy

gin to the division of the week and the nomenclature of each of the seven days.

Not the slightest reliance should be placed on them, even in the case of a nativity wherein Mercury or the Moon, or the planet ascending, may be in one of the decanates assigned to it. It is only in such cases that these assertions would apply, for the "lord of the ascendant and the dispositor of the Moon" can have nothing whatever to do with the disposition unless they happen to be either nearly rising or with Mercury or the Moon at the moment of birth, whatever Ramesey may say.

The "Part of Fortune" is that point of the heavens in which the Moon would be if the Sun were exactly rising. Claudius Ptolemy says:

"The Part of Fortune is ascertained by computing the number of degrees between the Sun and Moon; and it is placed at an equal number of degrees distant from the ascendant in the order of the signs. It is in all cases, both by night and day, to be so computed and set down that the Moon may hold with it the same relation as that which the Sun may hold with the ascendant; and it thus becomes, as it were, a lunar horoscope or ascendant."

Prior to the teaching of Negusantius, this was understood to mean that the Part of Fortune is to be placed as many degrees distant from the degree ascending as the Moon is from the Sun; below the horizon before full Moon, and above the horizon between full and new Moon. At new Moon the part of Fortune would have the same longitude as the ascendant; at full Moon, the same as the descendant. This method is still employed in mundane and horary astrology, and in elections, by those who mark in the Part of Fortune; and it was taught by the late Zadkiel in his "Handbook of Astrology," vol. i. For example: If the Sun be in ♏ 18° 6′, the Moon in ♉ 27° 7′, and the ascendant ♐ 10° 29′, the Part of Fortune would be in ♊ 19° 30′.

The author has already declared his opinion that the Part of Fortune must be discarded from a rational system of genethliacal astrology. As, however, reference is made to the position of the Part of Fortune in figures of the heavens for elections, in the rules of the ancients, a few remarks on the subject may be considered necessary. However, the student may at once be informed that the author would reject the Part of Fortune from mundane astrology and elections; in fact altogether, for it is a purely imaginary thing, and therefore can have neither influence nor signification.

The student will be surprised to learn that although the common method of determining the place of the Part of Fortune is still used by some astrologers in horary figures, a different method is adopted by them in nativities, although both methods cannot be right.

Placidus confessed that he had never been able to find any truth in the Part of Fortune, although he diligently studied it and very properly assigned to it the same latitude as that of the Moon. As James Wilson, in his "Dictionary of Astrology," observed, "there can scarcely be stronger proof of the truth of astrology than this, he [Placidus] could find truth in the planetary configurations because they are founded on the immutable laws of Nature; but when he came to investigate the Part of Fortune he could find no truth in it, because there was none."

Unfortunately for the reputation of Placidus, who was a most painstaking scientific man, he became charmed with the method of Negusantius (which received also the assent of the late Zadkiel, a greater astrologer than either), and finding one nativity in which, according to Ptolemy, neither the Sun nor the Moon was hyleg, but the Part of Fortune, he accepted it as conformable to reason, although in another page of his work ("Primum Mobile") he had written that "all these things must be confirmed by reason and experience." In the thirty remarkable nativities of eminent men published by Placidus, he had wisely omitted to mark the place of the Part of Fortune. After writing his comments on those nativities he received the new method of Negusantius, because it coincided with his preference for mundane positions and aspects to zodiacal, and because he found one nativity which appeared to support it. Placidus thus describes the method:

"When this work was finished, the very illustrious D. Adrian Negusantius, of Fanum, a man not only very well versed in astrology according to the true doctrine of Ptolemy, but also in Physics and the sublime secrets of Nature, having transmitted to me a method to calculate the Part of Fortune perfectly agreeable to reason and experience, I thought proper to set it down here, word for word, that everyone might see a secret in this art, invented by so great a man, truly worthy the pen of the greatest astrologers; for I willingly confess that with regard to the Part of Fortune, I have laboured a long time and have not been able to find any truth in it.

"'The Part of Fortune,' says Negusantius, 'if we may credit the precepts of Ptolemy, who asserts that it has the same position to the Moon as the Sun has to the horizon, ought to be described and defined in the lunar parallels; for neither, if it be constituted in the ecliptic, according to the intentions of the common astrologers, or in the Moon's orbit as was the opinion of a very eminent professor, will it be found to preserve that order and similitude which the respective conversions of two luminaries, both diurnal and annual, denote.' This man subscribes to the truth of everything I lately mentioned in my Celestial Philosophy, wherein I said that the Part of Fortune moves upon the orbit or way of the Moon's latitude, and therefore not in the ecliptic.

"But as I have shown that the distances and rays to the angles are, by no means, made in the zodiac, but upon the parallel of every star, he argues that the Sun in like manner is elongated from the east, viz., upon his parallel; also the Moon, who has not by any other method nor way different than when the Sun is in the horizon, by her real presence, posited the place of the Part of Fortune; for no other fundamental principle is seen to constitute this part in Nature, unless by such an assignation and impression of virtue, exhibited by the Moon at sunrise. Negusantius adds: 'For when the Sun comes to the cardinal sign of the east, then it is necessary the Moon be found in its horizon; afterwards, in an equal space of time, the Sun digressing, he is removed from it according to his ascension.' Wherefore, if we study the matter with accuracy, we shall find that, entirely in the same manner as the Sun departs from the east, the Moon is likewise separated from the Part of Fortune, that is, both upon their parallels, so that as many degrees as the Sun, in his parallel circle, is elongated from the east, so many is the Moon in her parallel distant from the Part of Fortune; whence it follows, that the true place of the Part of Fortune does not always remain in the zodiac, but always under the Moon's parallel circle, that is, with the Moon's declination the same both in number and name, and therefore the Part of Fortune does not receive any aspects from the stars in the zodiac, but only *in mundo*. We may make a calculation of its place in various ways, but it will be shorter as well as easier if, in the diurnal geniture, the Sun's true distance from the east be added to the Moon's right ascension, and in the nocturnal, subtracted, for the number thence arising will be the place and right ascension of the Part of Fortune; and it has always the same declination as the Moon, both in number and name, wherever it is found. Again, let the Sun's oblique ascension, taken in the ascendant, be subtracted always from the oblique ascension of the ascendant, as well in the day as in the night, and the remaining difference be added to the Moon's right ascension, the Sun will be the right ascension of the Part of Fortune, which will have the Moon's declination. He who has a mind to make its directions, will accomplish it only by motions in the world, that is to the aspects *in mundo*," etc.

In the example already given, the place of the Part of Fortune, by the common method, is ♊ 19° 30′. According to the method of Negusantius, its *mundane* position (as in a nativity) must be thus computed (the Moon's latitude being 4° 59′ N.):

Oblique ascension of the ascendant	279 28 14
Subtract Sun's oblique ascension	248 35 28
	30 52 46
Add Moon's right ascension	53 33 50
The Part of Fortune's right ascension =	84 26 36

The declination of the Part of Fortune must be, according to Negusantius, the same as that of the Moon; in this instance the Moon's declination is 24° 23′ 2″ N. Its semi-arc (the birthplace being in lat. 51° 30′ 35″ N.) is therefore 124° 45′ 13″, which is the opposite to that of the Moon because the Part of Fortune is above and the Moon is below the horizon.

Wilson says that:[1] "The longitude and latitude of the Part of Fortune may, if required, be found by trigonometry from its right ascension and declination, like that of any star." Let us proceed to test the truth of this assertion. The rule is given in Appendix I. of this work: *The R.A. and Dec. of a Heavenly Body being given, to find its Longitude and Latitude.*

Log. Sine of R.A.	84 26 36,	9.9979544
Log. co-tang of Dec.	24 23 2N,	0.3436324
Log. tang. ∠A	65 30 52.1 =	0.3415868
Add	23 27 43.4	
∠ B. =	88 58 35.5	

Log. Co-sine ∠ A. (a.c.)	0.3825139
Log. Co-sine ∠ B.	8.2519893
Log. Sine Dec.	9.6157905
Log. Sine *lat.* 1° 1′ 11″ N. =	8.2502937

Log. Sine ∠ A. (a.c.)	0.0409271
Log Sine ∠ B.	9.9999307
Log. tang. R.A.	1.0119437
Log. tang. long. 84° 56′ 22″=	1.0528015

[1] "A Complete Dictionary of Astrology." By James Wilson, London, 1819. Page 312.

The result is, then, that the Part of Fortune is in (geocentric) *longitude* 84° 56′ 22″, or Gemini (♊) 24° 56′ 22″ and *latitude* 1° 1′ 11″ N. It will be observed, that this *longitude* differs widely from that found by the common method, viz., ♊ 19° 30′. But, which is of much greater importance, this *latitude* differs largely from that of the Moon, viz., 4° 59′ 9″ N., whereas it should be the same.

The common method cannot be right because the places of the Sun and Moon are taken in the zodiac while that of the ascendant is taken in the world. The method of Negusantius cannot be right because it assigns to the Part of Fortune always the same declination as the Moon, whereas it cannot have the same declination as the Moon unless the Sun be exactly rising or setting or in parallel declination with that of the ascending degree—for "the Moon is to the Part of Fortune as the Sun is to the horoscope," *ergo* if the Sun be not in parallel declination with the ascendant the Moon cannot be in par. dec. with the Part of Fortune.

It is evident, therefore, that the whole thing is an absurdity. If the place of the Part of Fortune be taken by the common method, without reference to the Moon's latitude, as is still done in *horary* astrology, its place will differ from that found by the method of Negusantius, as in the case of a nativity. In *horary* astrology, in *elections*, and in *mundane* astrology, wherein the common method is still used, great importance is attached to the *trine* aspect of the Moon with the Part of Fortune, for when this connexion is found it is held to promise success in affairs relating to money; but the horary astrologers do not appear to have observed that when the Moon is in *trine* with the Part of Fortune, the SUN is in *trine* with the *ascending degree*; to this *zodiacal trine of the* SUN *to the ascendant* is to be attributed the good fortune wrongly ascribed to the trine of the Moon with the Part of Fortune.

Lest this should be considered by some as insufficient proof, let us refer to the nativity of Pope Urban VIII., published by Placidus in the Addenda to his "Primum Mobile." In this nativity the ascendant is ♌ 26°, the Sun is in ♈ 25° 42′ and in the ninth house. This trine aspect of the Sun to the ascendant must be the presignification of the good fortune of Urban VIII., for the nativity is not otherwise fortunate, with the exception of the Sun being near the mundane parallel with Jupiter.

It is true that the late Zadkiel I. wrote,[2] in the year 1840, in favour

[2] "Grammar of Astrology," chap, xiv.

of the Part of Fortune even in nativities; but down to that year he had but a comparatively short experience, and twenty-four years later[3] he made no such declaration in favour of it. The obvious conclusion is that his later and more extended experience did not confirm his first impression, which was no doubt greatly due to his respect for Ptolemy and Placidus.

Had the existence of Uranus and Neptune been known to Ptolemy, Placidus, and Negusantius, it is probable that the first named would not have *invented* the Part of Fortune and the others would not have thought of it—they found that something was wanting to account for occasional discrepancies. At the present day, it must be rejected; its retention can only bring discredit on astrology and its votaries, just as the extravagancies of horary astrologers in the past brought about the decline of *astrologia sana*. No science encumbered by superstition can nourish any more than a garden overrun by weeds.

HORARY ASTROLOGY is a system of divination by means of the celestial bodies, their relative positions and mutual configurations; the figure of the heavens being cast for the moment of consultation, and the question being propounded.

In my "Science of the Stars" the student who may wish to investigate *horary* astrology will find a sufficient description of it. As applied to questions it is not really worth serious consideration, except in cases of the deepest anxiety and perturbation of mind on the part of the querent, and when the horary figure harmonises with the horoscope of the querent, and when it also is in accord with the primary directions, falling due at the time, in his nativity.

[3] "Handbook of Astrology."

APPENDIX II.

TABLES OF HOUSES.

1 R. A. of the Meridian	LONDON. Lat. 51° 30′ 49″ North.							NORTHAMPTON. Lat. 52° 11′ 0″ North.						
	10th	11th	12th	Ascendant.		2nd	3rd	10th	11th	12th	Ascendant.		2nd	3rd
	♈	♉	♊	♋		♌	♍	♈	♉	♊	♋		♌	♍
H. M. S.	°	°	°	°	′	°	°	°	°	°	°	′	°	°
0 0 0	0	9	22	26	35	12	3	0	9	23	27	9	13	3
0 3 40	1	10	23	27	16	13	4	1	10	24	27	49	14	4
0 7 20	2	11	24	27	56	14	4	2	11	24	28	29	14	4
0 11 1	3	12	25	28	36	15	5	3	12	25	29	8	15	5
0 14 41	4	13	25	29	16	15	6	4	13	26	29	48	16	6
0 18 21	5	14	26	29	56	16	7	5	15	27	0♌	27	17	7
0 22 2	6	15	27	0♌	36	17	8	6	16	28	1	7	18	8
0 25 42	7	17	28	1	16	18	9	7	17	29	1	46	18	9
0 29 23	8	18	29	1	55	18	9	8	18	30	2	26	19	9
0 33 4	9	19	♋	2	35	19	10	9	19	♋	3	5	19	10
0 36 45	10	20	1	3	15	20	11	10	20	1	3	44	20	11
0 40 27	11	21	1	3	54	20	12	11	21	2	4	23	21	12
0 44 8	12	22	2	4	34	21	13	12	22	3	5	3	22	13
0 47 50	13	23	3	5	13	22	14	13	23	4	5	42	22	14
0 51 32	14	24	4	5	53	23	14	14	24	5	6	21	23	14
0 55 14	15	25	5	6	32	23	15	15	25	5	7	0	24	15
0 58 57	16	26	6	7	12	24	16	16	26	6	7	39	24	16
1 2 40	17	27	6	7	51	25	17	17	27	7	8	18	25	17
1 6 24	18	28	7	8	31	26	18	18	28	8	8	57	26	18
1 10 7	19	29	8	9	10	26	19	19	29	9	9	37	27	19
1 13 51	20	♊	9	9	50	27	19	20	♊	9	10	16	27	19
1 17 36	21	1	10	10	29	28	20	21	1	10	10	55	28	20
1 21 21	22	2	10	11	9	28	21	22	2	11	11	34	29	21
1 25 6	23	3	11	11	49	29	22	23	3	12	12	13	30	22
1 28 52	24	4	12	12	28	♍	23	24	4	13	12	53	♍	23
1 32 38	25	5	13	13	8	1	24	25	5	13	13	32	1	24
1 36 25	26	6	14	13	48	1	25	26	6	14	14	12	2	25
1 40 13	27	7	14	14	28	2	25	27	7	15	14	51	3	25
1 44 1	28	8	15	15	8	3	26	28	8	16	15	31	3	26
1 47 49	29	9	16	15	48	4	27	29	9	17	16	10	4	27
1 51 38	30	10	17	16♌	28	4	28	30	10	17	16♌	50	5	28

TABLES OF HOUSES.

2 R. A. of the Meridian	LONDON. Lat. 51° 30′ 49″ North.							NORTHAMPTON. Lat. 52° 11′ 0″ North.						
	10th	11th	12th	Ascendant.		2nd	3rd	10th	11th	12th	Ascendant.		2nd	3rd
	♉	♊	♋	♌		♍	♍	♉	♊	♋	♌		♍	♍
H. M. S.	°	°	°	°	′	°	°	°	°	°	°	′	°	°
1 51 38	0	10	17	16	28	4	28	0	10	17	16	50	5	28
1 55 27	1	11	18	17	8	5	29	1	11	18	17	30	5	29
1 59 18	2	12	19	17	48	6	♎	2	12	19	18	10	6	♎
2 3 8	3	13	19	18	28	7	1	3	13	20	18	50	7	1
2 7 0	4	14	20	19	9	8	2	4	14	21	19	30	8	2
2 10 52	5	15	21	19	49	9	2	5	15	21	20	10	8	2
2 14 44	6	16	22	20	30	9	3	6	16	22	20	50	9	3
2 18 37	7	16	22	21	11	10	4	7	17	23	21	31	10	4
2 22 31	8	17	23	21	51	11	5	8	18	24	22	11	11	5
2 26 26	9	18	24	22	32	11	6	9	19	25	22	52	12	6
2 30 21	10	19	25	23	13	12	7	10	20	26	23	32	12	7
2 34 17	11	20	25	23	55	13	8	11	21	27	24	13	13	8
2 38 14	12	21	26	24	36	14	9	12	22	27	24	54	14	9
2 42 11	13	22	27	25	17	15	10	13	23	28	25	35	15	10
2 46 9	14	23	28	25	59	15	11	14	23	29	26	16	15	11
2 50 9	15	24	29	26	41	16	11	15	24	30	26	58	16	11
2 54 7	16	25	29	27	22	17	12	16	25	♌	27	39	17	12
2 58 8	17	26	♌	28	4	18	13	17	26	1	28	21	18	13
3 2 8	18	27	1	28	46	18	14	18	27	2	29	2	19	14
3 6 10	19	28	2	29	28	19	15	19	28	2	29	44	19	15
3 10 12	20	29	3	0 ♍	11	20	16	20	29	3	0 ♍	26	20	16
3 14 16	21	♋	3	0	53	21	17	21	♋	4	1	8	21	17
3 18 19	22	1	4	1	36	22	18	22	1	5	1	50	22	18
3 22 24	23	1	5	2	19	22	19	23	2	6	2	33	23	19
3 26 29	24	2	6	3	1	23	20	24	3	6	3	15	23	20
3 30 35	25	3	7	3	44	24	21	25	4	7	3	58	24	21
3 34 42	26	4	7	4	28	25	22	26	5	8	4	41	25	22
3 38 49	27	5	8	5	11	26	23	27	6	9	5	24	26	22
3 42 57	28	6	9	5	54	27	23	28	7	10	6	7	27	23
3 47 6	29	7	10	6	38	27	24	29	7	10	6	50	27	24
3 51 16	30	8	11	7 ♍	22	28	25	30	8	11	7 ♍	33	28	25

TABLES OF HOUSES.

3 R. A. of the Meridian	LONDON. Lat. 51° 30′ 49″ North.							NORTHAMPTON. Lat. 52° 11′ 0″ North.						
	10th	11th	12th	Ascendant.		2nd	3rd	10th	11th	12th	Ascendant.		2nd	3rd
	♊	♋	♌	♍		♍	♎	♊	♋	♌	♍		♍	♎
H. M. S.	°	°	°	°	′	°	°	°	°	°	°	′	°	°
3 51 16	0	8	11	7	22	28	25	0	8	11	7	33	28	25
3 55 26	1	9	12	8	5	29	26	1	9	12	8	17	29	26
3 59 37	2	10	12	8	49	♎	27	2	10	13	9	0	♎	27
4 3 48	3	11	13	9	33	1	28	3	11	14	9	44	1	28
4 8 1	4	12	14	10	18	2	29	4	12	15	10	28	2	29
4 12 13	5	13	15	11	2	2	♏	5	13	15	11	12	2	♏
4 16 27	6	14	16	11	46	3	1	6	14	16	11	56	3	1
4 20 41	7	15	17	12	31	4	2	7	15	17	12	40	4	2
4 24 55	8	15	17	13	16	5	3	8	16	18	13	24	5	3
4 29 11	9	16	18	14	0	6	4	9	17	19	14	9	6	4
4 33 26	10	17	19	14	45	7	5	10	17	19	14	53	7	5
4 37 22	11	18	20	15	30	8	6	11	18	20	15	38	7	6
4 41 59	12	19	21	16	16	8	7	12	19	21	16	23	9	7
4 46 17	13	20	21	17	1	9	8	13	20	22	17	7	9	8
4 50 34	14	21	22	17	46	10	9	14	21	23	17	52	10	8
4 54 52	15	22	23	18	32	11	10	15	22	24	18	37	11	9
4 59 11	16	23	24	19	17	12	10	16	23	24	19	23	12	10
5 3 30	17	24	25	20	3	13	11	17	24	25	20	8	13	11
5 7 49	18	25	26	20	48	14	12	18	25	26	20	53	13	12
5 12 9	19	26	27	21	34	14	13	19	26	27	21	38	14	13
5 16 29	20	27	28	22	20	15	14	20	27	28	22	24	15	14
5 20 49	21	28	28	23	6	16	15	21	28	29	23	9	16	15
5 25 10	22	29	29	23	52	17	16	22	29	♍	23	55	17	16
5 29 30	23	♌	♍	24	37	18	17	23	♌	1	24	40	18	17
5 33 51	24	1	1	25	23	19	18	24	1	1	25	26	19	18
5 38 13	25	1	2	26	10	20	19	25	2	2	26	11	19	19
5 42 34	26	2	3	26	56	20	20	26	3	3	26	57	20	20
5 46 55	27	3	4	27	42	21	21	27	4	4	27	43	21	21
5 51 17	28	4	4	28	28	22	22	28	5	5	28	29	22	22
5 55 38	29	5	5	29	14	23	23	29	5	6	29	14	23	23
6 0 0	30	6	6	30♍	0	24	24	30	6	6	30♍	0	24	24

TABLES OF HOUSES.

4 R. A. of the Meridian	LONDON. Lat. 51° 30′ 49″ North.							NORTHAMPTON. Lat. 52° 11′ 0″ North.						
	10th	11th	12th	Ascendant.		2nd	3rd	10th	11th	12th	Ascendant.		2nd	3rd
	♋	♌	♍	♎		♎	♏	♋	♌	♍	♎		♎	♏
H. M. S.	°	°	°	°	′	°	°	°	°	°	°	′	°	°
6 0 0	0	6	6	0	0	24	24	0	6	6	0	0	24	24
6 4 22	1	7	7	0	46	25	25	1	7	7	0	46	25	25
6 8 43	2	8	8	1	32	26	26	2	8	8	1	31	25	26
6 13 5	3	9	9	2	18	27	27	3	9	9	2	17	26	27
6 17 26	4	10	10	3	4	27	28	4	10	10	3	3	27	28
6 21 47	5	11	10	3	50	28	29	5	11	11	3	49	28	28
6 26 9	6	12	11	4	37	29	29	6	12	11	4	34	29	29
6 30 30	7	13	12	5	23	♏	♐	7	13	12	5	20	♏	♐
6 34 50	8	14	13	6	8	1	1	8	14	13	6	5	1	1
6 39 11	9	15	14	6	54	2	2	9	15	14	6	51	2	2
6 43 31	10	16	15	7	40	2	3	10	16	15	7	36	2	3
6 47 51	11	17	16	8	26	3	4	11	17	16	8	22	3	4
6 52 11	12	18	16	9	12	4	5	12	18	17	9	7	4	5
6 56 30	13	19	17	9	57	5	6	13	19	17	9	52	5	6
7 0 49	14	20	18	10	43	6	7	14	20	18	10	17	6	7
7 5 8	15	21	19	11	28	7	8	15	21	19	11	23	6	8
7 9 26	16	21	20	12	14	8	9	16	22	20	12	8	7	9
7 13 43	17	22	21	12	59	8	10	17	23	21	12	53	8	10
7 18 1	18	23	22	13	44	9	11	18	23	22	13	27	9	11
7 22 18	19	24	22	14	30	10	12	19	24	23	14	22	10	12
7 26 34	20	25	23	15	15	11	13	20	25	23	15	7	11	13
7 30 49	21	26	24	16	0	12	14	21	26	24	15	51	11	13
7 35 5	22	27	25	16	44	13	15	22	27	25	16	36	12	14
7 39 19	23	28	26	17	29	13	15	23	28	26	17	20	13	15
7 43 33	24	29	27	18	14	14	16	24	29	27	18	4	14	16
7 47 47	25	♍	28	18	58	15	17	25	♍	28	18	48	15	17
7 51 59	26	1	28	19	42	16	18	26	1	28	19	32	16	18
7 56 12	27	2	29	20	27	17	19	27	2	29	20	16	16	19
8 0 23	28	3	♎	21	11	18	20	28	3	♎	21	0	17	20
8 4 34	29	4	1	21	55	18	21	29	4	1	21	43	18	21
8 8 44	30	5	2	22♎	38	19	22	30	5	2	22	27	19	22

TABLES OF HOUSES.

5 R. A. of the Meridian.			LONDON. Lat. 51° 30′ 49″ North.							NORTHAMPTON. Lat. 52° 11′ 0″ North.						
			10th	11th	12th	Ascendant.		2nd	3rd	10th	11th	12th	Ascendant.		2nd	3rd
			♌	♍	♎	♎		♏	♐	♌	♍	♎	♎		♏	♐
H.	M.	S.	°	°	°	°	′	°	°	°	°	°	°	′	°	°
8	8	44	0	5	2	22	38	19	22	0	5	2	22	27	19	22
8	12	54	1	6	3	23	22	20	23	1	6	3	23	10	20	23
8	17	3	2	7	3	24	6	21	24	2	7	3	23	53	20	24
8	21	11	3	8	4	24	49	22	25	3	8	4	24	36	21	25
8	25	19	4	8	5	25	32	23	26	4	9	5	25	19	22	26
8	29	25	5	9	6	26	16	23	27	5	9	6	26	2	23	27
8	33	31	6	10	7	26	59	24	28	6	10	7	26	45	24	27
8	37	36	7	11	8	27	41	25	29	7	11	7	27	27	25	28
8	41	41	8	12	8	28	24	26	29	8	12	8	28	10	25	29
8	45	44	9	13	9	29	7	27	♑	9	13	9	28	52	26	♑
8	49	48	10	14	10	29	49	27	1	10	14	0	29	34	27	1
8	53	50	11	15	11	0♏	32	28	2	11	15	11	0♏	16	28	2
8	57	52	12	16	12	1	14	29	3	12	16	11	0	58	28	3
9	1	52	13	17	12	1	56	♐	4	13	17	12	1	39	29	4
9	5	53	14	18	13	2	38	1	5	14	18	13	2	21	♐	5
9	9	51	15	19	14	3	19	2	6	15	19	14	3	2	1	6
9	13	51	16	19	15	4	1	2	7	16	19	15	3	44	1	6
9	17	49	17	20	16	4	43	3	8	17	20	15	4	25	2	7
9	21	46	18	21	16	5	24	4	9	18	21	16	5	6	3	9
9	25	43	19	22	17	6	5	5	10	19	22	17	5	47	4	10
9	29	39	20	23	18	6	47	5	11	20	23	18	6	28	5	11
9	33	34	21	24	19	7	28	6	12	21	24	19	7	8	6	11
9	37	29	22	25	19	8	9	7	13	22	25	19	7	49	6	12
9	41	23	23	26	20	8	49	8	14	23	26	20	8	29	7	13
9	45	16	24	27	21	9	30	9	14	24	27	21	9	10	8	14
9	49	8	25	28	22	10	11	9	15	25	28	22	9	50	9	15
9	53	0	26	28	23	10	51	10	16	26	28	22	10	30	9	16
9	56	52	27	29	23	11	32	11	17	27	29	23	11	10	10	17
10	0	42	28	♎	24	12	12	12	18	28	♎	24	11	50	10	18
10	4	33	29	1	25	12	52	12	19	29	1	24	12	30	11	19
10	8	22	30	2	26	13♏	32	13	20	30	2	25	13	10	12	20

TABLES OF HOUSES.

6 R. A. of the Meridian	LONDON. Lat. 51° 30′ 49″ North.							NORTHAMPTON. Lat. 52° 11′ 0″ North.						
	10th	11th	12th	Ascendant.		2nd	3rd	10th	11th	12th	Ascendant.		2nd	3rd
	♍	♎	♎	♏		♐	♑	♍	♎	♎	♏		♐	♑
H. M. S.	°	°	°	°	′	°	°	°	°	°	°	′	°	°
10 8 22	0	2	26	13	32	13	20	0	2	25	13	10	12	20
10 12 11	1	3	26	14	12	14	21	1	3	26	13	40	13	21
10 15 59	2	4	27	14	52	15	22	2	4	27	14	29	14	22
10 19 47	3	5	28	15	32	16	23	3	5	28	15	9	14	23
10 23 35	4	5	29	16	12	16	24	4	5	28	15	48	15	24
10 27 22	5	6	29	16	52	17	25	5	6	29	16	28	16	25
10 31 8	6	7	♏	17	32	18	26	6	7	♏	17	7	17	26
10 34 54	7	8	1	18	12	19	27	7	8	1	17	47	18	27
13 38 39	8	9	2	18	51	20	28	8	9	1	18	26	19	28
10 42 24	9	10	2	19	31	20	29	9	10	2	19	5	20	29
10 46 9	10	11	3	20	10	21	♒	10	11	3	19	44	21	♒
10 49 53	11	11	4	20	50	22	1	11	11	4	20	23	21	1
10 53 36	12	12	4	21	29	23	2	12	12	4	21	3	22	2
10 57 20	13	13	5	22	9	24	3	13	13	5	21	42	23	3
11 1 3	14	14	6	22	49	24	4	14	14	6	22	21	24	4
11 4 46	15	15	7	23	28	25	5	15	15	6	23	0	25	5
11 8 28	16	16	7	24	7	26	6	16	16	7	23	39	26	6
11 12 10	17	16	8	24	47	27	7	17	17	8	24	18	27	7
11 15 52	18	17	9	25	26	28	8	18	18	9	24	57	28	8
11 19 33	19	18	10	26	6	29	9	19	18	9	25	37	28	9
11 23 15	20	19	10	26	45	30	10	20	19	10	26	16	29	10
11 26 56	21	20	11	27	25	♑	11	21	20	10	26	55	30	11
11 30 37	22	21	12	28	5	1	12	22	21	11	27	34	♑	12
11 34 18	23	21	13	28	44	2	13	23	21	12	28	14	1	13
11 37 58	24	22	13	29	24	3	15	24	22	13	28	53	2	14
11 41 39	25	23	14	0 ♐	4	4	16	25	23	14	29	33	3	15
11 45 19	26	24	15	0	44	5	17	26	24	14	0 ♐	12	4	17
11 48 59	27	25	15	1	24	5	18	27	25	15	0	52	5	18
11 52 40	28	26	16	2	4	6	19	28	26	16	1	31	6	19
11 56 0	29	26	17	2	44	7	20	29	26	16	2	11	6	20
12 0 0	30	27	17	3 ♐	25	8	21	30	27	17	2 ♐	51	7	21

TABLES OF HOUSES.

7 R. A. of the Meridian			LONDON. Lat. 51° 30′ 49″ North							NORTHAMPTON. Lat. 22° 11′ 0″ North.						
			10th	11th	12th	Ascendant.		2nd	3rd	10th	11th	12th	Ascendant.		2nd	3rd
			♎	♎	♏	♐		♑	♒	♎	♎	♏	♐		♑	♒
H.	M.	S.	°	°	°	°	′	°	°	°	°	°	°	′	°	°
12	0	0	0	27	17	3	25	8	21	0	27	17	2	51	7	21
12	3	40	1	28	18	4	5	9	22	1	28	18	3	31	8	22
12	7	20	2	29	19	4	46	10	23	2	29	19	4	11	9	23
12	11	1	3	♏	20	5	26	11	24	3	♏	19	4	52	10	24
12	14	41	4	1	20	6	7	12	26	4	1	20	5	32	11	25
12	18	21	5	1	21	6	48	13	27	5	1	21	6	13	12	27
12	22	2	6	2	22	7	29	14	28	6	2	21	6	54	13	28
12	25	42	7	3	23	8	11	15	29	7	3	22	7	35	14	29
12	29	23	8	4	23	8	52	16	♓	8	4	23	8	16	15	♓
12	33	4	9	5	24	9	34	17	1	9	5	24	8	57	16	1
12	36	45	10	5	25	10	16	18	2	10	5	24	9	39	17	2
12	40	27	11	6	25	10	58	19	4	11	6	25	10	20	18	4
12	44	8	12	7	26	11	41	20	5	12	7	26	11	2	19	5
12	47	50	13	8	27	12	24	21	6	13	8	26	11	45	20	6
12	51	32	14	9	28	13	7	22	7	14	9	27	12	27	21	7
12	55	14	15	10	28	13	50	23	8	15	10	28	13	10	22	8
12	58	57	16	10	29	14	33	24	10	16	10	29	13	53	23	10
13	2	40	17	11	♐	15	17	25	11	17	11	29	14	37	24	11
13	6	24	18	12	1	16	1	26	12	18	12	♐	15	20	25	12
13	10	7	19	13	1	16	46	27	13	19	13	1	16	4	26	13
13	13	51	20	14	2	17	31	28	15	20	14	2	16	49	27	14
13	17	36	21	15	3	18	16	29	16	21	14	2	17	34	28	16
13	21	21	22	15	4	19	2	♒	17	22	15	3	18	19	29	17
13	25	6	23	16	4	19	48	1	18	23	16	4	19	4	♒	18
13	28	52	24	17	5	20	34	2	20	24	17	5	19	51	2	19
13	35	38	25	18	6	21	21	4	21	25	18	5	20	37	3	21
13	36	25	26	19	7	22	9	5	22	26	19	6	21	24	4	22
13	40	13	27	19	7	22	57	6	23	27	19	7	22	11	5	23
13	44	1	28	20	8	23	45	7	25	28	20	8	22	59	6	25
13	47	49	29	21	9	24	34	8	26	29	21	8	23	48	8	26
13	51	38	30	22	10	25 ♐	24	10	27	30	22	9	24 ♐	37	9	27

TABLES OF HOUSES.

8 R. A. of the Meridian	LONDON. Lat. 51° 30′ 49″ North.							NORTHAMPTON. Lat. 52° 11′ 0″ North.						
	10th	11th	12th	Ascendant		2nd	3rd	10th	11th	12th	Ascendant.		2nd	3rd
	♏	♏	♐	♐		♒	♓	♏	♏	♐	♐		♒	♓
H. M. S.	°	°	°	°	′	°	°	°	°	°	°	′	°	°
13 51 38	0	22	10	25	24	10	27	0	22	9	24	37	9	27
13 55 27	1	23	11	26	14	11	28	1	23	10	25	26	10	28
13 59 18	2	24	11	27	5	12	♈	2	24	11	26	16	12	♈
14 3 8	3	24	12	27	56	14	1	3	24	12	27	7	13	1
14 7 0	4	25	13	28	48	15	2	4	25	12	27	59	14	2
14 10 52	5	26	14	29	41	16	4	5	26	13	28	51	16	4
14 14 44	6	27	15	0 ♑	34	18	5	6	27	14	29	44	17	5
14 18 37	7	28	15	1	28	19	6	7	28	15	0 ♑	37	18	6
14 22 31	8	29	16	2	23	20	8	8	29	16	1	32	20	8
14 26 26	9	30	17	3	19	22	9	9	29	16	2	27	21	9
14 30 21	10	♐	18	4	16	23	10	10	♐	17	3	23	23	10
14 34 17	11	1	19	5	13	25	12	11	1	18	4	20	24	12
14 38 14	12	2	20	6	12	26	13	12	2	19	5	18	26	13
14 42 11	13	3	20	7	11	28	14	13	3	20	6	17	27	14
14 46 9	14	4	21	8	12	29	15	14	4	21	7	17	29	16
14 50 9	15	5	22	9	13	♓	17	15	5	21	8	18	♓	17
14 54 7	16	6	23	10	16	3	18	16	5	22	9	20	2	18
14 58 8	17	6	24	11	20	4	19	17	6	23	10	23	3	19
15 2 8	18	7	25	12	25	6	21	18	7	24	11	27	5	21
15 6 10	19	8	26	13	31	8	22	19	8	25	12	33	7	22
15 10 12	20	9	27	14	39	9	23	20	9	26	13	40	9	23
15 14 16	21	10	27	15	48	11	25	21	10	27	14	49	10	25
15 18 19	22	11	28	16	58	13	26	22	11	28	15	59	12	26
15 22 24	23	12	29	18	10	14	27	23	12	29	17	10	14	27
15 26 29	24	13	♑	19	24	16	29	24	13	29	18	23	15	29
15 30 35	25	14	1	20	39	17	♉	25	13	♑	19	38	17	♉
15 34 32	26	14	2	21	56	19	1	26	14	1	20	55	19	1
15 38 49	27	15	3	23	15	21	2	27	15	2	22	13	21	3
15 42 57	28	16	4	24	36	22	4	28	16	3	23	38	23	4
15 47 6	29	17	5	25	58	24	5	29	17	4	24	56	24	5
15 51 16	30	18	6	27 ♑	23	26	6	30	18	5	26 ♑	20	26	6

TABLES OF HOUSES.

9 R.A. of the Meridian			LONDON. Lat. 51° 30′ 49″ North.							NORTHAMPTON. Lat. 52° 11′ 0″ North.						
			10th	11th	12th	Ascendant.		2nd	3rd	10th	11th	12th	Ascendant.		2nd	3rd
			♐	♐	♑	♑		♓	♉	♐	♐	♑	♑		♓	♉
H.	M.	S.	°	°	°	°	′	°	°	°	°	°	°	′	°	°
15	51	16	0	18	6	27	23	26	6	0	18	5	26	20	26	6
15	55	26	1	19	7	28	50	28	8	1	19	6	27	47	28	8
15	59	37	2	20	8	0 ♒	19	♈	9	2	20	7	29	16	♈	9
16	3	48	3	21	9	1	50	1	10	3	21	8	0 ♒	47	2	10
16	8	1	4	22	10	3	24	3	11	4	22	9	2	21	4	11
16	12	13	5	23	11	5	0	5	13	5	23	10	3	57	5	13
16	16	27	6	24	12	6	38	7	14	6	24	11	5	36	7	14
16	20	41	7	25	13	8	20	9	15	7	25	13	7	18	9	15
16	24	55	8	26	14	10	4	11	16	8	26	14	9	2	11	16
16	29	11	9	27	16	11	51	12	18	9	26	15	10	50	13	18
16	33	26	10	28	17	13	41	14	19	10	27	16	12	40	15	19
16	37	42	11	29	18	15	34	16	20	11	28	17	14	34	16	20
16	41	59	12	♑	19	17	29	18	21	12	29	18	16	31	18	21
16	46	17	13	1	20	19	28	20	22	13	♑	19	18	31	20	23
16	50	34	14	1	21	21	30	21	24	14	1	20	20	34	22	24
16	54	52	15	2	22	23	35	23	25	15	2	22	22	41	24	25
16	59	11	16	3	24	25	43	25	26	16	3	23	24	51	25	26
17	3	30	17	4	25	27	54	27	27	17	4	24	27	5	27	27
17	7	49	18	6	26	0 ♓	8	28	28	18	5	25	29	21	29	28
17	12	9	19	7	27	2	25	♉	♊	19	6	27	1 ♓	41	♉	♊
17	16	29	20	8	29	4	45	2	1	20	7	28	4	0	2	1
17	20	49	21	9	♒	7	8	3	2	21	8	29	6	30	4	2
17	25	10	22	10	1	9	33	5	3	22	9	♒	8	59	6	3
17	29	30	23	11	3	12	1	7	4	23	10	2	11	30	7	4
17	33	51	24	12	4	14	31	8	5	24	12	3	14	4	9	5
17	38	13	25	13	5	17	3	10	6	25	13	5	16	40	10	6
17	42	34	26	14	7	19	36	11	7	26	14	6	19	18	12	8
17	46	55	27	15	8	22	11	13	9	27	15	7	21	57	14	9
17	51	17	28	16	10	24	47	14	10	28	16	9	24	37	15	10
17	55	38	29	17	11	27	23	16	11	29	17	10	27	18	17	11
18	0	0	30	18	13	30 ♓	0	17	12	30	18	12	30 ♓	0	18	12

TABLES OF HOUSES.

10 R.A. of the Meridian.			LONDON. Lat. 51° 30′ 49″ North.							NORTHAMPTON. Lat. 52° 11′ 0″ North.						
			10th	11th	12th	Ascendant.		2nd	3rd	10th	11th	12th	Ascendant.		2nd	3rd
			♑	♑	♒	♈		♉	♊	♑	♑	♒	♈		♉	♊
H.	M.	S.	°	°	°	°	′			°	°	°	°	′		
18	0	0	0	18	13	0	0	17	12	0	18	12	0	0	18	12
18	4	22	1	19	14	2	37	19	13	1	19	13	2	42	20	13
18	8	43	2	20	16	5	13	20	14	2	20	15	5	23	21	14
18	13	5	3	21	17	7	49	22	15	3	21	16	8	3	23	15
18	17	26	4	22	19	10	24	23	16	4	22	18	10	42	24	16
18	21	47	5	23	20	12	57	25	17	5	23	20	13	20	25	17
18	26	9	6	25	22	15	29	26	18	6	25	21	15	56	27	18
18	30	30	7	26	23	17	59	28	19	7	26	23	18	30	28	19
18	34	50	8	27	25	20	27	29	20	8	27	24	21	1	♊	21
18	39	11	9	28	27	22	52	♊	21	9	28	26	23	30	1	22
18	43	31	10	29	28	25	15	1	22	10	29	28	25	56	2	23
18	47	51	11	♒	♓	27	35	2	23	11	♒	♓	28	19	3	24
18	52	11	12	2	2	29	52	4	25	12	2	1	0 ♉	39	5	25
18	56	30	13	3	3	2 ♉	6	5	26	13	3	3	2	55	6	26
19	0	49	14	4	5	4	17	6	27	14	4	5	5	9	7	27
19	5	8	15	5	7	6	25	8	28	15	5	6	7	19	8	28
19	9	26	16	6	9	8	30	9	29	16	6	8	9	26	10	29
19	13	43	17	8	10	10	32	10	♋	17	7	10	11	29	11	♋
19	18	1	18	9	12	12	31	11	1	18	9	12	13	29	12	1
19	22	18	19	10	14	14	26	12	2	19	10	14	15	26	13	2
19	26	34	20	11	16	16	19	13	3	20	11	15	17	20	14	3
19	30	49	21	12	18	18	9	14	4	21	12	17	19	10	15	4
19	35	5	22	14	19	19	56	16	5	22	14	19	20	58	16	4
19	39	19	23	15	21	21	40	17	5	23	15	21	22	42	17	5
19	43	33	24	16	23	23	21	18	6	24	16	23	24	24	19	6
19	47	47	25	17	25	25	0	19	7	25	17	25	26	3	20	7
19	51	59	26	19	27	26	36	20	8	26	18	26	27	39	21	8
19	56	12	27	20	28	28	10	21	9	27	20	28	29	13	22	9
20	0	28	28	21	♈	29	41	22	10	28	21	♈	0 ♊	44	23	10
20	4	34	29	22	2	1 ♊	10	23	11	29	22	2	2	13	24	11
20	8	44	30	24	4	2	37	24	12	30	24	4	3	40	25	12

TABLES OF HOUSES.

11 R.A. of the Meridian	LONDON. Lat. 51° 30′ 49″ North.							NORTHAMPTON. Lat. 52° 11′ 0″ North.						
	10th	11th	12th	Ascendant.		2nd	3rd	10th	11th	12th	Ascendant.		2nd	3rd
	♒	♒	♈	♊		♊	♋	♒	♒	♈	♊		♊	♋
H. M. S.	°	°	°	°	′	°	°	°	°	°	°	′	°	°
20 8 44	0	24	4	2	37	24	12	0	24	4	3	40	25	12
20 12 54	1	25	6	4	2	25	13	1	25	6	5	4	26	13
20 17 3	2	26	7	5	25	26	14	2	26	7	6	27	27	14
20 21 11	3	28	9	6	45	27	15	3	27	9	7	47	28	15
20 25 18	4	29	11	8	4	28	16	4	29	11	9	6	29	16
20 29 25	5	♓	13	9	21	29	16	5	♓	13	10	22	♋	17
20 33 31	6	1	14	10	36	♋	17	6	1	15	11	37	1	17
20 37 36	7	3	16	11	50	1	18	7	3	16	12	50	1	18
20 41 41	8	4	18	13	2	2	19	8	4	18	14	1	2	19
20 45 44	9	5	19	14	12	3	20	9	5	20	15	11	3	20
20 49 48	10	7	21	15	21	3	21	10	7	21	16	20	4	21
20 53 50	11	8	23	16	29	4	22	11	8	23	17	27	5	22
20 57 52	12	9	24	17	35	5	23	12	9	25	18	33	6	23
21 1 52	13	11	26	18	40	6	24	13	11	26	19	37	7	24
21 5 53	14	12	28	19	44	7	24	14	12	28	20	40	8	25
21 9 51	15	13	29	20	47	8	25	15	13	♉	21	42	9	25
21 13 51	16	15	♉	21	48	9	26	16	14	1	22	43	9	26
21 17 49	17	16	2	22	49	10	27	17	16	3	23	43	10	27
21 21 46	18	17	4	23	48	10	28	18	17	4	24	42	11	28
21 25 43	19	18	5	24	47	11	29	19	18	6	25	40	12	29
21 29 39	20	20	7	25	44	12	30	20	20	7	26	37	13	♌
21 33 34	21	21	8	26	41	13	♌	21	21	9	27	33	14	1
21 37 29	22	22	10	27	37	14	1	22	22	10	28	28	14	1
21 41 23	23	24	11	28	32	15	2	23	24	12	29	23	15	2
21 45 16	24	25	13	29	26	15	3	24	25	13	0 ♋	16	16	3
21 49 8	25	26	14	0 ♋	19	16	4	25	26	14	1	9	17	4
21 53 0	26	28	15	1	12	17	5	26	28	16	2	1	18	5
21 56 52	27	29	16	2	4	18	6	27	29	17	2	53	18	6
22 0 42	28	♈	18	2	55	19	6	28	♈	18	3	44	19	6
22 4 33	29	2	19	3	46	19	7	29	2	20	4	34	20	7
22 8 22	30	3	20	4 ♋	36	20	8	30	3	21	5 ♋	28	21	8

TABLES OF HOUSES.

12 R. A. of the Meridian	LONDON. Lat. 51° 30′ 49″ North.							NORTHAMPTON. Lat. 52° 11′ 0″ North.						
	10th	11th	12th	Ascendant.		2nd	3rd	10th	11th	12th	Ascendant.		2nd	3rd
	♓	♈	♉	♋		♋	♌	♓	♈	♉	♋		♋	♌
H. M. S.	°	°	°	°	′	°	°	°	°	°	°	′	°	°
22 8 22	0	3	20	4	36	20	8	0	3	21	5	23	21	8
22 12 11	1	4	21	5	26	21	9	1	4	22	6	12	22	9
22 15 59	2	5	23	6	15	22	10	2	6	24	7	1	22	10
22 19 47	3	7	24	7	3	23	11	3	7	25	7	48	23	11
22 23 35	4	8	25	7	51	23	11	4	8	26	8	36	24	11
22 27 22	5	9	26	8	39	24	12	5	9	27	9	23	25	12
22 31 8	6	10	28	9	26	25	13	6	11	28	10	10	25	13
22 34 54	7	12	29	10	12	26	14	7	12	29	10	56	26	14
22 38 39	8	13	♊	10	58	26	15	8	13	♊	11	41	27	15
22 42 24	9	14	1	11	44	27	16	9	14	2	12	26	28	16
22 46 29	10	15	2	12	29	28	16	10	16	3	13	11	28	16
22 49 53	11	17	3	13	14	29	17	11	17	4	13	56	29	17
22 53 36	12	18	4	13	59	29	18	12	18	5	14	40	♌	18
22 57 20	13	19	5	14	43	♌	19	13	19	6	15	23	1	19
23 1 3	14	20	6	15	27	1	20	14	20	7	16	7	1	20
23 4 46	15	22	7	16	10	2	20	15	22	8	16	50	2	20
23 8 28	16	23	8	16	53	2	21	16	23	9	17	33	3	21
23 12 10	17	24	9	17	36	3	22	17	24	10	18	15	4	22
23 15 52	18	25	10	18	19	4	23	18	25	11	18	58	4	23
23 19 33	19	26	11	19	2	5	24	19	26	12	19	40	5	24
23 23 15	20	28	12	19	44	5	25	20	28	13	20	21	6	24
23 26 56	21	29	13	20	26	6	25	21	29	14	21	3	7	25
23 30 37	22	♉	14	21	8	7	26	22	♉	15	21	44	7	26
23 34 18	23	1	15	21	49	7	27	23	1	16	22	25	8	27
23 37 58	24	2	16	22	31	8	28	24	2	17	23	6	9	28
23 41 39	25	3	17	23	12	9	29	25	3	18	23	47	9	29
23 45 19	26	4	18	23	53	9	29	26	5	19	24	28	10	29
23 48 59	27	6	19	24	34	10	♍	27	6	20	25	8	11	♍
23 52 40	28	7	20	25	14	11	1	28	7	21	25	49	11	1
23 56 20	29	8	21	25	55	12	2	29	8	22	26	29	12	2
24 0 0	30	9	22	26 ♋	35	12	3	30	9	23	27 ♋	9	13	3

TABLE OF RIGHT ASCENSION.

(N.B. For *Libra* add 180°: when the amount exceeds 360° subtract that sum.)

Aries, with *North* Latitude.—*Libra* with *South* Latitude.

	0°		1°		2°		3°		4°		5°		6°		7°	
D.	D.	M.	D.	M.	D.	M.	D.	M.	D.	M.	D.	M.	D.	M.	D.	M.
0	0	0	359	37	359	13	358	49	358	25	358	1	357	37	357	13
1	0	55	0	0	0	8	359	49	359	20	358	58	358	32	358	8
2	1	50	1	27	1	3	0	39	0	15	359	51	359	27	359	3
3	2	45	2	22	1	58	1	34	1	10	0	46	0	22	359	58
4	3	40	3	17	2	53	2	29	2	5	1	41	1	17	0	53
5	4	35	4	12	3	48	3	24	3	0	2	36	2	12	1	48
6	5	30	5	7	4	43	4	19	3	55	3	31	3	7	2	43
7	6	26	6	2	5	38	5	14	4	50	4	26	4	2	3	38
8	7	21	6	57	6	33	6	9	5	45	5	21	4	57	4	32
9	8	16	7	52	7	28	7	4	6	40	6	16	5	52	5	28
10	9	11	8	47	8	23	8	59	7	35	7	11	6	47	6	23
11	10	7	9	42	9	18	8	55	8	31	8	7	7	43	7	19
12	11	2	10	38	10	14	9	51	9	27	9	3	8	39	8	15
13	11	57	11	33	11	9	10	46	10	22	9	58	9	34	9	10
14	12	53	12	29	12	5	11	42	11	18	10	54	10	30	10	6
15	13	49	13	25	13	1	12	38	12	14	11	50	11	26	11	2
16	14	44	14	20	13	57	13	34	13	10	11	46	12	22	11	58
17	15	40	15	16	14	53	14	30	14	6	13	42	13	18	12	54
18	16	36	16	12	15	49	15	26	15	2	14	39	14	15	13	51
19	17	32	17	8	16	45	16	22	15	58	15	35	15	11	14	47
20	18	28	18	4	17	41	17	18	16	54	16	31	16	7	15	44
21	19	24	19	0	18	37	18	14	17	51	17	28	17	4	16	41
22	20	20	19	56	19	33	19	11	18	48	18	25	18	1	17	38
23	21	16	20	53	20	30	20	8	19	45	19	22	18	58	18	35
24	22	13	21	50	21	27	21	5	20	42	20	19	19	55	19	32
25	23	10	22	47	22	24	22	2	21	39	21	16	20	52	20	29
26	24	6	23	44	23	21	22	59	22	36	22	13	21	50	21	27
27	25	3	24	41	24	19	23	57	23	34	23	11	22	48	22	25
28	26	0	25	38	25	16	24	54	24	31	24	9	23	46	23	23
29	26	57	26	35	26	13	25	51	25	29	25	7	24	44	24	21
30	27	54	27	33	27	11	26	49	26	27	26	5	25	42	25	19

RULE.—*To find the Right-Ascension of the* SUN, *or any point in the heavens, or any planet without latitude, the longitude being given.* 1° Seek in the column marked 0° at the top the right-ascension corresponding to the even degree of longitude, which transcribe and mark A. 2°. Observe the increase of right-ascension caused by 1° of increase in longitude. Then say: "As 60 minutes of increase, so are the minutes of difference in right-ascension. 3°. Add this correction to A and the sum will be the right-ascension.

TABLE OF RIGHT ASCENSION.

(N.B. For *Scorpio* add 180°.

Taurus with *North* Latitude.—*Scorpio* with *South* Latitude.

	0°		1°		2°		3°		4°		5°		6°		7°	
D.	D.	M.	D.	M.	D.	M.	D.	M.	D.	M.	D.	M.	D.	M.	D.	M.
0	27	54	27	33	27	11	26	49	26	27	26	5	25	42	25	19
1	28	52	28	30	28	8	27	47	27	25	27	3	26	40	26	17
2	29	49	29	27	29	6	28	45	28	23	28	1	27	38	27	16
3	30	47	30	25	30	4	29	43	29	21	28	59	28	37	28	15
4	31	45	31	23	31	2	30	41	30	19	29	58	29	36	29	14
5	32	43	32	21	32	0	31	39	31	18	30	57	30	35	30	13
6	33	41	33	20	32	59	32	38	32	17	31	56	31	34	31	12
7	34	39	34	18	33	58	33	37	33	16	32	55	32	33	32	12
8	35	38	35	17	34	57	34	36	34	15	33	54	33	33	33	12
9	36	36	36	16	35	56	35	36	35	15	34	54	34	33	34	12
10	37	35	37	15	36	55	36	35	36	15	35	54	35	33	35	12
11	38	34	38	14	37	54	37	35	37	15	36	54	36	33	36	13
12	39	33	39	14	38	54	38	35	38	15	37	55	37	34	37	14
13	40	33	40	13	39	54	39	35	39	15	38	56	38	35	38	15
14	41	32	41	13	40	54	40	35	40	16	39	57	39	36	39	16
15	42	32	42	13	41	54	41	36	41	17	40	58	40	38	40	18
16	43	32	43	13	42	54	42	36	42	18	41	59	41	39	41	19
17	44	32	44	13	43	55	43	37	43	19	43	0	42	40	42	21
18	45	32	45	14	44	56	44	38	44	20	44	1	43	42	43	23
19	46	33	46	14	45	57	45	39	45	21	45	3	44	44	44	25
20	47	33	47	15	46	58	46	40	46	23	46	5	45	46	45	28
21	48	34	48	16	47	59	47	42	47	25	47	7	46	49	46	31
22	49	35	49	17	49	0	48	44	48	27	48	9	47	52	47	34
23	50	36	50	18	50	2	49	46	49	29	49	12	48	55	48	37
24	51	37	51	20	51	4	50	48	50	32	50	15	49	58	49	41
25	52	39	52	22	52	6	51	51	51	35	51	18	51	2	50	45
26	53	40	53	24	53	9	52	54	52	38	52	22	52	6	51	49
27	54	42	54	27	54	12	53	57	53	42	53	25	53	10	52	54
28	55	44	55	29	55	15	55	0	54	45	54	30	54	14	53	58
29	56	46	56	32	56	18	56	3	55	49	55	34	55	18	55	3
30	57	49	57	35	57	21	57	7	56	53	56	38	56	23	56	8

RULE.—*To find the Right-Ascension of any celestial body whose longitude and latitude are given.* 1°. Look for the even degree of longitude and even degree of latitude, at the head of the table, and in the angle of meeting will be found the right-ascension for those even degrees, which transcribe and mark A. 2°. In the same column of latitude, seek the right-ascension of the next degree of longitude and mark the increase. Then say "As the minutes of increase, so are the minutes of difference in the longitude given to the first correction." 3°. Observe the difference of right-ascension caused by one degree of increase in the latitude Then say "As 60′ are to the minutes of difference *plus* or *minus*," so are the minutes of difference in the latitude to the second correction. *plus* or *minus*. 4°. If the second correction be *plus*, then the sum of the two corrections added to A will be the right-ascension ; but if the second correction be *minus* then the difference of the two corrections applied to A, plus or minus, will give the right-ascension required.

TABLE OF RIGHT ASCENSION.

(N.B. For *Sagittary* add 180°.)

Gemini with *North* Latitude.—*Sagittarius* with *South* Latitude.																
	0°		1°		2°		3°		4°		5°		6°		7°	
D.	D.	M.	D.	M.	D.	M.	D.	M.	D.	M.	D.	M.	D.	M.	D.	M.
0	57	49	57	35	57	21	57	7	56	53	56	38	56	23	56	8
1	58	51	58	38	58	24	58	10	57	57	57	42	57	28	57	13
2	59	54	59	41	59	27	59	14	59	1	58	47	58	33	58	19
3	60	57	60	44	60	31	60	18	60	5	59	52	59	38	59	25
4	62	0	61	47	61	35	61	22	61	10	60	57	60	44	60	31
5	63	3	62	51	62	39	62	27	62	15	62	2	61	50	61	37
6	64	7	63	55	63	43	63	32	63	20	63	8	62	56	62	44
7	65	10	64	59	64	47	64	37	64	25	64	13	64	2	63	50
8	66	14	66	3	65	52	65	42	65	30	65	19	65	8	64	56
9	67	18	67	7	66	57	66	47	66	36	66	25	66	14	66	3
10	68	22	68	11	68	2	67	52	67	42	67	31	67	21	67	10
11	69	26	69	16	69	7	68	57	68	48	68	38	68	28	68	18
12	70	30	70	21	70	12	70	3	69	54	69	45	69	35	69	26
13	71	34	71	26	71	17	71	9	71	0	70	51	70	42	70	33
14	72	38	72	31	72	22	72	15	72	6	71	58	71	49	71	41
15	73	43	73	36	73	28	73	21	73	13	73	5	72	57	72	49
16	74	48	74	41	74	33	74	27	74	19	74	12	74	4	73	57
17	75	52	75	46	75	39	75	33	75	26	75	19	75	12	75	5
18	76	57	76	51	76	45	76	39	76	33	76	27	76	20	76	14
19	78	2	77	56	77	51	77	45	77	40	77	34	77	28	77	22
20	79	7	79	2	78	57	78	52	78	47	78	41	78	36	78	30
21	80	12	80	8	80	3	79	59	79	54	79	49	79	44	79	39
22	81	17	81	13	81	9	81	5	81	1	80	56	80	52	80	48
23	82	23	82	18	82	15	82	11	82	8	82	4	82	0	81	57
24	83	28	83	24	83	21	83	18	83	15	83	11	83	9	83	6
25	84	33	84	30	84	27	84	25	84	22	84	20	84	17	84	15
26	85	38	85	36	85	33	85	32	85	29	85	28	85	25	85	24
27	86	44	86	42	86	40	86	39	86	37	86	36	86	34	86	33
28	87	49	87	48	87	46	87	46	87	44	87	44	87	42	87	42
29	88	55	88	54	88	53	88	53	88	52	88	52	88	51	88	51
30	90	0	90	0	90	0	90	0	90	0	90	0	90	0	90	0

RULE.—*To find the Right-Ascension of the* SUN, *or any point in the heavens, or any planet without latitude, the longitude being given.* 1° Seek in the column marked 0° at the top the right-ascension corresponding to the even degree of longitude, which transcribe and mark A. 2°. Observe the increase of right-ascension caused by 1° of increase in longitude. Then say: "As 60 minutes of increase, so are the minutes of difference in right-ascension. 3°. Add this correction to A and the sum will be the right-ascension.

TABLE OF RIGHT ASCENSION.

(N.B. For *Capricorn* add 180°.)

Cancer with *North* Latitude.—*Capricorn* with *South* Latitude.

	0°		1°		2°		3°		4°		5°		6°		7°	
D.	D.	M.	D.	M.	D.	M.	D.	M.	D	M.	D.	M.	D.	M.	D.	M.
0	90	0	90	0	90	0	90	0	90	0	90	0	90	0	90	0
1	91	5	91	6	91	7	91	7	91	7	91	8	91	9	91	9
2	92	11	92	12	92	14	92	14	92	15	92	16	92	18	92	18
3	93	16	93	18	93	20	93	21	93	23	93	24	93	26	93	27
4	94	22	94	24	94	27	94	28	94	30	94	32	94	35	94	36
5	95	27	94	30	95	33	95	35	95	38	95	40	95	43	95	45
6	96	32	96	36	96	39	96	42	96	45	96	48	96	51	96	54
7	97	37	97	42	97	45	97	49	97	52	97	56	98	0	98	3
8	98	43	98	47	98	51	98	55	99	0	99	4	99	8	99	12
9	99	48	99	52	99	57	100	1	100	7	100	11	100	16	100	21
10	100	53	100	58	101	3	101	8	101	14	101	19	101	24	101	30
11	101	58	102	4	102	9	102	15	102	21	102	26	102	32	102	38
12	103	3	103	9	103	15	103	21	103	27	103	33	103	40	103	46
13	104	8	104	14	104	21	104	27	104	34	104	41	104	38	104	55
14	105	12	105	19	105	27	105	33	105	41	105	48	105	56	106	3
15	106	17	106	24	106	33	106	39	106	47	106	55	107	3	107	11
16	107	21	107	29	107	38	107	45	107	53	108	2	108	11	108	19
17	108	26	108	34	108	43	108	53	108	59	109	9	109	18	109	27
18	109	30	109	39	109	48	109	57	110	5	110	15	110	25	110	34
19	110	34	110	44	110	53	111	3	111	12	111	22	111	32	111	42
20	111	38	111	49	111	58	112	8	112	18	112	29	112	35	112	50
21	112	42	112	53	113	3	113	13	113	24	113	35	113	46	113	56
22	113	46	113	57	114	8	114	18	114	30	114	41	114	52	115	4
23	114	50	115	1	115	13	115	23	115	35	115	47	115	58	116	10
24	115	53	116	5	116	17	116	28	116	41	116	52	117	4	117	17
25	116	57	117	9	117	21	117	33	117	46	117	58	118	10	118	23
26	118	0	118	13	118	25	118	38	118	51	119	3	119	16	119	29
27	119	3	119	16	119	29	119	42	119	55	120	8	120	22	120	35
28	120	6	120	19	120	33	120	46	120	59	121	13	121	27	121	41
29	121	9	121	22	121	36	121	50	122	3	122	18	122	32	122	47
30	122	11	122	25	122	39	122	53	123	7	123	22	123	37	123	52

RULE.—*To find the Right-Ascension of any celestial body whose longitude and latitude are given.* 1°. Look for the even degree of longitude and even degree of latitude, at the head of the table and in the angle of meeting will be found the right-ascension for those even degrees, which transcribe and mark A. 2°. In the same column of latitude, seek the right-ascension of the next degree of longitude and mark the increase. Then say "As the minutes of increase, so are the minutes of difference in the longitude given to the first correction." 3°. Observe the difference of right-ascension caused by one degree of increase in the latitude. Then say "As 60′ are to the minutes of difference *plus* or *minus*" so are the minutes of difference in the latitude to the second correction, *plus* or *minus*. 4°. If the second correction be *plus*, then the sum of the two corrections added to A will be the right-ascension; but if the second correction be *minus* then the difference of the two corrections applied to A, plus or minus, will give the right-ascension required.

TABLE OF RIGHT ASCENSION.

(N.B. For *Aquarius* add 180°.)

Leo with *North* Latitude.—*Aquarius* with *South* Latitude.

	0°		1°		2°		3°		4°		5°		6°		7°	
D.	D.	M	D.	M.	D.	M.	D.	M.	D.	M.	D.	M.	D.	M.	D.	M.
0	122	11	122	25	122	39	122	53	123	7	123	22	123	37	123	52
1	123	14	123	28	123	42	123	57	124	11	124	26	124	42	124	57
2	124	16	124	31	124	45	125	0	125	15	125	30	125	46	126	2
3	125	18	125	33	124	48	126	3	126	18	126	34	126	50	127	6
4	126	20	126	36	126	51	127	6	127	22	127	38	127	54	128	11
5	127	21	127	38	127	54	128	9	128	25	128	42	128	58	129	15
6	128	23	128	40	128	56	129	12	129	28	129	45	130	2	130	19
7	129	24	129	42	129	58	130	14	130	31	130	48	131	5	131	23
8	130	25	130	43	131	0	131	16	131	33	131	51	132	8	132	26
9	131	26	131	44	132	1	132	18	132	35	132	53	133	11	133	29
10	132	27	132	45	133	2	133	20	133	37	133	55	134	14	134	32
11	133	27	133	46	134	3	134	21	134	39	134	57	135	16	135	35
12	134	28	134	47	135	4	135	22	135	40	135	59	136	18	136	37
13	135	28	135	47	136	5	136	23	136	41	137	0	137	20	137	39
14	136	28	136	47	137	6	137	24	137	42	138	1	138	21	138	41
15	137	28	137	47	138	6	138	24	138	43	139	2	139	22	139	42
16	138	28	138	47	139	6	139	25	139	44	140	3	140	24	140	44
17	139	27	139	47	140	6	140	25	140	45	141	4	141	25	141	45
18	140	27	140	46	141	6	141	25	141	45	142	5	142	26	142	46
19	141	26	141	46	142	6	142	25	142	45	143	6	143	27	143	47
20	142	25	142	45	143	5	143	25	143	45	144	6	144	27	144	48
21	143	24	143	44	144	4	144	24	144	45	145	6	145	27	145	48
22	144	22	144	43	145	3	145	24	145	45	146	6	146	27	146	48
23	145	21	145	42	146	2	146	23	146	44	147	5	147	27	147	48
24	146	19	146	40	147	1	147	22	147	43	148	4	148	26	148	48
25	147	17	147	39	148	0	148	21	148	42	149	3	149	25	149	47
26	148	15	148	37	148	58	149	19	149	41	150	2	150	24	150	46
27	149	13	149	35	149	56	150	17	150	39	151	1	151	23	151	45
28	150	11	150	33	150	54	151	15	151	37	151	59	152	22	152	44
29	151	8	151	30	151	52	152	13	151	35	152	57	153	20	153	43
30	152	6	152	27	152	49	153	11	153	33	153	55	154	18	154	41

RULE.—*To find the Right-Ascension of the* SUN, *or any point in the heavens, or any planet without latitude, the longitude being given.* 1°. Seek in the column marked 0° at the top the right-ascension corresponding to the even degree of longitude. which transcribe and mark A. 2°. Observe the increase of right-ascension caused by 1° of increase in longitude. Then say: "As 60 minutes of increase, so are the minutes of difference in right-ascension. 3°. Add this correction to A and the sum will the right-ascension.

TABLE OF RIGHT ASCENSION.

(N.B. For *Pisces* add 180° : if the amount exceeds 360° subtract that sum.)

Virgo with *North* Latitude.—*Pisces* with *South* Latitude.

	0°		1°		2°		3°		4°		5°		6°		7°	
D.	D.	M.	D.	M.	D.	M.	D.	M.	D.	M.	D.	M.	D.	M.	D.	M.
0	152	5	152	27	152	49	153	11	153	32	153	55	154	18	154	41
1	153	3	153	25	153	47	154	9	153	31	154	52	155	16	155	39
2	154	0	154	22	154	44	155	6	155	29	155	51	156	14	156	37
3	154	57	155	19	155	41	156	3	156	26	156	49	157	12	157	35
4	155	54	156	16	156	39	157	1	157	24	157	47	158	10	158	33
5	156	50	157	13	157	36	157	58	158	21	158	44	159	8	159	31
6	157	47	158	10	158	33	158	55	159	18	159	41	160	5	160	28
7	158	43	159	7	159	30	159	51	160	15	160	38	161	2	161	25
8	159	40	160	4	160	27	160	49	161	12	161	35	161	59	162	22
9	160	36	161	0	161	23	161	46	162	9	162	32	162	56	163	19
10	161	32	161	56	162	19	162	42	163	6	163	29	163	53	164	16
11	162	28	162	52	163	15	163	38	164	2	164	25	164	49	165	13
12	163	24	163	50	164	11	164	34	164	58	165	21	165	45	166	9
13	164	20	164	44	165	7	165	30	165	54	166	18	166	42	167	6
14	165	16	165	40	166	3	166	26	166	50	167	14	167	38	168	2
15	166	11	166	35	166	59	167	22	167	46	168	10	168	34	168	58
16	167	7	167	31	167	55	168	18	168	42	169	6	169	30	159	54
17	168	2	168	27	168	51	169	14	169	38	170	2	170	26	170	50
18	168	58	169	23	169	46	170	9	170	33	170	57	171	21	171	45
19	169	53	170	18	170	42	171	5	171	29	171	53	172	17	172	41
20	170	49	171	13	171	37	172	1	172	25	172	49	173	13	173	37
21	171	44	172	8	172	32	172	56	173	20	173	44	174	8	174	32
22	172	39	173	3	173	27	173	51	174	15	174	39	175	3	175	27
23	173	34	173	58	174	22	174	46	175	10	175	34	175	58	176	22
24	174	30	174	53	175	17	175	41	176	5	176	29	176	53	177	17
25	175	25	175	48	176	12	176	36	177	0	177	24	177	48	178	12
26	176	20	176	43	177	7	177	31	177	56	178	19	178	43	179	7
27	177	15	177	38	178	2	178	26	178	50	179	14	179	38	180	2
28	178	10	178	33	178	57	179	21	179	45	180	9	180	33	180	57
29	179	5	179	28	179	52	180	16	180	40	181	4	181	28	181	52
30	180	0	180	23	180	47	181	11	181	35	181	59	182	23	182	47

RULE.—*To find the Right-Ascension of any celestial body whose longitude and latitude are given.* 1°. Look for the even degree of longitude and even degree of latitude, at the head of the table, and in the angle of meeting will be found the right-ascension for those even degrees, which transcribe and mark A. 2°. In the same column of latitude, seek the right-ascension of the next degree of longitude and mark the increase. Then say "As the minutes of increase, so are the minutes of difference in the longitude given to the first correction" 3°. Observe the difference of right-ascension caused by one degree of increase in the latitude. Then say "As 60′ are to the minutes of difference *plus* or *minus*," so are the minutes of difference in the latitude to the second correction, *plus* or *minus*. 4°. If the second correction be *plus*, then the sum of the two corrections added to A will be the right-ascension; but if the second correction be *minus* then the difference of the two corrections applied to A, plus or minus, will give the right-ascension required.

TABLE OF RIGHT ASCENSION

(N.B. For *Aries* subtract 180°.)

Libra with *North* Latitude.—*Aries* with *South* Latitude.

	0°		1°		2°		3°		4°		5°		6°		7°	
D.	D.	M.	D.	M.	D.	M.	D.	M.	D.	M.	D.	M.	D.	M.	D.	M.
0	180	0	180	23	180	47	181	11	181	35	181	59	182	23	182	47
1	180	55	181	18	181	42	182	6	182	30	182	54	183	18	183	42
2	181	50	182	13	182	37	183	1	183	25	183	49	184	13	184	37
3	182	45	183	8	183	32	183	56	184	20	184	44	185	8	185	32
4	183	40	184	3	184	27	184	51	185	15	185	39	186	3	186	27
5	184	35	184	58	185	22	185	46	186	10	186	34	186	58	187	22
6	185	30	185	54	186	18	186	42	187	6	187	30	187	53	188	17
7	186	26	186	49	187	13	187	37	188	1	188	25	188	48	189	12
8	187	21	187	44	188	8	188	32	188	56	189	20	189	43	190	7
9	188	16	188	39	189	3	189	27	189	51	190	15	190	38	191	2
10	189	11	189	34	189	58	190	22	190	46	191	10	191	33	191	57
11	190	7	190	29	190	53	191	17	191	41	192	5	192	28	192	52
12	191	2	191	25	191	48	192	13	192	36	193	0	193	23	193	47
13	191	57	192	20	192	43	193	8	193	31	193	55	194	18	194	41
14	192	53	193	16	193	39	194	3	194	26	194	50	195	13	195	36
15	193	49	194	12	194	35	194	58	195	21	195	45	196	8	196	31
16	194	44	195	7	195	30	195	53	196	16	196	40	197	3	197	26
17	195	40	196	2	196	25	196	48	197	11	197	35	197	58	198	21
18	196	36	196	58	197	21	197	44	198	7	198	30	198	53	199	16
19	197	32	197	54	198	17	198	40	199	2	199	25	199	48	200	11
20	198	28	198	50	199	13	199	36	199	58	200	21	200	43	201	7
21	199	24	199	46	200	9	200	32	200	54	201	16	201	39	202	2
22	200	20	200	42	201	5	201	28	201	50	202	12	202	34	202	57
23	201	17	201	38	202	1	202	24	202	46	203	8	203	30	203	52
24	202	13	202	35	202	57	203	20	203	42	204	4	204	26	204	48
25	203	10	203	31	203	53	204	16	204	38	205	0	205	21	205	43
26	204	6	204	29	204	50	205	12	205	34	205	56	206	17	206	39
27	205	3	205	25	205	47	206	9	206	30	206	52	207	13	207	35
28	206	0	206	22	206	43	207	5	207	26	207	48	208	9	208	30
29	206	57	207	19	207	40	208	1	208	22	208	44	209	5	209	26
30	207	54	208	16	208	37	208	58	209	19	209	40	210	1	210	22

RULE.—*To find the Right-Ascension of the* SUN, *or any point in the heavens, or any planet without latitude, the longitude being given.* 1° Seek in the column marked 0° at the top the right-ascension corresponding to the even degree of longitude, which transcribe and mark A. 2°. Observe the increase of right-ascension caused by 1° of increase in longitude. Then say: "As 60 minutes of increase, so are the minutes of difference in right-ascension. 3°. Add this correction to A and the sum will be the right-ascension.

TABLE OF RIGHT ASCENSION.

(N.B. For *Taurus* subtract 180°.)

Scorpio with *North* Latitude.—*Taurus* with *South* Latitude.																
	0°		1°		2°		3°		4°		5°		6°		7°	
D.	D.	M.	D.	M.	D.	M.	D.	M.	D.	M.	D.	M.	D.	M.	D.	M.
0	207	54	208	16	208	37	208	58	209	19	209	40	210	1	210	22
1	208	52	209	13	209	34	209	55	210	16	210	37	210	57	211	18
2	209	49	210	10	210	31	210	52	211	13	211	34	211	54	212	14
3	210	47	211	17	211	28	211	49	212	10	212	31	212	51	213	11
4	211	45	212	5	212	25	212	46	213	7	213	27	213	47	214	7
5	212	43	213	3	213	23	213	43	214	4	214	24	214	44	215	4
6	213	41	214	1	214	21	214	41	215	1	215	21	215	41	216	1
7	214	39	214	59	215	19	215	39	215	58	216	18	216	38	216	57
8	215	38	215	57	216	17	216	37	216	56	217	15	217	35	217	54
9	216	36	216	56	217	15	217	35	217	54	218	13	218	32	218	51
10	217	35	217	54	218	13	218	33	218	52	219	11	219	29	219	48
11	218	34	218	53	219	12	219	31	219	50	220	9	220	27	220	45
12	219	33	219	52	220	11	220	30	220	48	221	7	221	25	221	43
13	220	33	220	51	221	10	321	28	221	46	222	5	222	23	222	41
14	221	32	221	50	222	9	222	27	222	45	223	3	223	21	223	39
15	222	32	222	50	223	8	223	26	223	44	224	2	224	19	224	37
16	223	32	223	49	224	7	224	25	224	43	225	0	225	17	225	35
17	224	32	224	49	225	6	225	24	225	42	225	59	226	15	226	33
18	225	32	225	49	226	6	226	23	226	41	226	58	227	14	227	31
19	226	33	226	49	227	6	227	23	227	40	227	57	228	13	228	29
20	227	33	227	49	228	6	228	23	228	39	228	56	229	12	229	28
21	228	34	228	50	229	6	229	23	229	39	229	55	230	11	230	27
22	229	35	229	50	230	6	230	23	230	38	230	54	231	10	231	25
23	230	36	230	51	231	6	231	23	231	38	231	53	232	9	232	24
24	231	37	231	52	232	7	232	23	232	38	232	53	233	8	233	23
25	232	39	232	53	233	8	233	24	233	38	233	53	234	8	234	22
26	233	40	233	55	234	9	234	24	234	38	234	53	235	7	235	21
27	234	42	234	57	235	11	235	25	235	39	235	53	236	7	236	21
28	235	44	235	58	236	12	236	26	236	40	236	54	237	7	237	20
29	236	47	237	0	237	14	237	27	237	41	237	54	238	7	238	20
30	257	49	238	2	238	15	238	29	238	42	238	55	239	7	239	20

RULE.—*To find the Right-Ascension of any celestial body whose longitude and latitude are given.* 1°. Look for the even degree of longitude and even degree of latitude, at the head of the table. and in the angle of meeting will be found the right-ascension for those even degrees, which transcribe and mark A. 2°. In the same column of latitude seek the right-ascension of the next degree of longitude and mark the increase. Then say "As the minutes of increase, so are the minutes of difference in the longitude given to the first correction." 3°. Observe the difference of right-ascension caused by one degree of increase in the latitude. Then say "As 60′ are to the minutes of difference *plus* or *minus* " so are the minutes of difference in the latitude to the second correction, *plus* or *minus*. 4°. If the second correction be *plus*, then the sum of the two corrections added to A will be the right-ascension; but if the second correction be *minus* then the difference of the two corrections applied to A, plus or minus, will give the right-ascension required.

TABLE OF RIGHT ASCENSION.

(N.B. For *Gemini* subtract 180°.)

Sagittarius with *North* Latitude.—*Gemini* with *South* Latitude.

	0°		1°		2°		3°		4°		5°		6°		7°	
D.	D.	M.	D.	M.	D.	M.	D.	M.	D.	M	D.	M.	D	M.	D.	M.
0	237	49	238	2	238	15	238	29	238	42	238	55	239	7	239	20
1	238	51	239	4	239	17	239	30	239	43	239	55	240	7	240	20
2	239	54	240	6	240	19	240	31	240	44	240	56	241	8	241	20
3	240	57	241	9	241	21	241	33	241	45	241	57	242	9	242	21
4	242	0	212	11	242	23	242	35	242	46	242	58	243	9	243	21
5	243	3	243	14	243	25	243	37	243	48	243	59	244	10	244	21
6	244	7	244	17	244	28	244	39	244	50	245	1	245	11	245	22
7	245	10	245	20	245	31	245	41	245	52	246	2	246	12	246	22
8	246	14	246	23	246	34	246	44	246	54	247	4	247	13	247	23
9	247	18	247	27	247	37	247	47	247	56	248	6	248	15	248	24
10	248	22	248	30	248	40	248	49	248	58	249	7	249	16	249	25
11	249	26	249	34	249	43	249	52	250	0	250	9	250	17	250	26
12	250	30	250	38	250	46	250	55	251	3	251	11	251	19	251	27
13	251	34	251	42	251	49	251	58	252	5	252	13	252	21	252	28
14	252	38	252	46	252	53	253	1	253	8	253	15	253	23	253	30
15	253	43	253	50	253	57	254	4	254	11	254	18	254	25	254	32
16	254	48	254	54	255	1	255	7	255	14	255	20	255	27	255	33
17	255	52	255	58	256	5	256	11	256	17	256	22	256	29	256	35
18	256	57	257	3	257	9	257	15	257	20	257	25	257	31	257	37
19	258	2	258	7	258	13	258	18	258	23	258	28	258	33	258	38
20	259	7	259	12	259	17	259	21	259	26	259	31	259	35	259	40
21	260	12	260	17	260	21	260	25	260	29	260	34	260	38	260	42
22	261	17	261	21	261	25	261	28	261	32	261	36	261	40	261	44
23	262	23	262	25	262	29	262	32	262	35	262	39	262	42	262	46
24	263	28	263	30	263	33	263	36	263	39	263	42	263	45	263	48
25	264	33	264	35	264	37	264	40	264	42	264	45	264	47	264	50
26	265	38	265	40	265	41	265	44	265	45	265	48	265	49	265	52
27	266	44	266	45	266	46	266	48	266	49	266	51	266	52	266	54
28	267	49	267	50	267	50	267	52	267	52	267	54	267	54	267	56
29	268	55	268	55	268	55	268	56	268	56	268	57	268	57	268	58
30	270	0	270	0	270	0	270	0	270	0	270	0	270	0	270	0

RULE.—*To find the Right-Ascension of the* SUN, *or any point in the heavens, or any planet without latitude, the longitude being given.* 1°. Seek in the column marked 0° at the top the right-ascension corresponding to the even degree of longitude, which transcribe and mark A. 2°. Observe the increase of right-ascension caused by 1° of increase in longitude. Then say: "As 60 minutes of increase, so are the minutes of difference in right-ascension, 3°. Add this correction to A, and the sum will be the right-ascension.

TABLE OF RIGHT ASCENSION.

(N.B. For *Cancer* subtract 180°.)

Capicorn with *North* Latitude.—*Cancer* with *South* Latitude.

	0°		1°		2°		3°		4°		5°		6°		7°	
D.	D.	M.	D.	M.	D.	M.	D.	M.	D.	M.	D.	M.	D.	M.	D.	M.
0	270	0	270	0	270	0	270	0	270	0	270	0	270	0	270	0
1	271	5	271	5	271	5	271	4	271	4	271	3	271	3	271	2
2	272	11	272	10	272	10	272	8	272	8	272	6	272	6	272	4
3	273	16	273	15	273	14	273	12	273	11	273	9	273	8	273	6
4	274	22	274	20	274	19	274	16	274	15	274	12	274	11	274	8
5	275	27	275	25	275	23	275	20	275	18	275	15	275	13	275	10
6	276	32	276	30	276	27	276	21	276	21	276	18	276	15	276	12
7	277	37	277	35	277	31	277	28	277	25	277	21	277	18	277	14
8	278	43	278	39	278	35	278	32	278	28	278	24	278	20	278	16
9	279	48	279	43	279	39	279	35	279	31	279	26	279	22	279	18
10	280	53	280	48	280	43	280	39	280	34	280	29	280	25	280	20
11	281	58	281	53	281	47	281	42	281	37	281	32	281	27	281	22
12	283	3	282	57	282	51	282	45	282	40	282	34	282	29	282	23
13	284	8	284	2	283	55	283	49	283	43	283	37	283	31	283	25
14	285	12	285	6	284	59	284	53	284	46	284	40	284	33	284	27
15	286	17	286	10	286	3	285	56	285	49	285	42	285	35	285	28
16	287	21	287	14	287	7	286	59	286	52	286	45	286	37	286	30
17	288	26	288	18	288	11	288	2	287	55	287	47	287	39	287	32
18	289	30	289	22	289	14	289	5	288	57	288	49	288	41	288	33
19	290	34	290	26	290	17	290	8	290	0	289	51	289	43	289	34
20	291	38	291	30	291	20	291	11	291	2	290	53	290	44	290	35
21	292	42	292	33	292	23	292	13	292	4	291	55	292	45	291	36
22	293	46	293	37	293	26	293	16	293	6	292	56	292	47	292	37
23	294	50	294	40	294	29	294	19	294	8	293	58	293	48	293	38
24	295	53	295	43	295	32	295	21	295	10	294	59	294	49	294	38
25	296	57	296	46	296	35	296	23	296	12	296	1	295	50	295	39
26	298	0	297	49	297	37	297	25	297	14	297	2	296	51	296	39
27	299	3	298	51	298	39	298	27	298	15	298	3	297	51	297	39
28	300	6	299	54	299	41	299	29	299	16	299	4	298	52	298	40
29	301	9	300	56	300	43	300	30	300	17	300	5	299	53	299	40
30	302	11	301	58	301	45	301	31	301	18	301	5	300	53	300	40

RULE.—*To find the Right-Ascension of any celestial body whose longitude and latitude are given.* 1°. Look for the even degree of longitude and even degree of latitude, at the head of the table, and in the angle of meeting will be found the right-ascension for those even degrees, which transcribe and mark A. 2°. In the same column of latitude, seek the right ascension of the next degree of longitude and mark the increase. Then say "As the minutes of increase, so are the minutes of difference in the longitude given to the first correction." 3°. Observe the difference of right-ascension caused by one degree of increase in the latitude. Then say "As 60′ are to the minutes of difference *plus* or *minus*," so are the minutes of difference in the latitude to the second correction, *plus* or *minus*. 4°. If the second correction be *plus*, then the sum of the two corrections added to A will be the right-ascension; but if the second correction be *minus* then the difference of the two corrections applied to A, plus or minus, will give the right-ascension required.

TABLE OF RIGHT ASCENSION.

(N.B. For *Leo* substract 180°.)

Aquarius with *North* Latitude.—*Leo* with *South* Latitude.																
	0°		1°		2°		3°		4°		5°		6°		7°	
D.	D.	M.	D.	M.	D.	M.	D.	M.	D.	M.	D.	M.	D.	M.	D.	M.
0	302	11	301	58	301	45	301	31	301	18	301	5	300	53	300	40
1	303	13	303	0	302	47	302	33	302	19	302	6	301	53	301	40
2	304	16	304	2	303	48	303	34	303	20	303	6	302	53	302	40
3	305	18	305	3	304	50	304	35	304	21	304	7	303	53	303	39
4	306	20	306	5	305	51	305	36	305	22	305	7	304	53	304	39
5	307	21	307	7	306	52	306	36	306	22	306	7	305	52	305	38
6	308	23	308	8	307	53	307	37	307	22	307	7	306	52	306	37
7	309	24	309	9	308	54	308	37	308	22	308	7	307	51	307	36
8	310	25	310	10	309	54	309	37	309	22	309	6	308	50	308	35
9	311	26	311	10	310	54	310	37	310	21	310	5	309	49	309	33
10	312	27	312	11	311	54	311	37	311	21	311	4	310	48	310	32
11	313	28	313	11	312	54	312	37	312	20	312	3	311	47	311	31
12	314	28	314	11	313	54	313	37	313	19	313	2	312	46	312	29
13	315	28	315	11	314	54	314	36	314	18	314	1	313	45	313	27
14	316	28	316	11	315	53	315	35	315	17	315	0	314	43	314	25
15	317	28	317	10	316	52	316	34	316	16	315	58	315	41	315	23
16	318	28	318	10	317	51	317	33	317	15	316	57	316	39	316	21
17	319	27	319	9	318	50	318	32	318	14	317	55	317	37	317	19
18	320	27	320	8	319	49	319	30	319	12	318	53	318	35	318	17
19	321	26	321	7	320	48	320	29	320	10	319	51	319	33	319	15
20	322	25	322	6	321	47	321	27	321	8	320	49	320	31	320	12
21	323	24	323	4	322	45	322	25	322	6	321	47	321	28	321	9
22	324	22	324	3	323	43	323	23	323	4	322	45	322	25	322	6
23	325	21	325	1	324	41	324	21	324	1	323	42	323	22	323	3
24	326	19	325	59	325	39	325	19	324	59	324	39	324	19	323	59
25	327	17	326	57	326	37	326	17	325	56	325	36	325	16	325	56
26	328	15	327	55	327	35	327	14	326	53	326	33	326	13	325	53
27	329	13	328	53	328	32	328	11	327	50	327	30	327	10	326	49
28	330	11	329	50	329	29	329	8	328	47	328	27	328	6	327	46
29	331	8	330	47	330	26	330	5	329	44	329	25	329	3	328	42
30	332	6	331	44	331	23	331	2	330	41	330	20	329	59	329	38

RULE.—*To find the Right-Ascension of the* SUN, *or any point in the heavens, or any planet without latitude, the longitude being given.* 1°. Seek in the column marked 0° at the top the right-ascension corresponding to the even degree of longitude, which transcribe and mark A. 2°. Observe the increase of right-ascension caused by 1° of increase in longitude. Then say: "As 60 minutes of increase, so are the minutes of difference in right-ascension." 3°. Add this correction to A, and the sum will be the right-ascension.

TABLE OF RIGHT ASCENSION.

(N.B. For *Virgo* subtract 180°.)

Pisces with *North* Latitude.—*Virgo* with *South* Latitude.

	0°		1°		2°		3°		4°		5°		6°		7°	
D.	D.	M.	D.	M.	D.	M.	D.	M.	D.	M.	D.	M.	D.	M.	D.	M.
0	332	6	331	44	331	23	331	2	330	41	330	20	329	59	329	38
1	333	3	332	41	332	20	331	59	331	38	331	16	330	55	330	34
2	334	0	333	38	333	17	332	55	332	34	332	12	331	51	331	30
3	334	57	334	35	334	13	333	51	333	30	333	8	332	47	332	25
4	335	54	335	32	335	10	334	48	334	26	334	4	333	43	333	21
5	336	50	336	29	336	7	335	44	335	22	335	0	334	39	334	17
6	337	47	337	25	337	3	336	40	336	18	335	56	335	34	335	12
7	338	43	338	22	337	59	337	36	337	14	336	52	336	30	336	8
8	339	40	369	18	338	55	338	32	338	10	337	48	337	26	337	3
9	340	36	340	14	339	51	339	28	339	6	338	43	338	21	337	58
10	341	32	341	10	340	47	340	24	340	2	339	39	339	17	338	54
11	342	28	342	6	341	43	341	20	340	58	340	35	340	12	339	49
12	343	24	343	2	342	39	342	16	341	53	341	30	341	7	340	44
13	344	20	343	58	343	35	343	12	342	49	342	25	342	2	341	39
14	345	16	344	53	344	30	344	7	343	44	343	20	342	57	342	34
15	346	11	345	58	345	25	345	2	344	39	344	15	343	52	343	29
16	347	7	346	44	346	21	345	57	345	34	345	10	344	47	344	24
17	348	3	347	40	347	17	346	52	346	29	346	5	345	42	345	19
18	348	58	348	35	348	12	347	47	347	24	347	0	346	37	346	13
19	349	53	349	31	349	7	348	43	348	19	347	55	347	32	347	8
20	350	49	350	26	350	3	349	38	349	14	348	50	348	27	348	3
21	351	44	351	21	350	57	350	33	350	9	349	45	349	22	348	58
22	352	39	352	16	351	52	351	28	351	4	350	40	350	17	349	53
23	353	34	353	11	352	47	352	23	351	59	351	35	351	12	350	48
24	354	30	354	6	353	42	353	18	352	54	352	30	352	7	351	43
25	355	25	355	1	354	38	354	14	353	50	353	26	353	2	352	38
26	356	20	355	57	355	33	355	9	354	45	354	21	353	57	353	33
27	357	15	356	52	356	28	356	4	355	40	355	16	354	52	354	28
28	358	10	357	47	357	23	356	59	356	35	356	11	355	47	355	23
29	359	5	358	42	358	18	357	54	357	30	357	6	356	42	356	18
30	360	0	359	37	359	13	358	49	358	25	358	1	357	37	357	13

Rule.—*To find the Right-Ascension of any celestial body whose longitude and latitude are given.* 1°. Look for the even degree of longitude and even degree of latitude, at the head of the table, and in the angle of meeting will be found the right-ascension for those even degrees, which transcribe and mark A. 2°. In the same column of latitude, seek the right-ascension of the next degree of longitude and mark the increase. Then say "As the minutes of increase, so are the minutes of difference in the longitude given to the first correction." 3°. Observe the difference of right-ascension caused by one degree of increase in the latitude. Then say "As 60′ are to the minutes of difference *plus* or *minus*," so are the minutes of difference in the latitude to the second correction, *plus* or *minus*. 4°. If the second correction be *plus*, then the sum of the two corrections added to A will be the right-ascension; but if the second correction be *minus*, then the difference of the two corrections applied to A, plus or minus, will give the right-ascension required.

Mean Obliquity of the Ecliptic, January 1st, 1912, 23° 27′ 2·64″.

TABLE OF DECLINATION.

Cancer.	Degrees of North Latitude.																Gemini.
	0°		1°		2°		3°		4°		5°		6°		7°		
D.	D.	M.	D.	M.	D.	M.	D.	M.	D.	M.	D.	M.	D.	M.	D.	M.	D.
0	23	27	24	27	25	27	26	27	27	27	28	27	29	27	30	27	30
1	23	27	24	27	25	27	26	27	27	27	28	27	29	27	30	27	29
2	23	26	24	26	25	26	26	26	27	26	28	26	29	26	30	26	28
3	23	25	24	25	25	25	26	25	27	25	28	25	29	25	30	25	27
4	23	23	24	23	25	23	26	23	27	23	28	23	29	23	30	23	26
5	23	21	24	21	25	21	26	21	27	21	28	21	29	21	30	21	25
6	23	19	24	19	25	19	26	19	27	19	28	19	29	19	30	19	24
7	23	17	24	16	25	16	26	16	27	16	28	16	29	16	30	16	23
8	23	13	24	13	25	13	26	13	27	13	28	13	29	13	30	13	22
9	23	9	24	9	25	9	26	9	27	9	28	9	29	9	30	9	21
10	23	4	24	4	25	4	26	4	27	4	28	4	29	4	30	4	20
11	23	0	24	0	25	0	26	0	27	0	28	0	29	0	30	0	19
12	22	55	23	56	24	56	25	56	26	56	27	56	28	56	29	55	18
13	22	49	23	49	24	49	25	49	26	49	27	49	28	49	29	49	17
14	22	44	23	44	24	43	25	43	26	43	27	42	28	42	29	41	16
15	22	37	23	37	24	36	25	36	26	36	27	35	28	35	29	34	15
16	22	30	23	30	24	29	25	29	26	29	27	28	28	28	29	27	14
17	22	23	23	23	24	22	25	22	26	21	27	20	28	19	29	18	13
18	22	15	23	15	24	14	25	14	26	13	27	12	28	11	29	10	12
19	22	7	23	7	24	6	25	6	26	5	27	4	28	3	29	2	11
20	21	58	22	58	23	57	24	56	25	55	26	54	27	53	28	52	10
21	21	49	22	49	23	48	24	47	25	46	26	45	27	44	28	43	9
22	21	40	22	40	23	39	24	38	25	37	26	36	27	35	28	35	8
23	21	30	22	30	23	29	24	28	25	27	26	26	27	25	28	25	7
24	21	19	22	19	23	18	24	17	25	16	26	15	27	14	28	13	6
25	21	8	22	8	23	7	24	6	25	5	26	4	27	3	28	2	5
26	20	58	21	56	22	55	23	54	24	53	25	52	26	51	27	50	4
27	20	47	21	44	22	43	23	42	24	41	25	40	26	39	27	38	3
28	20	35	21	33	22	31	23	30	24	29	25	28	26	26	27	25	2
29	20	23	21	21	22	19	23	18	24	17	25	16	26	14	27	13	1
30	20	10	21	8	22	6	23	5	24	4	25	2	26	0	26	59	0

Apparent Obliquity of the Ecliptic, January 1st, 1795, 23° 27′ 50·5″.

Rule.—*To find the Declination of the* Sun, *or any point in the Ecliptic* (*without latitude*), *the longitude being given.*—1°. Look for the even degree of longitude and in the column marked 0° at the top, note the declination corresponding thereto, and mark it A. 2°. In the same column, observe the difference of declination caused by one degree of longitude. Then say: "As 60′ are to the minutes of difference, so are the minutes of difference in the longitude to the *correction*." 3°. This correction added to, or subtracted from A, according to whether the declination is increasing or decreasing, will give the required *declination*.

TABLE OF DECLINATION.

LEO.	DEGREES OF NORTH LATITUDE.																TAURUS.
	0°		1°		2°		3°		4°		5°		6°		7°		
D.	D.	M.	D.	M.	D.	M.	D.	M.	D.	M.	D.	M.	D.	M.	D.	M.	D.
0	20	10	21	8	22	6	23	5	24	4	25	2	26	0	26	59	30
1	19	57	20	56	21	54	22	53	23	51	24	50	25	48	26	46	29
2	19	44	20	42	21	41	22	39	23	37	24	36	25	34	26	32	28
3	19	31	20	28	21	27	22	25	23	23	24	22	25	20	26	18	27
4	19	17	20	14	21	13	22	11	23	9	24	8	25	6	26	4	26
5	19	2	20	0	20	59	21	57	22	55	23	53	24	51	25	49	25
6	18	48	19	46	20	44	21	42	22	40	23	38	24	36	25	34	24
7	18	33	19	31	20	29	21	27	22	25	23	23	24	21	25	19	23
8	18	17	19	15	20	13	21	11	22	9	23	7	24	5	25	3	22
9	18	2	18	59	19	57	20	55	21	53	22	51	23	49	24	46	21
10	17	46	18	43	19	41	20	38	21	36	22	34	23	31	24	28	20
11	17	29	18	26	19	24	20	22	21	19	22	17	23	14	24	11	19
12	17	13	18	9	19	7	20	5	21	2	22	0	22	57	23	54	18
13	16	56	17	52	18	50	19	47	20	44	21	42	22	39	23	36	17
14	16	39	17	35	18	33	19	30	20	27	21	25	22	22	23	19	16
15	16	21	17	18	18	15	19	12	20	9	21	7	22	4	23	1	15
16	16	3	17	0	17	57	18	54	19	51	20	49	21	46	22	43	14
17	15	45	16	42	17	39	18	36	19	33	20	30	21	27	22	24	13
18	15	27	16	23	17	20	18	17	19	14	20	11	21	8	22	5	12
19	15	9	16	4	17	1	17	58	18	55	19	52	20	49	21	46	11
20	14	50	15	45	16	41	17	38	18	35	19	32	20	29	21	26	10
21	14	31	15	26	16	22	17	19	18	16	19	13	20	10	21	7	9
22	14	11	15	7	16	3	17	0	17	56	18	53	19	50	20	47	8
23	13	52	14	47	15	43	16	40	17	36	18	33	19	29	20	26	7
24	13	32	14	27	15	23	16	19	17	15	18	12	19	8	20	5	6
25	13	12	14	7	15	3	16	0	16	56	17	53	18	49	19	45	5
26	12	52	13	47	14	43	15	39	16	35	17	32	18	28	19	24	4
27	12	32	13	27	14	23	15	19	16	15	17	12	18	8	19	4	3
28	12	11	13	6	14	2	14	58	15	54	16	51	17	47	18	43	2
29	11	50	12	45	13	41	14	37	15	33	16	30	17	26	18	22	1
30	11	29	12	24	13	20	14	16	15	12	16	8	17	4	18	0	0

RULE.—*To find the Declination of any heavenly body whose longitude and latitude are given.*—1°. Look for the even degree of longitude and under the even degree of latitude, at the head of the Table; at the angle of meeting will be found the declination for those even degrees, which transcribe and call A. 2°. In the same column of latitude, seek the declination for the next even degree of longitude, and note the difference. Then say: "As 60′ are to the minutes of difference, so are the minutes of difference in the *longitude* given to the *first correction.*" 3°. Observe the *difference* of declination caused by one degree of increase in the *latitude.* Then say: "As 60′ are to the minutes of difference, so are the minutes of difference in the *latitude* given to the *second correction.*" 4°. If both corrections be *plus* or *minus*, then the *sum* of the two corrections, added to or subtracted from A, will give the required *declination.* But, if one be *plus* and the other *minus*, then the *difference* of the two corrections added to or subtracted from A, will give the *declination* required.

TABLE OF DECLINATION.

VIRGO.	DEGREES OF NORTH LATITUDE.																ARIES.
	0°		1°		2°		3°		4°		5°		6°		7°		
D.	D.	M.	D.	M.	D.	M.	D.	M.	D.	M.	D.	M.	D.	M.	D.	M.	D.
0	11	29	12	24	13	20	14	16	15	12	16	8	17	4	18	0	30
1	11	7	12	4	13	0	13	56	14	51	15	47	16	43	17	39	29
2	10	46	11	42	12	38	13	33	14	29	15	25	16	21	17	17	28
3	10	25	11	21	12	17	13	12	14	8	15	4	16	0	16	56	27
4	10	3	10	59	11	55	12	51	13	47	14	43	15	39	16	35	26
5	9	41	10	37	11	35	12	30	13	26	14	22	15	18	16	14	25
6	9	19	10	17	11	11	12	6	13	2	13	58	14	54	15	50	24
7	8	57	9	53	10	49	11	44	12	40	13	35	14	31	15	26	23
8	8	35	9	31	10	27	11	22	12	18	13	13	14	9	15	4	22
9	8	12	9	8	10	4	10	59	11	54	12	49	13	44	14	39	21
10	7	50	8	46	9	41	10	36	11	31	12	26	13	21	14	16	20
11	7	27	8	22	9	17	10	12	11	7	12	2	12	57	13	52	19
13	7	4	8	0	8	55	9	50	10	45	11	40	12	35	13	30	18
13	6	41	7	36	8	31	9	26	10	21	11	16	12	11	13	6	17
14	6	18	7	13	8	8	9	3	9	58	10	53	11	48	12	43	16
15	5	55	6	51	7	46	8	41	9	36	10	31	11	26	12	21	15
16	5	32	6	28	7	23	8	18	9	13	10	8	11	3	11	58	14
17	5	8	6	4	6	59	7	54	8	49	9	44	10	39	11	34	13
18	4	45	5	41	6	36	7	31	8	26	9	21	10	16	11	11	12
19	4	21	5	17	6	12	7	7	8	2	8	57	9	52	10	47	11
20	3	58	4	54	5	49	6	44	7	39	8	34	9	29	10	24	10
21	3	34	4	30	5	25	6	20	7	15	8	10	9	5	10	0	9
22	3	11	4	7	5	2	5	57	6	52	7	47	8	42	9	37	8
23	2	47	3	43	4	38	5	33	6	28	7	23	8	18	9	13	7
24	2	23	3	19	4	14	5	9	6	4	6	59	7	54	8	49	6
25	1	59	2	55	3	50	4	45	5	40	6	35	7	30	8	25	5
26	1	36	2	31	3	26	4	21	5	16	6	11	7	6	8	1	4
27	1	12	2	7	3	2	3	57	4	52	5	47	6	42	7	37	3
28	0	48	1	43	2	38	3	33	4	28	5	23	6	18	7	13	2
29	0	24	1	19	2	14	3	9	4	4	4	59	5	54	6	49	1
30	0	0	0	55	1	50	2	45	3	40	4	35	5	30	6	25	0

RULE.—*To find the Longitude of the* SUN, *or body without latitude, corresponding to a given declination.*—1°. Seek in the column marked 0° at the top, the declination nearest to that given, and transcribe the degree of longitude corresponding thereto, marking it A. 2°. Observe the difference of declination caused by one degree of longitude. Then say: "As the minutes of difference of declination are to 60′ of longitude, so are the minutes of difference (between the given declination and that corresponding to the degree of longitude transcribed) to the *correction.*" 3°. Add the correction to A if it be *plus*, subtract it if it be *minus*, and the required *longitude* will be obtained.

[*Note.*—The longitude *and latitude* of the Moon, or a planet, corresponding to a given declination, must be computed from an *Ephemeris*, or the *Nautical Almanac* for the year of birth.]

TABLE OF DECLINATION.

SOUTH.

LIBRA.	DEGREES OF NORTH LATITUDE.																PISCES.
	0°		1°		2°		3°		4°		5°		6°		7°		
D.	D.	M.	D.	M.	D.	M.	D.	M.	D.	M.	D.	M.	D.	M.	D.	M.	D.
0	0	0	0	55	1	50	2	45	3	40	4	35	5	30	6	25	30
1	0	24	0	31	1	27	2	21	3	16	4	11	5	6	6	1	29
2	0	48	0	7	1	3	1	57	2	52	3	47	4	42	5	37	28
3	1	12	0	17	0	39	1	34	2	29	3	24	4	19	5	14	27
4	1	36	0	41	0	15	1	10	2	5	3	0	3	55	4	50	26
5	1	59	1	5	0	10	0	46	1	41	2	36	3	31	4	26	25
6	2	23	1	28	0	33	0	22	1	17	2	12	3	7	4	2	24
7	2	47	1	52	0	57	0	2	0	53	1	48	2	43	3	34	23
8	3	11	2	16	1	21	0	26	0	29	1	25	2	20	3	15	22
9	3	34	2	39	1	44	0	49	0	6	1	2	1	57	2	52	21
10	3	58	3	3	2	8	1	13	0	18	0	38	1	33	2	28	20
11	4	21	3	26	2	31	1	36	0	41	0	14	1	9	2	4	19
12	4	45	3	50	2	55	2	0	1	5	0	10	0	46	1	41	18
13	5	8	4	13	3	18	2	23	1	28	0	33	0	24	1	18	17
14	5	32	4	37	3	42	2	46	1	51	0	56	0	0	0	55	16
15	5	55	5	0	4	5	3	9	2	14	1	18	0	23	0	32	15
16	6	18	5	23	4	27	3	31	2	36	1	40	0	45	0	9	14
17	6	41	5	45	4	50	3	54	2	59	2	3	1	8	0	13	13
18	7	4	6	9	5	14	4	18	3	23	2	27	1	32	0	36	12
19	7	27	6	31	5	36	4	40	3	45	2	49	1	54	0	58	11
20	7	50	6	54	5	58	5	2	4	6	3	10	2	15	1	19	10
21	8	12	7	16	6	20	5	24	4	28	3	32	2	37	1	41	9
22	8	35	7	39	6	43	5	47	4	51	3	56	3	0	2	4	8
23	8	57	8	1	7	5	6	9	5	13	4	18	3	22	2	26	7
24	9	19	8	23	7	27	6	31	5	35	4	49	3	45	2	49	6
25	9	41	8	45	7	49	6	53	5	58	5	2	4	6	3	10	5
26	10	3	9	7	8	11	7	15	6	19	5	24	4	28	3	32	4
27	10	25	9	30	8	34	7	38	6	42	5	46	4	50	3	54	3
28	10	46	9	51	8	55	8	1	7	4	6	8	5	12	4	16	2
29	11	7	10	13	9	17	8	21	7	24	6	28	5	32	4	36	1
30	11	29	10	33	9	37	8	41	7	45	6	49	5	53	4	57	0

NORTH.

SOUTH.

RULE.—*To find the Declination of the* SUN, *or any point in the Ecliptic (without latitude) the longitude being given.* 1°. Look for the even degree of longitude and in the column marked 0° at the top, note the declination corresponding thereto, and mark it A. 2°. In the same column, observe the difference of declination caused by one degree of longitude. Then say: "As 60′ are to the minutes of difference, so are the minutes of difference in the longitude to the *correction.*" 3°. This correction added to, or subtracted from A, according to whether the declination is increasing or decreasing, will give the required *declination.*

TABLE OF DECLINATION.

SCORPIO.	DEGREES OF NORTH LATITUDE.																AQUARIUS.
	0°		1°		2°		3°		4°		5°		6°		7°		
D.	D.	M.	D.	M.	D.	M.	D.	M.	D.	M.	D.	M.	D.	M.	D.	M.	D.
0	11	29	10	33	9	37	8	41	7	45	6	49	5	53	4	57	30
1	11	50	10	54	9	58	9	2	8	6	7	10	6	14	5	18	29
2	12	11	11	15	10	18	9	22	8	26	7	29	6	32	5	36	28
3	12	32	11	36	10	39	9	43	8	47	7	50	6	54	5	58	27
4	12	52	11	56	10	58	10	1	9	5	8	8	7	12	6	16	26
5	13	12	12	16	11	19	10	22	9	26	8	29	7	33	6	37	25
6	13	32	12	36	11	39	10	42	9	46	8	49	7	52	6	55	24
7	13	52	12	56	11	59	11	2	10	5	9	8	8	11	7	14	23
8	14	11	13	14	12	17	11	20	10	23	9	26	8	29	7	32	22
9	14	31	13	34	12	37	11	40	10	43	9	46	8	49	7	52	21
10	14	50	13	53	12	56	11	59	11	2	10	5	9	8	8	11	20
11	15	9	14	12	13	15	12	18	11	21	10	23	9	26	8	29	19
12	15	27	14	30	13	33	12	36	11	39	10	41	9	44	8	47	18
13	15	45	14	47	13	50	12	53	11	56	10	58	10	1	9	4	17
14	16	3	15	5	14	8	13	11	12	14	11	16	10	19	9	22	16
15	16	21	15	23	14	26	13	29	12	34	11	34	10	37	9	40	15
16	16	39	15	41	14	44	13	46	12	49	11	51	10	54	9	57	14
17	16	56	15	58	15	1	14	3	13	6	12	8	11	11	10	14	13
18	17	13	16	15	15	18	14	20	13	22	12	24	11	27	10	30	12
12	17	29	16	31	15	33	14	35	13	37	12	39	11	42	10	45	11
20	17	46	16	48	15	50	14	52	13	54	12	56	11	59	11	1	10
21	18	2	17	4	16	6	15	8	14	10	13	12	12	15	11	17	9
22	18	17	17	19	16	21	15	23	14	25	13	26	12	28	11	30	8
23	18	33	17	35	16	36	15	38	14	40	13	41	12	43	11	45	7
24	18	48	17	50	16	52	15	54	14	56	13	57	12	59	12	0	6
25	19	2	18	4	17	6	16	8	15	10	14	11	13	15	12	14	5
26	19	17	18	19	17	20	16	22	15	24	14	25	13	27	12	29	4
27	19	31	18	33	17	34	16	36	15	37	14	39	13	40	12	42	3
28	19	44	18	45	17	47	16	48	15	49	14	51	13	52	12	54	2
29	19	57	18	58	17	59	17	1	16	2	15	4	14	5	13	7	1
30	20	10	19	11	18	12	17	14	16	15	15	16	14	17	13	18	0

RULE.—*To find the Declination of any heavenly body whose longitude and latitude are given.*—1°. Look for the even degree of longitude and under the even degree of latitude, at the head of the Table; at the angle of meeting will be found the declination for those even degrees, which transcribe and call A. 2°. In the same column of latitude, seek the declination for the next even degree of longitude, and note the difference. Then say: "As 60′ are to the minutes of difference, so are the minutes of difference in the *longitude* given to the *first correction*." 3°. Observe the *difference* of declination caused by one degree of increase in the *latitude*. Then say: "As 60′ are to the minutes of difference, so are the minutes of difference in the *latitude* given to the *second correction*." 4° If both corrections be *plus* or *minus*, then the *sum* of the two corrections, added to or subtracted from A, will give the required *declination*. But, if one be *plus* and the other *minus*, then the *difference* of the two corrections added to or subtracted from A, will give the *declination* required.

TABLE OF DECLINATION.

Mean Obliquity of the Ecliptic, January 1st, 1912, 23° 27′ 2·64″.

SAGITTARY.	DEGREES OF NORTH LATITUDE.																CAPRICORN.
	0°		1°		2°		3°		4°		5°		6°		7°		
D.	D.	M.	D.	M.	D.	M.	D.	M.	D.	M.	D.	M.	D.	M.	D.	M.	D.
0	20	10	19	11	18	12	17	14	16	15	15	16	14	17	13	18	30
1	20	23	19	24	18	25	17	26	16	27	15	29	14	30	13	31	29
2	20	35	19	36	18	37	17	38	16	39	15	41	14	42	13	43	28
3	20	47	19	48	18	49	17	50	16	52	15	53	14	54	13	55	27
4	20	58	19	59	19	0	18	1	17	2	16	3	15	5	14	6	26
5	21	8	20	9	19	10	18	11	17	12	16	14	15	15	14	16	25
6	21	19	20	20	19	21	18	22	17	23	16	24	15	25	14	26	24
7	21	30	20	31	19	32	18	33	17	34	16	34	15	35	14	36	23
8	21	40	20	41	19	42	18	43	17	44	16	43	15	44	14	44	22
9	21	49	20	50	19	51	18	52	17	53	16	53	15	54	14	54	21
10	21	58	20	59	20	0	19	1	18	2	17	2	16	2	15	3	20
11	22	7	21	8	20	9	19	10	18	11	17	11	16	11	15	12	19
12	22	15	21	16	20	17	19	18	18	19	17	19	16	19	15	20	18
13	22	23	21	24	20	25	19	25	18	26	17	26	16	26	15	27	17
14	22	30	21	31	20	32	19	32	18	33	17	33	16	33	15	34	16
15	22	37	21	37	20	37	19	37	18	38	17	38	16	38	15	39	15
16	22	44	21	44	20	44	19	44	18	45	17	45	16	45	15	46	14
17	22	49	21	49	20	49	19	49	18	50	17	51	16	51	15	52	13
18	22	56	21	56	20	56	19	56	18	57	17	57	16	57	15	58	12
19	23	0	22	0	21	0	20	0	19	1	18	2	17	2	16	2	11
20	23	4	22	4	21	4	20	4	19	4	18	4	17	4	16	4	10
21	23	9	22	9	21	9	20	9	19	9	18	9	17	9	16	9	9
22	23	13	22	13	21	13	20	13	19	13	18	13	17	13	16	13	8
23	23	17	22	16	21	16	20	16	19	16	18	16	17	16	16	16	7
24	23	19	22	19	21	19	20	19	19	19	18	19	17	19	16	19	6
25	23	21	22	21	21	21	20	21	19	21	18	21	17	21	16	21	5
26	23	23	22	24	21	24	20	24	19	24	18	24	17	24	16	24	4
27	23	25	22	25	21	25	20	25	19	25	18	25	17	25	16	25	3
28	23	26	22	26	21	26	20	26	19	26	18	26	17	26	16	26	2
29	23	27	22	27	21	27	20	27	19	27	18	27	17	27	16	27	1
30	23	27	22	27	21	27	20	27	19	27	18	27	17	27	16	27	0

Apparent Obliquity of the Ecliptic, January 1st, 1795, 23° 27′ 50·5″.

RULE.—*To find the Longitude of the* SUN *or body without latitude, corresponding to a given declination.*—1°. Seek in the column marked 0° at the top, the declination nearest to that given, and transcribe the degree of longitude corresponding thereto, marking it A. 2°. Observe the difference of declination caused by one degree of longitude. Then say: "As the minutes of difference of declination are to 60′ of longitude, so are the minutes of difference (between the given declination and that corresponding to the degree of longitude transcribed) to the *correction.*" 3°. Add the correction to A if it be *plus*, subtract it if it be *minus*, and the required *longitude* will be obtained.

[*Note.*—The longitude *and latitude* of the Moon, or a planet, corresponding to a given declination, must be computed from an *Ephemeris*, or the *Nautical Almanac* for the year of birth.]

Mean Obliquity of the Ecliptic, January 1st, 1912, 23° 27′ 2·64″.

TABLE OF DECLINATION.

Cancer.	Degrees of South Latitude.																Gemini.
	0°		1°		2°		3°		4°		5°		6°		7°		
D.	D.	M.	D.	M.	D.	M.	D.	M.	D.	M.	D.	M.	D.	M.	D.	M.	D.
0	23	27	22	27	21	27	20	27	19	27	18	27	17	27	16	27	30
1	23	27	22	27	21	27	20	27	19	27	18	27	17	27	16	27	29
2	23	26	22	26	21	26	20	26	19	26	18	26	17	26	16	26	28
3	23	25	22	25	21	25	20	25	19	25	18	25	17	25	16	25	27
4	23	23	22	24	21	25	20	25	19	25	18	25	17	25	16	25	26
5	23	21	22	21	21	21	20	21	19	21	18	21	17	21	16	21	25
6	23	19	22	19	21	19	20	19	19	19	18	19	17	19	16	19	24
7	23	17	22	16	21	16	20	16	19	16	18	16	17	16	16	16	23
8	23	13	22	13	21	13	20	13	19	13	18	13	17	13	16	13	22
9	23	9	22	9	21	9	20	9	19	9	18	9	17	9	16	9	21
10	23	4	22	4	21	4	20	4	19	4	18	4	17	4	16	4	20
11	23	0	22	0	21	0	20	0	19	1	18	2	17	2	16	2	19
12	22	56	21	56	20	56	19	56	18	57	17	57	16	57	15	58	18
13	22	49	21	50	20	50	19	50	18	51	17	51	16	51	15	52	17
14	22	44	21	44	20	44	19	44	18	45	17	45	16	45	15	46	16
15	22	37	21	37	20	37	19	37	18	38	17	38	16	38	15	39	15
16	22	30	21	31	20	32	19	32	18	33	17	33	16	33	15	34	14
17	22	23	21	24	20	25	19	25	18	26	17	26	16	26	15	27	13
18	22	15	21	16	20	17	19	18	18	19	17	19	16	19	15	20	12
19	22	7	21	8	20	9	19	10	18	11	17	11	16	11	15	12	11
20	21	58	20	59	20	0	19	1	18	2	17	2	16	2	15	3	10
21	21	49	20	50	19	51	18	52	17	53	16	53	15	54	14	54	9
22	21	40	20	41	19	42	18	43	17	44	16	43	15	44	14	44	8
23	21	30	20	31	19	32	18	33	17	34	16	34	15	35	14	36	7
24	21	19	20	21	19	22	18	23	17	24	16	25	15	25	14	26	6
25	21	8	20	10	19	11	18	12	17	12	16	14	15	15	14	16	5
26	20	58	19	59	19	0	18	1	17	2	16	3	15	5	14	6	4
27	20	47	19	48	18	49	17	50	16	52	15	53	14	54	13	55	3
28	20	35	19	36	18	37	17	38	16	39	15	41	14	42	13	43	2
29	20	23	19	24	18	25	17	26	16	27	15	29	14	30	13	31	1
30	20	10	19	11	18	12	17	14	16	15	15	16	14	17	13	18	0

Apparent Obliquity of the Ecliptic, January 1st, 1795, 23° 27′ 50·5″.

Rule.—*To find the Declination of the* Sun, *or any point in the Ecliptic (without latitude) the longitude being given.*—1°. Look for the even degree of longitude and in the column marked 0° at the top, note the declination corresponding thereto, and mark it A. 2°. In the same column, observe the difference of declination caused by one degree of longitude. Then say: "As 60′ are to the minutes of difference, so are the minutes of difference in the longitude to the *correction.*" 3°. This correction added to, or subtracted from A, according to whether the declination is increasing or decreasing, will give the required *declination.*

TABLE OF DECLINATION.

Leo.	Degrees of South Latitude.																Taurus.
	0°		1°		2°		3°		4°		5°		6°		7°		
D.	D.	M.	D.	M.	D.	M.	D.	M.	D.	M.	D.	M.	D.	M.	D.	M.	D.
0	20	10	19	11	18	12	17	14	16	15	15	16	14	17	13	18	30
1	19	57	18	58	17	59	17	1	16	2	15	14	14	5	13	7	29
2	19	44	18	45	17	47	16	48	15	49	14	51	13	52	12	54	28
3	19	31	18	33	17	34	16	36	15	37	14	39	13	40	12	42	27
4	19	17	18	19	17	20	16	22	15	24	14	25	13	27	12	29	26
5	19	2	18	4	17	6	16	8	15	10	14	11	13	13	12	14	25
6	18	48	17	50	16	52	15	54	14	56	13	57	12	59	12	0	24
7	18	33	17	35	16	36	15	38	14	40	13	41	12	43	11	45	23
8	18	17	17	19	16	21	15	23	14	25	13	26	12	28	11	30	22
9	18	2	17	4	16	6	15	8	14	10	13	12	12	15	11	17	21
10	17	46	16	48	15	50	14	52	13	54	12	56	11	59	11	1	20
11	17	29	16	31	15	33	14	35	13	37	12	39	11	42	10	45	19
12	17	13	16	15	15	18	14	20	13	22	12	24	11	27	10	30	18
13	16	56	15	58	15	1	14	3	13	6	12	8	11	11	10	14	17
14	16	39	15	41	14	44	13	46	12	49	11	51	10	54	9	57	16
15	16	21	15	23	14	26	13	29	12	32	11	34	10	37	9	40	15
16	16	3	15	5	14	8	13	11	12	14	11	16	10	19	9	22	14
17	15	45	14	47	13	50	12	53	11	56	10	58	10	1	9	4	13
18	15	27	14	30	13	33	12	36	11	39	10	41	9	44	8	47	12
19	15	9	14	12	13	15	12	18	11	21	10	23	9	26	8	29	11
20	14	50	13	53	12	56	11	59	11	2	10	5	9	8	8	11	10
21	14	31	13	34	12	37	11	40	10	43	9	46	8	49	7	52	9
22	14	11	13	14	12	17	11	20	10	23	9	26	8	29	7	32	8
23	13	52	12	56	11	59	11	2	10	5	9	8	8	11	7	14	7
24	13	32	12	36	11	39	10	42	9	46	8	49	7	52	6	55	6
25	13	12	12	16	11	19	10	22	9	26	8	29	7	33	6	37	5
26	12	52	11	56	10	58	10	1	9	5	8	8	7	12	6	16	4
27	12	32	11	36	10	39	9	43	8	47	7	50	6	54	6	58	3
28	12	11	11	15	10	18	9	22	8	26	7	29	6	32	6	36	2
29	11	50	10	54	9	58	9	2	8	6	7	10	6	14	5	18	1
30	11	29	10	33	9	37	8	41	7	45	6	49	5	53	4	57	0

Rule.—*To find the Declination of any heavenly body whose longitude and latitude are given.*—1°. Look for the even degree of longitude and under the even degree of latitude, at the head of the Table; at the angle of meeting will be found the declination for those even degrees, which transcribe and call A. 2°. In the same column of latitude, seek the declination for the next even degree of longitude, and note the difference. Then say: "As 60′ are to the minutes of difference, so are the minutes of difference in the *longitude* given to the *first correction*." 3°. Observe the *difference* of declination caused by one degree of increase in the *latitude*. Then say: "As 60′ are to the minutes of difference, so are the minutes of difference in the *latitude* given to the *second correction*." 4°. If both corrections be *plus* or *minus*, then the *sum* of the two corrections, added to or subtracted from A, will give the required *declination*. But, if one be *plus* and the other *minus*, then the *difference* of the two corrections added to or subtracted from A, will give the *declination* required.

TABLE OF DECLINATION.

VIRGO.	DEGREES OF SOUTH LATITUDE.								ARIES.
	0°	1°	2°	3°	4°	5°	6°	7°	
D.	D. M.	D. M.	D. M.	D. M.	D. M.	D. M.	D. M.	D. M.	D.
0	11 29	10 33	9 37	8 41	7 45	6 49	5 53	4 57	30
1	11 8	10 13	9 17	8 21	7 24	6 28	5 32	4 36	29
2	10 46	9 51	8 55	8 0	7 4	6 8	5 12	4 16	28
3	10 25	9 30	8 34	7 38	6 42	5 46	4 50	3 54	27
4	10 3	9 7	8 11	7 15	6 19	5 24	4 28	3 32	26
5	9 41	8 45	7 49	6 53	5 57	5 2	4 6	3 10	25
6	9 19	8 23	7 27	6 31	5 35	4 40	3 45	2 49	24
7	8 57	8 1	7 5	6 9	5 13	4 18	3 22	2 26	23
8	8 35	7 39	6 43	5 47	4 51	3 56	3 0	2 4	22
9	8 12	7 16	6 20	5 24	4 28	3 32	2 37	1 41	21
10	7 50	6 54	5 58	5 2	4 6	3 10	2 15	1 19	20
11	7 27	6 31	5 36	4 40	3 45	2 49	1 54	0 58	19
12	7 4	6 9	5 14	4 18	3 23	2 27	1 32	0 36	18
13	6 41	5 45	4 50	3 54	2 59	2 3	1 8	0 13	17
14	6 18	5 22	4 27	3 31	2 36	1 40	0 45	0 9	16
15	5 55	5 0	4 5	3 9	2 14	1 18	0 23	0 32	15
16	5 32	4 37	3 42	2 46	1 51	0 56	0 0	0 55	14
17	5 8	4 13	3 18	2 23	1 28	0 33	0 23	1 19	13
18	4 45	3 50	2 55	2 0	1 5	0 10	0 46	1 41	12
19	4 21	3 26	2 31	1 36	0 41	0 14	1 9	2 4	11
20	3 58	3 3	2 8	1 13	0 18	0 38	1 33	2 28	10
21	3 34	2 39	1 44	0 49	0 6	1 2	1 57	2 52	9
22	3 11	2 16	1 21	0 26	0 29	1 25	2 20	3 15	8
23	2 47	1 52	0 57	0 2	0 53	1 48	2 43	3 38	7
24	2 23	1 28	0 33	0 22	1 17	2 12	3 7	4 2	6
25	1 59	1 5	0 10	0 46	1 41	2 36	3 31	4 26	5
26	1 36	0 41	0 15	1 10	2 5	3 0	3 55	4 50	4
27	1 12	0 17	0 39	1 34	2 29	3 24	4 19	5 14	3
28	0 48	0 7	1 3	1 57	2 52	3 47	4 42	5 37	2
29	0 24	0 31	1 27	2 21	3 16	4 11	5 6	6 1	1
30	0 0	0 55	1 50	2 45	3 40	4 35	5 30	6 25	0

NORTH. SOUTH.

NORTH.

RULE.—*To find the Longitude of the* SUN, *or body without latitude, corresponding to a given declination.*—1°. Seek in the column marked 0° at the top, the declination nearest to that given, and transcribe the degree of longitude coresponding thereto, marking it A. 2°. Observe the difference of declination caused by one degree of longitude. Then say: "As the minutes of difference of declination are to 60′ of longitude, so are the minutes of difference (between the given declination and that corresponding to the degree of longitude transcribed) to the *correction.*" 3°. Add the correction to A if it be *plus*, subtract it if it be *minus*, and the required *longitude* will be obtained.

[*Note.*—The longitude *and latitude* of the Moon, or a planet, corresponding to a given declination, must be computed from an *Ephemeris*, or the *Nautical Almanac* for the year of birth.]

TABLE OF DECLINATION.

LIBRA.	DEGREES OF SOUTH LATITUDE.																PISCES.
	0°		1°		2°		3°		4°		5°		6°		7°		
D.	D.	M.	D.	M.	D.	M.	D.	M.	D.	M.	D.	M.	D.	M.	D.	M.	D.
0	0	0	0	55	1	50	2	45	3	40	4	35	5	30	6	25	30
1	0	24	1	19	2	14	3	9	4	4	4	59	5	55	6	49	29
2	0	48	1	43	2	38	3	33	4	28	5	23	6	18	7	13	28
3	1	12	2	7	3	2	3	57	4	52	5	47	6	42	7	37	27
4	1	36	2	31	3	26	4	21	5	16	6	11	7	6	8	1	26
5	1	59	2	55	3	50	4	45	5	40	6	35	7	30	8	25	25
6	2	23	3	19	4	14	5	9	6	4	6	59	7	54	8	49	24
7	2	47	3	43	4	38	5	33	6	28	7	23	8	18	9	13	23
8	3	11	4	7	5	2	5	57	6	52	7	47	8	42	9	37	22
9	3	34	4	30	5	25	6	20	7	15	8	10	9	5	10	0	21
10	3	58	4	54	5	49	6	44	7	39	8	34	9	29	10	24	20
11	4	21	5	17	6	12	7	7	8	2	8	57	9	52	10	47	19
12	4	45	5	41	6	36	7	31	8	26	9	21	10	16	11	11	18
13	5	8	6	4	6	59	7	54	8	49	9	44	10	39	11	34	17
14	5	32	6	28	7	23	8	18	9	13	10	8	11	3	11	58	16
15	5	55	6	51	7	46	8	41	9	30	10	31	11	26	12	21	15
16	6	18	7	13	8	8	9	3	9	58	10	53	11	48	12	43	14
17	6	41	7	36	8	31	9	26	10	21	11	16	12	11	13	6	13
18	7	4	8	0	8	55	9	50	10	45	11	40	12	35	13	30	12
19	7	27	8	22	9	17	10	12	11	7	12	2	12	57	13	52	11
20	7	50	8	46	9	41	10	36	11	31	11	26	13	21	14	16	10
21	8	12	9	8	10	4	10	59	11	54	12	49	13	44	14	39	9
22	8	35	9	31	10	27	11	22	12	18	13	13	14	9	15	4	8
23	8	57	9	53	10	49	11	44	12	40	13	35	14	31	15	26	7
24	9	19	10	15	11	11	12	6	13	2	13	58	14	54	15	50	6
25	9	41	10	39	11	35	12	29	13	26	14	22	15	18	16	14	5
26	10	3	10	59	11	55	12	51	13	47	14	43	15	39	16	35	4
27	10	25	11	21	12	17	13	12	14	8	15	4	16	0	16	56	3
28	10	46	11	42	12	38	13	33	14	29	15	25	16	21	17	17	2
29	11	7	12	4	13	0	13	56	14	51	15	47	16	43	17	39	1
30	11	29	12	24	13	20	14	16	15	12	16	8	17	4	18	0	0

TABLE OF DECLINATION.

SCORPIO.	Degrees of South Latitude.																AQUARIUS.
	0°		1°		2°		3°		4°		5°		6°		7°		
D.	D.	M.	D.	M.	D.	M.	D.	M.	D.	M.	D.	M.	D.	M.	D.	M.	D.
0	11	29	12	24	13	20	14	16	15	12	16	8	17	4	18	0	30
1	11	50	12	45	13	41	14	37	15	33	16	30	17	26	18	22	29
2	12	11	13	6	14	2	14	58	15	54	16	51	17	47	18	43	28
3	12	32	13	27	14	23	15	19	16	15	17	12	18	8	19	4	27
4	12	52	13	47	14	43	15	39	16	35	17	32	18	28	19	24	26
5	13	12	14	7	15	3	16	0	16	56	17	53	18	49	19	45	25
6	13	32	14	27	15	23	16	19	17	15	18	12	19	8	20	5	24
7	13	52	14	47	15	43	16	40	17	36	18	33	19	29	20	26	23
8	14	11	15	7	16	3	17	0	17	56	18	53	19	50	20	47	22
9	14	31	15	26	16	22	17	19	18	16	19	13	20	10	21	7	21
10	14	50	15	45	16	41	17	38	18	35	19	32	20	29	21	26	20
11	15	9	16	4	17	1	17	58	18	55	19	52	20	49	21	46	19
12	15	27	16	23	17	20	18	17	19	14	20	11	21	8	22	5	18
13	15	45	16	42	17	39	18	36	19	33	20	30	21	27	22	24	17
14	16	3	17	0	17	57	18	54	19	51	20	49	21	46	22	43	16
15	16	21	17	18	18	15	19	12	20	9	21	7	22	4	23	1	15
16	16	39	17	35	18	33	19	30	20	27	21	25	22	22	23	19	14
17	16	56	17	52	18	50	19	47	20	44	21	42	22	39	23	36	13
18	17	13	18	9	19	7	20	5	21	2	22	0	22	57	23	54	12
19	17	29	18	26	19	24	20	22	21	19	22	17	23	14	24	11	11
20	17	46	18	43	19	41	20	38	21	36	22	34	23	31	24	28	10
21	18	2	18	59	19	57	20	55	21	53	22	51	23	49	24	46	9
22	18	17	19	15	20	13	21	11	22	9	23	7	24	5	25	3	8
23	18	33	19	31	20	29	21	27	22	25	23	23	24	21	25	19	7
24	18	48	19	46	20	44	21	42	22	40	23	38	24	36	25	34	6
25	19	2	20	0	20	59	21	57	22	55	23	53	24	51	25	49	5
26	19	17	20	14	21	13	22	11	23	9	24	8	25	6	26	4	4
27	19	31	20	28	21	27	22	25	23	23	24	22	25	20	26	18	3
28	19	44	20	42	21	41	22	39	23	37	24	37	25	34	26	32	2
29	19	57	20	56	21	54	22	53	23	51	24	50	25	48	26	46	1
30	20	10	21	8	22	6	23	5	24	4	25	2	26	0	26	59	0

TABLE OF DECLINATION.

SAGITTARY.	DEGREES OF SOUTH LATITUDE.																CAPRICORN
	0°		1°		2°		3°		4°		5°		6°		7°		
D.	D.	M.	D.	M.	D.	M.	D.	M.	D.	M.	D.	M.	D.	M.	D.	M.	D.
0	20	10	21	8	22	6	23	5	24	4	25	2	26	0	26	59	30
1	20	23	21	20	22	19	23	18	24	17	25	16	26	14	27	13	29
2	20	35	21	32	22	31	23	30	24	29	25	28	26	26	27	25	28
3	20	47	21	44	22	43	23	42	24	41	25	40	26	39	27	38	27
4	20	58	21	56	22	55	23	54	24	53	25	52	26	51	27	50	26
5	21	8	22	8	23	7	24	6	25	5	26	4	27	3	28	2	25
6	21	19	22	19	23	18	24	17	25	16	26	15	27	14	28	13	24
7	21	30	22	30	23	29	24	28	25	27	26	26	27	25	28	25	23
8	21	40	22	40	23	39	24	38	25	37	26	36	27	35	28	35	22
9	21	49	22	49	23	48	24	47	25	46	26	45	27	44	28	43	21
10	22	58	22	58	23	57	24	56	25	55	26	54	27	53	28	52	20
11	22	7	23	7	24	6	25	6	26	5	27	4	28	3	29	2	19
12	22	15	23	15	24	14	25	14	26	13	27	12	28	11	29	10	18
13	22	23	23	23	24	22	25	22	26	21	27	20	28	19	29	18	17
14	22	30	23	30	24	29	25	29	26	29	27	28	28	28	29	27	16
15	22	37	23	37	24	36	25	36	26	36	27	35	28	35	29	34	15
16	22	44	23	44	24	43	25	43	26	43	27	42	28	42	29	41	14
17	22	49	23	50	24	50	25	50	26	50	27	50	28	50	29	48	13
18	22	56	23	56	24	56	25	56	26	56	27	56	28	56	29	55	12
19	23	0	24	0	25	0	26	0	27	0	28	0	29	0	30	0	11
20	23	4	24	4	25	4	26	4	27	4	28	4	29	4	30	4	10
21	23	9	24	9	25	9	26	9	27	9	28	9	29	9	30	9	9
22	23	13	24	13	25	13	26	13	27	13	28	13	29	13	30	13	8
23	23	17	24	16	25	16	26	16	27	16	28	16	29	16	30	16	7
24	23	19	24	19	25	19	26	19	27	19	28	19	29	19	30	19	6
25	23	21	24	21	25	21	26	21	27	21	28	21	29	21	30	21	5
26	23	23	24	23	25	23	26	23	27	23	28	23	29	23	30	23	4
27	23	25	24	25	25	25	26	25	27	25	28	25	29	25	30	25	3
28	23	26	24	26	25	26	26	26	27	26	28	26	29	26	30	26	2
29	23	27	24	27	25	27	26	27	27	27	28	27	29	27	30	27	1
30	23	27	24	27	25	27	26	27	27	27	28	27	29	27	30	27	0

Table I. Of Ascensional Difference for the Latitude of London, 51° 30′ 49″ North. Obliquity of the Ecliptic, 23° 27′.

Declin.	0′		5′		10′		15′		20′		25′		30′		35′		40′		45′		50′		55′	
°	°	′	°	′	°	′	°	′	°	′	°	′	°	′	°	′	°	′	°	′	°	′	°	′
0	0	0	0	6	0	13	0	19	0	25	0	31	0	38	0	44	0	50	0	57	1	3	1	9
1	1	15	1	22	1	28	1	34	1	41	1	47	1	53	2	0	2	6	2	12	2	18	2	25
2	2	31	2	37	2	44	2	50	2	56	3	3	3	9	3	15	3	22	3	28	3	34	3	40
3	3	47	3	53	3	59	4	6	4	12	4	18	4	25	4	31	4	37	4	44	4	50	4	56
4	5	3	5	9	5	15	5	22	5	28	5	35	5	41	5	47	5	54	6	0	6	6	6	13
5	6	19	6	25	6	32	6	38	6	45	6	51	6	57	7	4	7	10	7	17	7	23	7	29
6	7	36	7	42	7	49	7	55	8	1	8	8	8	14	8	21	8	27	8	34	8	40	8	47
7	8	53	9	0	9	6	9	12	9	19	9	25	9	32	9	38	9	45	9	51	9	58	10	4
8	10	11	10	17	10	24	10	30	10	37	10	42	10	50	10	57	11	3	11	10	11	16	11	23
9	11	29	11	36	11	43	11	49	11	56	12	2	12	9	12	16	12	22	12	30	12	36	12	42
10	12	49	12	55	13	2	13	9	13	15	13	22	13	29	13	36	13	42	13	49	13	56	14	2
11	14	9	14	16	14	23	14	29	14	36	14	43	14	50	14	56	15	3	15	10	15	17	15	24
12	15	30	15	37	15	44	15	51	15	58	16	5	16	11	16	18	16	25	16	32	16	39	16	46
13	16	53	17	0	17	7	17	14	17	21	17	28	17	35	17	42	17	49	17	56	18	3	18	10
14	18	17	18	24	18	31	18	38	18	45	18	52	18	59	19	6	19	13	19	20	19	27	19	35
15	19	42	19	49	19	56	20	3	20	10	20	18	20	25	20	32	20	39	20	47	20	54	21	1
16	21	8	21	16	21	23	21	30	21	38	21	45	21	52	22	0	22	7	22	15	22	22	22	29
17	22	37	22	44	22	52	22	59	23	7	23	14	23	22	23	29	23	37	23	45	23	52	24	0
18	24	7	24	15	24	23	24	30	24	38	24	46	24	53	25	1	25	9	25	16	25	24	25	32
19	25	40	25	48	25	55	26	3	26	11	26	19	26	27	26	35	26	43	26	51	26	59	27	7
20	27	15	27	23	27	31	27	39	27	47	27	55	28	3	28	11	28	19	28	28	28	36	28	44
21	28	52	29	0	29	9	29	17	29	25	29	34	29	42	29	50	29	59	30	7	30	16	30	24
22	30	33	30	41	30	50	30	58	31	7	31	15	31	24	31	33	31	41	31	50	31	59	32	7
23	32	16	32	25	32	34	32	43	32	51	33	0	33	9	33	18	33	27	33	36	33	45	33	54
24	34	3	34	12	34	22	34	31	34	40	34	49	34	58	35	8	35	17	35	26	35	36	35	45
25	35	55	36	4	36	14	36	23	36	33	36	42	36	52	37	2	37	11	37	21	37	31	37	41
26	37	50	38	0	38	10	38	20	38	30	38	40	38	50	39	0	39	10	39	21	39	31	39	39
27	39	51	40	2	40	12	40	23	40	33	40	44	40	54	41	5	41	15	41	26	41	37	41	48
28	41	58	42	9	42	20	42	31	42	42	42	53	43	4	43	16	43	27	43	38	43	49	44	1

Table II. Of Ascensional Difference for the Latitude of Washington, D.C., 38° 53' 20'' North. Obliquity of the Ecliptic, 23° 27'.

Declin.	0'		5'		10'		15'		20'		25'		30'		35'		40'		45'		50'		55'	
°	°	'	°	'	°	'	°	'	°	'	°	'	°	'	°	'	°	'	°	'	°	'	°	'
0	0	0	0	4	0	8	0	12	0	16	0	20	0	24	0	28	0	32	0	36	0	40	0	44
1	0	48	0	52	0	56	1	1	1	5	1	9	1	13	1	17	1	21	1	25	1	29	1	33
2	1	37	1	41	1	45	1	49	1	53	1	57	2	1	2	5	2	9	2	13	2	17	2	21
3	2	25	2	29	2	33	2	38	2	42	2	46	2	50	2	54	2	58	3	2	3	6	3	10
4	3	14	3	18	3	22	3	26	3	30	3	34	3	38	3	42	3	47	3	51	3	55	3	59
5	4	3	4	7	4	11	4	15	4	19	4	23	4	27	4	31	4	35	4	40	4	44	4	48
6	4	52	4	56	5	0	5	4	5	8	5	12	5	16	5	20	5	25	5	29	5	33	5	37
7	5	41	5	45	5	49	5	53	5	57	6	2	6	6	6	10	6	14	6	18	6	22	6	26
8	6	31	6	35	6	39	6	43	6	47	6	51	6	55	7	0	7	4	7	8	7	12	7	16
9	7	20	7	25	7	29	7	33	7	37	7	41	7	45	7	50	7	54	7	58	8	2	8	6
10	8	11	8	15	8	19	8	23	8	27	8	32	8	36	8	40	8	44	8	49	8	53	8	57
11	9	1	9	5	9	10	9	14	9	18	9	22	9	27	9	31	9	35	9	39	9	44	9	48
12	9	52	9	57	10	1	10	5	10	9	10	14	10	18	10	22	10	27	10	31	10	35	10	40
13	10	44	10	48	10	53	10	57	11	1	11	6	11	10	11	14	11	19	11	23	11	27	11	32
14	11	36	11	40	11	45	11	49	11	54	11	58	12	2	12	7	12	11	12	16	12	20	12	24
15	12	39	12	33	12	38	12	42	12	47	12	51	12	56	13	0	13	4	13	9	13	13	13	18
16	13	22	13	27	13	31	13	36	13	40	13	45	13	49	13	54	13	58	14	3	14	7	14	12
17	14	17	14	21	14	26	14	30	14	35	14	39	14	44	14	49	14	53	14	58	15	2	15	7
18	15	12	15	16	15	21	15	25	15	30	15	35	15	39	15	44	15	49	15	53	15	58	16	3
19	16	7	16	12	16	17	16	22	16	26	16	31	16	36	16	41	16	45	16	50	16	55	17	0
20	17	4	17	9	17	14	17	19	17	23	17	28	17	33	17	38	17	43	17	48	17	52	17	57
21	18	2	18	7	18	12	18	17	18	22	18	27	18	32	18	36	18	41	18	46	18	51	18	56
22	19	1	19	6	19	11	19	16	19	21	19	26	19	31	19	36	19	41	19	46	19	51	19	56
23	20	1	20	6	20	11	20	17	20	22	20	27	20	32	20	37	20	42	20	47	20	52	20	58
24	21	3	21	8	21	13	21	18	21	24	21	29	21	34	21	39	21	44	21	50	21	55	22	0
25	22	6	22	11	22	16	22	21	22	27	22	32	22	38	22	43	22	48	22	54	22	59	23	5
26	23	10	23	15	23	21	23	26	23	32	23	37	23	43	23	48	23	54	23	59	24	5	24	10
27	24	16	24	22	24	27	24	33	24	38	24	44	24	50	24	55	25	1	25	7	25	12	25	18
28	25	24	25	29	25	35	25	41	25	47	25	53	25	58	26	4	26	10	26	16	26	22	26	28

www.ingramcontent.com/pod-product-compliance
Lightning Source LLC
Chambersburg PA
CBHW020356100426
42812CB00001B/81

* 9 7 8 0 8 6 6 9 0 5 6 0 2 *